Structured BASIC Programming

Structured BASIC Programming

Second Edition

Harry Moriber
Greater Hartford Community College

Merrill Publishing Company
A Bell & Howell Information Company
Columbus Toronto London Melbourne

To my son Kurt

Cover: Computer art copyright © Robert Bowers

Published by
Merrill Publishing Company
A Bell & Howell Information Company
Columbus, Ohio 43216

This book was set in Times Roman.

Administrative Editor: Vernon R. Anthony
Cover Designer: Cathy Watterson

Library of Congress Catalog Card Number: 88–62547
International Standard Book Number: 0–675–20715–0
Printed in the United States of America
1 2 3 4 5 6 7 8 9—92 91 90 89

PREFACE

While there have been many additions and revisions in this new edition of *Structured BASIC Programming,* my basic goal in writing it has remained unchanged: to help students reach a level of proficiency in BASIC programming that will enable them to create useful programs for practical application in real-world settings. The text assumes no previous experience with BASIC or any other programming language. It is designed for the first course in BASIC programming or as part of the programming component of an Introduction to Computers class. It can also be used by any individual outside the classroom who is seeking to learn and use BASIC programming. The accent in the second edition is on a user-friendly approach, which includes many interesting case studies and a wealth of hands-on exercises.

New Features in the Second Edition

- [ ] Color is used as a teaching tool to enhance the format of the text, promote understanding, and reinforce concepts.
- [ ] All the advanced structures of new BASICA are included in the problems and cases. New graphics have been added.
- [ ] New case studies highlight improvements in BASIC and modern applications programs. Cases and problems are expanded to include full-screen formatting and error trapping.
- [ ] Revised problem definitions are easier to follow than in the previous edition, especially the input and output specifications.
- [ ] Building Block problems are now included in the Instructor's Manual as additional programs, rather than in the problems-for-solution sections of the text.
- [ ] A new appendix details necessary source code changes and/or differences for compiled versus interpreted problems using Microsoft's QuickBASIC.

Each chapter begins with a chapter outline and learning objectives and concludes with summaries, review questions, and problems for solution. In addition, the text is heavily illustrated with flowcharts, structure charts (VTOC's), and problem definition sheets.

The text progresses through the introductory concepts of computers and computer programming and concludes with sophisticated file processing techniques, including indexed sequential access. This technique was founded on the I/O buffer techniques of the direct access file programming methods of earlier texts. It is an important topic, not covered in many BASIC texts.

Students can become expert in developing realistic business systems by progressing through the ten chapters, or beginners can grasp and use the foundational concepts of programming by studying the material through Chapter 6. Instructors are afforded the flexibility to either treat Chapters 7 through 10 as a separate course on advanced programming topics or incorporate selected portions from these chapters into a complete one-semester course in programming.

All case studies and programs have been tested and proven on an IBM-PC with error-free interpretation and execution. Students and teachers can be confident of their accuracy.

Acknowledgments

Many thanks are due to the reviewers of the manuscript who provided so many helpful suggestions for refining the second edition. They are as follows: John Trifiletti, Florida Junior College; Darlene Hunt, Powassan, Ontario; Karen Braunstein, Renton Vocational Technical Institute; George Thompson, Southern Ohio College; Jim Sherrad, Jefferson Community College; Donald Musselman, James Madison University; and Herbert Morris, Bradley University.

CONTENTS

Structured BASIC Programming

CHAPTER ONE

INTRODUCTION TO COMPUTER PROGRAMMING

OUTLINE

WHAT IS A MICROCOMPUTER SYSTEM?
The Central Processing Unit | The Keyboard |
The CRT Display | The Printer | Disk Drives and
Disks | The Disk Operating System (DOS)

THE BASIC PROGRAMMING LANGUAGE
History | Compiling vs. Interpreting BASIC | How to
LOAD and RUN a BASIC Program

WRITING AND RUNNING PROGRAMS
Programming Computers vs. Instructing
People | Practice in Writing and Running BASIC
Programs

**THE FIVE STEPS IN PREPARING A COMPUTER
PROGRAM**
Define the Problem | Develop a Method of
Solution | Code the Algorithm | Run and Test the
Program | Document the Program

COMMON PROGRAMMING ERRORS

**A FEW SUGGESTIONS BEFORE YOU BEGIN
WRITING PROGRAMS**

LEARNING OBJECTIVES

Upon completion of this chapter, you will be able to:

☐ Understand the functions of the components of a
microcomputer system.

☐ Understand the features and advantages of BASIC,
including the pros and cons of using compilers and
interpreters.

☐ Understand the differences between writing instructions for people and programming computers.

☐ Understand the purpose of each of the five steps in
preparing a computer program.

☐ Understand and be able to avoid the four most
common types of errors made while writing and
running BASIC programs.

WHAT IS A MICROCOMPUTER SYSTEM?

Many historians regard the introduction of computers in the late 1940s as the beginning of a sociological and cultural revolution as significant as the Industrial Revolution. The impact of large-scale computer systems developed for the military in the 1940s and introduced in business in the early 1950s is well documented. The affordable, compact, and inexpensive microcomputer perfected in the mid 1970s has changed the way people live, work, and play, and so has become an integral part of many homes, schools, and small businesses. Tens of millions now own small computers. Schools (from elementary through college) use computers as teaching aids. Newspapers and magazines include special sections on computers, and hundreds of computer publications are available to hobbyists, business owners, and the general public. Indeed, the microcomputer is everywhere you look.

Because of their high cost, for more than 30 years computer systems were owned primarily by large businesses. A computer that rented for $50,000 to $100,000 per year 10 years ago can now be replaced by an equivalent or better microcomputer that can be purchased for less than $5,000. Industry analysts estimate that computer systems decrease in price by one-half every two years. Thus, a system that sells for $3,000 today (a reasonable price for a complete functional computer system for home, school, or business) is conservatively estimated to cost less than $1,000 in five years.

Beyond the dramatic reductions in price, the enhanced capabilities of newer systems brought about by improvements in the physical components of the computer system (hardware) and the increased power and flexibility in the programs that are executed by the computer (software) make their use increasingly attractive to individuals and small businesses. New systems have been so simplified that even a novice can learn a few commands and use the computer to accomplish the most sophisticated accounting, mathematical, word processing, or business tasks. This development is no accident. Computer manufacturers have long realized the potential market for machines that everyone can use. After reducing the price of system components—memory, logic units, input and output devices—the manufacturer's next step was to make the computer as simple to operate as an automobile. Few of us fully understand how an electronic ignition system functions or a fuel injection system works. As consumers, we are primarily concerned with whether the automobile serves its purpose, if it is dependable, and if it is reasonably priced. Computer manufacturers, considering the same types of issues, ushered in the current revolution in microcomputer marketing.

Because the introduction of microcomputers in the workplace has freed many workers from repetitive tasks, many people have been displaced from their jobs. However, the computer revolution also has created new jobs through increased productivity, many of which are more challenging, enjoyable, and financially rewarding than the jobs they eliminated.

The microcomputer also frees small business owners from routine paperwork, recordkeeping, and manual accounting. The tight control of inventory so crucial to the success of retail and manufacturing businesses can now be accomplished easily by microcomputers. Microcomputers give managers time to plan marketing strategies, develop new products, supervise production, and investigate new and better manufacturing techniques or product mix.

Independent and federal government studies show that prior to introduction of microcomputers, small business owners spent one-third of their time in routine functions and in preparing accounting and tax reports required by state, municipal, and federal government. Because these tasks do not allow them time to implement the money-making and money-saving techniques used in big businesses, many new businesses fail before the end of their fifth year. Although sufficient statistics are not yet available to establish a trend, failure ratios should drop as microcomputers relieve owners and managers from nonproductive activities.

Sometimes computers are intimidating. People tend to think that unless they understand the function of each and every integrated circuit and key, they are likely to do damage to the computer or get hurt. Chances are good that neither will happen. A computer system is rarely damaged by what is typed in. So, you can relax as you sit down at your computer. You should keep in mind that your goal at this point is to become familiar with the computer, not to thoroughly understand how every piece of equipment works.

Figure 1–1 shows five visible parts of the computer system. The central processing unit and disk drives are found in the large cabinet and the keyboard is located in front of a display (cathode Ray Tube or CRT), which looks like a television screen. The small envelopes contain information storage disks, and the printer, which looks like a typewriter with no keyboard, appears at the right. These separate devices are all connected by special cables, and together form a microcomputer system.

The Central Processing Unit

The central processing unit (CPU) stores the memory and logic units (that portion of the CPU where all processing takes place); a power supply; special connectors for the other devices, such as the CRT display and printer; and a number of other less important components. The front panel of the CPU contains at least one (and often two) disk drives, which are used to store data. Disk drives give the computer extra space to store information, much the way people use filing cabinets to store records and other pertinent data they may need to refer to later.

In storing information, the computer uses two kinds of storage devices: primary or main memory and secondary storage. Primary memory is made up of RAM (Random Access Memory) and ROM (Read Only Memory). RAM is the part of primary memory used to temporarily retrieve and store information for use by the CPU. Information held in RAM will be erased when the power to the computer is turned off. ROM, unlike RAM, is the part of memory that cannot be changed unless new instructions are physically rewired into the machine. ROM contains the instructions the computer uses to operate when it is turned on. It is not erased when the power is turned off.

Secondary storage permits additional storage space through the use of diskettes or built-in hard disks. Information must be transferred from these sources to primary memory by using the LOAD command before it can be used by the computer.

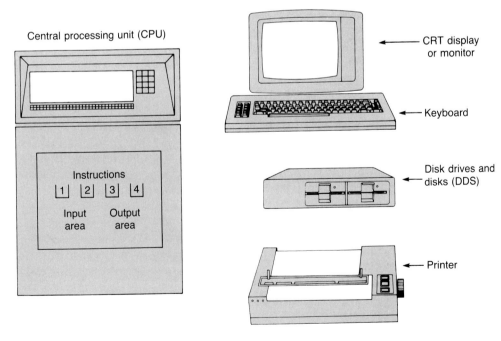

FIGURE 1–1
Components of a computer system.

3

The operation of data storage and disk drives is important but complex, so it will be discussed in detail in another section. For now, it is enough to know that nearly all of your programs and data will be saved on or loaded from the disks you will place in the computer's disk drives.

The Keyboard

The cabinet that resembles a typewriter is called the keyboard. It is the primary method by which you will communicate to the computer. Although enormous strides have been made in the past few years in getting computers to understand and respond to spoken commands, such systems are still unreliable and expensive. For at least the next few years, you can expect to have to type all your commands in. Touch typing skills are desirable if you will be doing much work with a computer.

The keyboard is not much different from a typewriter except for the extra keys on the left, top, and right depending on the style of keyboard you are using. Letters, numbers, and special characters on most keyboards are fairly standard, although the location and number of Function keys, and the numeric and control keys on the right vary widely. The purpose and location of these keys for your computer can be found in your computer's operation manual.

The CRT Display

The monitor located above the CPU is one of the two common output devices found on most microcomputer systems. The monitor is often referred to as the CRT (Cathode Ray Tube) or the video display terminal (VDT). Letters, numbers, pictures, and graphs will appear on the display in any combination, depending on the program running. Displays can produce images in color or in monochrome (such as green or amber letters on a black background). The type of display depends on what the computer system will be used for. For example, if a computer will be used mainly to process words and numbers, the system will probably include a monochrome display. On the other hand, if a computer will be used for producing diagrams and pictorial output, a high-resolution color display should be purchased. The recent trend is towards monitors that can produce color output. Recent advances in high resolution color monitors make text and graphics easy to read.

Many computer systems will actually permit the use of a standard television set as the display, although the resolution on television screens makes text difficult to read. Most serious computer users will acquire a computer monitor after comparing its output to a television set.

The Printer

The other output device found on microcomputer systems is the printer. Although you may find simply displaying information on the display satisfactory if you don't need a permanent record of its contents, sometimes a display is difficult to use. For instance, you may want a permanent form of output (hard copy) of bills, invoices, paychecks, accounting reports, letters, and tables of figures and data. Further, program development is more efficient when programs are printed, as most programs will be too long to fit on the screen. Viewing information on a display by moving from section to section is called scrolling. Scrolling up and down from one part of the program to another can be tedious and time consuming. For these reasons, anyone who does serious program development needs a printer, as does anyone who uses a computer to prepare paperwork for business, government, and education.

Disk Drives and Disks

In the front of the CPU cabinet you will find one or two disk drives. The disk drives *read* information from and *write* information to the diskettes (disks) which are contained in sealed vinyl or solid plastic envelopes depending on the type of disk drive your computer has, as shown in figure 1–2. The information is stored to the diskette as magnetized spots of iron oxide called bits (short for "BInary digiTs"). Special care must be used in handling disks to avoid damaging them or the information they store. You should never bend a floppy disk nor touch the record part of the diskette because you will destroy the information written on it.

The Disk Operating System (DOS)

Programs and data are loaded into the computer from the disks via disk drives. A series of special programs called the disk operating system (DOS) tells the computer how to organize and use the information on the disks. The disks may contain prewritten commercial programs, your own programs, or the data to be processed by a program. Working with the CPU, DOS tells your computer both how to take information from a disk (read the disk) and how to put information on the disk (write to the disk). Most computer systems require that DOS be loaded into the computer before you can run any other programs, and sometimes before you can run many versions of BASIC. It is a good idea to obtain and read your own DOS manual to become familiar with the important procedures and commands needed to run your programs and make duplicate copies of your programs, data file, or entire disks.

THE BASIC PROGRAMMING LANGUAGE

History

BASIC, which stands for Beginner's All-Purpose Symbolic Instruction Code, was developed at Dartmouth College between 1962 and 1965 when John G. Kemeny and Thomas E. Kurtz made a decision to help make computers accessible to all students. They designed

FIGURE 1–2
Floppy diskette.

and implemented what turned out to be the beginning of interactive time-sharing computing, where more than one person can communicate with the same computer while it is processing. This is the type of system used widely in airline reservation systems, banking systems, and department store cash register terminals. In 1962, the idea was quite revolutionary. To make this system functional to students in many fields and at many levels of understanding, a new and simple language called BASIC was developed. True to its name, BASIC was easy to learn yet useful for almost any programming problem, from abstract mathematics to real-world business.

From its beginning, BASIC was developed according to carefully chosen pedagogical principles. Although originally designed for beginners, by 1970 the language had grown to solve the most sophisticated and complex applications in business, science, and mathematics. During the 1970s, three major changes were made in BASIC. First, graphics were added to the language, greatly facilitating the use of pictures, charts, and animation. Second, structured commands were developed, which enabled programmers to write better designed and more easily maintained programs. Finally, a compiler version virtually eliminated the execution speed limitation traditionally associated with selecting BASIC for many business and scientific applications.

Because BASIC was never copyrighted, many versions of the language evolved from the original. These ''dialects'' often do not contain all the commands that are needed for comprehensive problem solving. Also, many are not compatible with each other, and, therefore, cannot be used on a variety of machines. Because of these drawbacks, BASIC lost favor with professional programmers between the late 1970s and early 1980s, relegating it to hobbyists and beginning students.

In 1984 and 1985, the Programming Language subcommittee of the American National Standards Institute (ANSI), chaired by Dr. Thomas Kurtz, helped get BASIC back on track. The new ANSI standard for BASIC offers a format for all BASIC developers and programmers to follow, thus eliminating dialects. This new BASIC standard, followed by most major software companies, adds powerful graphics and more commands as well as the statements needed for true structured-design programs compatible on all computer systems. Although not yet implemented by all computer-system manufacturers, the ANSI standard for BASIC is being adopted by most major computer companies. This new BASIC combines the power of ''mainframe'' languages such as COBOL (the standard language used on large computer systems since 1960) and FORTRAN (the traditional scientific and engineering applications language since 1960), while at the same time retaining the ease of use and convenience of a microcomputer.

The Microsoft BASIC (IBM BASICA, Advanced BASIC, and QuickBASIC) used in this text closely compares to the sophisticated versions of BASIC being adopted throughout the world. Although the current version of Microsoft BASIC does not meet all the ANSI standards, it is quite easy to convert.

Compiling vs. Interpreting BASIC

No computer can process BASIC statements directly. The only instructions a microcomputer can execute are its own machine-language instructions, special codes of zeroes and ones (Binary Code).

The computer needs a way to have statements translated into its own machine language. There are two methods by which this translation is accomplished: interpreting and compiling. Both are done by special computer programs written by computer scientists. These special translation programs save you from the tedious process of learning and memorizing hundreds of special numeric codes (the computer's machine language) to accomplish simple tasks such as accepting data from the keyboard, printing results, and doing arithmetic. It takes special programs inside the computer to translate your BASIC programs into information that the computer can recognize and process. In other words, BASIC is really a program in itself!

There are several key differences between an interpreter and a compiler. An interpreter reads and executes a line before advancing to the next. Each statement is checked for proper grammar and spelling during execution. If an error is detected, execution is immediately halted. On the other hand, a compiler examines all instructions for errors before execution is possible. If no errors are detected, the program is translated into machine code.

The compilation process proceeds no matter how many errors are found in the program and gives the user or program author a complete list of errors at the end. Sometimes this results in a staggering list of errors, which can slow down a program's development. Therefore, many programmers prefer to test their programs with an interpreter and then compile them for faster execution when the program is error free. (Appendix B explores this process in more detail.)

When you execute an interpreted program such as BASIC, the following steps are performed (assuming no errors):

1. Read the instruction
2. Check syntax
3. Interpret instruction
4. Execute instruction

When you execute a compiled program, only two steps are performed:

1. Read the instruction
2. Execute the instruction

The reduced steps make a compiled program's execution much faster.

You will see later that BASICA programs contain statements that must be numbered to be processed by an interpreter. This means that the computer examines every statement to determine if it is asked to jump to another section of the program (branching) or return to an earlier part of the program (looping). The line numbers show the computer the "right place" to go in the program. This is similar to searching through a telephone directory *page by page* until you find a particular person's name. Even though computers are much faster at searching than you are, it still is not a very efficient process.

In contrast, a compiler sets up a special table of unique memory addresses for each statement so that when a branch is encountered, the computer looks for the address and knows immediately where to go. This is similar to having mailboxes with names and addresses on them, as opposed to having mailboxes with only names. Lacking addresses, the postman, like a computer, would have to "search" each box for a number until the correct address was located.

So, more than in any other programming language, BASICA allows you to develop programs with the ease and convenience of an interpreter, which finds mistakes immediately. Then you can convert the corrected program to machine language with a compiler to obtain the benefit of quicker program execution. In fact, every program in this text can be compiled using a Microsoft BASIC compiler with a resulting improvement in execution time of one-third to one-tenth the original execution time. Be sure to check for minor differences between the programs in the text and the compiler you are using.

In Appendix B, a number of the advanced case studies presented throughout the text have been converted to run with the Microsoft Quick BASIC compiler. You will note the improved execution speed and better design of these converted programs.

How to LOAD and RUN a BASIC Program

Loading your program.   Your instructor (or your computer manual) will explain how to load the required disk operating system on your particular system, as well as the command needed to load your version of BASIC. The following instructions apply to the IBM series of computers using Microsoft BASIC and floppy disks. (IBM compatible computers may have varying commands and procedures, so check your manual if you are working on one.)

Getting your computer ready to run BASIC programs.

Writing and running BASIC programs means you are going to be communicating with your computer in a new language. As you learn, you will be practicing by writing many programs. No doubt, you will want to save these programs and maybe even have some of your friends try them out.

You don't need your own computer to save and run your programs, but you will need a place to save them if you use a computer at school. Therefore, it is a good idea to buy at least one diskette on which you can save your work. Be sure the disk you purchase is compatible with the computer you will be working with. The disks are inexpensive and are available in most bookstores or computer stores.

Also, as you progress in your studies, you will find that many statements and commands designed to accomplish the same task are quite different on different computer systems. To learn all the features of the BASIC statements and operating system commands you will be using, you should obtain copies of the BASIC and DOS manuals for your computer system. While these usually accompany computer systems at schools, you may find it desirable to have your own copies to study and mark if you are working on a computer you don't own. If you own your computer, the manuals you need probably came with the computer.

Finally, you will want to become familiar with the hardware on which you are working so that you know where the important switches are to turn on and off the machines, load the printer with paper, replace the ribbon if it runs out, and adjust the brightness and contrast of the monitor. This information is usually found in the *Guide to Operations* that accompanies new computers. Unlike the BASIC and DOS manuals that are a good investment even if you don't own the computer on which you are working, a "one-shot" reading of the *Guide to Operations* should be sufficient as long as the material is available to you for reference purposes.

Using and understanding DOS.

The key to unlocking the full potential of your computer system is in an understanding of its disk operating system. Fortunately, with BASIC only an overview of DOS and DOS commands is required. As you progress, you may find the DOS summary of commands in table 1–1 useful. For now, you will find that DOS is only needed in a limited number of situations.

1. To format your new disk, on which you will save your programs.
2. To see what is on your disk and how much space is available to store programs and/or data.
3. To make copies of the programs you write for safekeeping or for back-up purposes.
4. To make copies of your programs so that you can share them with others. (Remember, copying copyrighted software is a serious crime, so make sure the copies you make are allowed. Of course, you can make as many copies of your own programs as you like.)
5. To properly name data files and program files so that DOS can find and process them.
6. To set the date and time in the computer's clock so that you can access them through your BASIC program.
7. To check your disk for flaws or faults (bad sectors) so that you can decide whether to use it.
8. To erase files and/or programs you no longer want or need on your disk to make room for more.
9. To set or reset your computer's display mode (characters on the screen) or printer features like line width, or reroute output to other devices connected to your computer.

As you start out, it is likely that the only feature of DOS you will need is FORMAT, and perhaps date and time entries.

TABLE 1–1

Important DOS commands you will utilize in conjunction with BASIC programming.

Command	Description
CHKDSK	Will inspect the status of your disk and report how many files there are, how much space remains available, and most importantly, how many defective sectors there are on your disk.
DATE	Is used to change DOS's record of the current date. You can issue this command any time if you need the date but forgot to set it in the DOS welcome procedure.
DEL	Will delete a file from your disk to make room for others. Be careful with DEL because once a file is deleted, it cannot be recovered by ordinary DOS methods.
DIR	Lets you see a directory of your disk. It will show the files by name and tell how much space they take up on your disk. If you forget the name of a program you have written, this is a good way to remind yourself. A similar BASIC language command is FILES although only file names are displayed
DISKCOPY	Makes a complete copy of a disk, providing the disk is not ''copy protected'' or copyrighted. You can physically copy some disks, but it may be against the law. Be sure to check the copyright notice that comes with the software.
ERASE	Is the same command as DELETE. Be careful how you use it. Many useful programs have been irreversibly lost with this command.
FORMAT	Is a very important (and somewhat dangerous) command. It is needed every time you place a new blank disk into your computer, but it erases *everything* on that disk if the disk is not blank. If it is your first time at the computer, it is probably best to have someone show you how to format your new disks. Most disks can be recovered from the original if they are accidently erased.
RENAME	Is used to change the name of a program or data file if, after you assign a name to it, you think of a better name.
TIME	Is used to display or change the current time in the computer. Normally the time is entered when you load DOS, but you may decide later to correct it or add it to your programs.

Note: These are not BASIC commands but rather commands from the DOS level ''A:'' prompt.

Loading and starting DOS and BASIC.   The procedure described in this section is the one used on most versions of the IBM computer system using DOS and Advanced BASIC (BASICA). Your system may use a slightly different sequence of commands and have some command differences. Consult the manual that comes with the computer on which you are working if the procedure described here does not work. (This sequence is designed for a computer with two disk drives, and with DOS and BASICA on the same disk. It also assumes that you will want to save your programs on your own disk, which will be placed in the ''B'' drive.) To begin using DOS and BASIC, you will do the following.

1. Place the diskette containing DOS in the ''A'' drive, shut the disk drive latch, and turn on the computer. Be sure you place the disk in the disk drive correctly, usually with the label facing the drive latch and the cigar-shaped read area entered first.
2. When the date request appears, simply press Return (or Enter) to skip over it unless you will be accessing the date in your program. If you do want to enter the correct date, make sure to enter it in the format specified in the message on the screen: MM/DD/YY, where MM is the number of the month, DD is the day, and YY is the year.
3. Follow the same procedure when the time request appears unless you will be using the time in your programs. Here again, make sure to enter the time in the correct format: HH:MM:SS, where HH is hours in 24-hour notation, MM is the minutes, and SS is the seconds. Most people omit the seconds.

9

4. When the A> appears on the screen, this means that DOS has been properly loaded and the computer is awaiting your next command. Type in BASICA and press Return (or Enter) to load advanced BASIC into memory.

5. The screen will show the BASIC welcome message, which looks something like the following depending on the exact version of BASIC you will be using.

```
IBM ADVANCED BASIC VERSION 2.0
COPYRIGHT 198_ IBM
OK
```

or

```
GW = BASIC 3._
(c) Copyright Microsoft 198_
OK
```

Now you are ready to begin writing your BASIC program or to load in one that has already been written. A summary of BASIC commands follows in table 1–2. These are useful for a variety of tasks, but only a small number of these is required for beginning to program

TABLE 1–2
Summary of commonly used system commands.

Operating System Commands	Digital (DEC) BASIC Plus, Basic Plus-2 VAXII BASIC	IBM Advanced	TRS-80 Model II, 12
AUTOMATIC line numbering of program statements	AUTO	AUTO	AUTO
CLEAR memory for new program	NEW	NEW	CLEAR
CONTINUE execution of a program within program after a STOP statement halted execution	CONTINUE	CONT	CONT
CONTINUE scrolling display on CRT	CONTROL-Q	Any key	Any key except BREAK
CURSOR control commands	Cursor keys	Cursor keys	Cursor keys
DELETE a disk file from disk storage	KILL or UNSAVE	KILL 'fname'	KILL, PURGE 'fname'
DELETE current program from memory	NEW	NEW	NEW
DELETE program lines	DEL or EDIT mode	Line, enter key or EDIT	DELETE ln or ln-ln
EDIT a program in special edit mode	EDT	EDIT MODE	EDIT
ENTER data or statements on the CRT	RETURN or EN-TER	RETURN, ENTER	ENTER
EXECUTE a program (all or at specific line number)	RUN or RUN ln	RUN or RUN ln	RUN or RUN ln
HALT the execution of a program	CONTROL-C	CONTROL-BREAK	BREAK
LIST a directory of files on disk	DIR, CAT	DIR	DIR
LIST a program on the cRT	LIST (many options)	LIST (many options)	LIST (many options)
LIST a program on the printer	QU pname	LLIST	LLIST
LOAD a program into memory from disk	OLD pname	LOAD ''pname''	LOAD 'pname'
RENAME a file with a new name	RENAME	SAVE with new fname, RENAME	RENAME
RESUME execution of program after command stop	CONTINUE	RESUME (after error)	CONT
SAVE a program on disk	SAVE or REPLACE	SAVE	CSAVE
STOP display from scrolling on CRT	CONTROL-S	ALT NUM LOCK KEY	HOLD
TERMINATE BASIC programming session	BYE (many options)	SYSTEM	SYSTEM
TRACE execution of a program OFF	—	TROFF	TROFF
TRACE execution of a program ON	—	TRON	TRON

in BASIC. If a particular command gives the wrong result, or simply doesn't work, consult your manual.

When you write and run your programs in BASIC, you will find that there are a number of special commands that are not DOS commands or BASIC statement keywords. These fall into a special category called system commands. These commands are useful for listing, loading, executing, saving, printing, and displaying your program. System commands vary depending on your particular BASIC compiler or interpreter, so it is important to have a BASIC manual for the version of BASIC you are using.

WRITING AND RUNNING PROGRAMS

Programming Computers vs. Instructing People

Programs written for a computer to accomplish some task are really not much different from the instructions given to a person to accomplish the same task. Both processes consist of a series of steps to be performed in a logical order. The instructions intended for a person may not need to be as meticulous and error free as a computer program because if a word is misspelled or an instruction is out of order, a person can usually infer the correct word or sequence. Computers are not smart or intuitive. Therefore, preparing a computer program and verifying that it is error free is more complicated and time-consuming. Fortunately, the computer makes up in speed and accuracy what it lacks in deductive powers.

A computer never really solves any problem. Instead, a person devises a solution through a series of carefully planned instructions, known as the program. Consequently, the burden of solving problems does not rest on the computer, but rather on the programmer or analyst. Computers may provide solutions to problems previously thought to be "unsolvable" because of their speed, accuracy, and dependability, but computers must rely on a person's intellect for instruction.

Practice in Writing and Running BASIC Programs

This section gives two simple BASIC programs for you to try on your computer. They will help you see the simplicity and structure of a BASIC program.

To type in the program in figure 1–3, you must type the command NEW and press the return key. This command tells the computer to erase any program that is already in RAM. If you do not use the NEW command and there is already a program in RAM, the computer will assume you are still working on the old program and the commands from both programs will be mixed together.

Next, you type in the program or load it from your program disk.* After it is completely entered and you have checked it for typing errors, you should type RUN and press the return key. The RUN command tells the computer that you are ready to have the program executed. Look at the results on the screen in front of you. Are they correct? If not, check your program, correct any errors, and run it again.

You will note that most of the lines in the input contain remarks, or REM statements. These are statements the programmer uses to document or "explain" the program, or what is to occur in it. Without these REMs the program would be much shorter (these lines are printed in color), but would be less useful because subsequent users would not know what the original programmer meant for the program to do. Remark statements will be discussed completely in a later chapter.

The PRINT command tells the computer to display the results on the screen. To send the results to the printer (if your system is equipped with one), you must change the

---

*A disk is available with all case studies, already typed and ready to load and run.

Input

```
10    REM    THIS EXAMPLE PROGRAM ACCEPTS AS INPUT FROM THE
20    REM    KEYBOARD, TWO NUMBERS, A AND B, AND THEN ADDS THESE
30    REM    TOGETHER TO GIVE THE SUM, C.
40    REM
50    REM    THE RESULT, C, IS THEN PRINTED ON THE SCREEN
60    REM
70    REM    INPUT A NUMBER FROM THE KEYBOARD, AND STORE IT IN A
80    REM    MEMORY LOCATION (VARIABLE) CALLED A.
90           PRINT "Enter the first number"
100          INPUT A
110   REM
120   REM    INPUT THE SECOND NUMBER, AND STORE IT IN A MEMORY
130   REM    LOCATION CALLED B.
140          PRINT "Enter the second number"
150          INPUT B
160   REM
170   REM    ADD THE TWO NUMBERS TOGETHER (A + B), AND ASSIGN THE RESULT
180   REM    TO ANOTHER MEMORY LOCATION (VARIABLE) CALLED C.
190          C = A + B
200   REM
210   REM    PRINT THE RESULT C, ON THE SCREEN
220          PRINT "The sum is"; C
230   REM
240   REM    SIGNAL THE END OF THE PROGRAM WITH 'END'
250          END
```

Output

```
RUN
Enter the first number
? 12
Enter the second number
? 23
The sum is 35
OK
```

FIGURE 1–3
A simple BASIC program and its output.

PRINT statement to LPRINT. You also may wish to print the values of A and B along with the result C. If you do, you should change the print statement to

```
200 PRINT A,B,C
```

This will print the input values along with the results in evenly spaced columns called print zones. Note how any minor mistake you make typing in this program affects the results.

Figure 1–4 gives a more complicated program which contains titles, headings, and other details. To execute this program, you will again first use the NEW command to clear the memory. Then you will type the program into memory or load it from your program disk. After the "OK" prompt comes up, you will type RUN and press the return key. Then you will enter a number for MILES and then a number for GALLONS. If you have a printer attached to your computer, you can change all the PRINT statements to LPRINT statements. The LPRINT command is used to direct the output to the printer. If you use the LPRINT command without the printer being operational, an error will result.

A nice feature of the IBM PC is the Control-Print Screen (Ctrl/PrtSc) key sequence which takes all display output and sends a copy to the printer. With this command ON, you can use PRINT to display *and* print your output. If you are using an IBM PC,

Input

```
10   REM   THIS EXAMPLE PROGRAM COMPUTES MILES PER GALLON WITH DATA
20   REM   INPUT FROM THE KEYBOARD. THE INPUT CONSISTS OF TWO NUMBERS
25   REM   ONE FOR MILES DRIVEN, AND THE OTHER FOR GALLONS OF FUEL
30   REM   USED. MILES PER GALLON IS COMPUTED BY DIVIDING MILES BY
40   REM   GALLONS.
50   REM   THE RESULT IS THEN PRINTED ON THE SCREEN WITH TITLES
60   REM
70   REM   INPUT THE NUMBER OF MILES DRIVEN AND STORE IT IN A
80   REM   MEMORY LOCATION (VARIABLE) CALLED MILES.
90         PRINT "Enter the number of miles driven"
100        INPUT MILES
110  REM
120  REM   INPUT THE GALLONS USED AND STORE IT IN A MEMORY
130  REM   LOCATION CALLED GALLONS.
140        PRINT "Enter the number of gallons consumed"
150        INPUT GALLONS
160  REM
170  REM   DIVIDE GALLONS INTO MILES TO GET MILES PER GALLON AND STORE
180  REM   THIS RESULT IN ANOTHER MEMORY LOCATION CALLED MPG.
190        MPG = MILES/GALLON
200  REM
210  REM   PRINT TITLES AND THE RESULT (MPG) ON THE SCREEN
220        PRINT "               PROGRAM OUTPUT"
230        PRINT "MILES          GALLONS        MILES PER GALLON"
240        PRINT MILES,GALLONS,MPG
250  REM
260  REM   SIGNAL THE END OF THE PROGRAM WITH 'END'
270        END
```

Output

```
RUN
Enter the number of miles driven
? 125
Enter the number of gallons consumed
? 11
           PROGRAM OUTPUT
MILES   GALLONS     MILES PER GALLON
 125       11            11.36364
OK
```

FIGURE 1-4
A more complicated BASIC program and its output.

you can just hold down the CTRL key and press the PRTSC key, and everything that appears on the screen will be printed. Use the same key sequence to turn off the Print Screen option.

THE FIVE STEPS IN PREPARING A COMPUTER PROGRAM

When Sigmund Freud said "Only when one understands the problem can one attempt to solve it," he didn't know he was stating the key to writing successful computer programs. You must know what you want the computer to do before you can instruct it. For those new to computers and programming, this section is intended to clarify misconceptions about what a computer can and cannot do.

The procedures for efficient computer problem solving are summarized in the following list.

1. *Define the problem* by studying and understanding the input data, the organization (structure, content, etc.), the outputs desired, and the equations and decisions needed to go from input to output.
2. *Develop a method of solution,* called an algorithm, by drawing a pictorial or graphic representation of all the logical steps in proper sequence.
3. *Code the algorithm* in a programming language chosen on the basis of the type of problem, the computer languages and equipment available, and the needs of your environment.
4. *Run and test the program* to ensure that the results are valid and accurate. Find and remove computer language and logic errors, called bugs. Verify output results with hand-processed test data.
5. *Document the program* so that others can understand what the program does and how it does it. This is an important step because many programs must be modified or used by someone other than the author. However, unfortunately, this step is frequently overlooked, resulting in confusion and frustration.

The rest of this chapter will detail these five steps.

Define the Problem

A computer program is defined as a series of instructions that directs the computer to use specified data to solve a particular problem to produce useful information called output. This output may be a single numerical answer, a complex report, pictures or graphs, voice or music, or information on a variety of media (paper, disk, display, etc.). Before you write the instructions for a program, you must know the answers to the following questions. The answers provide the problem definition.

1. What output is desired from the program? Is it a simple numerical result? Is it a lengthy table or report? What information, aside from the computer's results, is needed to complete the output (titles, headings, special forms, etc.)? What are the possible output media (display, printer, disk, etc.), and how will the optimum one be selected?
2. What data needs to be entered into the program to give us the desired output? Is the data alphabetic, numeric, or alphanumeric (containing both numbers and letters)? From where is the data obtained (e.g., tape, disk, keyboard)? Is the data reliable, or will you need to include error routines in the program so that it will not terminate abnormally or produce useless output?
3. What calculations (formulas and equations) or data manipulations are needed to obtain the output desired? Which calculations or routines can be performed automatically by the computer, and which must be written by the programmer? Do the solutions require extreme accuracy or unusual precision, or can good approximations be used if exact formulas are not available?

Because programmers frequently write programs requested or used by others, everyone involved must agree completely on exactly what the problem consists of. To ensure thorough understanding, programmers use standard procedures to describe the problem in ways clear both to themselves and to the user (who may not be a data-processing professional). Input and output specifications like those in figures 1–5 and 1–6 help define the input needed and output expected. Usually, the programmer and the user agree what a computer report should look like and what data is available to and needed by the program.

Figure 1–5 shows that input data consists of records subdivided into fields. Each record contains information pertaining to one transaction (a sale, for example, or time card). The fields are the actual data elements such as name, address, hours worked. The fields consist of characters that can be numbers, letters, and combinations of numbers and letters. These are called numeric fields, alphabetic fields, and alphanumeric fields, respectively. The three types of fields compose one record. Many records stored or processed together make up a data file, and data files may consist of a few or thousands of records.

Field	Field Description	Type	Example
1	Employee Name	Character	John C. Jones
2	Employee Address	Character	125 Main Street
3	Hours Worked	Numeric	40.00
4	Pay Rate	Numeric	12.50
5	Tax Rate	Numeric	.25

FIGURE 1-5
Input specifications.

The output specifications usually consist of describing what results are to be printed, and where they are to appear on the output document. Titles are usually shown as they are to appear on the output, while actual results, which will be inserted in the output by the computer, are shown as x's (xxxxx) for alphabetic output, or 9's (99999) if the results are numeric. In figure 1-6 the actual output is shown for simplicity.

After agreeing on the input and output specifications, the programmer and user must arrive at the processing decisions and formulas. This may require extensive investigation (to come up with correct formulas) and elaborate decisions in case data errors or exceptional results arise. With this research complete, the programmer documents the findings. For the example shown in figures 1-5 and 1-6, the processing decisions and formulas would be:

$$\text{Gross Pay} = \text{Hours Worked} \times \text{Pay Rate}$$
$$\text{Tax} = \text{Gross} \times \text{Tax Rate}$$
$$\text{Net Pay} = \text{Gross Pay} - \text{Tax}$$

Processing decisions, such as paying an employee for 35 hours even if he or she didn't work 35 hours, might also be included.

Very simple programs such as this contain minimum information (such as a simple formula) and no provisions for recovery from data errors. More complex problems may require that many rules, formulas, decision tables, and error routines be defined.

In describing the error routines, the programmer and user describe what they want the computer to do about errors in the input data. The possibilities are infinite. Programs can be designed to tolerate nearly any data error without terminating. Erroneous data is disregarded and the program continues. This is essentially the principle of error recovery routines. Some specific rules to follow in writing these routines are listed below.

1. Do not permit one error to halt the execution of the program.
2. If possible, program the computer to correct the error or allow the user to correct the error. (This is actually done, as later chapters show).
3. Program the computer to display the erroneous record so that it can be processed later after correction or by hand.
4. Program the computer to describe what type of error it found in the data if you are using a computer language that has the means to do this.

```
                         SAMPLE PAYROLL PROGRAM

EMPLOYEE NAME    ADDRESS        HOURS    PAY RATE    GROSS PAY   TAX   NETPAY
JOHN C. JONES    125 MAIN ST    40       12.5        500         125   375
```

FIGURE 1-6
Output specifications.

5. Program the computer to print a report listing all errors encountered in the program run. This is an exception report or error report and is frequently as important as the intended output.

Not all types of data errors *can* be detected by the computer through programming logic. For example, numbers can be checked to see that they fall within a certain range—for example, a pay rate that should not exceed $99.99 per hour nor be less than $1.00 per hour. A rate outside these limits would be detected and the computer programmed to issue an error message. However, a rate of $12.50 instead of $13.50 per hour would not be as easily detected as an error.

In many companies, new programmers find such detail already prepared in their first programming assignments. However, this is not always the case. As a new programmer, you may have to research formulas and devise error recovery routines. In fact, as you advance to programmer analyst or systems analyst positions, you will notice that problem definitions become less precise. This should encourage you to become more innovative and to suggest processing alternatives.

Develop a Method of Solution

Simply defining a problem does not provide a method of solution. So, your next step is to develop a series of logical, concise steps that lead toward a solution. This series of steps is called an algorithm. Two widely used aids in developing algorithms are structure charts and flowcharts. Both structure charts and program flowcharts are usually drawn using standardized symbols and conventions, as shown in figures 1–7 and 1–8.

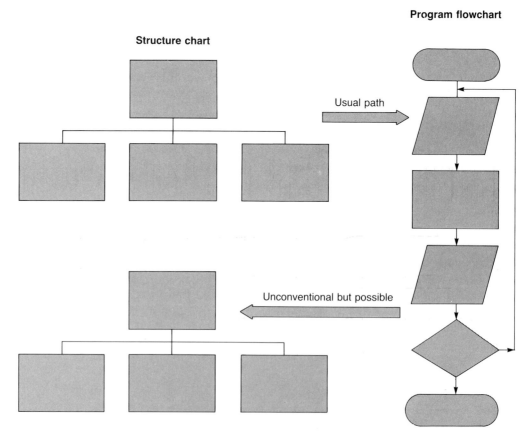

FIGURE 1–7
Structure chart and program flowchart.

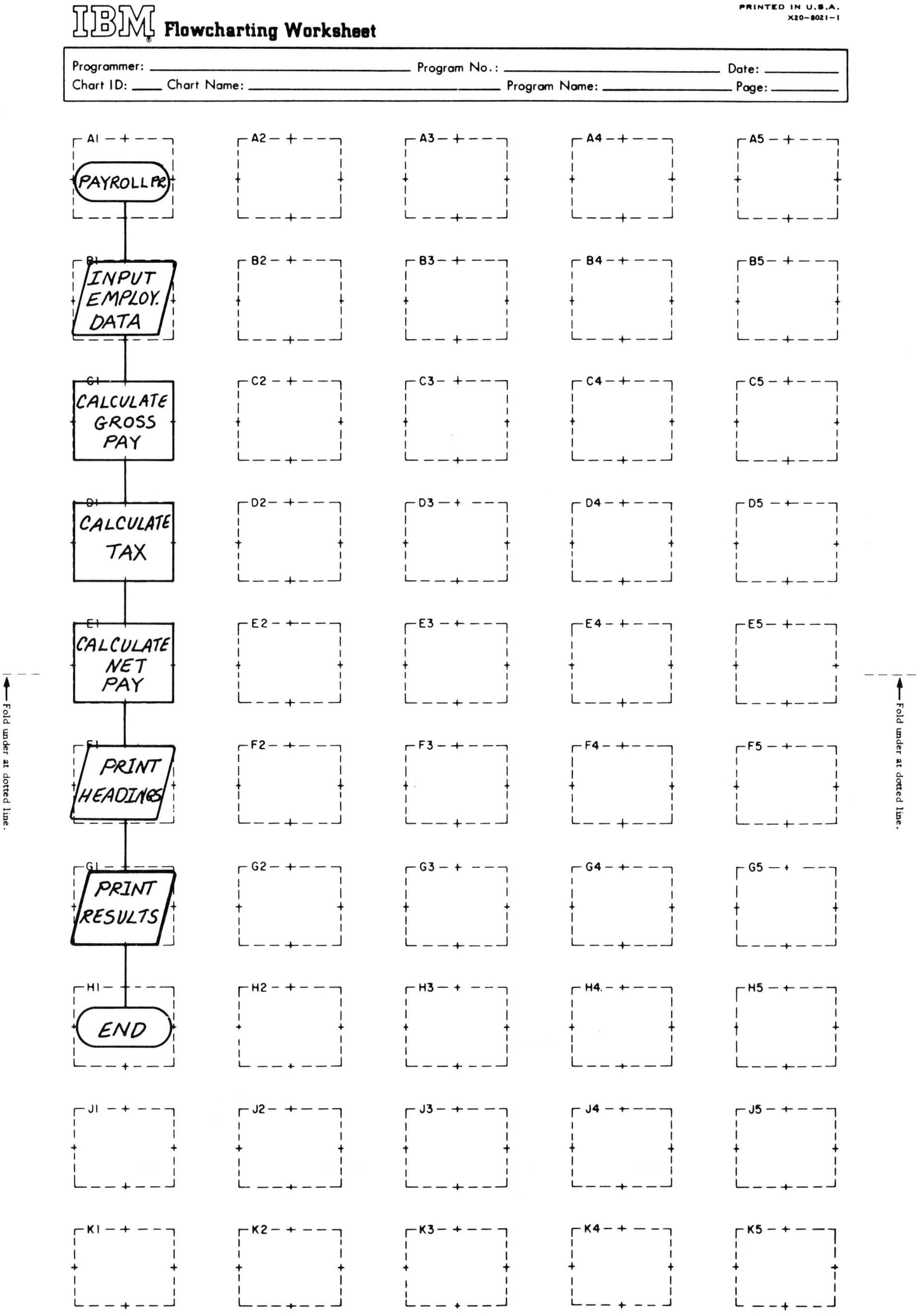

IBM Flowcharting Worksheet

| Programmer: _____ | Program No.: _____ | Date: _____ |
| Chart ID: _____ Chart Name: _____ | Program Name: _____ | Page: _____ |

A1
(PAYROLL PR)

B1
INPUT
EMPLOY.
DATA

C1
CALCULATE
GROSS
PAY

D1
CALCULATE
TAX

E1
CALCULATE
NET
PAY

F1
PRINT
HEADINGS

G1
PRINT
RESULTS

H1
(END)

Fold under at dotted line.

FIGURE 1–8
Standard program flowchart for payroll program.

17

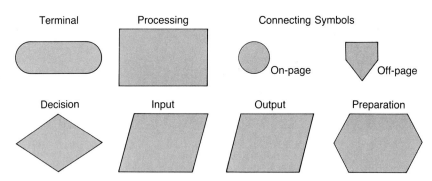

FIGURE 1–9
American National Standards Institute flowchart symbols.

Structure charting is a way of representing the key parts of an algorithm in organizational chart form. It is known by two popular names: VTOC (Visual Table of Contents) or PHC (Program Hierarchy Charts). Structure charts evolved with the science of structured problem solving (breaking a complex problem into modules, each with a particular function or objective). Structure charts are used to show the general steps that will be needed to solve a programming problem.

On the other hand, flowcharts are used to express in detail how and when the general steps in the structure chart will be accomplished. The program flowchart shows all the key steps in a program or process with standardized symbols that have precise meanings. The term *flow* indicates that there is a direction of logic from top to bottom and left to right on such a chart. For many years this was how algorithms developed. Currently, the program flowchart evolves from the VTOC or other structure chart.

Many symbols used in structure charts and flowcharts have been standardized by the American National Standards Institute (as shown in figure 1–9) and within companies.

Standard program flowcharts have been the primary communications link between a programmer and the user. They are among the most widely used graphic algorithmic techniques and a programmer may spend many more hours on developing it than in writing the actual program. This flowchart helps develop the logic of the program by reducing complex problems to finite ordered steps. For example, look at the flowchart of a nonprogrammable problem in figure 1–10. Note how the complex process is subdivided into concise, logical steps having a sequential relationship to one another.

Flowcharting is invaluable in the early stages of programming. You need training in logic not because you are illogical, but because you probably are not used to expressing, in detail, all the logical and inferential aptitudes you have as a human being. However, flowcharting doesn't make you logical; rather, it simply reflects how logical you already are! With time and practice you may find that flowcharting is a great aid in solving difficult problems because you may need to develop algorithms with complex logical alternatives. The proper combination of VTOC charts and standard flowcharts greatly reduces a programmer's design and testing problems in most business environments.

Code the Algorithm

Flowchart symbols and structure show the steps and the sequence of tasks needed to solve a problem. Discussion of what each symbol means and how the programmer translates each into a programming language starts in chapter 2 and continues in the case studies in each of the subsequent chapters. For now, you just need to know that each symbol ultimately becomes one or more program instructions in BASIC. This step of converting a symbol to a command is called coding. BASIC programmers write code on a standard form like that shown in figure 1–11, which makes it easier to type into the computer.

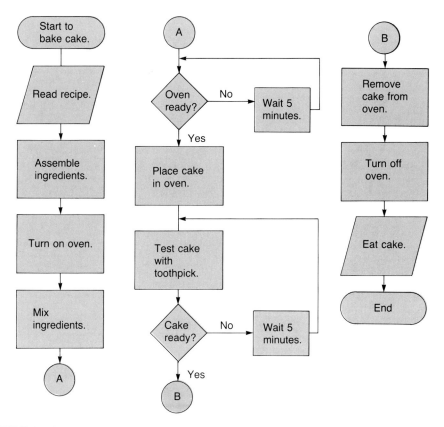

FIGURE 1-10
Flowchart for baking a cake.

Often a programmer needs only to consult a program library for an acceptable algorithm. However, many problems are unique, and in these cases the programmer must develop the algorithm. Beginners are wise to write their own algorithms to develop technique and proficiency in this crucial skill. You will find, for example, that a number of the case study problems in this text have long been solved in the literature and you may feel tempted to search out these solutions rather than work them out yourself. However, you should avoid this temptation because you will deprive yourself of the training to think logically. Of course, you can compare your solution's creativity and logic to that of the published solution's after you have given the problem your best effort.

Run and Test the Program

A newly written program will usually contain errors. So, for programmers, running and testing programs can be intensely frustrating because they want to believe the computer has done something wrong. However, computers rarely make errors, and the computer usually tells us to disregard its results in such instances. You should overcome the desire to look elsewhere for the error: it is almost certainly a human error. (Specific errors and how to deal with them will be covered in the next section.)

Document the Program

Although it is often overlooked at many computer installations, documenting the program is an important step in program development. Most computer programs are never really completed, and, therefore, if another programmer is to make revisions, documentation is critical.

19

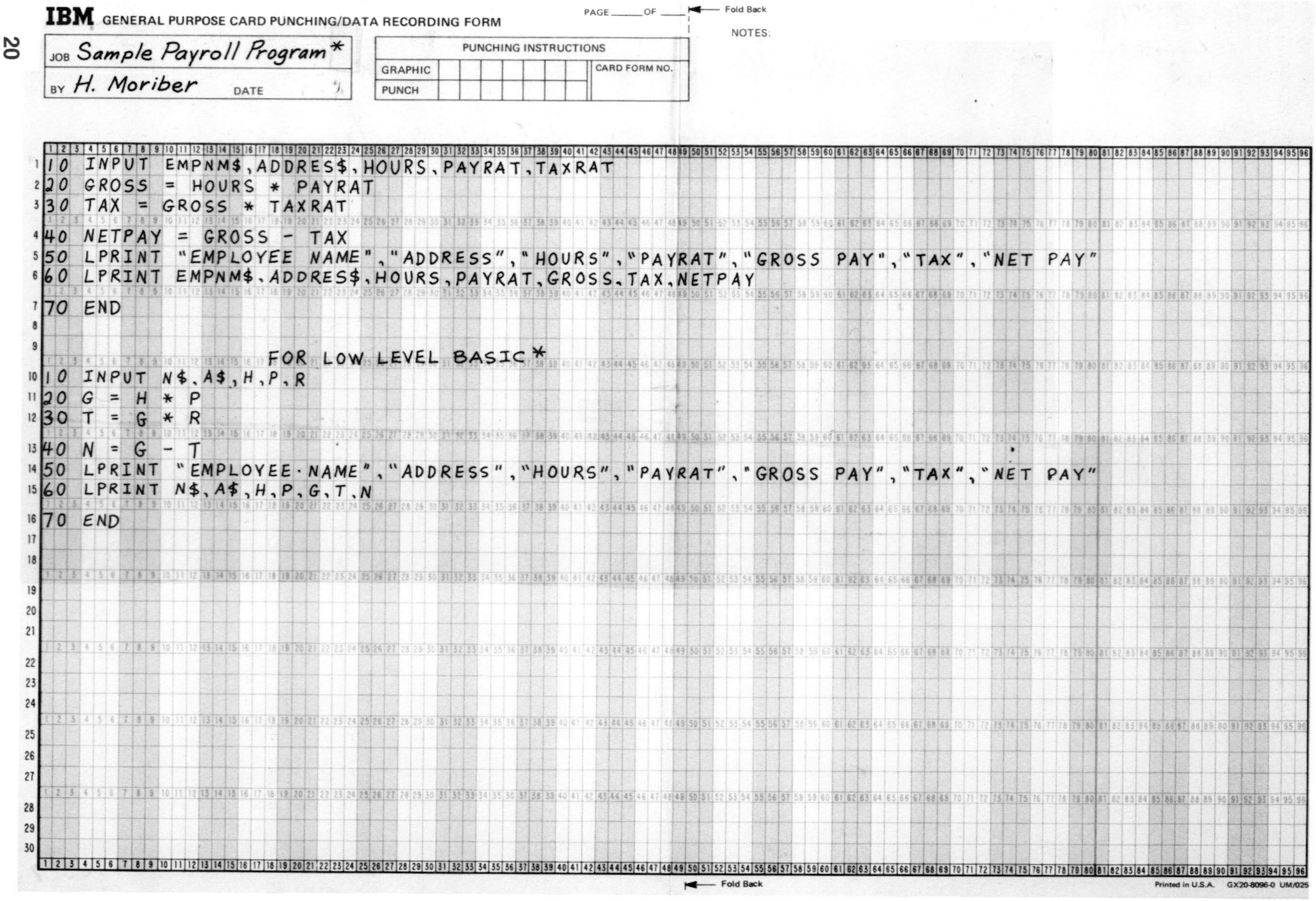

IBM GENERAL PURPOSE CARD PUNCHING/DATA RECORDING FORM

PAGE ____ OF ____ — Fold Back

NOTES:

JOB Sample Payroll Program*

BY H. Moriber DATE

PUNCHING INSTRUCTIONS — GRAPHIC / PUNCH — CARD FORM NO.

```
10 INPUT EMPNM$,ADDRES$,HOURS,PAYRAT,TAXRAT
20 GROSS = HOURS * PAYRAT
30 TAX = GROSS * TAXRAT
40 NETPAY = GROSS - TAX
50 LPRINT "EMPLOYEE NAME","ADDRESS","HOURS","PAYRAT","GROSS PAY","TAX","NET PAY"
60 LPRINT EMPNM$,ADDRES$,HOURS,PAYRAT,GROSS,TAX,NETPAY
70 END

          FOR LOW LEVEL BASIC*
10 INPUT N$,A$,H,P,R
20 G = H * P
30 T = G * R
40 N = G - T
50 LPRINT "EMPLOYEE NAME","ADDRESS","HOURS","PAYRAT","GROSS PAY","TAX","NET PAY"
60 LPRINT N$,A$,H,P,G,T,N
70 END
```

Fold Back

Printed in U.S.A. GX20-8096-0 UM/025

FIGURE 1–11
Coding form.

There are many conventions for documenting programs, depending on the preferences of those responsible. It is always a good idea to provide VTOCs and flowcharts as documentation for your programs and to clearly document within the program itself by using REM statements. These statements are not executed by the computer, but are intended to be used for internal program documentation.

COMMON PROGRAMMING ERRORS

The four most common types of programming errors are system command errors, syntax errors, data errors, and logic errors. These are illustrated in a simple BASIC payroll program modeled after the example in figure 1–11. Figures 1–12 through 1–15 show the effects of the four types of errors on program results.

You may wish to verify these results with your own computer system. (At this point do not be concerned with specific BASIC instructions in the program; these are described in detail in chapters 2, 3, and 4.)

```
Input

OK
10      REM     SAMPLE PAYROLL PROGRAM TO ILLUSTRATE SYSTEM COMMAND ERROR
20      REM
30      REM     VARIABLES USED:
40      REM
50      REM             N$ = EMPLOYEE NAME
60      REM             A$ = EMPLOYEE'S ADDRESS
70      REM             H  = HOURS WORKED
80      REM             P  = HOURLY PAY RATE
90      REM             R  = TAX RATE
100     REM             G  = GROSS PAY
110     REM             T  = TAX
120     REM             N  = NET (TAKE-HOME) PAY
130     REM
140         INPUT "ENTER EMPLOYEE NAME          ";N$
150         INPUT "ENTER EMPLOYEE ADDRESS       ";A$
160         INPUT "ENTER HOURS WORKED           ";H
170         INPUT "ENTER PAY RATE ($/HOUR)      ";P
180         INPUT "ENTER TAX RATE AS DECIMAL    ";R
190         G = H * P
200         T = G * R
210         N = G - T
220         PRINT
230         PRINT "         PROGRAM OUTPUT FOLLOWS"
240         PRINT "EMPLOYEE NAME    ";N$
250         PRINT "ADDRESS          ";A$
260         PRINT "HOURS WORKED     ";H
270         PRINT "PAY RATE         ";P
280         PRINT "TAX RATE         ";R
290         PRINT "GROSS PAY =    $ ";G
300         PRINT "TAX       =    $ ";T
310         PRINT "NET PAY   =    $ ";N

Output

RUM
SYNTAX ERROR
```

FIGURE 1–12
System command error—BASIC RUN command misspelled.

21

Input

```
10    REM  SAMPLE PAYROLL PROGRAM TO ILLUSTRATE SYSTEM COMMAND ERROR
20    REM
30    REM  VARIABLES USED:
40    REM
50    REM           N$ = EMPLOYEE NAME
60    REM           A$ = EMPLOYEE'S ADDRESS
70    REM           H  = HOURS WORKED
80    REM           P  = HOURLY PAY RATE
90    REM           R  = TAX RATE
100   REM           G  = GROSS PAY
110   REM           T  = TAX
120   REM           N  = NET (TAKE-HOME) PAY
130   REM
140        IMPUT "ENTER EMPLOYEE NAME        ";N$
150        INPUT "ENTER EMPLOYEE ADDRESS     ";A$
160        INPUT "ENTER HOURS WORKED         ";H
170        INPUT "ENTER PAY RATE ($/HOUR)    ";P
180        INPUT "ENTER TAX RATE AS DECIMAL  ";R
190        G = H * P
200        T = G * R
210        N = G - T
220        PRINT
230        PRINT "        PROGRAM OUTPUT FOLLOWS"
240        PRINT "EMPLOYEE NAME    ";N$
250        PRINT "ADDRESS          ";A$
260        PRINT "HOURS WORKED     ";H
270        PRINT "PAY RATE         ";P
280        PRINT "TAX RATE         ";R
290        PRINT "GROSS PAY = $ ";G
300        PRINT "TAX       = $ ";T
310        PRINT "NET PAY   = $ ";N
```

Output

```
RUN
140        INPUT "ENTER EMPLOYEE NAME        ";N$  Syntax error in 140
```

FIGURE 1–13
System command error—syntax error.

When a BASIC system command error occurs, you have not clearly defined what is to be done by the computer (run, list, save, etc.). BASIC system command errors prevent program execution or perform incorrect loading or saving of programs because the computer does not recognize what you want to do (see figure 1–12). You can correct these errors by studying your BASIC and system manual to determine the correct commands.

Syntax errors are errors in spelling or grammar of BASIC instructions. Syntax errors (see figure 1–13) prevent the computer from executing your program because the compiler or interpreter cannot understand what one or more instructions mean. Syntax errors can be typing mistakes, incorrect punctuation, key words in the wrong sequence, or incorrect spacing in a program statement.

Data errors occur when you use wrong numbers, letters, or letters instead of numbers. Data errors (see figure 1–14) prevent the computer from producing the correct output, although the program will run. Later chapters discuss how to correct data errors, but essentially, *you* must verify that the results are correct. You should not assume that just because your program produces a result or output that it is correct.

```
Input

10    REM    SAMPLE PAYROLL PROGRAM TO ILLUSTRATE DATA ERROR
20    REM
30    REM    VARIABLES USED:
40    REM
50    REM              N$ = EMPLOYEE NAME
60    REM              A$ = EMPLOYEE'S ADDRESS
70    REM              H  = HOURS WORKED
80    REM              P  = HOURLY PAY RATE
90    REM              R  = TAX RATE
100   REM              G  = GROSS PAY
110   REM              T  = TAX
120   REM              N  = NET (TAKE-HOME) PAY
130   REM
140          INPUT "ENTER EMPLOYEE NAME           ";N$
150          INPUT "ENTER EMPLOYEE ADDRESS        ";A$
160          INPUT "ENTER HOURS WORKED            ";H
170          INPUT "ENTER PAY RATE ($/HOUR)       ";P
180          INPUT "ENTER TAX RATE AS DECIMAL     ";R
190          G = H * P
200          T = G * R
210          N = G - T
220          PRINT
230          PRINT "        PROGRAM OUTPUT FOLLOWS"
240          PRINT "EMPLOYEE NAME     ";N$
250          PRINT "ADDRESS           ";A$
260          PRINT "HOURS WORKED      ";H
270          PRINT "PAY RATE          ";P
280          PRINT "TAX RATE          ";R
290          PRINT "GROSS PAY =    $ ";G
300          PRINT "TAX       =    $ ";T
310          PRINT "NET PAY   =    $ ";N


Output

RUN
ENTER EMPLOYEE NAME          ? JOHN C. JONES
ENTER EMPLOYEE ADDRESS       ? 125 MAIN STREET
ENTER HOURS WORKED           ? 40
?Redo from start               ↑
ENTER HOURS WORKED           ? |
                               |
```

O (oh) instead of 0 (zero) was entered, causing execution to terminate and a request for new data to be made

FIGURE 1–14
System command error—data error.

Logic errors are mistakes in formulas, order of instructions, general format, and so on. The cause of an error is often difficult to find if the mistake is due to faulty logic. Using an incorrect formula, translating a correct formula incorrectly, using a correct formula out of sequence, using an incorrect command, or any one of hundreds of possible errors in the desired sequence of instructions can cause a logic error (see figure 1–15). Ironically, the more quickly you progress from command, syntax, and data errors to logic errors, the better you are doing. However, developing proficiency in finding logic errors is critical to programming success, and is not at all simple.

```
Input

10      REM   SAMPLE PAYROLL PROGRAM TO ILLUSTRATE LOGIC ERROR
20      REM
30      REM   VARIABLES USED:
40      REM
50      REM              N$  = EMPLOYEE NAME
60      REM              A$  = EMPLOYEE'S ADDRESS
70      REM              H   = HOURS WORKED
80      REM              P   = HOURLY PAY RATE
90      REM              R   = TAX RATE
100     REM              G   = GROSS PAY
110     REM              T   = TAX
120     REM              N   = NET (TAKE-HOME) PAY
130     REM
140          INPUT "ENTER EMPLOYEE NAME            ";N$
150          INPUT "ENTER EMPLOYEE ADDRESS         ";A$
160          INPUT "ENTER HOURS WORKED             ";H
170          INPUT "ENTER PAY RATE ($/HOUR)        ";P
180          INPUT "ENTER TAX RATE AS DECIMAL      ";R
190          N = G - T
200          T = N * R        ⟵——Formulas in incorrect logical order
210          G = H * P
220          PRINT
230          PRINT "          PROGRAM OUTPUT FOLLOWS"
240          PRINT "EMPLOYEE NAME    ";N$
250          PRINT "ADDRESS          ";A$
260          PRINT "HOURS WORKED     ";H
270          PRINT "PAY RATE         ";P
280          PRINT "TAX RATE         ";R
290          PRINT "GROSS PAY =   $ ";G
300          PRINT "TAX       =   $ ";T
310          PRINT "NET PAY   =   $ ";N


Output

RUN
ENTER EMPLOYEE NAME          ? JOHN C. JONES
ENTER EMPLOYEE ADDRESS       ? 125 MAIN STREET
ENTER HOURS WORKED           ? 40
ENTER PAY RATE ($/HOUR)      ? 12.50
ENTER TAX RATE AS DECIMAL    ? .25
          PROGRAM OUTPUT FOLLOWS
EMPLOYEE NAME    JOHN C. JONES
ADDRESS          125 MAIN STREET
HOURS WORKED        40
PAY RATE            12.5
TAX RATE            .25
GROSS PAY =     $ 500
TAX       =     $ 0
NET PAY   =     $ 500
OK
```

FIGURE 1–15
System command error—logic error.

You can use three methods to find logic errors.

1. Go over the program statement by statement, calculating, branching, and looping just as if the computer were executing the program. When using this method of correcting errors (debugging), you can use test data that produces a known result. If you do not reach the correct answer, then you have a logic error. If the program has many deci-

sions and calculations, you should check intermediate results. Usually this pinpoints the incorrect formula or decision.

2. To detect logic errors in long and complex programs where it may not be practical to analyze a program statement by statement, you can insert instructions at key points in the program to tell the computer to print out the answers to formulas within the program. From these you may be able to determine how far the program progressed before it produced incorrect results. PRINT statements can also be placed temporarily in the program to indicate at what point the program stopped executing. For example, if a program stopped executing at a statement containing the formula $A = B/C$, you could place a PRINT instruction before the statement containing the formula to determine if B and C contained reasonable values. For example, if $C = 0$, the program would stop running since the value of A would be infinite.

3. Use one of the debugging aids provided by computer software manufacturers to help trace the execution of your program. These aids can usually be called in to help you by using certain special commands of your operating system or within your program itself. The aids generally provide an indication of the path of execution and some even permit you to see the contents of the computer's memory at the time execution stopped. The most widely used of these aids is called the TRace ON option (TRON), and it will be discussed in later chapters.

Figure 1–16 shows a correct program with output.

Once the program has been tested and debugged (a term that means all errors have been removed), it must be verified and documented. Verification is usually done in testing, since the test data's results are known. The user or analyst often provides the programmer test data specifications like those shown below.

```
JOHN C.JONES,125 MAIN ST.,45.00,12.50,.25

MARY B. SMITH,2 SOUTH ST.,40.00,17.50,.33
```

Often the calculations are done by hand and compared with the results produced by the computer. This procedure is recommended for all assigned problems.

As you begin programming, remember that a computer does only three things: (1) recalls information with perfect accuracy; (2) performs mathematical calculations with incredible speed; and (3) stores a large amount of information for nearly instantaneous retrieval. A programmer can write instructions that permit a computer to perform all three of these activities in one program; however, the beginning business programs in the text generally stress each of these activities in different programs. Beginning with chapter 7, you will see all three operations performed in the case programs as the problems become more realistic and complex.

A FEW SUGGESTIONS BEFORE YOU BEGIN WRITING PROGRAMS

The first few programming examples are meant to be simple. In fact, you could find the results without a computer in a fraction of the time it would take to write the programs. Careful planning, logical design, and meticulous attention to detail are not easily learned. So, where and how do you begin? These questions stump not only the beginner, but professionals as well.

First, *be patient*. Learning a programming language is very much like learning to speak a foreign language. It requires lots of studying and practice. Practice is the key in programming. The more time you spend working on your computer programs, the better you will get.

Second, *avoid the temptation to blame mistakes,* faulty output, and incorrect answers from your programs *on the computer.* Remember that it has simply followed your instructions, and if there is an error, most likely *you, not the computer,* made it.

Input

```
10    REM    SAMPLE PAYROLL PROGRAM CORRECTED AND ERROR FREE
20    REM
30    REM    VARIABLES USED:
40    REM
50    REM            N$ = EMPLOYEE NAME
60    REM            A$ = EMPLOYEE'S ADDRESS
70    REM            H  = HOURS WORKED
80    REM            P  = HOURLY PAY RATE
90    REM            R  = TAX RATE
100   REM            G  = GROSS PAY
110   REM            T  = TAX
120   REM            N  = NET (TAKE-HOME) PAY
130   REM
140        INPUT "ENTER EMPLOYEE NAME          ";N$
150        INPUT "ENTER EMPLOYEE ADDRESS       ";A$
160        INPUT "ENTER HOURS WORKED           ";H
170        INPUT "ENTER PAY RATE ($/HOUR)      ";P
180        INPUT "ENTER TAX RATE AS DECIMAL    ";R
190        G = H * P
200        T = G * R
210        N = G - T
220        PRINT
230        PRINT "        PROGRAM OUTPUT FOLLOWS"
240        PRINT "EMPLOYEE NAME    ";N$
250        PRINT "ADDRESS          ";A$
260        PRINT "HOURS WORKED     ";H
270        PRINT "PAY RATE         ";P
280        PRINT "TAX RATE         ";R
290        PRINT "GROSS PAY =    $ ";G
300        PRINT "TAX       =    $ ";T
310        PRINT "NET PAY   =    $ ";N
```

Output

```
RUN
ENTER EMPLOYEE NAME          ? JOHN C. JONES
ENTER EMPLOYEE ADDRESS       ? 125 MAIN STREET
ENTER HOURS WORKED           ? 40
ENTER PAY RATE ($/HOUR)      ? 12.50
ENTER TAX RATE AS DECIMAL    ? .25
           PROGRAM OUTPUT FOLLOWS
EMPLOYEE NAME    JOHN C. JONES
ADDRESS          125 MAIN STREET
HOURS WORKED     40
PAY RATE         12.5
TAX RATE         .25
GROSS PAY =    $ 500
TAX       =    $ 125
NET PAY   =    $ 375
OK
```

FIGURE 1–16
Correct, error-free program.

Third, *resist the temptation to immediately ask another person for help* if your program is not working correctly. The more time *you* spend debugging your programs, the better you will get at finding your own (and other programmers') errors. The ability to debug a program is just as important as the ability to write it. *Both* skills take practice.

Finally, if you get stumped and can't solve a programming problem or eliminate a bug in your program, *take a break for a while*. If you clear your mind and then come back to the problem, the solution is often apparent.

SUMMARY

The microcomputer is creating a revolution in the way information and data are processed in homes, businesses, and schools. Enhancements of the BASIC programming language now make it possible to employ this language in a wide range of important and realistic applications. BASIC is no longer merely a language used to teach programming; rather, it can be used to produce sophisticated business systems and solve a wide variety of complex calculations.

BASIC has been revised by the American National Standards Institute and is now a fully structured language. This should reduce the number of BASIC dialects so that the BASIC programs written on most microcomputer and minicomputer systems will be compatible with one another. This fully structured language contains the needed statements for true structured design programs. Many manufacturers are already supporting enhanced, structured BASIC.

Programming the computer to solve a problem involves five steps: (1) define the problem; (2) develop a method of solution; (3) code the solution (algorithm); (4) test and debug the program; and (5) document the program.

A computer program is a logical series of instructions that directs a computer to solve a particular problem by using available input to produce useful output. In developing the program, a complete problem definition is used to simplify and standardize the programming process. The definition includes input and output specifications, processing decisions and formulas, error recovery routine specifications, and a validation procedure. In addition, two popular graphical representations of the structured program algorithm are used: the visual table of contents (VTOC) chart and the program flowchart.

VTOC chart and program flowchart preparation methods have been standardized. Special forms and symbols are used to describe the essential parts of the computer program. Also, special coding sheets are used to write down the BASIC statements in the program for easy entry into the computer system.

Testing and debugging programs is a crucial step. To ensure proper results, validation and verification procedures (along with appropriate test data) are provided on validation and test data worksheets. Since many different types of errors can prevent a computer program from executing properly, four of the most common types of errors must be recognized: (1) system command errors; (2) syntax errors; (3) data errors; and (4) logic errors. Learning to eliminate errors, which can be a challenging task, is a crucial part of programming.

Once a program is designed, coded, and tested, it should be documented so that other programmers can maintain and modify it easily. Documentation consists of assembling the problem definition, the program listing, and the program output plus any program run instructions in an easily understood format.

Writing instructions for the computer in BASIC is a much more tedious task than writing instructions for people. Computers cannot infer or guess, but must be given instructions that are letter perfect. The computer cannot solve any problem that the programmer does not understand.

REVIEW QUESTIONS

1. Describe some of the ways in which microcomputers and the BASIC programming language are contributing to a revolution in data processing.
2. Describe some of the features of BASIC that have caused its increased popularity.
3. Describe some of the problems arising from the current nonstandard nature of the BASIC used by many microcomputer systems.

4. What agency is responsible for the standardization of computer programming languages and what efforts are currently being made to standardize BASIC?

5. Define the term *computer program*.

6. Name and describe the five key phases in preparing a computer program.

7. What are the function and purpose of the problem definition?

8. Describe why input and output specifications are important to the programmer and program user.

9. Who is responsible for determining the formulas and decisions to be incorporated in a computer program? Why is it beneficial to list these?

10. Why are error recovery routines essential in a computer program?

11. Describe the features of a comprehensive error recovery routine in a computer program.

12. What are the two most widely used graphical methods for developing a program algorithm (method of solution)?

13. Compare and contrast structure charts and flowcharts.

14. Describe the coding step in preparing a computer program. Why is it helpful to write the program in a standard coding sheet?

15. Why is it necessary to test a computer program?

16. Name the four most common types of errors encountered during a computer program test.

17. For each of the types of errors referred to in question 16, what methods can be used to eliminate or reduce the possibility of an occurrence of such an error?

18. Define the term *program documentation* and list all of the items usually included in a properly documented program.

19. Why is program documentation important?

20. Why is the documentation step frequently overlooked? How does overlooking it cause problems?

21. Compare and contrast the ways in which people and computers follow instructions.

22. Do you think it is possible for computers to be programmed to solve every type of problem?

23. The responsibility for an error-free computer program rests with the programmer. How does this fact relate to the instances of ''computer error'' frequently encountered.

CHAPTER TWO

STRUCTURED DESIGN PROBLEM SOLVING

OUTLINE

INTRODUCTION TO STRUCTURED DESIGN
The Outline and Structured Design | Cue-Card Outlines and Structure Charts | The Visual Table of Contents (VTOC) | Advantages of Structured Design | Structured vs. Standard Design Programming

APPLYING STRUCTURED DESIGN WITH VTOCs TO PROBLEM SOLVING
Coding the Program | Structured Program Conventions

LEARNING OBJECTIVES

Upon completion of this chapter, you will be able to:

☐ Understand the concepts of structured design problem solving.

☐ Understand the relationship between outlines, structure charts, and VTOCs.

☐ Develop your own VTOC charts for manual and computer problems.

☐ Understand the advantages of structured design compared to standard design problem solving.

☐ Apply structured design problem-solving principles to a simple computer program.

INTRODUCTION TO STRUCTURED DESIGN

Writing a computer program with a structured design is very much like writing an outline for a speech or paper. In such an outline, you can break down the main topic into subtopics, which are then subdivided into even more detailed subtopics. By doing this, you are able to determine the proper order of subtopics, and you can include as many relevant details as you wish. Structured design in programming accomplishes these same objectives, and the result is a clearly written, organized computer program. This chapter begins by discussing the outline form as it relates to structured design and ends by showing you how structured design helps in writing computer programs.

The Outline and Structured Design

To illustrate how an outline works, suppose that you are going to prepare a speech or paper on how to write a computer program. The five main parts will be those discussed in chapter 1:

1. Define the problem.
2. Develop a method of solution (algorithm).
3. Code the algorithm into a computer language.
4. Test the program.
5. Document the program.

Each of the five subtopics will have a number of secondary concepts. For example, within "Define the problem," you will have "Define the inputs"; "Define the processing decisions and formulas"; and "Define the outputs." Finally, within each of these subparts you will have more specific breakdowns. For example, you might break down "Define the inputs" into "Input media" (e.g., disk, tape, keyboard, etc.) and "Description of input data" (e.g., alphabetic or numeric).

If you use a well-known scheme to organize the material, you should get an outline that looks like that in figure 2–1, where:

Roman numerals are the main topics	I. Define the problem
Letters are the subordinate topics	A. Inputs
Arabic numerals are the details	1. type of input media
	2. description of input data

In the outline shown in figure 2–1, notice how easy it is to get an overall picture of what it takes to write a computer program by looking at the topics labeled with Roman numerals. Also, note that each topic is concisely defined by the subordinate items that are labeled with capital letters. Finally, the details comprising each subordinate item, which are indicated by numbers, serve to complete each main topic.

Cue-Card Outlines and Structure Charts

In addition to helping you plan a speech or paper, the outline also can help you *write* the paper or deliver the speech. Many professional speakers will transfer an outline to cue cards, as shown in figure 2–2. The cue-card method permits quick, easy reference to the main topics and subtopics. It is especially useful in political discussions or debates, where the audience (or opponents) may alter a planned sequence of topics by asking questions. The speaker need only find or remember the appropriate card to help answer the questions.

The Visual Table of Contents (VTOC)

If you take the cue-card outline cards and arrange them in order from left to right, you will arrive at a configuration remarkably similar to the visual table of contents (VTOC) chart

I. Define the problem
    A. Inputs
        1. type of input media (e.g., keyboard, disk, tape, etc.)
        2. description of input fields (e.g., alphabetic or numeric)
    B. Processing decisions and formulas
        1. formulas needed to arrive at output
        2. when to use each formula
        3. procedures in case of errors
    C. Outputs
        1. types of output media (e.g., printer, display, etc.)
        2. description of titles
        3. description of output fields (e.g., alphabetic, numeric)
II. Develop a method of solution
    A. Draw a pictorial representation
        1. visual table of contents (VTOC) chart
        2. structured program flowcharts
    B. Review all logical steps
        1. check logical flow, step to step
III. Code the algorithm into a computer language
    A. Select the programming language
        1. type of problem (e.g., scientific, business, etc.)
        2. hardware considerations
    B. Write the program
        1. sketch the program out
        2. write the program on coding sheet
IV. Test the program
    A. Obtain test data
        1. realistic data for actual results
        2. data to test error conditions
    B. Test run program to find errors
        1. system command errors
        2. syntax errors
        3. data errors
        4. logic errors
    C. Debug the program
        1. hand calculate and verify results
        2. ''dummy'' output statements
        3. standard debugging aids
V. Document the program
    A. Problem definition
        1. input specifications
        2. output specifications
        3. processing decisions and formulas
        4. test data
        5. error recovery routines
        6. validation procedure
    B. Algorithm
        1. visual table of contents (VTOC) chart
        2. structured program flowcharts
    C. Solution
        1. program listing
        2. program output
    D. validation
        1. ''hand-calculated'' results
        2. results with known data

FIGURE 2–1
Outline for how to write a computer program.

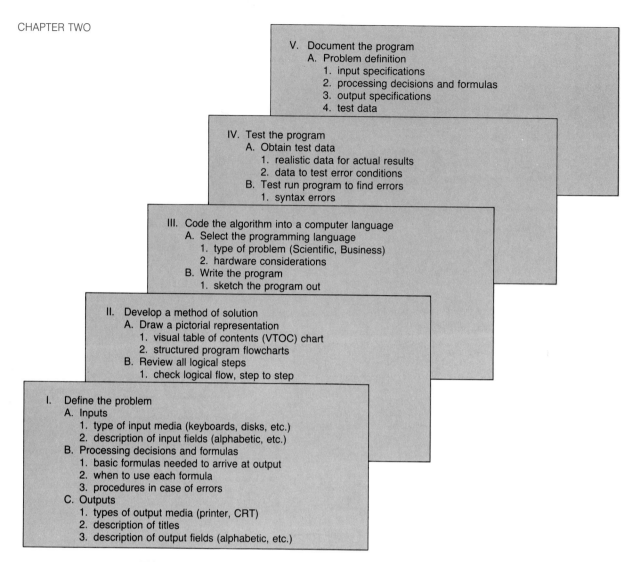

FIGURE 2–2
Cue-card outline.

used extensively in structured design programming. With the addition of a few conventions and an elaboration of the subtopics using individual symbols, you can make the chart look almost exactly like the VTOC. The conventions are as follows:

1. Assign a level number 0 to the main title.
2. Assign a level number 1 to the key topics that were previously indicated with Roman numerals.
3. Assign a level number 2 to those subtopics previously indicated by capital letters.
4. Assign a level number 3 to those individual contributing items with numbers.

Figure 2–3 illustrates the cue-card chart without these conventions and figure 2–4 shows the same chart with standard VTOC chart conventions. As you can see, the differences are relatively minor.

Structured design as applied to computer problem solving may seem like a new technique, but, as you can see, the principles upon which it is founded have been used long before the need for programming even existed.

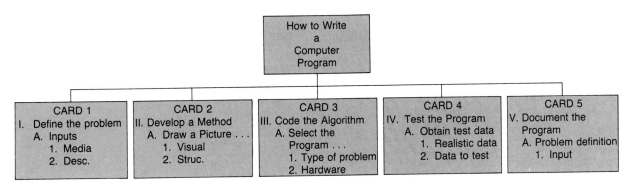

FIGURE 2–3
The cue-card structure chart.

Advantages of Structured Design

Whether you construct your outline nongraphically, as shown in figure 2–1, or in the graphical VTOC manner, as shown in figure 2–4, you have a means to logically organize your thoughts. Furthermore, by organizing a project into main tasks and subtasks, you are less likely to omit an important step.

    The concept of structured design is relatively new in the field of programming. The need for it arose mainly because of the ever-increasing complexity of business data processing systems which makes it virtually impossible for one programmer to design and develop such a system without assistance.

Structured vs. Standard Design Programming

Like an outline, structured programming follows the principles of modular design in that it consists of a main program that calls upon subroutines to perform individual tasks needed to accomplish the goal of the program. This design improves self-documentation, reduces

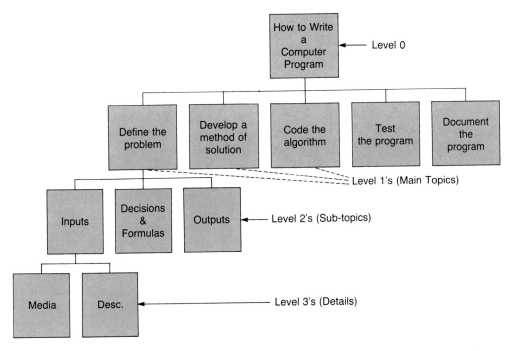

FIGURE 2–4
The cue-card structure chart with VTOC conventions.

design and testing time, and permits the division of labor and the delegation of responsibility, which is important for large programs.

By contrast, a standard design program is not modular, but instead consists of a continuous sequence of instructions not grouped for specific tasks. Standard design programming is most useful when you are developing short, simple programs where the logic is straightforward and there are only a few steps. In fact, a simple program that requires only a few instructions in standard design requires many more instructions in structured design. However, most functional, realistic computer programs do not fall into this category.

If structured design techniques are not followed for typical business programs that require hundreds of statements, they usually suffer serious shortcomings in design, coding, testing, modification, and documentation. The programmer is free to determine in what sequence he or she will code routines and in what sequence these routines will be placed in the program. Thus, sometimes essential routines are omitted and important details overlooked, especially in programs that include elaborate branching and looping instructions. (Branching and looping will be discussed in detail in later chapters.)

When you use structured design, your program flowchart (from chapter 1) is supplemented with a structured chart, which divides the program into its major functional modules. These modules, in turn, are divided into their subordinate modules, and so on. The structured chart displays all of the modules in the program and shows the relationships between them. It is used as a guide for coding. You should have one subroutine in the program for each module in the structured chart.

The benefits of structured programming become most obvious at the testing stage. The structured program is almost guaranteed to have fewer bugs than the standard design program, and bugs present are likely to be simple spelling or syntax errors rather than complex logic errors. Errors will be relatively easy to find and correct because you can examine modules independently. As each new module is added to the others in the program, if it contains an error it is reasonably easy to find so you can correct it. A standard design program is tested in its entirety regardless of the number of bugs it contains, making these errors much more difficult to isolate and correct.

Structured programs also increase programmer productivity. It is often necessary to make changes rapidly in computer programs in order to meet the changing needs of businesses. With structured design, such changes can be accomplished by simply adding, eliminating, or modifying a subroutine within the program rather than rewriting the entire program.

Structured design also provides more complete documentation because structured charts are by nature more thorough than standard program flowcharts, and a modular program is much easier to follow. This is particularly important in large businesses where over 90 percent of programs are maintained or revised by a programmer other than the person who originally wrote the program!

So, although a structured program requires more lines of written instruction than an equivalent program written in standard design, its overall superiority makes it a more practical means of both designing and writing computer programs. For a programmer to be marketable in today's business environment, he or she *must* know structured design.

APPLYING STRUCTURED DESIGN WITH VTOCs TO PROBLEM SOLVING

Structured problem solving entails taking a complex task and breaking it down into subtasks. Each subtask is then divided into smaller tasks so that all uncertainty about how to get the overall job done is eventually removed. The procedure is the same whether you are creating an involved computer program or writing a series of instructions on how to build a sailboat.

To illustrate the process of structured problem solving, apply it to housecleaning, which is, on one hand, very simple because you have probably practiced it, yet, on the other hand, is quite complex because it requires the performance of a great number of tasks in some specific order. You can either approach this routine in a random fashion, or you can perform the tasks in a step-by-step sequence that allows you to get the job done efficiently and without omission.

To begin your routine, you can make a partial list of housecleaning tasks, but not concern yourself with their logical order. Instead, you can merely write down the tasks, as shown below.

1. Vacuum carpet in living room and bedroom
2. Dust furniture in living room and bedroom
3. Clean windows in living room, bedroom, and dining room
4. Clean TV and stereo in living room
5. Make bed in bedroom
6. Clean floors in kitchen, bathroom, and dining room
7. Clean appliances in kitchen
8. Clean sink in bathroom
9. Clean shower in bathroom
10. Clean tables and chairs in dining room

Table 2–1 shows how subdividing the job into room-by-room instructions helps ensure that all of the tasks are performed. This structured approach to housecleaning is clearly more detailed than the standard list shown above.

Notice how the VTOC chart in figure 2–5 gives an overview of this complex task of housecleaning. What may seem like an endless succession of chores is broken down into modules that are clearly defined and can be delegated to other people. Each module is defined clearly and is separated from the others. It is, therefore, possible to accomplish the overall task sequentially if one person is doing it, or concurrently if several persons are involved.

So, drawing a chart of the tasks involved in cleaning the entire house provides an accurate overall picture of the complexity of the project. A project that was large and difficult to describe at the start has now been broken down into more simple, easily understood subtasks that can be delegated to others.

This technique of visualizing complex tasks with a diagram is used extensively by programmers and systems analysts. In fact, the chart shown in figure 2–5 is nearly identical to the VTOC charts that are widely used today in structured program design. (The key difference is that the tasks in regular program designs are performed by the computer, not by people.)

Many computer programs can be represented by the general VTOC chart shown in figure 2–6. This figure illustrates the three main steps in nearly all computer programs: input, processing, and output. In this simplified illustration, the program will process only one input. Of course, in a complete program, there will usually be many input, processing, and output steps arranged in various orders. However, for now use this simple form to help you solve a very simple problem: calculating your checking account balance at the end of the month. To do this, you need to provide the computer with the information

TABLE 2–1
Housecleaning as a structured task.

Living Room	Bedroom	Kitchen	Bathroom	Dining Room
Vacuum carpet	Make bed	Clean floor	Clean floor	Clean floor
Dust furniture	Vacuum carpet	Clean appliances	Clean sink	Clean tables and chairs
Clean TV, stereo	Dust furniture	Clean windows	Clean shower	Clean windows
Water plants	Clean windows			
Clean windows				

36

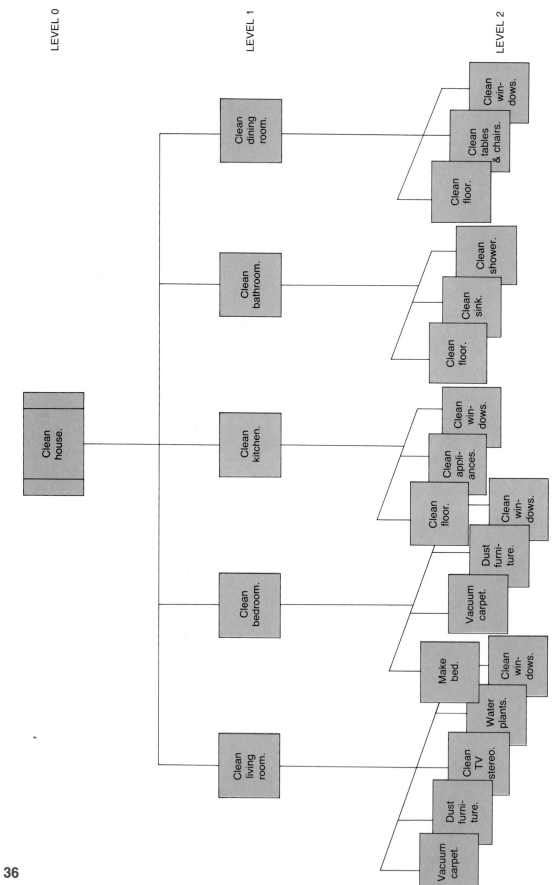

LEVEL 0

LEVEL 1

LEVEL 2

FIGURE 2–5
Housecleaning as a structured task.

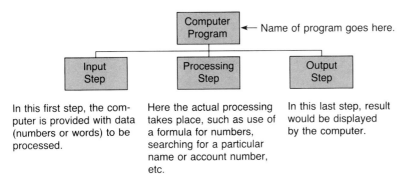

FIGURE 2–6
Input/processing/output VTOC.

shown in the table below. (This is a simplified example with no service charge or interest on the account and no unreconciled checks.)

The Input Needed	The Calculation Formula (Processing)	What You Want (Output)

1. Balance from last month
2. Total amount of all checks written
3. Total amount of all deposits made
	New balance =
	Balance from last month
	  + Total amount of deposits
	  − Total amount of checks
		New balance

The first step in solving this problem is to create a VTOC to help you visualize the significant parts needed for the program. The VTOC for this simple problem is shown in figure 2–7. As you can see, the module (or ''box'') at Level 0 is the main program, and it is responsible for controlling the order of input, calculations, and print modules found on Level 1. It is important to note that each module at Level 1 is mutually exclusive of the others. You can think of the VTOC as a map that shows the hierarchy or control structure of a program, as well as the general function of each module. Note on the VTOC chart that the specifics are *not* shown, as this is usually done on the flowcharts for the individual subroutines (Level 1 modules). The chart is read from left to right.

The next step in solving this problem is to create a flowchart. The flowchart will put more detail into the functions outlined in the VTOC. You can begin by analyzing the main module at Level 0, which will call, in order, the input, calculate, and output (print) modules. The flowchart for the main module is illustrated in figure 2–8.

Notice that each module is placed in the order that it will be executed by the main program. The terminal symbol ⬭ is used to indicate the beginning and end of the main program, while a slightly different terminal symbol ▭ shows the beginning and end of each subroutine referred to by the main program. The process/annotation symbol ▭ is used to represent the ''calling'' or use of another

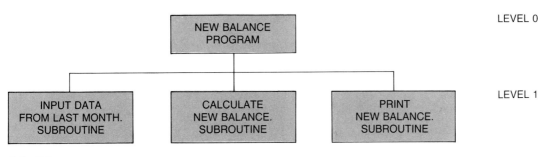

LEVEL 0

LEVEL 1

FIGURE 2–7
Checking account VTOC.

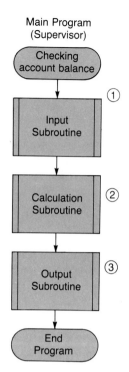

FIGURE 2–8

Checking account program—main module flowchart.

module or program segment. (When the process/annotation symbol is used, a programmer can expect that those subroutines will be represented by individual flowcharts.) In this example, the main program first uses the input subroutine of the program. After this subroutine is finished, the main program will use the calculating subroutine, and, finally, it will use the output subroutine. When the output subroutine has been completed, this program will be at its logical end, as indicated by the terminal symbol at the end of the flowchart.

After Level 0 has been completely flowcharted, your next step is to create a flowchart for each module in Level 1 of the VTOC. The flowcharts for the input, calculate, and output modules are shown in figure 2–9.

Notice that the terminal symbol is used to identify the subroutine as indicated on Level 1 of the VTOC. The number 1 on the side indicates that the flowchart represents a task assigned in Level 1 of the VTOC. Next the input/output symbol ⟋▭⟋ is used to indicate the specific information your program will need to have input before the calculations module can begin. The calculations are represented by the processing symbol ▭ and the output is shown by the input/output symbol. Again, the terminal symbol is used to indicate the logical end of each subroutine and the return of control back to the main module.

If the problem has been flowcharted properly, each logical instruction on the flowchart should be easily translated into a BASIC statement. The next section will show you how to write a simple program using the flowcharts from the checking account example.

Coding the Program

To write a BASIC program with structured design, you have to:

1. Write a main program that will control the overall sequence and logic by calling subroutines in their proper order.
2. Write the logic for the Level 1 subroutines on the VTOC chart.

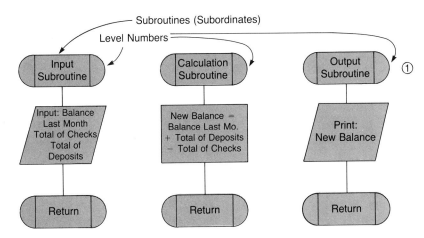

FIGURE 2–9
Subroutine flowcharts for checking account program.

The checking account VTOC in figure 2–7 shows you that the main program calls three subroutines to perform the required task. The BASIC instruction used to call a subroutine is the GOSUB command. The proper syntax for this command is:

```
line# GOSUB new-line#
```

When the computer reads this command, it will stop executing the program in sequence and skip down to the "new-line number." It will continue in sequence from the new line until the RETURN command is entered, at which time program control will return to the line immediately following the GOSUB command just executed. The format for the RETURN command is:

```
line# RETURN
```

The END statement is used to show the end to a program and, therefore, should always be the last statement in the main program. In effect, it tells the computer that processing is complete. The form of the END statement is:

```
line# END
```

With this information, you can write the program for the main module of the checking account balancing problem. It is shown in figure 2–10.

The INPUT command must be used to write the program for the INPUT module of the VTOC. The format for the INPUT command is: line# INPUT variable-name, variable-name(s).

Using the INPUT statement is one way you can enter data into a program. It is used when the data is needed from the person who is using the computer. When the INPUT command is executed, the computer will print a question mark (?) on the screen and then wait for the data to be entered. After the data is entered, the computer will continue processing. (In this example, the prompt will be "ENTER YOUR PREVIOUS BALANCE, TOTAL CHECKS, AND THE TOTAL DEPOSITS".)

A variable name is a name used to represent a value that will need to change or be changed during the processing of a program or upon reprocessing the program. For example, in this program, you need to enter your balance from last month. Next month that value will change, so it is necessary to use a variable to represent that value. Using the variable name PB (for *Previous Balance*) will allow you to change that value each time the program is run. Similarly, TC will be used to hold the value of the *Total Checks* and TD will be used to represent the *Total Deposits*. The input, calculation and output subrou-

39

Flowchart

Main Program
(Supervisor)

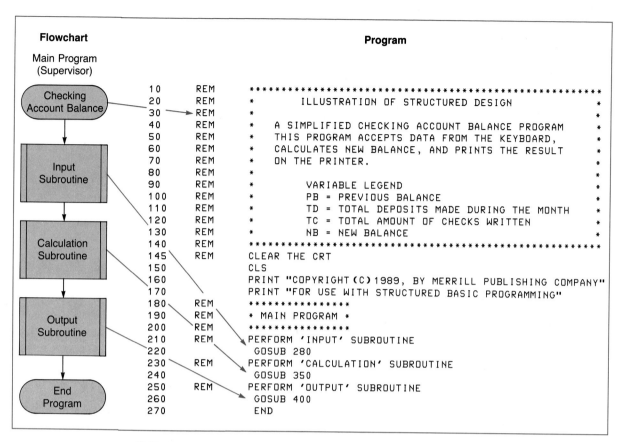

```
 10   REM   ****************************************************
 20   REM   *        ILLUSTRATION OF STRUCTURED DESIGN         *
 30   REM   *                                                  *
 40   REM   *    A SIMPLIFIED CHECKING ACCOUNT BALANCE PROGRAM *
 50   REM   *    THIS PROGRAM ACCEPTS DATA FROM THE KEYBOARD,  *
 60   REM   *    CALCULATES NEW BALANCE, AND PRINTS THE RESULT *
 70   REM   *    ON THE PRINTER.                               *
 80   REM   *                                                  *
 90   REM   *         VARIABLE LEGEND                          *
100   REM   *         PB = PREVIOUS BALANCE                    *
110   REM   *         TD = TOTAL DEPOSITS MADE DURING THE MONTH*
120   REM   *         TC = TOTAL AMOUNT OF CHECKS WRITTEN      *
130   REM   *         NB = NEW BALANCE                         *
140   REM   ****************************************************
145   REM   CLEAR THE CRT
150         CLS
160         PRINT "COPYRIGHT(C)1989, BY MERRILL PUBLISHING COMPANY"
170         PRINT "FOR USE WITH STRUCTURED BASIC PROGRAMMING"
180   REM   ***************
190   REM   * MAIN PROGRAM *
200   REM   ***************
210   REM   PERFORM 'INPUT' SUBROUTINE
220         GOSUB 280
230   REM   PERFORM 'CALCULATION' SUBROUTINE
240         GOSUB 350
250   REM   PERFORM 'OUTPUT' SUBROUTINE
260         GOSUB 400
270         END
```

FIGURE 2–10
Flowchart with corresponding BASIC statements.

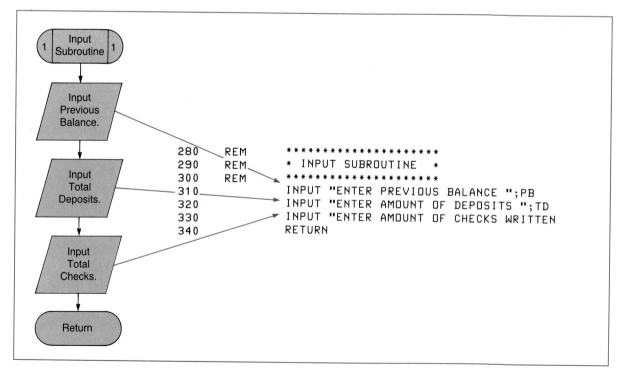

```
280   REM   *********************
290   REM   * INPUT SUBROUTINE  *
300   REM   *********************
310         INPUT "ENTER PREVIOUS BALANCE ";PB
320         INPUT "ENTER AMOUNT OF DEPOSITS ";TD
330         INPUT "ENTER AMOUNT OF CHECKS WRITTEN
340         RETURN
```

FIGURE 2–11
Input module flowchart and corresponding BASIC statements.

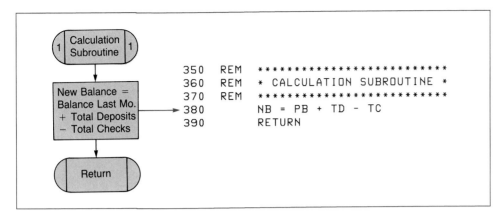

```
350   REM   * * * * * * * * * * * * * * * * * * * * * * * * * * *
360   REM   * CALCULATION SUBROUTINE *
370   REM   * * * * * * * * * * * * * * * * * * * * * * * * * * *
380         NB = PB + TD - TC
390         RETURN
```

FIGURE 2–12
Calculation module flowchart and corresponding BASIC statements.

tine flowcharts and programs are shown in figures 2–11, 2–12, and 2–13. The complete program is shown in figure 2–14.

The command statements discussed here will be covered in more detail later. For now, they are presented to illustrate the importance of how the VTOC, flowcharts, and the process of coding a program all go together.

Structured Program Conventions

Regardless of the program's complexity, a structured program uses only three logical structures for design and coding: sequence, selection, and iteration. The three structures are represented by the simple flowcharts shown in figure 2–15.

The sequence structure is any straightforward operation that does not feature decision making or looping. Sequence structure includes calculations, input and output, data movement, and assignments. Sequence symbols (operations) can be combined without changing the basic structure of the program.

The selection structure constitutes a choice made between two actions based on a condition. If the condition is true, one function is performed; if it is false, the other function is performed.

The iteration structure is essentially a looping structure that continues for as long as the test condition remains true. If the condition is false, execution will pass to the next sequential structure. Iteration structures can be formulated so that termination occurs when the test condition is true.

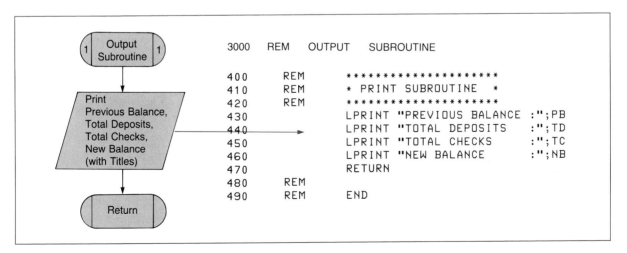

```
3000   REM   OUTPUT   SUBROUTINE

400    REM   * * * * * * * * * * * * * * * * * * * * *
410    REM   * PRINT SUBROUTINE   *
420    REM   * * * * * * * * * * * * * * * * * * * * *
430          LPRINT "PREVIOUS BALANCE :";PB
440          LPRINT "TOTAL DEPOSITS   :";TD
450          LPRINT "TOTAL CHECKS     :";TC
460          LPRINT "NEW BALANCE      :";NB
470          RETURN
480    REM
490    REM   END
```

FIGURE 2–13
Output module flowchart and corresponding BASIC statements.

FIGURE 2–14
Completed structured program.

```
Input

10    REM   *************************************************************
20    REM   *          ILLUSTRATION OF STRUCTURED DESIGN              *
30    REM   *                                                          *
40    REM   *    A SIMPLIFIED CHECKING ACCOUNT BALANCE PROGRAM        *
50    REM   *    THIS PROGRAM ACCEPTS DATA FROM THE KEYBOARD,         *
60    REM   *    CALCULATES NEW BALANCE, AND PRINTS THE RESULT        *
70    REM   *    ON THE PRINTER.                                      *
80    REM   *                                                          *
90    REM   *         VARIABLE LEGEND                                 *
100   REM   *         PB = PREVIOUS BALANCE                           *
110   REM   *         TD = TOTAL DEPOSITS MADE DURING THE MONTH       *
120   REM   *         TC = TOTAL AMOUNT OF CHECK WRITTEN              *
130   REM   *         NB = NEW BALANCE                                *
140   REM   *************************************************************
150         CLS
160         PRINT "COPYRIGHT (C) 1989, BY MERRILL PUBLISHING COMPANY"
170         PRINT "FOR USE WITH STRUCTURED BASIC PROGRAMMING"
180   REM   ***************
190   REM   * MAIN PROGRAM *
200   REM   ***************
210   REM   PERFORM 'INPUT' SUBROUTINE
220         GOSUB 280
230   REM   PERFORM 'CALCULATION' SUBROUTINE
240         GOSUB 350
250   REM   PERFORM 'OUTPUT' SUBROUTINE
260         GOSUB 400
270         END
280   REM   *********************
290   REM   * INPUT SUBROUTINE  *
300   REM   *********************
310         INPUT "ENTER PREVIOUS BALANCE ";PB
320         INPUT "ENTER AMOUNT OF DEPOSITS ";TD
330         INPUT "ENTER AMOUNT OF CHECKS WRITTEN ";TC
340         RETURN
350   REM   *************************
360   REM   * CALCULATION SUBROUTINE *
370   REM   *************************
380         NB = PB + TD - TC
390         RETURN
400   REM   *********************
410   REM   * PRINT SUBROUTINE  *
420   REM   *********************
430         LPRINT "PREVIOUS BALANCE :";PB
440         LPRINT "TOTAL DEPOSITS   :";TD
450         LPRINT "TOTAL CHECKS     :";TC
460         LPRINT "NEW BALANCE      :";NB
470         RETURN
480   REM
490   OK    END OF PROGRAM

Screen Output

RUN
COPYRIGHT (C) 1989, BY MERRILL PUBLISHING COMPANY
FOR USE WITH STRUCTURED BASIC PROGRAMMING
ENTER PREVIOUS BALANCE ? 250
ENTER AMOUNT OF DEPOSITS ? 100
ENTER AMOUNT OF CHECKS WRITTEN ? 50
```

```
Printed Output

PREVIOUS BALANCE : 250
TOTAL DEPOSITS   : 100
TOTAL CHECKS     : 50
NEW BALANCE      : 300
```

SUMMARY

Structured programming and structured problem solving are not new concepts for most people. The principle for both is the same: to break a complex task or operation into component modules called subroutines. Writing an outline for a speech or paper is a good example of structured design problem solving. An outline helps organize thoughts, reduces the possibility of omissions, and provides a logical overview of the problem.

The visual table of contents (VTOC) chart is similar to an outline. It can be used to help solve manual as well as computer problems. A structured program is designed with a VTOC chart, which serves as a guide. When the program is designed and written in this way, the program produced has several advantages because of its modular nature:

1. It is usually more complete.
2. Omissions of important logic are rarely made.
3. Coding takes place more efficiently because there is a clear ''road map'' to follow.
4. Testing and debugging are much simpler because subroutines can be studied and sometimes tested individually. This permits straightforward location of errors.
5. Modifications are simpler because only the affected subroutines usually need to be rewritten.
6. Documentation is clearer because design charts illustrate the sequence of important steps.
7. Programs can be prepared quickly because complex problems can be broken down into simpler modules that can then be distributed to a team of programmers for concurrent coding, testing, and debugging.

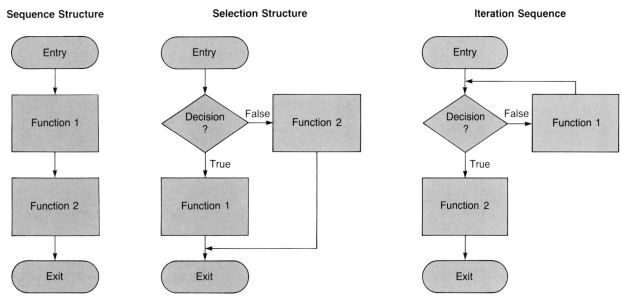

FIGURE 2–15
Program structures.

43

The creation of structured programs in BASIC involves the use of subroutines. These fall frequently into one of three main categories: input, processing, and output. In BASIC structured design, a main program consists of GOSUB statements. A typical main program branches to input, processing, and output subroutines, usually in that order. The subroutines are placed after the main program, and each ends with a RETURN statement, which allows the main program to proceed. The main program ends with an END statement.

The program development cycle proceeds from the VTOC chart to individual logic flowcharts and from there to coding in BASIC. The main program is usually coded first, followed by coding the subroutines.

Some errors to watch for in BASIC programming are listed in the following table. Study its contents carefully to avoid making some very common, but easily avoided, mistakes.

COMMON ERRORS IN PROGRAMMING—GENERAL

Error Type	Example	Solution
1. Failure to clear memory for a new program	No "NEW" typed.	Parts of old program with new program. Delete old program lines.
2. Failure to save the program once it is written.	No "SAVE" or "REPLACE" typed.	Program lost, no solution.
3. Failure to save a revised version of a program after a debugging session.	No "SAVE" typed.	Revisions lost unless program still in memory.
4. Failure to assign line numbers to BASIC statements as they are entered.	Print "HELLO."	Instruction is executed immediately and is not part of program. Retype instructions.
5. Failure to load in an old program before beginning modification or correction.	No "LOAD" or "OLD" typed.	Only modifications are saved. Begin again after load.
6. Failure to return or enter statements after typing them.	NO "RETURN" or "ENTER."	Type return or enter
7. Misspelling or misusing system commands.	RUM, SABE, etc., message. (syntax error)	Type return or enter. Retype correct command.
8. Inputting data with errors.	1O instead of 10. (Redo from start)	Run program again or re-enter data line.
9. Misspelled keywords, improper variable names, improper punctuation in INPUT, PRINT or OTHER statements.	PRIMT (syntax error)	Check BASIC manual for correct keyword spelling and statement punctuation.

REVIEW QUESTIONS

1. Define structured problem solving.
2. List the advantages and disadvantages of writing computer programs in structured design.
3. What type of graphical representation is used to define a problem in structured form? Draw a simple example.
4. When a complex task is structured, what do you call the component parts of the task?
5. When a problem is structured for eventual solution by a computer, what step usually follows the development of the structure chart? Why is it important?
6. Structured design is similar to what process used to prepare a speech or paper?
7. What are the advantages to structuring tasks such as housecleaning?
8. Describe a complex manual (noncomputer) task not described in the chapter for which structuring could prove beneficial. Explain the benefits.
9. In structured design computer programming, the main task can usually be subdivided into three key parts. What are these?
10. In BASIC, a structured program would consist of one main program and many subroutines. Explain.
11. What BASIC instruction in the main program causes the program to branch to and begin processing a subroutine?
12. What BASIC instruction returns control to the main program after the subroutine has been processed? To where is control returned?

13. The main program in a BASIC program is analogous to whose performance in a manual task or project?
14. The subroutine can be compared with whose performance in a manual task or project?
15. Does a structured design computer program contain more or fewer instructions than a comparable program of unstructured design? Explain.
16. In computer programs that are very long and complex, structured design proves particularly helpful. Explain why.
17. Name the three key constructs upon which all structured design computer programs are based.

PROBLEMS FOR SOLUTION

1. Write a VTOC chart using one of two alternative methods of cleaning, by task or by room. Tasks can include things such as dusting, vacuuming, straightening up, cleaning windows, etc. (*Hint:* If you choose to create a VTOC by task, the tasks would become the main modules and the rooms would become the submodules.)
2. Make up your own VTOC chart for a problem or task that has proved difficult for you to start. Examine the chart when you are finished and then describe the ways in which the VTOC chart has helped you to understand the problem and, perhaps, solve it in a more efficient manner.
3. Using the information in this problem, construct a VTOC chart that represents the key points described.

Anyone who has ever performed or watched a complete automobile tune-up knows that it is a rather complex and usually expensive procedure. There are many parts to be changed, cleaned, and repaired, and complicated adjustments must be made. There are also critical disassembly and reassembly procedures to be followed. Here is an abbreviated list of the tune-up tasks usually performed:

1. Check spark plugs. Replace if necessary, or clean and regap old plugs.
2. Check the electronic ignition system.
3. Adjust the ignition timing. Clean and adjust the carburetor.
4. Clean and adjust the automatic choke.
5. Check the air filter. Clean or replace if necessary.
6. Check the fuel filter. Clean or replace if necessary.
7. Check the battery.
8. Clean battery terminals.
9. Check battery cables. Replace if necessary.
10. Check the alternator and voltage regulator.
11. Check the radiator for leaks. Check the coolant level and add coolant if necessary. Verify temperature protection.
12. Check cooling system hoses.

Just looking at this partial list is intimidating. However, through use of structured design, you can feel assured that you will not forget important steps or perform them prematurely. If you begin by listing the individual tasks within the "system" to which they belong, you will make a good start. For example, you can think of a car as having a number of functional modules (or systems) that together contribute to its proper operation. A partial list of these systems would include:

1. The fuel system—those elements that control the proper supply and mixture of fuel and air to the engine for efficient combustion.
2. The ignition system—the elements that cause and control the proper timing of high-voltage electricity to the spark plugs in a gasoline engine, which ignite the fuel and air mixture at exactly the right instant.

3. The electrical system—the elements that supply low-voltage electricity to the ignition system, light, radio, horn, heater fan, and other accessories.
4. The cooling system—those elements that ensure that the burning of fuel does not overheat the metal parts of the engine, and also provide hot water to the heating system to heat the interior of the car in the winter.

Other systems that are equally important to the safe and proper operation of a car, such as the brakes, the exhaust system, and the suspension and steering system, could be (and usually are) included in a thorough tune-up or are covered by a dealer's maintenance inspection. Other systems such as these are omitted here for the sake of simplifying the problem. Those of you who do work on your own cars may wish to expand this over-simplified analysis (and by so doing, you will create an excellent reference source for future repair work!).

CHAPTER THREE

INPUT/OUTPUT OPERATIONS

OUTLINE

INTRODUCTION TO INPUT AND OUTPUT
Data Input Using the Keyboard | Output on a CRT Display | Output to a Printer | Special Purpose Printers and Plotters

CONVERTING KEYBOARD INPUT TO DISPLAYED AND PRINTED OUTPUT
General BASIC Language Conventions | The BASIC Character Set | BASIC Reserved Words | Line Numbers | Program Self-Documentation—Using REMarks | Structured Design Statements—GOSUB and RETURN | Variables and Variable Names | INPUT and READ/DATA Statements

OUTPUT ON THE CRT AND PRINTER
PRINT Statements

CASE 3–1: NAME AND PHONE NUMBER LISTING PROGRAM

INPUT/OUTPUT ENHANCEMENTS
Inputting Data with Prompts | Printing Titles and Headings | Editing Output with PRINT USING and LPRINT USING

CASE 3–2: PERSONNEL DATA INPUT AND LISTING PROGRAM ADDING A PROFESSIONAL LOOK TO YOUR PROGRAMS

ADDING A PROFESSIONAL LOOK TO YOUR PROGRAMS
Using Color

FULL-SCREEN FORMATTING FOR INPUT
The LOCATE Statement

DATA ERROR TRAPPING AND RECOVERY

CASE 3–3: FULL-SCREEN FORMATTING: PAYROLL AND PERSONNEL DATA INPUT AND LISTING

LEARNING OBJECTIVES

Upon completion of this chapter, you will be able to:

☐ Understand the principles of input and output in BASIC.

☐ Use the keyboard to input data and programs.

☐ Use the printer to obtain listings.

☐ Use the INPUT, READ/DATA, GOSUB, RETURN, and END statements to write structured design input/output programs.

☐ Understand the concepts of string variables and know string variable input, output, and naming conventions.

☐ Understand input and output of decimal and integer numbers using proper variable naming conventions.

☐ Understand input and output of decimals, integer numbers, and strings.

☐ Understand and use the COLOR, TAB, PRINT USING, and LPRINT USING statements to obtain professional-looking output on the display and printer.

☐ Understand the concepts and advantages of full-screen formatting for data input.

☐ Understand the concept and importance of data error detection and trapping during input.

☐ Use the CLS, LOCATE, COLOR, BEEP, and SOUND statements to control and enhance the data input operation.

☐ Create professional data input screens for your programs, complete with error detection and trapping routines.

INTRODUCTION TO INPUT AND OUTPUT

Computers use input devices to receive information for subsequent processing and use output devices to communicate results to people or to other computers. Keyboards (input devices), along with displays and printers (output devices), form an integral part of most microcomputer systems that support BASIC. In fact, many models of microcomputers incorporate the display, keyboard, central processing unit (CPU), main memory, and auxiliary memory in one cabinet. Whether the system is contained in one unit or comprised of several individual parts, the keyboard will be the primary method used to input the program statements and to enter data while the program is being run.

Most microcomputer systems have separate components that permit movement of the keyboard, the display, and the CPU for more comfortable operation and viewing. Having individual parts also allows buyers to pick from a wide variety of displays and auxiliary storage devices.

Data Input Using the Keyboard

The keys on most computer keyboards are very similar to those on an electric typewriter. Some models have supplemental keys called function and control keys located above the top row or along the left and right sides of the keyboard. Many models have a numeric keypad (similar to an adding machine) to the right of the standard keys. Most microcomputers also have two special keys, usually called the control key and escape key, which are essential to the operation of the computer or the terminal. These keys are used to issue operating system commands which typically control nonprogramming operations such as loading, saving, stopping, and editing programs, and loading in the BASIC interpreter or compiler. Since the operating system may vary with different computers, the use of the special keys and operating system commands also will differ, and these must be learned by studying the owner's or operator's manual that accompanies the computer. The appendix to this text provides a brief summary of some common operating system commands, as well as the BASIC system commands needed to run, stop, save, list, and load BASIC programs.

Output on the CRT Display

Once you have learned the fundamental operating system commands, you will be ready to learn how to enter and run BASIC programs. This involves typing the required BASIC instructions on the keyboard and observing what you have typed on the display, much the same way you would type on an electric typewriter and check the results of your typing on paper. However, it is easier to correct errors on a computer than it is on an electric typewriter because most operating systems permit quick and easy editing corrections of BASIC statements. But again, the commands will vary from system to system, and you must learn them by studying the pertinent operating system and BASIC manuals. The appendix to this text also provides an overview of some of the more commonly used editing commands and procedures in BASIC.

Output to a Printer

Most business systems require that permanent records be made of computer output. These hard copy outputs are produced by a variety of printing devices, some of which are similar to a standard typewriter and some of which are more complex and much faster. Charge account statements, bills, event tickets, tax bills, airline tickets, sales reports, and inventory listings are but a few of the many examples of hard copy output produced by high-speed computer printers. For most microcomputer systems using BASIC, printed output can be directed to either daisy wheel impact printers or to dot matrix printers, which are both slower than the high-speed line printers used in large systems, but are significantly cheaper. A high-speed line printer is used with most mainframe computer systems.

Hard copy output also is important to programmers because programmers often need permanent printed records of programs for error detection, as well as for program modifications and documentation. It is much easier to study a program in complete printed form than it is to examine small portions of it one segment at a time on the display. With the cost of high-speed dot matrix printers dropping below $300, nearly every owner of a microcomputer system can now enjoy the benefits of an on-line printer.

Figure 3–1 shows a sample printout from a daisy wheel letter-quality printer. To be letter quality, the print must be indistinguishable from the print typed on a regular typewriter. Daisy wheel letter-quality printers usually print at a slower speed than printers that offer a lower-quality draft print. For example, daisy wheel letter-quality printers print 12 to 60 characters per second (CPS) compared with 80 to 200 CPS for dot matrix printers.

Figure 3–2 shows the output from a dot matrix printer. Dot matrix printers are the most widely used microcomputer printers because of their high speed, low cost, and durability. A typical dot matrix printer could print this entire page of text in about half a minute, while it would take a daisy wheel letter-quality printer about 3 minutes.

Recent advances in laser and ink jet printers combine high-speed printing with letter-quality type. With these, it is difficult to distinguish the fast, printed output from true letter-quality output produced by daisy wheel printers.

Special Purpose Printers and Plotters

In addition to the standard printers just mentioned, a wide variety of special printers and plotters have been introduced into the business world. Some of these devices have been used in science and engineering for many years, but with the microcomputer revolution, the price of such special devices has dropped so much that they are now common in business. For example, it is now possible to buy a full-color printer/plotter for about $300. You can draw color graphs, bar charts, histograms, and even line charts with these machines. These machines also are capable of printing text, figures, and graphs in color. While their speed is not fast, the results are striking. Many dot matrix printers also can be used to produce charts and graphs, but they are not as clear as those done with a plotter. Figure 3–3 illustrates a graph produced by a plotter.

```
********************************************************************************
*  EMPLOYEE RECORD:                                                           *
*                    EARNINGS:                        TAX DEDUCTIONS:         *
*  EMP NO.  HOURS   REGULAR  OVERTIME  TOTAL GROSS  FEDERAL  FICA   TOTAL NET *
*                                                                             *
*  54321    44      416.00   62.40     478.40       95.68   29.33    353.39   *
*----------------------------------------------------------------------------*
* PAYROLL CHECK                                                               *
*                                                                             *
*                                                                             *
*    PAY TO THE ORDER OF   ANNE MENARD                 AMOUNT   $ 353.39      *
*                          --------------------                 -------       *
*                                                                             *
*                                                                             *
*                                                                             *
*                                       _____                *
*                                       JOHN SMITH, TREASURER                 *
*                                                                             *
********************************************************************************
```

FIGURE 3–1
Sample printouts from a letter-quality printer.

```
DATE            LOAN AMT,            INT, RATE          MONTHS TO PAY
22 FEB          $2,000,00               18                  24
+ + + + + + + + + + + + + + + + + + + + + + + + + + + + + + + + + + + + + + + + + +
+ + + + + + + + + + + + + + + + + + + + + + + + + + + + + + + + + + + + + + + + + +
            TOTAL AMT, PAID BACK      TOTAL INTEREST PAID
                $   2,396,36           $     396,36
+ + + + + + + + + + + + + + + + + + + + + + + + + + + + + + + + + + + + + + + + + +
MONTH       PAYMENT       INTEREST        PRINC,        REM, BALANCE
+ + + + + + + + + + + + + + + + + + + + + + + + + + + + + + + + + + + + + + + + + +
  1         $ 99,85       $ 30,00       $ 69,85         $2296,51
  2         $ 99,85       $ 28,95       $ 70,90         $2196,67
  3         $ 99,85       $ 27,89       $ 71,96         $2096,82
  4         $ 99,85       $ 26,81       $ 73,04         $1996,97
  5         $ 99,85       $ 25,71       $ 74,13         $1897,12
  6         $ 99,85       $ 24,60       $ 75,25         $1797,27
  7         $ 99,85       $ 23,47       $ 76,38         $1697,42
  8         $ 99,85       $ 22,33       $ 77,52         $1597,58
  9         $ 99,85       $ 21,16       $ 78,68         $1497,73
 10         $ 99,85       $ 19,98       $ 79,86         $1397,88
 11         $ 99,85       $ 18,79       $ 81,06         $1298,03
 12         $ 99,85       $ 17,57       $ 82,28         $1198,18
 13         $ 99,85       $ 16,34       $ 83,51         $1098,33
 14         $ 99,85       $ 15,08       $ 84,76         $ 998,49
 15         $ 99,85       $ 13,81       $ 86,04         $ 898,64
 16         $ 99,85       $ 12,52       $ 87,33         $ 798,79
 17         $ 99,85       $ 11,21       $ 88,64         $ 698,94
 18         $ 99,85       $  9,88       $ 89,97         $ 599,09
 19         $ 99,85       $  8,53       $ 91,32         $ 499,24
 20         $ 99,85       $  7,16       $ 92,69         $ 399,39
 21         $ 99,85       $  5,77       $ 94,08         $ 299,55
 22         $ 99,85       $  4,36       $ 95,49         $ 199,70
 23         $ 99,85       $  2,93       $ 96,92         $  99,85
 24         $ 99,85       $  1,48       $ 98,37         $   0,00
                    ****TABLE COMPLETED****
```

FIGURE 3–2
Sample printout from dot matrix printer.

Another type of printer, called near letter quality, has recently become available. These are high-resolution dot matrix printers (there are many more dots in the print head matrix), which are becoming more popular as prices drop.

CONVERTING KEYBOARD INPUT TO DISPLAYED AND PRINTED OUTPUT

General BASIC Language Conventions

Program lines in a BASIC program have the following general format.

```
line# statement [:statement. . .]["comment"]
```

The portions of the statement that are in brackets are optional. In other words, a program line may have more than one BASIC statement and may terminate with a comment. The statements themselves are either executable or nonexecutable. The executable statements tell the computer what to do while the program is running, while the nonexecutable statements, such as the comments (REMarks in BASIC), contain only information used to document the program. Comments do not cause program action when BASIC processes them.

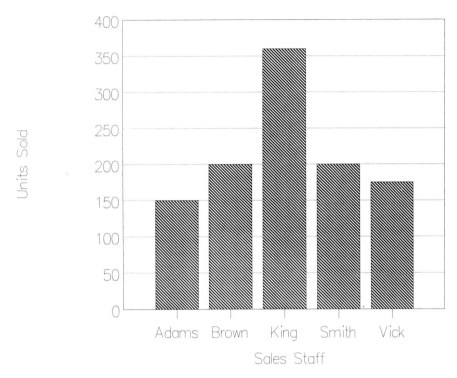

Product Sales for First Quarter

FIGURE 3-3
A graph produced by a laser printer or plotter.

You may have many executable and nonexecutable statements on one line, but they must be separated from one another by colons (:). Any letter (upper or lower case), number, or special character may be used in a BASIC statement. The total number of characters in any line may not exceed 255.

The BASIC Character Set

The reserved keywords in BASIC and all BASIC statements are made up from the BASIC character set shown in table 3–1. Use of any other character will usually cause errors in your programs. Check your keyboards because not all characters are available on all keyboards, and some have extra ''non-standard'' characters.

BASIC Reserved Words

In addition to the special characters that have specific meaning in BASIC statements, there are combinations of letters, words, and special characters that are reserved for certain use. These are called the BASIC reserved words or BASIC keywords. The reserved words include all BASIC commands, statement parts (except variable names), function names, and operators. They are separated from other keywords, variables data, etc., by blanks as dictated by the specific statement syntax.

Reserved words must be spelled exactly as they appear. If one small error is made, your program will not run properly. Also, reserved words cannot be used as variable names in your programs because the program will not run properly once the computer

TABLE 3–1
BASIC character set.

Character	Name
	blank or space
=	equal sign or assignment symbol
+	plus sign or concatenation symbol
−	minus sign
*	asterisk or multiplication symbol
/	slash or division symbol
^	caret or exponentiation symbol
(	left parenthesis
)	right parenthesis
%	percent sign or integer number declaration
#	number (or pound) sign or double precision
$	dollar sign or string type declaration character
!	exclamation point or single-precision number declaration
&	ampersand
,	comma
.	period or decimal point
'	single quotation mark (apostrophe) or remark
;	delimiter semicolon
:	colon or statement separator
?	question mark or PRINT abbreviation
<	less than
>	greater than
"	double quotation mark or string delimiter

encounters the word. Therefore, it is best to familiarize yourself with the list in table 3–2 and refer to it if you have any doubt about using a word as a variable name.

Table 3–2 gives a subset of the approximately 175 reserved words used in IBM BASICA (Microsoft BASIC). These are the words used in the programs and cases that you will need for the Problems for Solution sections in this text. Other words and their uses can be found in the BASIC manual for your computer. Remember that while this list is extensive, it is only partial. There are many BASIC functions and special graphics words and other keywords that make up commands not used in traditional business programming.

If you use a variable name that gives you a keyword error, or if you would like to become familiar with the words not on this list, consult the appendix to this text where *all* keywords, their functions, and example syntax are explained.

Line Numbers

Each line of a BASIC program is preceded by a number from 1 to 65529. The digits identify the line and its sequential relationship to other lines. In most systems, the lines can be entered in any order, but are automatically sequenced by the BASIC interpreter prior to execution. This is a very helpful feature of BASIC because it permits easy program modification and editing in that new or revised statements can be added after the program has been typed and then inserted automatically into the program according to their assigned numbers. Although it is possible to number lines in increments of one (e.g., 1, 2, 3, 4, etc.), this is not a good practice since it inhibits program modification. A better procedure is to number the program statements in increments of 10 (e.g., 10, 20, 30, 40, etc.). This will permit you to add nine lines between each of the original ones. BASIC has automatic line numbering commands that are useful for renumbering when desired.

It is not necessary to leave a space after line numbers; however, good programming practice usually calls for at least one space between the number and the keyword beginning the statement. Since BASIC is a free-form language, the programmer decides on the number of spaces to maintain between a line number and the first word of an instruction or between the words or parts of an instruction. This permits programs to be designed with indented margins, which greatly facilitates reading.

A BASIC program showing a good layout of REMarks, the main program, and subroutines appears in the program in figure 3–4.

```
10      REM     *****************************************
20      REM     *        INPUT/OUTPUT OPERATION         *
30      REM     *         CASE STUDY: C3-2              *     Remarks to identify
40      REM     *   PERSONNEL DATA LISTING PROGRAM      *     program
50      REM     * THIS PROGRAM ACCEPTS DATA FROM THE    *
60      REM     * KEYBOARD AND PRINTS THE DATA WITH A   *
70      REM     * TITLE TO THE PRINTER.                 *
80      REM     *           VARIABLE LEGEND             *
90      REM     *        ENO = EMPLOYEE NUMBER          *
100     REM     *        NAM$ = EMPLOYEE NAME           *
110     REM     *        ADDS$ = ADDRESS               *
120     REM     *        AGE = AGE                      *
130     REM     *        MS$ = MARITAL STATUS           *
140     REM     *        PRAT = PAY RATE                *
150     REM     *****************************************
160             PRINT "COPYRIGHT (C) 1989, BY MERRILL PUBLISHING
                COMPANY"
170             PRINT "FOR USE WITH STRUCTURED BASIC PROGRAMMING"
180     REM     ****************
190     REM     * MAIN PROGRAM *
200     REM     ****************
210     REM     PERFORM 'INPUT DATA' SUBROUTINE        Main program logic with
220             GOSUB 280                              remarks identifying key
230     REM     PERFORM 'PRINT TITLE LINE' SUBROUTINE  subroutines
240             GOSUB 330
250     REM     PERFORM 'PRINT OUTPUT' SUBROUTINE
260             GOSUB 380
270             END
280     REM     ********************
290     REM     * INPUT SUBROUTINE *   Subroutine identification
300     REM     ********************
310             INPUT ENO,NAM$,ADDS$,AGE,MS$,PRAT   Subroutine logic
320             RETURN
330     REM     ***********************************
340     REM     * PRINT TITLE LINE SUBROUTINE *
350     REM     ***********************************
360             LPRINT "EMPLOYEE NO.     NAME      ADDRESS
  AGE   MAR.ST.   PAYRATE"
370             RETURN
380     REM     ****************************
390     REM     * PRINT OUTPUT SUBROUTINE *
400     REM     ****************************
410             F1$ = "  #####        \              \\
  ##   \ \   ##.##"
420             LPRINT USING F1$;ENO,NAM$,ADDS$,AGE,MS$,PRAT
430             RETURN
440     REM
450     REM     END OF PROGRAM
```

FIGURE 3–4
Typical BASIC program layout.

TABLE 3–2
BASIC reserved words and their functions.

Reserved Word	Function
ABS	finds the absolute value of an expression
AND	logically joins two conditions
AUTO	automatically numbers BASIC statements
BEEP	causes the speaker to sound
CLEAR	clears all number variables to zero and strings to blank
CLOSE	concludes input/output to a device or file
CLS	clears the screen
COLOR	sets the colors for foreground, background, and border
CONT	resumes program execution after a break
CVD CVI CVS	converts a string variable to numeric for certain direct access file operations
DATA	stores the numeric and string constants that are accessed by READ
DATE$	sets or retrieves the date
DEF FN	defines and names a function that you write
DELETE	deletes program lines
DIM	specifies the maximum value for an array variable subscript and allocates storage for that variable
EDIT	displays a line for editing
ELSE	separates imperatives in an IF statement
END	terminates program execution and closes all files
EOF	indicates an end-of-file condition
ERASE	eliminates arrays from a program
ERR ERL	returns the error code and line number associated with the error
ERROR	simulates the occurrence of an error or allows you to define your own error codes
EXP	calculates the exponential function
FIELD	allocates space for variables in a random file buffer used in direct access file processing
FILES	displays all files on the current drive
FIX	truncates X to an integer
FOR NEXT	performs a series of instructions in a loop bounded by the FOR and NEXT statements
GET	reads a record from a direct access file
GOSUB RETURN	branches to and returns from a subroutine
GOTO	branches unconditionally to a specified line number
IF	makes a decision regarding program flow based on the results of a condition or expression
INKEY$	reads a character from the keyboard without return or enter pressed
INPUT	receives data from the keyboard during program execution
INPUT#	reads data from a file
INT	returns the largest integer less than or equal to X
KEY	sets or displays the soft (Function) keys
KILL	deletes a file from disk (like the ERASE in DOS)
LET	assigns value to a variable from constant or expression
LINE	draws a line or box on the screen in graphics mode
LINE INPUT	reads an entire line (less than 256 characters) from the keyboard into a string variable
LIST	lists the program currently in memory on the screen

TABLE 3–2 *continued*
BASIC reserved words and their functions.

Reserved Word	Function
LLIST	lists the program on the printer
LOAD	loads a program into memory (usually from disk)
LOCATE	positions the cursor on the screen
LOG	returns the natural log of X
LPRINT	prints data onto a connected printer
LPRINT USING	formats data and edits while printing on the printer
LSET ⎫ RSET ⎭	moves data into a random file buffer in preparation for output with the PUT statement. Used in direct access file processing
MERGE	merges program files together in memory
MKI\$ ⎫ MK\$\$ ⎬ MKD\$ ⎭	converts numeric-type variables to string for direct files
NAME	changes the name of a file (like RENAME in DOS)
NEW	deletes the program currently in memory and clears variables
ON ERROR	enables error trapping and specifies the first line of the error trapping routine
ON GOSUB	branches to one of several line numbers, depending on a value, and returns
ON GOTO	branches to one of several line numbers depending on a value
OPEN	allows input or output on a file or device
PLAY	plays music on the speaker, specified by a string
PRINT	displays data on the screen
PRINT USING	formats and edits output for display on the screen
PRINT#	prints to a file or device specified in an OPEN statement
PUT	writes a record from a random buffer to a direct-access file
READ	reads values from a DATA statement and assigns them to variables
REM	inserts explanatory remarks into a program
RENUM	renumbers line numbers in a program
RESET	closes all files and clears the system buffer
RESTORE	allows DATA statements to be reread
RESUME	continues program execution after an error routine
RETURN	returns after a GOSUB
RND	returns a random number between 0 and 1
RUN	begins execution of a program
SAVE	saves a BASIC program on disk
SOUND	generates a specific sound through the speaker
SQR	returns the square root of X
STEP	provides an increment for the FOR/NEXT loop
STOP	stops execution of a program
SWAP	exchanges the values of two variables
SYSTEM	exits BASIC and returns to DOS
TAB	tabs to a position in a print-type statement
TIME\$	sets or retrieves the current time (if set in DOS)
TIMER	returns the number of seconds since midnight
TRON	turns on the program execution tracing system
TROFF	turns off the tracing system
USING	(see PRINT USING or LPRINT USING)
WAIT	suspends program execution
WHILE ⎫ WEND ⎭	executes a series of statements in a loop while a condition is true
WIDTH	sets the number-of-characters width for the printer or screen
WRITE	outputs data to the screen (similar to PRINT), but with commas
WRITE#	writes data to a sequential file, but with commas between values

57

Program Self-Documentation—Using REMarks

Whenever possible, a computer program should contain sufficient informative remarks so that a reader or another programmer assigned to modify the program can easily understand each logical module of the program as well as ascertain the program's overall structure. In BASIC, this is easily accomplished by including REMark statements (also referred to as REM statements). REM statements often are placed at the beginning of a program to identify it and at key points within a program to describe the beginning of each new module as well as the processing taking place. Since REMs are not executed by the computer, any words, numbers, or special characters can be included in them. For instance, REMs may contain special characters to highlight key parts of the program, such as a line of asterisks or blanks. They may also be added to the end of any BASIC statement by preceding the remark with an apostrophe. One example of a REM statement would be

```
10  REM  *** GAS MILEAGE CALCULATION ***
```

Thus, a REM statement usually contains a short verbal description of the purpose of the logic following the remark. Where variable names are shortened to a few characters to save typing time, a REM often is used to identify what the variable stands for. This is called a variable legend. Often, remarks are preceded and followed by asterisks for easy identification and for locating key logical sections and subroutines in the program, as follows.

```
10 REM * VARIABLE LEGEND      *
20 REM * NM$ IS NAME          *
30 REM * PHO$ IS PHONE NUMBER *
```

You should be careful not to clutter your programs with so many REM statements that it actually makes it harder to read. Only use REMs when it will help clarify your program.

Structured Design Statements—GOSUB and RETURN

Although GOSUB and RETURN statements usually are introduced later in most BASIC texts, they are so essential to structured design in BASIC programs that a detailed discussion of them is in order now. As with all BASIC statements, GOSUB must be preceded by a line number and must be followed by another line number that tells the computer where to continue its processing, as shown here.

```
40 GOSUB 100
```

In this example, when the GOSUB is executed the computer will immediately skip down to line 100 and continue processing from there. The computer will continue to process in sequence until it encounters a RETURN statement, at which time the computer will go to the first statement following the GOSUB command and continue processing from there.

The format for the RETURN statement is simply

```
RETURN
```

Relating this to the visual table of contents charts described in chapter 2, each level 1 module is usually replaced in the program by a GOSUB statement, as shown in figure 3–5. Obviously, GOSUB statements themselves will not tell you the function or purpose of the routines because they are identified only by number. For this reason, good structured programming practice requires that a REM statement precede each GOSUB to identify what routine is being executed by the GOSUB. The following illustrates the execution process of a GOSUB statement.

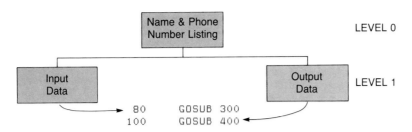

FIGURE 3–5
Structured chart with GOSUBs.

```
              70     REM  PERFORM "INPUT DATA" ROUTINE
GOSUB ──→     80     GOSUB 300
encountered  300     REM *************       REMs are used to
             310     REM * INPUT DATA *       conspicuously
             320     REM *************       identify routine
             330     INPUT NM$, PHO$          330
             340     RETURN
```

When line 80 is executed control is sent to line 300. After the return statement in line 340 is executed, control is returned to line 90.

The same REM convention is used to indicate the location and function of a subroutine, and the routine title itself can be "blocked" in asterisks for easy recognition and location (as shown above and in various program examples in the text).

When subroutines become complex, briefly describing the important elements of the subroutine with REMs at the beginning or at key points in the subroutine can be helpful. (This will be illustrated in later case studies.)

Subroutines do not have to be called in the same order that they appear in the program. While it is less confusing to number the routines in the order in which the main program processes them, this is not always possible with more complex programs (nor is it necessary). Some later case studies will serve to illustrate this point.

The newer compiler BASICs permit identification by number or label. For example, you will note later in Case 3–1 that instead of GOSUB 400, the programmer can write GOSUB PRINTOUT to obtain the same results.

Variables and Variable Names

Variable names are names assigned to computer storage locations. These storage locations will eventually hold the data input or to be read by the computer. The computer must know in advance what type of data (either alphabetic or numeric) it will be storing. This information is conveyed by the particular form used for the variable names.

Conventions for variable names vary among the machines that support BASIC; however, some rules of syntax do apply. (Consult Appendix A to this text for variable naming conventions or computers of different manufacturers.) Generally, for alphabetic or alphanumeric data, variable names (called string variables) should consist of a maximum of 40 letters (from A to Z) and/or numbers,* followed by a dollar sign. For example, N$ would be a variable name for name, ADDRESS$ for address, and P$ for phone number. Be careful not to use BASIC keywords like TIME$. When in doubt about the validity of a variable name, consult the table of BASIC reserved words (table 3–2) or the reserved list for your computer system.

*Must begin with a letter.

Most expanded BASIC systems, such as the BASIC used for the case studies in this text, permit from 1 to 40 letters in a variable name. However, many do not, so it is often necessary to abbreviate and write descriptive and meaningful variable names such as:

PNAME$ or PERSONSNAME$ for person's name
PHONE$ or PHONENUMBER$ for phone number

Writing abbreviated variable names also will save time in typing and in memory space since long variable names take up more memory than short names. Programmers often sacrifice the clarity that long descriptive variable names give for the time saved by using a rather short abbreviation such as

NM$ for name
PHO$ for phone number

Some systems differentiate between integer data (e.g., whole numbers such as 1, 6, or 2,364) and decimal numbers (e.g., 135.34 or 0.00001) by allowing a special symbol after the variable name. This feature permits speedier handling of integer numeric data, which is desirable is some applications (as will be illustrated in later case studies). For now, all you need to know is that a % following a variable name represents integer numbers, a ! following represents single-precision numbers, and a # represents double-precision numbers. You will learn more about this later.

INPUT and READ/DATA Statements

BASIC has two main commands that allow you to enter data into the computer: INPUT and READ. The INPUT statement accepts data from the keyboard and causes the program to stop until the programmer or computer operator enters the data it is looking for. The READ statement, on the other hand, looks within the program itself for data. A READ statement must be used in conjunction with a DATA statement that contains the actual data for the program. Both INPUT and READ are preceded by, in order, a statement number; a blank; the keyword INPUT or READ, respectively; and a blank. These are then followed by variable names corresponding to the type of information to be input. Since the INPUT statement is actually asking the person at the keyboard to enter data into the computer, a prompt should be added to the statement. This prompt will serve as a reminder of what should be entered, and must be enclosed in double quotation marks. A semicolon must be placed after the second quotation mark and before the variable names. If there is more than one variable, the variable names are separated by commas. Examples of the proper format for these commands are provided below:

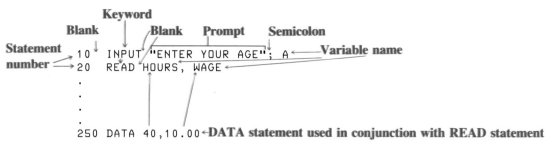

When the computer executes line 10, it will print the prompt "ENTER YOUR AGE" on the screen and stop processing. After a number has been entered and the return key pressed, that number will be stored under the variable name A.

Next, line 20 will be executed. When the READ statement is executed, the computer will immediately look for a corresponding DATA statement, which is found in line 250 in this example. The first number (40) will be read and assigned to the first variable name (HOURS). Then the second number (10.00) will be read and assigned to the second variable name (WAGE).

Once variable names are specified, a complete INPUT statement would look like this:

```
line# INPUT NM$, PHO$
```

Since no prompt has been included, the computer will display only a question mark on the CRT screen, indicating it is expecting data. A ? is always placed on the screen by INPUT. It's the machine's signal for a person to type in the data. The data is then entered after the ?. For example,

```
JOHN SMITH,233-4040
```

would cause JOHN SMITH to be stored in NM$ and 233-4040 in PHO$. Numbers can be entered without quotation marks and with or without decimal points, but large numbers such as 1,222.00 must be entered without commas, because since the comma is the field separator, a comma would indicate another field within this number.

The INPUT statement is referred to as an interactive instruction because the program pauses when an INPUT is encountered, and the computer waits for input from the keyboard. Sometimes, it is desirable to provide all the data within the program so that no human interaction is required. This is when the combination of READ and DATA instructions is used. The following illustrates this alternative input method.

```
100 REM *********************************
110 REM *           INPUT DATA          *
120 REM *********************************
130 READ NM$, PHO$
140 DATA "JOHN SMITH","234-5678"
150 RETURN
```

Actually, the DATA statement, which contains the input exactly as it would have been entered on the terminal with the interactive INPUT statement, could be placed anywhere in the program. However, good programming practice calls for placing small DATA statements (less than 5 lines) immediately below the READ statement that refers to them and large DATA statements at the end of the program. The program's purpose determines when READ/DATA statements are used as opposed to an INPUT statement. However, there are no hard-and-fast rules. Generally, most of the interactive programs described in this chapter use INPUT. Programs that produce tables, single numerical answers, or scientific computations often use the READ/DATA combination. You will encounter many examples of both INPUT and READ/DATA commands in later case examples.

OUTPUT ON THE CRT AND PRINTER

PRINT Statements

Although the PRINT statement is really the only display output instruction in BASIC, there are many variations of it. For example, the simplest form of the instruction contains the word PRINT preceded by a line number and followed by the variables or variable names to be printed. These values are separated by commas or semicolons. For example, the instruction

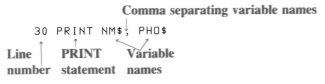

will cause the present contents of the memory locations NM$ (name) and PHO$ (phone number) to be displayed directly on the screen with automatic spacing (print zones) between the name and phone number. The comma separating the variables tells the computer to place their values in the corresponding print zones. The print zones will vary in the number of characters they contain (usually 14 characters) depending on the BASIC system being used. For example, the following is one output for the above program line.

Zone 1   **Zone 2**

`JOHN SMITH    242-8080`

14 characters long

A similar instruction, which sends output directly to the printer (assuming a printer is connected to your computer) instead of the screen is the LPRINT command. LPRINT functions the same as the PRINT instruction except that output is directed to the printer instead of the screen.

Enter the programs shown next and experiment with the PRINT and LPRINT commands. Note how both the screen and printed page are automatically divided into sections so that the output is evenly spaced (output is shown in color). When you do not want automatic spacing, you can use the PRINT USING and/or TAB command instead. (Because these statements are more complicated than the PRINT and LPRINT instructions, they will be discussed later.)

Screen Output   **Printed Output**

Normal print zone spacing with comma between variables.

```
10   N$="JOHN"                    10   N$="JOHN"
20   PH$="242-8080"               20   PH$="242-8080"
30   PRINT N$,PH$                 30   LPRINT N$,PH$
50   END                          50   END
     RUN                               RUN
JOHN      242-8080                JOHN        242-8080
OK                                OK
```

Compressed print zones with semicolon between variables.

```
10   N$="JOHN"                    10   N$="JOHN"
20   PH$="242-8080"               20   PH$="242-8080"
30   PRINT N$;PH$                 30   LPRINT N$;PH$
50   END                          50   END
     RUN                               RUN
JOHN242-8080                      JOHN242-8080
OK                                OK
```

Print zone exceeded by long name; therefore, print zone 2 is skipped.

```
10   N$="JONATHAN CORNELIUS JONES"   10   N$="JONATHAN CORNELIUS JONES"
20   PH$="242-8080"                  20   PH$="242-8080"
30   PRINT N$,PH$                    30   LPRINT N$,PH$
50   END                             50   END
     RUN                                  RUN
JONATHAN CORNELIUS JONES   242-8080  JONATHAN CORNELIUS JONES   242-8080
OK                                   OK
```

Print zone exceeded, but semicolon causes phone number to be shifted to the left.

```
10   N$="JONATHAN CORNELIUS JONES"   10   N$="JONATHAN CORNELIUS JONES"
20   PH$="242-8080"                  20   PH$="242-8080"
30   PRINT N$;PH$                    30   LPRINT N$;PH$
50   END                             50   END
     RUN                                  RUN
JONATHAN CORNELIUS JONES242-8080     JONATHAN CORNELIUS JONES242-8080
OK                                   OK
```

Name and Phone Number Listing Program

CONCEPTS TO BE ILLUSTRATED

This program illustrates the concepts of inputting data with the keyboard and then converting this input onto a permanent record on the printer. The program is elementary in that no data is stored and only one input is processed. It is designed to help familiarize you with BASIC's most widely used input and output statements.

PROBLEM DEFINITION

Input Specifications

Use the computer keyboard to input data consisting of records subdivided into two data fields containing alphanumeric characters. The two fields are a person's name and eight-character phone number.

Processing Decisions and Formulas

No processing of the data records is required. The input is taken as is and transferred to your printer.

Output Specifications

The actual output appears below for the three versions of the program given here.

PROGRAM C3-1 Output

```
Screen Output
COPYRIGHT (C) 1989, BY MERRILL PUBLISHING COMPANY
FOR USE WITH STRUCTURED BASIC PROGRAMMING

PLEASE MAKE SURE THE PRINTER IS ON.
ENTER NAME AND PHONE NUMBER, SEPARATED BY A COMMA.
PRESS THE RETURN WHEN DATA IS PROPERLY ENTERED. ? JOHN SMITH, 123-4567

Printer Output
JOHN SMITH     123-4567
```

PROGRAM C3–2 Output

```
Screen Output

OK
RUN
COPYRIGHT (C) 1989, BY MERRILL PUBLISHING COMPANY
FOR USE WITH STRUCTURED BASIC PROGRAMMING
OK

Printer Output

JOHN SMITH     234-5678
```

PROGRAM C3–3 Output

```
Screen Output

COPYRIGHT (C) 1989, BY MERRILL PUBLISHING COMPANY
FOR USE WITH STRUCTURED BASIC PROGRAMMING
PLEASE MAKE SURE THAT THE PRINTER IS ON.
ENTER NAME AND PHONE NUMBER, SEPARATED BY A COMMA.
PRESS RETURN WHEN DATA IS ENTERED PROPERLY. ? JOHN SMITH,123-4567

Printer Output

JOHN SMITH     123-4567
```

Test Data

Use your own name and phone number, or the names and phone numbers of friends. Phone numbers will be input as alphanumeric data since the hyphen will be included in the number (e.g., 242-8050).

Error Recovery Routines

None.

Validation Procedures

After you receive results from the printer, verify that the output results are identical with the data that you input by visually inspecting the printout. If they are not, rerun the program, carefully retyping the data.

Figure C3–1 shows a structure chart for Case 3–1 and Figure C3–2 shows the flowcharts.

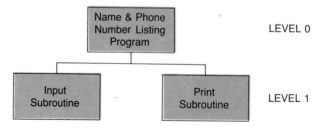

FIGURE C3–1
Structure chart for Case 3–1 showing program subroutines.

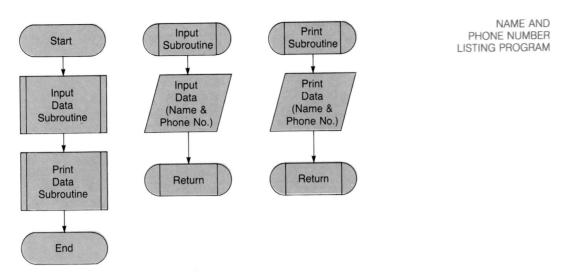

FIGURE C3-2

Flowchart for Case 3-1 showing main program and subroutines.

[handwritten: & ed   prog C3-1.bas]

[handwritten: Rem - Remark.]

CASE STUDY SOLUTION

PROGRAM C3-1

```
10      REM       ********************************************************
20      REM       *              INPUT/OUTPUT OPERATION                  *
30      REM       *                 CASE STUDY: C3-1                     *
40      REM       *        NAME & PHONE NUMBER LISTING PROGRAM           *
50      REM       *        THIS PROGRAM READS IN FROM THE TERMINAL       *
60      REM       *        A PERSON'S NAME AND PHONE NUMBER, AND         *
70      REM       *        PRINTS THEM OUT ON THE PRINTER.               *
80      REM       *                                                      *
90      REM       *              VARIABLE LEGEND                         *
100     REM       *            NM$  = NAME                               *
110     REM       *            PHO$ = PHONE NUMBER                       *
120     REM       ********************************************************
130               CLS       [handwritten: omit]
140               PRINT "COPYRIGHT (C) 1989, BY MERRILL PUBLISHING COMPANY"
150               PRINT "FOR USE WITH STRUCTURED BASIC PROGRAMMING"
160     REM       ****************
170     REM       * MAIN PROGRAM *
180     REM       ****************       [handwritten: →185 open "Printer.Lis" for output as File 1]
190     REM       PERFORM 'INPUT' SUBROUTINE
200               GOSUB 240
210     REM       PERFORM 'PRINT' SUBROUTINE
220               GOSUB 380       [handwritten: 225 close #1]
230               END       [handwritten: → Go to 999]
240     REM       ********************
250     REM       * INPUT SUBROUTINE *
260     REM       ********************
270               PRINT
280               PRINT
290               PRINT "PLEASE MAKE SURE THE PRINTER IS ON."
300               PRINT
310               PRINT "ENTER NAME AND PHONE NUMBER"
320               PRINT
330               PRINT "PRESS THE RETURN WHEN DATA IS PROPERLY ENTERED. "
340               PRINT
350               INPUT "ENTER NAME    ";NM$
360               INPUT "ENTER PHONE # ";PHO$
370               RETURN
```

```
380        REM        ********************
390        REM        *  PRINT SUBROUTINE  *
400        REM        ********************
410                   LPRINT NM$,PHO$            → 410 Print #1, NM$, PHO$
420                   RETURN
430        REM
440        REM        END OF PROGRAM
                                                   Control Z
                                                    * EX
```

PROGRAM C3-2 $ Ed prog c3-2.Bas

```
10         REM        ********************************************
20         REM        *          INPUT/OUTPUT OPERATION           *
30         REM        *            CASE STUDY: C3-2               *
40         REM        *     NAME & PHONE NUMBER LISTING PROGRAM    *
50         REM        *     THIS VERSION USED THE READ AND DATA    *
60         REM        *     STATEMENTS FOR INPUT                   *
70         REM        *                                           *
80         REM        *     VARIABLE LEGEND                        *
90         REM        *     NM$ = NAME                             *
100        REM        *     PHO$ = PHONE NUMBER                    *
110        REM        ********************************************
120                   PRINT "COPYRIGHT (C) 1989, BY MERRILL PUBLISHING COMPANY"
130                   PRINT "FOR USE WITH STRUCTURED BASIC PROGRAMMING"
140        REM        ****************
150        REM        * MAIN PROGRAM *
160        REM        ****************            → 165 open "Printer.lis" ForOutput as File 1
170        REM        PERFORM 'INPUT DATA' SUBROUTINE
180                   GOSUB 220
190        REM        PERFORM 'PRINT OUTPUT' SUBROUTINE
200                   GOSUB 280
210                   END                         → 205 close #1
220        REM        ********************
230        REM        * INPUT SUBROUTINE *
240        REM        ********************
250                   READ NM$,PHO$
260                   DATA "JOHN SMITH","234-5678"
270                   RETURN
280        REM        ********************
290        REM        * PRINT SUBROUTINE *
300        REM        ********************          → Print #2, NM$, PHO$
310                   LPRINT NM$,PHO$
320                   RETURN
330        REM
340        REM        END OF PROGRAM
           999        END
```

PROGRAM C3-3 $ ed c-3-3 .bas

```
10         REM        ********************************************
20         REM        *          INPUT/OUTPUT OPERATION           *
30         REM        *            CASE STUDY: C3-3               *
40         REM        *     NAME & PHONE NUMBER LISTING PROGRAM    *
50         REM        *     THIS PROGRAM READS IN FROM THE TERMINAL *
60         REM        *     A PERSON'S NAME AND PHONE NUMBER, AND   *
70         REM        *     PRINTS THEM OUT ON THE PRINTER.         *
80         REM        *                                           *
90         REM        *     AN "ENDLESS" LOOP HAS BEEN ADDED        *
100        REM        *       NM$ = NAME                           *
110        REM        *       PHO$ = PHONE NUMBER                   *
120        REM        ********************************************
130                   CLS       open "Printer.lis" For Output as File 1
```

```
140     REM      * * * * * * * * * * * * * * * *
150     REM      * MAIN PROGRAM *
160     REM      * * * * * * * * * * * * * * * *
170     REM      PERFORM 'INPUT' SUBROUTINE
180              GOSUB 220
190     REM      PERFORM 'PRINT' SUBROUTINE
200              GOSUB 390
210              GOTO 170                              210 IF NM$ = "STOP"
                   (CTRLC - to shutdown)               then GOTO 435 ELSE GOTO 170
220     REM      * * * * * * * * * * * * * * * * * * *
230     REM      * INPUT SUBROUTINE *
240     REM      * * * * * * * * * * * * * * * * * * *
250              PRINT "COPYRIGHT (C) 1989, BY MERRILL PUBLISHING COMPANY"
260              PRINT "FOR USE WITH STRUCTURED BASIC PROGRAMMING"
270              PRINT
280              PRINT
290              PRINT "PLEASE MAKE SURE THAT THE PRINTER IS ON."
300              PRINT
310              PRINT "ENTER NAME AND PHONE NUMBER"
320              PRINT
330              PRINT "PRESS RETURN WHEN DATA IS ENTERED PROPERLY."
340              PRINT
350              INPUT "ENTER NAME    ";NM$
360              INPUT "ENTER PHONE #";PHO$
370              CLS         omit
380              RETURN
390     REM      * * * * * * * * * * * * * * * * * * *
400     REM      * PRINT SUBROUTINE *
410     REM      * * * * * * * * * * * * * * * * * * *
420              LPRINT NM$,PHO$           Print #1, NM$, PHO$
430              RETURN              435 Close #1
440     REM
450     REM      END OF PROGRAM
```

PROG1. Basic - ED Prog1.Bas
- EDIT EDITOR

INPUT/OUTPUT ENHANCEMENTS

Inputting Data with Prompts

Often all fields in a record are input from a single INPUT command. However, it is possible, and often advantageous, to input the data with separate INPUT commands, each one containing a statement (prompt) to the programmer or to the data entry operator requesting the data the program is looking for, as shown below. Note how they reduce the potential of not understanding what data should be entered and when.

```
330     INPUT "ENTER EMPLOYEE NUMBER"; IDNO
340     INPUT "ENTER EMPLOYEE NAME"; ENAME$
350     INPUT "ENTER EMPLOYEE ADDRESS"; ADDS$
360     INPUT "ENTER EMPLOYEE AGE"; AGE
370     INPUT "ENTER MARITAL STATUS"; MS$
380     INPUT "ENTER EMPLOYEE PAY RATE"; RATE
```

This series of input instructions would produce the following display instead of a single question mark.

```
ENTER EMPLOYEE NUMBER?      63151
ENTER EMPLOYEE NAME?        JOHN C. JONES
ENTER EMPLOYEE ADDRESS?     125 MAIN ST. HARTFORD CONN.
ENTER EMPLOYEE AGE?         31
ENTER MARITAL STATUS?       S
ENTER EMPLOYEE PAY RATE?    7.50
```

The input data is entered on the screen and the next prompt automatically appears. In most programming situations, an INPUT statement with a prompt is essential since most program users are not the actual programmers and, therefore, may have little idea of what a ? on the screen means.

Printing Titles and Headings

Printing titles in BASIC is simple. You use the PRINT command (or the LPRINT if you want to send the title or heading to the printer) followed by your title or heading enclosed in quotation marks. The title can be any word, phrase, or series of numbers as long as it is enclosed in quotation marks. Placing the literal (title) in the proper location on the screen or paper can be accomplished in a number of ways.

First, you can place the title in quotation marks, leaving the desired number of spaces before the first title word and between each successive title word. An example of this is shown below where the numbers shown in color denote spaces.

```
430 PRINT " EMPLOYEE NO   NAME     ADDRESS    AGE     MAR ST    PAY RATE "
            2          3       5       5      5       5     1    1
```

If the output is to be printed on a printer, be careful not to exceed the maximum number of available print positions. This is determined by the type of printer being used.

Another method, which is less subject to space counting errors, uses the TAB function available on most BASIC interpreters. Here, the programmer specifies the column that each word in the title is to start in by placing that column number in parentheses behind the word TAB. For example, titles could be printed using the following PRINT statement where the statements shown in color denote spaces:

```
line# PRINT "EMPLOYEE NO." TAB(15) "NAME" TAB(32) "ADDRESS"
      TAB(53) "AGE" TAB(60) "MAR ST" TAB(70) "PAY RATE"
```

Editing Output with PRINT USING and LPRINT USING

The PRINT USING instruction in itself provides a powerful method of printing titles and data, and of editing output with $, commas, and decimal places. The key to understanding this instruction is in the USING which follows PRINT. USING refers to a "format string" which determines where and how the variables or literals following it are to be printed.

The string (or image, as it is sometimes called) is the heart of the PRINT USING statement. It is the part that determines *how* the variables that are named in the statement will appear when they are printed on the display or printer (for LPRINT USING).

The general form for PRINT USING is

line#	PRINT USING	{string or "image"}	variable 1, variable 2, etc.
↑	↑	↑	↑
Required	**Required key word must appear as written except the PRINT may be substituted with LPRINT, which will direct the output to a printer instead of the screen**	**This string (or image) determines *how* the variables named on the right should appear when they are printed out. The string controls such things as position on screen, number of decimal places, location of special characters like $, *, or commas.**	**The variables are named here. These will be printed according to the string (or image). The string will tell the computer how and where to print the variables, and whether to limit decimal places to one, two, or no places.**

The string (or image) may be placed directly in the PRINT USING statement like this:

```
line# PRINT USING "$ ###.##";AMOUNT
```

or it may be defined elsewhere in the program as a separate string and referred to by the PRINT USING statement, like this:

```
190 F$ = " $ ###.##"
200 PRINT USING F$;AMOUNT
```

In either case, the string is formatted with a combination of editing characters and data-accepting characters. The editing characters are the dollar sign and the decimal point. The data-accepting character is the pound sign (#). The editing characters usually do not get changed when the PRINT USING is executed, but rather appear on the output as they do in the string. On the other hand, the data-accepting characters *do change according to the values of the variable being printed*. For example, if the variable AMOUNT had contained the value 105.6312 in memory, then both PRINT USING statements 100 and 200 would produce the result

```
$ 105.63
```

Notice that the dollar sign and the decimal editing characters came out unchanged, while the numbers in AMOUNT replaced the pound signs. Also, notice that there were more digits in memory for AMOUNT, but that this particular string ($ ###.##) limited the number of digits after the decimal point to two. Thus, the variable AMOUNT was edited and presented in a more useful form. Without PRINT USING, a PRINT statement like

```
300 PRINT AMOUNT
```

would produce the output

```
105.6312
```

In the next section, you will see that by choosing the appropriate editing characters and writing the string with some useful conventions and techniques, you will be able to do many sophisticated editing and data placement operations, including the following:

1. Suppressing zeros
2. Placing decimal points where desired
3. Leaving off unnecessary decimal places
4. Putting in dollar signs and floating dollar signs
5. Putting in asterisks and floating asterisks
6. Placing commas in large numbers
7. Adding titles and labels to output numbers
8. Printing string variables in desired locations
9. Printing all or part of string variables
10. Spacing titles and output results as desired for good layout
11. Other operations specific to the needs of your programs

Table 3–3 illustrates the characters used in the string format portion of the PRINT USING statement and their functions on a variety of variables. Table 3–4 shows how these string formats, built from combinations of editing and data-accepting characters, allow you to format your output for realistic business and financial applications programs.

Take a look at the examples in figure 3–6. Try these out to test the power of PRINT USING on your computer, since different BASIC systems vary quite a bit in using this statement.

TABLE 3–3

PRINT USING format characters.

Editing and Data-Accepting Characters	Accepts or Edits
#	A number
\ \	String data
.	Places a decimal point
,	Places a comma
+, −	Places a plus/minus sign
$	Places a $
$$	Places a floating $
**	Places a floating *

TABLE 3–4

Examples of PRINT USING formats.

Data	Format	Results
Numbers		
6	#	6
56	##	56
4.56	#.##	4.56
34.56	##.##	34.56
1234.56	#,###.##	1,234.56
0.56	#,###.##	0.56
*Strings**		
EMPLOYEE	_____\	EMPLOYEE
AGE	_\	AGE
MAR. ST.	_____\	MAR. ST.
**	\\	**
*	!	*
*	_____\	*____
Plus or Minus		
+56	+##	+56
−56	−##	−56
+56	##+	56+
−56	##−	56−
+56	##+	56
−56	##−	56−
Dollar Signs		
34.56	$###.##	$ 34.56
34.56	$$###.##	$34.56
.05	$$###.##	$0.05
1234.56	$$####.##	$1234.56
Asterisk and Asterisk + $		
34.56	**##.##	**34.56
234.56	**##.##	*234.56
1234.56	**###.##	*1234.56
34.56	**$###.##	***$34.56

*Data edited by string formats can also be variables, for example,
```
TITLE = "ABC COMPANY"
PRINT USING "_____\"; TITLE
```
gives:
```
ABC COMPANY
```

FIGURE 3–6
PRINT USING examples.

```
5    REM THE PRINT USING STATEMENT TO CONTROL DECIMAL PLACES
10       N = 6
20       LPRINT N
30       LPRINT USING "#";N
40   REM
50       N = 56                                    6
60       LPRINT N                                  6
70       LPRINT USING "##";N                       56
80   REM                                           56
90       N = 4.56                                  4.56
100      LPRINT N                                  4.56
110      LPRINT USING "#.##";N                     34
120  REM                                           34.00
130      N = 34!                                   1234
140      LPRINT N                                  1,234.00
150      LPRINT USING "##.##";N                    .56
160  REM                                           0.5600
170      N = 1234!
180      LPRINT N
190      LPRINT USING"#,###.##";N
200  REM
210      N = .56
220      LPRINT N
230      LPRINT USING "##.####";N
240  END

100  REM THE PRINT USING TO INSERT PLUS AND MINUS SIGNS
110      N = + 56
120      LPRINT N                                  56
130      LPRINT USING "+##";N                      +56
140      LPRINT USING "##+";N                      56+
150      LPRINT USING "-##";N                      +56
160      LPRINT USING "##-";N                      56
170  REM                                           -56
180      N = - 56                                  -56
190      LPRINT N                                  56-
200      LPRINT USING "+##";N                      -56
210      LPRINT USING "##+";N                      56-
220      LPRINT USING "-##";N
230      LPRINT USING "##-";N
240  END

90   REM ASTERISKS AND DOLLAR SIGNS WITH PRINT USING
100      N = 34.56
110      LPRINT N                                  34.56
120      LPRINT USING "**##.##";N
125  REM                                           **34.56
130      N = 234.56
140      LPRINT N                                  234.56
150      LPRINT USING "**##.##";N
155  REM                                           *234.56
160      N = 1234.56
170      LPRINT N                                  1234.56
180      LPRINT USING "**###.##";N
185  REM                                           *1234.56
190      N = 34.56
200      LPRINT N                                  34.56
210      LPRINT USING "**$###.##";N
220  REM                                           ***$34.56
230      N = 34.56

240      LPRINT N                                  34.56
250      LPRINT USING "$###.##";N                  $ 34.56
```

```
260 REM
270     N = 34.56
280     LPRINT N                              ─────────→ 34.56
290     LPRINT USING "$$###.##";N ─────────
300 REM                                        ─────→ $ 34.56
310     N = .05
320     LPRINT N                              ─────────→ .05
330     LPRINT USING "$$###.##";N ─────────
340 REM                                        ─────→ $0.05
350     N = 1234.56
360     LPRINT N                              ─────────→ 1234.56
370     LPRINT USING "$$###,###.##";N ─────
380 REM                                        ─────→ $1,234.56
390     N = 0
400     LPRINT N                              ─────────→ 0
410     LPRINT USING "$$###,###.##";N ─────
420 END                                        ─────→ $0.00
```

Personnel Data Input and Listing Program

CONCEPTS TO BE ILLUSTRATED

This case study illustrates that BASIC stores different types of data in different ways in the program. All of the types of data listed previously are not used, since some of them are not common to the business environment. (Exponential numbers and double-precision numbers will be dealt with in chapter 4.) Since many business reports would be difficult to read without titles, headings, and edited numbers (such as the floating dollar sign and asterisks to show rounded off decimal places), these concepts are illustrated in this case.

All data processed by a computer is alphanumeric. In fact, data can be a combination of any of the following:

1. Alphabetic—letters only
2. Alphanumeric—letters, numbers, and special characters
3. Numeric (integers)—whole or counting numbers
4. Numeric (decimals)—scientific numbers or numbers of measurement
5. Exponential numeric—large or very small numbers

Most computer programs process many types of data from one record. With normal billing programs, such as those for charge accounts or utility bills, a variety of information is gathered consisting of numeric, alphanumeric, and alphabetic information. The following table lists some sample data with the type of data identified.

Data	Data Type
Customer name	alphabetic
Customer address	alphanumeric
Customer account number	alphanumeric
Hours and days	numeric (integer)
Dollar and cents amounts	numeric (decimal)
Text	alphanumeric

In this case, five common types of data are input and printed out. They are listed below.

Data	Data Type
ID number	numeric (integer)
Employee name and marital status	alphabetic
Address	alphanumeric
Age	numeric (integer)
Hourly pay rate	numeric (decimal)

No calculations are performed on the data, but you should be able to recognize the different data types.

The structure of Case 3–2 is nearly identical to that of Case 3–1: one input routine and two output routines, one for titles and the other for edited output.* The major difference is the type of output (namely, a combination of numeric, alphabetic, and alphanumeric data) and the way in which the output is printed (specifically, with headings to identify each field and with editing so that the fields can be printed how and where you would like them).

---

*Editing output involves placing dollar signs, commas, decimal points, etc., where desired, and it will be described later on in detail.

PROBLEM DEFINITION

Input Specifications

Field No.	Field Description	Type	Example
1	Employee Number	Integer	65151
2	Employee Name	Alphabetic	John C. Jones
3	Address	Alphanumeric	123 Main St. Hartford CT
4	Age of Employee	Integer	31
5	Marital Status	Alphabetic	S
6	Employee Pay Rate	Decimal Number	7.50

Processing Decisions and Formulas

None.

Output

```
Screen Output

RUN
COPYRIGHT (C) 1989, BY MERRILL PUBLISHING COMPANY
FOR USE WITH STRUCTURED BASIC PROGRAMMING
? 65151,JOHN C. JONES, 123 MAIN ST. HARTFORD CT, 31, S, 7.50

Printed Output

EMPLOYEE NO.      NAME              ADDRESS              AGE   MAR.ST.   PAYRATE
    65151     JOHN C. JONES   123 MAIN ST. HARTFORD CT    31      S         7.50
```

Test Data

65151, John C. Jones, 123 Main St. Hartford CT, 31, S, 7.50

Error Routines

None.

Validation Procedure

Examine the output and verify that it is identical to the input data. Check for proper spacing and alignment under headings.

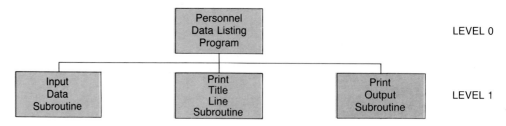

FIGURE C3–3
Visual table of contents—personnel data listing program.

74

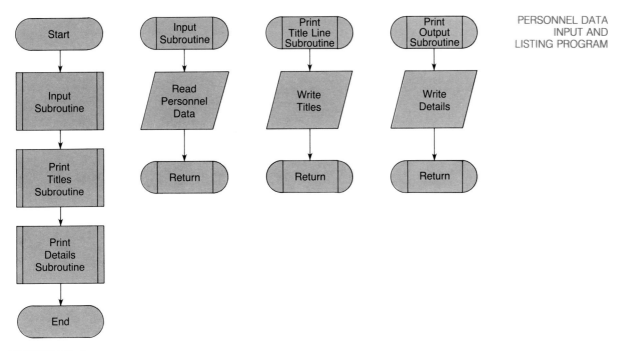

FIGURE C3–4
Program flowchart showing main program and subroutines.

CASE STUDY SOLUTION

```
10      REM       ********************************************
20      REM       *          INPUT/OUTPUT OPERATION         *
30      REM       *            CASE STUDY: C3-2             *
40      REM       *    PERSONNEL DATA LISTING PROGRAM       *
50      REM       * THIS PROGRAM ACCEPTS DATA FROM THE      *
60      REM       * KEYBOARD AND PRINTS THE DATA WITH A     *
70      REM       * TITLE ON THE PRINTER.                   *
80      REM       *          VARIABLE LEGEND                *
90      REM       *         ENO = EMPLOYEE NUMBER           *
100     REM       *         NAM$ = EMPLOYEE NAME            *
110     REM       *         ADDS$ = ADDRESS                 *
120     REM       *         AGE = AGE                       *
130     REM       *         MS$ = MARITAL STATUS            *
140     REM       *         PRAT = PAY RATE                 *
150     REM       ********************************************
160               PRINT "COPYRIGHT (C) 1989, BY MERRILL PUBLISHING COMPANY"
170               PRINT "FOR USE WITH STRUCTURED BASIC PROGRAMMING"
180     REM       ****************
190     REM       * MAIN PROGRAM *
200     REM       ****************
210     REM       PERFORM 'INPUT DATA' SUBROUTINE
220               GOSUB 280
230     REM       PERFORM 'PRINT TITLE LINE' SUBROUTINE
240               GOSUB 330
250     REM       PERFORM 'PRINT OUTPUT' SUBROUTINE
260               GOSUB 380
270               END
280     REM       *******************
290     REM       * INPUT SUBROUTINE *
300     REM       *******************
310               INPUT ENO, NAM$,ADDS$,AGE,MS$,PRAT
320               RETURN
```

```
330        REM       *****************************
340        REM       * PRINT TITLE LINE SUBROUTINE *
350        REM       *****************************
360                  LPRINT "EMPLOYEE NO.      NAME                    ADDRESS
   AGE    MAR.ST.  PAYRATE"
370                  RETURN
380        REM       **************************
390        REM       * PRINT OUTPUT SUBROUTINE *
400        REM       **************************
410                  F1$ = "  #####         \            \ \
   ##      \ \    ##.##"
420                  LPRINT USING F1$;ENO,NAM$,ADDS$,AGE,MS$,PRAT
430                  RETURN
440        REM
450        REM       END OF PROGRAM
```

ADDING A PROFESSIONAL LOOK TO YOUR PROGRAMS

Using Color

If your computer system contains a color monitor, you can add a more professional look as well as some variety to your program by using color. The COLOR statement sets the colors for the foreground (letters, numbers, and special characters), the background (screen), and the border. The exact syntax you use to specify these depends on whether you are in the text or graphics mode. The color statements and keywords are specific to IBM's BASICA, so check your BASIC manual for differences if you are using another version of BASIC.

When you first begin using BASIC, the color is set to white on black. The format for using the COLOR command is

```
line# COLOR (Foreground number), (Background number), (Border number)
```

The foreground number represents a number between 0 to 15. Each number represents a different color (see table 3–5). The foreground color is set by choosing one of the 15 numbered options. To choose a background or border color, you also insert a number from 0 to 15. The following table shows the usable number ranges for the COLOR command.

Setting	Number
Foreground	0 to 15
	16 to 31 (character blink)
Background	0 to 15
Border	0 to 15

Colors and intensity can vary depending on your display device. You might like to think of colors 8 to 15 as ''light'' or ''high-intensity'' values of colors 0 to 7. You can make the color characters blink by setting foreground equal to 16 *plus* the number of the desired color. That is, values of 16 through 31 cause blinking characters. You can select only color 0 through 7 for the background in the text mode.

If you have the IBM monochrome display and parallel printer adapter, the following values can be used for setting foreground colors

Number	Foreground Color
0	Black
1	Underline character with standard foreground color
2 through 7	Standard foreground color

TABLE 3–5
Foreground colors and corresponding numbers.

Number	Color
0	Black
1	Blue
2	Green
3	Cyan
4	Red
5	Magenta
6	Brown
7	White
8	Gray
9	Light Blue
10	Light Green
11	Light Cyan
12	Light Red
13	Light Magenta
14	Yellow
15	High-intensity White

With the color/graphics monitor, adding 8 to the number of the desired color gives you the color in high intensity. For example, an attribute of 15 gives you the standard color in high intensity (7 white + 8 = 15, high-intensity white). With the color/graphics monitor adapter, you can make the character blink by adding 16 to the attribute. Thus, 31 gives you high-intensity standard color characters.

For background with the IBM monochrome display and parallel printer adapter, you can select the following values:

Number	Background Color
0 through 6	Black
7	Standard foreground color

Attribute 7 as a background attribute appears as the standard color in the IBM monochrome display only when it is used with a foreground attribute of 0, 8, 16, or 24 (black). Conversely, black (attribute 0, 8, 16, or 24) as a foreground attribute shows up as black only when used with a background attribute that creates reverse image characters. Black used with a background of 0 makes the characters invisible. Other combinations of foreground and background attributes produce standard results on the IBM monochrome display.

For either adapter, the following general rules apply.

1. Foreground attribute can equal background attribute, which makes any character displayed invisible. Changing the foreground or background color makes subsequent characters visible again.
2. Any color number can be omitted. Omitted values assume the old value.
3. If the COLOR statement ends in a comma, you get a missing operand error, but the color changes. For example, the following is invalid

```
COLOR 1,7,
```

4. Any values entered outside the range 0 to 255 result in an illegal function call error. Previous values are retained.

The following is a complete and correct COLOR statement which sets a yellow foreground, a blue background, and a black border screen. It can be used with either the color/graphics monitor adapter or the IBM monochrome display and parallel printer adapter.

```
10   REM *** HIGH INTENSITY PROGRAM ***
20   COLOR 15
30   PRINT "CAPTAIN AHAB"
40   COLOR 7
50   END

150  REM *** BLINKING PROGRAM ***
160  COLOR 23
170  PRINT "STEVES ICE CREAM COMPANY!"
180  COLOR 7
190  END
```

Notice that lines 40 and 180 return the color setting to its original colors. Be careful not to use the COLOR 0 command because you will not be able to see your cursor or the letters you type since both the cursor and the background will be set to black.

FULL-SCREEN FORMATTING FOR INPUT

Often you will find it desirable to enter data on the screen with the keyboard as if you are filling out a form. Prompts for all the information to be entered are displayed on the screen at the same time. Then, all the data is typed in response to the cursor position, which is aligned with the appropriate prompt. As data is typed in and entered with the enter key, the cursor moves automatically to the next prompt until the screen (or form) is completed.

This method, sometimes called ''forms entry,'' has a number of psychological advantages as well as tangible differences when compared to the more elementary method of displaying a prompt, entering the data, displaying another prompt, and so on. First, when the screen is set up like a form, it is clear to you at the outset exactly how much data and in what order the data is to be entered. This makes the job of entering data discrete and tangible, eliminating the sometimes distressing ''surprises'' of having to re-type large amounts of data. Also, since the order of data fields is clearly shown, the user is less likely to inadvertently switch the order in which the data is entered. Second, screen formatting, when combined with some simple programming techniques, permits graphic displays of required field sizes. You know before entering a field how long or short it must be, and even what an acceptable range of values is. Third, screen formatting encourages you to use error trapping logic as the data is being entered, thus permitting you to correct incorrect data entries prior to actual data processing steps during program execution. A number of error-signalling techniques, which make use of sound, color, and cursor position, make it possible to prepare programs that won't be halted by entering erroneous data. (However, program results will not always be correct in these cases.)

The LOCATE Statement

Full-screen formatting makes use of the new BASIC command

```
LOCATE R, C
```

where R is the row number (the vertical positioning, with 25 being the standard for most BASIC system CRTs) and C is the column number (with 80 being the standard) that the cursor is moved back to for an INPUT statement that follows it. The following is an example of a LOCATE and INPUT command sequence that places the cursor at line 12 and column 25, and then requests an employee name:

```
LOCATE 12, 25: INPUT "ENTER EMPLOYEE NAME ........";NM$
```

This INPUT statement has the same function as an INPUT without the LOCATE preceding it, except that the cursor and the question mark will appear on line 12 at column 25 after the literal, as follows:

```
ENTER EMPLOYEE NAME ........?
```

Data errors can be signaled using commands such as SOUND, COLOR, and IF/THEN. They can be used to signal the user and trap erroneous data before it is "passed" to the program for processing. Of course, not all errors can be trapped. Typing in a pay rate of $9.00 per hour instead of $6.00 per hour can go undetected if $9.00 per hour is an acceptable pay rate. This, in turn, would result in the employee receiving a higher than normal paycheck, and would not be easy for the programmer to catch. Examples of data errors that are more easily trapped are inputting a month number greater than 12, a date number greater than 31, or a marital status that is not one of the defined codes of married (M), single (S), divorced (D), and so on. True numeric errors that are within acceptable ranges are almost impossible to detect in a program. This is why you sometimes get bills that are off slightly or have omissions of deposits or checks in your bank statements.

Error trapping entails including logic in your program for finding errors before processing begins. It saves a great deal of time and effort. Some error detection, trapping, and correction can be accomplished in BASIC with ON ERROR statements, which have the following format:

```
line# ON ERROR GOTO error-routine-line#
```

The error-routine line# is the first line number of the error-trapping routine. If the line number does not exist, an undefined line number error results.

Once error trapping has been enabled, *all* errors detected will cause a jump to the specified error handling subroutine. To disable error trapping, you execute an ON ERROR GOTO 0. Subsequent errors print an error message and halt execution.

The BASIC program stops normal execution from the time an error occurs and branches to the line specified by the ON ERROR statement until a RESUME statement is found which permits an exit from the error trapping routine (see "RESUME statement" below). The following example tests to see whether data is available when the program needs to access it.

```
10 ON ERROR GOTO 100
20 READ A,B,C,D,E,F,G
30 END
40 DATA 10,20,5,4
      .
      .
      .
100 IF ERR = 4 THEN LOCATE 23,1:
      PRINT "DATA IS NOT AVAILABLE"
110 RESUME NEXT
```

Errors trapped during input and output fall into one of the categories listed in table 3-6. Each error and its corresponding error routine must be specifically designed and written so that the data is reentered, a message displayed, and/or program execution continues at the proper location as indicated by the RESUME statement, as shown below. The format for RESUME can be any one of the following:

```
line# RESUME
line# RESUME NEXT
line# RESUME line#
RESUME or RESUME 100
```

This means that execution resumes at the statement that caused the error. (If you try to renumber a program containing a RESUME statement, you will get an undefined line number error.)

TABLE 3–6
Basic error codes and descriptions (input/output).

BASIC Error Code	Description
4 Out of data	A READ statement tried to read more than is in the DATA statements.
6 Overflow	A number is too large to be represented in BASIC's number format. Integer overflow is the only type of overflow that can be trapped. To correct integer overflow, use single- or double-precision variables.
13 Type mismatch	You gave a string value where a numeric value was expected. This may also be caused by trying to SWAP variables of different types, such as single and double precision.
14 Out of string space	BASIC allocates string space dynamically until it runs out of memory. This message means that string variables caused BASIC to exceed the amount of free memory remaining.
15 String too long	You tried to create a string more than 255 characters long. To correct this error, break the string into shorter strings.
24 Device timeout	BASIC did not receive information from an input/output device within a predetermined amount of time. Most often, the printer was not turned on in the specified period of time. Retry the operation after turning on your printer.
25 Device fault	A hardware error indication was returned by an interface adapter. This message can occur when data is transmitted to a communications file and the file is not available. In this case, it indicates that one or more of the signals being tested (specified on the OPEN ''COM...statement) were found in the specified time period.
27 Out of paper	The printer is out of paper or is not switched on. You should make sure that the power is on, verify that the printer is properly connected, insert paper if necessary, and then continue the program.
68 Device unavailable	You tried to open a file to a device that is not installed. Either you do not have the hardware to support the device (such as printer adapters for a second or third printer) or you have disabled the device.

This means that execution resumes at the statement immediately following the one that caused the error.

```
RESUME line#
```

This means that execution resumes at the specified line number.

In the following example, line 1000 is the beginning of the error trapping routine.

```
10    ON ERROR GOTO 1000
      .
      .
      .
1000 IF (ERR = 40) AND (ERL = 20) THEN PRINT "ENTER A
NUMBER, NOT A STRING and TRY AGAIN": RESUME 20
```

Note from table 3–6 that most of the error codes that can be detected by the ON ERROR statement in BASIC involve hardware and/or variable problems. The built-in error statements are very useful in helping the programmer recognize and correct oversights and system problems. Using the wrong type of variable, leaving the printer off or letting it run out of paper, leaving a disk drive door open or a write protect tape on a disk, etc., can all be detected with the ON ERROR/RESUME statements. Errors regarding insufficient memory, little data in the READ/DATA statements, strings that are too long, branching to a nonexistent statement, and many other syntactical problems can also be detected with the ON ERROR/RESUME. In fact, it may seem that almost every type of error can be detected and corrected with the built-in statements in BASIC, but in practice very few business programs rely on these.

While it is important for professional programmers to "protect" the user from oversights and errors like those described above, it is more important in business programming to recognize and, if possible, prevent the entry of invalid numeric or string data. Therefore, most business program error routines are custom tailored to a particular program, and sometimes to the needs of specific users. Error trapping that limits the hours-worked input for employees to a reasonable maximum value or places a ceiling on the pay rate of company employees is typical. Making sure that accrued sick days and vacation days are within reasonable limits and payments and credits are not excessive (or fraudulent) are common in business programs.

In Case 3–3, error trapping might be used to check the vacation days, sick days, hourly pay rate, FICA code, and years worked for the company to make sure they are within reasonable limits. These error routines are not shown in this chapter because the logic needed uses complex and often compound IF statements (to be covered in chapter 6).

Remember that although the important error trapping and recovery routines are omitted in many of the early case programs and illustrations because the syntax has not been covered yet, these routines are vital in business programming to reduce the incidence of incorrect program output and fraudulent use of computer systems.

Full-Screen Formatting: Payroll and Personnel Data Input and Listing

CONCEPTS TO BE ILLUSTRATED

This case incorporates the enhancements to input and output described in the chapter, including use of full-screen formatting, color, and error-trapping and correction routines.

This case expands on Case 3-2, Personnel Data Input and Listing Program, to include 14 realistic employee data fields which are entered onto a display form which is presented on the screen in color (if a color monitor is used), with field size indicators and descriptive prompts for each field. The actual data is entered in a different color and the completed "form" is printed on the printer.

Logic is included to perform some elementary error trapping. In this case, if the printer is inadvertently left off, the program error logic reminds the user to turn on the printer and the output is printed. Without this logic, the program would have to be rerun and all the data (14 fields) would have to be retyped. More advanced error routines that trap data errors are included in some of the later cases since the syntax needed is not covered until chapter 6.

PROBLEM DEFINITION

Input Specifications

Field No.	Field Description	Type	Example
1	Employee Name	Alphabetic	John C. Jones
2	Employee Address	Alphanumeric	125 Main Street
3	Home Phone Number	Alphanumeric	203-569-1234
4	Work Phone Number	Alphanumeric	203-233-1234
5	Number of Dependents	Integer	3
6	Allocated Vacation	Integer	14
7	Allocated Sick Days	Integer	14
8	Hourly Pay Rate	Decimal Number	9.50
9	FICA code (1 2 or 3)	Integer	3
10	Employee Extension	Integer	234
11	Department	Alphabetic	Production
12	Supervisor Name	Alphabetic	Bob M. Smith
13	Job Title	Alphabetic	Production Supervisor
14	Years Employed	Integer	8

Processing Decisions and Formulas

None.

Output

FULL SCREEN
FORMATTING:
PAYROLL AND
PERSONNEL DATA
INPUT AND
LISTING

Screen Layout Before Data Entry Output

```
            PAYROLL AND PERSONNEL DATA LISTING
            AN EXAMPLE OF FULL SCREEN FORMATTING

ENTER EMPLOYEE NAME.........?  _____
ENTER EMPLOYEE ADDRESS......   _____
ENTER HOME PHONE NUMBER.....   (__) __-___
ENTER WORK PHONE NUMBER.....   (__) __-___
ENTER NUMBER OF DEPENDENTS..   __
ENTER ALLOCATED VACATION....   __
ENTER ALLOCATED SICK DAYS...   __
ENTER HOURLY PAY RATE.......   __.__
ENTER FICA CODE (1 2 OR 3)..   _
ENTER EMPLOYEE EXTENSION....   __
ENTER DEPARTMENT............   _____
ENTER SUPERVISORS NAME......   _____
ENTER JOB TITLE.............   _____
ENTER YEARS EMPLOYED........   __
```

Screen after Input

```
COPYRIGHT (C) 1989, BY MERRILL PUBLISHING COMPANY
          FOR USE WITH STRUCTURED BASIC PROGRAMMING

      PLEASE MAKE SURE THE PRINTER IS ON

      PAYROLL AND PERSONNEL DATA LISTING
      AN EXAMPLE OF FULL SCREEN FORMATTING

ENTER EMPLOYEE NAME........? JOHN C. JONES_____
ENTER EMPLOYEE ADDRESS.....? 125 MAIN STREET_____
ENTER HOME PHONE NUMBER....? (203)569-1234_
ENTER WORK PHONE NUMBER....? (203)233-1234_
ENTER NUMBER OF DEPENDENTS.? 3_
ENTER ALLOCATED VACATION...? 14
ENTER ALLOCATED SICK DAYS..? 14
ENTER HOURLY PAY RATE......? 9.50_
ENTER FICA CODE (1 2 OR 3).? 3
ENTER EMPLOYEE EXTENSION...? 234
ENTER DEPARTMENT...........? PRODUCTION_____
ENTER SUPERVISORS NAME.....? BOB M. SMITH_____
ENTER JOB TITLE............? PRODUCTION SUPERVISOR
ENTER YEARS EMPLOYED.......? 8___
```

```
Printed Output
EMPLOYEE NAME.........JOHN C. JONES
EMPLOYEE ADDRESS......125 MAIN STREET
HOME PHONE NUMBER.....(203)569-1234
WORK PHONE NUMBER.....(203)233-1234
NUMBER OF DEPENDENTS.. 3
ALLOCATED VACATION.... 14
ALLOCATED SICK DAYS... 14
HOURLY PAY RATE....... 9.5
FICA CODE (1 2 OR 3).. 3
EMPLOYEE EXTENSION....234
DEPARTMENT...........PRODUCTION
SUPERVISORS NAME......BOB M. SMITH
JOB TITLE............PRODUCTION SUPERVISOR
YEARS EMPLOYED........8
```

Test Data

John C. Jones
125 Main Street
203-569-1234
203-233-1234
3
14
14
9.50
3
234
Production
Bob M. Smith
Production Supervisor
8

Error Routines

Include logic to recover from a ''device fault'' output error (printer not turned on), so that the user can turn the printer on and get the output without having to re-enter all the data. Use sound and a reminder message in the error routine.

Validation Procedure

Check to see that all input prompts are located properly on the screen, and that the data appears in the proper location near the prompts. Check for color and color changes (if you have a color monitor), and verify that all input is correctly printed on the printer. To validate the error routine, run the program with the printer off and check for the warning beep and reminder message. When these appear, turn the printer on and check the output for correctness.

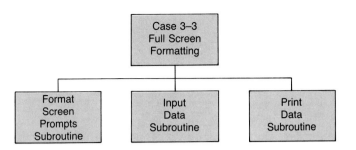

FULL SCREEN
FORMATTING:
PAYROLL AND
PERSONNEL DATA
INPUT AND
LISTING

FIGURE C3–5
Table of contents for Case 3–3.

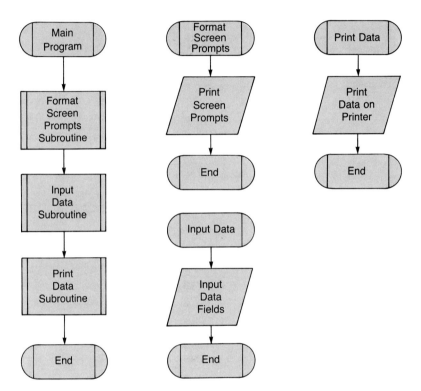

FIGURE C3–6
Detailed program flowcharts for Case 3–3.

CASE STUDY SOLUTION

```
10      REM     ****************************************************
20      REM     *  PAYROLL AND PERSONNEL DATA INPUT AND LISTING *
30      REM     *          WITH FULL SCREEN FORMATTING          *
40      REM     *               CASE STUDY: C3-3                *
50      REM     *    THIS PROGRAM FORMATS THE SCREEN FOR DATA    *
60      REM     * INPUT, ACCEPTS 14 FIELDS ON THE SCREEN, AND   *
70      REM     * PRINTS THESE ON THE PRINTER.                  *
80      REM     *    ONE ERROR TRAPPING ROUTINE WARNS IF THE    *
90      REM     * PRINTER IS OFF SO THAT THE USER CAN TURN IT   *
100     REM     * ON WITHOUT HAVING TO RERUN THE PROGRAM AND    *
110     REM     * RE-ENTER ALL THE DATA.                        *
120     REM     ****************************************************
130     REM
```

```
140     REM      ****************
150     REM      * MAIN PROGRAM *
160     REM      ****************
170     REM      THE ERROR TRAPPING STATEMENT
180              ON ERROR GOTO 960
190     REM
200     REM      CLEAR THE SCREEN-SET THE TEXT AND BACKGROUND COLORS
210              CLS:COLOR 14,1
220     REM
230     REM      PERFORM 'FORMAT SCREEN PROMPTS' SUBROUTINE
240              GOSUB 310
250     REM      PERFORM 'OBTAIN INPUT DATA' SUBROUTINE
260              GOSUB 580
270     REM      PERFORM 'PRINT DATA' SUBROUTINE
280              GOSUB 760
290              END
300     REM
310     REM      ************************************
320     REM      * FORMAT SCREEN PROMPTS SUBROUTINE *
330     REM      ************************************
340              PRINT " COPYRIGHT (C) 1989, BY MERRILL PUBLISHING COMPANY"
350              PRINT " FOR USE WITH STRUCTURED BASIC PROGRAMMING"
360              PRINT
370              PRINT "                    PLEASE MAKE SURE THE PRINTER IS ON"
380              PRINT
390              PRINT "                    PAYROLL AND PERSONNEL DATA LISTING"
400              PRINT "                    AN EXAMPLE OF FULL SCREEN FORMATTING "
410              PRINT
420              PRINT " ENTER EMPLOYEE NAME........ _____"
430              PRINT " ENTER EMPLOYEE ADDRESS..... _____"
440              PRINT " ENTER HOME PHONE NUMBER.... (_____) _____-_____"
450              PRINT " ENTER WORK PHONE NUMBER.... (_____) _____-_____"
460              PRINT " ENTER NUMBER OF DEPENDENTS. _____"
470              PRINT " ENTER ALLOCATED VACATION... _____"
480              PRINT " ENTER ALLOCATED SICK DAYS.. _____"
490              PRINT " ENTER HOURLY PAY RATE...... _____._____"
500              PRINT " ENTER FICA CODE (1 2 OR 3). _"
510              PRINT " ENTER EMPLOYEE EXTENSION... _____"
520              PRINT " ENTER DEPARTMENT........... _____"
530              PRINT " ENTER SUPERVISORS NAME..... _____"
540              PRINT " ENTER JOB TITLE............ _____"
550              PRINT " ENTER YEARS EMPLOYED....... _____"
560              RETURN
570     REM      ********************************
580     REM      * OBTAIN INPUT DATA SUBROUTINE *
590     REM      ********************************
600              COLOR 4,1
610              LOCATE 9,29 : INPUT NM$
620              LOCATE 10,29 : INPUT ADD$
630              LOCATE 11,29 : INPUT HPHO$
640              LOCATE 12,29 : INPUT WPHO$
650              LOCATE 13,29: INPUT NODEPS
660              LOCATE 14,29: INPUT VACA
670              LOCATE 15,29: INPUT SICK
680              LOCATE 16,29: INPUT PAYRATE
690              LOCATE 17,29: INPUT FICA
700              LOCATE 18,29: INPUT PHOEXT$
710              LOCATE 19,29: INPUT DEPT$
720              LOCATE 20,29: INPUT SUPV$
730              LOCATE 21,29: INPUT JOB$
740              LOCATE 22,29: INPUT YEARS
750              RETURN
760     REM
```

```
770        REM         ************************
780        REM         * PRINT DATA SUBROUTINE *
790        REM         ************************
800                    LPRINT " EMPLOYEE NAME.........";NM$
810                    LPRINT " EMPLOYEE ADDRESS......";ADD$
820                    LPRINT " HOME PHONE NUMBER.....";HPHO$
830                    LPRINT " WORK PHONE NUMBER.....";WPHON$
840                    LPRINT " NUMBER OF DEPENDENTS..";NODEPS
850                    LPRINT " ALLOCATED VACATION....";VACA
860                    LPRINT " ALLOCATED SICK DAYS...";SICK
870                    LPRINT " HOURLY PAY RATE.......";PAYRATE
880                    LPRINT " FICA CODE (1 2 OR 3)..";FICA
890                    LPRINT " EMPLOYEE EXTENSION....";PHOEXT$
900                    LPRINT " DEPARTMENT............";DEPT$
910                    LPRINT " SUPERVISORS NAME......";SUPV$
920                    LPRINT " JOB TITLE.............";JOB$
930                    LPRINT " YEARS EMPLOYED........";YEARS
950        REM
960        REM         ERROR CONDITION TESTING (ERR 25 IS A DEVICE FAULT)
970        REM
980                    IF ERR = 25 THEN BEEP:LOCATE 24,1:PRINT " THE PRINTER
                       IS OFF OR NOT READY- PLEASE TURN IT ON AND PRESS ANY
                       KEY THEN ENTER TO CONTINUE ":INPUT A
$:RESUME 800
990        REM
1000       REM         END OF PROGRAM
```

Programming the computer to accept input and produce output in BASIC most often involves the use of three hardware devices: the keyboard, the screen, and the printer. Program instructions and data that are entered into the computer can be displayed on the screen while they are being entered. Results from the program may be displayed on a screen, by a printer, or through a variety of special purpose output devices. Frequently, programs and data are stored permanently on an auxiliary storage device, such as magnetic tape or disk (these operations are studied in chapters 9 and 10).

Special instructions are needed to tell the computer how and where you would like your data entered and stored. These are INPUT, READ, DATA, PRINT, LPRINT, TAB, PRINT USING, LOCATE, ON ERROR, and RESUME.

Writing a BASIC program requires knowledge of BASIC syntax; that is, you must know the rules that dictate how each BASIC statement is constructed, what keywords are required, proper punctuation, and the meanings of a number of special characters.

Each BASIC statement must be preceded by a line number and a keyword such as INPUT, PRINT, REM (for REMark), IF, or GOSUB. Because BASIC is a free-form language, the spacing between keywords and/or mathematical expressions is fixed arbitrarily as long as there are no spaces within keywords.

A BASIC program should have a remarks section (REM) explaining the program and identifying variable names, a main program, and all subroutines. The keyword END terminates the main program segment. Statement numbering should be flexible enough that statements can be added later between existing statements. Increments of 10 are usually used within the main program, while subroutines are numbered beginning with hundreds and thousands, with increments of 10 within them, also.

A variable legend should be included in the REM section of the main program to explain exactly what the abbreviated BASIC variable names mean. This is especially important on some less enhanced versions of BASIC that permit only one- or two-character names. Memory location (variable) names ending with a dollar sign ($) signify the storage of alphabetic or alphanumeric data, often referred to as string data in BASIC. Variable names may end with %, !, or #, but the exact characters for integers, single- or double-precision numbers, and arrangement of the letters and special characters permitted to signify the variable are functions of the computer system with which you are working. Most systems permit about 40 characters for the variable name, beginning with a letter, and containing numbers (consult the appendix or your system manual for details). For advanced mathematical and financial calculations, many BASIC systems also support variables for decimal numbers, integers (whole numbers), and "extended" precision numbers (numbers with many significant digits). (Again, consult your reference manual.)

Data can be entered into a BASIC program by using the INPUT or the READ/DATA commands. The general form of the INPUT instruction is: line# INPUT variable 1, variable 2, etc., and the data requested by the computer is entered on the CRT. The READ statement obtains data from within the program by means of a DATA statement. The general form for this pair of instruction is:

```
line# READ variable-name 1, variable-name 2
line# DATA value 1, value 2
```

Alphabetic and alphanumeric data need not be enclosed in double quotation marks unless there is a comma in the field. Also, numbers are entered without any commas or dollar signs, but they may contain a decimal point. A variable can contain only one value at a time. When a new value is input or read, the previous value is erased.

The primary output keyword in BASIC is PRINT, and this keyword can be modified and combined with a variety of other keywords and punctuation characters to produce desired output. PRINT preceded by a line number and followed by variable names will print the contents of those variables on the screen. If a comma is used to separate the variable names, the output will appear in print zones on the screen, each of which are approximately 14 columns wide. If a semicolon is used, the results will be compressed to the left, and variables appear directly after one another.

To direct output results to a printer for a permanent copy, the LPRINT keyword is used on many BASIC systems. Some large computer systems do not support the LPRINT statement; rather, results must first be directed to a file for storage and then printed out using special operating system commands. (This is covered in chapters 9 and 10.)

The keyword TAB followed by a number in parentheses directs output to specific print positions both on the screen and on the printer. This option is handy for producing output with the results, titles, and headings all properly centered or located, as desired. A type of PRINT statement with the TAB option looks like this:

```
line# PRINT TAB(10);A TAB(20);B
```

With the PRINT USING keywords, titles as well as numeric and string data can be edited and placed in any desired location on the screen or printer. A wide variety of special PRINT USING formats is available for special editing purposes, such as specifying decimal places, placing floating dollar signs and asterisks in front of numeric data, and specifying positive and negative numbers.

COMMON ERRORS AND SOLUTIONS

Error	Example	Solution
1. Improperly spelled reserved words, such as INPUT, PRINT, REM, READ, DATA, END, etc., or spaces within these words.	10 IMPUT (syntax error)	Check manual for correct spelling, statement form, etc.
2. Failure to enclose alphanumeric data in quotation marks (on some systems) or to enclose strings with commas in quotation marks (all systems).	INPUT ADDS$? LOS ANGELES, CA (no diagnostic)	Place strings in double quotes: "LOS ANGELES, CA"
3. Placing *numeric* containing dollar signs, commas, or other special characters in a DATA statement or INPUT list.	INPUT GROSS ? $1,565.35 (redo from start)	INPUT GROSS ? 1565.35
4. Forgetting to place commas between data in DATA statements, or when inputting more than one item in an INPUT variable list.	READ A,B,C,D DATA 10 20 15 9 (redo from start)	READ A,B,C,D DATA 10,20,15,9
5. Placing data in a different order than that specified in a READ or INPUT statement.	INPUT HOURS, RATE ? 12.50, 40 (incorrect results)	INPUT HOURS, RATE ? 40, 12.50
6. Placing improper or incorrect line numbers on statements, thereby changing the order of execution (when the statements are sorted by the interpreter or compiler prior to execution).	10 PRINT A 20 INPUT A	Correct order to reflect proper logic: 10 INPUT A 20 PRINT A
7. Using incorrect format specifications for numeric and/or string variables in the PRINT USING instruction.	05 F$ = "\ \" 10 PRINT USING F$;A (type mismatch in 10) 20 F$ = "###.##" 30 PRINT USING F$,A$ (type mismatch in 10)	F$ = "###.##" PRINT USING F$;A F$ = "\ \" PRINT USING F$;A$
8. Improper assignment of variable names to string or numeric variables.	10 A$ = 10000 (type mismatch in 10) 20 A = "HELLO" (type mismatch in 20)	A$ = "HELLO" A = 1000 Check variable names and types continuously.
9. Using variable names with improper characters or names that are too long (on some systems).	30 GROSSPAY = 400.00 40 Employee.NAME$ = "JOHN"	Check your manual for maximum variable name length and shorten accordingly. Include a variable legend in program if names are not self-explanatory.
10. Forgetting the END statement at the logical end (or physical end) of the program.	No END at logical end	Check manuals, as some systems tolerate these errors.
11. Forgetting the RETURN statement at the end of a subroutine.	10 GOSUB 100 100 INPUT A,B,C PRINT A B C (on some systems no diagnostic)	10 GOSUB 100 20 STOP 100 INPUT A,B,C 110 RETURN 200 PRINT A,B,C
12. Branching to the wrong line number in a GOSUB statement, especially after the program has been modified to include additional statements.	10 GOSUB 110 120 INPUT N$ 130 RETURN (undefined line number in 110)	Correct GOSUB line number to reflect start of subroutine referenced: GOSUB 120

Error	Example	Solution
13. Failure to include proper REMARK statements, so that the program is well documented and easy to debug or modify.	10 REM MAIN PROG 20 GOSUB 200 30 END 200 INPUT A,B$	Example is nearly impossible to understand. Include REMark before each GOSUB statement and subroutine referenced.

14. Not providing an INPUT statement or READ statement with enough data.	10 INPUT A,B,C
	     ? 10,20 CR
	20 READ A,C,C
	30 DATA 10,20
	    (redo from start)
		Check that the number of data items and number of variables requesting data are the same (see "restore" for exception).

15. Providing an INPUT statement or READ statement with too much data. (Usually the result of forgetting a variable name in the INPUT or READ statement.)	10 INPUT A
	     ? 10,20
	    (redo from start)
	20 READ A
	30 DATA 10,20
	    (20 is ignored, no error)
		If there is simply extra data, this data will be ignored with no error; however, this is usually the result of forgetting a variable name in the INPUT or READ list, which will produce error later in program.

16. Failure to RETURN or ENTER data after typing these on the CRT.	?John, 10,4.5 NO RETURN (program halts)	Make sure to "enter" all data for INPUT instruction.
17. Referring to a line number (statement) that has been deleted in a previous editing or debugging operation.	10 GOSUB 100 110 REM SUB 150 RETURN (undefined line number)	Check all statement numbers after program modification to ensure consistency.
18. Placing a program in an endless loop, and not knowing the system command to terminate execution.	10 INPUT A$ 20 PRINT A$ 30 GOTO 10 (continuous execution)	Become familiar with system command needed to terminate program execution (usually the CONTROL-C).
19. For systems that require files to store output before printing, failure to properly declare, open, print to, and close that file.	(See chapter 9)	Consult chapter 9 for the proper declaration, use, and saving of files.
20. Using single quotation marks in place of double quotation marks to enclose strings, file names, program names, etc.	10 A$ = 'JOHN' 20 PRINT A$ (system-dependent; e.g., missing operand in 10)	Consult your manual. Most systems require double quotes for strings: A$ = "JOHN"

21. Typing a zero instead of the letter "O", or letter "O" instead of a zero.	10 INPUT NM$
	     ? J0hn
	(no error, wrong data)
	20 INPUT N
	     ? 1O)
	(zero used instead of the letter "O" in second line, letter "O" used instead of zero in fourth line—redo from start)
		The first error is not serious; the second will cause a data-type error. Be careful with O's and 0's

22. When using the TAB option, failure to count the columns accurately so that output and titles are properly aligned.	TAB(20) "NAME" TAB(23) N$ NAME JOHN C. JONES	Check the integer value used with the TAB to ensure proper alignment. Use output layout sheets to simplify counting. There should be no spaces between the command TAB and the left parenthesis.

23. When using the format specifications in the PRINT USING, failure to allow enough positions for the largest string or numeric variable in the data.	10 A$ = JOHN
	20 PRINT USING "\ \";A$
	    Joh
	30 A = 100.00
	40 PRINT USING "##.##";A
	    %100.00
		Alphabetic fields will be truncated; numeric fields will have a percent sign placed before the number output. Ensure that the format is large enough to account for the largest alphanumeric or numeric data.

COMMON ERRORS AND SOLUTIONS

Error	Example	Solution
24. Improper use of editing characters in the PRINT USING statement format, or improper placement of the editing characters, such as $, ##, **, ;, ., etc.	Many unpredictable results are common. See text for examples.	Study the variety of PRINT USING images available and practice with small program segments to become familiar with results obtained.
25. Improper punctuation between the key parts of the PRINT USING or PRINT (to a file) statement.	Examples are system-dependent.	Consult your manual for proper punctuation (e.g.,.,;:, etc.) for your PRINT and PRINT USING instructions.

REVIEW QUESTIONS

 1. Why are INPUT and OUTPUT operations important in computer programs?
 2. What are the primary methods used for computer input and output in conventional business applications?
 3. Describe the two most common types of printers used with microcomputer BASIC systems. What are the advantages and disadvantages of both?
 4. Why is hard copy important in business programming?
 5. Each BASIC statement must be preceded by a line number. Why is it beneficial to number statements in increments of 10 on programs written in structured design?
 6. Self-documentation of BASIC programs is accomplished by what type of statement? Why is this important? Give a few examples of how the statement can be used to identify key points in BASIC programs.
 7. Explain how a variable legend in BASIC programs helps identify what the variables represent and improves program documentation.
 8. Why is it good practice to precede GOSUB statements with a REM in structured BASIC programs?
 9. Name and describe the two primary data input statements in BASIC. Compare and contrast the two.
10. Why do different types of variables have different naming conventions in BASIC?
11. Describe the naming conventions for integer numeric, decimal numeric, double-precision decimal numeric, and character (string) variables on your BASIC system (if your system supports these variables).
12. Write an INPUT statement to accept your name, address, and age from the keyboard. (Remember that name and address are alphanumeric (string) fields and age is numeric field.)
13. Write a READ/DATA statement to read in the same data in question 12. Include your name, address, and age in the DATA statement as required by your BASIC system. (Remember that some systems require quotes around string variables, and all systems require quotes if the data field contains a comma—e.g.,"Jones, John C.")
14. Write a PRINT statement to print the data from question 13 on the screen using the normal print zones to space the output.
15. Write a PRINT statement to print the data in question 13 on the screen, but with no spaces between the output fields.
16. Explain what occurs when the first field to be printed is too large to fit one print zone. Where does the second field appear on the screen?
17. Explain the use of the TAB option in printing fields.
18. Using the TAB option, write a BASIC PRINT statement that will print your name beginning in column 10, your address beginning in column 30, and your age beginning in column 60.
19. Write a PRINT statement that will print the titles "SAMPLE PROGRAM OUTPUT" beginning in column 25 on the screen.

20. Write a PRINT statement that will print titles above your name, address, and age (from question 18) so that the titles "NAME", "ADDRESS", and "AGE" begin in column 15, 40, and 60, respectively.

21. Repeat questions 18 through 20 so that the output is directed to your printer (assuming your system supports LPRINT or a similar instruction).

22. What character cannot be typed as data in a program? Why will it cause a problem if it is typed?

23. What is the purpose of a prompt that results from an INPUT statement? What are two methods that can be used to indicate which data is being requested by the INPUT instruction?

24. Write a PRINT statement to prompt the input of an employee name, and follow this statement with a correct INPUT statement.

25. Write the prompt directly in the INPUT statement (if your system permits this feature) to accomplish the same result as in question 24.

26. Using the line continuation feature of your system (if available), write a long title as a literal. Use the title "This Is a Long Title Used to Illustrate the Line Continuation Feature".

27. What are the advantages of the PRINT USING statement?

28. Write the editing and data-accepting characters for your system to print the following: a number, string data, a decimal point in a field, a comma in a field, a minus sign before a number, a dollar sign in front of a number, an asterisk in front of a number, a floating dollar sign and a floating asterisk in front of a number.

29. Write the PRINT USING formats (sometimes referred to as images) to print the number 36 as $36.00, 1200 as $1,200.00 and −56 as −$56.00.

30. Write the PRINT USING formats to print the following alphanumeric or alphabetic fields: Employee Name (20 characters), Employee Address (30 characters), Employee Social Security Number (11 characters), and Marital Status (1 character abbreviation M, S, or D).

31. Using the format from question 29, write the correct PRINT USING statement to print the data on the display and the printer in the desired format, spacing the output neatly on the CRT or printer page.

32. Using the formats from question 30, write the correct PRINT USING statements to print the data on the display and the printer in the desired format, spacing the output neatly on the screen or printer page.

PROBLEMS FOR SOLUTION

Note: In some of these problems, an "incorrect" looping method can be used to produce a list of more than one data record. This method, which involves the use of the GOTO instruction, is not commonly used in structured design programming. (Correct looping methods are described in chapter 5.) The PRINT statement with the TAB option can be used to place the output in proper locations, or the PRINT USING instruction can be used.

1. Prepare a list of your classmates that includes their names, addresses, phone numbers, and ages using the terminal to input the data and the printer to provide permanent hardcopy output. See the following definition for details.

Input Specifications

Field No.	Field Description	Type	Example
1	Student Name	Alphabetic	John Smith
2	Street Address	Alphanumeric	3 John St
3	City and State	Alphabetic	Vernon, CT
4	Zip Code	Integer	09876
5	Phone Number	Alphanumeric	867-5524

Processing Decisions and Formulas

Use the unconditional branching statement GOTO to produce a listing of as many records as needed, although this looping method will be described later in chapter 5.

Output

```
     NAME           STREET        CITY-STATE   ZIP CODE   PHONE NUMBER
JOHN SMITH       3 JOHN ST       VERNON CT      09876       867-5524
```

Test Data

John Smith, 3 John St, Vernon, CT, 09876, 867-5524
(Add the data for your classmates.)

Error Routines

None.

Validation Procedure

Visually check that the titles and data are accurately reproduced on the printer listing, and that the data is correctly centered under the titles as specified.

2. Produce the same list as in problem 1, but use the READ/DATA statement combination to input the data.
3. Prepare a list of your record, tape, or compact disc collection that contains each recording artist's name, the name of each album, tape, or CD, the cost of the album, tape, or CD, the date of its release, and the date you bought it as shown in the problem definition. Use the INPUT instruction and input data on the terminal.

Input Specifications

Field No.	Field Description	Type	Example
1	Artist Name	Alphabetic	Wagner
2	Title of Album, Tape, or CD	Alphabetic	The Flying Dutchman
3	Cost of Album, Tape, or CD	Decimal Number	24.99
4	Date Released (Julian Date)	Integer	12060
5	Date Purchased (Julian Date)	Integer	23062
6	Type of Recording	Alphabetic	A

Processing Decisions and Formulas

Use the unconditional branching statement GOTO to produce a listing of as many data records as desired, although this looping method will be described in detail later in chapter 5.

Output

```
   ARTIST NAME    TITLE OF ALBUM OR TAPE OR CD    COST   DATE RELEASED DATE PURCHASED TYPE
   WAGNER         THE FLYING DUTCHMAN            $24.99     12060          23062        A
```

Test Data

Wagner, The Flying Dutchman, 24.99, 12060, 23062, A
(Add data for your own record, tape, and CD collection.)

Error Routines

None.

Validation Procedure

Visually check that the titles and data are accurately reproduced on the printer listing, and that the data is correctly centered under the titles, as specified above.

4. Prepare the same list as in problem 3 using the READ/DATA statement combination to input the data.

5. Prepare a list of your approximate monthly expenses in the categories listed in the problem definition. This problem will process only one month's expenses and will be enhanced later to include monthly totals and more than one month's data. Note the horizontal form of the output as well as the alignment of expense numbers and the dollar sign.

Input Specifications

Field No.	Field Description	Type	Example
1	Rent or Mortgage Expenses	Decimal Number	200.00
2	Food Expenses	Decimal Number	125.00
3	Entertainment Expenses	Decimal Number	50.00
4	Car or Transportation Expenses	Decimal Number	382.00
5	Utility Expenses	Decimal Number	75.00

Processing Decisions and Formulas

In this version of the program, input only one month's data.

Output

```
            MONTHLY EXPENSE LISTING

        CATEGORY                 AMOUNT

        RENT                     $200.00
        FOOD                     $125.00
        ENTERTAINMENT             $50.00
        CAR                      $382.00
        CLOTHING                  $75.00
```

Test Data

200.00
125.00
 50.00
382.00
 75.00

Error Routines

None.

Validation Procedure

Visually check that the output is printed in the vertical format specified in the output example above. Also, be sure the dollar sign is aligned in the proper column.

6. Program the typewriter simulation example illustrated in the chapter and experiment with various forms of text on your system. Note the special characters and string-handling capabilities of your computer system, and the ease with which you can correct errors if you catch them before you print each line of input. You may find that this small program allows you to do some simple word processing, or at least allows you to use your terminal as a "memory" typewriter for one line at a time.

Input Specifications

Field No.	Field Description	Type	Example
1	Student Name	Alphabetic	John Jones
2	First Class	Alphabetic	Biology
3	First Room	Integer	125
4	First Time	Integer	1000
5	Second Class	Alphabetic	Physics
6	Second Room	Integer	234
7	Second Time	Integer	1100
8	Third Class	Alphabetic	History
9	Third Room	Integer	110
10	Third Time	Integer	1200

Processing Decisions and Formulas

None.

Output

```
STUDENT NAME     1ST CLASS ROOM TIME    2ND CLASS ROOM TIME    3RD CLASS ROOM TIME
JOHN JONES       BIOLOGY    125 1000    PHYSICS    234 1100    HISTORY    110 1200
```

Test Data

Make up your own test data.

Error Routines

None.

Validation Procedure

Visually compare titles and format with output specifications.

CHAPTER FOUR

CALCULATIONS

OUTLINE

LEARNING OBJECTIVES

Upon completion of this chapter, you will be able to:

☐ Understand the importance of calculations in BASIC business programs.

☐ Develop your own calculation construct charts.

☐ Write formulas and equations in BASIC.

☐ Understand the order of execution of the BASIC mathematical operators.

☐ Understand the difference between formulas written with algebra and formulas written with BASIC.

☐ Understand all BASIC numeric variables (i.e., integer, decimal, and extended-precision decimal).

☐ Understand the importance and use of accumulators.

☐ Apply the concepts of numeric-type variables to a realistic business problem.

☐ Understand the concept and use of built-in numeric functions and user-defined functions.

☐ Understand some of the techniques for writing user-friendly programs.

CALCULATIONS IN COMPUTER PROGRAMS

Calculations in Business Programs

Calculations are a vital part of many business programs. Table 4–1 shows some typical formulas used in business systems. All the formulas in the table involve addition, subtraction, multiplication, or division, or some combination of these basic mathematical operations. While this table does not list all the formulas for business systems, from those shown you can see that many of the calculations are built upon very simple algebraic expressions. This chapter will explore how such formulas can be represented in BASIC.

Calculations in Structured Design Programming

A structured program, regardless of its complexity, uses only three logical structures (building blocks) for design and coding: sequence, iteration, and selection. The sequence structure constitutes any straightforward operation that includes calculations and does not feature decision making or looping. The sequence structure can be used to represent the calculations shown in table 4–1. Sequence symbols (operations) can be combined without changing the basic sequential structure of the program. This chapter deals with programs with this structure. The selection structure constitutes a choice made between two actions based on a condition. If the condition is true, one function is performed; if it is false, the other function is performed. This structure is covered in chapter 6. The iteration structure is essentially a looping structure that continues for as long as the "test" condition remains true. This structure is covered in chapter 5.

These three structures are represented by the simple flowcharts shown in figure 4–1. Note that all of the structures have only one entry and exit point, which is important because one of the primary principles of structured design states that any of the three structures can be substituted in the function box of *any other* structure. Most of the new interpreters and compilers for BASIC have statements that cater specifically to these three logical structures.

TABLE 4–1

Applications, formulas, and results for some typical business systems.

Application	Formulas	Results
Payroll	Regular pay = hours × pay rate	Base pay
	Overtime pay = (hours − 40) × pay rate	Overtime pay
	Gross pay = regular pay + overtime pay	Total pay
	Tax = gross pay × tax rate	Tax
	Net pay = gross pay − tax	Net pay
	Adjusted net pay = net pay − deductions	Take home pay
Billing	Total purchased = purchase 1 + purchase 2 + . . .	Total purchased
	Total payments = payment 1 + payment 2 + . . .	Total paid
	Amount due = total purchased − total paid	Amount due
	Interest = amount due × interest rate	Interest due
	Total amount due = amount due + interest	Total account balance
	Minimum payment + total amount due × %	Minimum payment due
Inventory control	Current QOH = initial QOH − number sold + number received (QOH = quantity on hand)	Current stock level
	Profit = price of item − cost of item	Profit per sale
	Total number sold = item sold + item sold + . . .	Total items sold
	Profit on item = profit per item × total sold	Total profit earned on item

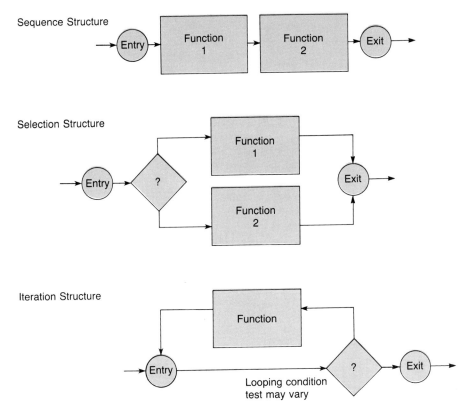

FIGURE 4–1
The sequence, selection, and iteration structure used in structured programming.

The Sequence Structure

The three basic structures often are referred to as constructs, and the terms *sequence structure* and *sequence construct* are often interchanged. The sequence construct for simple formulas is written by placing the formula (or expression) within a rectangle, with an entry and exit symbol on the left and right respectively, as shown in figure 4–2. This representation is called a sequence chart or sequence structure chart.

In a computer program, a sequence construct that represents a formula is preceded by an input operation that assigns values to the variables in the equation and is followed by an output operation so that you can learn the results of the calculation.

In most business programs, the sequence construct need not be (and should not always be) interpreted as representing one operation. A perfectly valid sequence construct could represent more than one operation. For example, the sequence chart in figure 4–3 calculates net "take-home" pay. To arrive at the final output, the sequence must go through three prior calculations.

Illustration—The Sum and Average of Two Numbers

The following is an illustration of a two-part sequence construct, combined with input and output operations. For this program illustration, you will input two numbers from the key-

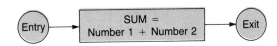

FIGURE 4–2
Sequence chart.

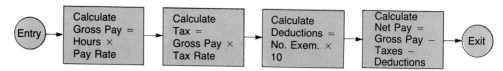

FIGURE 4–3
A sequence chart for net "take-home" pay.

board, add the two numbers together to get the sum, and then divide the sum by 2, giving the average. Then you will print the two original numbers, including their sum and average, along with a heading.

The two calculation charts look like this:

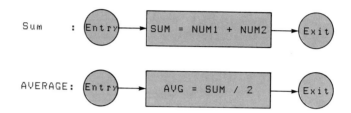

The complete VTOC chart for this example, including the input, calculation, and output routines, would look like this:

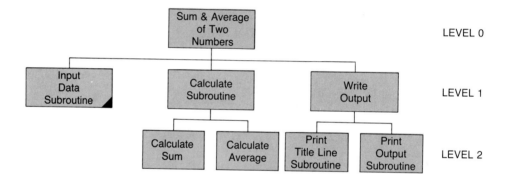

Since all symbols on the VTOC are sequence constructs, with one entry point and one exit point each, the chart can be readily converted to a standard program flowchart, as shown in figure 4–4. From this detailed flowchart, you can write the program shown in figure 4–5, where the two calculation steps appear at lines 490 and 500 in the calculations subroutine.

CALCULATIONS USING BASIC

Writing BASIC Expressions from Formulas and Equations

The preceding example of the sum and average sequence construct is straightforward because the formulas used in such elementary calculations are identical in both BASIC and mathematics. This is not the case for all calculations. In fact, there are many conventions in BASIC that depart significantly from "standard" algebraic and mathematical notation.

First, the symbols used to represent multiplication, division, exponentiation, and roots are different (see table 4–2). Secondly, very precise rules of syntax must be followed when writing formulas that are to become BASIC expressions. For example, only one

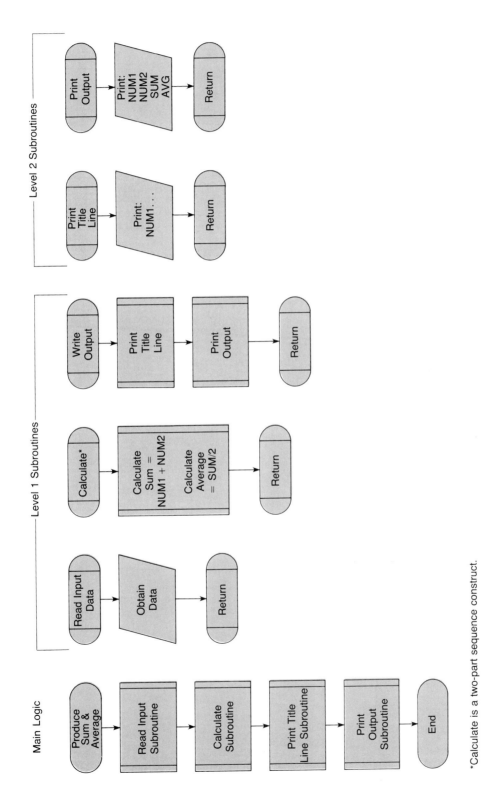

Main Logic

Level 1 Subroutines

Level 2 Subroutines

*Calculate is a two-part sequence construct.

FIGURE 4–4
Detailed program flowchart for complete program (input, calculation, output).

101

FIGURE 4–5

Detailed program, sum and average of two numbers.

Input

```
10     REM     ************************************************
20     REM     *              SIMPLE CALCULATIONS              *
30     REM     *                 ILLUSTRATION                  *
40     REM     *          SUM & AVERAGE OF TWO NUMBERS         *
50     REM     *   THIS PROGRAM ACCEPTS TWO NUMBERS FROM       *
60     REM     *   THE KEYBOARD, ADDS THEM TOGETHER            *
70     REM     *   AND DIVIDES THEM BY 2.                      *
80     REM     *   THE SUM AND AVERAGE ARE THEN PRINTED        *
90     REM     *             VARIABLE LEGEND                   *
100    REM     *             NUMB1 = FIRST NUMBER              *
110    REM     *             NUMB2 = SECOND NUMBER             *
120    REM     *               SUM = TOTAL                     *
130    REM     *               AVE = AVERAGE                   *
140    REM     ************************************************
150            CLS
160            PRINT "COPYRIGHT (C) 1989, BY MERRILL PUBLISHING COMPANY"
170            PRINT "FOR USE WITH STRUCTURED BASIC PROGRAMMING"
180            PRINT
190            PRINT "THIS PROGRAM WILL ADD TWO NUMBER TOGETHER"
200            PRINT "COMPUTE THEIR AVERAGE AND PRINT THEM OUT."
210            PRINT
220            PRINT "PLEASE MAKE SURE THE PRINTER IS ON."
230    REM     ****************
240    REM     * MAIN PROGRAM *
250    REM     ****************
260    REM     PERFORM 'INPUT DATA' SUBROUTINE
270            GOSUB 350
280    REM     PERFORM 'CALCULATIONS' SUBROUTINE
290            GOSUB 460
300    REM     PERFORM 'PRINT TITLE LINE' SUBROUTINE
310            GOSUB 520
320    REM     PERFORM 'PRINT OUTPUT' SUBROUTINE
330            GOSUB 580
340            END
350    REM     ************************
360    REM     *INPUT DATA SUBROUTINE *
370    REM     ************************
380            PRINT
390            PRINT
400            PRINT "ENTER FIRST NUMBER"
410            PRINT
420            PRINT "ENTER SECOND NUMBER"
430            LOCATE 10,21: INPUT NUMB1
440            LOCATE 12,21: INPUT NUMB2
450            RETURN
460    REM     **************************
470    REM     * CALCULATIONS SUBROUTINE *
480    REM     **************************
490            SUM = NUMB1 + NUMB2
500            AVG = SUM / 2
510            RETURN
520    REM     ********************************
530    REM     * PRINT TITLE LINE SUBROUTINE *
540    REM     ********************************
550            LPRINT"
560            LPRINT "NUMB1          NUMB2          SUM          AVERAGE"
570            RETURN
580    REM     ****************************
590    REM     * PRINT OUTPUT SUBROUTINE *
600    REM     ****************************
610            LPRINT NUMB1,NUMB2,SUM,AVG
```

```
620              RETURN
630     REM
640     REM   END OF PROGRAM
```

Output

NUMB1	NUMB2	SUM	AVERAGE
12	34	46	23

variable may be written on the left of the equal sign in BASIC (so a + b = c would be invalid). Also, no two variables can be written in the expression without a mathematical symbol separating them (that is, in BASIC A = BC is not the same as A = B*C). Furthermore, and most confusing of all the conventions, the equal sign in BASIC really means ''replace the variable on the left with the expression on the right''! Thus, the expression A = A + 1, which is meaningless in math, is perfectly valid (and quite useful) in BASIC.

All these syntactical rules and conventions are covered in detail in the latter sections of this chapter. For now, you should be on the lookout for errors in syntax as you convert your mathematical formulas to BASIC expressions.

Order of Priority in Expressions—Mathematical Hierarchy

In BASIC expressions converted from math, the order in which operations are performed is dictated by precise rules of priority, as shown in table 4–3. People can interpret a formula like X = 1 + Y/Z * 50 in a variety of ways, but the BASIC interpreters always follow the same consistent order and will *always get the same answer*. If *you* were to calculate this equation for X given values for Y and Z, would you add 1 to Y and then divide by Z or would you divide Y by Z and then add 1? There are obviously a number of ways for you to arrive at a value for X, but BASIC will always divide Y by Z, multiply by 50, and then add 1 because the priority of operations is consistently obeyed.

Why that happens is not as important as recognizing that sometimes you will interpret (and write) equations and expressions that mean one thing to you and something else to the computer. Sometimes the results from your programs can be surprisingly different from what you would have calculated using the same formulas.

Later, you'll look at some complex formulas that are converted to BASIC expressions and see that the priority of calculations is very important for you to understand if you are to get correct results in programs that feature calculations.

TABLE 4–2
Algebraic operators and BASIC equivalents.

Operation	In Mathematics	In BASIC
Addition	+	+
Subtraction	−	−
Multiplication	× or · or ()()	*
Division	÷ or /	/
Exponentiation*	A^n(power)	ô or **
Square root	$\sqrt{}$	SQR or ↑ (1/2)
Any root	$\sqrt[n]{}$	↑ (1/n)
MOD	Int Quotient A/B	\

Note: The caret listed for BASIC here is not available on some keyboards (see appendix A).

TABLE 4–3
Mathematical hierarchy in BASIC.

---

1. Function calls (to be discussed later)
2. Expressions in parentheses
3. ^ Exponentiation
4. *, / Multiplication and division (left to right)*
5. +, − Addition and subtraction (left to right)*
6. = Assignment to variable on left with equal sign

Operations at the same level are performed left to right. To change the order from the above, simply place the operation you want done in parentheses. These are *always* done first. Inside parentheses the usual order is maintained.

Differences between Algebra and BASIC

For most calculations in business problems, BASIC expressions provide an easy way to arrive at results; however, formulas must be written following very specific syntax rules to eliminate any possibility of getting wrong answers or no answers at all.

For example, when using the equal sign in writing expressions for the computer, you must remember that in BASIC (and almost all programming languages) it does not mean "equal to." Instead, it means *evaluate the expression on the right side of the equal sign and place the result in the memory location signified by the variable name to the left of the equal sign.* As short and simple as this statement is, failure to understand and adhere to it results in many of the programming errors found in computer programs that feature calculations. The rules that arise out of this new definition are:

1. Only one variable name may appear on the left side of the equal sign.
2. Any arithmetic operation (addition, subtraction, multiplication, division, and exponentiation) must be on the right side of the equal sign.
3. Any constants (such as tax rate, pay rate, or coefficient) also must be on the right, together with any variable and mathematical operators needed.
4. Multiplication is never assumed, but must be indicated with an asterisk between variables or between variables and constants.
5. You may place *as many* spaces in the equation as you like for ease of reading *except* there can be no spaces within variable names or within constants.

So, according to these rules, the right side of a BASIC formula (called the evaluation segment) can consist of any combination of variable names, constants, and mathematical operations or built-in functions. The complete BASIC formula consists of the line number, the variable name to which the result is to be assigned, the equal sign, and the evaluation segment. On some BASIC interpreters, the word LET must appear before the formula, but on most newer interpreters LET is optional. The format for using the LET statement is:

```
line# LET variable-name = expression
```

The variable name is a numeric variable name when the expression on the right contains a calculation expression that is mathematical. Some acceptable mathematical expressions in BASIC are:

Expression	Meaning
100 N1 = 10	variable N1 gets the value 10
110 N2 = 20	20 is added to variable N1, and the result is assigned to variable N2
120 SM = N1 + N2	variable N1 is added to variable N2, and the result is assigned to variable SM

130 DF = N1 − N2   variable N2 will be subtracted from variable N1 and the result assigned to variable DF

140 PD = N1 * N2 − 30   variable N1 will be multiplied by variable N2, then 30 will be subtracted from the product. The result will then be assigned to PD

150 QR = N1/N2 − 50   variable N1 will be divided by variable N2, then 50 will be subtracted from the result. The final value will be assigned to variable QR. (A zero value assigned to N2 will cause an error.)

In the above expressions, the values for N1 and N2 must be input as data or assigned values with assignment statements before a result can be computed in lines 110 and 120. Regardless of whether the values of N1 and N2 are assigned or input as data, the BASIC operating system will send the contents of memory locations N1 and N2 to the arithmetic and logic unit, where they will be added together.

Unlike mathematics outside the computer, most computer languages, including BASIC, permit some unusual, but useful, expressions. For example, in BASIC it is perfectly logical to write

```
160 N = N + 1
```

Although in mathematics there is no solution for this equation, to the computer this equation means "take the value stored in the memory location called N, add 1 to it, and assign the new value to N, replacing the old value for the new value." In BASIC, this rather strange expression is very useful to accumulate number of items sold, number of customers billed, number of lines printed, and the like. The memory location, N, is referred to as an *accumulator* or *counter* and the expression N = N + 1 is called an accumulation formula because each time it is executed, the value held in N will be increased (incremented) by the added number.

Not only is it possible to accumulate the number of items or occurrences with an accumulation formula, but it is also possible to accumulate profit, commission, sales tax, and any other desired quantity. An expression which accumulates profit on all sales looks like this:

```
TP = TP + P
```

where TP is total profit and P is the profit on each sale.

You can also decrease the quantity in a memory location (decrement) with an accumulation formula, which is useful in monitoring the quantity on hand of a particular item sold. The equation for this looks like

$$Q1 = Q1 − NS$$

where Q1 is the quantity on hand of a product and NS is the number sold during a particular sales transaction. When processing is complete the final value in Q1 would indicate the remaining inventory level. Of course, it would be important to test Q1 constantly to make sure it was never less than zero (which actually would be impossible). Methods of testing for this are described in chapter 6.

Hierarchy in Complex Expressions

BASIC allows you to use complex formulas, which greatly simplifies the calculation involved in many business programs. For example, if you want to calculate the average of two numbers, you can do it in one statement, as shown here.

```
10   AVG = (NUM1 + NUM2) / 2
```

Notice that NUM1 and NUM2 are enclosed by parentheses because hierarchy of arithmetic operations must be followed. If the parentheses were not included, NUM1 would be added to 1/2 of NUM2. As another example, if you need to compute an employee's earnings for the week, you could add the hours for all days and multiply by PAYRATE, as shown below. Again, the absence of the parentheses would cause BASIC to multiply the hours on Friday only by the pay rate!

```
10    TOTAL = (MON + TUES + WED + THURS + FRI)*PAYRATE
```

You also can combine variables and constants in one formula, as in the following formulas for computing sales tax.

```
20    TAX = PURCH1*0.075 + PURCH2*0.075 + PURCH3*0.075  or
20    TAX = (PURCH1 + PURCH2 + PURCH3)*0.075
```

In all expressions, the sequence of scanning for mathematical operations takes place from left to right, so that a complex expression like

```
10    ANS = A + B / C * D ^ N
```

would be evaluated as follows:

1. Variable D would be raised to the N power.
2. Variable B would be divided by C.
3. The result in step 2 would be multiplied by the step 1 result.
4. Variable A would then be added to the result from step 3.

Examples like the one above dramatically illustrate the importance of using parentheses to remove the ambiguity from the formula and ensure that both the computer and the programmer are using the same calculation logic.

Take a look at a common formula that converts temperature measurements from Fahrenheit to Celsius, which shows the importance of the hierarchy of operations.

```
C = (5/9)*(F - 32)
```

Here 32 is subtracted from degrees Fahrenheit, and the result is multiplied by 5/9. If the parentheses were left out, the formula would look like

```
C = 5/9*F-32
```

Here 5 is divided by 9, then that result is multiplied by degrees Fahrenheit, then 32 is subtracted from the second result. Try a few calculations with both formulas to show yourself the importance of understanding and correctly specifying the order of operations in mathematical calculation.

Take a few sample temperatures ($32°F = 0°C$). If you used the second formula, the result would be

$$5/9 = 0.5555556, \text{ then}$$
$$0.5555556 * 32 = 17.77778, \text{ then}$$
$$17.77778 - 32 = -14.22222$$

The first operation is performed as follows:

$$5/9 = 0.5555556, \text{ then}$$
$$(32 - 32) = 0, \text{ then}$$
$$0.555 * 0 = 0$$

Notice that by putting expressions in parentheses, you can control the sequence of operations. This is especially important for using compound expressions whether they are used for complex mathematical calculation or for simple business calculation.

Try inputting the following programs with and without the parentheses and note the different results.

```
10      INPUT F              10      INPUT F
20      C=(5/9)*(F-32)       20      C=5/9*F-32
30      LPRINT C             30      LPRINT C
40      END                  40      END
?60         Data, °F         ?60         Data, °F
15.5556                      1.33333
CORRECT!                     INCORRECT!
```

Numeric Data and Numeric Variable Types

Many versions of BASIC permit a useful distinction between numeric variable types. This distinction facilitates greater efficiency in memory allocation and allows greater execution speed and extended precision* for realistic financial business programs. There are three types of numeric variable options: integers, single-precision numbers, and double-precision numbers.

Integers.   Integers are whole numbers between -32767 and $+32767$, inclusive. Numbers that can be input reasonably as integers should be input with variable names that tell the computer the numbers are integers. To tell the computer that the memory location is reserved for an integer value, a percent sign is used as the last character of the variable name. Some examples of this would be:

$$NDEP\% = \text{number of dependents in a family}$$
$$NPGS\% = \text{number of pages in a book}$$
$$NSTD\% = \text{number of students in a class}$$

Assigning variable names for integer representation varies with different BASIC systems, so check appendix A or the language manual for rules for assignment on your BASIC system.

Single-Precision Numbers.   Single-precision numbers are numbers with decimal points that can be very large or small (approximately 10^{38} to 10^{-38}), but usually the computer will only store numbers with seven-digit precision and print numbers with only six significant digits. For example, in BASIC the answer to this expression

$$10/3 = 3.333333333. \ . \ .$$

would be stored as 3.3333333 and printed as 3.333333, with the rest of the number truncated and lost. This method of rounding off is correct since the decimal places after the sixth 3 contain all 3s. However, if the number 6.6666666. . . . were rounded to 6.666666, this result would clearly be incorrect since the rounded result should be 6.666667.

Although you can compensate for rounding errors with programming logic, there is another problem with single-precision numbers. Suppose the figures represent corporate or government expenditures or the total number of parts manufactured during the life of a company. Precision to only six digits and the rounding and truncation errors that result could, after repetitive calculations involving large figures, become significant and troublesome. Try to imagine a balance sheet and income statement for one of America's largest corporations that permitted only six-digit precision!

Single-precision or "normal" decimal numbers may or may not have a special character included as the last character in the variable name. If the special character is included, it serves only as program documentation to remind the programmer or user that the variable is single precision. The special character and its use also vary on BASIC systems (consult appendix A to this text or your BASIC manual). For example, variable names might be written as

```
HR    or HR!     = Hours
WAGES or WAGES!  = Wages
PAYRT or PAYRT!  = Pay rate
```

*Up to 16 significant digits in a variable, compared to 7 for standard.

Double-Precision Numbers. Double-precision numbers are decimal numbers in the range of approximately 10^{+36} to 10^{-36}, but with *16* significant digits of precision. Some examples are

$$1,000,003,526,957,635$$
$$123456.7898765436$$
$$9.99999234396082 \times 10^{-36}$$

Double-precision number variable names are indicated by placing a pound sign (#) at the end. Some examples are as follows:

GNP# = Gross National Product (4565645342132123)
DIST# = Distance to a star (8877996675645345 miles)
SIZE# = Size of a small item (1.23456789345467 inches)

Double-precision variables often are used in financial applications, where numbers (dollars and cents figures) may become very large and where high precision is required. Double-precision variables also are useful in scientific calculations involving very large or very small numbers. (For most of the case studies in this text, integers and single-precision decimal variables are sufficient.) Further, using double-precision variables where they are not actually needed may make a problem, known as a "floating-point error," worse. This problem occurs in the accumulation of decimal numbers. It results because some decimal numbers become repeating fractions in binary form and digits are lost when these binary fractions are converted back to decimal form for printing. For example a floating point error occurs when the computer takes a decimal number like 3.0, converts it to binary, then converts it back to decimal and gives you 2.9999999999. . . .

Illustrations of Variable Types

Figures 4–6 through 4–8 give programs that illustrate how BASIC handles integer, single-precision, and double-precision numbers, and how these different numeric data variable types can be used to your advantage. It would be a good idea to try these programs on

```
Input

10   REM   FIRST SET THE NUMBERS INTO THE VARIABLES
20         A=1.23456
30         B=.1234567890123456#
40         C=1234567890123456#
50   REM
60   REM   PRINT THE ABOVE NUMBERS WITH SINGLE
70   REM   PRECISION VARIABLES TO SEE THE EFFECT
80   REM   FIRST SET THE NUMBERS INTO THE VARIABLES
90   REM
100        LPRINT A,B,C
110  REM
120        END

Output

   1.23456        .1234568      1.234568E+15

                          Note lost digits
```

FIGURE 4–6
Program showing storing and printing large and small numbers in "normal" precision variables.

```
Input

10       A%=32767
20       B!=1.23456 * 10^38
30       C#=1.23456789012345# * 10^36
40  REM
50  REM  PRINT THE ABOVE NUMBERS WITH DIFFERENT
60  REM  VARIABLE TYPES
70  REM  FIRST ASSIGN NUMBERS INTO THE VARIABLES
80  REM
90       LPRINT A%,B!,C#
100 REM
110      END

Output

32767          1.23456E+38    1.23456794064009D+36
```

FIGURE 4–7
Program showing the effect on precision of different variable types.

your computer system to see if the results are consistent with these examples. If results vary, check your BASIC manual before writing programs that use integer or double-precision numbers.

In Case 4–1, the example program uses single-precision decimal number variables; therefore, you will be limited in the accuracy and precision of your answer.

```
Input

10  REM  ARITHMETIC WITH DIFFERENT VARIABLE TYPES
20  REM  AND THE EFFECT ON PRECISION
30       A=10
40       B=3
50  REM
60       ANS%=A/B
70       ANS!=A/B
80       ANS =A/B
90       ANS#=A/B
100 REM
110      LPRINT ANS%,ANS!,ANS,ANS#
120 REM
130      END

Output

3          3.333333    3.333333    3.333333253860474
```

FIGURE 4–8
Program showing the effect on precision of different variable types.

Salvage Value of an Investment

Most investments (such as cars, stereo equipment, business machinery) have a limited useful life, after which time they must be scrapped or sold and replaced with newer models. The steadily decreasing value of buildings and equipment is called *depreciation*, and the rate at which items depreciate depends on many factors. Typically, cars, computers, and stereo equipment depreciate rapidly, whereas business machines and factory equipment depreciate at a slower rate. Some items, such as houses and jewelry, may actually appreciate in value.

The salvage value of an item (the amount of money it is worth after a period of time) depends on the original investment amount, the depreciation rate for that item, and the age of the item. This value is computed with the following formula:

$$S = P(1 - R/100)Y$$

where S is the salvage value, P is the original investment price, R is the depreciation rate in percent per year, and Y is the age of the item in years since purchase.

CONCEPTS TO BE ILLUSTRATED

The instructions needed to program Case 4-1 are similar to those provided in the cases in chapter 3, except that Case 4-1 asks you to input numeric data and calculate results using a formula. The main program has one additional routine, the CALCULATION subroutine, and it appears (as you would expect) after the INPUT routine and before the OUTPUT routine. The OUTPUT routine consists of two subroutines, one that prints titles and another that prints the actual output result. This is done to separate the printing of titles from the printing of results, a common practice in business programming.

PROBLEM DEFINITION

Input Specifications

Field No.	Field Description	Type	Example
1	Item Description	Alphabetic	Tractor
2	Original Investment Amount	Numeric	10000
3	Depreciation Rate in %	Numeric	20
4	# of Years Held	Numeric	10

Processing Decisions and Formulas

$S = P \cdot [1 - (R/100)]^y$
$S =$ Salvage Value in Dollars
$P =$ Initial Investment in Dollars
$R =$ Depreciation Rate in %
$Y =$ Number of Years (Age) Held

SALVAGE VALUE OF
AN INVESTMENT

```
      ITEM        PRICE       RATE        YEARS       SALVAGE VALUE
    TRACTOR       10000       20          10            1073.742

      ITEM        PRICE       RATE        YEARS       SALVAGE VALUE
    CAR            7500       20           5            2457.6

      ITEM        PRICE       RATE        YEARS       SALVAGE VALUE
    STEREO          805       10          20            97.86914
```

Test Data

Item	Price	Rate %	Years
Tractor	10000	20.	10
Car	7500	20.	10
Stereo	805	10.	10

Error Routines

None required, but be sure there are no commas in the numeric dollars fields. Try to figure out what would happen if a comma were inadvertently included.

Validation Procedure

Select one input data record, and use a hand calculator to find the value of S, the salvage amount. Verify that the computer program and calculated results are approximately equal (small errors are usual).

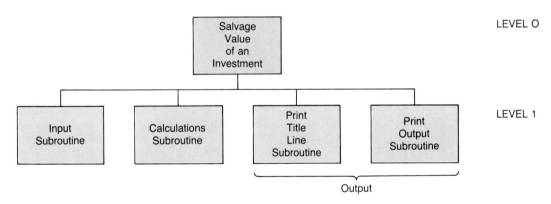

FIGURE C4–1
UTOC chart—salvage value.

111

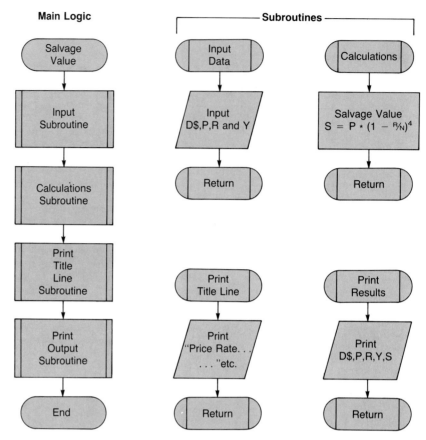

FIGURE C4–2
Detailed program flowchart—salvage value.

CASE STUDY SOLUTION

```
10      REM     ********************************************
20      REM     *            SIMPLE CALCULATIONS           *
30      REM     *             CASE STUDY: C4-1             *
40      REM     *    THE SALVAGE VALUE OF AN INVESTMENT     *
50      REM     * THIS PROGRAM USES AS INPUT THE ORIGINAL*
60      REM     * PURCHASE PRICE OF AN INVESTMENT,P, THE  *
70      REM     * DEPRECIATION RATE IN % PER YEAR, AND    *
80      REM     * THE NUMBER OF YEARS THE INVESTMENT IS   *
90      REM     * HELD.  THE SALVAGE VALUE IS COMPUTED    *
100     REM     * BY:   S = P * ( 1 - (R/100 )) ^ Y       *
110     REM     *    D$= ITEM DESCRIPTION                 *
120     REM     *    P = INITIAL INVESTMENT IN DOLLARS    *
130     REM     *    R = DEPRECIATION RATE IN % PER YEAR  *
140     REM     *    Y = NUMBER OF YEARS                  *
150     REM     *    S = SALVAGE VALUE IN DOLLARS         *
160     REM     ********************************************
170             CLS
180             PRINT "COPYRIGHT (C) 1989, BY MERRILL PUBLISHING COMPANY"
190             PRINT "FOR USE WITH STRUCTURED BASIC PROGRAMMING"
200             PRINT
210             PRINT
220             PRINT "THIS PROGRAM WILL CALCULATE THE DEPRECIATION RATE AND"
230             PRINT "THE NUMBER OF YEARS THE INVESTMENT IS HELD."
240             PRINT "ALSO, THE SALVAGE VALUE."
250             PRINT
260             PRINT
```

```
270       REM      * * * * * * * * * * * * * * *
280       REM      * MAIN PROGRAM *
290       REM      * * * * * * * * * * * * * * *
300       REM      PERFORM 'INPUT' SUBROUTINE
310                GOSUB 390
320       REM      PERFORM 'CALCULATIONS' SUBROUTINE
330                GOSUB 550
340       REM      PERFORM 'PRINT TITLE LINE' SUBROUTINE
350                GOSUB 600
360       REM      PERFORM 'PRINT OUTPUT' SUBROUTINE
370                GOSUB 660
380                END
390       REM      * * * * * * * * * * * * * * * * * *
400       REM      * INPUT SUBROUTINE *
410       REM      * * * * * * * * * * * * * * * * * *
420                PRINT
430                PRINT "PLEASE MAKE SURE THE PRINTER IS ON"
440                PRINT
450                PRINT
460                PRINT "ENTER ITEM DESCRIPTION............_____"
470                PRINT "ENTER THE ORIGINAL INVESTMENT PRICE....._____"
480                PRINT "ENTER THE DEPRECIATION RATE IN PERCENT.._____"
490                PRINT "ENTER THE NUMBER OF YEARS HELD........._____"
500                LOCATE 14,39: INPUT D$
510                LOCATE 15,39: INPUT P
520                LOCATE 16,39: INPUT R
530                LOCATE 17,39: INPUT Y
540                RETURN
550       REM      * * * * * * * * * * * * * * * * * * * * * * * *
560       REM      * CALCULATIONS SUBROUTINE *
570       REM      * * * * * * * * * * * * * * * * * * * * * * * *
580                S = P * (1 - (R/100)) ^ Y
590                RETURN
600       REM      * * * * * * * * * * * * * * * * * * * * * * * * * * *
610       REM      * PRINT TITLE LINE SUBROUTINE *
620       REM      * * * * * * * * * * * * * * * * * * * * * * * * * * *
630                LPRINT"
640                LPRINT " ITEM          PRICE      RATE      YEARS
          SALVAGE VALUE"
650                RETURN
660       REM      * * * * * * * * * * * * * * * * * * * * * * * *
670       REM      * PRINT OUTPUT SUBROUTINE *
680       REM      * * * * * * * * * * * * * * * * * * * * * * * *
690                LPRINT D$,P,R,Y,S
700                RETURN
710       REM
720                END
```

ADVANCED FEATURES

Built-In and Programmer-Defined Functions

In addition to doing your calculations with formulas that you convert from mathematical expressions to BASIC expressions, you may find the eleven built-in math functions available in BASIC useful. These functions are shown in table 4–4. Many programmers who use BASIC for scientific, mathematical, and business calculations use these extensively. In particular, those functions involving the absolute value sign, integer, and square root have widespread use.

TABLE 4–4
Built-in math functions.

Function	Description	Argument
ABS(X)	Absolute value of x	any number
ATN(X)	Arctangent of x	x in radians
COS(X)	cosine of x	x in radians
EXP(N)	e to the n power	e defined, n = number
FIX(X)	integer,truncated	x any number
INT(X)	value $<\,=$ x	x any number
LOG(X)	natural log of x	x any number
SGN(X)	sign (+ or −) of x	x any number
SIN(X)	trig sine of x	x in radians
SQR(X)	square root of x	x positive number
TAN(X)	tangent of x	x in radians

Like with the integer and extended-precision features described previously, it's a good idea to check your BASIC manual before using built-in functions because the exact spelling of the function, its input requirements, and its output may vary from those shown in the table. Also, when using functions on another system, pay particular attention to the requirements of the argument (the data variable that is given to the function for evaluation) because these often differ. Also, in these functions the arguments may be different from what you are used to if you have used math functions in another programming language. For example, the arguments for the trigonometric functions are in radians, not degrees; therefore, your program will have to convert degrees to radians before using the function. (Trig functions are not used in any of the cases or illustrations in this text, but are included here for those programmers who may need them in mathematical or scientific applications of BASIC.)

The user-defined function feature of BASIC is an enhanced feature of newer interpreters and compilers which allows you to write powerful single-statement functions similar in operation to the built-in functions, but with the logic and calculations *you* want to write. They are useful when you have calculations you use frequently in a program on different data variables. The code you must write is minimal, but powerful. To define your own function, you use the DEF FN statement, which has the form

```
line# DEF FN name (arg,arg,arg etc.) = expression
```

where

name is a valid BASIC variable name that becomes the name of the function. For numeric functions, a variable name is used corresponding to the numeric precision that you want in the result of the function (string functions are not covered).

arg,arg,etc. are the names of the argument variables used in the function. These names are replaced by program variables during execution of the function, and they must be defined at that time. You can have 1 or many arguments depending on the needs of your function.

expression is any valid BASIC formula that conforms to the syntactical rules for writing calculation expressions. The arguments will appear in the expression as variables.

The definition of the function is limited to *one* statement. You cannot join together two or more statements with the colon, as can be done with many other multiple statement per line expressions in BASIC.

To use the function you have created with the DEF FN, simply refer to it by name as with any other BASIC function, but remember to precede the name with the letter FN. You also must have placed the DEF FN statement before any reference to your function, and it must be in the logical execution path prior to its use. In other words, you must execute the DEF FN before you call your function, unlike the DATA statement which is called by the READ in the READ/DATA pair.

These rules of syntax and construction are illustrated in the following example for a defined function that finds the volume of any sphere of radius, R.

```
10   PI =3.14159
20   DEF FNVOL(R)=PI*R^3
30   INPUT "ENTER THE RADIUS OF THE SPHERE";RAD
40   V=FNVOL(RAD)
50   PRINT"THE VOLUME OF THE SPHERE IS " ;V
60   END
```

Output

```
ENTER THE RADIUS OF THE SPHERE? 5
THE VOLUME OF THE SPHERE IS  392.6988
```

The function name is FNVOL (for volume). The one and only argument is R, the radius of any sphere. The expression computes the volume as PI*R^3 (PI × R cubed in math). When RAD is input, its value is given to the function by referring to the function name in V = FNVOL(RAD) and placing RAD in parentheses as the argument. The resulting volume is calculated by the function and then printed in statement 50.

Notice that the DEF FN and the assignment statement for PI are placed before the reference to the function. If this were not done, an "undefined user function" error would result.

The following more business-oriented function rounds any number representing a number up to the next whole number. It could be used for billing programs, tax programs, and numerous applications where arriving at a whole dollar amount rather than a dollars and cents amount is desired.

```
10      REM DOLLAR ROUNDING FUNCTION
20          DEF FNROUND(AMT)=INT(AMT+.5)
30          INPUT "ENTER NUMBER TO BE ROUNDED UP ";D
40          PRINT FNROUND(D)
50          END
```

Output

```
ENTER NUMBER TO BE ROUNDED UP ? 3.4679
 3
```

Notice two interesting things about this example. First, the function uses one of BASIC's built-in functions as part of the expression. This is perfectly valid since the syntax requires only that the expression be a valid BASIC expression. Also, note that the value of the function can be referred to and retrieved directly in the output statement. There is no need to assign the actual function to another variable.

Another example of this type of function is shown below. This function rounds any dollars and cents number up to the appropriate cents amount. Note that it duplicates one of the very useful features of the PRINT USING statement, which also does automatic rounding. The results of this user-defined function (the PRINT USING with a ###.## format and the standard PRINT statement) are all printed on the same line for comparison. Keep this function in mind in the later financial problems. It might come in handy.

Input

```
10      REM USER DEFINED FUNCTION TO ROUND UP DOLLARS AND CENTS
20          DEF FNRNDUP(D)=INT((D*100)+.5)/100
30          INPUT "ENTER DOLLARS AND CENTS TO BE ROUNDED ";N
```

```
40    REM PRINT N THREE WAYS FOR COMPARISON
50        PRINT "            FUNCTION RNDUP          PRINT USING        REGULAR PRINT"
60        PRINT "               ";FNRNDUP(N);:PRINT "            ";
70        PRINT USING "  ###.##               ";N;
80        PRINT N
90        GOTO 10
```

Output

```
RUN
ENTER DOLLARS AND CENTS TO BE ROUNDED ? 12.344
        FUNCTION RNDUP          PRINT USING          REGULAR PRINT
            12.34                   12.34           12.344
ENTER DOLLARS AND CENTS TO BE ROUNDED ? 12.345
        FUNCTION RNDUP          PRINT USING          REGULAR PRINT
            12.35                   12.35           12.345
ENTER DOLLARS AND CENTS TO BE ROUNDED ? 100.005
        FUNCTION RNDUP          PRINT USING          REGULAR PRINT
           100.01                  100.01          100.005
ENTER DOLLARS AND CENTS TO BE ROUNDED ? 100.004
        FUNCTION RNDUP          PRINT USING          REGULAR PRINT
            100                   100.00           100.004
ENTER DOLLARS AND CENTS TO BE ROUNDED ? 99.944
        FUNCTION RNDUP          PRINT USING          REGULAR PRINT
           99.94                   99.94           99.944
ENTER DOLLARS AND CENTS TO BE ROUNDED ? 99.945
        FUNCTION RNDUP          PRINT USING          REGULAR PRINT
           99.95                   99.95           99.945
ENTER DOLLARS AND CENTS TO BE ROUNDED ?
```

Making Your Programs User Friendly

BASIC contains the features and statements needed for you to make your programs *user-friendly*. This term implies that the user of your program will be assisted in running your program by logic included in the program. User-friendly programs do the following:

1. guide the user through the steps needed to run the program without error.
2. remind the user how to and where and when to enter data.
3. remind the user of what type of data is to be entered.
4. help with error trapping and assist in locating data entries out of reasonable bounds.
5. give the user the opportunity to correct common oversights that occur when running programs, such as forgetting to turn on the printer, not placing a required program disk or data disk in a disk drive, forgetting to get the disk ready to accept data, and others. The correcting procedure would involve alerting the user to the oversight and giving him/her the opportunity to correct it before program execution continues.
6. give the user a diverse and interesting presentation on the CRT or monitor that uses color and/or sound to add variety and interest.
7. present the user with output that is useful, easy to read and interpret, and correctly formatted.

Items 2, 5, and 6 on prompts, full-screen formatting, and device error trapping and color, were presented in chapter 3. Item 5, data error trapping, will be covered in chapter 6. In this chapter, you will find out how to prepare a proper welcome message and series of instructions for the user of your program (item 1) and how to provide the user with meaningful printed output, expanding a bit on the material in chapter 3.

Welcome message and instructions.   Since computer program users usually do not (and should not need to) have a copy of the program they are using accessible as they run it, the instructions for that program should be presented as the program is being run. A well-written program should present everything that the user needs to know for proper execution at the beginning of the program or during key steps in the execution. Tutorials and menus are common in computer programs and a description of how to write these will be given in chapter 6.

Prompts and full-screen formatting were covered in chapter 3. These are excellent sources of information for the user. However, by adding some general instructions at the beginning of the program the user will be able to proceed more smoothly and with less apprehension. You should ask yourself whether users need to know information such as that listed below when completing an interactive program (the type you are writing in this text):

1. When entering string data, are capital letters required for "Yes" and "No" answers to procedural questions? Can answers be abbreviated?
2. Should the Enter key be pressed after each data entry, or will you be using other input statements to enter data (like INKEY$, which requires no return—see chapter 6).
3. Are any disks needed for the data input or output from the program? If so, must these be formatted and non-write protected?
4. Will the printer be needed? If so, can standard paper be used for the output? Are any special forms or printer operating instructions required before producing the output, as in the case of mailing labels (covered in chapters 5 and 6)?

You will not have to answer all these questions for every program. These are presented to give you an overview of what programmers should take into account when preparing the instructions for a user-friendly program. The most direct way of presenting this important information to the user is to prepare a "Welcome Message" routine in your program so that it is the first subroutine called by the main program *if* the user needs it. The user will not need detailed instructions every time he/she runs your program. After a few runs, probably most of the features and requirements will be memorized. Therefore, you will need a way to allow the user to bypass the welcome message and/or instructions. (Logic for doing this will be presented in chapter 6.) For now, you will explore how to present the welcome message and instructions using the PRINT statements, color, and/or sound. An example of such a message follows:

Input

```
10    REM ******************************
20    REM * WELCOME MESSAGE SUBROUTINE *
30    REM ******************************
40    REM
50        CLS
60        COLOR 14,1
70        PRINT "HELLO! WELCOME TO THE CHECKING ACCOUNT BALANCE"
80        PRINT "PROGRAM WRITTEN IN CHAPTER 4. THE PURPOSE OF THIS"
90        PRINT "PROGRAM IS TO COMPUTE YOUR NEW BALANCE AFTER YOU"
100       PRINT "ENTER LAST MONTH'S BALANCE, THE TOTAL AMOUNT OF"
110       PRINT "CHECKS YOU WROTE, AND TOTAL OF ALL DEPOSITS MADE."
120       PRINT "LET'S BEGIN!"
130       PRINT
140       END
```

Output

```
HELLO! WELCOME TO THE CHECKING ACCOUNT BALANCE
PROGRAM WRITTEN IN CHAPTER 4.  THE PURPOSE OF THIS
PROGRAM IS TO COMPUTE YOUR NEW BALANCE AFTER YOU
ENTER LAST MONTH'S BALANCE, THE TOTAL AMOUNT OF
CHECKS YOU WROTE, AND TOTAL OF ALL DEPOSITS MADE.
LET'S BEGIN!
```

Remember that the computer does not inspect literals (those letters, numbers, and special characters enclosed in quotation marks) for syntax errors, so be careful! It is discouraging to see an otherwise well-written and well-designed program that has misspellings throughout prompts, titles, and headings, as in the following.

```
Input

10     REM MAIN PROGRAM
20     REM PERFORM "WELCOME MESSAGE" ROUTINE
30     GOSUB 100
          .
          .
          .
       END
100    REM WELCOME MESSAGE SUBROUTINE
110    PRINT "HELO WELCOM TO THE CHECKING ACCONT"
120    PRINT "BALANCE POGRAM WRITTEN IN CHAPTER 4"
130    PRINT "THE PURPOSE OF DIS PROGRAM IS TO COMPOOT"
          .
          .           (Remainder of welcome message)
          .
160    RETURN

Output

HELO! WELCOM TO THE CHECKING ACCONT BALANCE
POGRAM WRITTEN IN CHAPTER 4. THE PURPOSE OF
DIS PROGRAM IS TO COMPOOT
```

Notice that the message appears on many lines of the screen. This occurs because most BASIC system terminals display only 80 characters or less on one line. So, it is best to limit messages to 80 characters or less. But keep in mind that the statement number, the word PRINT, and the open quote use from 8 to 12 characters (depending on the number of digits in the statement number) that won't be used in the displayed message. Usually, there are 80 usable characters per line of output to a CRT screen. Therefore, it may be necessary to continue a literal beyond what could be typed on one line of the CRT. The methods for doing this vary on BASIC systems, but most systems allow entry of longer literals or statements, automatically continuing on the next line or scrolling the display to the left. The WIDTH function may permit variations in screen display on your system. Check your manual for details on how to use this statement if you need to compress or expand CRT and printer character limits.

Charge Account Monthly Statement

This case will illustrate mathematical calculations, including addition, subtraction, multiplication, and division with a simple business problem. Titles will be used to produce an output report that resembles a customer's charge account bill.

Referring to the VTOC and subroutine flowcharts for Case 4–2, you can see that this program has a number of new features. Most prominent is the new welcome message routine (a Level 1 subroutine called by the main program). Also, CALCULATE STATEMENT FIGURES and OUTPUT MONTHLY STATEMENT consist of three unique operations each. When this is true, and the operations are short and simple, it is acceptable to write these within one subroutine each.

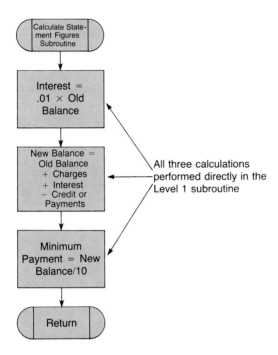

In this program the calculation is simple logic. However, the individual steps in a calculation subroutine may be complex and may involve many statements for each part of a calculation. However, in complex and large programs, combining all formulas for the operations into one routine can lead to problems in design, documentation, understanding, and program modification.

119

PROBLEM DEFINITION

Input Specifications

Field No.	Field Description	Type	Example
1	Account Number	Numeric	61251
2	Customer Name	Alphabetic	Mary B. Smith
3	Address (not used in Output)	Alphabetic	123 Main St.
4	Old Balance	Numeric	250.00
5	Charges/Purchases	Numeric	50.00
6	Payments/Credits/Returns	Numeric	25.00

Processing Decisions and Formulas

Interest $= .01 \times$ Old Balance

New Balance $=$ Old Balance $+$ Interest $+$ Charges/Purchases $-$ Payments/Credits/Returns

Minimum Payment $=$ New Balance/10.

Output

```
                         MONTHLY STATEMENT
                       ABC DEPARTMENT STORE
                       HARTFORD CONN 06105
ACCOUNT NO.        NAME       OLD BAL  CHARGES  CREDITS  NEW BAL  MIN PAYMENT
  61251    MARY B. SMITH      $250.00  $ 50.00  $ 25.00  $277.50   $ 27.75
```

Test Data

61251, Mary B. Smith, 250.00, 50.00, 25.00

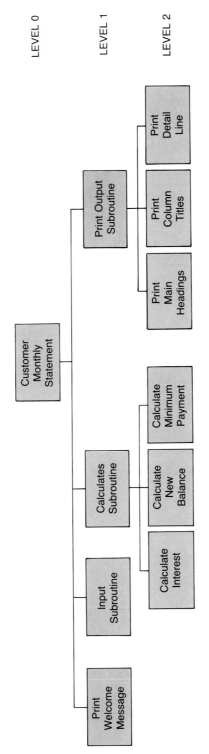

LEVEL 0

LEVEL 1

LEVEL 2

FIGURE C4−3
Visual table of contents.

121

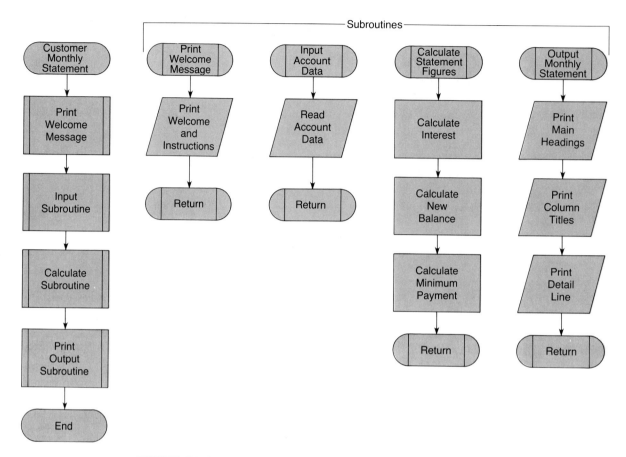

FIGURE C4–4
Program flowchart showing main program and subroutines.

CASE STUDY SOLUTION

```
10      REM     *******************************************************
20      REM     *                SIMPLE CALCULATIONS                  *
30      REM     *                 CASE STUDY:C4-2                     *
40      REM     *             MONTHLY STATEMENT PROGRAM               *
50      REM     *        THIS PROGRAM CALCULATES INTEREST ON A        *
60      REM     * CUSTOMER'S OLD BALANCE, ADDS THE CHARGES FOR        *
70      REM     * THE MONTH, SUBTRACTS THE CREDITS AND PAYMENTS       *
80      REM     * AND PRINTS A MONTHLY STATEMENT FOR THE ACCOUNT      *
90      REM     *                                                     *
100     REM     *                 VARIABLE LEGEND                     *
110     REM     * ACNO = ACCOUNT NO.      NM$ = NAME                  *
120     REM     * AD$ = ADDRESS           OBAL = OLD BALANCE          *
130     REM     * CHG = CHARGES           CRT = CREDITS               *
140     REM     * INRT = INTEREST         NBAL = NEW BALANCE          *
150     REM     * MINPAY = MINIMUM PAYMENT DUE                        *
160     REM     *******************************************************
170     CLS
180     PRINT "COPYRIGHT (C) 1989, BY MERRILL PUBLISHING COMPANY"
190     PRINT "FOR USE WITH STRUCTURED BASIC PROGRAMMING"
200     PRINT
210     PRINT
220     PRINT
230     PRINT "THIS PROGRAM WILL CALCULATE INTEREST ON CUSTOMERS'
240     PRINT "OLD BALANCE, ADD THE CHARGES FOR THE MONTH,
```

```
250                  PRINT "SUBTRACT THE CREDITS AND BILLS THE CUSTOMER FOR
260                  PRINT "THE NEW BALANCE AMOUNT."
270                  PRINT
280        REM       ****************
290        REM       * MAIN PROGRAM *
300        REM       ****************
310        REM        PERFORM 'INPUT DATA' SUBROUTINE
320                  GOSUB 380
330        REM        PERFORM 'CALCULATIONS' SUBROUTINE
340                  GOSUB 580
350        REM       PERFORM 'PRINT OUTPUT' SUBROUTINE
360                  GOSUB 650
370                  END
380        REM       ********************
390        REM       * INPUT SUBROUTINE *
400        REM       ********************
410                  PRINT "PLEASE MAKE SURE THE PRINTER IS ON"
420                  PRINT
430                  PRINT
440                  PRINT
450                  PRINT "ACCOUNT NUMBER......._____"
460                  PRINT "NAME................_____"
470                  PRINT "ADDRESS............._____"
480                  PRINT "OLD BALANCE........._____.__"
490                  PRINT "CHARGES............._____.__"
500                  PRINT "PAYMENTS + CREDITS...._____.__"
510                  LOCATE 15,21: INPUT ACNO
520                  LOCATE 16,21: INPUT NM$
530                  LOCATE 17,21: INPUT ADDR$
540                  LOCATE 18,21: INPUT OBAL
550                  LOCATE 19,21: INPUT CHG
560                  LOCATE 20,21: INPUT CRT
570                  RETURN
580        REM       *************************
590        REM       * CALCULATIONS SUBROUTINE *
600        REM       *************************
610                  INTR = .01 * OBAL
620                  NBAL = OBAL + INTR + CHG - CRT
630                  MINPAY = .1 * NBAL
640                  RETURN
650        REM       *************************
660        REM       * PRINT OUTPUT SUBROUTINE *
670        REM       *************************
680                  LPRINT
690                  LPRINT "                          MONTHLY STATEMENT"
700                  LPRINT "                          ABC DEPARTMENT STORE"
710                  LPRINT "                          HARTFORD CONN  06105"
720                  LPRINT
730                  LPRINT "ACCOUNT NO.      NAME      OLD BAL   CHARGES   CREDITS
    NEW BAL MIN PAYMENT"
740                  F1$ = "  #####    \                \ $###.##  $###.##  $###.##
$###.##  $###.##"
750                  LPRINT USING F1$;ACNO,NM$,OBAL,CHG,CRT,NBAL,MINPAY
760                  RETURN
770        REM
780        REM       END OF PROGRAM

ACCOUNT NUMBER..........? 61251_____
CUSTOMER NAME...........? MARY B. SMITH__
ADDRESS.................? 123 MAIN ST._____
OLD BALANCE.............? 250.00
CHARGES/PURCHASES.......?  50.00
PAYMENTS/CREDITS/RETURNS?  25.00
```

SUMMARY

Calculations are important in business programs because nearly every application involves some form of calculation (e.g., payroll, billing, and inventory control). Sometimes, the calculations involve one simple formula or a series of more complex formulas. However, in all cases, the sequence construct is used to program the desired mathematical operation when writing programs in structured design. A sequence construct should have only one entry and one exit point, regardless of the complexity of the calculation. In BASIC, this is accomplished by writing the calculation sequence as one subroutine or a series of subroutines.

In most BASIC programs, the calculation subroutine follows an INPUT subroutine and precedes OUTPUT subroutine. The calculations within the subroutine may be programmed with programmer-written formula statements, built-in functions, or programmer-defined functions. Programmer-constructed formulas (statements) are the most common method used in BASIC business programs, and they use the following symbols to represent key arithmetic operations: + for addition; − for subtraction; * for multiplication; / for division; and ** or for exponentiation.

A BASIC statement that performs a mathematical operation consists of a statement number followed by one variable name on the left of an equal sign, and then the mathematical evaluation expression, constant, or another variable on the right side of the equal sign. The information on the right is called the evaluation segment. It is evaluated first, and the result is then stored in the memory location (variable name) named to the left of the equal sign. Therefore, the equal sign in BASIC does not mean literally "equal to," and it does not have the same meaning as it does in mathematics. This makes it possible to construct valid BASIC statements like:

```
COUNT = COUNT + 1
```

and

```
TOTAL = TOTAL + SALE
```

The reserved word LET, previously required before BASIC computational statements, is now optional on most BASIC systems and is most often omitted from BASIC calculation statements. (It may be required again in new BASIC interpreters and compilers.)

Some BASIC systems allow for storage and manipulation of different types of numeric data using various variable-naming conventions to distinguish the numeric variable types. Integers (whole numbers that range between −32767 and +32767) can be designated by adding a percent sign at the end of the variable name (e.g., PART%). Normal single-precision numbers are the default, so no special character is needed for single-precision variable names, although an exclamation mark is optional on many systems (e.g., PRICE!). Single-precision numbers may contain only six significant digits, although the magnitude can range from approximately 10^{-38} to 10^{+38} (see appendix A). Double-precision numbers, important for precise scientific, financial, and accounting applications, are designated by adding a # to the end of the variable name (e.g., INCOME#). Variables of this type may store 16 significant digits with a magnitude of approximately 10^{-36} to 10^{+36}.

Because of the conversion process involved in representing decimal numbers in binary form for computer processing, results in BASIC calculations may not be accurate in the sixth decimal place (e.g., 2.99999 versus 3.00000). This error can be corrected through a number of algorithms or by use of double-precision variables, when available. More serious errors can result if care is not taken in understanding the hierarchy of arithmetic operations in BASIC calculation statements. This hierarchy is exponentiation; multiplication and division; and addition and subtraction—all scanning of the statement from left to right. Enclosing expressions with parentheses overrides the normal hierarchy and is recommended whenever expressions are unclear or when desired operations must be isolated in the order to be executed in the sequence intended by the programmer.

124

In addition to expressions converted from algebra to BASIC, there are eleven built-in functions that can be used advantageously in programs involving calculations. Also, BASIC permits you to write your own function definitions and use that function wherever you need to in your program logic.

The syntactical rules for using and defining functions are extensive, but logical and exact. You should be careful using functions on different versions of BASIC since function names and syntax may vary.

COMMON ERRORS AND SOLUTIONS

Error	Example	Solution
1. Improper use of parentheses to direct hierarchy in calculations.	10 C = 5/9 *F − 32 should be . . . 10 C = (5/9)*(F − 32) (no diagnostic given, only incorrect answer!)	Check sections on use of parentheses to direct proper order in calculating.
2. Placing more than one variable on left of equal sign.	10 A + B = C should be . . . 10 C = A + B (syntax error in 10)	Remember that the equal sign does not mean "equal to" in BASIC, but rather "place result in variable to left of equal sign."
3. Producing a numeric result greater than 10^{38}.	10 A = 10 ^ 50 (overflow) (system-dependent)	Check the approximate value of large results and compare to maximum permissible numbers on your system.
4. Division by zero.	10 B = B/C, C = 0 (division by zero)	In cases where the divisor may be zero, check before performing division.
5. Unbalanced parentheses in complex numeric BASIC expression.	10 B = (C + 1)*(A ^ 2) + N) (syntax error in 10)	Count the number of left- and right-facing parentheses. They should always be the same, although this, in itself, does not guarantee the correctness of the BASIC expression.
6. Incorrect variable type for data being INPUT or READ.	10 INPUT A,B\$,C ? 10,John, 125 Main St. (redo from start)	Check the variable list against the data types being processed, and make sure they correspond.
7. PRINT USING formats (images) too small for numbers produced as result of expressions.	10 A = 236 20 PRINT USING"##";A (%236—error)	Estimate the maximum size of numbers calculated in expressions, and make images at least as large.
8. PRINT USING formats (images) incorrect for field being printed.	10 A = 236 20 PRINT USING "\\;"A (type mismatch in 20)	Check the variable types against each image in the image string for compatibility.
9. Entering O for 0, I for 1, Z for 2, etc.	10 A = 2l (should be) 10 A = 21 (syntax error in 10)	Pay particular attention to the 0, 1, and 2 when keying in these numbers, specifications, or reading input containing them.
10. Forgetting to use the * for multiplication, and using · or ().	10 A = B·C or 10 A = (B)(C) (syntax error in 10)	Just remember: multiplication in BASIC is done by indicating the asterisk (*).

11. Trying to take the square root of a negative number.	10 A = −1
	20 B = SQR(A)
	    or
	    B = A$^{(1/2)}$
	(illegal function call in 20)
		Test the argument of the square root function, or the number raised to an even power to see if it is negative before proceeding.

12. Misuse of a counter or accumulator expression.	10 A = A + 1 or 10 TPROF = TPROF + PROF where A and TPROF are not properly initialized (no diagnostic—incorrect results if misused)	Remember: the values of A and TPROF will continue to increase as they are executed unless reset in the program logic (assuming PROF is positive).
13. Formulas in wrong logical order in calculations with more than one formula.	10 A = 10 20 B = C + A 30 C = 30 (no diagnostic—incorrect results for B)	Check the logical order of BASIC expressions which are dependent on one another for proper results.

1. Explain why calculations are important in business programs and give some typical business calculation formulas.
2. Calculations fall into which category of the three key constructs in structured design programming?
3. Give examples of BASIC formulas that may consist of many more than one calculation step.
4. What type of operation usually precedes and follows calculation of results?
5. Explain why it is desirable to write the calculation operation as a separate subroutine.
6. What property makes the computer outstanding in its calculation of results in programs? Give evidence of this property.
7. Name and describe the three ways in which results can be calculated in BASIC programs.
8. Describe what the equal sign means in BASIC. Why is it important that only one variable name appear to the left of the equal sign?
9. List the symbols used in BASIC for addition, subtraction, multiplication, division, and exponentiation.
10. Is the reserved word LET needed on most BASIC systems? Explain why or why not.
11. Given two decimal numbers called NUM1 and NUM2, write five BASIC statements that will add, subtract, multiply, divide, and exponentiate (exponentiate Num2 by Num1) the two numbers and store the result in a variable called "ANSWER."
12. The expression $N = N + 1$ is a special expression valid only in programming languages. What is N called in this case? Why is this type of statement important?
13. Give examples of business program applications where the expression in question 12 is useful and important.
14. Describe the hierarchy of mathematical operations in BASIC. Explain why it is important for programmers to understand the order in which operations take place.
15. In the following example BASIC statements, $A = 1$, $B = 2$, and $C = 3$, what will be the results for D in each case?

```
D = A + B / C
D = (A + B) / C
D = (A + B / C)
D = A + (B / C)
```

16. On many BASIC systems, integers, decimal numbers, and double-precision decimal numbers are stored differently and require specific variable-naming conventions. Describe the variable-naming conventions for these data types on your system, and explain why this knowledge may be important.
17. Are results from a computer calculation in BASIC always exact? Explain why or why not.
18. Give three examples of situations in which it might be necessary to use double-precision numbers.
19. After designing the VTOC chart, what is the next step in developing a program with a calculation? Give an example.
20. Programmers can make errors in some BASIC statements that have no effect on the execution of the program or the correctness of the results. Explain where these errors can occur and why they have no effect.
21. Explain why prompts before INPUT statements and titles before or within PRINT statements become increasingly important as programs become more complex.
22. Many BASIC programs feature calculations that require many separate steps (formulas). When is it desirable to include these steps as separate subroutines? When can the steps be combined?

127

PROBLEMS FOR SOLUTION

1. One of the most popular beginning calculation problems for programmers is the compound interest calculation, because this type of calculation involves laborious hand calculation compared to the speed with which a result can be obtained with a computer.

The problem is to find T, final value (not counting any inflationary loss) of an investment P earning interest at rate i for y years, where the interest is compounded (added into the principal) N times per year. The formula is:

$$T = P\left(1 + \frac{i}{N}\right)^{y \cdot N}$$

Input Specifications

Field No.	Field Description	Type	Example
1	Initial Investment	Decimal Number	10000.00
2	Interest Rate in Decimal Form	Decimal Number	.12
3	Number of Compounding Periods	Integer	365 (daily)
4	Number of Years of Investment	Integer	20

Processing Decisions and Formulas

$$T = P \times (1 + (i/N))^{y \cdot N}$$

T = Final Value of Investment
P = Original Principal Invested
i = Annual Interest Rate as Decimal
N = Number of Compounding Periods/Year
y = Number of Years of Investment

Output

```
ORIGINAL INVEST.   INT.RATE,% COMP. PER. NO. OF YEARS   TOTAL VALUE OF INVEST.
    $10,000.00         0.12      365       20.0              $110,203.00
```

Test Data

```
10000.00, .12, 365, 20
10000.00, .15, 365, 20
10000.00, .18, 365, 20
```

Error Routines

None required.

Validation Procedure

Although tedious and time-consuming, validate at least one record by calculating T with a calculator by hand. Check to see that the results are nearly equal. Also check alignment of output results under the titles, and proper editing of numeric fields.

2. Whenever an item is manufactured, there are many factors that management must consider in pricing and in establishing facilities for manufacturing. One of the most important of these is the break-even quantity, which is the level of production that covers not only the variable costs (raw materials and direct manufacturing costs such as labor), but also the overhead costs associated with the manufacturing process, such as the plant and machinery, and so forth. These latter costs are referred to as *fixed* costs, and they exist regardless of how many items are produced.

Assuming that the selling price of the manufactured item, the overhead (or fixed costs), and the variable costs are known and can be input as data, write a program to compute the break-even quantity that will produce enough revenue to cover all costs. The formulas needed are described in the problem definition, as well as the output desired.

Input Specifications

Field No.	Field Description	Type	Example
1	Fixed Cost (Overhead)	Decimal Number	15000.00
2	Item Selling Price	Decimal Number	25.00
3	Variable Cost per Item	Decimal Number	10.00

Processing Decisions and Formulas

Break-Even Quantity = Fixed Cost/(Item Selling Price − Variable Cost per Unit)
Total Variable Cost = Variable Cost per Unit × Break-Even Quantity
Total Revenue = Item Selling Price × Break-Even Quantity
Total Cost = Fixed Cost + Total Variable Cost
Cost per Unit = Total Cost / Break-Even Quantity

Output

```
              ITEM                    VALUE
     BREAKEVEN QUANTITY      :           1000
     TOTAL VARIABLE COST     :     $10,000.00
     TOTAL REVENUE           :     $25,000.00
     TOTAL COST              :     $25,000.00
     COST PER UNIT           :         $25.00
     PRICE PER UNIT          :         $25.00


     BREAKEVEN QUANTITY      :           3333
     TOTAL VARIABLE COST     :   $106,666.70
     TOTAL REVENUE           :   $116,666.70
     TOTAL COST              :   $116,666.70
     COST PER UNIT           :         $35.00
     PRICE PER UNIT          :         $35.00


     BREAKEVEN QUANTITY      :            333
     TOTAL VARIABLE COST     :      $1,666.67
     TOTAL REVENUE           :      $6,666.67
     TOTAL COST              :      $6,666.67
     COST PER UNIT           :         $20.00
     PRICE PER UNIT          :         $20.00
```

Test Data

15000.00, 25.00, 10.00
10000.00, 35.00, 32.00
5000.00, 20.00, 5.00

Error Routines

None. However, note the effect of having a high fixed cost and a selling price and variable cost that are close in value.

Validation Procedure

Calculate one test example by hand and verify the results obtained in your program. Also, check alignment of titles and headings and proper editing of dollars and cents fields.

3. Using the information and formulas given in problem 2, input the quantity to be manufactured and calculate the selling price necessary to equate all costs with revenue. This involves some rewriting of the formulas in the problem definition provided for problem 2; however, the output will be nearly the same with the exception of the price per unit (which should now be called the "break-even" price), and the break-even quantity should now be called the "manufactured" quantity, which is INPUT. Rewrite the problem definition accordingly, and write the structured BASIC program to solve the revised problem.

Input Specifications

Field No.	Field Description	Type	Example
1	Fixed Cost	Decimal Number	15000.00
2	Item Selling Price	Decimal Number	25.00
3	Variable Cost per Item	Decimal Number	10.00
4	Manufactured Quantity	Integer	100

Processing Decisions and Formulas

$$\text{Total Variable Cost} = \text{Variable Cost per Item} \times \text{Manufactured Quantity}$$
$$\text{Total Cost} = \text{Fixed Cost} + \text{Total Variable Cost}$$
$$\text{Break-Even Price} = \text{Total Cost/Manufactured Quantity}$$
$$\text{Total Revenue} = \text{Item Selling Price} \times \text{Manufactured Quantity}$$

Output

```
             ITEM                      VALUE
MANUFACTURED QUANTITY :  100
TOTAL VARIABLE COST   :  $10.00
TOTAL REVENUE         :  $2,500.00
TOTAL COST            :  $16,000.00
BREAKEVEN PRICE       :  $160.00
```

Test Data

15000.00, 25.00, 10.00, 100

Error Routines

None. However, note the effect of having a high fixed cost and a selling price and variable cost that are close in value.

Validation Procedure

Calculate the test example by hand and verify the results obtained in your program. Also, check alignment of titles and headings and proper editing of dollars and cents fields.

4. Often we are interested in how close to our budgeted monthly expenses we actually come when paying our bills each month. Assume that we have established budget amounts for rent, car expenses, food, entertainment, and clothing, and have kept a record of these same expenses for the month. Write a program to add up the budgeted expenses and the actual expenses for these items, and compare the total budgeted amount to the actual amount expressed as percent under or over budget, as shown in the problem definition.

Input Specifications

Field No.	Field Description	Type	Example
1 + 2	Rent or Mortgage Expense, Budget, Actual	Decimal Number	200.00, 200.00
3 + 4	Food Expenses, Budget, Actual	Decimal Number	125.00, 175.00
5 + 6	Entertainment Expenses, Budget, Actual	Decimal Number	50.00, 25.00
7 + 8	Car Expenses, Budget, Actual	Decimal Number	382.00, 382.00
9 + 10	Clothing Expenses, Budget, Actual	Decimal Number	75.00, 125.00

Processing Decisions and Formulas

Total Budgeted Expenses = Rent + Car + Food + Entertainment + Clothing

Total Actual Expenses = Act. Rent + Act. Car + Act. Food + Act. Entertainment + Act. Clothing

$$\text{Percent over Budget} = \left(\frac{\text{Total Actual Expenses} - \text{Total Budgeted Expenses}}{\text{Total Budgeted Expenses}} \right) * 100$$

Output

```
                    MONTHLY EXPENSE ANALYSIS

            CATEGORY        BUDGETED AMOUNT      ACTUAL AMOUNT

     RENT                       $200.00            $200.00
     FOOD                       $125.00            $175.00
     ENTERTAINMENT               $50.00             $25.00
     CAR                        $382.00            $382.00
     CLOTHING                    $75.00            $125.00

            TOTALS              $832.00            $907.00

         PERCENT OVER BUDGET  :   +9.0%
```

Test Data

200.00, 200.00, 125.00, 175.00, 50.00, 25.00, 382.00, 382.00, 75.00, 125.00

(Make up your own data for a typical month.)

Error Routines

None.

Validation Procedure

Calculate one month's expenses by hand and check your result against the program output results. Also, verify that numeric fields are properly edited and centered under the titles and headings as shown.

5. Often in costing jobs, it is necessary in business to compute the area and volume of various shapes and items. The series of formulas given in this problem can be used to compute these areas and volumes in a fraction of the time normally spent using calculators or calculating by hand, especially when the parameters that affect volume or area change and the computations are repeated for several alternatives. Write a structured BASIC program to compute the areas and volumes described, in accordance with the problem definition that follows.

Input Specifications

Field No.	Field Description	Type	Example
1	Radius of Sphere	Decimal Number	6.00

Processing Decisions and Formulas

Volume is

$$V = \tfrac{4}{3} \pi R^3$$

Where R is the radius. Assuming that there are 7.48 gallons per cubic foot, find the number of cubic feet in a sphere *six* feet in radius and print out the number of gallons a water tower that size could hold.

Output

```
RADIUS OF SPHERE IS :  6.00

VOLUME IS           :  904.78

GALLONS HELD ARE    :  6767.76
```

Test Data

6.00

Error Routines

None.

Validation Procedure

Calculate the results by hand and verify the program output.

CHAPTER FIVE

LOOPING

OUTLINE

LEARNING OBJECTIVES

Upon completion of this chapter, you will be able to:

☐ Understand the importance of looping in BASIC business programs.

☐ Program the WHILE loop in BASIC using the WHILE and WEND statements.

☐ Program the WHILE loop in BASIC using the FOR/NEXT statements.

☐ Combine WHILE loops and FOR/NEXT loops to produce interesting and useful looping programs.

☐ Program the DO UNTIL construct in BASIC by rearranging the routines in the WHILE loop.

Looping occurs when a statement within a program tells the computer to move back to a previously executed statement and execute it again. Looping is important because it permits the computer to repeat a program (or a section of a program) automatically, thus saving the time and effort that would be needed to repeat the logic in the loop. For example, it would be time-consuming and wasteful to execute a separate payroll program for every employee a company pays. With looping, the same program can be used to process each employee's paycheck. The program would repeat after the computer is signalled (with a program statement) to do so, and it would stop when the payment process is complete. Almost every computer language features a way to tell the computer to repeat logical steps like those in a payroll program. This chapter will explore the features of the looping, or iteration, structure.

While almost every business application program has a looping provision in it, looping causes the greatest problems for programmers because it is not as simple as it seems. Thus, the proper understanding of looping principles and statements can help you avoid wasted time and effort, and help you write efficient and realistic business programs.

LOOPING IN STRUCTURED DESIGN PROGRAMMING—WHILE LOOP

There are two statements used to represent looping in structured design programs: the DO WHILE and DO UNTIL. Although these statements appear similar, use of the wrong one can cause program errors that will generate excessive or even false output.

The DO WHILE and DO UNTIL constructs are represented by the charts in figure 5–1. The flowcharts show that in the DO WHILE structure, as long as the condition is true, the program operation will repeat. If any subsequent condition returns false, the looping ends and the program continues with the statements after the loop. On the other hand, the DO UNTIL processes the operation first, and then the condition is evaluated. If the condition is true, the loop is exited, and program execution continues with the statements after the loop. Figure 5–2 illustrates these constructs with a familiar process and condition.

Writing the WHILE Loop with WHILE/WEND

DO WHILE loops can be created in BASIC with WHILE/WEND, the statements that were designed for performing the DO WHILE loop (or with FOR/NEXT on systems that do not support the WHILE/WEND). The WHILE and WEND statements determine, respectively,

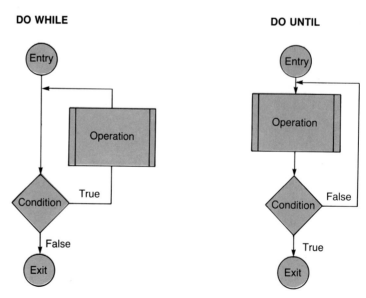

FIGURE 5–1

The DO WHILE and DO UNTIL structures.

DO WHILE (I am hungry) **DO UNTIL** (I am full; not hungry)

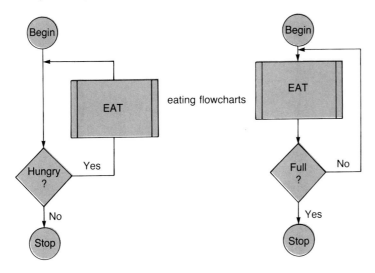

eating flowcharts

FIGURE 5–2
The DO WHILE and DO UNTIL structures illustrated with a simple example.

the beginning and end of a WHILE loop. The computer checks the condition specified after the word WHILE before it executes any instructions placed between WHILE and WEND statements. The format of the WHILE is:

```
line# WHILE (any expression)
```

An example of a WHILE statement would be

```
10 WHILE A>10
```

If the expression is true (or not zero), the statements in the loop execute until the WEND is reached. Control then returns to WHILE where the condition is tested again. If it is still true, then the processes are repeated. If it is false, execution resumes at the first statement after WEND.

WHILE loops do not have built-in counters, so if these are needed in the program logic, they must be provided by the programmer. Also, WHILE loops may be placed inside one another. The following program shows a simple example of a WHILE loop using WHILE and WEND statements.

```
10   C = 1
20   WHILE C < 101
30   PRINT C
40   C = C + 1
50   WEND
60   PRINT "WHILE LOOP COMPLETED"
70   END
```

In this program, C will start off at 1 and be incremented by line 40 in the program. Each value of C will be printed until C reaches 101, at which time the loop will end.

An example that uses an INPUT statement to change the condition in the WHILE loop and terminate the loop is

```
10   NA$ = "ANYTHING"
20   WHILE NA$<>"END"
30   INPUT "ENTER A PERSON'S NAME....";NA$
40   LPRINT NA$
45   WEND
50   END
```

135

In this program, any name that is entered as data for the INPUT statement at line 30 will be printed on the printer. When the word "END" is input, the program will print it out. Then the loop will be exited and the program will end.

Writing the WHILE Loop with FOR/NEXT

The FOR/NEXT statements also can be used to program a WHILE loop, but with the added advantage of providing a built-in counter that can be set, altered, and incremented in special ways. This allows you to use FOR/NEXT to actually generate data for tables and other applications. The syntactical rules for these statements are

```
line# FOR (variable) = A TO B [STEP C] (where [ ] is optional)
```

where: (variable) = an integer or single-precision number used as the built-in counter
        A = another variable or a numeric value or expression that becomes the initial value of the counter
        B = another variable, number, or expression that becomes the final value of the counter
        C = a variable, number, or numeric expression that is used to increment the counter in each loop cycle (optional)

Like the WHILE/WEND, FOR/NEXT sets up the boundary for the loop, and all statements inside are executed until the NEXT statement is encountered. The STEP can be omitted, making the default value 1 for each loop cycle. When the NEXT is encountered, BASIC checks to see if the current value of the counter has reached the ending value, and if it has, the loop is exited. Interestingly, the STEP value can be negative, so that the values of the counter go in reverse (larger to smaller) until the value of the counter is less than the final value. If C is zero, you create an infinite loop, so be careful when using the STEP. Finally, program speed is improved if the counter variables are assigned as integers because these take less time to calculate in the computer.

The NEXT statement has the format:

```
line# NEXT variable
```

where: variable = the same name as that used for the counter.

On many BASIC versions the variable can be omitted. This has the advantage of speeding up execution time, but may result in more confusing logic when you have more than one FOR/NEXT loop in your program.

Figure 5–3 shows a short, but useful, program that prints out the squares, square roots, cubes, and cube roots of all the numbers between 1 and 25.

NESTED LOOPS—COMBINING WHILE/WEND AND FOR/NEXT

The mailing label program in figure 5–4 illustrates how two loops can be effectively combined in one program to produce useful results with a small amount of code. The "outer" loop, a WHILE/WEND loop, executes as long as the name being entered in the INPUT statements (lines 60–90) is not END. This will allow the program to proceed to the "inner loop," a FOR/NEXT loop, which prints any number of mailing labels for the person whose name and address were entered in the INPUT statements. A FOR/NEXT loop controls the number of labels for each person, which can be any number as long as there are label forms in the printer to satisfy the request.

This process of "nesting" one loop inside the other also is very useful when producing tables of financial and other data, as you will see in the upcoming case studies.

Input

```
10      REM     ************************************************************
20      REM     * PROGRAM USING FOR/NEXT LOOP TO GENERATE                  *
30      REM     * A TABLE OF SQUARES, CUBES, SQUARE ROOTS, AND CUBE ROOTS *
40      REM     ************************************************************
50      REM     PRINT TITLE LINE
60              LPRINT "                          TABLE OF VALUES "
70              LPRINT "   X       X SQUARED       X CUBED    SQUARE ROOT X   CUBE R
OOT X"
80              FOR X = 1 TO 25 STEP 1
90                   XSQUARED = X * X
100                  X CUBED = X * X * X
110                  SQROOTX = SQR(X)
120                  CUBERTX = X ^ (1/3)
130                  F1$ = "   ##.##     ###.##     ##,###.##     ##.###     ##.###"
140                  LPRINT USING F1$;X,XSQUARED,XCUBED,SQROOTX,CUBERTX
150             NEXT X
160             LPRINT "                TABLE FINISHED"
170             END
```

Output

```
                          TABLE OF VALUES
   X       X SQUARED       X CUBED    SQUARE ROOT X   CUBE ROOT X
 1.00        1.00             1.00        1.000         1.000
 2.00        4.00             8.00        1.414         1.260
 3.00        9.00            27.00        1.732         1.442
 4.00       16.00            64.00        2.000         1.587
 5.00       25.00           125.00        2.236         1.710
 6.00       36.00           216.00        2.449         1.817
 7.00       49.00           343.00        2.646         1.913
 8.00       64.00           512.00        2.828         2.000
 9.00       81.00           729.00        3.000         2.080
10.00      100.00         1,000.00        3.162         2.154
11.00      121.00         1,331.00        3.317         2.224
12.00      144.00         1,728.00        3.464         2.289
13.00      169.00         2,197.00        3.606         2.351
14.00      196.00         2,744.00        3.742         2.410
15.00      225.00         3,375.00        3.873         2.466
16.00      256.00         4,096.00        4.000         2.520
17.00      289.00         4,913.00        4.123         2.571
18.00      324.00         5,832.00        4.243         2.621
19.00      361.00         6,859.00        4.359         2.668
20.00      400.00         8,000.00        4.472         2.714
21.00      441.00         9,261.00        4.583         2.759
22.00      484.00        10,648.00        4.690         2.802
23.00      529.00        12,167.00        4.796         2.844
24.00      576.00        13,824.00        4.899         2.884
25.00      625.00        15,625.00        5.000         2.924
                        TABLE FINISHED
```

FIGURE 5–3

Program and output of a program that generates squares and cubes.

LOOPING IN STRUCTURED PROGRAMMING—DO UNTIL LOOPS

Problems with the WHILE Loop

You might have a problem with the WHILE loop, particularly when it comes to the last record being processed, as is true in the mailing label program in figure 5–4. The last input in that program was the word END, which was used to signal that the program is

137

Input

```
10    REM ****************************************************************
20    REM * THIS PROGRAM PRINTS ONE COLUMN OF MAILING LABELS ON STANDARD *
30    REM * MAILING LABEL FORMS. MAKE SURE YOU HAVE THE CORRECT LABEL     *
40    REM * PAPER LOADED BEFORE PRINTING.                                 *
50    REM ****************************************************************
60         CLS
70         PRINT "COPYRIGHT (C) 1989, BY MERRILL PUBLISHING COMPANY"
80         PRINT "FOR USE WITH STRUCTURED BASIC PROGRAMMING"
90            N$ = "OK"   ' TO INITIALIZE THE WHILE LOOP
100   WHILE N$ <> "END"
110        PRINT
120        PRINT "THIS PROGRAM PRINTS ONE COLUMN OF MAILING LABELS ON STANDARD"
130        PRINT "MAILING LABEL FORMS. MAKE SURE YOU HAVE THE CORRECT LABEL"
140        PRINT "PAPER LOADED BEFORE PRINTING"
150        PRINT
155        PRINT "PLEASE MAKE SURE PRINTER IS ON"
156        PRINT
160        PRINT "ENTER NAME..........................."
170        PRINT "ENTER STREET........................."
180        PRINT "ENTER CITY STATE AND ZIP - NO COMMAS.."
190        PRINT "HOW MANY LABELS FOR THIS PERSON......."
200        LOCATE 10,39: INPUT N$
210        LOCATE 11,39: INPUT S$
220        LOCATE 12,39: INPUT C$
230        LOCATE 13,39:INPUT N
240            FOR I = 1 TO N
250                    LPRINT N$
260                    LPRINT S$
270                    LPRINT C$
280                    LPRINT
290                    LPRINT
300                    LPRINT
310            NEXT I
320    WEND
330    END
```

Screen Output

```
COPYRIGHT (C) 1989, MERRILL PUBLISHING COMPANY
FOR USE WITH STRUCTURED BASIC PROGRAMMING

THIS PROGRAM PRINTS ONE COLUMN OF MAILING LABELS ON STANDARD
MAILING LABEL FORMS. MAKE SURE YOU HAVE THE CORRECT LABEL
PAPER LOADED BEFORE PRINTING

PLEASE MAKE SURE PRINTER IS ON

ENTER NAME...........................? JOHN C. JONES
ENTER STREET.........................? 125 MAIN STREET
ENTER CITY STATE AND ZIP - NO COMMAS...? HARTFORD CT 06105
HOW MANY LABELS FOR THIS PERSON........? 2
```

Printer Output

```
JOHN C. JONES
125 MAIN STREET
HARTFORD CT 06105
JOHN C. JONES
125 MAIN STREET
HARTFORD CT 06105
```

FIGURE 5–4
A program combining WHILE/WEND and FOR/NEXT statements.

supposed to end. However, once inside the WHILE/WEND statements, the program proceeded to ''ask'' for the person's address, even though END had been entered as the name. Also, a label for that signal record was printed, even though it made no sense to do so. Although not a serious problem when printing mailing labels (you could just throw away the extras), in some applications this processing on the last signal record could cause trouble and, in some cases, result in false output.

You can modify the mailing label program in figure 5–4 so this problem is eliminated by a slight relocation of some of the statements. In doing so, you arrive at what is called a DO UNTIL loop, one of the most important features in most commercial business programs where a lot of data records are processed. All you have to do is relocate the INPUT N$ statement to two places: to outside the loop before the WHILE and to the very end of the WHILE loop right before the WEND. This program and its output is shown in figure 5–5.

FIGURE 5–5
Program input and output for program with relocated INPUT statement.

```
Input

 10      REM ****************************************************************
 20      REM * THIS PROGRAM PRINTS ONE COLUMN OF MAILING LABELS ON STANDARD *
 30      REM * MAILING LABEL FORMS. MAKE SURE YOU HAVE THE CORRECT LABEL     *
 40      REM * PAPER LOADED BEFORE PRINTING                                  *
 50      REM ****************************************************************
 60      CLS
 70      PRINT "COPYRIGHT (C) 1989, BY MERRILL PUBLISHING COMPANY"
 80      PRINT "FOR USE WITH STRUCTURED BASIC PROGRAMMING"
 90              PRINT
100              PRINT "THIS PROGRAM PRINTS ONE COLUMN OF MAILING LABELS ON"
110              PRINT "STANDARD MAILING LABEL FORMS.  MAKE SURE YOU HAVE"
120              PRINT "THE CORRECT LABEL PAPER LOADED BEFORE PRINTING"
130              PRINT
140              PRINT "PLEASE MAKE SURE THE PRINTER IS ON"
150              PRINT
160              PRINT "ENTER NAME.........................."
170              LOCATE 10,39: INPUT N$
180      WHILE N$ <> "END"
190              PRINT "ENTER STREET........................"
200              PRINT "ENTER CITY STATE AND ZIP - NO COMMAS.."
210              PRINT "HOW MANY LABELS FOR THIS PERSON......."
220              LOCATE 11,39: INPUT S$
230              LOCATE 12,39: INPUT C$
240              LOCATE 13,39: INPUT N
250                  FOR I = 1 TO N
260                      LPRINT N$
270                      LPRINT S$
280                      LPRINT C$
290                      LPRINT
300                      LPRINT
310                      LPRINT
320                  NEXT I
330              CLS
340              PRINT
350              PRINT
360              PRINT
370              PRINT
380              PRINT "PLEASE MAKE SURE THE PRINTER IS ON"
390              PRINT
400              PRINT
410              PRINT
420              PRINT
```

```
430                     PRINT "ENTER NAME........................."
440                     LOCATE 10,39: INPUT N$
450        WEND
460        END
```

Output

```
THIS PROGRAM PRINTS ONE COLUMN OF MAILING LABELS ON
STANDARD MAILING LABEL FORMS.  MAKE SURE YOU HAVE
THE CORRECT LABEL PAPER LOADED BEFORE PRINTING

PLEASE MAKE SURE THE PRINTER IS ON

ENTER NAME..........................? JOHN C. JONES
ENTER STREET........................? 125 MAIN STREET
ENTER CITY STATE AND ZIP - NO COMMAS...? HARTFORD CT 06105
HOW MANY LABELS FOR THIS PERSON........? 2

JOHN C. JONES
125 MAIN STREET
HARTFORD CT 06105


JOHN C. JONES
125 MAIN STREET
HARTFORD CT 06105


PLEASE MAKE SURE THE PRINTER IS ON


ENTER NAME..........................? MARY B. SMITH
ENTER STREET........................? 12 SOUTH STREET
ENTER CITY STATE AND ZIP - NO COMMAS...? EAST HARTFORD CT 06118
HOW MANY LABELS FOR THIS PERSON........? 3


MARY B. SMITH
12 SOUTH STREET
EAST HARTFORD CT 06118

MARY B. SMITH
12 SOUTH STREET
EAST HARTFORD CT 06118


MARY B. SMITH
12 SOUTH STREET
EAST HARTFORD CT 06118
```

In this program, when you input END and control is returned to the WHILE, no other steps are processed and the WHILE loop stops. The purpose of placing one INPUT before the WHILE is to give the program a name for the very first label. Without it, the program would attempt to print a name that had not been defined, and it would stop with an error.

As stated, using the original WHILE loop to produce labels didn't create a serious problem—it caused just one wasted label to be printed per run. Now take a look at figure 5–6 where the results are more serious—a mathematical result is completely wrong. In

FIGURE 5-6
DO WHILE loop for test averages.

```
Input
10      REM     *********************************
20      REM     * THIS PROGRAM WILL AVERAGE TEST *
30      REM     * SCORES, BUT WITH AN ERROR       *
40      REM     *********************************
50              TEST=100
60                PRINT "COPYRIGHT (C) 1989, BY MERRILL PUBLISHING COMPANY"
70                PRINT "FOR USE WITH STRUCTURED BASIC PROGRAMMING"
80              WHILE TEST <> -1
90                CLS
100               PRINT
110               PRINT "ENTER TEST SCORES.  WHEN ALL SCORES ARE ENTERED"
120               PRINT "ENTER -1 AS THE LAST SCORE AND THE AVERAGE WILL BE"
130               PRINT "PRINTED OUT"
140               PRINT
150               PRINT "MAKE SURE THE PRINTER IS ON"
160               PRINT
170               PRINT "ENTER TEST SCORE......"
180               LOCATE 10,24: INPUT TEST
190               ACCUM=ACCUM + TEST
200               NTEST=NTEST + 1
210             WEND
220               AVG=ACCUM/NTEST
230               PRINT
240               PRINT "THE AVERAGE IS...";AVG
250               END
```

Output

```
ENTER TEST SCORES. WHEN ALL SCORES ARE ENTERED
ENTER -1 AS THE LAST SCORE AND THE AVERAGE WILL BE
PRINTED OUT.

MAKE SURE THE PRINTER IS ON

ENTER A TEST SCORE...? 90

ENTER TEST SCORES. WHEN ALL SCORES ARE ENTERED
ENTER -1 AS THE LAST SCORE AND THE AVERAGE WILL BE
PRINTED OUT.

MAKE SURE THE PRINTER IS ON

ENTER A TEST SCORE...? 80

ENTER TEST SCORES. WHEN ALL SCORES ARE ENTERED
ENTER -1 AS THE LAST SCORE AND THE AVERAGE WILL BE
PRINTED OUT.

MAKE SURE THE PRINTER IS ON

ENTER A TEST SCORE...? 70

ENTER TEST SCORES. WHEN ALL SCORES ARE ENTERED
ENTER -1 AS THE LAST SCORE AND THE AVERAGE WILL BE
PRINTED OUT.
```

```
MAKE SURE THE PRINTER IS ON

ENTER A TEST SCORE...? -1

THE AVERAGE IS... 59.75 ◄————————Wrong Answer
```

this program, you use a WHILE loop to find the average of test scores, which are input via the keyboard. You will signal the end of ''real'' test score data to end the processing and produce the answer by inputting a −1 as a score (assume that a −1 cannot be a real score). The ACCUM variable will contain the sum of all scores and the NTEST variable will contain the number of tests. Dividing ACCUM by NTEST should then give the average. But, what went wrong? The average is clearly too low because the lowest ''real'' test score is 70. What happened was that the −1 was included in the sum and the counter was incremented accordingly.

Now, modify this program as you did the mailing label example to create an UNTIL loop, and then look at the results as shown in figure 5–7.

The UNTIL loop is important in business because it is often desirable to process a large number of records without counting them or knowing how many there are in advance. In these applications, having a signal (often called a *data flag*) at the end of all the ''real'' records signals the computer to end loop processing and proceed with the remaining logic, if any. Clearly, in these programs the data flag should not be processed along with the other records, which is the reason the unmodified WHILE is inadequate. Rearranging the steps to produce an UNTIL loop solves these problems.

The following summarizes the steps needed to convert a WHILE loop to an UNTIL loop.*

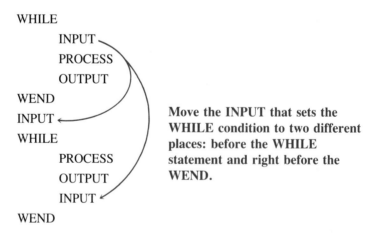

WHILE
    INPUT
    PROCESS
    OUTPUT
WEND
INPUT
WHILE
    PROCESS
    OUTPUT
    INPUT
WEND

Move the INPUT that sets the WHILE condition to two different places: before the WHILE statement and right before the WEND.

*Some versions of BASIC do have an UNTIL statement pair like WHILE/WEND which terminates a program loop as soon as a condition becomes true, greatly simplifying the built-up versions demonstrated in the chapter. However, the systems that support this statement pair currently are rare so consult your manual for more information. It is anticipated that future versions of BASIC will support the UNTIL loop directly.

Input

```
10      REM     ********************************
20      REM     * THIS PROGRAM WILL AVERAGE TEST *
30      REM     * SCORES, WITH NO ERROR          *
40      REM     ********************************
50      REM
60              TEST=100
70              CLS
80              PRINT "COPYRIGHT (C) 1989, BY MERRILL PUBLISHING COMPANY"
90              PRINT "FOR USE WITH STRUCTURED BASIC PROGRAMMING"
100             PRINT
110             PRINT "ENTER TEST SCORES.  WHEN ALL SCORES ARE ENTERED"
120             PRINT "ENTER -1 AS THE LAST SCORE AND THE AVERAGE WILL BE PRINTED"
130             PRINT
140             PRINT "ENTER A TEST SCORE..."
150             LOCATE 7,24: INPUT TEST
160         WHILE TEST<>-1
170             ACCUM=ACCUM + TEST
180             NTEST =NTEST + 1
190             CLS
230             PRINT "ENTER TEST SCORES. WHEN ALL SCORES ARE ENTERED"
240             PRINT "ENTER -1 AS THE LAST SCORE AND THE AVERAGE WILL BE PRINTED"
250             PRINT
260             PRINT "ENTER A TEST SCORE..."
270             LOCATE 7,24: INPUT TEST
280         WEND
290             AVG = ACCUM/NTEST
300             PRINT
310             PRINT "THE AVERAGE IS...";AVG
320             END
```

Output

```
RUN

COPYRIGHT (C) 1989, BY MERRILL PUBLISHING COMPANY
FOR USE WITH STRUCTURED BASIC PROGRAMMING

ENTER TEST SCORES. WHEN ALL SCORES ARE ENTERED
ENTER -1 AS THE LAST SCORE AND THE AVERAGE WILL BE PRINTED

ENTER A TEST SCORE...

ENTER A TEST SCORE...? 90

ENTER TEST SCORES. WHEN ALL SCORES ARE ENTERED
ENTER -1 AS THE LAST SCORE AND THE AVERAGE WILL BE PRINTED

ENTER A TEST SCORE...? 80

ENTER TEST SCORES. WHEN ALL SCORES ARE ENTERED
ENTER -1 AS THE LAST SCORE AND THE AVERAGE WILL BE PRINTED

ENTER A TEST SCORE...? 70

ENTER TEST SCORES. WHEN ALL SCORES ARE ENTERED
ENTER -1 AS THE LAST SCORE AND THE AVERAGE WILL BE PRINTED

ENTER A TEST SCORE...? -1

THE AVERAGE IS... 80
```

FIGURE 5-7
DO UNTIL loop for test averages.

Sales Tax Tables

CONCEPTS TO BE ILLUSTRATED

Many state governments generate revenue by collecting a sales tax on most goods and services sold by merchants. This tax, which is a function of a sales tax rate and the dollar amount of the retail purchase, is calculated with the following formula:

$$\text{sales tax} = \text{sales tax rate} \times \text{purchase amount}$$

For large purchases, such as a car, the tax is substantial, whereas for smaller purchases, the tax is obviously less.

Write a structured BASIC program that will accept the sales tax rate as input and then generate a sales tax table (as shown in the problem definition) for purchases between $1 and $10 in increments of $1. Use the WHILE and FOR/NEXT statements to generate the table.

PROBLEM DEFINITION

Input Specifications

Field No.	Field Description	Type	Example
1	Sales Tax Rate	Numeric	0.075

Processing Decisions and Formulas

$$\text{sales tax} = \text{sales tax rate} \times \text{purchase amount}$$

Round the tax up to the nearest penny with PRINT USING and for a rounding function. Continue to prepare tables for various tax rates until a -1 is input to end the processing.

Output

```
                    SALES TAX TABLE

                 SALES TAX RATE =0.075

          DOLLARS                    SALES TAX
    ---------------            ---------------
       $     1.00                 $     0.08
       $     2.00                 $     0.15
       $     3.00                 $     0.23
       $     4.00                 $     0.30
       $     5.00                 $     0.38
       $     6.00                 $     0.45
       $     7.00                 $     0.53
       $     8.00                 $     0.60
       $     9.00                 $     0.68
       $    10.00                 $     0.75
                    END OF TABLE
```

```
                SALES TAX TABLE
               SALES TAX RATE =0.095
          DOLLARS                   SALES TAX

        ---------------           ---------------
          $    1.00                 $     0.10
          $    2.00                 $     0.19
          $    3.00                 $     0.29
          $    4.00                 $     0.38
          $    5.00                 $     0.48
          $    6.00                 $     0.57
          $    7.00                 $     0.66
          $    8.00                 $     0.76
          $    9.00                 $     0.86
          $   10.00                 $     0.95
                   END OF TABLE
        END OF SALES TAX TABLE PROGRAM
```

Test Data

Use a tax rate of 0.075 (dollars tax/dollars spent) and 0.095. Vary dollars spent from 1 to 10 in increments of $1.

Validation Procedure

Calculate a few sales tax values and verify the program output. Also, check that the dollars and cents figures are properly edited, and that the results are centered under the titles and headings.

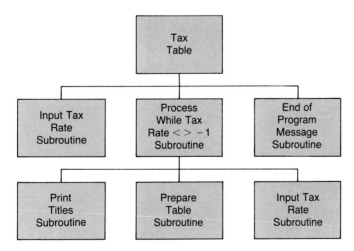

FIGURE C5–1
Visual table of contents—tax table program.

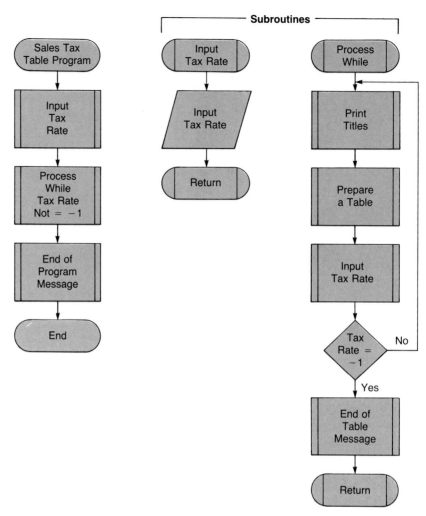

FIGURE C5-2
Detailed program flowchart—tax tables example.

CASE STUDY SOLUTION

Input

```
10    REM     **********************************************
20    REM     *              LOOPING                       *
30    REM     *           CASE STUDY: C5-1                 *
40    REM     *        SALES TAX TABLE PROGRAM             *
50    REM     *     THIS PROGRAM DEMONSTRATES THE          *
60    REM     *     DO WHILE AND DO UNTIL CONSTRUCTS.      *
70    REM     *                                            *
80    REM     *              VARIABLE LEGEND               *
90    REM     *     TAX  = SALES TAX                        *
100   REM     *     RATE = TAX RATE IN DECIMAL             *
110   REM     *                                            *
120   REM     *     D = LOOP COUNTER AND DOLLARS           *
130   REM     *                                            *
140   REM     *                                            *
150   REM     **********************************************
```

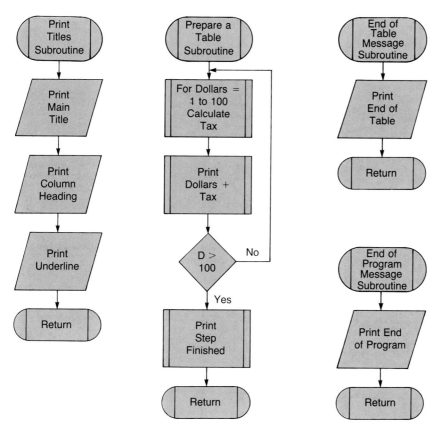

FIGURE C5–2 (continued)

```
160     REM        * * * * * * * * * * * * * * * *
170     REM        * MAIN PROGRAM *
180     REM        * * * * * * * * * * * * * * * *
190     REM        PERFORM 'INPUT TAX RATE' SUBROUTINE
200                GOSUB 260
210     REM        PERFORM 'PROCESS WHILE TAX RATE NOT = -1' SUBROUTINE
220                GOSUB 390
230     REM        PERFORM 'END OF PROGRAM MESSAGE' SUBROUTINE
240                GOSUB 810
250                END
260     REM        * * * * * * * * * * * * * * * * * * * * * * * * * *
270     REM        * INPUT TAX RATE SUBROUTINE *
280     REM        * * * * * * * * * * * * * * * * * * * * * * * * * *
290                CLS
300                PRINT "COPYRIGHT (C) 1989, BY MERRILL PUBLISHING COMPANY"
310                PRINT "FOR USE WITH STRUCTURED BASIC PROGRAMMING"
320                PRINT
330                PRINT "TO END THIS PROGRAM, TYPE IN A MINUS 1 (-1) FOR"
340                PRINT "TAX RATE ."
350                PRINT
```

```
360              PRINT "PLEASE ENTER TAX RATE "
370              LOCATE 7,22: INPUT RATE
380              RETURN
390       REM    ***********************************************
400       REM    * PROCESS RECORDS WHILE RATE <> -1 SUBROUTINE *
410       REM    ***********************************************
420       REM
430              WHILE RATE <> -1
440       REM      PERFORM 'PRINT TITLES' SUBROUTINE
450              GOSUB 520
460       REM    PERFORM 'PREPARE A TABLES' SUBROUTINE
470              GOSUB 650
480       REM    PERFORM 'INPUT TAX RATE' SUBROUTINE
490              GOSUB 260
500              WEND
510              RETURN
520       REM    ***************************
530       REM    * PRINT TITLES SUBROUTINE *
540       REM    ***************************
550              LPRINT
560              LPRINT
570              LPRINT "                              SALES TAX TABLE "
580              LPRINT
590              F1$ = "                        SALES TAX RATE =#.###"
600              LPRINT USING F1$;RATE
610              LPRINT
620              LPRINT "                      DOLLARS           SALES TAX"
630              LPRINT "                    _____       _____"
640              RETURN
650       REM    *****************************
660       REM    * PREPARE A TABLE SUBROUTINE *
670       REM    *****************************
680                  FOR D = 1 TO 10
690                     TAX = D * RATE
700                     F2$ = "              $###.##           $###.## "
710                     LPRINT USING F2$;D,TAX
720                  NEXT D
730       REM    PERFORM 'END OF TABLE' ROUTINE
740              GOSUB 760
750              RETURN
760       REM    ****************
770       REM    * END OF TABLE *
780       REM    ****************
790              LPRINT "                        END OF TABLE"
800              RETURN
```

148

```
810      REM       ***********************************
820      REM       * END OF PROGRAM MESSAGE SUBROUTINE *
830      REM       ***********************************
840                LPRINT
850                LPRINT "                    END OF SALES TAX TABLE PROGRAM
860                RETURN
870      REM
880                END
```

Output

```
COPYRIGHT (C) 1989, BY MERRILL PUBLISHING COMPANY
FOR USE WITH STRUCTURED BASIC PROGRAMMING

TO END THIS PROGRAM, TYPE IN A MINUS 1 (-1) FOR
TAX RATE .

PLEASE ENTER TAX RATE? .075


                         SALES TAX TABLE

                     SALES TAX RATE 0.075

               DOLLARS                 SALES TAX
            ---------------         ---------------
            $     1.00              $      0.08
            $     2.00              $      0.15
            $     3.00              $      0.23
            $     4.00              $      0.30
            $     5.00              $      0.38
            $     6.00              $      0.45
            $     7.00              $      0.53
            $     8.00              $      0.60
            $     9.00              $      0.68
            $    10.00              $      0.75
                          END OF TABLE

COPYRIGHT (C) 1989, BY MERRILL PUBLISHING COMPANY
FOR USE WITH STRUCTURED BASIC PROGRAMMING

TO END THIS PROGRAM, TYPE IN A MINUS 1 (-1) FOR
TAX RATE.

PLEASE ENTER TAX RATE? .095
```

```
                        SALES TAX TABLE

                     SALES TAX RATE 0.095

            DOLLARS                    SALES TAX
      ----------------            ----------------
          $    1.00                    $    0.10
          $    2.00                    $    0.19
          $    3.00                    $    0.29
          $    4.00                    $    0.38
          $    5.00                    $    0.48
          $    6.00                    $    0.57
          $    7.00                    $    0.66
          $    8.00                    $    0.76
          $    9.00                    $    0.86
          $   10.00                    $    0.95
                        END OF TABLE
```

Currency Exchange Tables

CONCEPTS TO BE ILLUSTRATED

As shown in Case 5–1, the WHILE/WEND and FOR/NEXT statements combined make it possible to generate tables of useful data. In fact, in many business applications where tables are generated, the table values are a result of generated data (such as dollar amounts) combined with changing parameters (such as interest rates, payback periods for loans, amounts initially borrowed). In this case study, the changing parameters are the currency exchange rates in various countries. These rates fluctuate according to how much a country's currency can be exchanged for in dollars. The currency names also differ from country to country. Currency exchange tables are used by consumers and bankers to determine a given currency's exact equivalent in dollars without calculation. Mortgage and loan payment tables are used for the same reason.

You will be constructing currency exchange tables by combining the DO WHILE construct (which will generate the desired dollar amounts) with the DO UNTIL construct (which will allow tables to be generated for different currencies and exchange rates). This program will convert to any desired currency once the proper exchange rate or the country name ends the DO UNTIL condition.

Currency exchange rates for many countries are shown in table C5–1. Note that although these rates are useful, a great deal of arithmetic would be needed to calculate the equivalent of any specific dollar amount into other currencies. With a table of dollar amounts ranging from $1 to $1000, a traveler could find exact converted amounts instantly.

TABLE C5–1
Currency exchange rates.

Country	Monetary Unit	Price in U.S. Dollars	Units per U.S. Dollar
Austria	Schilling	.0641	15.60
Czechoslovakia	Koruna	.1600	6.25
Egypt	Pound	1.2300	.81
Germany, West	Mark	.4488	2.20
Hong Kong	Dollar	.1287	7.77
Ireland	Pound	1.3660	.73
Jamaica	Dollar	.1825	5.48
Japan	Yen	.005557	179.95
Mexico	Peso	.00218	458.72
Norway	Krone	.1427	7.01
Philippines	Peso	.0460	21.74
Soviet Union	Ruble	1.3924	.72
Taiwan	Dollar	.0265	37.74
Zimbabwe	Dollar	.6528	1.53

PROBLEM DEFINITION

Input Specifications

The input consists of data containing the exchanged currency name, the exchange rate in "number" per U.S. dollar, and the name of the country using the "new" currency.

Field No.	Field Description	Type	Example
1	Foreign Currency Name	Alphabetic	D—Marks
2	Exchange Rate (Foreign Currency/Dollar)	Numeric	2.42
3	Foreign Country Name	Alphabetic	West Germany

Processing Decisions and Formulas

Print an exchange table for each currency (country) with values corresponding to 1 U.S. dollar to 10 U.S. dollars in every table. Put new titles on each table.

$$\text{exchange value} = \text{dollars} \times \text{exchange rate}$$

Generate dollar amounts from 1 to 10 for each table.

Output

```
            CURRENCY EXCHANGE TABLE - GERMANY
                    DOLLARS TO MARKS
    EXCHANGE RATE =        2.00   MARKS        PER DOLLAR

              DOLLARS                  MARKS

               1.00                     2.00
               2.00                     4.00
               3.00                     6.00
               4.00                     8.00
               5.00                    10.00
               6.00                    12.00
               7.00                    14.00
               8.00                    16.00
               9.00                    18.00
              10.00                    20.00

                 END OF DOLLARS TO MARKS

            CURRENCY EXCHANGE TABLE - MEXICO
                    DOLLARS TO PESOS
    EXCHANGE RATE = 1,500.00   PESOS         PER DOLLAR

              DOLLARS                  PESOS

               1.00                 1,500.00
               2.00                 3,000.00
               3.00                 4,500.00
               4.00                 6,000.00
               5.00                 7,500.00
               6.00                 9,000.00
               7.00                10,500.00
               8.00                12,000.00
               9.00                13,500.00
              10.00                15,000.00

                 END OF DOLLARS TO PESOS
            END OF CURRENCY EXCHANGE PROGRAM
```

Test Data

For Table 1	Currency	Exchange Rate	Country
	Marks	2.00	Germany
For Table 2	Pesos	1500	Mexico

Error Routines

None required.

Validation Procedure

Calculate a few exchange currency values by hand to verify the program results. Also, check for proper editing of numeric fields, and see values are centered under titles and headings.

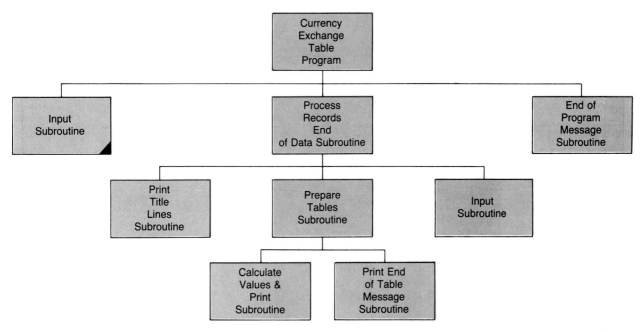

FIGURE C5–3
Visual table of contents—Currency exchange program.

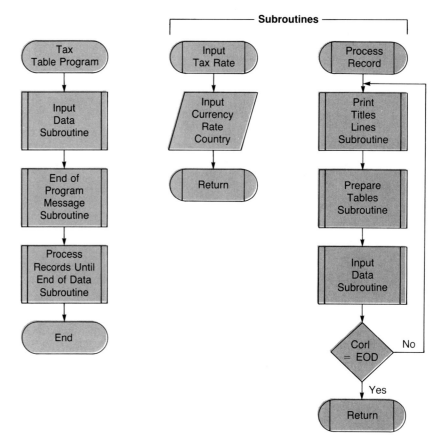

FIGURE C5–4
Detailed program flowchart—currency exchange program.

CASE STUDY SOLUTION

```
Input

10    REM    **********************************************
20    REM    *              LOOPING                       *
30    REM    *          CASE STUDY: C5-2                  *
40    REM    *    CURRENCY EXCHANGE TABLE PROGRAM         *
50    REM    *      THIS PROGRAM DEMONSTRATES THE         *
60    REM    *      DO WHILE AND DO UNTIL CONSTRUCTS.     *
70    REM    *                                            *
80    REM    *              VARIABLE LEGEND               *
90    REM    *    CUR$ = CURRENCY NAME                    *
100   REM    *    RATE = EXCHANGE RATE TO US DOLLAR       *
110   REM    *    CNTRY$ = COUNTRY NAME                   *
120   REM    *    D = LOOP COUNTER FOR US DOLLAR          *
130   REM    *    EXCH = AMOUNT EQUAL TO US DOLLAR        *
140   REM    *                                            *
150   REM    **********************************************
160   REM
170   REM    ****************
180   REM    * MAIN PROGRAM *
190   REM    ****************
200   REM    PERFORM 'READ INPUT DATA' SUBROUTINE
210          GOSUB 270
220   REM    PERFORM 'PROCESS RECORDS UNTIL END OF DATA' SUBROUTINE
230          GOSUB 470
240   REM    PERFORM 'END OF PROGRAM MESSAGE' SUBROUTINE
```

```
250                 GOSUB 990
260                 END
270      REM        ********************
280      REM        * INPUT SUBROUTINE *
290      REM        ********************
300                 CLS
310                 PRINT "COPYRIGHT (C) 1989, BY MERRILL PUBLISHING COMPANY"
320                 PRINT "FOR USE WITH STRUCTURED BASIC PROGRAMMING"
330                 PRINT
340                 PRINT "TO END PROGRAM, TYPE IN 'EOD' FOR CURRENCY NAME,"
350                 PRINT "FOLLOWED BY ZERO FOR EXCHANGE RATE AND ANY "
360                 PRINT "CHARACTER FOR COUNTRY NAME - PRESS RETURN AFTER"
370                 PRINT "EVERY DATA ENTRY."
380                 PRINT
390                 PRINT
400                 PRINT "ENTER CURRENCY NAME......................"
410                 PRINT "ENTER EXCHANGE RATE IN UNITS PER DOLLAR.."
420                 PRINT "ENTER NAME OF COUNTRY...................."
430                 LOCATE 10,41: INPUT CUR$
440                 LOCATE 11,41: INPUT RATE
450                 LOCATE 12,41: INPUT CNTRY$
460                 RETURN
470      REM        ************************************************
480      REM        * PROCESS RECORDS UNTIL END OF DATA SUBROUTINE *
490      REM        ************************************************
500                 WHILE CUR$ <> "EOD"
510      REM        PERFORM 'PRINT TITLE LINES' SUBROUTINE
520                 GOSUB 590
530      REM        PERFORM 'PREPARE TABLES' SUBROUTINE
540                 GOSUB 750
550      REM        PERFORM 'INPUT' SUBROUTINE
560                 GOSUB 270
570                 WEND
580                 RETURN
590      REM        ********************************
600      REM        * PRINT TITLE LINES SUBROUTINE *
610      REM        ********************************
620                 LPRINT " "
630                 LPRINT " "
640                 F1$ = "                    CURRENCY EXCHANGE TABLE - \    \"
650                 F2$ = "                         DOLLARS TO \        \"
660                 F3$ = "                 EXCHANGE RATE = ##,###.##  \       \ PER DOLLAR"
670                 F4$ = "                       DOLLARS            \              \"
680                 LPRINT USING F1$;CNTRY$
690                 LPRINT USING F2$;CUR$
700                 LPRINT USING F3$;RATE,CUR$
710                 LPRINT " "
720                 LPRINT USING F4$;CUR$
730                 LPRINT " "
740                 RETURN
750      REM        *****************************
760      REM        * PREPARE TABLES SUBROUTINE *
770      REM        *****************************
780                     FOR D = 1 TO 10
790      REM                PERFORM 'CALCULATE VALUES AND PRINT' SUBROUTINE
800                         GOSUB 850
810                     NEXT D
820      REM                PERFORM 'END OF TABLE MESSAGE' SUBROUTINE
830                         GOSUB 920
840                 RETURN
850      REM        ****************************************
860      REM        * CALCULATE VALUES AND PRINT SUBROUTINE *
870      REM        ****************************************
880                 EXCH = D * RATE
890                 F5$ = "               ###.##           ##,###.##"
900                 LPRINT USING F5$;D,EXCH
```

155

```
910              RETURN
920     REM      ************************************
930     REM      * PRINT END OF TABLE MESSAGE SUBROUTINE *
940     REM      ************************************
950              LPRINT
960              F6$ = "                        END OF DOLLARS TO \        \ "
970              LPRINT USING F6$;CUR$
980              RETURN
990     REM      ************************************
1000    REM      * END OF PROGRAM MESSAGE SUBROUTINE *
1010    REM      ************************************
1020             LPRINT
1030             LPRINT "                    END OF CURRENCY EXCHANGE PROGRAM"
1040             RETURN
1050    REM
1060             END
```

Output

```
        CURRENCY EXCHANGE TABLE - GERMANY
              DOLLARS TO MARKS
EXCHANGE RATE =      2.00  MARKS       PER DOLLAR


           DOLLARS              MARKS
            1.00                 2.00
            2.00                 4.00
            3.00                 6.00
            4.00                 8.00
            5.00                10.00
            6.00                12.00
            7.00                14.00
            8.00                16.00
            9.00                18.00
           10.00                20.00


           END OF DOLLARS TO MARKS



        CURRENCY EXCHANGE TABLE - MEXICO
              DOLLARS TO PESOS
EXCHANGE RATE =  1,500.00  PESOS        PER DOLLAR


           DOLLARS              PESOS

            1.00             1,500.00
            2.00             3,000.00
            3.00             4,500.00
            4.00             6,000.00
            5.00             7,500.00
            6.00             9,000.00
            7.00            10,500.00
            8.00            12,000.00
            9.00            13,500.00
           10.00            15,000.00


           END OF DOLLARS TO PESOS

        END OF CURRENCY EXCHANGE PROGRAM
```

COMMON ERRORS AND SOLUTIONS		
Error	**Example**	**Solution**
1. Writing a FOR/NEXT and forgetting the NEXT or the variable name after NEXT.	10 FOR I = 1 TO 10 20 PRINT I,I^2 (no NEXT) or 30 NEXT (no I)	Every loop must have a beginning and end. The variable name (counter) must be repeated in the NEXT statement.
2. Deleting a FOR instruction and forgetting to delete the NEXT	20 INPUT A 30 NEXT I (NEXT without FOR)	When modifying or documenting your programs, be sure that both statements in a loop construct are deleted or changed.
3. Writing a WHILE loop without including WHILE loop-terminating instruction.	10 WHILE ENDSW = 0 20 INPUT A 30 PRINT A (WHILE without WEND)	The ending statement for a WHILE loop is system dependent. Some systems use WEND, some use END WHILE, and others use NEXT. Be sure you know the correct statement for your system, and have placed it at the logical end of your WHILE loop. (See appendix A.)
4. Deleting or changing a WHILE instruction and forgetting to delete or change the WHILE ending instruction.	10 INPUT A 20 PRINT A 30 WEND (WEND without WHILE)	(See solution 2, above.)
5. Improper nesting of FOR/NEXT loops.	10 FOR I = 1 TO 10 20 FOR D = 1 TO 100 30 TAX = D * 0.75 40 PRINT D, TAX 50 NEXT I 60 NEXT D (50,60 should be switched—no diagnostic)	Make sure that inner FOR/NEXT loops are complete within outer FOR/NEXT loops.
6. Failure to exit a DO UNTIL construct (i.e., program remains in loop).	10 INPUT A$ 20 WHILE A$<>"END DATA" 30 INPUT A 40 WEND (value for A, END DATA, mistyped or never entered)	Be sure to check which value is needed to end the UNTIL construct, and make sure that it is typed correctly and entered at the logical time.

SUMMARY

Looping is important in BASIC business programs because in most applications the same logic is repeated for many input records. In structured design programming, looping is accomplished with two constructs, the DO WHILE and DO UNTIL. BASIC contains a number of statements to use in these constructs, including the WHILE/WEND and FOR/NEXT statements.

    The DO WHILE is programmed with a condition. If the condition tested is true, some desired logic is repeated. The WHILE/WEND and FOR/NEXT statements are the most common statements used to formulate the DO WHILE construct. The DO WHILE construct is useful for generating data tables without inputting or reading in the data.

The other important looping construct is the DO UNTIL construct, in which the condition that controls looping is tested after the program logic segment is executed. If the condition is true, the looping logic is exited. This construct is available on only a very small number of BASIC systems as an UNTIL statement. However, the DO UNTIL construct can be readily fabricated with DO WHILE by starting with an INPUT statement and placing another INPUT statement within the DO WHILE construct as the last logical operation.

The DO UNTIL construct forms the basis for the majority of business application programs where it is not feasible or desirable to count or specify the number of records in advance of the looping construct. Examples are payroll processing, billing, point-of-purchase sales processing, and the like, wherein the number of records to be processed is either unknown or too large to count accurately. The DO UNTIL construct allows the programmer to specify that processing continue until a specific data record (signal) is encountered, at which time the looping stops.

Care must be taken in writing DO WHILE and DO UNTIL constructs because, although they appear quite similar, an erroneous substitution of one for the other can lead to disastrous program results, especially when accumulation or counting logic is included in the iteration loop.

Often, a structured BASIC program contains a combination of DO WHILE and DO UNTIL constructs, sometimes with one nested within the other, such as in the currency exchange table program. Usually the WHILE loop (written with FOR/NEXT statements) is used to generate data and within the FOR/NEXT other related values are calculated and printed to produce the table. The DO UNTIL construct establishes parameters for the table, such as the tax rate and currency exchange rate examples.

REVIEW QUESTIONS

1. Describe why looping is important in computer programs. Give some examples of programs with loops.
2. What term is used specifically to describe looping in structured design programs?
3. Name and describe the two looping constructs used in structured design programs.
4. Describe DO WHILE statements for BASIC systems that support the DO WHILE. Write a short example program segment.
5. Describe how to write a DO UNTIL construct using the WHILE statements. Write a short example program segment illustrating the DO UNTIL construct.
6. Give an example of a problem that would effectively use the WHILE loop.
7. Give an example of a problem that would benefit from a DO UNTIL loop.
8. In problems where the number of loop cycles is known in advance, which type of looping construct would be applicable? Why?
9. In problems where the number of data records is unknown in advance, which type of loop would be applicable? Why?
10. What signals were used to signal the end of data in a DO UNTIL loop?
11. The FOR/NEXT loop is which type of loop?
12. Since the WHILE loop is now standard on most BASIC systems, consult your manual and write a program that uses your version of these WHILE instructions. If these statements are not available on your system, construct a WHILE program loop with FOR/NEXT loop.
13. In the following FOR/NEXT loop, what will be the starting and the ending values of N, and how many times would this loop be executed on your system?

```
100    FOR N = 2 TO 20 STEP 2
110    NEXT N
```

14. In the following FOR/NEXT loop, what will be the starting and ending values of M on your system?

15. Write a FOR/NEXT loop that will start with D (dollars) equal to 1, and then increase to 100 by increments of 10 cents (0.10 dollars).

PROBLEMS FOR SOLUTION

1. Driving in many European countries can be an interesting experience for many reasons, not the least of which is the difference in measuring distance and speed. Although an attempt has been made to convert American measurements to metric, the changeover has been slow, thus making a conversion table useful. Such a table is quite simple to generate with a BASIC program. Given that 1 mi. = 1.609 km and 1 mi./hr. = 1.609 km/hr., prepare a table that

  1. relates miles per hour between 10 and 1000 to kilometers in increments of 100
  2. relates miles per hour between 10 and 100 to kilometers per hour in increments of 10.

   Use the format given in the problem definition worksheet, and write the program so that no data need be input but, rather, data are generated using a looping structure available on your system (e.g., FOR/NEXT or WHILE loop).

   For added interest, add nautical miles (NM), which are used for navigation with ships and aircraft, to the table, where:

$$1 \text{ NM} = 1.853 \text{ km}$$

Input Specifications

None.

Processing Decisions and Formulas

$$1 \text{ mile} = 1.609 \text{ kilometers}$$
$$1 \text{ nautical mile} = 1.853 \text{ kilometers}$$

Output

```
          AMERICAN TO METRIC SPEED AND DISTANCE CONVERSION TABLE

   MILES    KILOMETERS        MILES PER HOUR   KILOMETERS PER HOUR

    100       160.7                10                16.1
    200       321.4                20                32.1
    300       482.1                30                48.2
    400       642.8                40                64.3
    500       803.5                50                80.4
    600       964.2                60                96.4
    700      1124.9                70               112.5
    800      1285.6                80               128.6
    900      1446.3                90               144.6
   1000      1607.0               100               160.7
```

Test Data

Made up in program loop.

Error Routines

None.

Validation Procedure

Calculate a few converted distances and speeds by hand and verify the program output. Also check for proper editing of numeric decimal number and centering of results under titles and headings.

2. Converting recipes written with metric weights and volumes to American equivalents, and vice versa, can be challenging when neither a conversion table nor a calculator is at hand. With a simple BASIC program it is possible to produce a conversion table for most of the common weights and measures used in cooking. Given the following data:

> Weights: 1 ounce = 28.35 grams
> 1 pound = 0.454 kilograms (or 454 grams)
> Volume: 1 fluid ounce = 0.0296 liters
> 1 pint = 0.4732 liters
> 1 quart = 0.9463 liters

write a BASIC program that will help convert recipes. Do not input any data; rather, define the formulas needed with your program and generate the amounts in the table using a loop supported by your system (e.g., FOR/NEXT or WHILE).

Input Specifications

None.

Processing Decisions and Formulas

> 1 pound = 0.454 kilograms or 454 grams
> 1 ounce = 28.35 grams
> 1 fluid ounce = 0.0296 liters
> 1 pint = 0.4732 liters
> 1 quart = 0.9463 liters

Output

OUNCES	GRAMS	POUNDS	GRAMS	OUNCES	LITERS	PINTS	LITERS	QUARTS	LITERS
1	28.4	1	454.0	1	0.03	1	0.47	1	0.95
2	56.7	2	908.0	2	0.06	2	0.95	2	1.89
3	85.1	3	1362.0	3	0.09	3	1.42	3	2.84
4	113.4	4	1816.0	4	0.12	4	1.89	4	3.79
5	141.8	5	2270.0	5	0.15	5	2.37	5	4.73
6	170.1	6	2724.0	6	0.18	6	2.84	6	5.68
7	198.5	7	3178.0	7	0.21	7	3.31	7	6.62
8	226.8	8	3632.0	8	0.24	8	3.79	8	7.57
9	255.2	9	4086.0	9	0.27	9	4.26	9	8.52
10	283.5	10	4540.0	10	0.30	10	4.73	10	9.46
11	311.9	11	4994.0	11	0.33	11	5.21	11	10.41
12	340.2	12	5448.0	12	0.36	12	5.68	12	11.36
13	368.6	13	5902.0	13	0.38	13	6.15	13	12.30
14	396.9	14	6356.0	14	0.41	14	6.62	14	13.25
15	425.3	15	6810.0	15	0.44	15	7.10	15	14.19
16	453.6	16	7264.0	16	0.47	16	7.57	16	15.14

Test Data

None.

Error Routines

None.

Validation Procedure

Calculate a few weights-and-measures conversions by hand and verify the results in the output table. Also check to see that the decimal numbers are properly edited and results are centered under column headings as indicated above.

3. Clothes shopping in countries that use metric sizing standards is not as simple as you might expect. Sizes for suits, shirts, dresses, and other clothing items cannot be determined by multiplying metric conversion factors and the American size numbers. Instead, metric sizes are related to American sizes by the following formulas:

$$\text{For women's suits and dresses: metric size} = \text{American size} + 8$$
$$\text{For misses' suits and dresses: metric size} = \text{American size} + 28$$
$$\text{For men's suits and jackets: metric size} = \text{American size} + 10$$
$$\text{For men's shirts: metric size} = 2 * \text{American size} + 8$$

Using these formulas, write a structured BASIC program that will prepare conversion tables for clothing items in each of the categories listed. Generate the American sizes specified in the problem definition worksheet using a FOR/NEXT loop or a WHILE construct, and prepare titled conversion tables according to the output specifications.

Input Specifications

No input is used. Values are generated in program loops.

Processing Decisions and Formulas

$$\text{Women's Suits and Dresses: Metric Size} = \text{American Size} + 8$$
$$\text{Misses' Suits and Dresses: Metric Size} = \text{American Size} + 28$$
$$\text{Men's Suits and Jackets: Metric Size} = \text{American Size} + 10$$
$$\text{Men's Shirts: Metric Size} = 2 \times \text{American Size} + 8$$

Output

```
          WOMEN'S SUITS AND DRESSES

        AMERICAN          METRIC

           32               40
           34               42
           36               44
           38               46
           40               48
           42               50
           44               52


          MISSES' SUITS AND DRESSES

        AMERICAN          METRIC

           10               38
           12               40
           14               42
           16               44
           18               46
           20               48
           22               50
```

```
                    MENS' SUITS AND JACKETS

            AMERICAN              METRIC

                36                  46
                38                  48
                40                  50
                42                  52
                44                  54
                46                  56
                48                  58


                        MENS' SHIRTS

            AMERICAN              METRIC

               14.5                 37
               15.0                 38
               15.5                 39
               16.0                 40
               16.5                 41
               17.0                 42
               17.5                 43
```

Test Data

Generate the metric sizes for the 4 conversion tables using FOR/NEXT or WHILE loop constructs.

Error Routines

None.

Validation Procedure

Check at least 1 metric size in each table by hand-calculating the conversion. Also, check that output is properly edited and centered under the titles and headings.

4. Referring to the problem definition in Case 4–2, ''Customer Monthly Statement,'' rewrite the program so that any number of customer accounts can be processed and a statement be issued for each customer (as described in the output specifications).

In addition, add logic that will accumulate the total receivables (total of all outstanding customer balances) due the company and the average customer balance, as shown in the problem definition worksheet that follows. Use a DO UNTIL construct to process customer records. Make up your own test data. Remember to include a last record that will signal the end of processing.

Input Specifications

Field No.	Field Description	Type	Example
1	Account Number	Integer	12345
2	Customer Name	Alphabetic	Joe Smith
3	Customer Address	Alphanumeric	29 Main St
4	Last Month's Balance	Decimal Number	300.00
5	Charges Made	Decimal Number	40.00
6	Credits and Payments	Decimal Number	100.00

Processing Decisions and Formulas

$$\text{Interest} = 0.01 \times \text{Old Balance from Last Month}$$
$$\text{New Balance} = \text{Old Balance} + \text{Interest} + \text{Charges} - \text{Credits}$$
$$\text{Total Due Company} = \text{Sum of All NEW Balances}$$
$$\text{Average per Customer} = \text{Total Due Co.} / \text{Number of Customers}$$
$$\text{Minimum Payment} = \text{New Balance} / 10$$

Output

```
                    ABC DEPARTMENT STORE
                     SPRINGFIELD, MASS.

ACCT NO    NAME      ADDRESS    OLD BAL   CHARGES INTEREST   NEW BAL  MIN PAYMENT
 12345  JOE SMITH 29 MAIN ST    $300.00   $40.00   $3.00    $243.00    $24.30
```

Test Data

12345, Joe Smith, 29 Main St, 300.00, 40.00, 100.00

Error Routines

None.

Validation Procedure

Hand-calculate the results for one customer and check your program output.

5. In this problem, a carpet salesperson would like to be able to give customers an immediate estimate of the costs of carpeting rooms of various sizes with any of the carpet materials selected by a customer.

    You will assume that all the rooms are rectangular and measured in feet. The following formula will determine the cost:

    $$\text{cost} = \text{length of room} \times \text{width of room} \times \text{carpet cost per yard}/9$$

    Input the dimensions of the room and the carpet cost per square yard on the keyboard, and print the estimate as shown below.

```
        FOR YOUR ROOM OF 999 FEET BY 999 FEET
        THE TOTAL CARPET COST IS; $9,999.99
```

6. When homebuyers shop for mortgages, they are often astounded at the effect of small interest-rate differences on both monthly payments and the total amount paid back on the loan. Write, in tabular form, a BASIC program that will show the effect of interest rates on monthly mortgage payments, total interest, and the total amount paid back, as shown below. Input the mortgage amount desired and the number of years, and print the monthly payment for interest rates that range from 6% up to 15%, as shown in the problem definition. Use a looping method supported by your BASIC system (e.g., the FOR/NEXT) to vary the interest rate in your program.

Input Specifications

Field No.	Field Description	Type	Example
1	Mortgage Amount	Decimal Number	60000.00
2	Number of Years	Integer	30

Processing Decisions and Formulas

$$I^* = I/(12 \times 100)$$
$$\text{Monthly Interest Factor} = I^*/[(1+I)^{(y \times 12)} - 1[\ + I$$
$$\text{Monthly Payment} = \text{Monthly Interest Factor} \times \text{Amount}$$
$$\text{Total Paid Back} = \text{Years} \times 12 \times \text{Monthly Payment}$$
$$I^* = \text{Annual Interest Rate Converted to Monthly Rate}$$

Output

```
             MORTGAGE INTEREST COMPARISON TABLE
                MORTGAGE :  $60,000.00
                YEARS    :    30

       INTEREST RATE    MONTHLY PAYMENT    TOTAL PAID BACK

            6              $359.73          $129,502.90
            7              $399.18          $143,705.20
            8              $440.26          $158,493.10
            9              $482.77          $173,798.20
           10              $526.54          $189,555.60
           11              $571.39          $205,701.80
           12              $617.17          $222,180.40
           13              $663.72          $238,939.00
           14              $710.92          $255,932.40
           15              $758.67          $273,119.80
```

Test Data

60000.00, 30

Make up your own test data if you are interested in a particular amount and time.

Error Routines

None.

Validation Procedure

Calculate the output values for one input record and one interest rate, and compare your results with the program output. Also, check that numeric fields are properly edited and that results are centered below headings in the output.

CHAPTER SIX

PROGRAMMING DECISIONS

LEARNING OBJECTIVES

Upon completion of this chapter, you will be able to:

☐ Understand the importance of decision making in business computer programs.

☐ Program the computer to make decisions using IF/THEN, IF/THEN/ELSE, ON/GOTO, and ON/GOSUB.

☐ Understand the use of the six most commonly-used relational operators and AND, OR, and NOT logic.

☐ Write programs that perform computer-assisted tutorials and tests.

☐ Understand and write simplified inventory control programs.

COMPUTER DECISION MAKING

Most people readily accept that computers can perform rapid input, output, and calculation functions, but find it more difficult to believe that computers can be programmed to make very complex decisions. However, without the capability to select the correct logic under varying conditions, most programs would have only limited usefulness. Therefore, selection, or logical decision making, is a critical inclusion in the majority of computer applications programs, especially in business. The decision-making capabilities in BASIC programs rely on the following statements:

1. IF/THEN
2. IF/THEN/ELSE
3. ON/GOTO
4. ON/GOSUB

Each of these statements is covered in the sections that follow. You may find it surprising how much power and usefulness the programs have that use just these four relatively straightforward statements. With these, you can program the computer to perform tasks and make complex decisions that most people tend to think could only be done by humans. Furthermore, when these decision-making programs are carefully and logically designed and written, the results are reliable, accurate, and more quickly produced than if done by humans. The following are some traditional business applications and systems based on computer decisions and the decision-making logic that they include.

In a payroll program, the computer is programmed to account for:

1. overtime worked—to apply an overtime pay rate and to compute pay.
2. number of dependents—to adjust deductions.
3. health and life insurance—to adjust deductions.
4. contributions to a credit union or charity—to adjust deductions.
5. used vacation time—to adjust vacation allowance.

In a charge account billing program, the computer is programmed to determine:

1. if a customer should get a normal bill or a special notice that an account payment is past due or the credit limit has been exceeded.
2. if a customer's name and phone number should be placed on a delinquency list used for telephone contact.

In an inventory control program, the computer is programmed to determine:

1. which part or item has been sold by part or item number, name, or description so the inventory level can be updated.
2. whether the remaining quantity on hand (QOH) in the inventory is adequate, or whether it has fallen below the reorder point (sometimes called the minimum quantity on hand (MQOH)).
3. if the QOH is less than the MQOH, whether a reorder message should be printed, and if so, to whom.

In a ranking inquiry and accounting system, the computer is programmed to:

1. retrieve account balances, savings and checking transaction data, interest and service charge data, and so on, by customer name or account number.
2. determine whether checking accounts are overdrawn, and if so, which special reports or documents need to be produced.
3. determine whether minimum balances are in effect so that customers need not pay a service charge on special accounts.

In addition to these traditional applications, many businesses are incorporating computers into employee training using computer-assisted instruction (CAI). In this application, the computer is programmed to present information (usually on a display) and guide the person being trained through lessons, quizzes, reviews, and tests covering the material presented. These systems have the primary advantage of being self-paced, which means that the user can proceed at a comfortable rate based on his or her individual needs. Also, CAI systems are usually programmed to review and repeat information until a high level of understanding and competence has been achieved. Most commercial applications software now include this type of training on disks packaged with the applications software, and many programmers now concentrate their skills on developing these programs.

In the CAI session, after information is presented to the user, questions are displayed and the user's response is evaluated or tested with the IF/THEN or another selection logic. For example, if the user's answer is correct, the program responds with the verbal reward and proceeds to the next question or lesson segment. If the response is incorrect, the user may be guided back to review material or given more examples and illustrations. Tests also can be administered in the CAI session, and the results tabulated, compiled, and stored on disk for all program users.

The IF/THEN Statement

The most often used and simplest selection statement is the IF/THEN, which has two forms

```
line# IF expression THEN statement or line#
line# IF expression GOTO line#
```

where:

1. the expression can be a variable or any valid BASIC numeric expression, which may include variables, constants, simple and complex mathematical operations, and combinations of the six relational operators shown in table 6-1 (equal, less than or equal to, greater than or equal to, greater than, less than, and the logical operators AND, OR, and NOT).
2. the statement can be any executable BASIC statement, including another IF statement, or a sequence of statements separated by colons. This sequence is sometimes referred to as multiple imperatives because more than one operation takes place when the IF condition (expression) is true.
3. the line number (the one after the THEN or GOTO) is the number of any statement that exists in the program except the number of the current IF statement itself, which would cause an endless loop in the program. For example

```
100 IF A = B THEN 100
```

is invalid.

TABLE 6-1
Relational operators.

Condition	BASIC Symbol Used	Example 1	Example 2
Equal to	=	IF A=B THEN 10	IF A=B THEN PRINT A
Greater than	>	IF A>B THEN 10	IF A>B THEN C=A
Less than	<	IF A<B THEN 10	IF A<B THEN C=C+1
Greater than or equal to	>=	IF A$>=B$ THEN 10	IF A$>=B$ THEN PRINT "END"
Less than or equal to	<=	IF A$<=B$ THEN 10	IF A$<=B$ THEN INPUT IN
Not equal to	<>	IF A<>B THEN 10	IF A<>B THEN B=A

167

If the variable in the expression is non-zero (when using a single variable as the expression) or if the expression is true, then the statement(s) or line number after the THEN or GOTO is executed. After that, control returns to the next executable statement after the IF, and execution resumes at that point in the program.

If the variable is zero, or the expression is false, control drops immediately to the statement following the IF, and the statement and/or line number following the THEN or GOTO is ignored.

The IF/THEN and its operation are represented by the flowchart in figure 6–1. Generally, in the IF/THEN structure when the condition is true, the operation to be performed is indicated to the right of the decision, and when the condition is false, the next operation in line (below) is normally executed. This is a frequently used convention. The following is an example of IF/THEN in a program segment:

```
10   REM   ****************************************
20   REM   * ILLUSTRATION OF IF/THEN IN BILLING *
30   REM   ****************************************
40         CLS
50         PRINT "COPYRIGHT (C) 1989, BY MERRILL PUBLISHING COMPANY"
60         PRINT "FOR USE WITH STRUCTURED BASIC PROGRAMMING"
70         PRINT
80         PRINT " ENTER ACCOUNT LIMIT "
90         PRINT " ENTER ACCOUNT BALANCE "
100        LOCATE 4,23: INPUT L
110        LOCATE 5,23: INPUT B
120        IF B > L  THEN PRINT " ACCOUNT OVER LIMIT"
130        IF B < L  THEN PRINT " ACCOUNT BELOW LIMIT"
140        IF B = L  THEN PRINT " ACCOUNT AT LIMIT"
150        END
```

Example Output

```
COPYRIGHT (C) 1989, BY MERRILL PUBLISHING COMPANY
FOR USE WITH STRUCTURED BASIC PROGRAMMING
ENTER ACCOUNT LIMIT  ?  1500
ENTER ACCOUNT BALANCE?  1600
ACCOUNT OVER LIMIT
ENTER ACCOUNT LIMIT ? 1500
ENTER ACCOUNT BALANCE ? 1200
ACCOUNT BELOW LIMIT
```

This is a simple example of the IF/THEN structure in a billing program where charge account customers receive special notification when they exceed their individual credit limits. If (*and only if*) the credit limits have been exceeded, then notification will be sent.

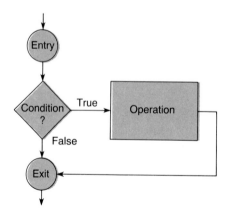

FIGURE 6–1
Looping-control structure.

The flowchart for this application is shown in figure 6–2. This illustrates that *if* the condition is true (if the account balance is over the limit), *then* the appropriate message is printed on the customer's bill. *If* the condition is not true (if the account balance is not over limit, i.e., is false), *then* no special message is issued and the structure is exited.

The IF/THEN/ELSE Statement

The general form of the IF/THEN/ELSE is

```
line# IF expression THEN statement
```

or

```
line# ELSE statement or line#
```

or

```
line# IF expression GOTO line# ELSE statement or line#
```

The expression, statement, and line number have exactly the same requirements as in the IF/THEN statement. In fact, the function of IF/THEN/ELSE is the same as that for the IF/THEN, except that when the expression following IF is false (or zero for a single variable), the statement(s) or line number following the ELSE is executed before the program returns to the next executable statement after the IF statement. This provides logic for choosing two discrete alternatives for any condition as part of the selection for any one condition or expression prior to program continuation. This is shown schematically in the flowchart in figure 6–3.

An example of the use of the IF/THEN/ELSE structure would be a payroll program in which an employee would receive overtime pay for time worked that exceeded 40 hours during one week. (For the time being, you should not be concerned with the exact formulas. These will be described in later case studies.) The IF/THEN/ELSE structure for this program would look like the one in figure 6–4. This flowchart goes through the following decision-making sequence: If the total hours worked exceed 40, then the overtime payroll calculation is executed; otherwise (ELSE), the normal payroll calculation is executed. The program for this is shown in figure 6–5.

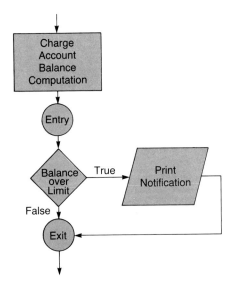

FIGURE 6–2
Billing applications flowcharts.

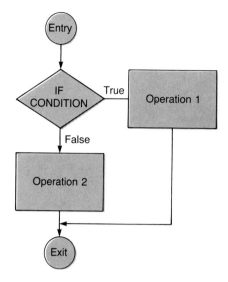

FIGURE 6–3
Flowchart for the IF/THEN/ELSE structure.

Naturally, the two possible sequences related to the IF condition are mutually exclusive; that is, only one or the other is executed, depending on the condition evaluated and its outcome. This does not imply, however, that only one operation (sequence) can be executed as the result of *either* alternative. For example, the flowchart in figure 6–6 illustrates the use of the IF/THEN/ELSE with a number of sequence structures. Here, if a particular condition is true, the program must perform operations A, B, *and* C. If it is false, it will perform operations D *and* E. Thus, in both cases, the sequences are completing more than one operation within themselves with such multiple sequence structures; the

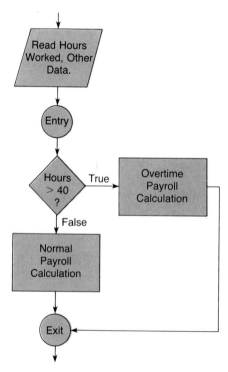

FIGURE 6–4
Structure for payroll example.

Input

```
10    REM   ********************************************************
20    REM   * ILLUSTRATION OF IF/THEN/ELSE IN PAYROLL CALCULATION *
30    REM   ********************************************************
40    REM
50          CLS
60          PRINT "COPYRIGHT (C) 1989, BY MERRILL PUBLISHING COMPANY"
70          PRINT "FOR USE WITH STRUCTURED BASIC PROGRAMMING"
80          PRINT
90          PRINT " ENTER HOURS WORKED "
100         PRINT " ENTER HOURLY PAYRATE "
110         LOCATE 4,25: INPUT H
120         LOCATE 5,25: INPUT P
130         IF H > 40 THEN GROSS = (1.5 * (H - 40 * P) + (40 * P)
                       ELSE GROSS = 40 * P
140         PRINT
150         PRINT "GROSS PAY EQUALS "GROSS
160   END
```

Output

```
COPYRIGHT (C) 1989, BY MERRILL PUBLISHING COMPANY
FOR USE WITH STRUCTURED BASIC PROGRAMMING
ENTER HOURS WORKED     ? 40
ENTER HOURLY PAYRATE   ? 10
GROSS PAY EQUALS   400
ENTER HOURS WORKED     ? 50
ENTER HOURLY PAYRATE   ? 10
GROSS PAY EQUALS 550
```

FIGURE 6–5
Program for payroll program.

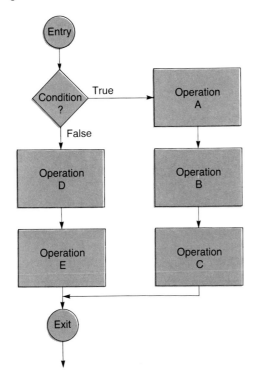

FIGURE 6–6
IF/THEN/ELSE—multiple conditions.

171

two sequences are exclusive of one another. Thus, in the flowchart, operations A, B, and C are exclusive of operations D and E—that is, all five operations will never be executed together.

An example of a short program that illustrates multiple operations in one IF/THEN/ELSE selection is when motorists input their current car insurance premiums and answer whether or not they have had accidents in the last year. If they have, the IF statement does the following:

1. Prints PLEASE BE CAREFUL
2. Calculates the new premium PREM = PREM * 1.10 (a 10 increase)
3. Prints out the new premium. If the drivers have not had accidents in the last year, the IF statement
   a. prints CONGRATULATIONS
   b. prints THE PREMIUM WILL REMAIN AS IT WAS

Figures 6–7 and 6–8, respectively, show the flowchart and program for this example.

Many times the sequence that follows a decision will be a calculation. Sometimes calculations are so complex that the sequence itself will be subdivided into many segments that are executed sequentially. Sometimes the sequence will even be written as a subroutine. This is particularly true of statistical calculations, where it can become difficult to represent an entire sequence of formulas. The fact that a formula, a series of formulas, or some other complex routine follows a decision in no way alters the operations themselves.

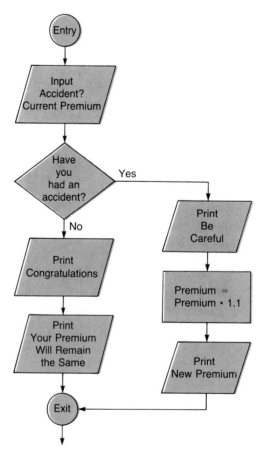

FIGURE 6–7
Multiple operation program flowchart.

```
10    REM   ************************************************************
20    REM   * ILLUSTRATION OF IF/THEN/ELSE WITH MULTIPLE OPERATIONS *
30    REM   * INSURANCE BILLING AND NOTIFICATION                    *
40    REM   ************************************************************
50    REM
60         CLS
70         PRINT "COPYRIGHT (C) 1989, BY MERRILL PUBLISHING COMPANY"
80         PRINT "FOR USE WITH STRUCTURED BASIC PROGRAMMING"
90         PRINT
100        PRINT
110        PRINT " HAVE YOU HAD A CAR ACCIDENT LAST YEAR? TYPE YES OR NO."
120        PRINT " ENTER YOUR CURRENT PREMIUM ...................."
130        LOCATE 5,55: INPUT A$
140        LOCATE 6,55: INPUT PREM
150        PRINT
160        IF A$ = "YES" THEN PRINT " PLEASE BE CAREFUL":PREM=PREM * 1.1:PRINT " YOUR
NEW PREMIUM IS ";PREM ELSE PRINT "CONGRATULATIONS ":PRINT "YOUR PREMIUM WILL REMAIN
THE SAME "
170        END
```

Output

```
COPYRIGHT (C) 1989, BY MERRILL PUBLISHING COMPANY
FOR USE WITH STRUCTURED BASIC PROGRAMMING
HAVE YOU HAD A CAR ACCIDENT LAST YEAR? TYPE YES OR NO? NO
ENTER YOUR CURRENT PREMIUM ..........................? 500

CONGRATULATIONS
YOUR PREMIUM WILL REMAIN THE SAME

HAVE YOU HAD A CAR ACCIDENT LAST YEAR? TYPE YES OR NO? YES
ENTER YOUR CURRENT PREMIUM ..........................? 500

PLEASE BE CAREFUL
YOUR NEW PREMIUM IS 550
```

FIGURE 6–8
Multiple operation program.

ON/GOTO and ON/GOSUB

The two statements that facilitate the case control selection (choosing between many alternatives) are the ON/GOTO and the ON/GOSUB statements. In structured programming, the ON/GOSUB is considered the preferable statement because it conforms to the principles of structured design (branching is to a subroutine with subsequent return rather than branching to a statement with no return). The general forms for the two statements are

```
line# ON n GOTO line#,line#,line#, etc.
```
and
```
line# ON n GOSUB line#, line#, line#, etc.
```

where n is a numeric integer variable or a decimal number rounded to an integer in the range 0 to 255.

The line number is the statement number that the program branches to depending on the value of n. For example, when n = 1, the first line number in the list after the GOTO or GOSUB is branched to; when n = 2, the second line number is branched to; and so on. If n = 0, control goes to the next executable statement after the ON/GOTO or ON/GOSUB, and no line number in the list is branched to. If n is greater than the number of lines referenced after the GOTO or GOSUB, control also goes to the next executable statement; however, if n is outside the range of 0 to 255, an illegal function call error occurs.

The primary difference between the two statements is that when the ON/GOSUB is used, after the branch occurs a return statement causes return to the next executable statement after it, and there must be a RETURN statement in the logic of the subroutine. Figure 6–9 shows an example of a program that uses the ON/GOSUB statement.

Input

```
10    REM   **************************************************
20    REM   * ON/GOSUB SEAT SELECTION ILLUSTRATION          *
30    REM   *                                               *
40    REM   * THERE ARE FIVE SEATS AVAILABLE AT A CONCERT   *
50    REM   *    SEAT PRICES ARE AS FOLLOWS:                *
60    REM   *              SEAT 1 = 25 DOLLARS              *
70    REM   *              SEAT 2 = 30 DOLLARS              *
80    REM   *              SEAT 3 = 35 DOLLARS              *
90    REM   *              SEAT 4 = 48 DOLLARS              *
100   REM   *              SEAT 5 = 50 DOLLARS              *
110   REM   **************************************************
120   REM
130       CLS
140       PRINT " COPYRIGHT (C) 1989, BY MERRILL PUBLISHING COMPANY"
150       PRINT " FOR USE WITH STRUCTURED BASIC PROGRAMMING"
160       PRINT
170       PRINT
180       PRINT " ENTER THE NUMBER OF THE SEAT YOU WOULD LIKE (1- 5)"
190       LOCATE 5,50: INPUT N
200   ON N GOSUB 220,240,260,280,300
210   END
220       PRINT " YOU CHOSE SEAT ";N;" THE PRICE IS 25 DOLLARS"
230       RETURN
240       PRINT " YOU CHOSE SEAT ";N;" THE PRICE IS 30 DOLLARS"
250       RETURN
260       PRINT " YOU CHOSE SEAT ";N;" THE PRICE IS 35 DOLLARS"
270       RETURN
280       PRINT " YOU CHOSE SEAT ";N;" THE PRICE IS 48 DOLLARS"
290       RETURN
300       PRINT " YOU CHOSE SEAT ";N;" THE PRICE IS 50 DOLLARS"
310       RETURN
320       END OF PROGRAM
```

Output

```
COPYRIGHT (C) 1989, BY MERRILL PUBLISHING COMPANY
FOR USE WITH STRUCTURED BASIC PROGRAMMING
ENTER THE NUMBER OF THE SEAT YOU WOULD LIKE (1-5? 1
YOU CHOSE SEAT  1   THE PRICE IS 25 DOLLARS

ENTER THE NUMBER OF THE SEAT YOU WOULD LIKE (1-5? 2
YOU CHOSE SEAT  2   THE PRICE IS 30 DOLLARS

ENTER THE NUMBER OF THE SEAT YOU WOULD LIKE (1-5? 3
YOU CHOSE SEAT  3   THE PRICE IS 35 DOLLARS

ENTER THE NUMBER OF THE SEAT YOU WOULD LIKE (1-5? 4
YOU CHOSE SEAT  4   THE PRICE IS 48 DOLLARS

ENTER THE NUMBER OF THE SEAT YOU WOULD LIKE (1-5? 5
YOU CHOSE SEAT  5   THE PRICE IS 50 DOLLARS
```

FIGURE 6–9
An example program that uses the ON/GOSUB.

Inventory Control Selection with the IF/THEN

Assume that a furniture store sells only four basic items (chairs, tables, couches, and lamps) and that each time a sale is made, the description of the item sold is entered into a program. If you further assume that there is one entry for each sale, then your program could accumulate the number of items in each of the four categories. If your program included logic so that the selling price and store's cost could be input along with the sale information (what was sold), it also could accumulate the profit made during any selling period for the four items.

The input would, therefore, consist of description, selling price, and store's cost. The selection logic needed to do the accounting is shown in the flowchart on figure 6–10. A complete program for this logic appears in figure 6–11.

Inventory Control Selection with the ON/GOSUB

Using the IF/THEN in the inventory example works fine if the store sells only the four items, but imagine what the chart and resulting program would be like if the store sold

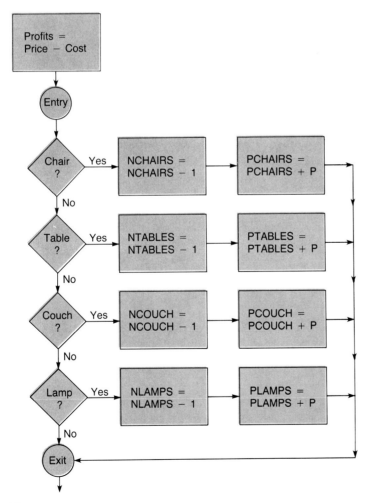

FIGURE 6–10
Program flowchart for inventory control illustration using IF/THEN.

FIGURE 6–11
Program for inventory control illustration using IF/THEN.

Input

```
10    REM     *********************************
20    REM     * INVENTORY CONTROL EXAMPLE IN A *
30    REM     * FURNITURE STORE WITH IF/THEN   *
40    REM     * THERE ARE FOUR ITEMS SOLD      *
50    REM     *         CHAIRS                 *
60    REM     *         TABLES                 *
70    REM     *         COUCHES                *
80    REM     *         LAMPS                  *
90    REM     * TOTAL SOLD IN EACH CATEGORY AND*
100   REM     * TOTAL EARNED PROFIT ARE:       *
110   REM     *   NCHAIRS           PCHAIRS *
120   REM     *   NTABLES           PTABLES *
130   REM     *   NCOUCHES          PCOUCHES*
140   REM     *   NLAMPS            PLAMPS  *
150   REM     * PROFIT = PRICE - COST         *
160   REM     * (PRICE AND COST ARE INPUT)    *
170   REM     *********************************
180           PRINT "COPYRIGHT (C) 1989, BY MERRILL PUBLISHING COMPANY"
190           PRINT "FOR USE WITH STRUCTURED BASIC PROGRAMMING"
200
210       I$ = "ANYTHING"
220       WHILE I$<> "END"
230           CLS
240           PRINT "COPYRIGHT (C) 1989, BY MERRILL PUBLISHING COMPANY"
250           PRINT "FOR USE WITH STRUCTURED BASIC PROGRAMMING "
260           PRINT
270           PRINT "ENTER ITEMS (CHAIR,TABLE,COUCH, OR LAMP)
280           PRINT "TO GET REPORT, TYPE 'END' FOR ITEM AND 0 FOR AMOUNTS"
290           PRINT
300           PRINT
310           PRINT "ENTER ITEM PURCHASED "
320           PRINT "ENTER THE SELLING PRICE "
330           PRINT "ENTER THE STORE'S COST "
340           LOCATE 8,25: INPUT I$
350           LOCATE 9,25: INPUT P
360           LOCATE 10,25:INPUT C
370           PROFIT = P - C
380                   IF I$="CHAIR" THEN NCHAIRS = NCHAIRS + 1:PCHAIRS = PCHAIRS + PROFIT
390                   IF I$="TABLE" THEN NTABLES = NTABLES + 1:
                                         PTABLES = PTABLES + PROFIT
400                   IF I$="COUCH" THEN NCOUCHES = NCOUCHES + 1:
                                         PCOUCHES = PCOUCHES + PROFIT
410                   IF I$="LAMP"  THEN NLAMPS = NLAMPS + 1:
                                         PLAMPS = PLAMPS + PROFIT
420       WEND
430           PRINT
440           PRINT "ITEM        TOTAL SOLD        TOTAL PROFIT"
450           PRINT "CHAIRS ",NCHAIRS,PCHAIRS
460           PRINT "TABLES ",NTABLES,PTABLES
470           PRINT "COUCHES",NCOUCHES,PCOUCHES
480           PRINT "LAMPS  ",NLAMPS,PLAMPS
490   END
```

Output

```
COPYRIGHT (C) 1989, BY MERRILL PUBLISHING COMPANY
FOR USE WITH STRUCTURED BASIC PROGRAMMING
```

```
ENTER ITEMS (CHAIR,TABLE,COUCH, OR LAMP)
TO GET REPORT, TYPE 'END' FOR ITEM AND 0 FOR AMOUNTS

ENTER ITEM PURCHASED    ? END
ENTER THE SELLING PRICE ? 0
ENTER THE STORE'S COST  ? 0

ITEM        TOTAL SOLD      TOTAL PROFIT
CHAIRS          1           30
TABLES          1           200
COUCHES         1           100
LAMPS           1           20
```

200 or 500 different categories of merchandise. Writing that many IF statements would be impractical. The ON/GOSUB provides a solution.

For the ON/GOSUB statement to work, the key field used in the selection of alternatives must be a number. If you assign codes to the chairs, tables, couches and lamps (say the numbers 1, 2, 3, and 4, respectively), you can perform this selection with only one ON/GOSUB statement. In fact, you could cover 255 possibilities with this statement, although you would still have to write that many subroutines. This is obviously better than using the IF/THEN to solve the problem. The flowchart and programs to illustrate this appear in figures 6–12 and 6–13, respectively.

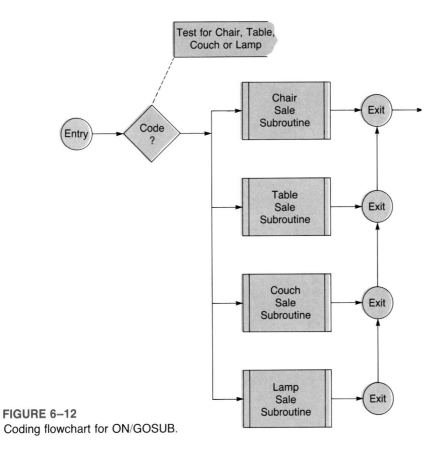

FIGURE 6–12
Coding flowchart for ON/GOSUB.

FIGURE 6-13

6-13 Program illustrating the ON/GOSUB.

```
Input

10    REM    ****************************************************************
20    REM    * INVENTORY CONTROL EXAMPLE IN A FURNITURE STORE              *
30    REM    *                   WITH ON/GOSUB                             *
40    REM    * THERE ARE FOUR ITEMS SOLD                                   *
50    REM    *         CHAIRS - WITH CODE NUMBER 1                         *
60    REM    *         TABLES - WITH CODE NUMBER 2                         *
70    REM    *         COUCHES- WITH CODE NUMBER 3                         *
80    REM    *         LAMPS  - WITH CODE NUMBER 4                         *
90    REM    * TOTAL SOLD IN EACH CATEGORY AND TOTAL EARNED PROFIT ARE:    *
100   REM    *    NCHAIRS                        PCHAIRS                   *
110   REM    *    NTABLES                        PTABLES                   *
120   REM    *    NCOUCHES                       PCOUCHES                  *
130   REM    *    NLAMPS                         PLAMPS                    *
140   REM    * PROFIT = PRICE - COST (PRICE AND COST ARE INPUT)            *
150   REM    ****************************************************************
160   REM
170       PRINT "COPYRIGHT (C) 1989, BY MERRILL PUBLISHING COMPANY"
180       PRINT "FOR USE WITH STRUCTURED BASIC PROGRAMMING"
190     CODE = 999
200     WHILE CODE <> 0
210         CLS
220         PRINT "COPYRIGHT (C) 1989, BY MERRILL PUBLISHING COMPANY"
230         PRINT "FOR USE WITH STRUCTURED BASIC PROGRAMMING"
240         PRINT
250         PRINT " CODES: 1 = CHAIR, 2 = TABLE, 3 = COUCH, 4 = LAMP"
260         PRINT " TO GET REPORT, TYPE 0 AS ITEM CODE"
270         PRINT
280         PRINT "ENTER THE CODE FOR ITEM PURCHASED "
290         PRINT "ENTER THE SELLING PRICE "
300         PRINT "ENTER THE STORE'S COST  "
310         LOCATE 7,35: INPUT CODE
320         LOCATE 8,35: INPUT P
330         LOCATE 9,35: INPUT C
340         PROFIT = P - C
350         ON CODE GOSUB 470,520,570,620
360     WEND
370             PRINT
380         PRINT "ITEM        TOTAL SOLD      TOTAL PROFIT"
390         PRINT "CHAIRS ",NCHAIRS,PCHAIRS
400         PRINT "TABLES ",NTABLES,PTABLES
410         PRINT "COUCHES",NCOUCHES,PCOUCHES
420         PRINT "LAMPS  ",NLAMPS,PLAMPS
430     END
440   REM    ************************
450   REM    * CHAIR SALE SUBROUTINE *
460   REM    ************************
470             NCHAIRS = NCHAIRS + 1:PCHAIRS = PCHAIRS + PROFIT
480             RETURN
490   REM    ************************
500   REM    * TABLE SALE SUBROUTINE *
510   REM    ************************
520             NTABLES = NTABLES + 1:PTABLES = PTABLES + PROFIT
530             RETURN
540   REM    ************************
550   REM    * COUCH SALE SUBROUTINE *
560   REM    ************************
570             NCOUCHES = NCOUCHES + 1:PCOUCHES = PCOUCHES + PROFIT
580             RETURN
```

```
590   REM   *************************
600   REM   * LAMP SALE SUBROUTINE *
610   REM   *************************
620         NLAMPS = NLAMPS + 1:PLAMPS = PLAMPS + PROFIT
630             RETURN
640      END
```

Output

```
COPYRIGHT (C) 1989, BY MERRILL PUBLISHING COMPANY
FOR USE WITH STRUCTURED BASIC PROGRAMMING

 CODES: 1 = CHAIR, 2 = TABLE, 3 = COUCH, 4 = LAMP
 TO GET REPORT, TYPE 0 AS ITEM CODE
ENTER THE CODE FOR ITEM PURCHASED ? 0
ENTER THE SELLING PRICE          ? 0
ENTER THE STORE'S COST           ? 0

ITEM      TOTAL SOLD      TOTAL PROFIT
CHAIRS        0           0
TABLES        1           200
COUCHES       1           100
LAMPS         1           20
```

COMPLEX SELECTION LOGIC

BASIC permits complex selection logic so sophisticated that it is possible to diagnose diseases, match real estate investments to client preferences, match people to one another (dating), and more. (These applications are discussed in chapters 7 and 8.) This section will explore the type of selection statements possible in these programs, and relate these to a few simple illustrations.

Compound Logic with AND, OR and NOT

When used in an expression in an IF statement, AND joins two or more conditions so that they both must be true for the expression as a whole to be considered true. For example

```
IF ACCOUNTBALANCE > LIMIT AND PASTDUE > 30 THEN PRINT "CANCEL ACCOUNT"
```

In this expression, both the account balance must exceed the credit limit and the past due payment must be more than 30 days late before the "cancel account" message is printed in this statement.

If OR were used to join the conditions, as shown in the following, then the "cancel account" message would be printed if either condition is true:

```
IF ACCOUNTBALANCE > LIMIT OR PASTDUE > 30 THEN PRINT "CANCEL ACCOUNT"
```

The NOT logic is used frequently to negate the equal sign, as in this example

```
IF PAYMENT NOT = REQUIREDAMOUNT THEN PRINT " INSUFFICIENT PAYMENT "
```

The same result also can be obtained with the combination of the greater than and less than signs (<>), and some programmers prefer to use these rather than the NOT in cases of selection for inequality.

```
IF PAYMENT <> REQUIREDAMOUNT THEN PRINT " INSUFFICIENT PAYMENT "
```

NOT has other uses in mathematical logic, and is often used to negate an entire condition, such as in this example

```
IF NOT (PAYMENT = 0 AND LATE$ = "YES") THEN PRINT " ACCOUNT IS FINE ! "
```

which means both the payment is non-zero and the payment is not late. However, this is complicated and confusing wording. A straightforward IF statement that could test the same two conditions would be

```
IF PAYMENT > 0 AND LATE$ = "NO" THEN PRINT " ACCOUNT IS FINE ! "
```

Avoid NOT if you are not sure what the compound statement really means, and try to formulate the condition you need with the six relational operators and AND and OR.

Comparing String Data

In selection constructs, string (alphanumeric) variables can be compared to one another or to string constants, called literals. The exact outcome of the comparison of alphanumeric or alphabetic data depends on the binary codes used to store the characters. Each character used in BASIC is represented by a binary number ranging from 010 0000 (for the blank) to 111 1010 (for the lower-case z) in the most common binary code, which is a standard seven-bit code called ASCII (American Standard Code for Information Interchange). Although other codes are used by various BASIC systems, the hierarchy of characters is generally as follows:

Binary Value	Characters
Lowest	Blanks
↓	Special characters (e.g., ! " # $, and numerals)
↓	Upper-case (capital) letters
Highest	Lower-case (small) letters

The examples that follow illustrate the outcomes of various comparisons that occur left to right.

Comparison	A	B	E
"ABE"<"BOB"	100 0001	100 0010	100 0101
	100 0010	100 1111	100 0010
	B	**O**	**B**

B is represented by a larger binary number than A; therefore, BOB is greater than ABE.

Generally, the lower the letter in the alphabet, the smaller its binary code; thus, words that begin with a capital letter A are always less than those that begin with other capital letters. Data with a mixture of upper- and lower-case letters should be entered with care. For example, a trivial mistake, such as typing in the name field

```
John l. Smith
```

instead of

```
John L. Smith
```

will make the equating of the two fields impossible, since the lower-case l is binary 110 1100, whereas the upper-case L is 100 1100. Therefore, "John l. Smith" is greater than "John L. Smith" when represented as a binary number.

All numeric characters stored in strings (for example, a part number such as PN$ = $ 124-A") have lower binary code values in ASCII than letters. For example,

"124-A" > "A-123"

whereas

$$A\text{-}000 > 9\text{-}000$$

The blank has the lowest code value; therefore, comparing strings of unequal size that are otherwise identical produces the following:

```
JOHN BROWN _____  <  JOHN BROWNSTONE
              ↑
          Blanks
```

Thus, you must be careful when entering and comparing string variables and constants; otherwise, you may obtain unpredictable and often incorrect results.

On some systems, string data may be entered with or without enclosing quotation marks. However, on other systems, the absence of enclosing quotation marks will cause any blanks in the field to be removed, thus compressing the stored data. For example, inputting the name ''Mary B. Smith'' as

```
ENTER NAME: "MARY B. SMITH"
```

would cause the data to be stored exactly as entered

```
MARY B. SMITH
```

But, entering the name without the enclosing quotation marks causes the name to be stored as

```
MARYB.SMITH
```

COMPUTER-ASSISTED INSTRUCTION

Computer-assisted instruction (CAI) is a rapidly growing application for microcomputers programmed in BASIC. BASIC lends itself beautifully to CAI because it is an interactive language with sound, color, and graphics capabilities, as well as traditional text and numeric data manipulation. The areas of application for CAI are becoming boundless, but the principles for developing CAI programs are expressed simply in this section.

Principles of Computer-Assisted Instruction

In computer-assisted instruction you program the computer to present information to the user and then test the user's understanding of the information presented. The presentation portion of the program presents information on the screen and then asks for user responses regarding understanding or desire for review. When the user is ready, the program moves on and presents additional information, tests, evaluates, and so on, until the lesson or section is completed or the user tires. At key points in the presentation, review questions may be asked, and an incorrect answer may cause the program to proceed to a review of the appropriate part of the presentation. An example of presentation logic would be:

```
10 PRINT "AN AUTOMOBILE ENGINE WILL MISFIRE IF THE SPARK PLUGS ARE FOULED,"
20 PRINT " OR IF THE IGNITION WIRES ARE WORN OR WET. ON CARS NOT EQUIPPED"
30 PRINT "WITH ELECTRONIC IGNITION, MISFIRING CAN ALSO OCCUR IF THE POINTS"
40 PRINT " ARE NOT PROPERLY ADJUSTED."
50 PRINT " "
55 CLS
60 INPUT "ENTER AN ENGINE PART THAT MAY CAUSE MISFIRING" ; N$
70 IF N$ = "SPARK PLUG" THEN 200
80 IF N$ = "IGNITION WIRES" THEN 200
90 IF N$ = "POINTS" THEN 200
100 PRINT "YOU DID NOT NAME AN ENGINE PART THAT CAN CAUSE MISFIRING. LET'S"
110 PRINT " REVIEW THAT PORTION OF THE LESSON"
120 GOTO 10
200  ........Rest of presentation
```

Note that the presentation provides the information in a brief, factual manner. The review question is geared to the points presented and appears very soon after the presentation. This immediate feedback is highly desirable and is recognized by learning specialists as one of the most attractive features of computer-assisted instruction.

Ideally, the review questions will appear after the presentation text has rolled off the screen or after a CLEAR SCREEN (CLS) command, so the answers are not obvious. In the example above, a CLEAR SCREEN command located at number 55 would be desired.

Sometimes, the presentation may become long and tedious to the user, causing him or her to become bored or restless. Therefore, it is considered good programming practice to provide the user with the opportunity to end a session at frequent intervals during the session. A PRINT statement which would alert the user to this option looks like this:

```
300 PRINT "YOU HAVE COMPLETED THE FIRST SESSION IN THE PRESENTATION OF THE"
310 PRINT " OPERATION OF THE INTERNAL COMBUSTION GASOLINE ENGINE"
320 PRINT " IF YOU WOULD LIKE, YOU CAN TAKE A BREAK NOW AND RESUME LATER."
330 PRINT "WHAT WOULD YOU LIKE TO DO? (ENTER 1 TO TAKE TEST, 0 TO WAIT)";A
340 IF A = 1 GOSUB 500 ELSE 600.....
```

Designing and Programming a Tutorial

The testing session in the following CAI consists of this sequence of BASIC statements: PRINT, INPUT, LET (the evaluation routine), and IF statements for each question on the test. The PRINT statement presents the question on the display, the INPUT statement accepts the answer from the keyboard, and the IF and LET statements evaluate the answer for correctness and accumulate points for each correct answer. The results are often scaled to 100% for the attained test grade.

Here is an example test session with the PRINT, INPUT, and IF/LET (evaluation outline logic) statements in their logical order.

```
10 PRINT "WHERE WAS THE BATTLE OF BUNKER HILL ACTUALLY FOUGHT?"
20 INPUT A$
30 IF A$ = "BREEDS HILL" THEN LET SCORE = SCORE + 10:PRINT "GOOD!!"
40 IF A$ <> "BREEDS HILL" THEN PRINT "SORRY THE CORRECT ANSWER IS BREEDS HILL"
50 REM NEXT QUESTION SEQUENCE
60 PRINT "THE ELECTRIC LIGHT BULB WAS INVENTED BY WHOM?"
70 INPUT A$
80 IF A$ = "JOSEPH SWAN" THEN SCORE = SCORE + 10:PRINT "EXCELLENT-MOST PEOPLE
 THINK IT WAS THOMAS EDISON":GOTO 110
90 IF A$ = "THOMAS EDISON"THEN PRINT "A COMMON ERROR! THE ELECTRIC LIGHT
BULB WAS ACTUALLY INVENTED BY SIR JOSEPH SWAN":GOTO 110
100 IF A$ <>"JOSEPH SWAN" THEN PRINT "SORRY, WRONG ANSWER"
110 REM NEXT QUESTION ROUTINE.....
```

Dress Shop Inventory Control

Computerized inventory control is a widespread computer application in businesses today. Now that the cost of microcomputers is down, even small businesses are able to automate their inventory control systems. By using this application, the store owner can ensure that items a customer may want are kept in adequate supply while at the same time not keeping an excess supply. Excess goods (surplus inventory) might spoil, go out of style, become obsolete, or tie up capital. Hence, a proper balance of not having too little or too much on hand is crucial to long-term business survival. Numerous businesses have failed primarily because the management did not have a good handle on inventory.

Inventory control systems use selection structures to keep track of current quantities on hand and sales of hundreds or even thousands of different items. It is possible to write simple inventory control systems using the IF/THEN and case control structures. Both of these structures are illustrated in this case study.

This case study is concerned with the inventory control of a dress shop. In this case study you will assume the following:

1. The dress shop carries only three dress sizes.
2. Inventory control by size only (not size and style) is the prime consideration.
3. Profit is equal to simply the selling price minus the store's cost.
4. The management is interested only in the sales of each size and the profit by size.
5. There is no reorder point.
6. Initial inventory is sufficient to meet demand.
7. Reorder messages are not printed.

Input Specifications

Input to this program consists of two different record types:

1. The first record sets up the initial inventory level for size 5, 7, and 9 dresses.
2. The second record type is a sales transaction, indicating the size of dress sold, its selling price, and store's cost. On this record a code is used to indicate the end of data.

Details of both record types are shown below.

	Field No.	Field Discription	Type	Example
Initial	1	Beginning Inventory, Size 5	Numeric	15
Inventory	2	Beginning Inventory, Size 7	Numeric	10
Records	3	Beginning Inventory, Size 9	Numeric	1
Sales	1	Customer's Name	Alphanumeric	Mary Smith
Transaction	2	Customer's Address	Alphanumeric	125 Main Street
Records	3	Size of Dress Sold	Numeric	05
	4	Retail (Selling)Price	Numeric	$150.00
	5	Cost to store	Numeric	$100.00

183

Processing Decisions and Formulas

The key processing decisions and formulas are designed to keep track of current inventory and profit by size. Inventory level for each size dress is reduced by 1 for each dress sold in that size. Profit is simply the selling price minus the store's cost for each dress, and is accumulated by size. Detailed formulas are shown below.

$$\text{Profit} = \text{Retail Price} - \text{Cost to Store}$$
$$\text{Number Sold} = \text{Number Sold} + 1$$
$$\text{Quantity on Hand} = \text{Quantity on Hand} - 1$$
$$\text{If Quantity on Hand} = 0, \text{Print ``Out of Stock''}$$

An "EOD" record will signal the end of sales transaction processing for the day.

Output

There are two outputs from this program. The first is a customer's bill, showing the price and size of the dress sold, and—as an option—the name and address of the customer who made the purchase. (If this option is included, the customer's name and address must be entered as data on the sales record above.) The second output is a management report which contains the number of size 5, 7, and 9 dresses sold, the ending inventory level, the total profit earned on each size, and the total profit for the period.

```
                        BEGINNING INVENTORY
                      INITIAL QUANTITY ON HAND
             SIZE 5            SIZE 7            SIZE 9
               15                10                 1

          INITIAL INVENTORY HAS BEEN PROCESSED



                             DRESS SHOP BILL
     CUSTOMER NAME              ADDRESS          PURCHASE      SALES PRICE

   MARY SMITH              125 MAIN STREET        SIZE 5        $150.00



                             DRESS SHOP BILL
     CUSTOMER NAME              ADDRESS          PURCHASE      SALES PRICE

   ALICE BROWN            100 NORTH AVENUE        SIZE 7         $98.00



                             DRESS SHOP BILL
     CUSTOMER NAME              ADDRESS          PURCHASE      SALES PRICE

   LANA ALMAN             255 SOUTH STREET        SIZE 9        $222.00



                         SIZE 9 OUT OF STOCK



          ALL CUSTOMER BILLS HAVE BEEN PROCESSED
```

```
                     MANAGEMENT  REPORT
                     SIZE 5          SIZE 7          SIZE 9        TOTAL
 NUMBER SOLD           1               1               1            3

 PROFIT EARNED        50.00           40.00          109.50      $199.50

 QUANTITY ON HAND      14              9               0           23



                   END OF DRESS SHOP PROGRAM
```

Test Data

Test data to be used is shown below.

> 15, 10, 1
> Mary Smith, 125 Main Street, 05, 150.00, 100.00
> Alice Brown, 100 North Avenue, 07, 98.00, 50.00
> Lana Alman, 255 South Street, 09, 222.00, 112.50
> Phyllis Cooley, 11 East Street, 09, 222.00, 112.50
> EOD, 0, 0, 0, 0

Error Recovery Routines

If the inventory level on any size falls below zero, the computer is to print an appropriate message, and eliminate that sale from the processing.

Validation Procedure

All totals sold, current inventory levels, profits, and totals are to be verified by hand calculating the results using the test data. The hand-calculated and computer-produced results should be identical.

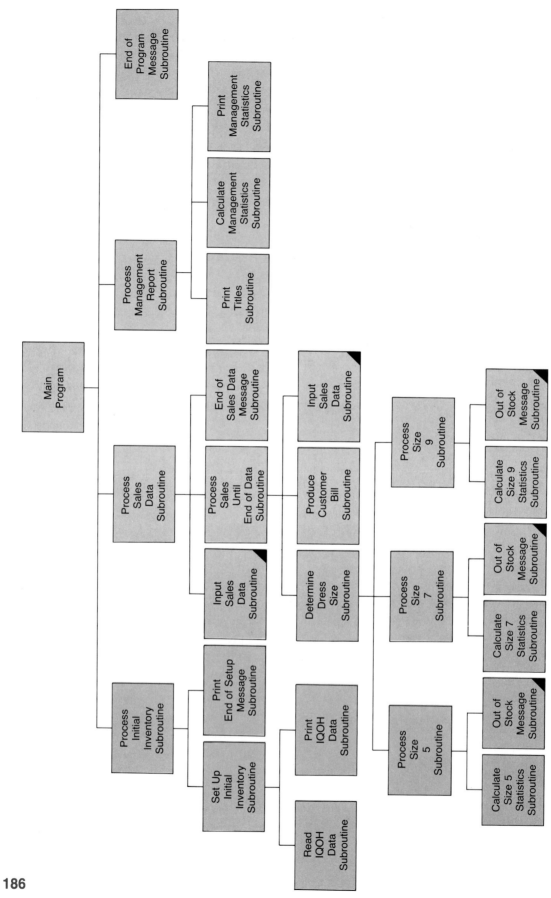

FIGURE C6–1
Visual table of contents—dress shop inventory program.

186

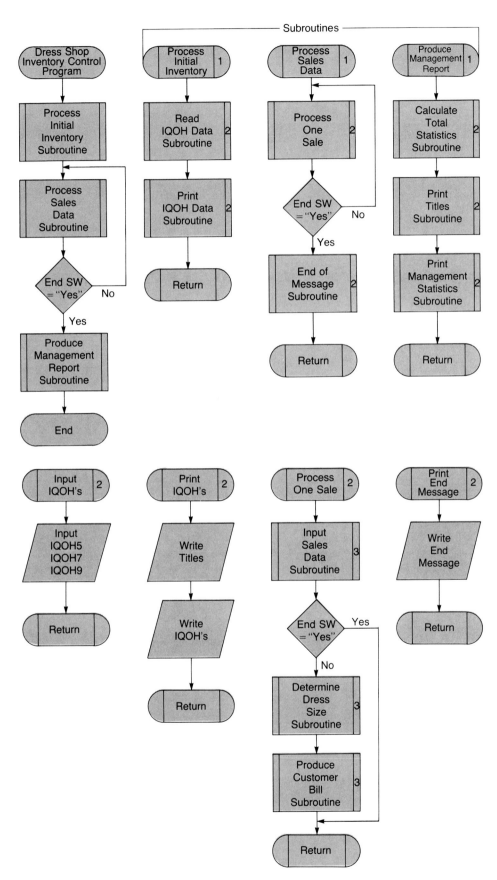

FIGURE C6-2
Program flowchart—dress shop inventory program.

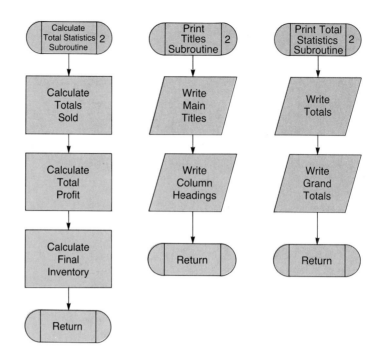

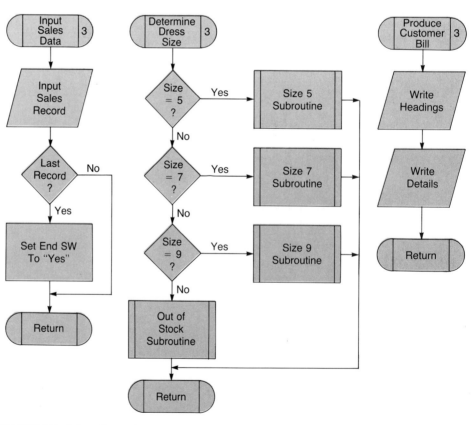

FIGURE C6–2 *(continued)*

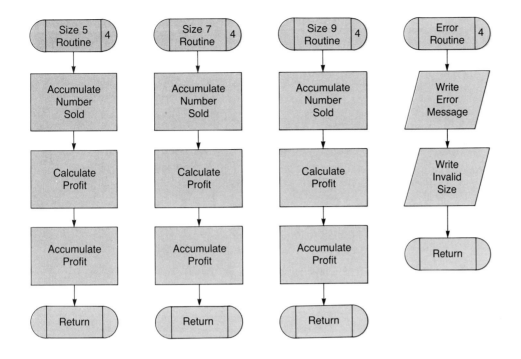

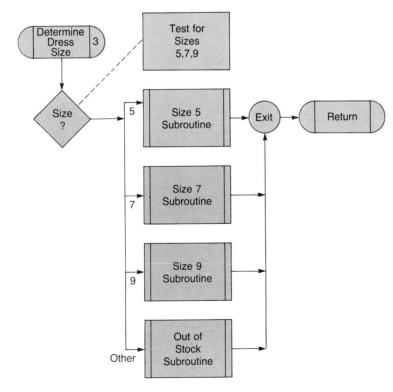

FIGURE C6–2 *(continued)*

```
10    REM   ********************************************************
20    REM   *          CALCULATIONS WITH LOGICAL DECISIONS         *
30    REM   *                  CASE STUDY:C6-1                      *
40    REM   *                  DRESS SHOP PROGRAM                   *
50    REM   *   THIS PROGRAM CALCULATES THE CURRENT INVENTORY       *
60    REM   *   LEVEL, PRODUCES AN OUT OF STOCK MESSAGE, A          *
70    REM   *   CUSTOMER BILL, AND A MANAGEMENT REPORT.             *
80    REM   *                                                       *
90    REM   *                    VARIABLE LEGEND                    *
100   REM   *           IQOH = INITIAL QUANTITY ON HAND             *
110   REM   *           SIZE = DRESS SIZE (5, 7, 9)                 *
120   REM   *           TQOH = TOTAL ALL QUANTITY ON HAND           *
130   REM   *           PRC = SALES PRICE                           *
140   REM   *           CST = WHOLESALE COST                        *
150   REM   *           PROF = PROFIT ON SALE (5,7,9)               *
160   REM   *           TPROF = PROFIT ON TOTAL SALES (5,7,9)       *
170   REM   *           NUM = NUMBER OF SALES (5,7,9)               *
180   REM   *           TNUM = TOTAL NUMBER OF SALES   (5+7+9)      *
190   REM   *           PROFIT = PROFIT ON TOTAL SALES (5+7+9)      *
200   REM   *           TQOH = TOTAL QUANTITY ON HAND  (5+7+9)      *
210   REM   *           ENDSW = END OF DATA SWITCH                  *
220   REM   *           BILLSW = PRINT BILL SWITCH                  *
230   REM   ********************************************************
240         PRINT "COPYRIGHT (C) 1989, BY MERRILL PUBLISHING COMPANY"
250         PRINT "FOR USE WITH STRUCTURED BASIC PROGRAMMING"
260   REM   ***************
270   REM   * MAIN PROGRAM *
280   REM   ***************
290   REM   PERFORM 'PROCESS INITIAL INVENTORY' SUBROUTINE
300         GOSUB 380
310   REM   PERFORM 'PROCESS SALES DATA' SUBROUTINE
320         GOSUB 900
330   REM   PERFORM 'PROCESS MANAGEMENT REPORT' SUBROUTINE
340         GOSUB 2270
350   REM   PERFORM 'END OF PROGRAM MESSAGE' SUBROUTINE
360         GOSUB 2650
370         END
380   REM   ******************************************
390   REM   * PROCESS INITIAL INVENTORY SUBROUTINE *
400   REM   ******************************************
410         LPRINT
420   REM   PERFORM 'SET UP INITIAL INVENTORY' SUBROUTINE
430         GOSUB 470
440   REM   PERFORM 'PRINT END OF SET UP MESSAGE' SUBROUTINE
450         GOSUB 810
460         RETURN
470   REM   ******************************************
480         * SET UP INITIAL INVENTORY SUBROUTINE *
490         ******************************************
500   REM   PERFORM 'READ IQOH DATA' SUBROUTINE
510         GOSUB 550
520   REM   PERFORM 'PRINT IQOH DATA' SUBROUTINE
530         GOSUB 710
540         RETURN
550   REM   ***************************
560   REM   * READ IQOH DATA SUBROUTINE *
570   REM   ***************************
580         CLS
620         PRINT "ENTER TOTAL AMOUNT OF ON HAND INVENTORY BY SIZE"
630         PRINT
640         PRINT "SIZE 5"
650         PRINT "SIZE 7"
660         PRINT "SIZE 9"
```

```
670         LOCATE 6,8: INPUT IQOH5
680         LOCATE 7,8: INPUT IQOH7
690         LOCATE 8,8: INPUT IQOH9
700         RETURN
710    REM  ****************************
720    REM  * PRINT IQOH DATA SUBROUTINE *
730    REM  ****************************
740         LPRINT
750         LPRINT "                                    BEGINNING INVENTORY"
760         LPRINT "                                    INITIAL QUANTITY ON HAND"
770         LPRINT "                        SIZE 5         SIZE 7         SIZE 9"
780         F$ = "                          ##             ##             ##
790         LPRINT USING F$;IQOH5,IQOH7,IQOH9
800         RETURN
810    REM  *********************************************
820    REM  * PRINT END OF SET UP MESSAGE SUBROUTINE *
830    REM  *********************************************
840         LPRINT
850         LPRINT "                    INITIAL INVENTORY HAS BEEN PROCESSED"
860         LPRINT
870         LPRINT
880         LPRINT
890         RETURN
900    REM  ********************************
910    REM  * PROCESS SALES DATA SUBROUTINE *
920    REM  ********************************
930    REM  PERFORM 'INPUT SALES DATA' SUBROUTINE
940         GOSUB 1000
950    REM  PERFORM 'PROCESS SALES UNTIL END OF DATA' SUBROUTINE
960         GOSUB 1230
970    REM  PERFORM 'END OF SALES DATA MESSAGE' SUBROUTINE
980         GOSUB 2170
990         RETURN
1000   REM  ******************************
1010   REM  * INPUT SALES DATA SUBROUTINE *
1020   REM  ******************************
1030        CLS
1070        PRINT "ENTER INFORMATION REGARDING SALES"
1080        PRINT "WHEN ALL SALES HAVE BEEN RECORDED TYPE 'EOD' FOR NAME"
1090        PRINT
1100        PRINT "NAME"
1110        PRINT "ADDRESS"
1120        PRINT "SIZE"
1130        PRINT "PRICE"
1140        PRINT "COST"
1150        LOCATE 7,10: INPUT NM$
1160        LOCATE 8,10: INPUT ADDR$
1170        LOCATE 9,10: INPUT SIZE
1180        LOCATE 10,10:INPUT PRC
1190        LOCATE 11,10:INPUT CST
1200        IF NM$ = "EOD" THEN ENDSW = 1
1210        BILLSW = 0
1220        RETURN
1230   REM  *************************************************
1240   REM  * PROCESS SALES UNTIL END OF DATA SUBROUTINE *
1250   REM  *************************************************
1260        ENDSW = 0
1270        WHILE ENDSW = 0
1280   REM  PERFORM 'DETERMINE DRESS SIZE' SUBROUTINE
1290        GOSUB 1360
1300   REM  PERFORM 'PRODUCE CUSTOMER BILL' SUBROUTINE
1310        IF BILLSW = 1 THEN GOSUB 2040
1320   REM  PERFORM 'INPUT SALES DATA' SUBROUTINE
```

```
1330          GOSUB 1000
1340          WEND
1350          RETURN
1360   REM    ************************************
1370   REM    * DETERMINE DRESS SIZE SUBROUTINE *
1380   REM    ************************************
1390   REM    PERFORM 'PROCESS SIZE 5' SUBROUTINE
1400          IF SIZE = 5 THEN GOSUB 1460
1410   REM    PERFORM 'PROCESS SIZE 7' SUBROUTINE
1420          IF SIZE = 7 THEN GOSUB 1530
1430   REM    PERFORM 'PROCESS SIZE 9' SUBROUTINE
1440          IF SIZE = 9 THEN GOSUB 1600
1450          RETURN
1460   REM    ****************************
1470   REM    * PROCESS SIZE 5 SUBROUTINE *
1480   REM    ****************************
1490   REM    IF IN STOCK = PERFORM 'CALCULATE SIZE 5 STATISTICS' SUBROUTINE
1500   REM    IF OUT OF STOCK = PERFORM 'OUT OF STOCK MESSAGE' SUBROUTINE
1510          IF IQOH5 > 0 THEN GOSUB 1770 ELSE GOSUB 1670
1520          RETURN
1530   REM    ****************************
1540   REM    * PROCESS SIZE 7 SUBROUTINE *
1550   REM    ****************************
1560   REM    IF IN STOCK = PERFORM 'CALCULATE SIZE 7 STATISTICS' SUBROUTINE
1570   REM    IF OUT OF STOCK = PERFORM 'OUT OF STOCK MESSAGE' SUBROUTINE
1580          IF IQOH7 > 0 THEN GOSUB 1860 ELSE GOSUB 1670
1590          RETURN
1600   REM    ****************************
1610   REM    * PROCESS SIZE 9 SUBROUTINE *
1620   REM    ****************************
1630   REM    IF IN STOCK = PERFORM 'CALCULATE SIZE 9 STATISTICS' SUBROUTINE
1640   REM    IF OUT OF STOCK = PERFORM 'OUT OF STOCK MESSAGE' SUBROUTINE
1650          IF IQOH9 > 0 THEN GOSUB 1950 ELSE GOSUB 1670
1660          RETURN
1670   REM    **********************************
1680   REM    * OUT OF STOCK MESSAGE SUBROUTINE *
1690   REM    **********************************
1700          LPRINT
1710          LPRINT
1720          F1$ = "                        SIZE # OUT OF STOCK"
1730          LPRINT USING F1$;SIZE
1740          LPRINT
1750          LPRINT
1760          RETURN
1770   REM    ******************************************
1780   REM    * CALCULATE SIZE 5 STATISTICS SUBROUTINE *
1790   REM    ******************************************
1800          PROF5 = PRC - CST
1810          TPROF5 = TPROF5 + PROF5
1820          NUM5 = NUM5 + 1
1830          BILLSW = 1
1840          IQOH5 = IQOH5 - 1
1850          RETURN
1860   REM    ******************************************
1870   REM    * CALCULATE SIZE 7 STATISTICS SUBROUTINE *
1880   REM    ******************************************
1890          PROF7 = PRC - CST
1900          TPROF7 = TPROF7 + PROF7
1910          NUM7 = NUM7 + 1
1920          BILLSW = 1
1930          IQOH7 = IQOH7 - 1
1940          RETURN
```

192

```
1950    REM   ********************************************
1960    REM   * CALCULATE SIZE 9 STATISTICS SUBROUTINE *
1970    REM   ********************************************
1980          PROF9 = PRC - CST
1990          TPROF9 = TPROF9 + PROF9
2000          NUM9 = NUM9 + 1
2010          BILLSW = 1
2020          IQOH9 = IQOH9 -1
2030          RETURN
2040    REM   **************************************
2050    REM   * PRODUCE CUSTOMER BILL SUBROUTINE *
2060    REM   **************************************
2070          LPRINT
2080          LPRINT
2090          LPRINT "                              DRESS SHOP BILL"
2100          LPRINT "     CUSTOMER NAME            ADDRESS  PURCHASE  SALES PRICE"
2110          LPRINT
2120          F1$ = "\                    \            \SIZE #     $\##.##"
2130          LPRINT USING F1$;NM$,ADDR$,SIZE,PRC
2140          LPRINT
2150          LPRINT
2160          RETURN
2170    REM   ****************************************
2180    REM   * END OF SALES DATA MESSAGE SUBROUTINE *
2190    REM   ****************************************
2200          LPRINT
2210          LPRINT
2220          LPRINT
2230          LPRINT "                    ALL CUSTOMER BILLS HAVE BEEN PROCESSED"
2240          LPRINT
2250          LPRINT
2260          RETURN
2270    REM   *********************************************
2280    REM   * PROCESS MANAGEMENT REPORT SUBROUTINE *
2290    REM   *********************************************
2300    REM   PERFORM 'PRINT TITLES' SUBROUTINE
2310          GOSUB 2370
2320    REM   PERFORM 'CALCULATE MANAGEMENT STATISTICS' SUBROUTINE
2330          GOSUB 2460
2340    REM   PERFORM 'PRINT MANAGEMENT STATISTICS' SUBROUTINE
2350          GOSUB 2530
2360          RETURN
2370    REM   ****************************
2380    REM   * PRINT TITLES SUBROUTINE *
2390    REM   ****************************
2400          LPRINT
2410          LPRINT
2420          LPRINT "               MANAGEMENT REPORT"
2430          LPRINT "               SIZE 5     SIZE 7     SIZE
9  TOTAL"
2440          LPRINT
2450          RETURN
2460    REM   ************************************************
2470    REM   * CALCULATE MANAGEMENT STATISTICS SUBROUTINE *
2480    REM   ************************************************
2490          TNUM = NUM5 + NUM7 + NUM9
2500          TPROFIT = TPROF5 + TPROF7 + TPROF9
2510          TQOH = IQOH5 + IQOH7 + IQOH9
2520          RETURN
2530    REM   ********************************************
2540    REM   * PRINT MANAGEMENT STATISTICS SUBROUTINE *
2550    REM   ********************************************
```

```
2560        F3$ = "              NUMBER SOLD           ##         ##         ##
###"
2570        F4$ = "              PROFIT EARNED       ###.##     ###.##     ###.##
$$#,###.##"
2580        F5$ = "              QUANTITY ON HAND       ##         ##         ##
###"
2590        LPRINT USING F3$;NUM5,NUM7,NUM9,TNUM
2600        LPRINT
2610        LPRINT USING F4$;TPROF5,TPROF7,TPROF9,TPROFIT
2620        LPRINT
2630        LPRINT USING F5$;IQOH5,IQOH7,IQOH9,TQOH
2640        RETURN
2650   REM  **********************************
2660   REM  * END OF PROGRAM MESSAGE SUBROUTINE *
2670   REM  **********************************
2680        LPRINT
2690        LPRINT
2700        LPRINT
2710        LPRINT "                        END OF DRESS SHOP PROGRAM"
2720   REM
2730   REM  END OF PROGRAM
```

Inventory Control and Accounting in an Automobile Dearlership

Often in business computer systems, the decisions that need to be made are not as simple as those in the dress shop example. Often, you need to write instructions to evaluate aspects of the incoming data and to perform various routines that will depend on the outcome of the decisions. As an introduction to this type of system, this case study will illustrate how the computer "interrogates" the data record and produces two distinctly different reports for management on the basis of the results of its interrogation. The first report, which is very similar to the dress shop inventory status report, shows the number of items sold by type, the profit earned by type, and the total profit earned on all items. The second report shows the status of the commissions earned by the salespeople in the dealership and lists the number of cars sold by each of them. To produce these two reports, the program must determine not only what item was sold, but also who sold it. This compound decision process can become quite elaborate, with the program checking literally hundreds of data characteristics.

PROBLEM DEFINITION

Input Specifications

Input consists of three record types. Record 1 sets up the initial inventory level of cars in stock by description. Record 2 contains the commission rates for the salespeople in the dealership. Record 3 is a sales transaction containing the code number of the salesperson who sold the car and the car's description, selling price, and dealer's cost.

	Field No.	Field Description	Type	Example
Initial	1	IQOH, Buick	Numeric	40
Inventory	2	IQOH, Ford	Numeric	60
Record	3	IQOH, Pontiac	Numeric	2
Sales	1	Salesman's Code Number	Numeric	1
Record	2	Car Description	String	Buick
	3	Selling Price	Numeric	5000.00
	4	Dealer's Cost	Numeric	3500.00

Processing Decisions and Formulas

Three key decisions must be made in the program. What car has been ordered? Is that car available? Who sold the particular car? The processing formulas under each situation are shown below.

Decisions

1. The description of the car sold will determine which processing routines will be followed.
2. If a particular car is out of stock, an "out of stock" message will be printed; otherwise the statistics for that car are to be calculated.
3. The code for the salesman who sold the car will determine which commission logic will be followed.

195

Formulas

1. Calculate Commission
   COMM = PRICE * COMM RATE
2. Calculate Profit
   PROFIT = PRICE − COST − COMM
3. Accumulate Profit
   TPROF = TPROF + PROFIT
4. Accumulate Commission
   TCOMM = TCOMM + COMM
5. Update Quantity on Hand
   QOH = QOH − 1

Formulas 3 and 5 apply to each car type sold. Formula 4 applies to each salesman. Variable names are modified to reflect this.

Output

```
                    BEGINNING INVENTORY
                  INITIAL QUANTITY ON HAND

        BUICK           FORD            PONTIAC
         40              60                2


     INITIAL QUANTITY ON HAND HAS BEEN PROCESSED



               OUT OF STOCK PONTIAC



          ALL SALES DATA HAS BEEN PROCESSED


                 AUTOMOBILE SALES REPORT
        DESCRIPTION      IQOH  SOLD  QOH     PROFIT

          BUICK           40    1    39   $ 1,000.00
          FORD            60    2    58   $   490.00
          PONTIAC          2    2     0   $   425.00
              TOTAL      102    5    97   $ 1,915.00


             SALESMAN   COMMISSION REPORT
          SALESMAN       COMMISSION      NUMBER SOLD
             1         $    500.00           1
             2         $  2,325.00           2
             3         $  3,660.00           2
          TOTAL        $  6,485.00           5


        END OF AUTOMOBILE DEALERSHIP PROGRAM
```

Test Data

40, 60, 2
1 BUICK, 5000, 3500
2 PONTIAC, 8500, 6800
3 PONTIAC, 8500, 6800
1 PONTIAC, 9500, 8000
2 FORD, 7000, 5500
3 FORD, 9800, 7800
End of Data 0

Error Recovery Routines

Include the same type of error routines described in the dress shop program for out of stock automobiles.

Validation Procedure

Hand calculate the results and verify the computer output.

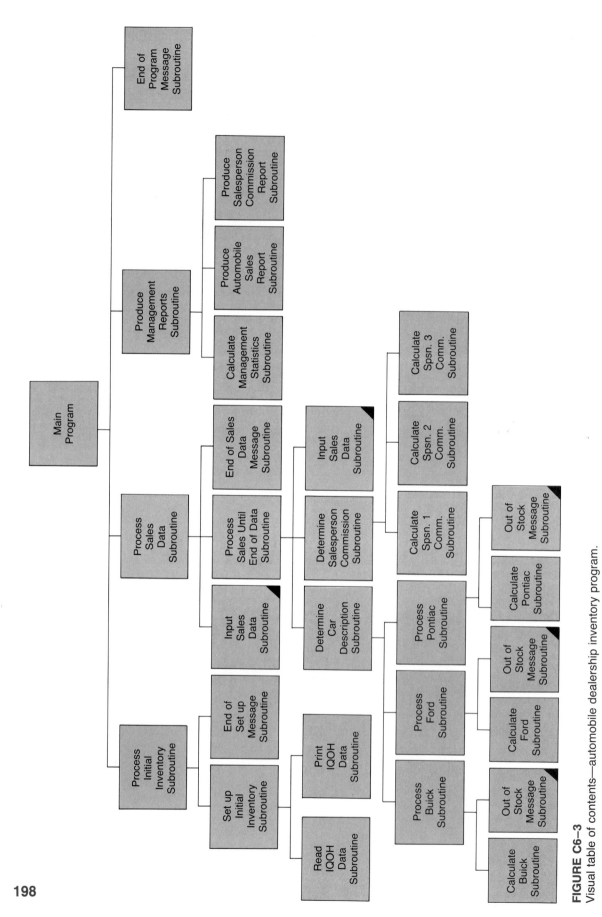

FIGURE C6–3
Visual table of contents—automobile dealership inventory program.

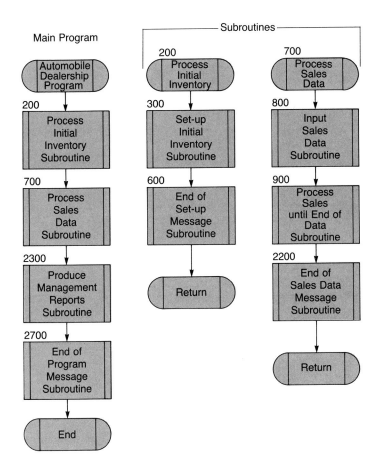

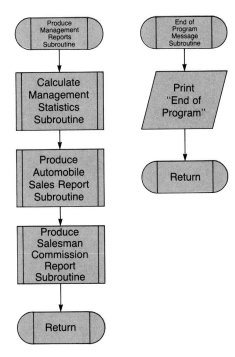

FIGURE C6–4
Program flowcharts—automobile dealership inventory program.

CASE STUDY SOLUTION

```
10    REM   ********************************************************
20    REM   *            CALCULATIONS WITH LOGICAL DECISIONS        *
30    REM   *                  CASE STUDY: C6-2                     *
40    REM   *              AUTOMOBILE DEALERSHIP PROGRAM             *
50    REM   * THIS PROGRAM CALCULATES THE CURRENT INVENTORY         *
60    REM   * LEVEL, PRODUCES AN 'OUT OF STOCK'  MESSAGE, AN        *
70    REM   * AUTOMOBILE SALES REPORT AND A SALESMANS REPORT        *
80    REM   *                                                       *
90    REM   *                  VARIABLE LEGEND                      *
100   REM   *         IQOH = INITIAL QUANTITY ON HAND               *
110   REM   *         QOH = QUANTITY ON HAND                        *
120   REM   *         SMAN = SALESMAN CODE                          *
130   REM   *         DES$ = CAR DESCRIPTION                        *
140   REM   *         PRC = SALE PRICE                              *
150   REM   *         CST = DEALER COST                             *
160   REM   *         COMM = SALESMAN COMMISSION                    *
170   REM   *         PROFIT = PROFIT ON SALE                       *
180   REM   *         TPROF = TOTAL PROFIT ALL SALES                *
190   REM   *         NUM = NUMBER OF CARS SOLD                     *
200   REM   *         SOLD = NO. OF CARS SOLD BY SALESMAN           *
210   REM   *         TIQOH = TOTAL INITIAL QUANTITY ON HAND        *
220   REM   *         TNUM = TOTAL ALL NUMBER OF CARS SOLD          *
230   REM   *         TQOH = TOTAL ALL QUANTITY ON HAND             *
240   REM   *         TPROFIT = TOTAL PROFIT ALL CARS SOLD          *
250   REM   *         TCOMM = TOTAL ALL COMMISSIONS PAID            *
260   REM   *         TSOLD = TOTAL CARS SOLD BY SALESMEN           *
270   REM   *         B = BUICK                                     *
280   REM   *         F = FORD                                      *
290   REM   *         P = PONTIAC                                   *
300   REM   *         ENDSW = END OF DATA SWITCH                    *
310   REM   *         CARSW = PROCESS SALE SWITCH                   *
320   REM   ********************************************************
330         PRINT  "COPYRIGHT (C) 1989, BY MERRILL PUBLISHING COMPANY"
340         PRINT  "FOR USE WITH STRUCTURED BASIC PROGRAMMING"
350   REM   ****************
360   REM   * MAIN PROGRAM *
370   REM   ****************
380   REM   PERFORM 'PROCESS INITIAL INVENTORY' SUBROUTINE
390         GOSUB 470
400   REM   PERFORM 'PROCESS SALES DATA' SUBROUTINE
410         GOSUB 1050
420   REM   PERFORM 'PRODUCE MANAGEMENT REPORTS' SUBROUTINE
430         GOSUB 2640
440   REM   PERFORM 'END OF PROGRAM MESSAGE' SUBROUTINE
450         GOSUB 3190
460         END
470   REM   **************************************
480   REM   * PROCESS INITIAL INVENTORY SUBROUTINE *
490   REM   **************************************
500   REM   PERFORM 'SET UP INITIAL INVENTORY' SUBROUTINE
510         GOSUB 550
520   REM   PERFORM 'END OF SET UP MESSAGE' SUBROUTINE
530         GOSUB 950
540         RETURN
550   REM   **************************************
560   REM   * SET UP INITIAL INVENTORY SUBROUTINE *
570   REM   **************************************
580   REM   PERFORM 'READ IQOH DATA' SUBROUTINE
590         GOSUB 630
600   REM   PERFORM 'PRINT IQOH DATA' SUBROUTINE
610         GOSUB 840
620         RETURN
```

200

```
630     REM   ******************************
640     REM   * READ IQOH DATA SUBROUTINE *
650     REM   ******************************
660           CLS
700           PRINT "ENTER STARTING INVENTORY FOR ALL MAKES"
710           PRINT
720           PRINT "PLEASE MAKE SURE PRINTER IS ON"
730           PRINT
740           PRINT "BUICK...."
750           PRINT "FORD....."
760           PRINT "PONTIAC.."
770           LOCATE 8,10:  INPUT IQOHB
780           LOCATE 9,10:  INPUT IQOHF
790           LOCATE 10,10: INPUT IQOHP
800           QOHB = IQOHB
810           QOHF = IQOHF
820           QOHP = IQOHP
830           RETURN
840     REM   ******************************
850     REM   * PRINT IQOH DATA SUBROUTINE *
860     REM   ******************************
870           LPRINT
880           LPRINT "                    BEGINNING INVENTORY"
890           LPRINT "                  INITIAL QUANTITY ON HAND"
900           LPRINT
910           LPRINT "              BUICK       FORD        PONTIAC"
920           F$ = "              ##          ##          ##"
930           LPRINT USING F$;IQOHB,IQOHF,IQOHP
940           RETURN
950     REM   **********************************
960     REM   * END OF SET UP MESSAGE SUBROUTINE *
970     REM   **********************************
980           LPRINT
990           LPRINT
1000          LPRINT " INITIAL QUANTITY ON HAND HAS BEEN PROCESSED"
1010          LPRINT
1020          LPRINT
1030          LPRINT
1040          RETURN
1050    REM   **********************************
1060    REM   * PROCESS SALES DATA SUBROUTINE *
1070    REM   **********************************
1080    REM   PERFORM 'INPUT SALES DATA' SUBROUTINE
1090          GOSUB 1150
1100    REM   PERFORM 'PROCESS SALES UNTIL END OF DATA' SUBROUTINE
1110          GOSUB 1360
1120    REM   PERFORM 'END OF SALES DATA MESSAGE' SUBROUTINE
1130          GOSUB 2540
1140          RETURN
1150    REM   ******************************
1160    REM   * INPUT SALES DATA SUBROUTINE *
1170    REM   ******************************
1180          CLS
1220          PRINT "ENTER INFORMATION, WHEN COMPLETE PRESS RETURN"
1230          PRINT "WHEN ALL SALES HAVE BEEN RECORDED TYPE 0 FOR SALESMAN"
1240          PRINT
1250          PRINT "SALESMAN ....."
1260          PRINT "DESCRIPTION..."
1270          PRINT "PRICE........."
1280          PRINT "COST.........."
1290          LOCATE 7,15: INPUT SMAN
1300          LOCATE 8,15: INPUT DES$
1310          LOCATE 9,15: INPUT PRC
```

```
1320        LOCATE 10,15:INPUT CST
1330        IF SMAN = 0 THEN ENDSW = 1
1340        CARSW = 0
1350        RETURN
1360   REM  *************************************************
1370   REM  * PROCESS SALES UNTIL END OF DATA SUBROUTINE *
1380   REM  *************************************************
1390        ENDSW = 0
1400        WHILE ENDSW = 0
1410   REM  PERFORM 'DETERMINE CAR DESCRIPTION' SUBROUTINE
1420        GOSUB 1490
1430   REM  PERFORM 'DETERMINE SALESMAN COMMISSION' SUBROUTINE
1440        IF CARSW = 1 THEN GOSUB 2280
1450   REM  PERFORM 'INPUT SALES DATA' SUBROUTINE
1460        GOSUB 1150
1470        WEND
1480        RETURN
1490   REM  *************************************************
1500   REM  * DETERMINE CAR DESCRIPTION SUBROUTINE *
1510   REM  *************************************************
1520   REM  PERFORM 'PROCESS BUICK' SUBROUTINE
1530        IF DES$ = "BUICK" THEN GOSUB 1590
1540   REM  PERFORM 'PROCESS FORD' SUBROUTINE
1550        IF DES$ = "FORD" THEN GOSUB 1660
1560   REM  PERFORM 'PROCESS PONTIAC' SUBROUTINE
1570        IF DES$ = "PONTIAC" THEN GOSUB 1730
1580        RETURN
1590   REM  ***************************
1600   REM  * PROCESS BUICK SUBROUTINE *
1610   REM  ***************************
1620   REM  IF "AVAILABLE " PERFORM 'CALCULATE BUICK STATISTICS'
1630   REM  IF "OUT OF STOCK" PERFORM 'OUT OF STOCK MESSAGE'
1640        IF QOHB > 0 THEN GOSUB 1920 ELSE GOSUB 1800
1650        RETURN
1660   REM  **************************
1670   REM  * PROCESS FORD SUBROUTINE *
1680   REM  **************************
1690   REM  IF "AVAILABLE " PERFORM 'CALCULATE FORD STATISTICS'
1700   REM  IF "OUT OF STOCK" PERFORM 'OUT OF STOCK MESSAGE'
1710        IF QOHF > 0 THEN GOSUB 2040 ELSE GOSUB 1800
1720        RETURN
1730   REM  *****************************
1740   REM  * PROCESS PONTIAC SUBROUTINE *
1750   REM  *****************************
1760   REM  IF "AVAILABLE " PERFORM 'CALCULATE PONTIAC STATISTICS'
1770   REM  IF "OUT OF STOCK " PERFORM 'OUT OF STOCK MESSAGE'
1780        IF QOHP > 0 THEN GOSUB 2160 ELSE GOSUB 1800
1790        RETURN
1800   REM  **********************************
1810   REM  * OUT OF STOCK MESSAGE SUBROUTINE *
1820   REM  **********************************
1830        LPRINT
1840        LPRINT
1850        LPRINT
1860        F1$ = "                        OUT OF STOCK \         \"
1870        LPRINT USING F1$;DES$
1880        LPRINT
1890        LPRINT
1900        LPRINT
1910        RETURN
1920   REM  **********************************************
1930   REM  * CALCULATE BUICK STATISTICS SUBROUTINE *
1940   REM  **********************************************
1950        IF SMAN = 1 THEN COMM = .1 * PRC
```

202

```
1960          IF SMAN = 2 THEN COMM = .15 * PRC
1970          IF SMAN = 3 THEN COMM = .2 * PRC
1980          PROFITB = PRC - CST - COMM
1990          TPROFB = TPROFB + PROFITB
2000          NUMB = NUMB + 1
2010          CARSW = 1
2020          QOHB = QOHB - 1
2030          RETURN
2040   REM    ******************************************
2050   REM    * CALCULATE FORD STATISTICS SUBROUTINE *
2060   REM    ******************************************
2070          IF SMAN = 1 THEN COMM = .1 * PRC
2080          IF SMAN = 2 THEN COMM = .15 * PRC
2090          IF SMAN = 3 THEN COMM = .2 * PRC
2100          PROFITF = PRC - CST - COMM
2110          TPROFF = TPROFF + PROFITF
2120          NUMF = NUMF + 1
2130          CARSW = 1
2140          QOHF = QOHF - 1
2150          RETURN
2160   REM    ******************************************
2170   REM    * CALCULATE PONTIAC STATISTICS SUBROUTINE *
2180   REM    ******************************************
2190          IF SMAN = 1 THEN COMM = .1 * PRC
2200          IF SMAN = 2 THEN COMM = .15 * PRC
2210          IF SMAN = 3 THEN COMM = .2 * PRC
2220          PROFITP = PRC - CST - COMM
2230          TPROFP = TPROFP + PROFITP
2240          NUMP = NUMP + 1
2250          CARSW = 1
2260          QOHP = QOHP - 1
2270          RETURN
2280   REM    ******************************************
2290   REM    * DETERMINE SALESMAN COMMISSION SUBROUTINE *
2300   REM    ******************************************
2310   REM    PERFORM 'CALCULATE SALESMAN COMMISSION' SUBROUTINE
2320          IF SMAN = 1 THEN GOSUB 2360
2330          IF SMAN = 2 THEN GOSUB 2420
2340          IF SMAN = 3 THEN GOSUB 2480
2350          RETURN
2360   REM    ******************************************
2370   REM    * CALCULATE SALESMAN 1 COMMISSION SUBROUTINE *
2380   REM    ******************************************
2390          COMM1 = COMM1 + COMM
2400          SOLD1 = SOLD1 + 1
2410          RETURN
2420   REM    ******************************************
2430   REM    * CALCULATE SALESMAN 2 COMMISSION SUBROUTINE *
2440   REM    ******************************************
2450          COMM2 = COMM2 + COMM
2460          SOLD2 = SOLD2 +1
2470          RETURN
2480   REM    ******************************************
2490   REM    * CALCULATE SALESMAN 3 COMMISSION SUBROUTINE *
2500   REM    ******************************************
2510          COMM3 = COMM3 + COMM
2520          SOLD3 = SOLD3 + 1
2530          RETURN
2540   REM    ******************************************
2550   REM    * END OF SALES DATA MESSAGE SUBROUTINE *
2560   REM    ******************************************
2570          LPRINT
2580          LPRINT
2590          LPRINT "                        ALL SALES DATA HAS BEEN PROCESSED"
```

```
2600       LPRINT
2610       LPRINT
2620       LPRINT
2630       RETURN
2640  REM  *****************************************
2650  REM  * PRODUCE MANAGEMENT REPORTS SUBROUTINE *
2660  REM  *****************************************
2670  REM  PERFORM 'CALCULATE MANAGEMENT STATISTICS' SUBROUTINE
2680       GOSUB 2740
2690  REM  PERFORM 'PRODUCE AUTOMOBILE SALES REPORT' SUBROUTINE
2700       GOSUB 2840
2710  REM  PERFORM 'PRODUCE SALESMAN COMMISSION REPORT' SUBROUTINE
2720       GOSUB 3020
2730       RETURN
2740  REM  ***********************************************
2750  REM  * CALCULATE MANAGEMENT STATISTICS SUBROUTINE *
2760  REM  ***********************************************
2770       TIQOH = IQOHB + IQOHF + IQOHP
2780       TNUM = NUMB + NUMF + NUMP
2790       TQOH = QOHB + QOHF + QOHP
2800       TPROFIT = TPROFB + TPROFF + TPROFP
2810       TCOMM = COMM1 + COMM2 + COMM3
2820       TSOLD = SOLD1 + SOLD2 + SOLD3
2830       RETURN
2840  REM  ***********************************************
2850  REM  * PRODUCE AUTOMOBILE SALES REPORT SUBROUTINE *
2860  REM  ***********************************************
2870       LPRINT "           AUTOMOBILE SALES REPORT"
2880       LPRINT " DESCRIPTION  IQOH   SOLD   QOH   PROFIT"
2890       LPRINT
2900       F2$ = "  BUICK          ##     ##     ##   $ #,###.##"
2910       F3$ = "  FORD           ##     ##     ##   $ #,###.##"
2920       F4$ = "  PONTIAC        ##     ##     ##   $ #,###.##"
2930       F5$ = "     TOTAL      ###    ###    ###   $##,###.##"
2940       LPRINT USING F2$;IQOHB,NUMB,QOHB,TPROFB
2950       LPRINT USING F3$;IQOHF,NUMF,QOHF,TPROFF
2960       LPRINT USING F4$;IQOHP,NUMP,QOHP,TPROFP
2970       LPRINT USING F5$;TIQOH,TNUM,TQOH,TPROFIT
2980       LPRINT
2990       LPRINT
3000       LPRINT
3010       RETURN
3020  REM  ***************************************************
3030  REM  * PRODUCE SALESMAN COMMISSION REPORT SUBROUTINE  *
3040  REM  ***************************************************
3050       LPRINT "       SALESMAN COMMISSION REPORT"
3060       LPRINT " SALESMAN       COMMISSION       NUMBER SOLD"
3070       LPRINT
3080       F6$ = "    1           $ #,###.##          ##"
3090       F7$ = "    2           $ #,###.##          ##"
3100       F8$ = "    3           $ #,###.##          ##"
3110       F9$ = "  TOTAL         $##,###.##         ###"
3120       LPRINT USING F6$;COMM1,SOLD1
3130       LPRINT USING F7$;COMM2,SOLD2
3140       LPRINT USING F8$;COMM3,SOLD3
3150       LPRINT USING F9$;TCOMM,TSOLD
3160       LPRINT
3170       LPRINT
3180       RETURN
3190  REM  **********************************
3200  REM  * END OF PROGRAM MESSAGE SUBROUTINE *
3210  REM  **********************************
3220       LPRINT
```

```
3230        LPRINT
3240        LPRINT "      END OF AUTOMOBILE DEALERSHIP PROGRAM"
3250        RETURN
3260   REM
3270        END
```

SUMMARY

The IF/THEN, IF/THEN/ELSE, ON/GOTO, and ON/GOSUB are decision-making statements used in structured design BASIC programs. Most business program applications use one or more of these to select formulas to be used or logical sequences to be followed under various conditions.

The IF/THEN is comprised of a condition portion followed by one or more imperatives. If the condition is true, the imperatives that follow the condition are executed; if the condition is false, the next executable instruction following the IF statement is executed. The IF/THEN/ELSE is similar to the IF except that when the condition is not true, the imperatives stated after ELSE are executed, and they are executed before the next executable instruction that follows the IF statement. For these two statements, both the number and the type of imperatives used are flexible. Most systems permit nearly any BASIC statement to be the imperative in an IF statement, such as INPUT, PRINT, GOSUB, GOTO, and so on, including another IF. Multiple imperatives (more than one statement is executed when the condition is true) are permitted in BASIC.

The condition evaluated in the IF can consist of BASIC variables, constants, relational operators, mathematical operators, and the logical operators AND and OR. Most BASIC systems include the following relational operators: =(equal to), > (greater than), <(less than), <> or NOT = (not equal to), >= (greater than or equal to), and <= (less than or equal to). These relational operators can be joined with the logical operators to construct all of the necessary evaluation condition statements.

Often, it is necessary to choose between more than two alternatives, which can make the IF/THEN and the IF/THEN/ELSE ineffective. For these applications, ON/GOTO or ON/GOSUB is used. These statements cause a branch to the appropriate statement or subroutine depending on the numeric value of the variable named after ON. The advantage of the ON/GOSUB or ON/GOTO may be offset by the disadvantage of having to use a numeric key field. Generally, if items, people, and so on are easily coded into integer identifications, ON/GOTO and ON/GOSUB are acceptable alternatives to numerous IF/THEN statements. The IF/THEN and the IF/THEN/ELSE are often used to compare alphabetic or numeric data and information to one another. In the computer's binary code the value that determines the outcome of comparisons proceeds on the basis of the following hierarchy: blank; special characters (!,@,#,$,%); numbers (1,2,3,4,5,6,7,8,9,0); uppercase letters (A,B,C,D,E, etc.); lower-case letters (a,b,c,d,e,etc.).

Care must be taken when comparing string alphabetic and alphanumeric data because some systems will eliminate the spaces between strings if the strings are not input with enclosing quotation marks. This problem can always be solved by placing strings in quotation marks on INPUT or in DATA statements.

Computer-assisted instruction (CAI) is a method whereby the computer can be programmed to teach, review, and test users on a variety of topics. The three principles of CAI are (1) present factual information, (2) quiz the user on the information and review and/or reward as appropriate, and (3) test the user on comprehension, retention, and skill by administering tests or quizzes.

BASIC is particularly suited to CAI because of the wide variety of features such as interactive statements, color, sound, and graphics, all of which can be programmed with relatively simple syntax and very concise commands.

205

COMMON ERRORS AND SOLUTIONS

Error	Example	Solution
1. Improper use or understanding of the relational operators, >, <, =, <>, >=, <=.	10 IF A > B THEN 100 20 IF A = B THEN 200 20 IF (A − B = 0.00001 THEN 200 (no diagnostics given, only incorrect results)	The expression evaluated tests the numeric value for A against B. If A and B are integers, there is no problem. Note: The computer system approximates decimal numbers so a match may not occur.
2. Misunderstanding of AND logic.	10 IF (A = B) and (C = D) THEN 100 (no diagnostic given, only incorrect results)	This means A must = B *and* C must = D for a branch to occur.
3. Misunderstanding of OR logic.	10 IF (A = B) OR (C = D) THEN 100	If *either* or both conditions are true, the branch will occur.

4. Attempting to compare variables of different types.	10 IF A$ = B THEN 20
	(Type mismatch)
		These types of comparisons are valid:
		Numeric varible to numeric literal
		   IF (A = 10)
		String variable to string literal
		   IF (A$ = 'YES')
		Numeric expression to numeric expression
		   IF (A + 1) > (B + 1)
		String variable to string variable
		   IF A$ < B$
		Numeric variable to numeric variable
		   IF A < B
		Numeric expression to numeric variable
		   IF A + 10 <= B
		Numeric variable to numeric expression
		   IF A <> B ^ 2

5. Improper use of multiple imperatives (statements) resulting from true condition.	10 IF A = B THEN C = C + 1 20 PRINT A should be 10 IF A = B THEN C = C + 1: PRINT A	Use the appropriate multiple statement per line symbol (if available) to link the imperatives.
6. Branching out of a subroutine from an IF statement.	100 IF A$ = "END" GOTO 1000 110 (Logic) 120 RETURN	Always branch to the end of the subroutine containing the IF. Set switches, if necessary, to signal occurrences to the main program.

7. Misunderstanding of values of characters in ASCII code, resulting in false condition results.	10 IF A$ > B$ THEN 100
	   where A$ = "23-1A1"
	          B$ = "AA-000"
	
	(numbers are less than letters)
		Check the ASCII code values for numbers, letters, and special characters so that you can select the correct conditional test for the logic you desire.

8. Misunderstanding and/or misuse of IF/THEN/ELSE statement	10 IF A = 10 THEN 50 ELSE 60 Same as 10 IF A = B THEN 50 30 GOTO 60 50 PRINT "EQUAL"	The ELSE option is executed if the condition tested is false, but never at any other time. It is easily simulated with IF/THEN logic and merely reduces coding.
9. Writing confusing compound logic statements that are hard to interpret and/or debug.	10 IF A = B OR C = 1 AND D = 10 OR E = 5 THEN 20	Place conditions in parentheses and around OR logical conditions: IF ((A = B) OR (C = 1)) AND ((D = 10) OR (C = 5)), etc.

COMMON ERRORS AND SOLUTIONS

Error	Example	Solution
10. False results due to incorrectly combined AND and OR logic.	In example 9, the conditions linked by OR are evaluated first. If neither is true, the entire expression is false.	Practice with examples of AND and OR logic, and check your interpretation with the results from your programs to be sure they are consistent.
11. Getting lost with IF/THEN logic, especially in programs with loops and conditional branching.		The use of the TRACE instructions in BASIC makes it possible to see exactly what sequence of instructions is being executed in your program. (See appendix A or your BASIC manual for the exact form of the TRACE ON and TRACE OFF statements.)

12. Branching to a line number that has been deleted or changed during program codification.	10 IF N\$ = "EOF"
	     THEN 100
	   .
	   .
	   .
	90 RETURN
	100 (next routine)
	
	(logic or syntax error if 100 does not exist in routine)
		When you modify your programs, i.e., add and delete statements or change the logic, be sure that the decision statments refer to the correct branch points and existing statement numbers.

13. Unexpected results when comparing string variables of different size.	N1\$ = John Smith N2\$ = John Smith II 10 IF N1\$ = Ns\$ THEN 100 (Condition is false)	Remember, the shorter string variable is "padded" with blanks, which have the lowest binary value. Therefore, the shorter field will always be less than the longer field.
14. Improper use or interpretations of the NOT operator.	10 IF NOT (A = B) THEN 100 Same as 10 IF A<>B THEN 100	The NOT operator reverses the condition. That is, if the condition is *false,* the imperative will be executed; if the condition is *true,* it will not. Avoid this operator and write the conditions in the usual manner.

REVIEW QUESTIONS

1. Give five examples of applications where decisions are programmed and then briefly describe the decisions to be made in the programs.
2. What is the name of the statements used for decision in structured design programs?
3. Draw a flowchart for the IF/THEN structure indicating the entry and exit points, the decision symbol, and an operation symbol.
4. For the IF/THEN structure in question 3, under what circumstances is the operation performed? Explain.
5. Give a specific example of an IF/THEN construct in a business program problem.
6. What occurs in an IF/THEN structure when the condition is false?
7. Explain the difference between the IF/THEN and the IF/THEN/ELSE constructs.
8. Give a specific example of a case in which an IF/THEN/ELSE construct would be preferred to an IF/THEN.
9. Draw an IF/THEN/ELSE construct for a typical business problem. Include the entry and exit points and the operations. State the condition alternatives.
10. Draw the IF/THEN/ELSE construct as a flowchart.
11. Can the IF/THEN/ELSE construct be fabricated on systems that do not support this statement? Explain with an example.

12. Write a complete BASIC statement to perform the IF/THEN in the case of a customer credit balance that exceeds a credit limit and necessitates a reminder letter. Use more than one statement, if necessary on your system.

13. Write the IF/THEN/ELSE construct to compute an employee's pay with and without overtime. Assume that the overtime pay rate is 1.5 times the normal pay rate and that overtime pay is computed when the employee has worked more than 40 hours and is applied only to those hours exceeding 40.

14. Convert the construct in question 13 to BASIC using the statements available on your system. Input the hours worked and pay rate from the terminal, and print the regular pay, the overtime pay, and the total pay.

15. Often, the IF/THEN and the IF/THEN/ELSE involve more than one operation for each condition. Draw an example of such constructs.

16. Draw the IF/THEN/ELSE construct for the following problem. A student has taken three exams. You must find the average of the three exams, print that average, and print the student's name. If the student has taken fewer than three exams, you must print the student's name and a message that states "MISSING EXAM(S)." (Consider each operation separately when you draw the construct.)

17. Write a BASIC program that will accomplish the construct in question 16. Input the student's name, the number of tests, and the test scores from the display. If your system permits multiple imperatives, use that feature. If not, devise a method of performing the separate operations for each condition.

18. What structure is often used when evaluating more than two alternatives? Describe when this type of structure would be useful in a business problem.

19. Use ON/GOSUB for an inventory control application where the items sold by a retail store are indicated by part numbers 1, 2, 3, 4, and 5.

20. If your system supports ON/GOSUB, write a BASIC statement to process the data in question 19 so that the computer will print what item was sold. Input to the program will consist of only the part number of the item sold.

21. Write a BASIC program that will accumulate the number of each type of item sold. Print out the total number of each type of item sold, and place the program in a loop where processing continues until a code (END-OF-DATA) is reached.

22. Write as many forms of the imperative as your system supports for the IF statement. For example:

```
IF [condition] THEN 500
IF [condition] GOTO 500
IF [condition] GOSUB 500
```

Use a specific condition for your examples, such as the account-over-limit condition described in the chapter.

23. In the ON/GOSUB statement, what type of number must the following expressions be? Why?

```
ON [expression] GOTO 100,200,300
ON [expression] GOSUB 100,200,300
```

24. Write the relational operators supported by your system to test the following conditions: equal to; greater than; less than; greater than or equal to; less than or equal to; not equal to.

25. Logical operators make it possible to join conditions for complex decisions. Give examples of the logical operators most often used.

26. Describe the following BASIC statement:

```
IF A = B and C = D THEN GOSUB 100
```

Under what condition will subroutine 100 be executed? When will it not be executed?

27. Describe under what condition(s) subroutine 200 will be executed. When will it *not* be executed?

```
IF LIMIT >1000 OR PASTDUE >30 GOSUB 200
```

28. What is the *key* difference between AND logic and OR logic?
29. When comparing string data in IF statements, explain the hierarchy of values for alphanumeric data; in other words, which have values greater than others on your system: numbers; capital letters; small letters; special characters?
30. In the following example, will subroutine 500 be executed? Why or why not?

```
IF [ROBERT > ROBERTA] GOSUB 500
```

31. Name the principles involved in writing a computer-assisted instruction tutorial.
32. Why has CAI become popular?
33. What properties of BASIC lend it to CAI programming?

PROBLEMS FOR SOLUTION

1. A pet store sells four different kinds of pets, and its management would like to know which pets are the biggest sellers, which contribute the most to profit, and when to reorder a particular type of pet when the supply drops below a certain level. The four types of animals are dogs, cats, birds, and tropical fish (within each species, of course, there are variations, but these are ignored in this simplified program).

    Data for each sale is entered on a sales terminal and then processed at the time of sale. The initial inventory level for each species is entered at the beginning of the program run as number of dogs, number of cats, number of birds, and number of tropical fish. Also entered at the beginning of the program run is the reorder point, which is the number of each species to which the supply on hand must drop before management will send a reorder message to the pet wholesaler.

    Write a structured BASIC program using the simple selection (IF/THEN) structure that will produce the desired output based on the specifications provided in the problem definition. During the business day, the data entered into the program will look like this:

Sale Number	Type of Animal	Selling Price	Cost to Store
1	Dog	$235.00	$100.00
2	Bird	17.00	9.00
3	Fish	6.50	0.80
4	Cat	160.00	12.00
5	Dog	95.00	32.00

The program will check the type of animal sold, compute the number of that species sold, compute the profit earned on that sale, list the new quantity on hand, check the quantity on hand against the reorder point (MQOH), and print a reorder message.

Input Specification

	Field No.	Field Description	Type	Example
Initial	1.2	QOH Cats, MQOH Cats	Integer	25,5
Inventory	3.4	QOH Dogs, MQOH Dogs	Integer	15,10
Record	5.6	QOH Birds, MQOH Birds	Integer	30,5
	7.8	QOH Fish, MQOH Fish	Integer	10,8
Sales	1	Discription of Pet Sold	Alphabetic	Bird
Record	2	Selling Price	Decimal Number	195.00
	3	Cost to Sore	Decimal Number	85.00

209

Processing Decisions and Formulas

For Each Pet Type:

$$\text{Number Sold} = \text{Number Sold} + 1$$
$$\text{QOH} = \text{QOH} - 1$$
$$\text{Profit Earned} = \text{Profit Earned} + \text{Profit on Sale}$$
$$(\text{Profit on Sale} = \text{Selling Price} - \text{Cost to Store})$$

General:

$$\text{Total Profit} = \text{sum of profits for all sales (or all pet types)}$$
$$\text{Total Pets Sold} = \text{sum of all sales (or number sold in all categories)}$$

Reorder message issued when QOH for pet type $<$ MQOH for pet type.

Output

```
CHICKEN (S) ARE NOT IN STOCK


                      SALES DATA REPORT

                   DOGS      CATS      BIRDS     FISH
QUANTITY SOLD        0         0         1         0
QUANTITY IN STOCK   15        25        29        10
PROFIT EARNED      $0.00     $0.00   $110.00    $0.00
                 TOTAL NUMBER OF PETS SOLD:      1
                 TOTAL PROFIT EARNED      :   $110.00
```

Error Routines

Print an error message if an attempt is made to sell an animal *not* in stock or not in normal inventory.

Validation Procedure

Check the statistics calculated by evaluating the sales transactions by hand. Check that the reorder messages appear when needed, and that the sale of a pet not in inventory results in the appropriate error message.

2. In many retail furniture stores, the commissions that the sales staff receive for items sold are based on a percentage of the retail price of each item and the commission rate. Therefore, in addition to keeping track of furniture inventory, sales, and profits, the management also would like to record the commission earned by each salesperson to ensure that appropriate payments are made (and, perhaps, that bonuses are awarded to the "top" salespeople).

Assume that the furniture store sells only four types of items (chairs, tables, couches, and lamps—coded 1, 2, 3, and 4, respectively) and that there are only three salespeople (Jones, Smith, and Rivera—1, 2, 3, respectively), each of whom receives a sales commission of 10% of the item selling price.

The initial inventory level and the reorder point for each type of item are input at the beginning of the week, and sales are processed each day on the store's point-of-purchase computer terminals. The sales transactions entered include not only the code number, the price, and the cost of each item of furniture sold, but also the code number of the salesperson who made the sale (so that commissions can be calculated and accumulated for each salesperson).

Since both the item sold and the salesperson who sold it have integer code numbers, write a structured BASIC program using the case control construct (ON/GO-SUB) to produce the inventory and commission reports that management requires.

Input Specifications

	Field No.	Field Description	Type	Example
Initial	1,2	QOH Couches, MQOH Couches	Integer	15,5
Inventory	3,4	QOH Tables, MQOH Tables	Integer	5,3
Record	5,6	QOH Chairs, MQOH Chairs	Integer	25,10
	7,8	QOH Lamps, MQOH Lamps	Integer	30,10
Sales	1	Code for Item Type Sold	Integer	1 (=Couch)
Transaction	2	Code for Salesperson Making Sale	Integer	3 (=Rivera)
Record	3	Selling Price of Item	Decimal Number	365.00
	4	Cost to Store of Item	Decimal Number	175.00

Processing Decisions and Formulas

For Each Furniture Type:

$$\text{Number Sold} = \text{Number Sold} + 1$$
$$\text{QOH} = \text{QOH} - 1.$$
$$\text{Profit} = \text{Profit} + \text{Profit on Sale}$$
$$(\text{Profit on Sale} = \text{Price} - \text{Cost})$$

General Sales Data:

$$\text{Total Profit} = \text{Sum of Profits for All Items}$$
$$\text{Total Items Sold} = \text{Sum of Numbers Sold, Each Item}$$

Reorder message issued when QOH < MQOH, each item.

For Each Salesperson:

$$\text{Commission on Sale} = \text{Price} * .10$$
$$\text{Total Commission} = \text{Total Commission} + \text{Commission on Sale}$$

Output

```
        REORDER MESSAGE
CURRENT LEVEL OF TABLE    (S) IS:  3
TIME TO REORDER TABLE     (S)
MINIMUM QUANTITY ON HAND IS:  3
WRONG NUMBER, TRY AGAIN!


           SALES DATA REPORT

               COUCHES   TABLES   CHAIRS   LAMPS
QUANTITY SOLD     0         2        2        1

QUANTITY IN STOCK 13        3        23       29

PROFIT EARNED    $50.00  $100.00  $215.00  $25.00
```

* Driver and car characteristics may be input as alphanumeric or alphabetic data if desired. Converting the classifications to numeric integer codes is designed to reduce coding and permit use of ON/GOSUB statements, if desired.

```
                          TOTAL NUMBER OF ITEMS SOLD:  7

                          TOTAL PROFIT EARNED      :  $390.00

                   SALESPERSON COMMISSION REPORT

          SALESPERSON CODE        COMMISSION EARNED
                 1                     $107.50

                 2                     $10.00

                 3                     $42.50

          TOTAL COMMISSION PAID :        $160.00
```

Test Data

QOH, MQOH	15, 5, 5, 3, 25, 10, 30, 10
Sales Record	1, 3, 365.00, 175.00
	2, 2, 100.00, 50.00
	3, 1, 75.00, 60.00
	4, 3, 60.00, 35.00
	2, 1, 400.00, 350.00
	3, 1, 600.00, 400.00
	1, 4, 200.00, 150.00

Error Routines

Print error messages under the following conditions:

Attempt is made to sell item other than code 1 through 4.

Attempt is made to credit sale to salesperson with code *other* than 1, 2, or 3.

Validation Procedure

Check program output by evaluating sales transactions by hand, particularly in the case of erroneous item or salesperson codes.

3. When insurance companies compute the premiums that a person pays for automobile accident and theft insurance, they take a great many factors into consideration. Generally, an applicant's driving record (number and severity of accidents and instances of moving violations, such as speeding), the characteristics of the car being insured (sports car, compact, or full size—in other words, its type and value), and the amount of liability coverage desired, especially in serious accident cases, are prime considerations.

If you reduce the factors to a reasonably simplified subset of the factors considered by insurance company rate-determination programs, you can simulate the relevant program concepts with a relatively straightforward BASIC program. In this example, then, you will include the following driver and car characteristics:

CAR CHARACTERISTICS
Value of car in dollars (<2000, 2000–6000, or >6000)
Type of car (full size, medium size, or compact)
Car use (pleasure, work, or work and pleasure)
Miles driven per year ($<10{,}000$, 10,000–20,000, or $>20{,}000$)

DRIVER CHARACTERISTICS
Number of accidents of driver (0, 1, 2, or more)
Number of moving violations (0, 1, 2, or more)
Age of driver (>25, 18–25, <18)
Liability coverage desired in dollars (100,000, 200,000, or 300,000)

Further, you will assume that the following rate factor table is used to multiply a base rate of $100 per year to arrive at the annual premium.

Driver and Car Characteristics	Rate Multiplication Factors Categories		
	1	2	3
Value of car	<2000 1.0	(2000–6000) 1.2	>6000 1.6
Type of car	Full size 1.0	Medium size 1.1	Compact size 1.2
Car use	Pleasure 1.0	Business 1.5	Business and pleasure 2.0
Miles driven per year	<10,000 1.0	10,000–20,000 1.2	>20,000 1.4
Number of accidents	None 1.0	One 2.0	Two or more 4.0
Number of moving violations	None 1.0	One 1.5	Two or more 2.0
Age of driver	>25 1.0	18–25 1.2	<18 1.4
Amount of coverage desired	$100,000 1.0	$200,000 1.3	$300,000 1.6

The data input and the desired output are shown below. To simplify coding and reduce the complexity of BASIC statements, you may input the car and driver characteristics with a numeric code (i.e., 1, 2, or 3, respectively) for each of the categories in the table. Remember that the total premium will be the result of repetitive multiplication of the base code rate ($100) by the factors in each of the eight categories.

Input Specifications

Field No.	Field Description	Type	Example
1	Driver's Name	Alphabetic	John Grath
2	Driver's Address (Number, Street)	Alphanumeric	125 South St.
3	Driver's Address (City, State, Zip)	Alphanumeric	Austin, Texas 43216
4	Value of Car	Integer	1
5	Type of Car	Integer	1
6	Car Use	Integer	2
7	Miles Driven/Year	Integer	1
8	Number of Past Accidents	Integer	3
9	Number of Past Moving Violations	Integer	1
10	Age of Driver	Integer	2
11	Amount of Liability Coverage Desired	Integer	2

Processing Decisions and Formulas

Use the "Rate Multiplication Factor Table" to multiply the basic insurance premium of $100 by the appropriate factors for each of the eight categories listed, e.g.

$$\text{Premium} = 100 * (\text{Rate Factor** for ``Value of Car''})$$
$$\text{Premium} = \text{Premium} * (\text{Rate Factor for ``Type of Car''})$$
$$\text{Premium} = \text{Premium} * (\text{Rate Factor for ``Car Use''})$$
$$\text{etc.}$$

Be sure to include all eight factors in the table. If you like, contact your insurance company and find out what other factors it considers, and add these to the program.

Output

```
         INSURANCE PREMIUM ESTIMATE
PREPARED FOR  :  JOHN GRATH
ADDRESS       :  125 SOUTH ST
                 AUSTIN TEXAS 43216

VALUE OF CAR   : 1 (1) < 2000 (2) 2000-6000 (3) > 6000
TYPE OF CAR    : 1 (1) FULL SIZE (2) MEDIUM SIZE (3) COMPACT SIZE
CAR USE        : 2 (1) PLEASURE (2) BUSINESS (3) BOTH
MILES/YEAR     : 1 (1) < 10,000 (2) 10,000-20,000 (3) > 20,000
NO. ACCIDENTS  : 3 (1) NONE (2) ONE (3) TWO OR MORE
NO. VIOLATIONS : 1 (1) NONE (2) ONE (3) TWO OR MORE
DRIVER'S AGE   : 2 (1) > 25 (2) 18-25 (3) < 18
COVERAGE       : 2 (1) $100,000 (2) $200,000 (3) $300,000
TOTAL ESTIMATED ANNUAL PREMIUM : $1,200.00
```

Test Data

John Grath, 125 South St, Austin Texas 43216, 1, 1, 2, 1, 3, 1, 2, 2
(Make up additional data if you like, perhaps for yourself or friends)

Error Routines

Provide error messages for classifications not included in the rate factor table, and skip the record being processed if this error occurs since this estimate would be inaccurate.

Validation Procedure

Calculate one final premium estimate by hand to verify the program output. Also check for proper editing of numeric fields and centering under titles and headings.

4. Most airline companies sell the majority of tickets through authorized travel agencies. In order to determine the frequency of visits by airline representatives to these agencies, incentives, and useful statistics, airlines categorize the agencies according to the volume of business (revenue) that such agencies provide.

In the following problem, you will assume that a category 1 agency produces over $100,000 in revenue per year for the airline, that a category 2 agency produces between $50,000 and $100,000, that a category 3 agency produces between $25,000 and $50,000, and that a category 4 agency produces less than $25,000. Further, you will assume that airline management would like to know the following information:

1. The number of agencies in each of the four revenue categories.
2. The average revenue in each category.
3. The total revenue in each category.
4. The total of all revenues from all agencies.
5. The total number of all agencies and the average revenue for all agencies.

**This program is a much simplified version of premium determination programs actually in use, and the rate factors used are purely fictitious for use in this simplified example.

Input for this program will consist of the total yearly revenue produced by each agency for the airline, as shown below. For this simple input, write a structured BASIC program that will produce the management report described by the output specifications.

Input Specifications

Field No.	Field Description	Type	Example
1	Total Annual Revenue for Agency	Integer	150000

Processing Decisions and Formulas

Class "1" Agency : Revenue $\geq$ $100,000 per year
Class "2" Agency : Revenue $\geq$ $50,000 but less than $100,000 per year
Class "3" Agency : Revenue $\geq$ $25,000 but less than $50,000 per year
Class "4" Agency : Revenue $<$ $25,000 per year

Output

```
                  AGENCY REVENUE REPORT
        TOTAL NUMBER OF AGENCIES IN EACH CATEGORY
            1         2         3         4
            2         3         3         2
                  TOTAL YEARLY REVENUE
        $350,000  $225,000  $95,000   $38,000

                  AVERAGE YEARLY INCOME
        $175,000   $75,000   $31,667   $19,000
           TOTAL NUMBER OF AGENCIES  :   10
           TOTAL REVENUE ALL AGENCIES: $708,000
        AVERAGE REVENUE ALL AGENCIES:  $70,800
```

Test Data

```
150000
200000
90000
75000
60000
40000
30000
25000
20000
18000
```

Error Routines

None required.

Validation Procedure

Verify the number of agencies in each category by evaluating the data by hand. Select one agency category, and calculate the total and average revenue in that category. Also, check for proper editing of numeric fields, and make sure that the output is centered under titles and headings.

215

5. A company would like to analyze and adjust the salaries of its employees to determine the total cost of salary increases based on merit and cost-of-living adjustments. Assume that the company is proposing a schedule of salary increases to adjust salary levels among its employees, and that according to it, all employees will receive a 6 across-the-board cost-of-living increase. Also, employees will receive additional percentage increases based on their current salaries, as shown below:

Employee's Current Salary per Year	Adjustment (Percentage Increase in Salary)
Greater than $60,000	4%
Greater than or equal to $40,000, but less than $60,000	6%
Greater than or equal to $20,000, but less than $40,000	8%
Greater than or equal to $15,000, but less than $20,000	9%
Less than $15,000	10%

Write a structured BASIC program that will (1) classify the number of employees in each salary group; (2) compute their individual increases; (3) total the increases in each salary group; and (4) compute the total cost of the salary adjustment program to the company.

Field No.	Field Description	Type	Example
1	Employee's I.D. Number	Integer	12345
2	Employee's Name	Alphabetic	John Jones
3	Current Salary ($/year)	Integer	65000

Processing Decisions and Formulas

Employee's New Salary = (Employee's current salary) * (1.06 + Adjustment)

Adjustment is based on current salary as described above.

Output

```
                     SALARY ADJUSTMENT TABLE
  EMP. NO      EMPLOYEE NAME  CURRENT SALARY  ADJUSTED SALARY  PERCENT INC.
  12345    JOHN JONES            $65,000         $650,000         10.0
   9751    MARY LINDY             $9,000         $144,000         16.0
  73452    FRANK SAMPSON         $26,640         $372,960         14.0
  33322    DAVID ROSE            $45,000         $540,000         12.0
  77777    IAN YORK              $59,500         $714,000         12.0

              COMPANY SALARY ADJUSTMENT STATISTICS
  SALARY GROUP              NUMBER OF EMPL.        TOTAL DOLLAR INCREASE
       1                          1                    $650,000
       2                          2                  $1,254,000
       3                          1                    $372,960
       4                          0                          $0
       5                          1                    $144,000
  TOTAL DOLLARS INCREASE FOR ALL EMPLOYEES:  $2,420,960
  TOTAL NUMBER OF EMPLOYEES AFFECTED     :          5
  AVERAGE PERCENT INCREASE - ALL EMPLOYEES:       12.8
  AVERAGE DOLLAR  INCREASE - ALL EMPLOYEES:    $484,192
```

Error Routines

None required.

Validation Procedure

Check the number of employees who fall into each salary group and verify the program output. Calculate a few salary increases based on the criteria described and verify the program calculations. Check for proper editing of numeric fields, and make sure that output is centered under the headings.

6. Academic achievement is rewarded at many schools by placing students with high performance records on the Dean's Honor List. The requirements vary, but generally if your grade point average (GPA) is equivalent to B (a 3.0 average, based on a maximum of 4.0) or higher, you are awarded this honor. GPA's are computed on the basis of the following equivalencies:

Grade	Quality Points
A	4
B	3
C	2
D	1

Quality points multiplied by the number of credit hours for the course yields the total number of points for the course. The total of all points received for all courses divided by the total number of credits taken then yields the GPA, or the quality point average, as it is sometimes also called.

Write a structured BASIC program that will accept data from the keyboard (for up to six courses), as shown in the problem definition, and that will produce the two Dean's List reports as illustrated.

Field No.	Field Description	Type	Example
1	Student Name	Alphabetic	Alice Watson
2	Grade in Course 1	Alphabetic	A
3	Number of Credits for Course 1	Integer	3
4	Grade in Course 2	Alphabetic	B
5	Number of Credits in Course 2	Integer	2
6	Grade in Course 3	Alphabetic	B
7	Number of Credits in Course 3	Integer	3
8	Grade in Course 4	Alphabetic	A
9	Number of Credits in Course 4	Integer	4

Processing Decisions and Formulas

Quality Points for Course = (Points for Grade) * Number of Credits for Course.

Quality Point Average = Sum of Quality Points/Total Credits

Dean's List of Quality Point Average ≥ 3.0

Output

```
              STUDENT NAME   GRADES AND CREDITS  DL
    ALICE WATSON             A 3 B 2 B 3 A 4   YES
    JOHN MORAN               A 3 A 3 A 3 A 3   YES
    VAN OLSON                B 2 B 3 A 4 C 4   YES
    JOYCE CHIN               A 3 B 3 A 2 C 2   YES
    CARMEN RIVERA            A 2 A 3 B 3 B 4   YES
    BILL WRIGHT              C 2 C 3 C 4 D 1   NO
```

```
      PHYLISS CHENEY          A 2 B 3 C 4 D 2   NO
      LARRY HOLMES            C 2 D 2 C 4 C 4   NO
      CAROL BRONSON           A 3 B 2 C 3 A 4   YES
      ED WOODHOUSE            A 3 A 3 B 2 C 4   YES
      DEAN'S LIST REPORT
      TOTAL NUMBER OF STUDENTS    :   10
      TOTAL NUMBER ON DEAN'S LIST:    7
      PERCENT ON DEAN'S LIST      : 70.0
```

Test Data

Alice Watson, A, 3, B, 2, B, 3, A, 4,
John Moran, A, 3, A, 3, A, 3, A, 3
Van Olson, B, 2, B, 3, A, 4, C, 4
Joyce Chin, A, 3, B, 3, A, 2, C, 2
Carmen Rivera, A, 2, A, 3, B, 3, B, 4
Bill Wright, C, 2, C, 3, C, 4, D, 1
Phyliss Cheney, A, 2, B, 3, C, 4, D, 2
Larry Holmes, C, 2, D, 2, C, 4, C, 4
Carol Bronson, A, 3, B, 2, C, 3, A, 4
Ed Woodhouse, A, 3, A, 3, B, 2, C, 4

Routines

None required.

Validation Procedure

Check the Grade Point Average calculation for one student and verify the program results. Verify the number and percent of students on the Dean's Honor List.

7. Using the eating and drinking test taken from the American Medical Association's *Family Medical Guide*,* write a structured BASIC program that will (1) ask the 14 questions on the display; (2) compute a score for the respondent based on the number of ''Yes'' answers; and (3) print out the following three messages, depending on the score: If score = 90% or higher: ''Your eating and drinking habits are excellent. Keep up the good work!''

   If score > 50, but < 90: ''Your eating and drinking habits could stand some modification. Check the questions to which you answered no, and consider changing your routine.''

   If score < 50: ''Your eating and drinking habits are not good! It is important that you consider a major change if you wish to stay healthy.''

   If score <25: ''Wow! You may be heading for big trouble if you don't change your eating and drinking habits promptly.''

---

*Reprinted from Jeffrey R. M. Kunz, M.D., The American Family Medical Guide (New York: Random House, 1982).

Are you eating and drinking sensibly?

This questionnaire tests the prudence of your current eating and drinking habits. For a questionnaire that deals specifically with drinking alcohol, read Are you drinking too much alcohol? (see p.32).

Answer YES or NO to the following questions

1 Is your weight within the normal range for your height (see the weight chart on p.28)?

YES ☐ NO ☐

2 Do you generally have two or three medium-sized meals a day rather than occasional snacks and one big meal?

YES ☐ NO ☐

3 Do you make a point of setting aside specific times for leisurely meals instead of eating hastily while continuing your other activities?

YES ☐ NO ☐

4 Do you limit your use of fats and use mainly polyunsaturated cooking oil and margarine?

YES ☐ NO ☐

5 Do you eat fried foods sparingly, and limit yourself to no more than three or four helpings of fried food a week?

YES ☐ NO ☐

6 Do you eat no more than four eggs a week?

YES ☐ NO ☐

7 Do you drink, on average, several glasses of water or skim milk each day?

YES ☐ NO ☐

8 Do you have a generous portion of at least two high-fiber foods every day?

YES ☐ NO ☐

9 Do you often choose to eat fish or poultry rather than red or fatty meats such as beef or pork?

YES ☐ NO ☐

10 For between-meal snacks and desserts do you eat fresh fruit rather than cakes, pies and cookies?

YES ☐ NO ☐

11 Do you avoid lavish use of salty foods such as pickles, pretzels and potato chips?

YES ☐ NO ☐

12 Do you limit your use of salt and always taste foods before salting them?

YES ☐ NO ☐

13 Do you drink tea or coffee without sugar, and do you avoid sweet soft drinks?

YES ☐ NO ☐

14 Do you limit your intake of coffee to five cups a day?

YES ☐ NO ☐

EVALUATION
The more YES answers you gave, the healthier your diet and the more sensible your eating habits. The following pages explain why. The more NO answers you gave, the more important it is that you consider a change in your eating habits.

CHAPTER SEVEN

INTRODUCTION TO TABLES AND ARRAYS

OUTLINE

LEARNING OBJECTIVES

Upon completion of this chapter, you will be able to:

☐ Understand why tables are important in business programming applications.

☐ Use the techniques for allocating memory space for tables and assigning variable names.

☐ Understand what subscripts are and how they are used.

☐ Use the techniques for loading, printing, and searching tables.

☐ Understand and use two important data retrieval techniques: sequential search and direct access.

TABLES—GENERAL CONCEPTS

You can compare a table (often called an array) to an apartment building, where the entire building represents the table and the individual apartments inside the building represent the records within the table. Within each apartment, there are rooms, which are like the fields that make up the records (see figure 7–1). Each apartment contains a livingroom, diningroom, bathroom, and two bedrooms, which are differentiated from other livingrooms, diningrooms, bathrooms, and bedrooms in the building by the apartment number that labels them as a group. Similarly, a record consists of fields that are grouped together within the record by a common identification, usually the record number. This record number differentiates one record from another and identifies the group of fields in that record from other groups of fields in other records. The identifying number for a record in a table is shown in parentheses after the field to which it refers (e.g., PAY RATE (1), PAY RATE (2), etc.). This identifying number is called a subscript.

Records are "loaded" into tables by inputting data from a keyboard, tape, or disk while varying the locating number (subscript) so that each field within each new record gets its own location in the table. Records also are retrieved from a table by varying the location number. This can be done in a variety of ways, as you will see shortly. Usually, computer memory must be allocated in advance for programs containing tables. The size of the table is usually determined by the maximum number of records expected, and may be larger than, but never smaller than, the records in the table.

So, before you continue with this chapter, you should know and fully understand the following key facts about tables.

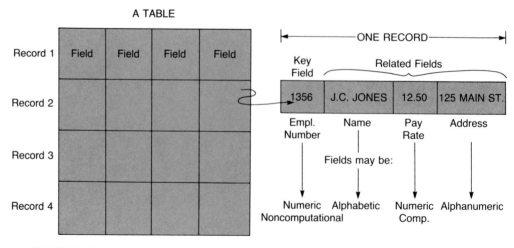

FIGURE 7–1
Apartment building analogy.

1. Tables can contain thousands of records. The number is limited only by the amount of random access memory (RAM) available on your BASIC system.
2. Records can consist of fields of numeric, alphabetic, or alphanumeric data.
3. Usually there is one key field and one or more related fields in each table record.
4. All fields that share the same location in each record have the same symbolic name. These fields are differentiated from the field(s) in other records by a subscript.
5. Subscript numbers designate a location in the table.
6. The key field of a record is usually the main field. It shows that the record belongs to a particular person, item, or place. It does not have to be the first field in the record, and there can be more than one key field.
7. Records in a table may be searched for and located by following three principal methods (to be discussed in detail in this chapter).

The Importance of Tables in Business Programming

In all case studies in chapters 1 through 6, each record was processed by the computer and when processing was complete, the storage location reserved for that record and its fields was replaced with data from the next record. In those cases, it was not important to store the records in memory before processing began because each record was independent of the next and sequential processing made sense. However, in a great many business applications, all data records must be available concurrently. For example, if you want to arrange records in a particular order (sorting) or if you want to quickly find a record (retrieve) containing a specific part number, flight number, account number, or customer name, it is necessary to have all records in storage at the same time. Processing time required to select a particular record is decreased significantly when all information is in main memory.

To illustrate the efficiency of tables and table processing more closely, consider the steps needed to load three records into memory and store them concurrently if table processing were not possible. Say that the three records consist of an account number field, a name field, and an account balance field. The records will require nine separate memory locations, all with unique variable names, to store the data. These are shown in figure 7–2.

Imagine how cumbersome and time consuming inputting and coding would be if you wanted to store 1,000 or 2,000 records of this type. That processing would require thousands of variable names, thousands of input instructions, and an inordinate amount of patience. It also would waste a large amount of computer time. Table processing eliminates these problems. The remainder of the chapter will deal with various methods of setting up tables.

SETTING UP TABLES

Table routines allow you to group like fields under one variable name, providing that you reserve a storage area at the beginning of your program sufficient to accommodate all the variables. To allocate storage you use the DIM statement.

Account Number 1	Name 1	Balance on Acct. 1
236	JONES	250.00

Account Number 2	Name 2	Balance on Acct. 2
165	SMITH	175.00

Account Number 3	Name 3	Balance on Acct. 3
869	BROWN	650.00

Variable Names

```
ACCOUNT1,NAME1,BALANCE1
ACCOUNT2,NAME2,BALANCE2
ACCOUNT3,NAME3,BALANCE3
```

FIGURE 7–2
Memory locations.

223

The DIM Statement

Whenever a table containing more than ten records is to be set up in your programs, you must include a DIM statement to allocate memory space for it (or any record within it) is referred to. The format for the DIM (DIMension) statement is:

```
line# DIM variable (subscript), variable (subscript), etc.
```

where the variable may be of any type.

When executed, the DIM statement not only allocates the required memory, but also sets all string variable space to blank and all numeric variables to 0. If a table is used without a DIM statement, the table variables are valid, but only ten records are permitted. Exceeding the maximum (subscript) number of a table produces a "subscript out of range" error. You may use a 0 as a subscript, but this has a special purpose (see Appendix A under option base).

So, if you set up a table of example records, the new variable names for the example in figure 7–2 would be:

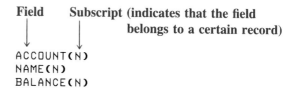

Field   **Subscript (indicates that the field belongs to a certain record)**

```
ACCOUNT(N)
NAME(N)
BALANCE(N)
```

Remember the variable N, which is the subscript, shows that a field belongs to a particular record. It then becomes possible to load any number of records and their respective fields into memory with simple logic where N is varied from 1 to 3 by the counter step N = N + 1. The flowchart and program for this processing is shown in figure 7–3. Note from the program that when the FOR/NEXT loop is completed, the table is loaded. (The purposes of statement 10, although not specifically required in this program, are explained below.)

Since in the program I, the FOR/NEXT loop counter, varies automatically from 1 to 3, it can replace N as the subscript. You then can use similar logic to vary the value of N to print all the records stored in the table. Figure 7–4 shows the flowchart, program, and output for this operation.

Using Counters and FOR/NEXT to Vary Subscripts

Another convenient method of varying the subscript is to use the FOR/NEXT loop. As described in chapter 5, if the FOR/NEXT STEP option is omitted, the default is +1. Starting and ending values can be constants or variables, which may be positive or negative decimal numbers or integers. But, for table processing, the constants or variables must be integers, and the STEP value is usually either +1 or −1. Here are some example statements for table processing with FOR/NEXT.

```
10 FOR N = 1 TO 100
20 NEXT N
10 FOR N = NS TO NE
20 NEXT N
10 FOR N = 1 TO NR
20 NEXT N
```

You can even process table records starting from the last record position to the first. The following FOR/NEXT instructions can be used to do this:

```
10 FOR N = 100 TO 1 STEP -1
   .
   .
   .
90 NEXT N
```

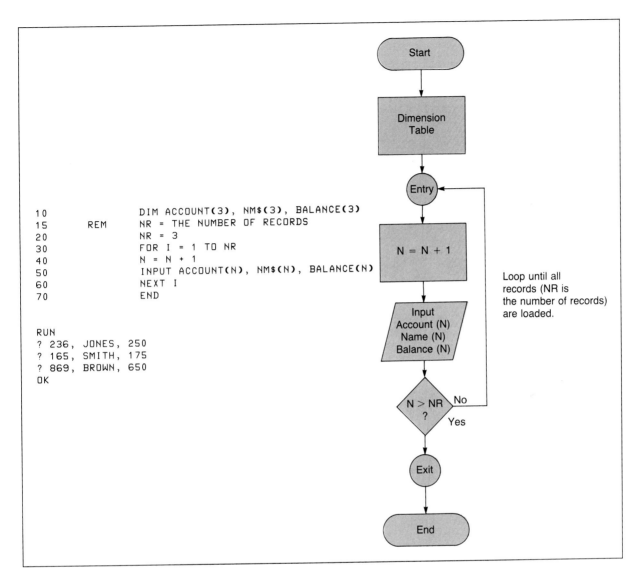

```
10          DIM ACCOUNT(3), NM$(3), BALANCE(3)
15    REM   NR = THE NUMBER OF RECORDS
20          NR = 3
30          FOR I = 1 TO NR
40          N = N + 1
50          INPUT ACCOUNT(N), NM$(N), BALANCE(N)
60          NEXT I
70          END


RUN
? 236, JONES, 250
? 165, SMITH, 175
? 869, BROWN, 650
OK
```

Loop until all records (NR is the number of records) are loaded.

FIGURE 7-3
Flowchart with result in memory.

It is important to print table contents before processing data in the table to make sure what you think is in the table is actually there.

For table programs with more than a few records in the table, it is wise to load the table using the READ/DATA combination instead of INPUT. This gives you the advantage of not having to retype the table data again if something occurs later in your program to cause it to stop before normal termination. This is especially true during program development, since an execution halting error followed by a run command causes all fields in the table to be lost.

SEQUENTIAL SEARCH

Theory of Sequential Search

Sequential searching of table data allows you to retrieve data easily and efficiently. The method is simple and is widely used in many business applications. After setting up and printing a table, the key field of a desired record is input. It then is compared to every key field for every record in the table until a match is found. When a match occurs, the matching record fields may be printed, updated, deleted, or transferred to another location de-

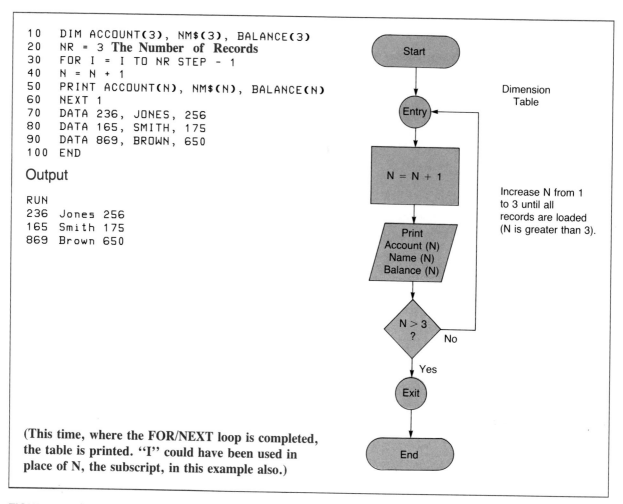

```
10   DIM ACCOUNT(3), NM$(3), BALANCE(3)
20   NR = 3 The Number of Records
30   FOR I = I TO NR STEP - 1
40   N = N + 1
50   PRINT ACCOUNT(N), NM$(N), BALANCE(N)
60   NEXT 1
70   DATA 236, JONES, 256
80   DATA 165, SMITH, 175
90   DATA 869, BROWN, 650
100  END
```

Output

```
RUN
236  Jones 256
165  Smith 175
869  Brown 650
```

(This time, where the FOR/NEXT loop is completed, the table is printed. "I" could have been used in place of N, the subscript, in this example also.)

FIGURE 7–4
Printing a table.

pending on program logic (see figure 7–5.) The key field can be any data type (numeric, alphabetic, or alphanumeric), and the records need not be in any special order. However, since every record in the table up to and including the desired record must be compared, this method of searching is slow. This is the only serious limitation of sequential search applications.

An example of a simple sequential search program is one in which you would input the names and phone numbers of all your friends, as shown in figure 7–6. Then, if

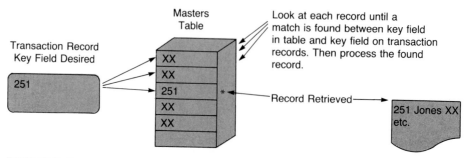

FIGURE 7–5
Simple sequential search summary.

226

you wanted to know one of their phone numbers, you would simply type in the name of the friend you wanted to phone, and the program would print the number on the display or print it on the printer. Such a program is not much different from the phone company's directory assistance system, except that you could set up your directory using first names or last names only, even nicknames. And, of course, your system would contain fewer records.

Naturally, the only phone numbers you could retrieve would be the numbers that you input, but you would avoid spending much time typing in lots of names and numbers because tables are lost when the computer is turned off.

FIGURE 7–6
Sequential search program.

```
Input

10      REM       *****************************************
20      REM       * THIS PROGRAM SETS UP, PRINTS, AND    *
30      REM       * SEARCHES A TABLE OF NAMES AND PHONE  *
40      REM       * NUMBERS.                             *
50      REM       *****************************************
60      REM
70      REM       ***************************
80      REM       * VARIABLE LEGEND:        *
90      REM       *  I    = SUBSCRIPT        *
100     REM       *  NM$  = NAME             *
110     REM       *  PHNO$ = PHONE NUMBER    *
120     REM       *  N$    = NAME TO SEARCH  *
130     REM       ***************************
140     REM
150     REM       ****************
160     REM       * MAIN PROGRAM *
170     REM       ****************
180     REM       PERFORM 'TABLE SET-UP' SUBROUTINE
190               GOSUB 250
200     REM       PERFORM 'TABLE PRINT' SUBROUTINE
210               GOSUB 470
220     REM       PERFORM 'TABLE SEARCH' SUBROUTINE
230               GOSUB 570
240               END
250     REM       ****************
260     REM       * TABLE SET-UP *
270     REM       ****************
290               DIM NM$(100),PHNO$(100)
300     REM       NOTE THAT THE TABLE HAS BEEN ALLOCATED FOR
310     REM       A MAXIMUM OF 100 ENTRIES (RECORDS), ALTHOUGH
320     REM       WE WILL PROBABLY INPUT FEWER THAN 100, THIS IS ACCEPTABLE
330               FOR I = 1 TO 10
340               READ NM$(I), PHNO$(I)
350               NEXT I
360               DATA JOHN,232-4040
370               DATA MARY, 666-7890
380               DATA AL, 456-2343
390               DATA BRIAN, 232-5555
400               DATA BILL, 888-5645
410               DATA ALICE, (212) 455-1212
420               DATA BIG JOHN, (303) 566-8888
430               DATA LITTLE JOHN, (303) 566-8877
440               DATA LOIS, 666-9988
450               DATA EASTWOOD, (807) 456-1234
460               RETURN
470     REM       **************
480     REM       * TABLE PRINT *
```

```
490      REM      * * * * * * * * * * * * * * *
500      REM      PRINT THE TELEPHONE "DIRECTORY" TO CHECK IT. THIS IS
510      REM      ALWAYS A GOOD PRACTICE WHEN SETTING UP TABLES
520      REM
530               FOR I = 1 TO 10
540               LPRINT NM$(I), PHNO$(I)
550               NEXT I
560               RETURN
570      REM      * * * * * * * * * * * * * * *
580      REM      * TABLE SEARCH *
590      REM      * * * * * * * * * * * * * * *
600      REM      INPUT THE NAME OF THE PERSON WHOSE PHONE NUMBER YOU WANT.
610               INPUT " ENTER NAME OF PERSON ";N$
620               LPRINT N$
630      REM      SEARCH THE TABLE UNTIL THE NAMES MATCH (N$ = NM$(I))
640               FOR I = 1 TO 10
650               IF N$ = NM$(I) THEN LPRINT NM$(I), PHNO$(I)
660               NEXT I
670      REM
680      REM      IF YOU WANT TO LOOK UP ANOTHER NUMBER, LOOP BACK.
690      REM
700               INPUT " WANT TO FIND ANOTHER ? (Y OR N) ";A$
710               IF A$ = "Y" THEN 610
720      REM      PRINT " END OF PROGRAM " MESSAGE
730               LPRINT " INQUIRIES COMPLETED - PROGRAM FINISHED"
740               RETURN
750      REM      END OF PROGRAM
```

Output

```
JOHN            232-4040
MARY            666-7890
AL              456-2343
BRIAN           232-5555
BILL            888-5645
ALICE           (212) 455-1212
BIG JOHN        (303) 566-8888
LITTLE JOHN     (303) 566-8877
LOIS            666-9988
EASTWOOD        (807) 456-1234
EASTWOOD
EASTWOOD        (807) 456-1234
 INQUIRIES COMPLETED - PROGRAM FINISHED
```

Phone Number Illustration—Set-Up, Print, and Search

The simple telephone number search program in figure 7–6 shows the three important steps in table processing in their logical sequence: table set-up, table print, and table search. The main program calls three subroutines to accomplish the three steps. Subroutine 1, TABLE SET-UP, reads ten names and phone numbers from DATA statements and places these in the table allocated in the DIM statement (line 290).

Subroutine 2, TABLE PRINT, prints the table records in the printer to verify the contents of the table. This is critical since many hours of debugging time might be wasted trying to find a logic error in a program that has incorrect data in the original table. Always verify the table's contents by printing the entire table after the INPUT or READ/DATA containing subroutine. Do not just put a PRINT statement after the INPUT or READ in the input routine because this may not always show what data has wound up in your table.

Subroutine 3, TABLE SEARCH, first inputs the name of the person whose phone number you're looking for and then does a sequential search of the entire table. When a match occurs in the IF statement (line 650), then the phone number for that person is displayed and/or printed.

If more than one match occurs, then more than one phone number is retrieved. That is not unrealistic because often there is more than one listing of popular or common names.

Payroll-Sequential Search

CONCEPTS TO BE ILLUSTRATED

Often sequential processing of table data involves more than simply retrieving information from the table. Tabular data may be updated, sorted, used for calculations and reports, and more. When a program involves these operations, it is called interactive processing and/or updating program. Figure C7–1 illustrates that in this case, the inquiry into the table will be made on the basis of an employee name and the pertinent payroll data will be retrieved from the table. The data retrieved will not just be displayed or printed. It will be used to calculate values for a paycheck and to update certain fields within the table, such as year-to-date (YTD) gross pay. Updating YTD gross pay involves calculating the current gross pay by multiplying the hours worked (from the transaction time sheet) by the hourly pay rate for the correct employee (located by sequentially searching the table). This value of gross pay is used not only in subsequent calculations (for numbers that appear on the paycheck), but it also is added back into the table value for current gross pay. In other words, the YTD gross pay in the master table becomes an accumulator which is increased every time each employee's time sheet is processed. That is why the arrow points in both directions from the program box to the table in figure C7–1. This represents a table update step.

The key field used in the access step may come from a time card or time sheet. It is the field used to locate the desired record in the table. In payroll, the key field is

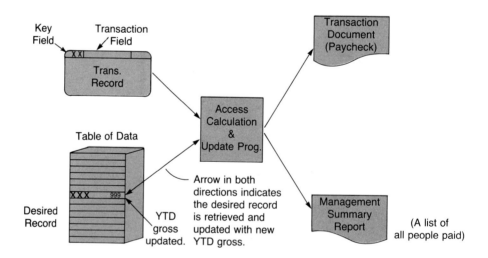

The transaction record may consist of a time card or time sheet, which indicates the employee's name and the number of hours that he or she worked:

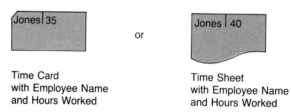

Time Card
with Employee Name
and Hours Worked

or

Time Sheet
with Employee Name
and Hours Worked

FIGURE C7–1
Accessing tables with updates.

usually the employee's name or identification number. The processing involves a sequential search of the master table until the name on the time card or time sheet is matched with a name in the table. When that occurs, processing of the pay figures can begin because the pay rate deductions and other information can be retrieved from the table record. Also, the table field YTD__GROSS can be updated to reflect the addition of the gross pay for the current pay period.

Although actual payroll records are usually stored on files and contain many more fields than indicated here, this example can show many payroll processing steps accurately enough.

Table C7–1 presents an abridged payroll master table consisting of eight records. These records are loaded into the table so that the employee number fields are in sequence (although any order would be satisfactory). The table has been set up this way so that it may be accessed directly by employee number or sequentially by employee name. (The direct access is illustrated later. The employee numbers appear in this example solely for consistency with the next case. They are *not* used here!)

Naturally one of the requirements of a payroll system is that a paycheck be produced. The table must also be updated with a new YTD GROSS. These steps are in addition to retrieving fields such as employee's address and pay rate, which is then multiplied by the hours worked (taken from the time card or time sheet) to compute the gross pay for the period. (You will ignore overtime and deduction calculations for this example.) So:

$$\text{Gross Pay} = \underset{\underset{\text{From Time Card}}{\uparrow}}{\text{Hours}} \quad * \quad \underset{\underset{\text{From Retrieved Table Record}}{\uparrow}}{\text{Pay Rate (I)}}$$

TABLE C7–1
Simplified payroll master table.

Record	Employee Number	Name	Address	Age	Marital Status	Pay Rate	YTD Gross Pay
1	001	Jones, C	12 S. Main	42	S	$12.50	$ 8,000.00
2	002	Smith, R	8 RT. 6	26	M	7.20	4,600.00
3	003	Brown, L	12 TR. 9	29	S	9.20	5,000.00
4	004	White, W	125 Oak	19	D	4.80	3,072.00
5	005	Black, O	10 Maple	31	M	15.60	10,560.00
6	006	East, M	North Ln.	48	M	6.30	4,032.00
7	007	West, D	RT. 30	22	S	5.90	3,776.00
8	008	North, S	1 Collins	19	S	6.00	3,890.00

PROBLEM DEFINITION

Input Specifications

The input consists of two types of records:
1. The master payroll table of payroll records.
2. Transaction cards for sequential search.
   These are shown below.

	Field No.	Field Description	Type	Example
Payroll	1	Employee Number	Integer	11234
Processing—	2	Employee Name	Alphabetic	Carol Jones
Master	3	Address	Alphanumeric	12 Main St.
Table	4	Age	Integer	42
Records	5	Marital Status	Alphabetic	S
	6	Pay Rate per Hour	Decimal Number	12.50
	7	Year-to-Date Gross Pay	Decimal Number	11,000.00
Time	1	Employee Name	Alphabetic	Carol Jones
Card	2	Hours Worked	Decimal Number	40.00

Processing Decisions and Formulas

1. Calculate the weekly gross pay for each employee.

$$\text{Gross Pay} = \text{Hours} * \text{Pay Rate}$$

2. Calculate the updated YTD-gross pay for each employee.

$$\text{YTD-Gross Pay} = \text{YTD-Gross Pay} + \text{Gross Pay}$$

3. Locate the desired record by sequential search.
4. Print a paycheck.
5. Update YTD-Gross Pay in Master Table.
6. Terminate processing with a last record containing "EOD".

Output

1. The master table printed with titles
2. Paychecks
3. Updated table with titles

PAYROLL MASTER TABLE

EMPLOYEE NUMBER	EMPLOYEE NAME	EMPLOYEE ADDRESS	AGE	MARITAL STATUS	PAY RATE	YTD GROSS
11234	CAROL JONES	12 MAIN ST	42	S	$12.50	$10,500.00
21345	BOB SMITH	RTE 6	26	M	$7.25	$4,600.00
32451	JOHN BROWN	29 AVON RD	29	S	$9.25	$5,000.00
56413	BILL WHITE	125 OAK ST	19	S	$4.50	$3,000.00
26845	ANNE JAMES	15 PRATT ST	34	M	$8.25	$6,500.00
46578	JACK NORTH	25 COLT RD	19	S	$6.00	$4,000.00
23612	JOAN WEST	RTE 30	27	S	$8.75	$6,800.00
85621	ELLEN KANE	10 GRAND ST	22	S	$7.50	$4,500.00
45376	MARY RAYE	14 MAPLE AVE	48	S	$8.00	$8,500.00
78231	JOE GREEN	54 NORTH ST	45	M	$14.00	$12,000.00

```
* PAYCHECK ISSUED TO EMPLOYEE CAROL JONES    *

******************************************************
*                                                    *
*    EMPLOYEE NO: 11234 HOURS WORKED: 40             *
*                                                    *
*                                                    *
* PAY TO THE ORDER OF: CAROL JONES   $500.00         *
*                                                    *
*                                                    *
******************************************************

   EMPLOYEE NAME NOT FOUND IN TABLE !R BLACK

* PAYCHECK ISSUED TO EMPLOYEE ELLEN KANE     *

******************************************************
*                                                    *
*    EMPLOYEE NO: 85621 HOURS WORKED: 35             *
*                                                    *
*                                                    *
* PAY TO THE ORDER OF: ELLEN KANE   $ 262.50         *
*                                                    *
*                                                    *
******************************************************

* PAYCHECK ISSUED TO EMPLOYEE JACK NORTH     *

******************************************************
*                                                    *
*    EMPLOYEE NO: 46578 HOURS WORKED: 30             *
*                                                    *
*                                                    *
* PAY TO THE ORDER OF: JACK NORTH   $ 180.00         *
*                                                    *
*                                                    *
******************************************************

* PAYCHECK ISSUED TO EMPLOYEE JOE GREEN      *

******************************************************
*                                                    *
*    EMPLOYEE NO: 78231 HOURS WORKED: 40             *
*                                                    *
*                                                    *
* PAY TO THE ORDER OF: JOE GREEN    $560.00          *
*                                                    *
*                                                    *
******************************************************

   ALL PAYCHECKS HAVE BEEN PROCESSED
```

233

```
                    UPDATED MASTER TABLE

EMPLOYEE      EMPLOYEE     EMPLOYEE                 MARITAL
NUMBER        NAME         ADDRESS        AGE       STATUS      PAY RATE      YTD GROSS

11234         CAROL JONES  12 MAIN ST     42        S           $12.50        $11,000.00
21345         BOB SMITH    RTE 6          26        M           $7.25         44,600.00
32451         JOHN BROWN   29 AVON RD     29        S           $9.25         $5,000.00
56413         BILL WHITE   125 OAK ST     19        S           $4.50         $3,000.00
26845         ANNE JAMES   15 PRATT ST    34        M           $8.25         $6,500.00
46578         JACK NORTH   25 COLT RD     19        S           $6.00         $4,180.00
23612         JOAN WEST    RTE 30         27        S           $8.75         $6,800.00
85621         ELLEN KANE   10 GRAND ST    22        S           $7.50         $4,762.50
45376         MARY RAYE    14 MAPLE AVE   48        S           $8.00         $8,500.00
78231         JOE GREEN    54 NORTH ST    45        M           $14.00        $12,560.00


                    END OF PAYROLL PROGRAM
```

Test Data

For sequential search, the data consists of employee name and number of hours worked.

Carol Jones, 40
Ellen Kane, 35
Jack North, 30
Joe Green, 40
EOD, 0

Error Recovery Routines

If the name is not found in the table, then a display message is to be printed containing the error type, the data that was in error, and a recovery feature to resume processing with the next record.

Validation Procedure

Hand calculate all of the figures that were computed for the gross pay and for the YTD-gross pay, and verify that they are correctly calculated. Intentionally attempt to process employees not in the table and verify that error messages are produced and that processing is resumed. Check for correct numeric field editing and centering under headings.

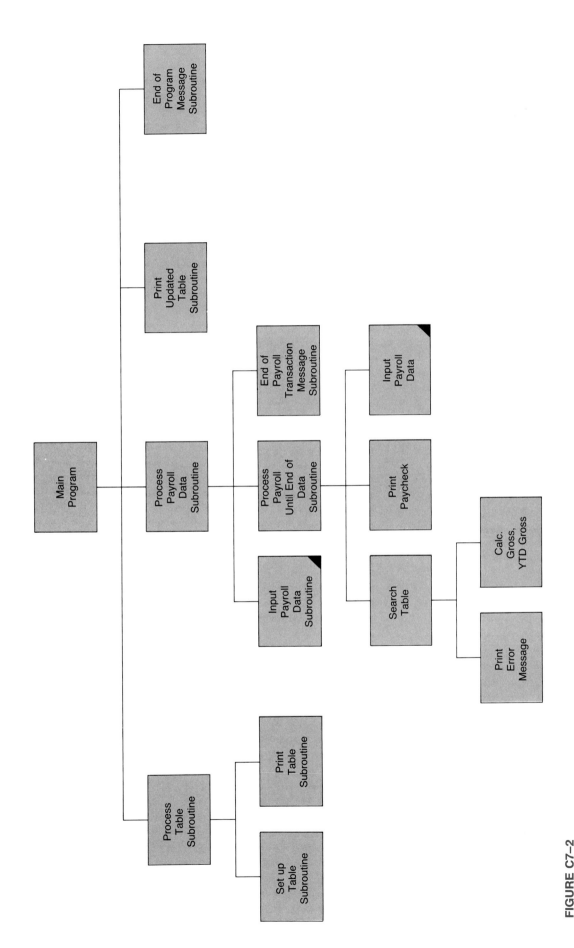

FIGURE C7–2
Visual table of contents—payroll program.

```
 10   REM   *****************************************************
 20   REM   *                    TABLES                         *
 30   REM   *          CASE STUDY: C7-1                          *
 40   REM   *              PAYROLL PROGRAM                       *
 50   REM   * THIS PROGRAM LOADS, PRINTS, AND UPDATES A          *
 60   REM   * MASTER TABLE USING SEQUENTIAL ACCESS               *
 70   REM   *                                                    *
 80   REM   *            VARIABLE LEGEND                         *
 90   REM   *       EMPNO = EMPLOYEE NUMBER                       *
100   REM   *        NM$ = EMPLOYEE NAME                          *
110   REM   *       ADDR$ = EMPLOYEE ADDRESS                      *
120   REM   *        AGE = EMPLOYEE AGE                           *
130   REM   *         M$ = MARITAL STATUS                         *
140   REM   *       PRAT = EMPLOYEE PAY RATE                      *
150   REM   *        YTD = YEAR TO DATE GROSS                     *
160   REM   *        ENO = EMPLOYEE NUMBER (TRANSACTION)          *
170   REM   *        HRS = NUMBER OF HOURS WORKED                 *
180   REM   *       GROSS = GROSS PAY                             *
190   REM   *       ENDSW = END OF DATA SWITCH                    *
200   REM   *       PAYSW = PRODUCE PAYCHECK SWITCH               *
210   REM   *****************************************************
220         PRINT "COPYRIGHT (C) 1989, BY MERRILL PUBLISHING COMPANY"
230         PRINT "FOR USE WITH STRUCTURED BASIC PROGRAMMING"
240   REM   ****************
250   REM   * MAIN PROGRAM *
260   REM   ****************
270   REM
280   REM   PERFORM 'PROCESS TABLE' ROUTINE
290         GOSUB 370
300   REM   PERFORM 'PROCESS PAYROLL DATA' ROUTINE
310         GOSUB 760
320   REM   PERFORM 'PRINT UPDATED TABLE' ROUTINE
330         GOSUB 1760
340   REM   PERFORM 'END OF PROGRAM MESSAGE' ROUTINE
350         GOSUB 1890
360         END
370   REM   ****************
380   REM   * PROCESS TABLE *
390   REM   ****************
400   REM   PERFORM 'SET UP TABLE' ROUTINE
410         GOSUB 450
420   REM   PERFORM 'PRINT TABLE' ROUTINE
430         GOSUB 630
440         RETURN
450   REM   ****************
460   REM   * SET UP TABLE *
470   REM   ****************
480         DIM EMPNO(10),NM$(10),ADDR$(10),AGE(10),M$(10),PRAT(10),YTD(10)
490         FOR I = 1 TO 10
500         READ EMPNO(I),NM$(I),ADDR$(I),AGE(I),M$(I),PRAT(I),YTD(I)
510         NEXT I
520         DATA 11234, CAROL JONES, 12 MAIN ST, 42, S, 12.5, 10500
530         DATA 21345, BOB SMITH, RTE 6, 26, M, 7.25, 4600
540         DATA 32451, JOHN BROWN, 29 AVON RD, 29, S, 9.25, 5000
550         DATA 56413, BILL WHITE, 125 OAK ST, 19, S, 4.5, 3000
560         DATA 26845, ANNE JAMES, 15 PRATT ST, 34, M, 8.25, 6500
570         DATA 46578, JACK NORTH, 25 COLT RD, 19, S, 6, 4000
580         DATA 23612, JOAN WEST, RTE 30, 27, S, 8.75, 6800
590         DATA 85621, ELLEN KANE, 10 GRAND ST, 22, S, 7.5, 4500
600         DATA 45376, MARY RAYE, 14 MAPLE AVE, 48, S, 8, 8500
610         DATA 78231, JOE GREEN, 54 NORTH ST, 45, M, 14, 12000
620         RETURN
```

```
630 REM ***************
640 REM  * PRINT TABLE *
650 REM  ***************
660        LPRINT TAB(30);"PAYROLL MASTER TABLE"
670        LPRINT
680        LPRINT "EMPLOYEE   EMPLOYEE   EMPLOYEE         MARITAL"
690        LPRINT "NUMBER       NAME      ADDRESS   AGE  STATUS  PAY RATE    YTD GROSS"
700        F$ = "#####     \        \\          \   ##    !     $$##.##    $$##,###.##
710        LPRINT
720        FOR I = 1 TO 10
730        LPRINT USING F$;EMPNO(I);NM$(I);ADDR$(I);AGE(I);M$(I);PRAT(I);YTD(I)
740        NEXT I
750        RETURN
760 REM    ***********************
770 REM    * PROCESS PAYROLL DATA *
780 REM    ***********************
790 REM    PERFORM 'PROCESS PAYROLL UNTIL END OF DATA' ROUTINE
800        GOSUB 860
810 REM    PERFORM 'PROCESS PAYROLL UNTIL END OF DATA' ROUTINE
820        GOSUB 1020
830 REM    PERFORM 'END OF PAYROLL TRANSACTION MESSAGE' ROUTINE
840        GOSUB 1680
850        RETURN
860 REM    *********************
870 REM    * INPUT PAYROLL DATA *
880 REM    *********************
890        PAYSW = 0
900        CLS
910        PRINT "ENTER THE DATA ON THE APPROPRIATE LINES AND PUSH "
920        PRINT "RETURN AFTER EACH ENTRY. WHEN YOU ARE FINISHED, "
930        PRINT "TYPE IN 'EOD' ON THE LINE OF THE EMPLOYEE'S NAME "
940        PRINT "AND A '0' FOR THE HOURS WORKED."
950        PRINT:PRINT:PRINT
960        PRINT "ENTER THE EMPLOYEE'S NAME: _____"
970        PRINT "ENTER THE HOURS WORKED:_____"
980        LOCATE 8,28 : INPUT NAM$
990        LOCATE 9,25 : INPUT HRS
1000       IF NAM$ = "EOD" THEN ENDSW = 1
1010       RETURN
1020 REM   ************************************
1030 REM   * PROCESS PAYROLL UNTIL END OF DATA *
1040 REM   ************************************
1050       ENDSW = 0
1060       WHILE ENDSW = 0
1070 REM   PERFORM 'SEARCH TABLE' ROUTINE
1080       GOSUB 1150
1090 REM   PERFORM 'PRINT PAYCHECK' ROUTINE
1100       IF PAYSW = 1 THEN GOSUB 1440
1110 REM   PERFORM 'INPUT PAYROLL DATA' ROUTINE
1120       GOSUB 860
1130       WEND
1140       RETURN
1150 REM   ***************
1160 REM   * SEARCH TABLE *
1170 REM   ***************
1180       FOR I = 1 TO 10
1190 REM   IF "MATCH" PERFORM 'CALCULATIONS' ROUTINE
1200       IF NAM$ =NM$(I) THEN PAYSW = 1:GOTO 1220
1210       NEXT I
1220 REM   IF "MATCH" PERFORM 'CALCULATIONS' ROUTINE
1230 REM             ELSE PERFORM 'ERROR' ROUTINE
1240       IF PAYSW = 1 THEN GOSUB 1370 ELSE GOSUB 1260
1250       RETURN
```

```
1260 REM     ***********************
1270 REM     * PRINT ERROR MESSAGE *
1280 REM     ***********************
1290       LPRINT
1300       LPRINT
1310       LPRINT
1320       LPRINT TAB(15);"EMPLOYEE NAME NOT FOUND IN TABLE !";NAM$
1330       LPRINT
1340       LPRINT
1350       LPRINT
1360       RETURN
1370 REM     *****************************
1380 REM     * CALCULATE GROSS, YTD GROSS *
1390 REM     *****************************
1400       GROSS = HRS * PRAT(I)
1410       YTD(I) = YTD(I) + GROSS
1420       PAYSW = 1
1430       RETURN
1440 REM     *****************
1450 REM     * PRINT PAYCHECK *
1460 REM     *****************
1470       F3$ = "            * PAYCHECK ISSUED TO EMPLOYEE \ \ *"
1480       F4$ = "            **********************************************"
1490       F5$ = "            *                                            *"
1500       F6$ = "            * EMPLOYEE NO: ##### HOURS WORKED: ##         *"
1510       F7$ = "            * PAY TO THE ORDER OF: \        \ $ ###.##    *"
1520       LPRINT
1530       LPRINT USING F3$;NAM$
1540       LPRINT
1550       LPRINT F4$
1560       LPRINT F5$
1570       LPRINT USING F6$;EMPNO(I),HRS
1580       LPRINT F5$
1590       LPRINT F5$
1600       LPRINT USING F7$;NM$(I),GROSS
1610       LPRINT F5$
1620       LPRINT F5$
1630       LPRINT F4$
1640       LPRINT
1650       LPRINT
1660       LPRINT
1670       RETURN
1680 REM     ***********************************
1690 REM     * END OF PAYROLL TRANSACTION MESSAGE *
1700 REM     ***********************************
1710       LPRINT "        ALL PAYCHECKS HAVE BEEN PROCESSED"
1720       LPRINT
1730       LPRINT
1740       LPRINT
1750       RETURN
1760 REM     ****************************
1770 REM     * PRINT UPDATED MASTER TABLE *
1780 REM     ****************************
1790       LPRINT TAB(30); "UPDATED MASTER TABLE"
1800       LPRINT
1810       LPRINT "EMPLOYEE   EMPLOYEE   EMPLOYEE               MARITAL"
1820       LPRINT "NUMBER     NAME       ADDRESS   AGE  STATUS    PAY RATE      YTD GROSS"
1830       F$ = "#####      \        \  \\         \ ##   !      $$###.##    $$##,###.##"
1840       LPRINT
1850       FOR I = 1 TO 10
1860       LPRINT USING F$;EMPNO(I);NM$(I);ADDR$(I);AGE(I);M$(I);PRAT(I);YTD(I)
1870       NEXT I
1880       RETURN
1890 REM     ***********************
1900 REM     * END OF PROGRAM MESSAGE *
1910 REM     ***********************
```

```
1920      LPRINT
1930      LPRINT
1940      LPRINT
1950      LPRINT "                    END OF PAYROLL PROGRAM"
1960      RETURN
1970 REM
1980 REM  END OF PROGRAM
```

Theory of Direct Access

Since records in the payroll table in Case 7–1 have a simple integer that can be used as the key field, the records can be loaded into a table so that the table location number (i.e., the subscript) is the same as the key field number. The employees in the company are numbered 1, 2, 3, etc., and the records are loaded into the table so that employee 1's record occupies record position 1 in the table, employee 2 occupies record position 2, and so on.

With the records loaded this way, if you want to retrieve or update any employee's record, you need only know the employee number and then specify this as the subscript (locator) for the record or for any field in that record. The pay rate for employee 2 is found by simply writing PAY RATE (2) or PAY__RATE (EMPLOYEE__NUMBER). There is no searching when a table subscript is specified explicitly [e.g., with (2) or with a symbolic name (e.g., EMPLOYEE__NUMBER)]. Instead, the correct field (or record) is retrieved directly. This is illustrated in figure 7–7.

The key field can actually be omitted from the table record descriptions (fields) since, by definition, the key field number and the position of the record in the table are identical. Such an omission, however, is not considered good programming practice because if an error in numbering is made, it is very difficult to find.

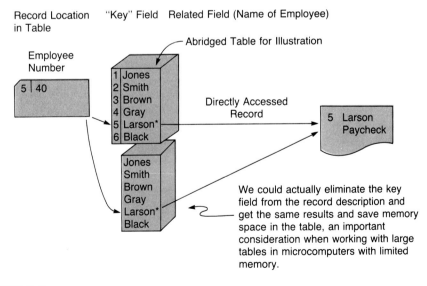

FIGURE 7–7
Direct access summary.

Direct Access Illustration

Consider table 7–1, which lists table customer account data. If you load this table so that each customer is in order according to his or her customer number, and each number corresponds exactly to the record position in the table, then you should be able to access directly any customer's account balance by simply inputting that customer's number and using it as the subscript in a direct access, as follows:

```
10        DIM CUSTNO(10), CUST$(10), ACCTBAL(10)
20        FOR I = 1 TO 10
30        READ CUSTNO(I), CUST$(I), ACCTBAL(I)
40        NEXT I
50        DATA 1,JONES,100
60        DATA 2,SMITH,200
70        DATA 3,BROWN,500
80        DATA 4,ABEL,50
90        DATA 5,CLARK,200
100       DATA 6,ALMAN,400
110       DATA 7,REED,600
120       DATA 8,RAMONE,100
130       DATA 9,BANE,20
140       DATA 10,LARK,100
150 REM   DIRECT ACCESS PORTION
160       FOR I = 1 TO 10
170       PRINT CUSTNO(I),CUST$(I),ACCTBAL(I)
180       NEXT I
190       INPUT "ENTER CUSTOMER ACCOUNT NUMBER ",N
200       PRINT "THE ACCOUNT BALANCE FOR "; CUST$(N)
210       PRINT " IS $";ACCTBAL(N)
220       END
```

Output

```
1             JONES          100
2             SMITH          200
3             BROWN          500
4             ABEL           50
5             CLARK          200
6             ALMAN          400
7             REED           600
8             RAMONE         100
9             BANE           20
10            LARK           100
ENTER CUSTOMER ACCOUNT NUMBER 2
THE ACCOUNT BALANCE FOR SMITH
 IS $ 200
```

TABLE 7–1

Master account table—Direct access illustration.

Customer Number (CUSTNO)	Customer Name (CUST$)	Account Balance (ACCTBAL)
1	Jones	100
2	Smith	200
3	Brown	500
4	Abel	50
5	Clark	200
6	Alman	400
7	Reed	600
8	Ramone	100
9	Bane	20
10	Lark	100

The program is so concise that it's hard to believe it works. Once the table is set up and verified by printing it, the access becomes simply a matter of using the N from INPUT (customer number) as the subscript to go directly to the desired record in the table.

Table 7–2 contains the revised payroll master file which consists of the eight records loaded into a table. These records were loaded into the table so that the employee number fields are in sequence and, in fact, occupy table positions that correspond exactly to the employee numbers. Consequently, this table may be accessed by employee number.

Remember, the employee's number can be used for direct access to the payroll master table only because the table was originally set up to permit this feature. In cases where records have been loaded into the table by employee number in random order, it is possible to sort the master records so that direct access is allowed. Ultimately, the table key field *must* be in strict numeric order. (Sorting will be described in Case 7–3.)

TABLE 7–2
Simplified payroll master table.

Record	Employee Number	Name	Address	Age	Marital Status	Pay Rate	YTD Gross Pay
1	001	Jones, C	12 S. Main	42	S	$12.50	$ 8,000.00
2	002	Smith, R	8 Rt. 6	26	M	7.20	4,600.00
3	003	Brown, L	12 Rt. 9	29	S	9.20	5,000.00
4	004	White, W	125 Oak	19	D	4.80	3,072.00
5	005	Black, O	10 Maple	31	M	15.60	10,560.00
6	006	East, M	North Ln.	48	M	6.30	4,032.00
7	007	West, D	Rt. 30	22	S	5.90	3,776.00
8	008	North, S	1 Collins	19	S	6.00	3,890.00

Payroll Direct Access

CONCEPTS TO BE ILLUSTRATED

This case uses nearly the same problem definition as the previous example, except that the time card or time sheet record now contains the employee number instead of name.

PROBLEM DEFINITION

Input Specifications

The input consists of two types of records:
1. A master payroll table of ten payroll records.
2. Five transactions for direct access search.

	Field No.	Field Description	Type	Example
Master	1	Employee Number	Numeric	01
Table	2	Employee Name	Alphabetic	Jones, C.
Records	3	Address	Alphanumeric	12 Main
	4	Age	Numeric	42
	5	Marital Status	Alphabetic	S
	6	Pay Rate per Hour	Numeric	12.50
	7	Year-to-Date Gross Pay	Numeric	8,000.00
Time	1	Employee Number	Numeric	01
Card	2	Hours Worked	Numeric	10.00

Processing Decisions and Formulas

1. Calculate the weekly gross pay for each employee.

$$\text{Gross Pay} = \text{Hours} * \text{Pay Rate}$$

2. Calculate the updated YTD-gross pay for each employee.

$$\text{YTD-Gross Pay} = \text{YTD-Gross Pay} + \text{Gross Pay}$$

3. Locate the desired record by direct access of master table.
4. Print a paycheck.
5. Update Year-to-Date Gross Pay in Master Table.
6. Terminate processing with a last record containing "EOD."

Output

1. The initial current table, printed with titles.
2. The printout of five paychecks, using sequential search.
3. The printout of five data lines, using direct access.
4. A complete update table, with titles.

```
                      PAYROLL MASTER TABLE

EMPLOYEE    EMPLOYEE        EMPLOYEE        MARITAL
NUMBER      NAME            ADDRESS    AGE  STATUS   PAY RATE    YTD GROSS

    1       JONES C     12 MAIN      42      S       $12.50      $8,000.00
    2       SMITH R     8 RT 6       26      M        $7.20      $4,600.00
    3       BROWN L     12 RT 9      29      S        $9.20      $5,000.00
    4       WHITE W     125 OAK      19      D        $4.80      $3,072.00
    5       BLACK O     10 MAPLE     31      M       $15.60     $10,560.00
    6       EAST M      NORTH LN     48      M        $6.30      $4,032.00
    7       WEST D      RT 30        27      S        $5.90      $3,776.00
    8       NORTH A     COLLINS      19      S        $6.00      $3,840.00
    9       SOUTH B     10 GRAND     22      S        $7.50      $4,500.00
   10       JAMES C     15 PRATT     34      M        $8.25      $6,400.00


        * PAYCHECK ISSUED TO EMPLOYEE NO       1           *

        ******************************************************
        *                                                    *
        *     EMPLOYEE NO:   1     HOURS WORKED: 10          *
        *                                                    *
        *                                                    *
        *   PAY TO THE ORDER OF: JONES C         $125.00     *
        *                                                    *
        *                                                    *
        ******************************************************


        * PAYCHECK ISSUED TO EMPLOYEE NO       3           *

        ******************************************************
        *                                                    *
        *     EMPLOYEE NO:    3 HOURS WORKED: 40             *
        *                                                    *
        *                                                    *
        *   PAY TO THE ORDER OF: BROWN L         $368.00     *
        *                                                    *
        *                                                    *
        ******************************************************


        * PAYCHECK ISSUED TO EMPLOYEE NO       10          *

        ******************************************************
        *                                                    *
        *   EMPLOYEE NO:    10 HOURS WORKED: 30             *
        *                                                    *
        *                                                    *
        * PAY TO THE ORDER OF: JAMES C         $247.50      *
        *                                                    *
        *                                                    *
        ******************************************************


        * PAYCHECK ISSUED TO EMPLOYEE NO       8           *

        ******************************************************
        *                                                    *
        *   EMPLOYEE NO:    8 HOURS WORKED: 35             *
        *                                                    *
        *                                                    *
        * PAY TO THE ORDER OF: NORTH A         $210.00      *
        *                                                    *
        *                                                    *
        ******************************************************
```

```
                    *  PAYCHECK ISSUED TO EMPLOYEE NO        4          *

     **************************************************************
     *                                                            *
     *    EMPLOYEE NO:       4 HOURS WORKED: 20                    *
     *                                                            *
     *                                                            *
     *  PAY TO THE ORDER OF: WHITE W          $ 96.00             *
     *                                                            *
     *                                                            *
     **************************************************************

          EMPLOYEE NUMBER NOT FOUND IN TABLE !! 294
```

Test Data

Use master table and transaction data as shown below.

Master	1,"Jones,C", 12 Main, 42, S, 12.5, 8000
Table	2, "Smith, R", 8 Rt 6, 26, M, 7.2, 4600
	3, "Brown, L", 12, Rt 9, 29, S, 9.2, 5000
	4, "White, W", 125 Oak, 19, D, 4.8, 3072
	5, "Black, D", 10 Maple, 31, M, 15.6, 10560
	6, "East, M", North Ln, 48, M, 6.3, 4032
	7, "West, D", Rt 30, 27, S, 5.9, 3776
	8, "North, A", Collins, 19, S, 6, 3840
	9, "South, B", 10 Grand, 22, 7.5, 4500
	10, "James, C", 15 Pratt, 34, M, 8.25, 6400

Time	1,10
Cards	3,40
	10,30
	8,35
	4,20
	294,40
	0,0

```
                    UPDATED MASTER TABLE
```

EMPLOYEE NUMBER	EMPLOYEE NAME	EMPLOYEE ADDRESS	AGE	MARITAL STATUS	PAY RATE	YTD GROSS
1	JONES C	12 MAIN	42	S	$12.50	$8,125.00
2	SMITH R	8 RT 6	26	M	$7.20	$4,600.00
3	BROWN L	12 RT 9	29	S	$9.20	$5,368.00
4	WHITE W	125 OAK	19	D	$4.80	$3,168.00
5	BLACK D	10 MAPLE	31	M	$15.60	$10,560.00
6	EAST M	NORTH LN	48	M	$6.30	$4,032.00
7	WEST D	RT 30	27	S	$5.90	$3,776.00
8	NORTH A	COLLINS	19	S	$6.00	$4,050.00
9	SOUTH B	10 GRAND	22	S	$7.50	$4,500.00
10	JAMES C	15 PRATT	34	M	$8.25	$6,647.50

```
                  END OF PAYROLL PROGRAM
```

Error Recovery Routines

If the number is not found in table, then a display message is to be printed containing the type error, the data that was in error, and a recovery feature to resume processing with the next record.

Validation Procedure

Hand calculate all of the figures that were computed for the gross pay and for the YTD Gross, and verify that they are correctly calculated. Intentionally attempt to process employees not in table and verify that error messages are produced and that processing is resumed. Check for correct numeric field editing and centering under headings.

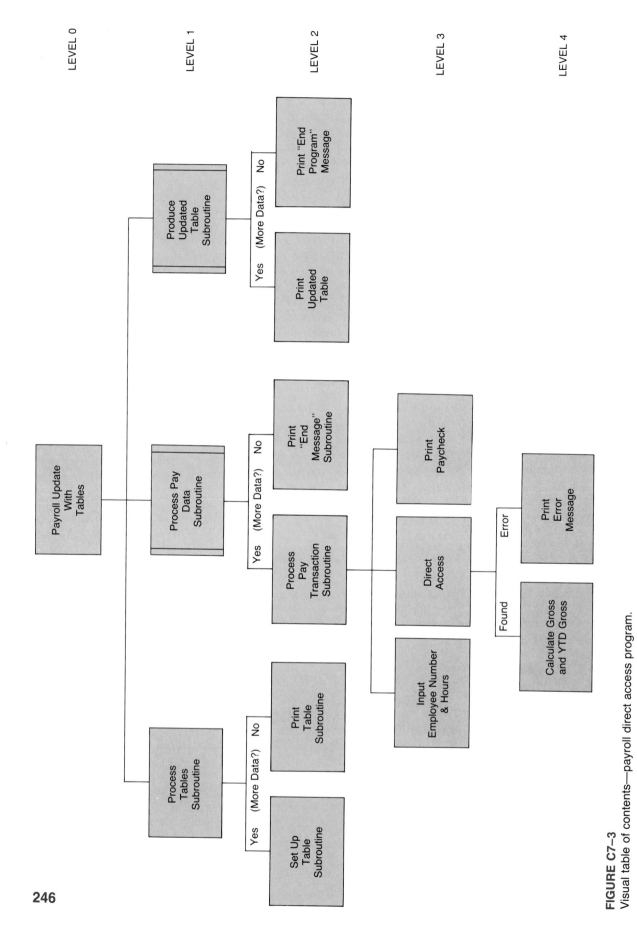

LEVEL 0

LEVEL 1

LEVEL 2

LEVEL 3

LEVEL 4

Payroll Update With Tables

Process Tables Subroutine

(More Data?) Yes

Set Up Table Subroutine

(More Data?) No

Print Table Subroutine

Process Pay Data Subroutine

(More Data?) Yes

Process Pay Transaction Subroutine

Input Employee Number & Hours

Direct Access

Found

Calculate Gross and YTD Gross

Error

Print Error Message

Print Paycheck

(More Data?) No

Print "End Message" Subroutine

Produce Updated Table Subroutine

(More Data?) Yes

Print Updated Table

(More Data?) No

Print "End Program" Message

246

FIGURE C7–3
Visual table of contents—payroll direct access program.

```
10    REM    ******************************************************
20    REM    *                    TABLES                          *
30    REM    *              CASE STUDY: 7-2                        *
40    REM    *               PAYROLL PROGRAM                       *
50    REM    *   THIS PROGRAM LOADS, PRINTS, AND UPDATES A         *
60    REM    *   MASTER TABLE USING A DIRECT ACCESS SEARCH         *
70    REM    *                                                     *
80    REM    *                VARIABLE LEGEND                      *
90    REM    *        EMPNO = EMPLOYEE NUMBER                       *
100   REM    *        NM$ = EMPLOYEE NAME                          *
110   REM    *        ADDR$ = EMPLOYEE ADDRESS                     *
120   REM    *        AGE = EMPLOYEE AGE                           *
130   REM    *        M$ = MARITAL STATUS                          *
140   REM    *        PRAT = EMPLOYEE PAY RATE                     *
150   REM    *        YTD = YEAR TO DATE GROSS                     *
160   REM    *        ENO = EMPLOYEE NUMBER (TRANSACTION)          *
170   REM    *        HRS = NUMBER OF HOURS WORKED                 *
180   REM    *        GROSS = GROSS PAY                            *
190   REM    *        ENDSW = END OF DATA SWITCH                   *
200   REM    *        PAYSW = PRODUCE PAYCHECK SWITCH              *
210   REM    ******************************************************
220          PRINT "COPYRIGHT (C) 1989, BY MERRILL PUBLISHING COMPANY"
230          PRINT "FOR USE WITH STRUCTURED BASIC PROGRAMMING"
240   REM    ****************
250   REM    * MAIN PROGRAM *
260   REM    ****************
270   REM
280   REM    PERFORM 'PROCESS TABLE' ROUTINE
290          GOSUB 370
300   REM    PERFORM 'PROCESS PAYROLL DATA' ROUTINE
310          GOSUB 760
320   REM    PERFORM 'PRINT UPDATED TABLE' ROUTINE
330          GOSUB 1730
340   REM    PERFORM 'END OF PROGRAM MESSAGE' ROUTINE
350          GOSUB 1860
360          END
370   REM    ****************
380   REM    * PROCESS TABLE *
390   REM    ****************
400   REM    PERFORM 'SET UP TABLE' ROUTINE
410          GOSUB 450
420   REM    PERFORM 'PRINT TABLE' ROUTINE
430          GOSUB 630
440          RETURN
450   REM    ****************
460   REM    * SET UP TABLE *
470   REM    ****************
480          DIM EMPNO(10),NM$(10),ADDR$(10),AGE(10),M$(10),PRAT(10),YTD(10)
490          FOR I = 1 TO 10
500          READ EMPNO(I),NM$(I),ADDR$(I),AGE(I),M$(I),PRAT(I),YTD(I)
510          NEXT I
520          DATA 1,JONES C,12 MAIN,42,S,12.5,8000
530          DATA 2 ,SMITH R,8 RT 6,26,M,7.2,4600
540          DATA 3 ,BROWN L,12 RT 9,29,S,9.2,5000
550          DATA 4 ,WHITE W,125 OAK,19,D,4.8,3072
560          DATA 5 ,BLACK O,10 MAPLE,31,M,15.6,10560
570          DATA 6 ,EAST M,NORTH LN,48,M,6.3,4032
580          DATA 7 ,WEST D,RT 30,27,S,5.9,3776
590          DATA 8 ,NORTH A,COLLINS,19,S,6,3840
600          DATA 9 ,SMITH B,10 GRAND,22,S,7.5,4500
610          DATA 10 ,JAMES C,15 PRATT,34,M,8.25,6400
620          RETURN
```

```
630     REM      ***************
640     REM      * PRINT TABLE *
650     REM      ***************
660              LPRINT TAB(30);"PAYROLL MASTER TABLE"
670              LPRINT
680              LPRINT "EMPLOYEE      EMPLOYEE      EMPLOYEE      MARITAL    "
690              LPRINT "NUMBER        NAME          ADDRESS   AGE STATUS  PAY
RATE    YTD GROSS"
700              F$    = "   ##       \          \  \          \  ##    !    $$##.##
$$###,##.##"
710              LPRINT
720              FOR I = 1 TO 10
730              LPRINT USING F$;EMPNO(I);NM$(I);ADDR$(I);AGE(I);M$(I);PRAT(I);YTD(I)
740              NEXT I
750              RETURN
760     REM      ***********************
770     REM      * PROCESS PAYROLL DATA *
780     REM      ***********************
790     REM      PERFORM 'INPUT PAYROLL DATA' ROUTINE
800              GOSUB 860
810     REM      PERFORM 'PROCESS PAYROLL UNTIL END OF DATA' ROUTINE
820              GOSUB 1020
830     REM      PERFORM 'END OF PAYROLL TRANSACTION MESSAGE' ROUTINE
840              GOSUB 1650
850              RETURN
860     REM      *********************
870     REM      * INPUT PAYROLL DATA *
880     REM      *********************
890              PAYSW = 0
900              CLS
910              PRINT "ENTER THE DATA ON THE APPROPRIATE LINES AND PUSH "
920              PRINT "RETURN AFTER EACH ENTRY.  WHEN YOU ARE FINISHED, "
930              PRINT "TYPE IN A '0' ON THE LINE OF THE EMPLOYEE'S NAME "
940              PRINT "AND FOR THE HOURS WORKED."
950              PRINT:PRINT:PRINT
960              PRINT "ENTER THE EMPLOYEE'S NUMBER:_____"
970              PRINT "ENTER THE HOURS WORKED.....:_____"
980              LOCATE 8,29 : INPUT ENO
990              LOCATE 9,29 : INPUT HRS
1000             IF ENO  = 0 THEN ENDSW = 1
1010             RETURN
1020    REM      **********************************
1030    REM      * PROCESS PAYROLL UNTIL END OF DATA *
1040    REM      **********************************
1050             ENDSW = 0
1060             WHILE ENDSW = 0
1070    REM      PERFORM 'SEARCH TABLE' ROUTINE
1080             GOSUB 1150
1090    REM      PERFORM 'PRINT PAYCHECK' ROUTINE
1100             IF PAYSW = 1 THEN GOSUB 1410
1110    REM      PERFORM 'INPUT PAYROLL DATA' ROUTINE
1120             GOSUB 860
1130             WEND
1140             RETURN
1150    REM      ***************
1160    REM      * SEARCH TABLE *
1170    REM      ***************
1180             I = ENO
1190    REM      IF "MATCH" PERFORM 'CALCULATIONS' ROUTINE
1200    REM          ELSE PERFORM 'ERROR' ROUTINE
1210             IF ENO < = 10 THEN GOSUB 1340 ELSE GOSUB 1230
1220             RETURN
```

```
1230    REM     ***********************
1240    REM     * PRINT ERROR MESSAGE *
1250    REM     ***********************
1260            LPRINT
1270            LPRINT
1280            LPRINT
1290            LPRINT TAB(15);"EMPLOYEE NUMBER NOT FOUND IN TABLE !"ENO
1300            LPRINT
1310            LPRINT
1320            LPRINT
1330            RETURN
1340    REM     *****************************
1350    REM     * CALCULATE GROSS, YTD GROSS *
1360    REM     *****************************
1370            GROSS = HRS * PRAT(I)
1380            YTD(I) = YTD(I) + GROSS
1390            PAYSW = 1
1400            RETURN
1410    REM     *****************
1420    REM     * PRINT PAYCHECK *
1430    REM     *****************
1440            F3$ = "            * PAYCHECK ISSUED TO EMPLOYEE NO #####              *"
1450            F4$ = "            ****************************************************"
1460            F5$ = "            *                                                  *"
1470            F6$ = "            *    EMPLOYEE NO: ##### HOURS WORKED: ##            *"
1480            F7$ = "            *  PAY TO THE ORDER OF: \              \ $ ###.##    *"
1490            LPRINT
1500            LPRINT USING F3$;ENO
1510            LPRINT
1520            LPRINT F4$
1530            LPRINT F5$
1540            LPRINT USING F6$;EMPNO(I),HRS
1550            LPRINT F5$
1560            LPRINT F5$
1570            LPRINT USING F7$;NM$(I),GROSS
1580            LPRINT F5$
1590            LPRINT F5$
1600            LPRINT F4$
1610            LPRINT
1620            LPRINT
1630            LPRINT
1640            RETURN
1650    REM     *********************************
1660    REM     * END OF PAYROLL TRANSACTION MESSAGE *
1670    REM     *********************************
1680            PRINT "               ALL PAYCHECKS HAVE BEEN PROCESSED"
1690            LPRINT
1700            LPRINT
1710            LPRINT
1720            RETURN
1730    REM     *****************************
1740    REM     * PRINT UPDATED MASTER TABLE *
1750    REM     *****************************
1760            LPRINT TAB(30); "UPDATED MASTER TABLE"
1770            LPRINT
1780            LPRINT "EMPLOYEE     EMPLOYEE      EMPLOYEE       MARITAL     "
1790            LPRINT "NUMBER       NAME          ADDRESS    AGE STATUS   PAY RATE     YTD GROSS"
1800            F$ =  "  ##      \        \ \           \ ##    !   $$###.##    $$###,##.##"
1810            LPRINT
1820            FOR I = 1 TO 10
1830            LPRINT USING F$;EMPNO(I);NM$(I);ADDR$(I);AGE(I);M$(I);PRAT(I);YTD(I)
1840            NEXT I
1850            RETURN
```

```
1860   REM    *************************
1870   REM    * END OF PROGRAM MESSAGE *
1880   REM    *************************
1890          LPRINT
1900          LPRINT
1910          LPRINT
1920          LPRINT "                    END OF PAYROLL PROGRAM"
1930          RETURN
1940   REM
1950   REM    END OF PROGRAM
```

Translating Languages

CONCEPTS TO BE ILLUSTRATED

This program sets up a table that consists of a series of word pairs (i.e., an English word with its corresponding meaning in a foreign language, such as German, Russian, or Spanish). The resulting table is a very simple dictionary (there is only one meaning for each word). Once the dictionary table is set up, you can input a sentence to be translated. The sentence can consist of one to eight words. For example, you might want to translate the sentence "I like school" into a foreign language. First, you will devise logic that will search the first sentence, word against word, in the dictionary until a match is found for each word. Then you will store the corresponding foreign language word in an "output" table. Specifically, if "sentence word (1)" equals "English word (1)", you retrieve the corresponding foreign language word and save it. If a match is found between the first sentence word and the ninth English word in the dictionary, the ninth foreign word from the dictionary will be saved in the first output table position. The logic is repeated to find a match for the second English word. Again, when a match is found, the subsequent corresponding foreign language word is stored in "output word (2)". This process is repeated until a match for every word in the sentence has been found and each of the corresponding foreign language words has been stored.

PROBLEM DEFINITION

Input Specifications

Set up a dictionary of at least twenty-five word pairs consisting of an English word and its foreign language equivalent. Choose enough words so that some simple sentences can be translated. Remember to include a blank in the dictionary. Then, input two or three sentences to be translated.

	Field No.	Field Description	Type	Example
Language	1	English Word	Alphabetic	A
Dictionary	2	Spanish Word	Alphabetic	Esto
Table				
Sentence	1	1st English Word	Alphabetic	This
to be	2	2nd English	Alphabetic	is
Translated	·	Word	·	
	·	·	·	
	·	·	·	
	8	8th English Word	Alphabetic	—

Processing Decisions and Formulas

Sequential search to find a match for each word in the sentence to be translated.

1. Load the original dictionary into a table.
2. Input a sentence (English) to be translated (eight words maximum).
3. Search the dictionary for each word.
4. Load the corresponding Spanish words into a table for output.
5. Print the English and Spanish sentences.

Output

Print the dictionary and then print each English sentence to be translated and its corresponding foreign language sentence after translation.

```
              DICTIONARY TABLE
              THIS                ESTO
              A                   UN
              IS                  ES
              LANGUAGE            LENGUAJE
              TRANSLATION         TRADUCCION
              PROGRAM             PROGRAMA
              SET-UP              CREACION
              TABLE               TABLA
              AND                 Y
              ENABLED             PERMITIDO
              US                  NOSOTROS
              SEARCH              BUSQUEDA
              OF                  DE
              THE                 LA
              TO                  A
              TRANSLATE           TRADUCIR
              SENTENCE            FRASE
              SPANISH             ESPANOL
              HAS                 HA
              ENGLISH             ENGLES
                   .                   .

                        ENGLISH SENTENCE
      THIS IS A LANGUAGE TRANSLATION PROGRAM .

                        SPANISH SENTENCE
      ESTO ES UN LENGUAJE TRADUCCION PROGRAMA .

                        ENGLISH SENTENCE
      THE SET-UP AND SEARCH OF A TABLE

                        SPANISH SENTENCE
      LA CREACION Y BUSQUEDA DE UN TABLA

                        ENGLISH SENTENCE
      HAS ENABLED US TO TRANSLATE THE ENGLISH SENTENCE

                        SPANISH SENTENCE
      HA PERMITIDO NOSOTROS A TRADUCIR LA ENGLES FRASE

                        ENGLISH SENTENCE
      TO A SPANISH SENTENCE .

                        SPANISH SENTENCE
      A UN ESPANOL FRASE . LA ENGLES FRASE


                   END OF TRANSLATION PROGRAM
```

Test Data

Choose a "dictionary" reflecting enough words to translate simple sentences, and select two or three simple sentences to translate. An example is shown below.

Dictionary

```
              THIS,ESTO
              A,UN
```

```
IS,ES
LANGUAGE,LENGUAJE
TRANSLATION,TRADUCCION
PROGRAM,PROGRAMA
SET-UP,CREATION
TABLE,TABLA
AND,Y
ENABLED,PERMITIDO
US,NOSOTROS
SEARCH,BUSQUEDA
OF,DE
THE,LA
TO,A
TRANSLATE,TRADUCIR
SENTENCE,FRASE
SPANISH,ESPANOL
HAS,HA
ENGLISH,ENGLES

.,.
" ","  "
```

Sentences to be translated:

> This, is, a, language, translation, program, .
> The, set-up, and, search, of, a, table, " ",
> has, enabled, us, to, translate, the, English, sentence,
> to, a, Spanish, sentence, . , ".", " ", " , "

Error Recovery Routines

Place a "*" or blank in the output (foreign) sentence if there is no word in your dictionary corresponding to a word in the input (English) sentence. It would be beneficial to include a provision if an English sentence word input for translation has no match in the dictionary. Placing a "*" in the output Spanish sentence might permit the reader to infer the meaning of the missing word.

Validation Procedure

Check the translation to see if it makes sense. Verify that the word-for-word translation proceeded properly, and that the correct foreign language words were selected from the dictionary.

Show the sentence to someone who speaks the foreign language, or check the translated sentence yourself if you know the language and see if the sentence comes close to the "true" meaning. Remember, this program is simplified and does not consider noun genders, word order, grammar, etc., which may vary from language to language. Nevertheless, it should be possible to deduce the meaning of the original sentence from the computer translation.

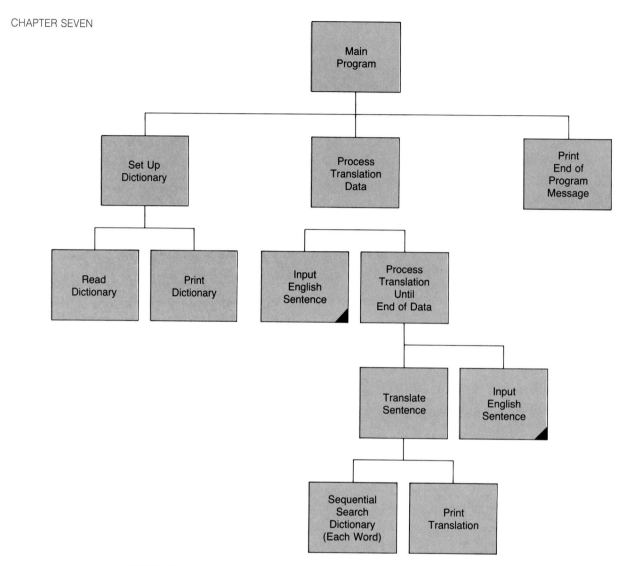

FIGURE C7–4
Visual table of contents—translation program.

```
10      REM     ***********************************************************
20      REM     *                         TABLES                          *
30      REM     *                   CASE STUDY:C7-3                        *
40      REM     *                 TRANSLATION PROGRAM                      *
50      REM     *   THIS PROGRAM SETS UP A DICTIONARY TABLE OF             *
60      REM     *   ENGLISH AND SPANISH WORDS. USING THE BUBBLE            *
70      REM     *   SORT AND BINARY SEARCH, WE WILL TRANSLATE              *
80      REM     *   THE ENGLISH SENTENCES INTO SPANISH.                    *
90      REM     *                                                          *
100     REM     *                    VARIABLE LEGEND                       *
110     REM     *         ENG$  = ENGLISH WORD INPUT TABLE                 *
120     REM     *         SPA$  = SPANISH WORD INPUT TABLE                 *
130     REM     *         SENT$ = ENGLISH SENTENCE WORD                    *
140     REM     *         SPAWD$ = SPANISH WORD OUTPUT                     *
150     REM     *         NREC  = NUMBER OF RECORDS                        *
160     REM     *         ENDSW = END OF DATA SWITCH                       *
170     REM     *         I,J,K = SUBSCRIPTS                               *
180     REM     *                                                          *
190     REM     *                                                          *
200     REM     *                                                          *
210     REM     ***********************************************************
220             PRINT "COPYRIGHT (C) 1989, BY MERRILL PUBLISHING COMPANY"
230             PRINT "FOR USE WITH STRUCTURED BASIC PROGRAMMING"
240     REM     NOTE: WHEN RUNNING THIS PROGRAM ON SOME SYSTEMS, IT IS
250     REM           NECESSARY TO ENTER THE 'BLANK'  SENTENCE WORDS IN
260     REM           QUOTATION MARKS TO BE COMPATIBLE WITH THE BLANK IN
270     REM           THE DATA STATEMENT DICTIONARY.
280     REM
290     REM     *****************
300     REM     * MAIN PROGRAM *
310     REM     *****************
320     REM     PERFORM 'SET-UP DICTIONARY' ROUTINE
330             GOSUB 390
340     REM     PERFORM 'PROCESS TRANSLATION DATA' ROUTINE
350             GOSUB 880
360     REM     PERFORM 'PRINT END OF PROGRAM MESSAGE' ROUTINE
370             GOSUB 1510
380             END
390     REM     *********************
400     REM     * SET UP DICTIONARY *
410     REM     *********************
420     REM     PERFORM 'READ DICTIONARY' ROUTINE
430             GOSUB 470
440     REM     PERFORM 'PRINT DICTIONARY' ROUTINE
450             GOSUB 780
460             RETURN
470     REM     *******************
480     REM     * READ DICTIONARY *
490     REM     *******************
500             DIM ENG$(22),SPA$(22)
510             FOR I = 1 TO 22
520             READ ENG$(I),SPA$(I)
530             PRINT ENG$(I),SPA$(I)
540             NEXT I
550             DATA THIS,ESTO
560             DATA A,UN
570             DATA IS,ES
580             DATA LANGUAGE,LENGUAJE
590             DATA TRANSLATION,TRADUCCION
600             DATA PROGRAM,PROGRAMA
610             DATA SET-UP,CREACION
620             DATA TABLE,TABLA
```

```
630                    DATA AND,Y
640                    DATA ENABLED,PERMITIDO
650                    DATA US,NOSOTROS
660                    DATA SEARCH,BUSQUEDA
670                    DATA OF,DE
680                    DATA THE,LA
690                    DATA TO,A
700                    DATA TRANSLATE,TRADUCIR
710                    DATA SENTENCE,FRASE
720                    DATA SPANISH,ESPANOL
730                    DATA HAS,HA
740                    DATA ENGLISH,ENGLES
750                    DATA ".","."
760                    DATA " "," "
770                    RETURN
780       REM          * * * * * * * * * * * * * * * * * * * *
790       REM          * PRINT DICTIONARY *
800       REM          * * * * * * * * * * * * * * * * * * * *
810                    LPRINT TAB(32);"DICTIONARY TABLE"
820                    FOR I = 1 TO  22
830                    LPRINT TAB(25);ENG$(I);TAB(45);SPA$(I)
840                    NEXT I
850                    LPRINT
860                    LPRINT
870                    RETURN
880       REM          * * * * * * * * * * * * * * * * * * * * * * * * *
890       REM          * PROCESS TRANSLATION DATA *
900       REM          * * * * * * * * * * * * * * * * * * * * * * * * *
910                    DIM SENT$(8),SPAWD$(8)
920       REM          PERFORM 'INPUT ENGLISH SENTENCE' ROUTINE
930                    GOSUB 970
940       REM          PERFORM 'PROCESS TRANSLATION UNTIL END OF DATA' ROUTINE
950                    GOSUB 1080
960                    RETURN
970       REM          * * * * * * * * * * * * * * * * * * * * * * * * *
980       REM          * INPUT ENGLISH SENTENCE *
990       REM          * * * * * * * * * * * * * * * * * * * * * * * * *
1000                   PRINT "ENTER AN ENGLISH SENTENCE"
1010                   PRINT "WITH A MAXIMUM OF 8 WORDS"
1020                   FOR I = 1 TO 8
1030                   PRINT "ENTER WORD ";I
1040                   INPUT SENT$(I)
1050                   IF SENT$(I) = "EOD" THEN ENDSW = 0
1060                   NEXT I
1070                   RETURN
1080      REM          * * * * * * * * * * * * * * * * * * * * * * * * * * * * * * * * * * * *
1090      REM          * PROCESS TRANSLATION UNTIL END OF DATA *
1100      REM          * * * * * * * * * * * * * * * * * * * * * * * * * * * * * * * * * * * *
1110      REM          ENDSW = 1
1120                   WHILE ENDSW = 1
1130      REM          PERFORM 'TRANSLATE SENTENCE' ROUTINE
1140                   GOSUB 1190
1150      REM          PERFORM 'INPUT ENGLISH SENTENCE' ROUTINE
1160                   GOSUB 970
1170                   WEND
1180                   RETURN
1190      REM          * * * * * * * * * * * * * * * * * * * * *
1200      REM          * TRANSLATE SENTENCE *
1210      REM          * * * * * * * * * * * * * * * * * * * * *
1220      REM          PERFORM 'PRINT TRANSLATION' ROUTINE
1230                   GOSUB 1270
1240      REM          PERFORM 'PRINT TRANSLATE' ROUTINE
1250                   GOSUB 1370
1260                   RETURN
```

256

```
1270      REM      * * * * * * * * * * * * * * * * * * * *
1280      REM      * SEARCH DICTIONARY *
1290      REM      * * * * * * * * * * * * * * * * * * * *
1300               FOR I = 1 TO 8
1310               NREC = 22
1320               FOR J = 1 TO NREC
1330               IF SENT$(I) = ENG$(J) THEN SPAWD$(I) = SPA$(J)
1340               NEXT J
1350               NEXT I
1360               RETURN
1370      REM      * * * * * * * * * * * * * * * * * * * *
1380      REM      * PRINT TRANSLATION *
1390      REM      * * * * * * * * * * * * * * * * * * * *
1400               LPRINT TAB(30) "ENGLISH SENTENCE"
1410               FOR I = 1 TO 8
1420               LPRINT SENT$(I);" ";
1430               NEXT I
1440               LPRINT
1450               LPRINT TAB(30) "SPANISH SENTENCE"
1460               FOR I = 1 TO 8
1470               LPRINT SPAWD$(I);" ";
1480               NEXT I
1490               LPRINT
1500               RETURN
1510      REM      * * * * * * * * * * * * * * * * * * * * * * * * * * * * * *
1520      REM      * PRINT END OF PROGRAM MESSAGE *
1530      REM      * * * * * * * * * * * * * * * * * * * * * * * * * * * * * *
1540               LPRINT
1550               LPRINT
1560               LPRINT
1570               LPRINT TAB(27);"END OF TRANSLATION PROGRAM"
1580               RETURN
1590      REM
1600      REM      END OF PROGRAM
```

SUMMARY

This chapter discusses the techniques for storing records as tables in the computer's main memory. Through the use of tables, it is possible to have a very large number of data records all available for processing at the same time, and with a dramatic reduction in the number of variable names and corresponding lines of code. This is accomplished by assigning the same variable name to each field within each record, but differentiating each field with an identifying number called a subscript. This scheme permits sorting and searching with a fraction of the coding, simply by varying the subscript to identify the desired field of any record. Records within a table are differentiated from one another by the subscript value.

Two common access methods are used to quickly retrieve and/or update data records in tables. These are (1) sequential search and (2) direct access.

In direct access, when inputting the transaction record, the key field must be an integer since it will be used as a subscript to locate the desired record fields directly. So, for example, a part number is used instead of a description field.

In a sequential search, any type of variable can be used as the key field (alphabetic, alphanumeric, numeric integer, or decimal), but every record in the table must be compared in sequence until the desired record is located. As a result, this method is slow.

COMMON ERRORS AND SOLUTIONS

Error	Example	Solution
1. Forgetting to dimension a variable used as a table (subscripted) variable. Ten is assumed on most systems without the dimension statement.	10 FOR I = 1 TO 25 20 INPUT N$(I),RATE(I) 30 NEXT I (10 inputs, then subscript out of range in 20)	It is probably best to get into the habit of using the dimension (DIM) statement even for a table variable with ten records or less, as you are less likely to make this error.
2. Redimensioning the same variable name later in your program, or using the undimensioned variable name later in the program *as* a dimensioned variable.	10 A = 10 20 PRINT A . . . 100 DIM A(20) 150 PRINT A(1), A(2), etc. (logic error—A ≠ A(1) or A(2), etc.)	This error is difficult to catch, since the original variable A and the dimensioned variable A(I) are different. Be sure to use distinct variable names for unsubscripted and subscripted variables, even though most BASIC systems allow use of the same name.
3. Redimensioning the same subscripted variable in a subroutine that was previously dimensioned in a calling routine or the main program.	10 DIM A(20) 20 REM PERFORM INPUT 30 GOSUB 100 . . . 100 REM INPUT SUBROUTINE 110 DIM A(20) 120 FOR I = 1 TO 20 130 INPUT A(I) 140 NEXT I 150 RETURN (duplicate definition in 110)	This error is frequently an oversight. It is probably best to dimension variables in your main program, as this permits transfer of information to all subroutines that may ''need'' the table data. Dimension variables in subroutines only if you can be sure about the logical order in which the information is needed.
4. Increasing the value of a subscript for a dimensioned variable beyond the number specified in the original dimension statement. This commonly occurs when using a counter for the subscript, and forgetting to re-initialize the counter before processing in another loop.	10 DIM NM$ (25) 30 FOR I = 1 TO 30 40 INPUT NM$ (1) 50 NEXT I (program will run up to I = 25, then stop—subscript out of range in 40) 05 N = 50 10 DIM NM$(25) 20 INPUT NM$(N) (subscript out of range in 20)	This can be a very troublesome and frustrating error because it usually occurs after you have input or processed a large amount of data. When the error occurs, all data is lost and must be reprocessed. Check your subscript values to ensure that they do not exceed the limit specified in your dimension statement.
5. Dimensioning tables that are too large to be stored in main memory at the same time, especially tables that store large alphabetic or alphanumeric data.	10 DIM NM$(1000), ADD$ (1000) 20 FOR I = 1 TO 1000 30 INPUT NM$(I), ADD$ (I) 40 NEXT I (subscript out of range in 30)	As in error 4, this error is frustrating because it will be ''picked up'' during execution; therefore, you will probably lose the data you have input. Always determine the amount of free memory available and estimate the amount of memory your table will use *before* executing your program.
6. Trying to locate a record in a direct access table by specifying a key field (subscript value) outside the range of the original dimensioned table.	10 DIM DESC$(100) 20 INPUT PARTNO 30 PRINT DESC$(PARTNO) (if part number > 100, then subscript out of range in 30)	Direct access can be tricky. Always check the key field *before* using it as a subscript to ensure that it is less than the table subscript maximum value.

Error	Example	Solution

7. Failure to check the contents of your table. Before processing, such as sequential or direct access, it is not sufficient to print the data *as* you load your table. It is better to print the entire table after loading (see solution).	05 DIM N$(100), PHON$(100)
	10 FOR I = 1 TO 20
	20 INPUT N$(I), PHON$(I)
	30 NEXT (I)
	40 INPUT TRNM$
	50 FOR I = 1 TO 100
	60 IF TRNM$ = N$(I)
	  GOSUB 100
	70 NEXT I
	100 REM FOUND RTN
	110 PRINT PHON$(I)
	120 RETURN
	  (possibly no phone number)
		Always print the contents of your tables before you attempt *any* operation on or with the table data. You may think all data was entered correctly, but you cannot be sure unless you print it out or display it! Place this logic after 30:
		
		32 FOR I = 1 TO 100
		34 PRINT N$(I), PHON$(I)
		36 NEXT I

8. Loading large multiple field arrays with input rather than READ/DATA. This is not really an error, but can result in much lost time inputting data if an error occurs (see errors 4 and 5).	10 DIM ENG$(I),GER$(I) 20 FOR I = 1 TO 100 30 INPUT ENG$(I), GER$(I) 40 NEXT I (not an error, but the following is preferred) 20 FOR I = 1 TO 100 30 READ ENG$(I), GER$(I) 40 NEXT I 50 DATA I, ICH 52 DATA CAR, AUTO	READ/DATA statements are great for loading tables where the data do not usually need to be updated, such as in a language dictionary, zip codes for addresses, etc. It saves re-entering data if an execution-halting error is encountered while inputting data.
9. Failure to provide an error routine or message when a record in a table cannot be located.	10 FOR I = 1 TO 25 20 IF N$ = NM$(I) THEN PRINT PHON$(I) 30 NEXT I	At the end of the search loop, if no match has occurred when I = 25, then print an appropriate message— for example: If FOUND$ = 'NO' AND I = 25 THEN PRINT "NAME NOT FOUND IN TABLE"
10. Endless loop in the binary search logic when a key field is not found. Program does not proceed or terminate.		

REVIEW QUESTIONS

1. Explain why tables are important in programming.
2. A table consists of component parts. Name these parts and explain their relationship to the table as a whole.
3. Using the apartment building analogy, explain how the table's component parts correspond to the units and rooms within an apartment building.
4. What identifies the individual records and fields within a table as unique items even though they have the same variable name?
5. What types of information can a table contain? Explain with examples.
6. Name and briefly describe the two methods by which records can be searched in a table.
7. How many records can a table contain?
8. What is meant by the term *key field?* Explain with an example.
9. Describe two methods for loading data into a table.
10. Why must the subscript value be increased as records are loaded into a table? Explain how this can be accomplished.

11. What BASIC statement allocates memory space for a table? Give an example.

12. Is a DIM statement needed on your system for tables with ten or fewer records?

13. Explain with an example how the FOR/NEXT loop can be used to load fields (records) into tables.

14. Why must the variable that is used as the counter in the FOR/NEXT loop be an integer (or contain an integer value) when used to load records into tables?

15. Write a program segment that will input five names, addresses, and phone numbers into a table. Use the FOR/NEXT loop.

16. Write the program in question 15 using a counter and increment the counter in your logic to accomplish the same table loading.

17. Print the results of the tables set up in questions 15 and 16 with a title placed above each field in the table listing.

18. Explain the principles of sequential searching and describe the key statement that locates the desired record in the table.

19. What are the advantages and disadvantages of the sequential search?

20. Write a simple telephone directory program listing using 15 or 20 names and phone numbers.

21. When searching a table, what is the record called that is used to search for the desired table record? Give an example of this type of record.

22. Why is the sequential search not a serious limitation for many business applications? Give some examples of systems that use this method effectively.

23. Draw a flowchart for a typical business system that processes data in tables. Include in your flowchart the inputs, the table, and typical outputs for such a system.

24. What is meant by the phrase "accessing tables with update"? Give some examples of update systems.

25. In Cases 7–1 and 7–2 (payroll), why is it possible to search the table by either the employee name or the employee number?

26. In the payroll example, you learned that some of the values calculated combined information from the transaction record and the table. Explain.

27. Describe the principles of direct access table processing.

28. Explain some of the advantages and disadvantages of direct access table processing.

29. In a table, why must the key field that is used for direct access be a simple integer?

30. What must be done in a direct access table for key field numbers that have no corresponding related fields?

31. What are some of the advantages and disadvantages of a computer language translation program like the one illustrated in Case 7–3?

32. What enhancements could be added to the language translation program in Case 7–3 to provide more acceptable results?

PROBLEMS FOR SOLUTION

1. A phone number retrieval program that can be written easily in BASIC will enable you to "instantly" retrieve the phone numbers (also addresses and birthdays or other special days) of family, friends, and business associates. Furthermore, it is possible to construct the logic so that you can search for information by phone number in the same way that police departments use a "reverse" directory to retrieve relevant information, such as a name and address, for a particular phone number.

   In this problem, it is best to load the table of phone numbers, addresses, and other desired information using the READ/DATA instruction so that during program development and debugging, the entire table need not be re-entered

   The table that you will set up for this problem should contain, at minimum, the following fields, as well as 15 or 20 names, to make the program somewhat realistic: Name, Address, Phone Number, Birthday, Other Special Days, Other Information.

   The name can be used as the input inquiry, and the information retrieved should be printed as shown in the output, using sequential search logic to retrieve the related fields.

Add the "reverse" directory feature to the program by programming the computer to ask what type of inquiry you wish to make: by name or by phone number. Then, to handle a response of "PHONE NUMBER", include logic in your program to print the second output report, as shown in the output.

TELEPHONE DIRECTORY

Input Specifications

Field No.	Field Description	Type	Example
1	Name	Alphabetic	David ONeill
2	Address	Alphanumeric	3 Nut Ln. East Hartford
3	Phone Number	Alphanumeric	(203) 568-8888
4*	Birthday	Alphanumeric	September 16
5*	Other Related Information	Alphabetic	Away

*optional

Processing Decisions and Formulas

Set up a table of 10* records containing the fields above, using the READ/DATA statements, and access this table by name to produce the output below.

Output

```
                    TELEPHONE DIRECTORY TABLE

CARL JONES                   2 GRANT ST. NEW YORK,NY        (212)454-9000
WILLIAM BROWN                25 WOODLAND ST. HARTFORD,CT    (203)549-4211
JAMES HOWELL                 5 MOUNTAIN ST. AVON,CT         (203)677-1233
GAYLE WHITTAKER              125 JAMES ST. AVON,CT          (203)659-4320
JOAN ROCK                    15 DREXEL ST. SPRINGFIELD,MA   (413)737-1187
DAVID ONEILL                 3 NUT LN. EAST HARTFORD,CT     (203)568-8888
ANN PERKINS                  33 CARP STREET MOSCOW,ID       (814)883-1234
ANNE MENARD                  45 LAUREL ST. CANTON,CT        (203)345-6789
PHIL BROWN                   12 SOUTH ST. VERNON,CT         (203)875-1222
TOM MOORE                    2 FIFTH AVE NEW YORK,NY        (212)549-1255


        INQUIRY DATA:  DAVID ONEILL

                      TABLE RECORD
              NAME                    ADDRESS              PHONE NO.
DAVID ONEILL        3 NUT LN. EAST HARTFORD,CT       (203)568-8888



        INQUIRY DATA:  ANN PERKINS

                      TABLE RECORD
              NAME                    ADDRESS              PHONE NO.
ANN PERKINS         33 CARP STREET MOSCOW,ID         (814)883-1234



        INQUIRY DATA:  (212)454-9000

                      TABLE RECORD
              NAME                    ADDRESS              PHONE NO.
CARL JONES          2 GRANT ST. NEW YORK,NY          (212)454-9000
```

*Add more records to make the program more realistic and useful.

Test Data

For this program, provide your own test data, as you may wish to use it for actual information retrieval.

Error Routines

Print a message "xxxxxxxxxx—x is not on table" if your inquiry does not produce a listing from your name, address and phone number table.

Validation Procedure

Verify that the names, addresses and phone numbers retrieved are correct, and that the correct record is retrieved from the table based on your inquiry.

REVERSE TELEPHONE DIRECTORY

Input Specifications

Field No	Field Description	Type	Example
1	Phone Number Inquiry	Alphanumeric	(213)692-1315

Processing Decisions and Formulas

Add logic to request "Type of Inquiry," and if phone number is used as the inquiry field, search the table to produce the same output as described in part one.

The Julian calendar uses a method of assigning a simple integer to each day of the year. It is based on a simple sequential numbering of each day, which starts with January 1 as day 1 and ends with December 31 as day 365 (except during a leap year, when it becomes day 366).

While not commonly used, the Julian system has some distinct advantages over the monthly day calendar. It permits quick calculation of the number of days separating any two dates (in the same year), and it represents any date in a short and easily read numeric form (e.g., July 12, 1983 = 18383). For programmers, the Julian calendar has another distinct advantage. It permits tables and files to be established so that dates can be used for direct access instead of the slower sequential search logic.

In this problem, simple conventional logic will be used to convert standard month and day dates to equivalent Julian dates. Write a BASIC program that uses tables to calculate Julian dates. Set up the table as shown below, but instead of using the 12 IF statements, use sequential search to find the month, and construct an algorithm that will add the correct number of days from the previous months to the date of the month you are converting.

Month	Number of Days	Conventional Logic	If Leap Year Add 1 after February 28
January	31	IF M$ = 'JAN' THEN JD = DAY	
February	28	IF M$ = 'FEB' THEN JD = DAY + 31	
March	31	IF M$ = 'MAR' THEN JD = DAY + 59	(+ 60)
April	30	IF M$ = 'APR' THEN JD = DAY + 90	(+ 91)
May	31	IF M$ = 'MAY' THEN JD = DAY +	(+121)
June	30	120	(+152)
July	31	IF M$ = 'JUNE' THEN JD = DAY +	(+182)
August	31	151	(+213)
September	30	IF M$ = 'JULY' THEN JD = DAY +	(+244)

October	31	181	(+274)
November	30	IF M\$ = 'AUG' THEN JD = DAY + 212	(+305)
December	31	IF M\$ = 'SEPT' THEN JD = DAY + 243	(+335)

IF M\$ = 'OCT' THEN JD = DAY + 273
IF M\$ = 'NOV' THEN JD = DAY + 304
IF M\$ = 'DEC' THEN JD = DAY + 334

You will find this program useful in solving problem 3, where you perform direct access by date for any date in the year.

3. The following shows a simplified example of a computerized appointment calendar. Although this version does not list more than one activity for each day, most BASIC systems permit large string entries that make numerous appointment listings possible. With the table set up using the Julian date as the key field (refer to problem 2), it is possible to directly access items (for both retrieving from and adding to the calendar), which permits speed and flexibility. Set up a table with 366 record positions (one for each day of the year, including leap year), the five fields shown, and information about each day. Then enhance it so that appointments can be scheduled or retrieved by date and time.

Julian Date	Activity	With Whom	Location	Time
001	Make list of resolutions	—	Home	11 A.M.
002	—	—	—	—
003	Register for classes	—	College	6:00 P.M.
004	Take car for repair	—	Dealer	1:00 P.M.
005	Check bus schedule	—	Depot	5:00 A.M.
006	Pick up car from dealer	—	Dealer	5:00 P.M.
.				
362				
363	Go shopping	—	New Mall	8:00 P.M.
364				
365	New Year's party	Jones'	San Francisco	10–??

4. Referring to problem 1 in Chapter 6, write a structured BASIC program that will process sales and produce a final inventory report as shown in the problem definition, but read the initial inventory data into memory as a table, as shown below.

Description	Price	Cost	QOH	MQOH
Dog, Shepherd	350	250	3	2
Dog, Collie	400	300	5	3
Cat, Siamese	90	60	5	2
Cat, Persian	110	80	3	3
Fish, Tropical	6	2	15	10
Fish, Gold	2	1	50	20
Bird, Parakeet	15	6	12	10
Bird, Parrot	1500	100	2	1

Since price, cost, quantity on hand (QOH), and reorder point (MQOH) will all be stored, they need not be entered as input data. Use the READ/DATA statements to set up a table like the one shown, and input a sales transaction containing the pet description and the customer's name. Update the inventory level (QOH) in the table, and then print a reorder message if the stock level falls below the reorder point (MQOH). Use the sequential search method to retrieve the proper data.

As in all problems that use tables for storage and retrieval of data, be sure to print out both the original inventory table (with titles) and the updated table after all sales have been processed for the day. The management report produced should look like the one featured in problem 1 in Chapter 6, but it should be expanded to show the increased product line.

Input Specifications

	Field No.	Field Description	Type	Example
Initial	1	Pet Description	Alphabetic	Dog, Shepherd
Inventory	2	Selling Price	Decimal Number	350.00
Record	3	Store's Cost	Decimal Number	250.00
	4	Current Quantity on Hand	Integer	3
	5	Minimum Quantity on Hand	Integer	2
Sales	1	Pet Description	Alphabetic	Dog, Collie
Record	2	Customer Name	Alphabetic	John C. Jones

Processing Decisions and Formulas

QOH = QOH − 1
Number of Pets Sold = Number of Pets Sold + 1
Gross Sale per Pet = Number of Pets Sold * Selling Price
Total Cost for Pet Type = Number of Pets Sold * Dealer's Cost
Total Profit per Pet = Gross Sale per Pet − Total Cost for Pet Type
Total Sales = Total Sales + Gross Sale per Pet
Total Cost = Total Cost + Total Cost for Pet Type
Total Profit = Total Profit + Total Profit per Pet
Reorder Message Issued When QOH for Pet Type < QOH for Pet Type

Output

```
            INVENTORY TABLE
DOG,SHEPHERD, 350 , 250 , 3 , 2 , 0
DOG,COLLIE, 400 , 300 , 5 , 3 , 0
CAT,SIAMESE, 90 , 60 , 5 , 2 , 0
CAT,PERSIAN, 110 , 80 , 3 , 3 , 0
FISH,TROPICAL, 6 , 2 , 15 , 10 , 0
FISH,GOLD, 2 , 1 , 50 , 20 , 0
BIRD,PARAKEET, 15 , 6 , 12 , 10 , 0
BIRD,PARROT, 1500 , 100 , 2 , 1 , 0


            PET SHOP
        CUSTOMER SALES SLIP

        SOLD TO JOHN C. JONES

    UNITS    DESCRIPTION      AMOUNT

      1    DOG,COLLIE           400.00


            PET SHOP
        CUSTOMER SALES SLIP

        SOLD TO ANN PERRY

    UNITS    DESCRIPTION      AMOUNT

      1    CAT,SIAMESE           90.00
```

```
                    PET SHOP
              CUSTOMER SALES SLIP

          SOLD TO DAVID ONEILL

UNITS    DESCRIPTION      AMOUNT

   1   BIRD,PARROT              %1500.00


REORDERBIRD,PARROT
QUANTITY ON HAND = 1

                    PET SHOP
              CUSTOMER SALES SLIP

          SOLD TO MIKE BLAIR

UNITS    DESCRIPTION      AMOUNT

   1   BIRD,PARROT              %1500.00

    ALL SALES DATA HAS BEEN PROCESSED

DOG,SHEPHERD, 350 , 250 , 3 , 2 , 0
DOG,COLLIE, 400 , 300 , 4 , 3 , 1
CAT,SIAMESE, 90 , 60 , 4 , 2 , 1
CAT,PERSIAN, 110 , 80 , 3 , 3 , 0
FISH,TROPICAL, 6 , 2 , 15 , 10 , 0
FISH,GOLD, 2 , 1 , 50 , 20 , 0
BIRD,PARAKEET, 15 , 6 , 12 , 10 , 0
BIRD,PARROT, 1500 , 100 , 0 , 1 , 2
PROGRAM EXECUTION COMPLETED
```

Test Data

"Dog, Collie", John C. Jones
"Cat, Siamese", Ann Perry
"Bird, Parrot", David ONeill
"Bird, Parrot", Mike Blair

Error Routines

Print an error message if the pet desired is not in the inventory table.

Validation Procedure

Check that the correct data is retrieved from the table for each sales input, and that profit figures are correctly computed and accumulated.

Verify an out-of-stock message for pets where QOH is less than QOH, and check the total number sold and total profit results.

5. Referring to the inventory control illustration in chapter 6, write a structured BASIC program that will process sales of furniture items and produce a final inventory and commission report, as shown below.

Description	Price	Cost	QOH	MQOH
Couch	365	175	15	15
Table	100	50	5	3
Chair	75	60	25	10
Lamp	60	35	30	10

Salesperson	Commission Rate
1	10%
2	15%
3	12%

For this program, however, load a table with the required inventory data shown. This table changes the previous commission calculation method (a straight 10% for every salesperson) to a variable rate, one which could be based, for example, on the number of years of employment with the company.

Both tables should be set up with the READ/DATA statement combination to save time during debugging, and both should be searched sequentially by item description. Use the salesperson's number to perform a direct access of the commission table.

Output reports should be similar to those shown in the problem definition. Provide your own input test data.

Input Specifications

	Field No.	Field Description	Type	Example
Inventory Table	1	Item Description	Alphabetic	Couch
	2	Selling Price	Numeric	365
	3	Store's Cost	Numeric	175
	4	Current Quantity on Hand	Numeric	15
	5	Minimum Quantity on Hand (Reorder Point)	Numeric	5
Salesperson Commission Table	1	Salesperson ID Number	Numeric	1
	2	Commission Rate in Percent	Numeric	15

Processing Decisions and Formulas

Same accumulation expression as problem 2 in chapter 6,

$$Profit = Price - Cost - Commission$$

Sequential search of inventory table by item description.
Direct access of commission rate table by salesperson ID number.

Output

```
           INVENTORY TABLE
COUCH, 365 , 175 , 15 , 15
TABLE, 100 , 50 , 5 , 3
CHAIR, 75 , 60 , 25 , 10
LAMP, 60 , 35 , 30 , 10
COMMISSION TABLE
 1 , .1
 2 , .15
 3 , .12


      REORDER MESSAGE

CURRENT LEVEL OF COUCH(S) IS:  15
TIME TO REORDER COUCH(S)

MINIMUM QUANTITY ON HAND IS: 15

ALL SALES DATA HAS BEEN PROCESSED
```

```
                 COUCHES    TABLES    CHAIRS    LAMPS

QUANTITY SOLD       1         2         1         3

PROFIT EARNED      329       173        64       180


        TOTAL NUMBER OF ITEMS SOLD:       7

        TOTAL PROFIT EARNED:          ` $724.85

    SALESPERSON COMMISSION REPORT


  SALESPERSON CODE      COMMISSION EARNED


    1                      $32.25

    2                      $26.25

    3                      $26.40


    TOTAL COMMISSION PAID:      $84.90


            INVENTORY TABLE
        COUCH, 365 , 175 , 14 , 15
        TABLE, 100 , 50 , 3 , 3
        CHAIR, 75 , 60 , 24 , 10
        LAMP, 60 , 35 , 27 , 10


    PROGRAM EXECUTION COMPLETED
```

Test Data

Make up your own data.

Error Routines

Print an error message if either the item description or salesperson ID number attempted in the sales transaction record is not in its respective table.

Validation Procedure

Check program output by evaluating sales transactions by hand, particularly in the case of erroneous item or salesperson codes.

6. Inventory control and pricing in retail stores that sell "seasonal" items, such as the ones listed in the following table, frequently discount these items depending on the time of year. Set up the following inventory and discount table in memory, and then process sales as you did in problem 4.

Description	Price	Cost	Monthly Discount Rate (Percentage Off List Price)												QOH	MQOH
			Jan.	Feb.	Mar.	April	May	June	July	Aug.	Sept.	Oct.	Nov.	Dec.		
Lawn Mower	350	200	0	0	.10	.20	.20	.10	.10	.10	.20	.20	0	0	15	10
Rototiller	600	400	0	0	.10	.20	.25	.30	.30	.25	.20	.10	0	0	5	3
Weed Trimmer	95	65	0	0	.10	.20	.20	.20	.20	.20	.10	0	0	0	35	20
Hedge Clipper	75	40	0	0	.10	.20	.20	.20	.20	.20	.10	0	0	0	40	35
Drill	45	35	.20	.20	.25	.30	.30	.35	.30	.30	.30	.20	.20	.20	60	15
Snow Blower	800	450	.20	.20	.10	0	0	0	0	0	0	0	.20	.20	3	3
Snow Shovel	12	8	.15	.15	.10	0	0	0	0	0	0	0	.15	.15	14	10
Ice Chopper	8	4	.15	.15	.10	0	0	0	0	0	0	0	.15	.15	10	5

Since the items are discounted according to month, sales transaction data should include the month of the sale as well as the item description and the customer's name. The selling price of an item is then computed on the basis of the list price, the appropriate percentage discount for the item, and the month in which it is sold. This will affect the profit earned on that item since profit = selling price − store's cost.

As in problem 4 and the inventory examples in chapter 6, the management report should reflect the number of items sold in each item category, the total profit earned for each item category, the total number of items sold, and the overall total gross profit. See problems 1 and 2 in chapter 6 and problem 4 in this chapter for detailed formulas and typical output.

Also, as in previous inventory control problems, include reorder message logic in your program that will print reorder or low stock messages when the QOH for any item falls below the reorder point (MQOH).

Use the READ/DATA statement combination to load the table, which will circumvent your having to reenter the inventory table should any syntax or logic errors occur in your program during program development and testing.

7. This problem requires that you write a structured BASIC program that will allow owners of an automobile dealership to process their automobile sales with a sophisticated computerized sales processing, inventory, and accounting system. For each sales request being processed, the data record entered into the terminal will contain the following: automobile description; customer's name; customer's address; customer's phone number; amount of deposit; maximum waiting period; and salesman's code numbers. This sales record is used to access and update three tables and to complete processing. The three tables are the automobile inventory data table, which contains important data about the vehicle ordered; the salesperson's data table, which contains pertinent sales data for each salesperson; and the customer account table, which stores data about past and present customers. These tables will look like this.

Automobile Inventory Data Table

Code Number	Description	Price	Cost	YTD Profit	Normal Time Delivery	Number in Stock	MQOH	Options	Maximum Discounts
1	Cheetah	10,500	7,500	0	30	5	1	Air Conditioning	8%
2	Leopard	12,000	8,000	0	30	5	1	Stereo	6%
3	Snake	23,000	17,000	0	60	8	1	—	4%
4	Superlark	16,000	11,000	0	60	3	1	Air Conditioning	8%
5	Zuess	22,000	16,000	0	45	1	1	Air Conditioning	10%
6	Cosmo	18,000	14,000	0	45	1	1	Stereo	10%
7	Flash	9,500	6,500	0	30	3	1	Standard Shift	4%
8	Lion Wagon	14,000	10,000	0	60	2	1	Air Conditioning	9%

Salesperson's Data Table

ID Number	Name	Commission Rate*	This Month's Commission
1	John Smith	0.08	0
2	Albert Logan	0.10	0
3	Phil West	0.12	0
4	Joyce Alverez	0.12	0
5	Arnold Brown	0.09	0

*Assume that the commission rate for each salesperson was based on seniority and past sales performance.

Customer Account Table

Name	Car Code Number	Deposit	Balance Remaining
Jones	3	300	22,700

Your program should provide the following information to the dealership's owners and manager:

1. Determine if the car is in stock.
2. Determine if the customer's waiting period will be exceeded for the car ordered if it is not in stock, and print an appropriate message.
3. Compute the selling price of the car by applying the appropriate maximum discount, print a customer bill, and enter the sale in the customer account table.
4. Update the master inventory table to reflect each car sold.
5. Compute the commission on the sale by multiplying the selling price by the appropriate salesperson's commission rate from the salesperson's data, and add the commission to the monthly total for the salesperson in the same table.
6. Compute the profit on the sale of the car and update the YTD profit for the vehicle sold in the inventory data table.
7. Print all tables before and after the day's processing, which will constitute the management report.

Access the inventory table by sequential search using the automobile description as the key field. Access the salesperson's data table by direct access, using the salesperson's ID code, which was input with the sales transaction data. Add the customer data for each sale to the customer accounts table, and then sort this table to produce an alphabetical listing by customer name. Make up your own customer sales data, and use the output of case 6–3 as a guide for your management report formats.

CHAPTER EIGHT

ADVANCED TABLE PROCESSING

OUTLINE

SORTING RECORDS WITH THE BUBBLE SORT METHOD

BINARY SEARCHING
Binary Search Illustration | Theory of Computer Matching Programs with Tables |

CASE 8–1: REAL ESTATE MATCHING

LEARNING OBJECTIVES

Upon completion of this chapter, you will be able to:

☐ Understand the principles of sorting records in tables.

☐ Be able to write and use the bubble sort method.

☐ Understand the principles and advantages of the binary search for locating table records.

☐ Be able to write and use the binary search to locate table records.

☐ Understand the theory and utility of matching programs.

☐ Be able to design and write matching programs.

SORTING RECORDS WITH THE BUBBLE SORT METHOD

A bubble sort places records in tables in order, either alphabetically (for names or descriptions) or numerically (for part numbers, employee numbers, etc.). Sorting records in order facilitates locating information in printed tables, such as in telephone directories or inventory listings, and allows you to use binary search, a very fast data retrieval method.

The bubble sort is one of the most widely used sorting algorithms because it permits a programmer to rearrange records in the same table in which the records were originally loaded, saving memory. Also, this sorting method proceeds only to the point where the records are in the desired order because the logic uses switches to determine when the desired results have been reached and then halts the looping logic. This is important because if a table were nearly in order, it would be wasteful to proceed unnecessarily through a lengthy and time-consuming algorithm.

To illustrate how the bubble sort works, you can set up a simple table of employee names and use the bubble sorting method to place the records in ascending alphabetical order. The data to be sorted will be examined so that the program will place the name with the highest (binary) value in the highest or topmost position in the table. To do this, the first name at the top of the table is compared to the name in the next lower position in the table. If the first name is greater than the second, the two are switched by the SWAP statement and the second name is moved into the first table position. If the first name is not greater than the second, no switching takes place. The procedure is repeated down through the table, comparing the second name to the third, the third to the fourth, and so on, until all names have been compared to the name below it or the end of the table is reached. This is illustrated in figure 8–1.

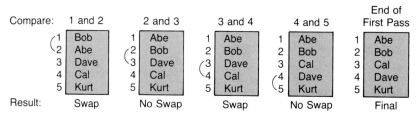

Because the records in this table were not badly out of order, the table was placed in order in just one pass. This is not always the case. Consider this example:

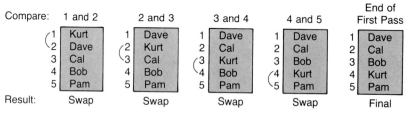

The table looks more ordered, but it is not in order. Another pass is needed:

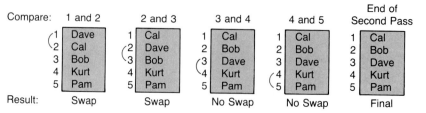

FIGURE 8–1
Bubble sort illustration.

272

So the number of necessary passes is a function of just how disordered the original table is. If there are three records and they are in reverse order, it takes two passes. For N records, it takes $N - 1$ passes to place the table in order.

The example in figure 8–2 shows that the table could be placed in order after only one pass if the records were not too badly disordered. To allow for this possibility, you can add some interesting logic in the form of a sort switch. This would be a signal value that could be set to 0 or 1, or "yes" or "no," respectively, depending on whether or not any switching took place in a pass through the table. For example, if your program compared records and did any swapping of adjacent records, you could set your sort switch to 1. However, if the program compared adjacent records and went from the first record to the last without switching, you could set the sort switch to 0. Better, you could set it before a pass to 0, and if no swapping took place it would *remain* at 0.

With that addition, you should provide logic to test the sort switch after each pass and before the next pass, and if it were still 0, no subsequent pass would be made (because it would be unnecessary—the table would already be in order).

In a large table, say one with 200 records, if the table is placed in order after the first pass, only one more pass is needed to find that out. You reduce the processing from 199 passes to 2—quite an improvement for such a small addition in logic! On the average, tables will be "half" out of order and the inclusion of the sort switch cuts processing time in half.

Figure 8–3 gives a BASIC program that uses the bubble sort with sort-switch logic to arrange a list of names in ascending alphabetical order. There are actually two versions of this program, one with SWAP and one with "swapping logic" that can be used on BASIC systems that don't support the SWAP statement. If your system supports SWAP, use it; if not, try the alternate version. In both cases be sure to include the logic that prints out the contents of the table before and after sorting.

In figure 8–3, line 20 allocates storage for 100 document names and their code designations for a manufacturing business. Sorting the documents by name will facilitate location of the corresponding codes. At lines 40 through 70, the table is loaded using the READ/DATA statements. Line 110 is the beginning of the "outer loop" for the search logic, which will control the number of complete passes through the table. In the outer loop, the sort switch is set to "NO," indicating that the table is not in order and the program should proceed to the inner loop, which does the comparing and swapping of adjacent table records (actually the key fields). The WHILE condition proceeds as long as the sort switch is equal to "NO." As soon as that loop is begun, the sort switch is set to "YES" so that if no swapping takes place in the inner loop (lines 140–170), it will remain "YES." (Swapping any record pair sets the switch to "NO.")

As adjacent record key fields are compared, with J always being one greater than I, the record locator, records will be swapped if they are out of order and left as is if they are not. The actual comparison, swapping, and resetting of the sort switch occur at line 160, which is the key statement in the program.

When the inner loop is exited after all adjacent pairs of key fields in the records have been compared, the WEND at line 180 transfers control back to WHILE.

If no swapping takes place in the inner comparison loop, the sort switch will remain "YES" and the entire outer WHILE loop will be exited. This is the feature that

FIGURE 8–2
A bubble sort with only one switch.

FIGURE 8-3

BASIC programs using a bubble sort with sort-switch logic.

```
10       REM      SET UP TABLES FOR DATA TO BE SORTED
20                DIM NM$(100),N$(100)
30       REM      LOAD THE TABLES
40                FOR J = 1 TO 100
50                    READ NM$(J), N$(J)
60                        IF NM$(J) ="END" THEN NR = J - 1: GOTO 80
70                NEXT J
80       REM      SET SORT SWITCH TO "NO". "YES" MEANS SORTED
90                SORTSW$ = "NO"
100      REM      BEGIN THE SORT
110               WHILE SORTSW$ = "NO"
120                  SORTSW$ = "YES"
130                  NP = NR - 1
140                  FOR I = 1 TO NP
150                      J = I + 1
160                        IF NM$(I) > NM$(J) THEN SWAP NM$(I),NM$(J)
                                      :SWAP N$(I),N$(J): SORTSW$ = "NO"
170                  NEXT I
180               WEND
190      REM      PRINT THE SORTED TABLE
200               LPRINT "    DOCUMENT FILE OR LEDGER        DESIGNATION CODE"
210               LPRINT "_____    _____"
220               LPRINT
230               FOR K = 1 TO NR
240                   LPRINT NM$(K);TAB(40);N$(K)
250               NEXT K
260               END
270      REM
280      DATA     CUSTOMER UPDATE INFORMATION,1
290      DATA     APPLICATION FOR CREDIT,2
300      DATA     CREDIT DENIAL OR CANCELLATION,7
310      DATA     SALES ORDER,3
320      DATA     CATALOG,4
330      DATA     CREDIT REPORT,5
340      DATA     A/R TRANSACTION NOTICE,6
350      DATA     CREDIT CARD,8
360      DATA     CUSTOMER INVOICE,9
370      DATA     MONTHLY STATEMENT,10
380      DATA     OVERDUE NOTICE,11
390      DATA     OVERCREDIT NOTICE,12
400      DATA     CUSTOMER COMPLAINT,13
410      DATA     WAREHOUSE TRANSFER NOTICE,14
420      DATA     SHIPPING NOTICE,15
430      DATA     BILL OF LADING,16
440      DATA     CUSTOMER PAYMENT,17
450      DATA     PAYMENT NOTICE,18
460      DATA     VENDOR INVOICE,19
470      DATA     MATERIAL REQUISITION,20
480      DATA     FINISHED GOODS TRANSFER CARD,21
490      DATA     PURCHASE REQUISITION,22
500      DATA     PURCHASE ORDER,23
510      DATA     INVENT RECEIVED AND TRANS NOTICE,24
520      DATA     RECEIVING REPORT,25
530      DATA     ACCOUNTS PAY. TRANS. NOTICE,26
540      DATA     BILL OF LADING (VENDOR),27
550      DATA     COMPANY PAYMENT,28
560      DATA     CUSTOMER,D-1
570      DATA     COLLECTION,D-2
580      DATA     BILLING,D-3
590      DATA     SALES,D-4
600      DATA     DISTRIBUTION,D-5
610      DATA     A/R SUPERVISOR,D-6
```

```
620     DATA    PRODUCTION SUPERVISOR,D-7
630     DATA    FINISHED PRODUCT INVENTORY,D-8
640     DATA    RAW MATERIALS INVENTORY,D-9
650     DATA    PRODUCTION,D-10
660     DATA    PURCHASING,D-11
670     DATA    RECEIVING,D-12
680     DATA    ACCOUNTS PAYABLE,D-13
690     DATA    VENDOR,D-14
700     DATA    A/R MASTER FILE,F-1
710     DATA    SALES ORDER FILE,F-2
720     DATA    PARTS EXPLOSION MASTER FILE,F-4
730     DATA    RAW MATERIALS INVENTORY FILE,F-5
740     DATA    VENDOR MASTER FILE,F-6
750     DATA    ACCOUNTS PAYABLE MASTER FILE,F-7
760     DATA    CASH RECEIPTS (CUSTOMER) JOURNAL,J-1
770     DATA    ACCOUNTS REC. TRANS REG,J-2
780     DATA    CASH PAYMENT (TO VENDOR) JOURNAL,J-3
790     DATA    END,END
```

makes the bubble sort efficient. Looping stops after no more swapping. If the table being sorted was nearly in order, just a few passes through the outer loop would determine this, and the program would be stopped.

Lines 200–260 print out the newly sorted table with titles and headings.

Note that the program in figure 8–3 has the relatively large number of records— 52 in this example—(lines 280–790). This large number, greater than the amount of data used in most of the illustrative programs, is designed to show how time-consuming sorting logic can be, even for a computer that takes only thousandths of a second to complete each individual comparison. There is actually a significant delay as this program is run! This is a feature of the bubble sort and other programs that contain nested loops, illustrating the need for providing logic to improve the processing efficiency, such as the sort switch.

Figure 8–4 shows the output from the sort program shown in figure 8–3.

The alternate version of the bubble sort program shown in figure 8–5 illustrates logic that can be used to accomplish swapping on versions of BASIC that do not support the SWAP statement. This new logic appears at lines 162–168. If the record key fields are out of order and need to be exchanged, you would move the ''top'' record key field to a ''holding area,'' as shown here:

$$NMHOLD\$ = NM\$(I)$$

where I designates the ''top'' record position. Then, you could move the key field below it in the table to the I position like this:

$$NM\$(I) = NM\$(J)$$

where J is one greater than I. Finally, you would move the data in the ''holding area'' to the location indicated by J, like this:

$$NM\$(J) = NMHOLD\$$$

Remember to provide this exchanging logic of three statements for every field in the record. In this example, there were only two fields per record, so there are only six statements in the switching routine. If you forget to do this for each field in the record, the result will look like the table is sorted; however, every record's related fields (those related to the key field) will be mismatched and the sorted table will be useless. A telephone directory where the names are in order alphabetically, but the phone numbers remain as they were is a good example of this kind of error.

275

```
        DOCUMENT FILE OR LEDGER                 DESIGNATION CODE
--------------------------------                ----------------

   A/R MASTER FILE                                    F-1
   A/R SUPERVISOR                                     D-6
   A/R TRANSACTION NOTICE                             6
   ACCOUNTS PAY. TRANS. NOTICE                        26
   ACCOUNTS PAYABLE                                   D-13
   ACCOUNTS PAYABLE MASTER FILE                       F-7
   ACCOUNTS REC. TRANS REG                            J-2
   APPLICATION FOR CREDIT                             2
   BILL OF LADING                                     16
   BILL OF LADING (VENDOR)                            27
   BILLING                                            D-3
   CASH PAYMENT (TO VENDOR) JOURNAL                   J-3
   CASH RECEIPTS (CUSTOMER) JOURNAL                   J-1
   CATALOG                                            4
   COLLECTION                                         D-2
   COMPANY PAYMENT                                    28
   CREDIT CARD                                        8
   CREDIT DENIAL OR CANCELLATION                      7
   CREDIT REPORT                                      5
   CUSTOMER                                           D-1
   CUSTOMER COMPLAINT                                 13
   CUSTOMER INVOICE                                   9
   CUSTOMER PAYMENT                                   17
   CUSTOMER UPDATE INFORMATION                        1
   DISTRIBUTION                                       D-5
   FINISHED GOODS TRANSFER CARD                       21
   FINISHED PRODUCT INVENTORY                         D-8
   INVENT RECEIVED AND TRANS NOTICE                   24
   MATERIAL REQUISITION                               20
   MONTHLY STATEMENT                                  10
   OVERCREDIT NOTICE                                  12
   OVERDUE NOTICE                                     11
   PARTS EXPLOSION MASTER FILE                        F-4
   PAYMENT NOTICE                                     18
   PRODUCTION                                         D-10
   PRODUCTION SUPERVISOR                              D-7
   PURCHASE ORDER                                     23
   PURCHASE REQUISITION                               22
   PURCHASING                                         D-11
   RAW MATERIALS INVENTORY                            D-9
   RAW MATERIALS INVENTORY FILE                       F-5
   RECEIVING                                          D-12
   RECEIVING REPORT                                   25
   SALES                                              D-4
   SALES ORDER                                        3
   SALES ORDER FILE                                   F-2
   SHIPPING NOTICE                                    15
   VENDOR                                             D-14
   VENDOR INVOICE                                     19
   VENDOR MASTER FILE                                 F-6
   WAREHOUSE TRANSFER NOTICE                          14
```

FIGURE 8-4

Output obtained from the program in figure 8-3.

FIGURE 8–5
Alternate version of the bubble sort program in figure 8–3 (without SWAP).

```
10      REM     SET UP TABLES FOR DATA TO BE SORTED
20              DIM NM$(100),N$(100)
30      REM     LOAD THE TABLES
40              FOR J = 1 TO 100
50                  READ NM$(J),N$(J)
60                      IF NM$(J) ="END" THEN NR = J - 1: GOTO 80
70              NEXT J
80      REM     SET SORT SWITCH TO "NO". "YES" MEANS SORTED
90              SORTSW$ = "NO"
100     REM     BEGIN THE SORT
110             WHILE SORTSW$ = "NO"
120                 SORTSW$ = "YES"
130                 NP = NR - 1
140                 FOR I = 1 TO NP
150                     J = I + 1
160                         IF NM$(I) < NM$(J) THEN GOTO 170
161     REM                 THIS IS AN ALTERNATE TO THE SWAP STATEMENT
162                             NMHOLD$ = NM$(I)
163                             NM$(I)  = NM$(J)
164                             NM$(J)  =NMHOLD$
165     REM
166                             NHOLD$  = N$(I)
167                             N$(I)   = N$(J)
168                             N$(J)   = NHOLD$
169                             SORTSW$ = "NO"
170                 NEXT I
180             WEND
190     REM     PRINT THE SORTED TABLE
200             PRINT "    DOCUMENT FILE ON LEDGER        DESIGNATION CODE"
210             PRINT "_____    _____"
220             PRINT
230             FOR K = 1 TO NR
240                 PRINT NM$(K);TAB(40);N$(K)
250             NEXT K
260             END
270     REM
280     DATA    CUSTOMER UPDATE INFORMATION,1
290     DATA    APPLICATION FOR CREDIT,2
300     DATA    CREDIT DENIAL OR CANCELLATION,7
310     DATA    SALES ORDER, 3
320     DATA    CATALOG,4
330     DATA    CREDIT REPORT,5
340     DATA    A/R TRANSACTION NOTICE,6
350     DATA    CREDIT CARD,8
360     DATA    CUSTOMER INVOICE,9
370     DATA    MONTHLY STATEMENT,10
380     DATA    OVERDUE NOTICE,11
390     DATA    OVERCREDIT NOTICE,12
400     DATA    CUSTOMER COMPLAINT,13
410     DATA    WAREHOUSE TRANSFER NOTICE,14
420     DATA    SHIPPING NOTICE,15
430     DATA    BILL OF LADING,16
440     DATA    CUSTOMER PAYMENT,17
450     DATA    PAYMENT NOTICE,18
460     DATA    VENDOR INVOICE,19
470     DATA    MATERIAL REQUISITION,20
480     DATA    FINISHED GOODS TRANSFER CARD,21
490     DATA    PURCHASE REQUISITION,22
500     DATA    PURCHASE ORDER,23
510     DATA    INVENT RECEIVED AND TRANS NOTICE,24
520     DATA    RECEIVING REPORT,25
```

```
530        DATA       ACCOUNTS PAY. TRANS. NOTICE,26
540        DATA       BILL OF LADING (VENDOR),27
550        DATA       COMPANY PAYMENT,28
560        DATA       CUSTOMER,D-1
570        DATA       COLLECTION,D-2
580        DATA       BILLING,D-3
590        DATA       SALES,D-4
600        DATA       DISTRIBUTION,D-5
610        DATA       A/R SUPERVISOR,D-6
620        DATA       PRODUCTION SUPERVISOR,D-7
630        DATA       FINISHED PRODUCT INVENTORY,D-8
640        DATA       RAW MATERIALS INVENTORY,D-9
650        DATA       PRODUCTION,D-10
660        DATA       PURCHASING,D-11
670        DATA       RECEIVING,D-12
680        DATA       ACCOUNTS PAYABLE,D-13
690        DATA       VENDOR,D-14
700        DATA       A/R MASTER FILE,F-1
710        DATA       SALES ORDER FILE,F-2
720        DATA       PARTS EXPLOSION MASTER FILE,F-4
730        DATA       RAW MATERIALS INVENTORY FILE,F-5
740        DATA       VENDOR MASTER FILE,F-6
750        DATA       ACCOUNTS PAYABLE MASTER FILE,F-7
760        DATA       CASH RECEIPTS (CUSTOMER) JOURNAL,J-1
770        DATA       ACCOUNTS REC. TRANS REG,J-2
780        DATA       CASH PAYMENT (TO VENDOR) JOURNAL,J-3
790        DATA       END,END
```

BINARY SEARCHING

Binary searching proceeds similarly to the way you look up information in a dictionary or the index of a text. Let's say, for example, that you want to find information on the GOSUB statement. Since G (in GOSUB) is near the beginning of the alphabet, you would instinctively not look in the last pages of the index, but probably concentrate in the first half (approximately). Let's say while you were searching for GOSUB you found that the page you opened to referred to IF. Knowing I in IF came after G, you could rule out all the pages after the one you found, and concentrate on the pages before IF. You would continue this splitting process until you found GOSUB.

Figure 8–6 shows a table in which you are looking for the number 6 in a table containing 10 numbers in ascending order (remember that for the search to work, the numbers must be in order). Since the midpoint is determined by a rounding algorithm, IF N = 1, it will be located as shown in the second chart in figure 8–6. However, since the rounding algorithm will produce a midpoint of 9 for an average of 9.5, if the last record is the one being searched for, then it will never be found. For this reason, when using this algorithm, it is important to check for the location of the record desired in the last table position before continuing with the algorithm. The complete program shown in figure 8–7 illustrates this important logical inclusion!

Note that binary search, unlike direct access, does not require numeric key fields. Alphabetic or alphanumeric will work just as well. However, for this to work the fields used must be sorted in ascending alphabetical order, A to Z, as shown previously.

One final note on speed of binary searching: it is obviously faster than sequential search because half of the table is eliminated with each comparison. What may not be obvious is that the speed advantage increases as the table size increases. For example, if the table size consists of four records, the desired record will be located, on average, in two passes. If the table has eight records, three passes may be required. If the table had

278

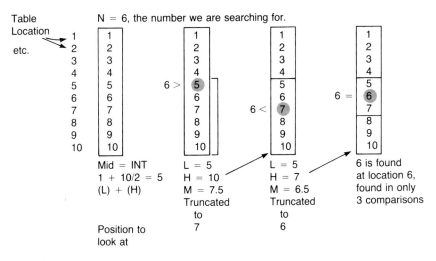

FIGURE 8–6
Binary search example.

sixteen records, four passes might be required. This trend should become apparent—it is really a function of the powers of 2, as shown in table 8–1. In other words, the relative speed is a function of table size—the larger the table, the greater the savings in access time.

When you combine binary search logic with the previous sort program, you come up with a very fast method for retrieving table records, as illustrated in figure 8–7. In this program, a WHILE loop was established at lines 990–1280 to continue searching for document names (the key field for searching) until the word END is entered as the "transaction search field." At lines 1000 and 1010, the initial beginning and end points (record positions) for the table to be searched were established, and the name of the document to be searched for was entered at line 1030. Line 1070 set a counter, which was used later in line 1180 to determine whether the document being searched for was in the table at all, and line 1090 branched to the end of the WHILE loop if END was entered to terminate the program.

At line 1130, the actual search logic began, with a comparison of the document name being searched for with the last document name in the table. This was necessary because of the truncation logic which calculates the midpoint of each table part, as explained earlier.

At line 1160, the midpoint of the table was calculated, and depending on whether the name of the document being searched for was greater or less than the name of the document located at the midpoint, the table was split by assigning new beginning and end points. This took place at lines 1220 and 1230.

TABLE 8–1
Relative speed advantage of binary searching compared to a sequential search.

Table Size	4096	2048	1024	512	256	128	64
Number of Passes to Find Record	12	11	10	9	8	7	6
Table Size	32	16	8	4	2		
Number of Passes to Find Record	5	4	3	2	1		

Thus the advantage is about 1/400 for a 4,096-record table, compared to sequential searching, and 4/16 (or 1/4) for a 16-record table, compared to sequential searching!

Binary Search Illustration

FIGURE 8–7

Binary search program.

```
Input
10      REM     SET UP TABLES FOR DATA TO BE SORTED
20              DIM NM$(100),N$(100)
30      REM     LOAD THE TABLES
40              FOR J = 1 TO 100
50                      READ NM$(J),N$(J)
60                      IF NM$(J) ="END" THEN NR = J - 1: GOTO 80
70              NEXT J
80      REM     SET SORT SWITCH TO "NO". "YES" MEANS SORTED
90              SORTSW$ = "NO"
100     REM     BEGIN THE SORT
110             WHILE SORTSW$ = "NO"
120                SORTSW$ = "YES"
130                NP = NR - 1
140                FOR I = 1 TO NP
150                   J = I + 1
160                   IF NM$(I) < NM$(J) THEN GOTO 260
170     REM             THIS IS AN ALTERNATE TO THE SWAP STATEMENT
180                         NMHOLD$ = NM$(I)
190                         NM$(I)  = NM$(J)
200                         NM$(J)  =NMHOLD$
210     REM
220                         NHOLD$  = N$(I)
230                         N$(I)   = N$(J)
240                         N$(J)   = NHOLD$
250                         SORTSW$ = "NO"
260                NEXT I
270             WEND
280     REM     PRINT THE SORTED TABLE
290             LPRINT "    DOCUMENT FILE OR LEDGER        DESIGNATION CODE"
300             LPRINT "_____   _____"
310             LPRINT
320             FOR K = 1 TO NR
330                 LPRINT NM$(K);TAB(40);N$(K)
340             NEXT K
342             GOSUB 880
345             END
350     REM
360     DATA    CUSTOMER UPDATE INFORMATION,1
370     DATA    APPLICATION FOR CREDIT,2
380     DATA    CREDIT DENIAL OR CANCELLATION,7
390     DATA    SALES ORDER, 3
400     DATA    CATALOG,4
410     DATA    CREDIT REPORT,5
420     DATA    A/R TRANSACTION NOTICE,6
430     DATA    CREDIT CARD,8
440     DATA    CUSTOMER INVOICE,9
450     DATA    MONTHLY STATEMENT,10
460     DATA    OVERDUE NOTICE,11
470     DATA    OVERCREDIT NOTICE,12
480     DATA    CUSTOMER COMPLAINT,13
490     DATA    WAREHOUSE TRANSFER NOTICE,14
500     DATA    SHIPPING NOTICE,15
510     DATA    BILL OF LADING,16
520     DATA    CUSTOMER PAYMENT,17
530     DATA    PAYMENT NOTICE,18
540     DATA    VENDOR INVOICE,19
550     DATA    MATERIAL REQUISITION,20
560     DATA    FINISHED GOODS TRANSFER CARD,21
```

```
570    DATA    PURCHASE REQUISITION,22
580    DATA    PURCHASE ORDER,23
590    DATA    INVENT RECEIVED AND TRANS NOTICE,24
600    DATA    RECEIVING REPORT,25
610    DATA    ACCOUNTS PAY. TRANS. NOTICE,26
620    DATA    BILL OF LADING (VENDOR),27
630    DATA    COMPANY PAYMENT,28
640    DATA    CUSTOMER,D-1
650    DATA    COLLECTION,D-2
660    DATA    BILLING,D-3
670    DATA    SALES,D-4
680    DATA    DISTRIBUTION,D-5
690    DATA    A/R SUPERVISOR,D-6
700    DATA    PRODUCTION SUPERVISOR,D-7
710    DATA    FINISHED PRODUCT INVENTORY,D-8
720    DATA    RAW MATERIALS INVENTORY,D-9
730    DATA    PRODUCTION,D-10
740    DATA    PURCHASING,D-11
750    DATA    RECEIVING,D-12
760    DATA    ACCOUNTS PAYABLE,D-13
770    DATA    VENDOR,D-14
780    DATA    A/R MASTER FILE,F-1
790    DATA    SALES ORDER FILE,F-2
800    DATA    PARTS EXPLOSION MASTER FILE,F-4
810    DATA    RAW MATERIALS INVENTORY FILE,F-5
820    DATA    VENDOR MASTER FILE,F-6
830    DATA    ACCOUNTS PAYABLE MASTER FILE,F-7
840    DATA    CASH RECEIPTS (CUSTOMER) JOURNAL, J-1
850    DATA    ACCOUNTS REC. TRANS REG,J-2
860    DATA    CASH PAYMENT (TO VENDOR) JOURNAL, J-3
870    DATA    END,END
880    REM     NM$ IS THE KEY FIELD THAT WILL BE SEARCHED FOR ⟵──────── **Binary Search Logic**
890    REM     N$  IS THE RELATED DOCUMENT CODE THAT WILL BE RETRIEVED          **Begins Here**
900    REM
910    REM     NR IS THE NUMBER OF TABLE RECORDS AS IN THE SORT
920    REM     TRXNM$ IS THE NAME OF THE DOCUMENT TO START THE SEARCH
930    REM
940    REM     L IS THE STARTING POINT OF THE 'SPLIT' TABLE
950    REM     H IS THE TOP OF THE 'SPLIT' TABLE OR NR AT THE START
960    REM
970    REM     LET L = 1 AND H = NR TO BEGIN (THE ENTIRE TABLE)
980            TRXNM$="ANYTHING"
990            WHILE TRXNM$ <> "END"
1000           L = 1
1010           H = NR
1020   REM
1030   REM     INPUT THE DOCUMENT NAME TO BE SEARCHED FOR
1040           TRXNM$="ANYTHING"
1050           LPRINT
1060           LPRINT
1070           COUNT = 0
1080           INPUT "ENTER THE DOCUMENT NAME "TRXNM$
1085           LPRINT "ENTER THE DOCUMENT NAME : "TRXNM$
1090           IF TRXNM$ = "END" THEN 1280
1100   REM
1110   REM     COMPARE WITH THE LAST RECORD BECAUSE OF TRUNCATION
1120   REM
1130           IF TRXNM$ = NM$(NR) THEN LPRINT NM$(NR),N$(NR):GOTO 1280
1140   REM
1150   REM
1160           MID = INT((L + H)/2):LPRINT MID
1170           COUNT = COUNT + 1
1180           IF COUNT > NR THEN LPRINT NO SUCH RECORD IN TABLE:GOTO 1280
1190           I = MID
```

281

```
1200              LPRINT TRXNM$,NM$(I)
1210              IF TRXNM$ = NM$(I) THEN 1250
1220              IF TRXNM$ > NM$(I) THEN L = MID:GOTO 1160
1230              IF TRXNM$ < NM$(I) THEN H = MID:GOTO 1160
1240      REM
1250      REM
1260      REM    PRINT THE LOCATED RECORD (NAME OF DOCUMENT AND ITS CODE)
1270              LPRINT NM$(I),N$(I)
1280              WEND
1290      RETURN
1300      REM END OF PROGRAM
```

Output

(Note: Output for the sorted table is the same as shown in figure 8–4.)

Output for the search logic

```
ENTER THE DOCUMENT NAME : CATALOG
  26
CATALOG          FINISHED GOODS TRANSFER CARD
  13
CATALOG          CASH RECEIPTS (CUSTOMER) JOURNAL
  19
CATALOG          CREDIT REPORT
  16
CATALOG          COMPANY PAYMENT
  14
CATALOG          CATALOG
CATALOG          4


ENTER THE DOCUMENT NAME : VENDOR
  26
VENDOR           FINISHED GOODS TRANSFER CARD
  38
VENDOR           PURCHASE REQUISITION
  44
VENDOR           SALES
  47
VENDOR           SHIPPING NOTICE
  49
VENDOR           VENDOR INVOICE
  48
VENDOR           VENDOR
VENDOR           D-14


ENTER THE DOCUMENT NAME : A/R MASTER FILE
  26
A/R MASTER FILE            FINISHED GOODS TRANSFER CARD
  13
A/R MASTER FILE            CASH RECEIPTS (CUSTOMER) JOURNAL
  7
A/R MASTER FILE            ACCOUNTS REC. TRANS REG
  4
A/R MASTER FILE            ACCOUNTS PAY. TRANS. NOTICE
  2
A/R MASTER FILE            A/R SUPERVISOR
  1
A/R MASTER FILE            A/R MASTER FILE
A/R MASTER FILE            F-1


ENTER THE DOCUMENT NAME : END
```

Of course, if the document being searched for matched the name found at the midpoint, then statement 1210 caused a branch to the output statements, which printed the results of the search (the found document code).

Theory of Computer Matching Programs with Tables

In chapter 7, you learned how tables are used for storing, retrieving, and updating large numbers of records quickly and efficiently. Often, these operations are not the foundation of table programs. Instead, sometimes tables are set up to form databases containing many records. In matching programs, the database consists of a store of information which can be searched and compared so that a "best match" can be found between the records in the table and an inquiry record. Matching systems are the foundation for many popular computerized applications such as real estate selection, job placement, disease diagnosis, police inquiry, and dating.

A matching system works like this: an inquiry record is input which contains many fields that have corresponding fields in the table records. Each field value in the inquiry record is compared to its corresponding field value in each table record (one record at a time). As each field value is compared to the table record field value, the computer is programmed to keep track of how closely the two field values match. If they match closely, points are added to an accumulator. These points will ultimately reflect the degree of similarity between the inquiry record and each table record. When all table records have been compared to the inquiry record, the table record having the highest accumulator value will be the best match.

A simplified job placement program will help illustrate the features just described. Table 8–2 lists some jobs available for programmers. In the table, each record pertains to one job, and the fields in each record describe some important characteristics of the job: its description; the programming languages needed; years of experience required; geographical location; and salary.

You will input one job applicant's preferences, containing the same fields. However, the fields will specify what the applicant *wants*, not the particular job characteristics. This is the inquiry record and it will be compared to every available job record in the job table to find the best match. The following shows an example of an inquiry record for an applicant.

Applicant	Job Desired	Best Programming Language	Years of Data Processing Experience	Preferred Location	Minimum Salary
1	Programmer	BASIC	2	Anywhere	$16,000

If you want to find the best match between what a person is looking for and what is available, you will compare all fields in the inquiry record to all the fields in each table

TABLE 8–2
Available data processing jobs.

Job Number	Job Description	Programming Language Needed	Minimum Years of Experience	Geographical Location	Starting Salary
1	Programmer	BASIC	2	N.Y.C.	$18,500
2	Programmer/Trainee	COBOL	1	Boston	17,000
3	Systems analyst	BASIC	4	Columbus	26,000
4	Scientific programmer	FORTRAN	3	Hartford	19,500
5	Analyst/programmer	BASIC	3	Los Angeles	22,000
6	Programmer	BASIC	2	Springfield	16,500

record. Notice that this is not a search, but rather a sequential evaluation of all the records in the entire table. Each field is important in the accumulator value assignment.

Usually, complex algorithms are used to assign points for various degrees of matching, but for now, you will consider the best job the one with the greatest number of matches (fields that meet minimum requirements or match exactly and all field matches will be weighted equally). So, since the applicant in the example is looking for a job as a programmer, has 2 years experience, would like a minimum starting salary of $16,000, and is willing to work anywhere, then job number 6 in the table is the best job for that person. It is the closest match to the applicant's needs compared to the other five jobs available (since it requires 2 years of experience in BASIC, is located in Springfield, and offers a starting salary of $16,500).

With such a small job table, you should have no trouble visually scanning it and arriving at this same conclusion. In reality, a job placement system would contain thousands of jobs with many more evaluation fields, making it virtually impossible for a person to make a good evaluation without a computer program.

The program you write to perform this matching for you must take two things into consideration. First, the evaluation procedure must include all table records, since you want your program to evaluate all possible jobs. Thus, a complete sequential (first-to-last) evaluation is desired. Second, each field in the job applicant's preference record should be compared to each corresponding field in the table record of job characteristics. But, you will need to answer some questions if you want to develop a meaningful program.

1. Should a job be considered if the job description preferred by the applicant does not match *exactly* the job description in the table, or can you allow some leeway?
2. Are the programming language requirements strict, or can you assume some flexibility is allowed?
3. Must the minimum number of years of experience required be strictly adhered to?
4. Does the location have to be a perfect match?
5. Is the salary requirement flexible?

For our first matching program, keep it simple. Assume that each field must match exactly and all fields are weighted equally, as shown in the following.

	Applicant Preferences		Job Characteristics	
IF	Job preferred	=	Job description	AND
	Program language preferred	=	Program language needed	AND
	Years of experience	=	Minimum years of experience needed	AND
	Location preferred	=	Actual location	AND
	Salary preferred	=	Starting salary	THEN PRINT
	JOB NO.___IS O.K.			

If you make these assumptions, you will obtain a listing of those jobs with perfect matches only. Obviously, the logic lacks sophistication and practicality. For example, jobs that called for less experience than our applicant possessed or jobs located in a town nearby would never be considered. To improve the evaluation criteria, you can modify the testing conditions slightly. For example, experience and salary considerations should be changed to:

```
IF Years of experience > = Minimum years of experience needed
     IF Preferred salary < = Starting salary ADD POINTS!
```

To refine further, rather than joining all selection criteria together in the form of one compound logical IF statement, suppose you add points to an accumulator for each field comparison in each job. If you assign these points on the basis of how good the match between the preference fields and characteristic fields is, the score at the end of each evaluation should reflect the extent of satisfactory matching. For example,

If years of experience are equal to minimum years of experience, then add five points.

If years of experience are greater than minimum years of experience, then add ten points.

or in BASIC:

```
IF YREXP = MYREXP THEN SCORE = SCORE + 5
IF YREXP > MYREXP THEN SCORE = SCORE + 10
```

Thus, you have used the number of points added to an accumulator for each job to indicate the degree of correspondence and also have taken into consideration the possibility that the job offers even more than the applicant might prefer. You can even reverse the logic and subtract points when the critical fields do not match, such as when the preferred location and the actual job location do not match:

If preferred location is not equal to geographical location, then subtract 10 points.

or in BASIC:

```
SCORE = SCORE - 10
```

Taking this situation one step further, if particularly critical evaluation criteria are not met, you could set the score to 0 (or negative), branch around the other evaluation fields, and go on to the next job record. For example, if the applicant's required salary is greater than the starting salary, you could skip that tab completely by writing the following:

```
IF SPREF > STSAL THEN SCORE = 0:GOTO (Next record in table)
```

A more sophisticated refinement might be to assign points in proportion to how close the preference and characteristic are, or in other words, in proportion to the magnitude of the difference between them. In the following example, points are assigned on the basis of difference in salary (DIFF).

```
Let:   DIFF = SPREF - STSAL
Then:  IF DIFF < = 0 THEN SCORE = SCORE + 0
       IF DIFF > 1000 THEN SCORE = SCORE + 5
       IF DIFF > 2000 THEN SCORE = SCORE + 10
```

Or, using a formula that differs from the preceding point-assignment algorithm:

```
IF DIFF > 0 THEN SCORE = SCORE + (DIFF/100)
```

In some cases, taking the absolute value (i.e., the positive difference between two numbers) of the difference might be sensible in numeric evaluation criteria.

With the refined evaluation scheme, the result will be a more meaningful table of available jobs, their characteristics, and sensible evaluation score for each job that reflects the degree of correspondence between what the applicant prefers and the jobs available. If you then sort this table by score in descending numerical order, the best jobs will appear at the top of the table and the worst at the bottom. You then need only print out the top five table records to get a realistic, useful, and sensible listing of the best jobs for the applicant.

The job characteristics' variables are subscripted variables comprising a table of available job characteristics. The variable names conform to BASIC and the dimension statement will have N = JOB,

```
***DIM NO(100), JDESC(100), JLANG(100) ...etc.
```

for 100 available jobs. An example data table is shown in table 8–3.

TABLE 8–3
Example data table for job example.

Field	Job Number and Description		Programming Language Needed	Minimum Years of Experience	Location	Starting Salary
BASIC Variable	NO(I)	JDESC$(I)	JLANG$(I)	JMINEX(I)	JLOC$(I)	JSTSAL(I)
I = 1	1	Programmer	BASIC	1	Boston	$16,000
I = 2	2	Jr. Programmer	BASIC	0	New York	14,000
I = 3	3	Prog./Analyst	BASIC	3	Los Angeles	19,500
I = 4	4	Analyst	BASIC	5	Denver	26,000

Inputting a long table of available jobs should be done with the READ/DATA instructions, and of course, you would print the table to verify that it is correct. This can save hours of debugging and retyping time if an error occurs during program development. Figure 8–8 shows the complete BASIC program for this example. This routine will produce a score of 100 for any job that matches an applicant's preferences exactly and a score of 0 for any job that meets none of an applicant's preferences. Next, it will sort the scores and job numbers in descending numerical order by score, and then print this information. This will yield a list of the job matches from best to worst for the applicant, as shown in the output.

FIGURE 8–8
Matching program for job selection example.

```
Input

 10   REM   ********************************************************
 20   REM   *            MATCHING PROGRAM ILLUSTRATION              *
 30   REM   *                  JOB SELECTION                        *
 40   REM   *                                                       *
 50   REM   *      THIS PROGRAM WILL TELL YOU WHAT JOBS ARE         *
 60   REM   *   AVAILABLE THAT BEST MEET THE GIVEN CRITERIA         *
 70   REM   *               USING A BUBBLE SORT                     *
 80   REM   *                                                       *
 90   REM   *                 VARIABLE LEGEND                       *
100   REM   *    ADESC$=PREFERRED JOB DESCRIPTION                   *
110   REM   *    ALANG$=PROGRAMMING LANGUAGE                        *
120   REM   *    AEXP  =YEARS OF EXPERIENCE                         *
130   REM   *    ALOC$ =PREFERRED LOCATION                          *
140   REM   *    ASAL  =STARTING SALARY REQUIREMENT                 *
150   REM   *    NO(I) =JOB NUMBER                                  *
160   REM   *    JDESC$=AVAILABLE JOB DESCRIPTIONS                  *
170   REM   *    JLANG$=AVAILABLE PROGRAMMING LANGUAGES             *
180   REM   *    JMINEX=MINIMUM YEARS OF EXPERIENCE REQUIRED        *
190   REM   *    JLOC$ =AVAILABLE LOCATIONS                         *
200   REM   *    JSTSAL=STARTING SALARIES                           *
210   REM   ********************************************************
220   REM   PERFORM 'LOAD AND INPUT TABLE' SUBROUTINE
230         GOSUB 330
240   REM   PERFORM 'INPUT APPLICANT DATA' SUBROUTINE
250         GOSUB 450
260   REM   PERFORM 'EVALUATE JOBS' SUBROUTINE
270         GOSUB 670
280   REM   PERFORM 'PLACE JOBS IN BEST ORDER' SUBROUTINE
290         GOSUB 780
300   REM   PERFORM 'PRINT BEST JOBS' SUBROUTINE
310         GOSUB 980
320         END
330   REM   ************************************
```

```
340   REM  * LOAD AND INPUT TABLE SUBROUTINE *
350   REM  **********************************
360        FOR I = 1 TO 4
370        READ JDESC$(I),JLANG$(I),JMINEX(I),JLOC$(I),JSTSAL(I)
380        NO(I) = I
390        NEXT I
400        LPRINT "NUMBER","DESCRIPT","LANGUAGE","MIN. EXP","LOCATION","START SAL."
410        FOR I = 1 TO 4
420        LPRINT NO(I),JDESC$(I),JLANG$(I),JMINEX(I),JLOC$(I),JSTSAL(I)
430        NEXT I
440        RETURN
450   REM  ***********************
460   REM  * INPUT APPLICANT DATA *
470   REM  ***********************
480        CLS
490        PRINT "COPYRIGHT (C) 1989, BY MERRILL PUBLISHING COMPANY"
500        PRINT "FOR USE WITH STRUCTURED BASIC PROGRAMMING"
510        PRINT
520        PRINT "ENTER APPLICANTS JOB DESCRIPTION, THE PROGRAMMING LANGUAGE"
530        PRINT "MINIMUM EXPERIENCE, LOCATION, STARTING SALARY"
540        PRINT
550        PRINT
560        PRINT "APPLICANTS JOB DESCRIPTION    _____"
570        PRINT "APPLICANTS PROG LANGUAGE      _____"
580        PRINT "APPLICANTS MIN EXPERIENCE     _____"
590        PRINT "APPLICANTS LOCATION           _____"
600        PRINT "APPLICANTS STARTING SALARY    _____"
610        LOCATE 8,28: INPUT ADESC$
620        LOCATE 9,28: INPUT ALANG$
630        LOCATE 10,28: INPUT AEXP
640        LOCATE 11,28: INPUT ALOC$
650        LOCATE 12,28: INPUT ASAL
660        RETURN
670   REM  ***************************
680   REM  * EVALUATE JOBS SUBROUTINE *
690   REM  ***************************
700        FOR I= 1 TO 4
710            IF ADESC$=JDESC$(I) THEN SCORE(I)=SCORE(I)+20
720            IF ALANG$=JLANG$(I) THEN SCORE(I)=SCORE(I)+20
730            IF AEXP  =JMINEX(I) THEN SCORE(I)=SCORE(I)+20
740            IF ALOC$ =JLOC$(I)  THEN SCORE(I)=SCORE(I)+20
750            IF ASAL  =JSTSAL(I) THEN SCORE(I)=SCORE(I)+20
760        NEXT I
770        RETURN
780   REM  ***************************************
790   REM  * PLACE JOBS IN BEST ORDER SUBROUTINE *
800   REM  ***************************************
810        SORTSW=1
820        WHILE SORTSW=1
830            IF SORTSW=0 THEN 900
840            SORTSW=0
850            FOR I= 1 TO 3
860                    J= I + 1
870            IF SCORE(J)<SCORE(I) THEN GOSUB 910
880            NEXT I
890        WEND
900        RETURN
910   REM  ******************
920   REM  * SWAP SUBROUTINE *
930   REM  ******************
940        SWAP SCORE(I),SCORE(J)
950        SWAP NO(I),NO(J)
960        SORTSW=1
```

```
970        RETURN
980  REM   ****************************
990  REM   * PRINT JOBS BEST TO WORST *
1000 REM   ****************************
1010       LPRINT
1020       LPRINT
1030       LPRINT " TABLE OF JOBS"
1040       LPRINT " BEST_TO_WORST"
1050       LPRINT "_____"
1060       LPRINT " JOB NUMBER","SCORE"
1070       FOR I= 1 TO 4
1080       LPRINT NO(I),SCORE(I)
1090       NEXT I
1100       RETURN
1110       DATA PROGRAMMER,BASIC,1,BOSTON,16000
1120       DATA JR.PROG,BASIC,0,NEW YORK,14000
1130       DATA PROG/ANALYST,BASIC,3,LOS ANGELES,19500
1140       DATA ANALYST,BASIC,5,DENVER,26000
1150 REM   END OF PROGRAM
```

Output

NUMBER	DESCRIPT	LANGUAGE	MIN. EXP	LOCATION	START SAL.
1	PROGRAMMER	BASIC	1	BOSTON	16000
2	JR.PROG	BASIC	0	NEW YORK	14000
3	PROG/ANALYST	BASIC	3	LOS ANGELES	19500
4	ANALYST	BASIC	5	DENVER	26000

```
ENTER APPLICANTS JOB DESCRIPTION, THE PROGRAMMING LANGUAGE
MINIMUM EXPERIENCE, LOCATION, STARTING SALARY

APPLICANTS JOB DESCRIPTION ? PROG/ANALYST___
APPLICANTS PROG LANGUAGE   ? BASIC_____
APPLICANTS MIN EXPERIENCE  ? 3_____
APPLICANTS LOCATION        ? LOS ANGELES____
APPLICANTS STARTING SALARY ? 18000_____
```

```
 TABLE OF JOBS
 BEST_TO_WORST

_____
 JOB NUMBER   SCORE
 1            20
 2            20
 4            20
 3            80
```

NUMBER	DESCRIPT	LANGUAGE	MIN. EXP	LOCATION	START SAL.
1	PROGRAMMER	BASIC	1	BOSTON	16000
2	JR.PROG	BASIC	0	NEW YORK	14000
3	PROG/ANALYST	BASIC	3	LOS ANGELES	19500
4	ANALYST	BASIC	5	DENVER	26000

```
ENTER APPLICANTS JOB DESCRIPTION, THE PROGRAMMING LANGUAGE
MINIMUM EXPERIENCE, LOCATION, STARTING SALARY


APPLICANTS JOB DESCRIPTION ? ANALYST_____
APPLICANTS PROG LANGUAGE   ? BASIC_____
APPLICANTS MIN EXPERIENCE  ? 4_____
APPLICANTS STARTING SALARY ? 25000_____


 TABLE OF JOBS
 BEST_TO_WORST
 _____
 JOB NUMBER   SCORE
 1             20
 2             20
 3             20
 4             60
```

Real Estate Matching

CONCEPTS TO BE ILLUSTRATED

This case illustrates the features of a matching program as they apply to the selection of homes. First, a table of characteristics of available homes is read into memory. This table then is printed to verify its accuracy. A record containing a given individual's preferences then is input. Next, a field-by-field comparison between each field on the preference record and each table record is made. This comparison yields a score for each table record which corresponds to the degree of matching obtained between the individual's preferences and the types of homes currently available.

The output from the program consists of the best three matches. Therefore, the table of available homes must be sorted by score in descending order. The bubble sort is used to do this. After sorting, the first three table records are printed, along with the individual's preferences.

The evaluation segment of the program is then repeated until the end of the preference records is reached, which signals the end of processing

PROBLEM DEFINITION

Input Specifications

Input consists of two record types. Record type 1 is used to set up a table of available homes having a variety of characteristics such as price, location, number of rooms, amount of land, etc. Record 2 contains a client's preferences for a home (also specifying price, location, number of rooms, etc.).

	Field No.	Field Description	Type	Example
Master	1	Address of Home	Alphanumeric	125 Main Street
Home	2	Town in Which Located	Alphabetic	Hartford
Directory	3	Phone Number	Alphanumeric	232-4040
Table	4	Number of Rooms	Integer	6
	5	Acres of Land	Decimal Number	.5
	6	Number of Bedrooms	Integer	3
	7	Number of Bathrooms	Integer	2
	8	Number of Automobile Garages	Integer	2
	9	Assumable Mortgage (1 = Yes, 0 = No)	Integer	0
	10	Asking Price	Integer	75000
Client	1	Client's Name	Alphabetic	John C. Smith
Preference	2	Town Preferred	Alphabetic	E. Hartford
	3	Client's Phone Number	Alphanumeric	242-7890
	4	Number of Rooms Desired	Integer	6
	5	Acres of Land Desired	Decimal Number	.3
	6	Number of Bedrooms Desired	Integer	3
	7	Number of Bathrooms Desired	Integer	1
	8	Garage(s) Desired (Number)	Integer	1
	9	Assumable Mortgage Desired (1 = Yes)	Integer	1
	10	Maximum Price Offered	Integer	80000

290

Processing Decisions and Formulas

After the "Available Homes" table has been set up and printed for verification, the client's preferences are input. A record-by-record sequential evaluation of all available homes is made, incrementing a "score" accumulator, when the client's preferences match the available property characteristics. When all table records have been evaluated, the table is sorted in high-to-low order by score, and when the best have been evaluated, the table is sorted in high-to-low order by score, and the best five matches—based on the five highest scores—are printed. The process is repeated until the end of the client preference file is reached.

Output

The original "Available Homes" table is to be printed with headings. The best three homes are printed as a report to the client for each client in the file.

```
                          TABLE OF AVAILABLE HOMES
             ----------------------------------------
RECORD     ADDRESS          TOWN        PHONE NO   RMS ACRE   BDRM BATH GAR MRTG PRICE
  1    125 MAIN STREET   HARTFORD      232-4040    6  0.50     3    2    2   0   $ 75,000
  2    60 SOUTH DRIVE    AVON          677-1111    1  1.00     4    3    2   0   $178,000
  3    10 NORTH AVENUE   W. HARTFORD   563-1234    7  0.50     3    1    1   0   $ 86,000
  4    15 EAST STREET    E. HARTFORD   569-6666    6  0.30     2    1    0   1   $ 68,000
  5    12 ARGOSY DRIVE   MANCHESTER    644-1313    8  0.40     2    2    1   1   $ 92,000
  6    1020 FOREST LANE  SIMSBURY      678-4131    9  2.00     2    2    2   0   $ 96,000
  7    4 WOODSTOCK AVE   HARTFORD      522-6100    5  0.20     2    1    0   1   $ 48,000
  8    1336 CHURCH ST.   S. WINDSOR    644-8080    7  0.50     3    2    2   0   $ 95,000
  9    45 SPRING STREE   BLOOMFIELD    244-1600    8  0.30     3    1    1   0   $ 72,000
 10    300 ROSE DRIVE    HARTFORD      232-1652    5  0.30     2    1    0   1   $ 49,000
```

```
                    CLIENT INQUIRY REPORT
                     A.D.P. REALTY CO.

         CLIENT: JOHN SMITH          PHONE:242-7890

    RATING   PREFERRED HOME ADDRESS   PHONE NO   EVALUATION SCORE    PRICE
    ------   ----------------------   --------   ----------------    -----
      1      125 MAIN STREET          232-4040         80          $ 75,000
      2      45 SPRING STREET         244-1600         60          $ 72,000
      3      300 ROSE DRIVE           232-1652         60          $ 49,000
```

```
                    CLIENT INQUIRY REPORT
                     A.D.P. REALTY CO.

         CLIENT: SUSAN BROWN          PHONE:322-4501

    RATING   PREFERRED HOME ADDRESS   PHONE NO   EVALUATION SCORE    PRICE
    ------   ----------------------   --------   ----------------    -----
      1      10 NORTH AVENUE          563-1234         80          $ 86,000
      2      125 MAIN STREET          232-4040         60          $ 75,000
      3      1336 CHURCH ST.          644-8080         60          $ 95,000
```

```
                    CLIENT INQUIRY REPORT
                     A.D.P. REALTY CO.

         CLIENT: CAROL JONES          PHONE:668-2323

    RATING   PREFERRED HOME ADDRESS   PHONE NO   EVALUATION SCORE    PRICE
    ------   ----------------------   --------   ----------------    -----
      1      1020 FOREST LANE         678-4131         70          $ 96,000
      2      45 SPRING STREET         244-1600         70          $ 72,000
      3      10 NORTH AVENUE          563-1234         60          $ 86,000
```

```
                        CLIENT INQUIRY REPORT
                          A.D.P. REALTY CO.

           CLIENT: DAVID CARTER              PHONE:422-1824

     RATING    PREFERRED HOME ADDRESS   PHONE NO   EVALUATION SCORE      PRICE
     ------    ----------------------   --------   ----------------      -----
       1       1020 FOREST LANE         678-4131          90          $ 96,000
       2       1336 CHURCH ST.          644-8080          60          $ 95,000
       3       125 MAIN STREET          232-4040          50          $ 75,000


                        CLIENT INQUIRY REPORT
                          A.D.P. REALTY CO.

           CLIENT: CECILE KANE              PHONE:525-1155

     RATING    PREFERRED HOME ADDRESS   PHONE NO   EVALUATION SCORE      PRICE
     ------    ----------------------   --------   ----------------      -----
       1       45 SPRING STREET         244-1600          60          $ 72,000
       2       1020 FOREST LANE         678-4131          40          $ 96,000
       3       125 MAIN STREET          232-4040          30          $ 75,000


                        CLIENT INQUIRY REPORT
                          A.D.P. REALTY CO.

           CLIENT: GEORGE CAREY              PHONE:628-5954

      THERE ARE NO HOMES AVAILABLE THAT MEET YOUR PREFERENCE


                        CLIENT INQUIRY REPORT
                          A.D.P. REALTY CO.

           CLIENT: THELMA BACH              PHONE:422-6300

     RATING    PREFERRED HOME ADDRESS   PHONE NO   EVALUATION SCORE      PRICE
     ------    ----------------------   --------   ----------------      -----
       1       60 SOUTH DRIVE           677-1111          30          $178,000
       2       45 SPRING STREET         244-1600          20          $ 72,000
       3       1020 FOREST LANE         678-4131          20          $ 96,000


                        CLIENT INQUIRY REPORT
                          A.D.P. REALTY CO.

           CLIENT: JAMES CLARK              PHONE:525-6360

     RATING    PREFERRED HOME ADDRESS   PHONE NO   EVALUATION SCORE      PRICE
     ------    ----------------------   --------   ----------------      -----
       1       4 WOODSTOCK AVE.         522-6100          20          $ 48,000
                       END OF REAL ESTATE MATCHING PROGRAM
```

Test Data

Available Homes Data

125 Main Street, Hartford, 232-4040, 6, .5, 3, 2, 2 ,0 , 75000
60 South Drive, Avon, 677-1111, 1, 1, 4, 3, 2, 0, 178000
10 North Avenue, W. Hartford, 563-1234, 7, .5, 3, 1, 1, 0, 86000
15 East Street, E. Hartford, 569-6666, 6, .3, 2, 1, 0, 1, 68000
12 Argosy Drive, Manchester, 644-1313, 8, .4, 2, 2, 1, 1, 92000
1020 Forest Lane, Simsbury, 678-4131, 9, 2, 2, 2, 2, 0, 96000

4 Woodstock Ave, Hartford, 522-6100, 5, .2, 2, 1, 0, 1, 48000
1336 Church St., S. Windsor, 644-8080, 7, .5, 3, 2, 2, 0, 95000
45 Spring Street, Bloomfield, 244-1600, 8, .3, 3, 1, 1, 0, 72000
300 Rose Drive, Hartford, 232-1652, 5, .3, 2, 1, 0, 1, 49000

Clients' Preferences

John Smith, Hartford, 242-7890, 6, .3, 3, 3, 1, 1, 80000
Susan Brown, W. Hartford, 322-4501, 5, .5, 2, 1, 1, 0, 50000
Carol Jones, E. Hartford, 668-2323, 8, 1, 3, 1, 0, 0, 100000
David Carter, Simsbury, 422-1824, 7, 2, 4, 2, 2, 0, 150000
Cecile Kane, Bloomfield, 525-1155, 8, 3, 5, 3, 3, 0, 175000
George Carey, Windsor, 628-5954, 12, 6, 8, 4, 4, 2, 45000
Thelma Bach, Enfield, 422-6300, 10, 4, 5, 3, 3, 2, 180000
James Clark, Enfield, 525-6360, 11, 5, 6, 4, 3, 2, 48000

Error Routines

None are required in this case, although traditional error trapping logic for invalid input data would be useful.

Validation Procedures

The hand comparisons and evaluation of one preference record against all table records would, of course, be desirable, although in tables with many records of large numbers of fields, this is really impractical.

A good scrutiny of the results, using sensible test data, as shown in this case, can often identify faulty logic. This is the method advocated here, and for the problems for solution at the end of chapter 8.

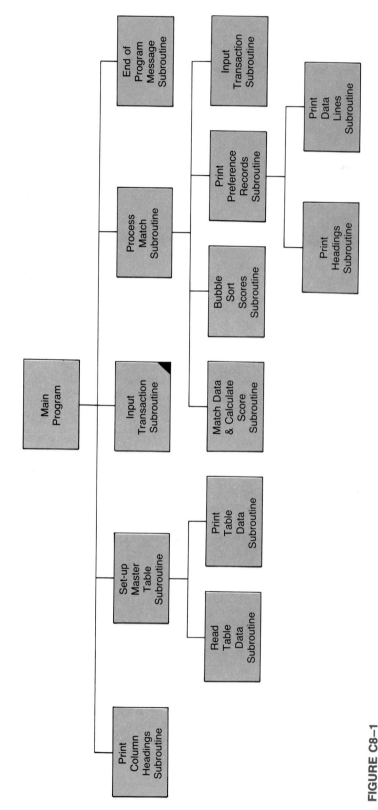

FIGURE C8–1
Visual table of contents—real estate matching program.

294

```
10      REM     *********************************************
20      REM     *           ADVANCED TABLE HANDLING          *
30      REM     *             CASE STUDY: C8-1               *
40      REM     *          REAL ESTATE MATCHING PROGRAM       *
41      REM     *                                            *
42      REM     *  THIS PROGRAM SETS UP A TABLE OF AVAILABLE *
43      REM     *  HOMES AND THEIR CHARACTERISTICS. IT THEN  *
44      REM     *  PERFORMS A SEQUENTIAL COMPARISON (MATCH)   *
45      REM     *  COMPARING A CLIENT'S PREFERENCES TO THE    *
46      REM     *  CHARACTERISTICS OF THE HOMES IN THE TABLE *
47      REM     *                                            *
48      REM     *  THE BEST MATCH IS INDICATED BY AN          *
49      REM     *  EVALUATION SCORE FOR EACH HOME, WHICH IS   *
50      REM     *  THEN USED AS THE KEY FIELD TO SORT (RANK) *
51      REM     *  THE HOMES FROM BEST MATCH TO WORST.        *
52      REM     *                                            *
53      REM     *  THE RESULTS ARE THEN PRINTED AS A CLIENT   *
54      REM     *  REPORT FOR THE BEST THREE MATCHES.         *
80      REM     *                                            *
90      REM     *                 VARIABLE LEGEND            *
100     REM     *    TABLE DATA:                             *
110     REM     *            ADR$ = ADDRESS                  *
120     REM     *            TWN$ = TOWN                     *
130     REM     *            PHON$= PHONE NUMBER             *
140     REM     *            RMS  = NUMBER OF ROOMS          *
150     REM     *            ACR$ = NUMBER OF ACRES          *
160     REM     *            BDRM = NUMBER OF BEDROOMS        *
170     REM     *            BTH  = NUMBER OF BATHS          *
180     REM     *            GAR  = GARAGE                   *
190     REM     *            MRTG = ASSUMABLE MORTGAGE        *
200     REM     *            PRC  = PRICE                    *
210     REM     *            SCORE= EVALUATION SCORE         *
220     REM     *    CLIENT PREFERENCE DATA:                 *
230     REM     *            TN$  = TOWN PREFERRED           *
240     REM     *            PNE$ = CLIENT PHONE NUMBER       *
250     REM     *            RM   = NUMBER OF ROOMS          *
260     REM     *            AC   = NUMBER OF ACRES          *
261     REM     *            BR   = NUMBER OF BEDROOMS        *
270     REM     *            BA   = NUMBER OF BATHS          *
280     REM     *            GA   = GARAGE                   *
290     REM     *            MGT  = ASSUMABLE MORTGAGE        *
300     REM     *            PRCE = MAXIMUM PRICE            *
310     REM     *********************************************
320             PRINT "COPYRIGHT (C) 1989, BY MERRILL PUBLISHING COMPANY"
330             PRINT "FOR USE WITH STRUCTURED BASIC PROGRAMMING"
340     REM     ***************
350     REM     * MAIN PROGRAM *
360     REM     ***************
370     REM     PERFORM 'PRINT COLUMN HEADINGS' SUBROUTINE
380             GOSUB 460
385     REM     PERFORM 'SETUP MASTER TABLE' SUBROUTINE
387             GOSUB 530
391     REM     PERFORM 'INPUT TRANSACTION' SUBROUTINE
392             GOSUB 880
393     REM     PERFORM 'PROCESS MATCH' SUBROUTINE WHILE NOT END OF DATA
394             GOSUB 1220
430     REM     PERFORM 'END OF PROGRAM MESSAGE' SUBROUTINE
440             GOSUB 2000
450             END
460     REM     ************************************
470     REM     * PRINT COLUMN HEADINGS SUBROUTINE *
480     REM     ************************************
```

```
490              LPRINT TAB(28);"TABLE OF AVAILABLE HOMES"
500              LPRINT TAB(28);"_____"
510              LPRINT "RECORD    ADDRESS    TOWN         PHONE NO  RMS ACRE  BDRM
      BATH GAR MRTG PRICE"
520              RETURN
530      REM     ******************************
540      REM     * SETUP MASTER TABLE SUBROUTINE *
550      REM     ******************************
560              DIM ADR$(100),TWN$(100),PHON$(100),RMS(100),ACR(100),BDRM(100),B
      TH(100),GAR(100),MRTG(100),PRC(100),SCORE(100)
570      REM     PERFORM 'READ TABLE DATA' SUBROUTINE
580              GOSUB 620
590      REM     PERFORM 'PRINT TABLE DATA' SUBROUTINE
600              GOSUB 700
610              RETURN
620      REM     ******************************
630      REM     * READ TABLE DATA SUBROUTINE *
640      REM     ******************************
650              FOR I = 1 TO 10
660                  READ ADR$(I),TWN$(I),PHON$(I),RMS(I),ACR(I),BDRM(I),BTH(I),G
      AR(I),MRTG(I),PRT(I)
670                  SCORE(I) = 0
680              NEXT I
690              RETURN
700      REM     ******************************
710      REM     * PRINT TABLE DATA SUBROUTINE *
720      REM     ******************************
730              FOR I = 1 TO 10
740                  F$ = " ## \            \ \          \ \        \## #.##
      #   #   #   #   $###,###"
750                  LPRINT USING F$;I,ADR$(I),TWN$(I),PHON$(I),RMS(I),ACR(I),BDR
      M(I),BTH(I),GAR(I),MRTG(I),PRC(I)
760              NEXT I
770              RETURN
880      REM     ******************************
890      REM     * INPUT TRANSACTION SUBROUTINE *
900      REM     ******************************
910              CLS
920              PRINT
930              PRINT
940              PRINT
950              PRINT "PLEASE ENTER YOUR PREFERENCES.  PRESS RETURN AFTER EACH E
      NTRY"
960              PRINT "TYPE 'EOD' INSTEAD OF CLIENT NAME, TO END THE PROGRAM"
970              PRINT
980              PRINT "PLEASE MAKE SURE THAT THE PRINTER IS ON"
990              PRINT
1000             PRINT "NAME......"
1010             PRINT "TOWN......"
1020             PRINT "PHONE #..."
1030             PRINT "ROOMS....."
1040             PRINT "ACRES....."
1050             PRINT "BEDROOMS.."
1060             PRINT "BATHS....."
1070             PRINT "GARAGE...."
1080             PRINT "MORTGAGE.."
1090             PRINT "PRICE....."
1100             LOCATE 9,11: INPUT NM$
1110             LOCATE 10,11: INPUT TN$
1120             LOCATE 11,11: INPUT PNE$
1130             LOCATE 12,11: INPUT RM
1140             LOCATE 13,11: INPUT AC
1150             LOCATE 14,11: INPUT BR
1160             LOCATE 15,11: INPUT BA
```

```
1170          LOCATE 16,11: INPUT GA
1180          LCOATE 17,11: INPUT MGT
1190          LOCATE 18,11: INPUT PRCE
1200          REPSW = 0
1210          RETURN
1220    REM   ****************************
1230    REM   * PROCESS MATCH SUBROUTINE *
1240    REM   ****************************
1245          WHILE NM$ <> "EOD"
1250    REM       PERFORM 'MATCH DATA & CALCULATE SCORE' SUBROUTINE
1260              GOSUB 1350
1270    REM       PERFORM 'BUBBLE SORT SCORES' SUBROUTINE
1280              GOSUB 1490
1290    REM       PERFORM 'INPUT TRANSACTION' SUBROUTINE
1300              GOSUB 1690
1301    REM       PERFORM 'INPUT TRANSACTION' SUBROUTINE
1302              GOSUB 880
1310                  FOR I = 1 TO 10
1320                  SCORE(I) = 0
1330                  NEXT I
1335          WEND
1340          RETURN
1350    REM   *********************************************
1360    REM   * MATCH DATA & CALCULATE SCORE SUBROUTINE *
1370    REM   *********************************************
1380          FOR I = 1 TO 10
1390          IF PRCE > = PRC(I) THEN SCORE(I) = SCORE(I) + 20
1400          IF TN$ = TWN$(I)    THEN SCORE(I) = SCORE(I) + 20
1410          IF RM < = RMS(I)    THEN SCORE(I) = SCORE(I) + 10
1420          IF AC < = ACR(I)    THEN SCORE(I) = SCORE(I) + 10
1430          IF BR < = BDRM(I)   THEN SCORE(I) = SCORE(I) + 10
1440          IF BA < = BTH(I)    THEN SCORE(I) = SCORE(I) + 10
1450          IF GA < = GAR(I)    THEN SCORE(I) = SCORE(I) + 10
1460          IF MGT = MRTG(I)    THEN SCORE(I) = SCORE(I) + 10
1470          NEXT I
1480          RETURN
1490    REM   ********************************
1500    REM   * BUBBLE SORT SCORES SUBROUTINE *
1510    REM   ********************************
1520          NREC = 10 - 1
1530          SORTSW = 1
1540          FOR K = 1 TO NREC
1550          IF SORTSW = 0 THEN 1660
1560              SORTSW = 0
1570              FOR I = 1 TO NREC
1580                  J = I + 1
1590                      IF SCORE(I) < SCORE(J) THEN SWAP ADR$(I),ADR$(J)
1600                      IF SCORE(I) < SCORE(J) THEN SWAP TWN$(I),TWN$(J):SWAP PH
ON$(I),PHON$(J):SWAP RMS(I),RMS(J):SWAP ACR(I),ACR(J)
1610                      IF SCORE(I) < SCORE(J) THEN SWAP BDRM(I),BDRM(J):SWAP BT
H(I),BTH(J)
1620                      IF SCORE(I) < SCORE(J) THEN SWAP GAR(I),GAR(J):SWAP MRTG
(I),MRTG(J):SWAP PRC(I),PRC(J):SWAP SCORE(I),SCORE(J)
1630                  SORTSW=1
1640              NEXT I
1650          NEXT K
1660          I = 1
1670          IF SCORE(I) > = 10 THEN REPSW = 1
1680          RETURN
1690    REM   *************************************
1700    REM   * PRINT PREFERENCE RECORDS SUBROUTINE *
1710    REM   *************************************
```

```
1720      REM       PERFORM 'PRINT HEADINGS' SUBROUTINE
1730                GOSUB 1770
1740      REM       PERFORM 'PRINT DATA LINES' SUBROUTINE
1750                IF REPSW = 1 THEN GOSUB 1920
1760                RETURN
1770      REM       ****************************
1780      REM       * PRINT HEADINGS SUBROUTINE *
1790      REM       ****************************
1800                LPRINT
1810                LPRINT
1820                LPRINT TAB(30)"CLIENT INQUIRY REPORT"
1830                LPRINT TAB(32)"A.D.P. REALTY CO."
1840                LPRINT
1850                F2$ = "               CLIENT: \              \ PHONE:\
          \"
1860                LPRINT USING F2$;NM$,PNE$
1870                LPRINT
1880                IF REPSW = 1 THEN LPRINT TAB(6);"RATING";TAB(15);"PREFERRED HOME
ADDRESS";TAB (39);"PHONE NO";TAB(49);"EVALUATION SCORE";TAB(69);"PRICE"
1890                IF REPSW = 1 THEN LPRINT TAB(6);"------";TAB(15);"--------------
--------";TAB (39);"--------";TAB(49);"----------------";TAB(69);"-----"
1900                IF REPSW = 0 THEN LPRINT TAB(14);"THERE ARE NO HOMES AVAILABLE T
HAT MEET YOUR PREFERENCE"
1910                RETURN
1920      REM       ******************************
1930      REM       * PRINT DATA LINES SUBROUTINE *
1940      REM       ******************************
1950                FOR I = 1 TO 3
1960                F3$ = "       #      \              \ \      \    ###
          $###,###"
1970                IF SCORE(I) > 0 THEN LPRINT USING F3$;I,ADR$(I),PHON$(I),SCORE(I
),PRC(I)
1980                NEXT I
1990                RETURN
2000      REM       **********************************
2010      REM       * END OF PROGRAM MESSAGE SUBROUTINE *
2020      REM       **********************************
2030                LPRINT
2040                LPRINT
2050                LPRINT
2060                LPRINT TAB(23);"END OF REAL ESTATE MATCHING PROGRAM"
2070                RETURN
2080      REM
2090                125 Main Street, Hartford, 232-4040, 6, .5, 3, 2, 2, 0, 75000
2100                60 South Drive, Avon, 677-1111, 1, 1, 4, 3, 2, 0, 178000
2110                10 North Avenue, W. Hartford, 563-1234, 7, .5, 3, 1, 1, 0, 86000
2120                15 East Street, E. Hartford, 569-6666, 6, .3, 2, 1, 0, 1, 68000
2130                12 Argosy Drive, Manchester, 644-1313, 8, .4, 2, 2, 1, 1, 92000
2140                1020 Forest Lane, Simsbury, 678-4131, 9, 2, 2, 2, 2, 0, 96000
2150                4 Woodstock Ave, Hartford, 522-6100, 5, .2, 2, 1, 0, 1, 48000
2160                1336 Church St., S. Windsor, 644-8080, 7, .5, 3, 2, 2, 0, 95000
2170                45 Spring Street, Bloomfield, 244-1600, 8, .3, 3, 1, 1, 0, 72000
2180                300 Rose Drive, Hartford, 232-1652, 5, .3, 2, 1, 0, 1, 49000
2190                END
```

SUMMARY

This chapter covered the sorting, binary searching, and matching logic table processing used in sophisticated and realistic business problem solving. Matching applications (i.e., programs that select the best matching record from a table of data records) form the basis for many useful and important business systems. Computerized home selection and job placement are two examples of matching applications covered in this chapter. These employ the concept of comparing a preference record (an individual's preferences for something) sequentially against a table containing certain characteristics. As comparisons are made, a counter (accumulator) is increased in proportion to the extent of matching between preference fields and characteristic fields from the table records. After all fields have been compared for one table record, a total score is stored in the table in the location corresponding to the record for which the score was computed, and the evaluation of the next table record begins.

After all of the table records have been compared against the preference record and all of the resulting scores have been calculated and stored in the table, the records are then sorted by score in high-to-low order. Printing the first "N" records in the table produces the best "N" matches for one preference record. The best-match records, which can be descriptions of homes, people, or employment opportunities, represent the best choices, assuming that the program decision logic is sound and the score-evaluation algorithms are reasonable.

COMMON ERRORS AND SOLUTIONS

Errors	Example	Solution
1. Failure to reset the score accumulators back to zero before processing additional transaction records. This results in inflated scores for all subsequent evaluations and incorrect matching results.	See Case 8–1 for details. Typically, all score accumulations increase in value, making this error easy to spot. The best match is always the last record, which is incorrect.	See Case 8–1 for logic and BASIC statements needed to reinitialize accumulators to zero for processing subsequent transaction records.
2. Including one specific condition as a true possibility in more than one IF statement.	IF SCORE >= 90 . . . IF SCORE <= 90 AND SCORE >= 80 . . . (IF SCORE = 90, the imperatives of both IF statements would be executed, making the results incorrect.)	Be careful with selection or evaluation criteria that use greater-than-or-equal-to, and less-than-or-equal-to in IF statements. Make sure that conditions which are supposed to be mutually exclusive are translated to be mutually exclusive IF conditions.
3. Improper use of AND logic in multiple evaluation IF statements used in matching logic.	IF Salary > 18000 AND LOCATE$ = "NYC" THEN . . . (Causes the execution of the imperative only if both conditions are true. When conditions become numerous, all must be true when combined with AND.)	Select AND logic constructs carefully, and only when both (or all) conditions are to be logically joined together. Treat separate evaluation criteria separately, and do not join them with AND logic to save coding. The results are almost always incorrect when this is done.
4. Improper use of OR logic in multiple evaluation IF statements used in matching logic.	IF FIRPL$ = "NO" OR ACRES < 2 THEN . . . (Causes execution of the imperative if either condition is true. This may not be what is desired.)	As with AND logic, select OR logic constructs carefully, and do not join criteria that should be separate. When in doubt, leave separate criteria in separate IF statements, as described above.
5. In indexed/sequential access programs. Failure to correctly extract the proper field and record number for the index table.	10 FOR I = 1 TO 10 20 INM$(I) = PARTNO(I) 30 IRECNO(I) = I 40 NEXT I (Statement 20 should be: 20 INM$(I) = MNM$(I)—(i.e., index name equals master name)	The index table key field should be the same as in the master table. This field should be the one that will ultimately be used to retrieve the entire master record. If the inquiry is to be done by name, for example, then name should be the key field in the index table. Remember, when inquiry is to be done by more than one key field, then separate index tables are needed, each containing the needed key field.
6. Failure to sort the index table in order by key field. (This is an error only if the binary search is used to locate the record in the index table.)	Results will be that an incorrect record is retrieved from the master table by direct access because the record number used for the subscript will be incorrect.	Consult chapter 7 for correct sorting logic. It is good practice to always print the contents of the index table before and after sorting, and certainly prior to use in an indexed sequential table access application.
7. Failure to use correct binary search logic when locating the desired record in the index table. (This is only an error if the binary search is used to locate the record.)	As with error 6, the incorrect record will be retrieved from the master table, or a program-halting error such as "subscript out of range" will occur.	As with solution 6, consult chapter 7 for correct binary search logic. It is good practice to test the routine separately, to be sure it works, before including it in a complex indexed sequential application.

1. Explain why matching-type systems and programs are useful in business.
2. Give some examples of matching systems. Explain, in general, how each system functions and describe the output produced.
3. Name the key BASIC statements used in matching programs and give three examples of these statements.
4. How is compound logic useful in matching decisions? Give three examples of compound logical IF statements.
5. An accumulator is used in matching programs to tally the extent of matching. Explain the concept of using an accumulator in these programs and describe how these variable expressions differ from the mathematical equations studied previously.
6. Explain the concept of absolute value of an expression. How can this function be used in matching programs?
7. Why is sorting important in matching programs?
8. Give five examples of matching systems not described in the chapter.
9. Write a VTOC chart and appropriate program for a disease-diagnosing matching system. (The table should contain disease symptoms and the transaction record should contain a person's symptoms.)

1. Computer dating programs involve reading in a preference record that contains traits that typify an individual whom another person would like to date, and then comparing these traits to the characteristics of available people.

   In this problem, you will set up a table of people's names and their characteristics in the areas listed in table 8–4. The characteristics scale is 0 = "dislike," 9 = "like very much". For the physical characteristics, actual words can be used.

   After evaluating characteristics against those preferences for the person seeking a partner, you will place the score obtained through your matching logic into your table and sort it by score in descending order. Then, you will print the first five records, which will represent the best five matches. The evaluation of preferences and available people's characteristics should follow the principles of matching described in the chapter. What will make the program you write interesting are additions to the characteristics

TABLE 8–4

Typical fields for characteristics, problem for solution 1.

Name	Build (1—10; how important	Dancing (ballroom)
Phone number	is this criteria by itself?)	Dancing (disco)
Age	Level of education (1–12, 13,	Movies
Height	14, etc.)	Eating
Weight	Annual salary (in increments of	TV viewing
Build (slender, normal, ample—	$1,000)	Theater (live performance)
S, N, A)	Type of dress (informal—I,	Art
Sex (M,F)	formal—F)	Travel
Eyes (brown—1, blue—2,	Own transportation (yes, no)	Children
green—3, hazel—4)	Parties*	Lower age limit
Hair (red—1, brown—2,	Music (rock—R, country—C,	Upper age limit
black—3, blonde—4,	jazz—J, classical—K, folk—F)	
gray—5)	Spectator sports	
Language (English—E,	Participation sports	
French—F, Spanish—S,		
German—G)		

*Any scaling device (0 = dislike, 9 = like) can be used.

```
NAME    SEX AGE PHONE NO FILM SPORT ROCK CLASSIC DANCE TV SKI TEN FISH HEIGHT

JOHN     M   20  663-3100   9    2     9    0        8   6   9   9    5   SHORT
MARY     F   21  223-1120   9    5     8    3        9   3   8   0    0   SHORT
FRED     M   30  524-3211   8    4     9    0        0   2   9   8    0   TALL
NANCY    F   25  395-4567   2    3     9    0        5   1   0   5    0   MEDIUM
BILL     M   32  247-5678   0    2     9    2        2   7   9   0    5   TALL
JEAN     F   29  462-7890   1    0     9    3        8   5   0   7    8   SHORT
BOB      M   24  432-0123   5    1     9    1        9   4   9   8    0   TALL
MIKE     M   21  867-1234   7    9     0    9        7   5   3   0    7   MEDIUM
ANNE     F   28  691-4321   9    5     2    9        2   8   2   0    8   TALL
PAULA    F   19  714-3214   6    7     0    9        0   2   8   7    5   MEDIUM


                    COMPUTER DATING SERVICE

                    CLIENT INQUIRY REPORT
           CLIENT: JOHN SMITH              PHONE: 233-6566

                        SELECTED RECORDS
       RATING    NAME      PHONE NO   MATCH SCORE        REMARKS
         1      NANCY      395-4567      170        AVERAGE MATCH
         2      PAULA      714-3214      160        AVERAGE MATCH
         3      ANNE       691-4321      150        AVERAGE MATCH
         4      MARY       223-1120      140        SEX IS YOUR ONLY MATCH
         5      JEAN       462-7890      140        SEX IS YOUR ONLY MATCH


                    COMPUTER DATING SERVCE

                    CLIENT INQUIRY REPORT
           CLIENT: SUSAN BROWN            PHONE: 244-9099

                        SELECTED RECORDS
       RATING    NAME      PHONE NO   MATCH SCORE        REMARKS
         1      JOHN       663-3100      170        AVERAGE MATCH
         2      FRED       524-3211      160        AVERAGE MATCH
         3      MIKE       867-1234      150        AVERAGE MATCH
         4      BOB        432-0123      140        SEX IS YOUR ONLY MATCH
         5      BILL       247-5678      140        SEX IS YOUR ONLY MATCH


                    COMPUTER DATING SERVICE

                    CLIENT INQUIRY REPORT
           CLIENT: ROBERT BLACK           PHONE: 311-1676

                        SELECTED RECORDS
       RATING    NAME      PHONE NO   MATCH SCORE        REMARKS
         1      ANNE       691-4321      160        AVERAGE MATCH
         2      NANCY      395-4567      150        AVERAGE MATCH
         3      MARY       223-1120      150        AVERAGE MATCH
         4      JEAN       462-7890      140        SEX IS YOUR ONLY MATCH
         5      PAULA      714-3214      140        SEX IS YOUR ONLY MATCH


                ALL DATA HAS BEEN PROCESSED


                PROGRAM EXECUTION COMPLETED
```

FIGURE 8–9

Sample output for problem 1.

TABLE 8–5

Simplified disease symptoms.

Disease/Illness	Fever	Chills	Cough	Nausea	Muscle Aches	Dizziness	Fatigue	Head Ache	Lung Congest.
Common cold	P	P	P	L	L	N	Y	P	N
Influenza	Y	Y	P	P	Y	P	Y	P	P
Mononucleosis	P	P	P	P	Y	P	Y	Y	P
Strep throat	Y	P	P	P	N	N	P	N	P
Bronchitis	P	P	Y	N	N	N	P	P	P
Pneumonia	Y	P	Y	P	P	P	Y	P	Y
Hepatitis	Y	P	N	Y	P	N	Y	P	N
Gastroenteritis	P	P	N	Y	P	N	P	N	N
Pancreatitis	Y	P	N	Y	P	N	P	N	N
Appendicitis	Y	P	N	Y	P	N	P	N	N
Peritonitis	Y	Y	N	Y	P	P	Y	N	N
Gastritis	Y	Y	N	Y	Y	Y	Y	Y	N

table and preference records. An example program for a simplified computer dating program is shown in figure 8–9.

2. In recent years, computers have been programmed to assist doctors in the diagnosis of diseases. While the actual systems in use are quite complex, it is possible to write a simplified version of this type of program using tables and the logical matching techniques described in this chapter.

For this problem, you can set up an abridged table of diseases or illnesses and their characteristics, as shown in table 8–5. To add realism and usefulness to your program,* you can set up another table with prognoses, remedies, and remarks, using the diagnosed disease as the key field, as shown in abridged form in table 8–6. Once your program matches the patient's symptoms to a disease, have your program print out the prognosis, recommended remedies, and any remarks for the diagnosis. As an example, note the expanded sample output for "influenza" in table 8–6 and the sample program output in figure 8–10.

TABLE 8–6

Disease/illness chart.

Disease/Illness	Prognosis, Remedies, and Remarks
Common cold	Bed rest, aspirin, fluid
Influenza	Bed rest, aspirin, fluid
Mononucleosis	Rest, careful blood test monitoring
Strep throat	Antibiotics, bed rest, aspirin
Bronchitis	Antibiotics, bed rest, cough medication
Pneumonia	Antibiotics, bed rest, cough therapy
(Etc.)	(Etc.)

DETAILED OUTPUT EXAMPLE

Influenza: Go to bed with temperature. Take aspirin or aspirin substitute. Drink as much water or juice as possible. If fever lasts for longer than four days, call doctor. You will probably feel weak and possibly depressed for about a week after your temperature drops. Rest as much as possible.

---

*Do not use this, or any other computer program to analyze or to diagnose your own or anyone else's illnesses—always consult a doctor!

FIGURE 8–10

Sample output for problem 2.

```
                          DISEASE SYMPTOM TABLE
       DISEASE     FEVER CHILL COUGH NAUSEA ACHE DIZZY FATIGUE HACHE CONG    DUR    SC
  COMMON COLD        P     P     P     P      P    P      P      P    N  < 2 WEEKS 0
  INFLUENZA          Y     Y     Y     P      Y    P      Y      Y    P  > 2 WEEKS 0
  MONONUCLEOSIS      Y     N     P     P      Y    P      Y      Y    P  > 6 WEEKS 0
  STREP THROAT       Y     P     P     P      N    N      P      N    N  > 2 WEEKS 0
  BRONCHITIS         Y     P     P     N      N    N      P      P    P  > 2 WEEKS 0
  PNEUMONIA          Y     Y     P     P      P    P      Y      P    Y  > 3 WEEKS 0

                          DISEASE REMEDY TABLE
             DISEASE                          REMEDY
        COMMON COLD          BED REST, ASPIRIN, FLUIDS
        INFLUENZA            BED REST, ASPIRIN, FLUIDS
        MONONUCLEOSIS        REST - CAREFUL BLOOD TEST MONITORING
        STREP THROAT         ANTIBIOTICS, BED REST, ASPIRIN
        BRONCHITIS           ANTIBIOTICS, BED REST, COUGH MEDICATION
        PNEUMONIA            ANTIBIOTICS, BED REST, COUGH THERAPY

                        DISEASE DIAGNOSIS
                        CLIENT INQUIRY REPORT
                        -----------------

          CLIENT: JOHN C. SMITH         PHONE NO: 233-7665

          YOUR SYMPTOMS INDICATE THE FOLLOWING POSSIBILITIES

DISEASE OR ILLNESS          PROGNOSIS, REMEDIES              REMARKS
-------------------------------------------------------------------------
   COMMON COLD      BED REST, ASPIRIN, FLUIDS           SYMPTOM.MATCH 60%
   BRONCHITIS       ANTIBIOTICS, BED REST, COUGH MEDICATION SYMPTOM.MATCH 15%

                        DISEASE DIAGNOSIS
                        CLIENT INQUIRY REPORT
                        -----------------

          CLIENT: THELMA JONES          PHONE NO: 333-9800

          YOUR SYMPTOMS INDICATE THE FOLLOWING POSSIBILITIES

DISEASE OR ILLNESS          PROGNOSIS, REMEDIES              REMARKS
-------------------------------------------------------------------------
   MONONUCLEOSIS    REST - CAREFUL BLOOD TEST MONITORING  SYMPTOM.MATCH 40%

                        DISEASE DIAGNOSIS
                        CLIENT INQUIRY REPORT
                        -----------------

          CLIENT: ROBERT BLACK          PHONE NO: 499-8765

          YOUR SYMPTOMS INDICATE THE FOLLOWING POSSIBILITIES

DISEASE OR ILLNESS          PROGNOSIS, REMEDIES              REMARKS
-------------------------------------------------------------------------
   PNEUMONIA        ANTIBIOTICS, BED REST, COUGH THERAPY  SYMPTOM.MATCH 55%
   MONONUCLEOSIS    REST - CAREFUL BLOOD TEST MONITORING  SYMPTOM.MATCH 20%
   COMMON COLD      BED REST, ASPIRIN, FLUIDS             SYMPTOM.MATCH 10%

                   ALL DATA HAS BEEN PROCESSED

                   PROGRAM EXECUTION COMPLETED
```

```
                    DISEASE SYMPTOM TABLE
  DISEASE      FEVER CHILL COUGH NAUSEA ACHE DIZZY FATIGUE HACHE CONG   DUR      SC
COMMON COLD      P     P     P     P     P    P      P      P    N  < 2 WEEKS  0
INFLUENZA        Y     Y     Y     P     Y    P      Y      Y    P  > 2 WEEKS  0
MONONUCLEOSIS    Y     N     P     P     Y    P      Y      Y    P  > 6 WEEKS  0
STREP THROAT     Y     P     P     P     N    N      P      N    N  > 2 WEEKS  0
BRONCHITIS       Y     P     P     N     N    N      P      P    P  > 2 WEEKS  0
PNEUMONIA        Y     Y     P     P     P    P      Y      P    Y  > 3 WEEKS  0

                    DISEASE REMEDY TABLE
         DISEASE                         REMEDY
      COMMON COLD        BED REST, ASPIRIN, FLUIDS
      INFLUENZA          BED REST, ASPIRIN, FLUIDS
      MONONUCLEOSIS      REST - CAREFUL BLOOD TEST MONITORING
      STREPP THROAT      ANTIBIOTICS, BED REST, ASPIRIN
      BRONCHITIS         ANTIBIOTICS, BED REST, COUGH MEDICATION
      PNEUMONIA          ANTIBIOTICS, BED REST, COUGH THERAPY



                    DISEASE DIAGNOSIS
                 CLIENT INQUIRY REPORT
                 ----------------


       CLIENT: JOHN JONES          PHONE NO: 233-9000

       YOUR SYMPTOMS INDICATE THE FOLLOWING POSSIBILITIES

 DISEASE OR ILLNESS        PROGNOSIS, REMEDIES              REMARKS
 ------------------------------------------------------------------------
    COMMON COLD      BED REST, ASPIRIN, FLUIDS      SYMPTOM.MATCH 100%



                 ALL DATA HAS BEEN PROCESSED


                 PROGRAM EXECUTION COMPLETED
```

3. Most poison control centers provide information to people who need to know what to do when poisonous substances are ingested or touched. Some substances become poisons because they are used improperly or because too much is taken (like aspirin), but are not normally considered poisons.

   In the majority of cases, the substance involved in the poisoning is known, and the corrective measures to be taken by first-aid personnel, doctors, or hospital staff are found by consulting files (often contained in special easy-to-locate microfilm documents). The search procedure must be rapid, and most remedies and corrective measures are determined in a matter of seconds or minutes.

   On some occasions, however, the poisonous substance is unknown and corrective measures can be taken only after determining what substance the patient has ingested, inhaled, or contacted. Only then can appropriate first-aid measures be applied, as in the case of a known poison. (Cases such as this are difficult since considerable time is needed for blood or other chemical analysis and because the comparison of patient symptoms and poison characteristics is a complex and time-consuming process.)

   Some poison control centers use computerized systems that can reduce the time needed to accomplish these comparisons to a fraction of time that was required in the past. These computerized programs generally rely on the matching principles that have been described in this chapter.

   Write a program, using these principles, that will accomplish the identification of an ''unknown'' poison by matching patient symptoms against the effects of various

305

TABLE 8–7

Symptoms of poison.

Poisonous Substance	Nausea	Vomiting	Abdominal Pain	Coughing/ Choking	Headache	Vertigo	Mental Confusion	Uncon- sciousness	Hyper- activity	Convul- sions	Respiratory Depression	Slurred Speech
Alcohol (isopropyl)	Yes	Yes	Yes	No	Yes	Yes	No	No	No	No	Yes	No
Bleach (Clorox type)	Yes	Yes	No	Yes	No	No	No	No	No	No	No	No
Aspirin	Yes	Yes	Yes	No	No	No	Yes	No	No	Yes	No	No
Rhubarb (leaves)	Yes	Yes	Yes	No	No	No	No	Yes	No	Yes	Yes	No
Nail polish remover	No	Yes	Yes	Yes	No	No	No	No	No	No	Yes	Yes
Fly paper	No	Yes	Yes	Yes	No	No	No	Yes	No	Yes	Yes	No
Contac	Yes	Yes	No	No	Yes	Yes	No	No	Yes	Yes	Yes	No
Pine-sol	Yes	Yes	No	No	No	No	No	No	Yes	Yes	No	No
Sominex	Yes	No	No	No	No	No	Yes	Yes	No	No	Yes	No
Turpentine	Yes	Yes	Yes	No	No	No	No	Yes	Yes	Yes	No	No
Gasoline	Yes	Yes	No	No	No	No	No	Yes	No	Yes	Yes	No
Caffeine	Yes	Yes	Yes	No	Yes	No	No	No	Yes	No	No	No
Oleander (shrub)	Yes	No	No	No	No	No	No	Yes	No	No	Yes	No
Campho-Phenique	No	Yes	Yes	No	Yes	Yes	Yes	Yes	No	Yes	Yes	No

household products if ingested, inhaled, or touched. Use the abridged (i.e., incomplete) information in table 8–7 table to test your program logic*, and use the example program output in figure 8–11 as a guide.

4. Finding the ideal vacation spot is not always easy. Although travel agents can be helpful, they may not take into consideration all the factors you might consider important. For example, some typical considerations might be:

   1. Amount of money available
   2. Amount of time available
   3. Climate
   4. Sports or special events available
   5. Points of scenic, historic, or other interest
   6. Domestic, European, Asian, or other geographic location
   7. Special interests, such as art, music, dance, etc.

   If potential vacation locations are researched with these or other considerations in mind, you can construct a master table of vacation locations that could be compared against your vacation preferences by using the matching principles that have been described in this chapter. The program logic will be similar to the real estate matching case study; however, instead of locating the best home, the output from the program will be the best vacation spot based on the preferences indicated, as shown in the example output in figure 8–12.

   Consult the travel section of your newspaper or your local travel agents and see if you can obtain data that can be used to establish a master table with considerations such as those listed. You may wish to add other factors that you feel are important, for example, data on transportation to and from (cruises, air, train, bus, etc.) to make your program realistic and practical.

   Construct your program so that it will print out the best three vacation selections for each individual using this program. After running your program, ask them if the vacation choices suggested by your logic seem appropriate and attractive.

*Never use your program to diagnose crisis situations! In any actual emergency you should consult the staff of your local poison control center and/or a qualified physician.

FIGURE 8–11

Sample output for problem 3.

```
                        POISON SYMPTOM TABLE
  RN    SUBSTANCE NA VOM PA COU HA VER CON UN HY CO RES SPE
   1  ,ALCOHOL,Y,Y,Y,N,Y,Y,N,N,N,N,Y,N
   2  ,BLEACH,Y,Y,N,Y,N,N,N,N,N,N,N,N,N
   3  ,ASPIRIN,Y,Y,Y,N,N,N,Y,N,N,Y,N,N
   4  ,RHUBARB,Y,Y,Y,N,N,N,Y,Y,N,Y,Y,N
   5  ,NAIL POLISH REM,N,Y,Y,Y,N,N,N,N,N,N,Y,Y
   6  ,FLY PAPER,N,Y,Y,Y,N,N,N,Y,N,Y,Y,N
   7  ,CONTAC,Y,Y,N,N,Y,Y,N,N,Y,Y,Y,N
   8  ,PINE-SOL,Y,Y,N,N,N,N,N,N,Y,Y,Y,N
   9  ,SOMINEX,Y,N,N,N,N,N,Y,Y,N,N,Y,N
  10  ,TURPENTINE,Y,Y,Y,N,N,N,N,Y,Y,Y,N,N
  11  ,GASOLINE,Y,Y,N,N,N,N,N,Y,N,Y,Y,N
  12  ,CAFFEINE,Y,Y,Y,N,Y,N,N,N,Y,N,N,N
  13  ,OLEANDER,Y,N,N,N,N,N,N,Y,N,N,Y,N
  14  ,CAMPHO-PHENIQUE,N,Y,Y,N,Y,Y,Y,Y,N,Y,Y,N
```

```
                   POISON INDEX TABLE
          REC NO      SUBSTANCE         SCORE
            1         ALCOHOL             0
            2         BLEACH              0
            3         ASPIRIN             0
            4         RHUBARB             0
            5         NAIL POLISH REM     0
            6         FLY PAPER           0
            7         CONTAC              0
            8         PINE-SOL            0
            9         SOMINEX             0
           10         TURPENTINE          0
           11         GASOLINE            0
           12         CAFFEINE            0
           13         OLEANDER            0
           14         CAMPHO-PHENIQUE     0
```

Before Logical Comparison of Symptoms

```
                   POISON INDEX TABLE
          REC NO      SUBSTANCE         SCORE
            1         ALCOHOL            12
            7         CONTAC              9
           12         CAFFEINE            9
            4         RHUBARB             8
           14         CAMPHO-PHENIQUE     8
            2         BLEACH              7
            3         ASPIRIN             7
            5         NAIL POLISH REM     7
           11         GASOLINE            7
           13         OLEANDER            7
            6         FLY PAPER           6
            8         PINE-SOL            6
            9         SOMINEX             6
           10         TURPENTINE          6
```

After Logical Comparison of Symptoms

```
         POISON CONTROL CENTER SIMULATION
                 DIAGNOSTIC REPORT
         CALLER:JOHN C. JONES PHONE NO: 322-9800


         THE COMPUTER SEARCH INDICATES THAT THE
         VICTIM INGESTED THE FOLLOWING SUBSTANCE
```

```
                    SCORE                          SUBSTANCE
        12 OUT OF THE 12 SYMPTOMS MATCH     ALCOHOL
         9 OUT OF THE 12 SYMPTOMS MATCH     CONTAC
         9 OUT OF THE 12 SYMPTOMS MATCH     CAFFEINE
         8 OUT OF THE 12 SYMPTOMS MATCH     RHUBARB
         8 OUT OF THE 12 SYMPTOMS MATCH     CAMPHO-PHENIQUE
         7 OUT OF THE 12 SYMPTOMS MATCH     BLEACH
         7 OUT OF THE 12 SYMPTOMS MATCH     ASPIRIN
         7 OUT OF THE 12 SYMPTOMS MATCH     NAIL POLISH REM
         7 OUT OF THE 12 SYMPTOMS MATCH     GASOLINE


            POISON INDEX TABLE
    REC NO      SUBSTANCE       SCORE
       4      RHUBARB            11
      11      GASOLINE           10
       6      FLY PAPER           9
      10      TURPENTINE          9
       3      ASPIRIN             8
       5      NAIL POLISH REM     8
      13      OLEANDER            8
       1      ALCOHOL             7
       8      PINE-SOL            7
       9      SOMINEX             7
      14      CAMPHO-PHENIQUE     7
       2      BLEACH              6
       7      CONTAC              6
      12      CAFFEINE            6


        POISON CONTROL CENTER SIMULATION
                DIAGNOSTIC REPORT
           CALLER:THELMA SMITH              PHONE NO: 122-8911

    THE COMPUTER SEARCH INDICATES THAT THE
    VICTIM INGESTED THE FOLLOWING SUBSTANCE

                    SCORE                          SUBSTANCE
        11 OUT OF THE 12 SYMPTOMS MATCH     RHUBARB
        10 OUT OF THE 12 SYMPTOMS MATCH     GASOLINE
         9 OUT OF THE 12 SYMPTOMS MATCH     FLY PAPER
         9 OUT OF THE 12 SYMPTOMS MATCH     TURPENTINE
         8 OUT OF THE 12 SYMPTOMS MATCH     ASPIRIN
         8 OUT OF THE 12 SYMPTOMS MATCH     NAIL POLISH REM
         8 OUT OF THE 12 SYMPTOMS MATCH     OLEANDER
         7 OUT OF THE 12 SYMPTOMS MATCH     ALCOHOL
         7 OUT OF THE 12 SYMPTOMS MATCH     PINE-SOL


            POISON INDEX TABLE
    REC NO      SUBSTANCE       SCORE
       5      NAIL POLISH REM     7
       6      FLY PAPER           6
       9      SOMINEX             6
      14      CAMPHO-PHENIQUE     6
       2      BLEACH              5
       3      ASPIRIN             5
       7      CONTAC              5
      11      GASOLINE            5
      13      OLEANDER            5
       1      ALCOHOL             4
       4      RHUBARB             4
       8      PINE-SOL            4
      12      CAFFEINE            3
      10      TURPENTINE          2
```

308

```
                 POISON CONTROL CENTER SIMULATION
                        DIAGNOSTIC REPORT

                 CALLER:ROBERT BLACK            PHONE NO: 223-4433

             THE COMPUTER SEARCH INDICATES THAT THE
             VICTIM INGESTED THE FOLLOWING SUBSTANCE

                        SCORE                   SUBSTANCE
             7 OUT OF THE 12 SYMPTOMS MATCH     NAIL POLISH REM
             6 OUT OF THE 12 SYMPTOMS MATCH     FLY PAPER
             6 OUT OF THE 12 SYMPTOMS MATCH     SOMINEX
             6 OUT OF THE 12 SYMPTOMS MATCH     CAMPHO-PHENIQUE


             ALL DATA HAS BEEN PROCESSED


             PROGRAM EXECUTION COMPLETED
```

FIGURE 8–12

Sample output for problem 4.

```
                      VACATION SELECTION TABLE
   REC NO TYPE  CLIMATE DAYS   LOCATION        S  T  SW G GA M A D TH H  PRICE

      1   DOM   COLD      5 ASPEN,COLORADO     1  0  0  0  0 0 1 1  0 0 $  950
      2   DOM   WARM      4 SAN JUAN, P.RIC    0  1  1  0  1 0 0 1  0 1 $  650
      3   EUROP WARM     14 PARIS, FRANCE      0  0  0  0  0 1 1 1  1 1 $2,250
      4   ASIAN WARM     14 CHINA TOUR         0  0  0  0  0 1 1 1  0 1 $1,549
      5   EUROP COLD     12 SWEDEN             1  0  0  0  0 1 1 1  0 1 $1,549
      6   EUROP WARM      7 MONACO             0  1  1  1  1 0 1 1  0 0 $1,250
      7   DOM   COLD      3 STOWE, VERMONT     1  0  0  0  0 0 0 1  0 1 $  495
      8   DOM   WARM      7 BAHAMAS            0  1  1  1  1 0 0 1  0 0 $  579
      9   EUROP COLD     10 SWISS ALPS         1  0  0  0  0 0 0 1  0 1 $1,895
     10   DOM   WARM     10 HAWAII             1  1  1  1  0 1 1 1  0 1 $  895



                  VARIABLE LEGEND FOR TABLE ABBREVIATIONS
                         S  = SKIING
                         T  = TENNIS
                         SW = SWIMMING
                         G  = GOLF
                         GA = GAMBLING
                         M  = MUSEUMS
                         A  = ART
                         D  = DANCING
                         TH = THEATER
                         H  = HISTORIC



                         IDEAL VACATION REPORT
                         --------------------

             CLIENT: JOHN C. SMITH          PHONE: 323-8767


   RATING    IDEAL VACATION SPOT      NO DAYS    EVALUATION SCORE    PRICE
   ------    -------------------      -------    ----------------    -----
     1          MONACO                   7              70          $1,250
     2          PARIS, FRANCE           14              40          $1,995
         EVALUATION SCORE OF 120 = A PERFECT MATCH!
```

309

```
                    IDEAL VACATION REPORT
                    --------------------

        CLIENT: THELMA WALKER              PHONE: 332-8777

  RATING    IDEAL VACATION SPOT      NO DAYS    EVALUATION SCORE    PRICE
  ------    -------------------      -------    ----------------    -----
     1         ASPEN,COLORADO           5              60          $  950
     2         STOWE, VERMONT           3              50          $  495
      EVALUATION SCORE OF 120 = A PERFECT MATCH!


             ALL INPUT DATA HAS BEEN PROCESSED

         PROGRAM EXECUTION COMPLETED
```

CHAPTER NINE

SEQUENTIAL AND DIRECT ACCESS FILES

LEARNING OBJECTIVES

Upon completion of this chapter, you will be able to:

☐ Understand the importance of files in business data processing applications and programs.

☐ Understand BASIC and DOS conventions when programming with files in BASIC.

☐ Understand sequential access and direct access processing.

☐ Incorporate the sequential statements and concepts to produce fully functional and realistic BASIC business systems.

☐ Incorporate direct access theory, statements, and special conversion functions to produce realistic business programs.

THE IMPORTANCE OF FILES IN BUSINESS

For the applications presented in chapters 7 and 8, many records were processed by loading data into the computer's main memory in the form of tables. As processing took place, the storage location reserved for each record was updated or records located in the table were used to provide important related information through a process of retrieval. Updating data records in tables was done as new information was simply "written over" old information in the desired fields of the table records. Retrieval speed was rapid in direct as well as sequential access methods because all records were in main memory.

Tables might seem to meet all the programming needs of business systems; but, actually, most business programs process volumes of data too large to reside in a computer's main memory at one time. Also, on microcomputers, main memory is volatile; that is, when the power is interrupted, the contents of the main memory are lost, along with it all the table data. Since many applications pass data from one program to another, it would be time consuming and wasteful to have to type in all that data each time a program is run. (Imagine a payroll program where every week the volumes of information about each employee would have to be re-entered.) A permanent method of storage is required, and files fill this need.

Being able to process many different applications on one computer is vital. The use of files to store data and programs permits this much-needed flexibility. Table 9–1 illustrates some of the many business system applications that use files to store information for retrieval and updating.

In this chapter you will learn how files can be used to greatly simplify the input, output, and permanent storage of large amounts of data. But, more importantly, you will discover how files make it possible to retrieve and update information quickly, even when files contain thousands of records.

TABLE 9–1
Some business system programs that use files.

Bookkeeping	Inventory Control
Post journal entries	As-required processing
Trial balance	End-of-period processing
Closing accounts	Inventory transaction recording
Account file printing	Updating inventory master file
Account display and correction	Printing inventory master file
Journal printing	Preparation of inventory reports
Income and expense comparison	Inventory analysis
	Reorder point computation
Accounts Receivable	Inventory turnover analysis
Accounts receivable processing	Inventory use projections
Accounts receivable reports	Asset control accounting
	Material locator
Financial—General	
Income statement	**Production**
Balance sheet	Job costing
Cash flow and budget analysis	Bill of materials
Income and expense analysis	Production scheduling
	Job routing
Sales Analysis and Forecasting	Equipment maintenance scheduling
Least squares regression forecasting	Production lot size computation
Moving average forecasting	Production cost computation
Exponential smoothing forecasting	Analysis of production alternatives
Ratio analysis	Production cost comparisons
Expense Analysis	
Equipment comparisons	
Expected value comparisons	
Property comparisons	
Job pricing/bidding	

File Nomenclature in BASIC

File Definition and File Names. A file is a collection of related records treated as a unit. Within the file there are records that contain fields. The fields within a record may be any type of variable used in BASIC: integer; single-precision number; double-precision number; and string.

An example of a file would be the names, addresses, and pay rates for a group of employees. Any one entry in this payroll file is called a payroll record, and the variables in the record are payroll fields. An example of this is

Data	**Data**	**Data**		
SUSAN,	35 HILL STREET,	3.50	←	**Record**
↑	↑	↑		
Name	**Address**	**Rate**	←	**Fields**

To be able to create, access, and update a file, the file must have a name. File-names must conform to DOS file naming conventions. The filename must be at least one character long and can be as long as eight characters. Filenames can be made up of letters, digits, and some punctuation characters, but cannot include a space or any character that is used by the system as commands or separators (such as the comma or semicolon). You can use upper- or lower-case letters, but all letters will be converted to upper case. The following are some acceptable filenames:

DATA	123
A	PAYROLL
A1	PAYROLL1

Following the name, a one- to three-character extension can be added to the name to help identify the type of file as a data file (.fil or .cat), a BASIC program (.BAS), or another type of file, such as machine code (.EXE). This extension is separated from the filename by a period. While using an extension is optional, it is recommended that you always do so to identify the type of file being referenced.

The filename with its extension is referred to as the file name. The first part (before the extension) is called the filename (with no space). This is confusing terminology, so we will use file name to refer to the two parts and always use an extension (this is good practice, anyway). Here are some "complete" file names:

DATA.FIL	PAYROLL.DAT	INCOME.FIL	A12345.DAT
A.DAT	1.DAT	MASTER.FYL	MY.FYL
PAYROLL.BAS	INTEREST.BAS	TEST.BAS	FIRST.BAS

Notice that the more complete the file name, the easier it is to tell what the file contains in it and whether the file is data or a program. The file names in the last line in this list are programs, so the extension .BAS was used.

Be sure to read your DOS manual and BASIC programming manual for the other variations permitted or encouraged in file naming. A properly named file can prevent problems in identifying output files, master files, programs, and the file type. The name usually describes the type of information and the extension its use. Some examples are CUST.IN (customer information for input) and EXPENS.OUT (expenses to be output). Examine the following file example.

EMPPAY.RAT is the file name with an extension.

```
SUSAN, 35 HILL ST., 3.50
JOHN, 47 BENTWOOD RD., 4.25
CRAIG, 44 PINEBROOK LA., 3.50
JILL, 55 FARMINTON AVE., 3.17
```

Within each of the records, there are three fields: name, address, and pay rate, respectively. The name EMPPAY.RAT stands for "employee's pay rates." In this file example, there are four records and three fields per record.

A delimiter is a symbol that designates where a field begins and ends. In the preceding file, EMPPAY.RAT, commas are used. Delimiters are important because without the commas, the computer would not be able to distinguish where one field ended and the next began. You will see that there are three ways to place the delimiters into your file records: editing; defining the commas as literals in a PRINT statement; or using the WRITE statement. This will be discussed in the next section.

SEQUENTIAL ACCESS AND DIRECT ACCESS FILES

Principles of Access Methods

File processing falls into two categories: sequential and direct access. Sequential files are easier to use and create than direct access files, but are much slower in retrieving data on the file. In sequential files, data is written and stored sequentially, one record after another. Each record must be read back or processed the same way, from the first record to the last. With sequential access, *each* record on the file is processed by the computer to determine if it is the desired record. Sequential files on direct access devices, such as a disk, do permit some flexibility in processing sequential records.

With random access (or direct access, as it is more correctly termed), a desired record can be obtained for processing without reading all previous records or searching through other records on the file. Updating can be done "in place" by rewriting the new revised record onto the original file in its original location. In addition, numbers in random files are stored in true binary format, while they are stored in ASCII format in sequential files. Therefore, direct files often save disk space for records with lots of numeric data.

Sequential access can best be compared to the way a conventional tape player works. If you want to hear a recording of a particular song, you must play through the tape until you recognize the song. In other words, you must search sequentially through the tape until you find something familiar, and when you have located the familiar sound pattern, you begin to listen. This procedure can be very time consuming, and sometimes you may switch your tape player to fast forward, then reverse, and so on, in an effort to speed it up. However, with sequential access files, this cannot be done to locate a specific record if that record has been passed.

If you wish to listen to the entire tape (which is usually the case), the sequence in which the music has been stored (and will be retrieved) presents no problem. Fortunately, in many computer applications, this procedure (reading all records) is also workable. Sequential file processing is adequate for many systems such as billing, payroll, and many accounting systems because most of the records in such systems, with few exceptions, need to be processed and speedy access to any one record is not usually required. Consequently, such applications can benefit from the simplicity and cost reductions of sequential file processing.

In contrast to sequential processing, direct access retrieval can be compared to the way in which music is stored and retrieved from a phonograph record. On a turntable, you can locate any song or selection by advancing the pick-up arm to the desired track on the record. You can figure out quite easily which track to move the arm to by consulting the contents listed on the record label. An analogous, but somewhat more complex, method is used to store the location (address) of information placed in and retrieved from a direct access computer file. This method will be described later in this chapter.

Applications of both sequential and direct file processing constitute the majority of programming applications in business systems since data and programs need to be saved for future runs.

Opening a File

Before a file can be created, accessed, or updated, it must be opened. To do so you use the OPEN statement, which has the general form:

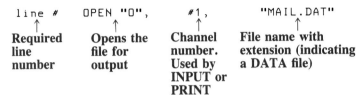

line #	OPEN "O",	#1,	"MAIL.DAT"
↑	↑	↑	↑
Required line number	**Opens the file for output**	**Channel number. Used by INPUT or PRINT**	**File name with extension (indicating a DATA file)**

Creating a Sequential File

There are two ways to create a file: (1) write the file directly using a word processing program or text editor or (2) write a program to write the file. Using word processors and editors requires practice and learning new commands. However, the time spent learning these is well spent compared to the time it might take to develop, write, test, and run a program to set up the file. Simple editors such as EDLIN* (which is available on the DOS diskette) are quite good for creating files for your BASIC programs, but most good word processors are easier to use and permit quicker editing of mistakes. It is not possible here to cover the use of word processors** to create files, so consult your manual if you are using a word processor for documents and would like to learn how to set up BASIC files and/or programs with it.

Writing a BASIC program to create the file is the method you will use in this chapter since it enhances understanding of BASIC file syntax.

Creating a Sequential File with a Program—Mailing Label Example

Figure 9–1 illustrates the steps in sequential file creation using a BASIC program. In this program, statement 50 opens a file called MAIL.DAT for output and assigns it to file number (channel) 1. Statements 70, 90 and 100 INPUT the names and addresses that you want to place on the file, and the WHILE/WEND continues to place these names and addresses on the file until END is entered as the NAME. Inside the WHILE/WEND loop, the data input in response to the INPUT statement is printed onto the file using the WRITE statement at line 110, which directs the output to the specified file number. Note that the file number functions like a nickname in that the filename need not be referred to in the WRITE statement. This shortens the amount of coding that needs to be done when doing input and output with files.

It is acceptable to use the PRINT statement instead of WRITE when placing the data on the MAIL.DAT file if a comma is placed as a literal between each field in the record. Use "," entries in the PRINT statement, as follows:

```
line# PRINT#1 N$;",";S$;",";C$
```

The WRITE statement is a better way to output data onto a sequential file since commas need not be entered in the PRINT statement as literals. The WRITE statement has the general form:

```
line# WRITE# filenumber, variable1, variable2, etc.
```

*See your DOS manual for details on use and features of EDLIN.
**If you use a word processor, be sure it allows for the creation of ASCII files without the special characters often inserted in word processed text. (Again, consult your word processing manual for the specific commands. They vary significantly.)

```
10      REM     MAILING LABEL ILLUSTRATION FOR SEQUENTIAL ACCESS FILE
20      REM     THIS PROGRAM SETS UP A SEQUENTIAL FILE CALLED MAIL.DAT
30      REM     WHICH WILL LATER BE ACCESSED TO PRODUCE MAILING LABELS
40      REM
50              OPEN "O",#1,"MAIL.DAT"
60      REM
70              INPUT " ENTER NAME - ('END' TO QUIT)";NM$
80              WHILE NM$ <> "END"
90              INPUT " ENTER STREET ADDRESS ";S$
100             INPUT " ENTER CITY STATE ZIP ";C$
110             WRITE #1,NM$,S$,C$
120             INPUT " ENTER NAME - ('END' TO QUIT)";NM$
130             WEND
140             CLOSE #1
150             END
```

Screen Output

```
ENTER NAME - ('END' TO QUIT)? JOHN C. JONES
ENTER STREET ADDRESS ? 125 MAIN STREET
ENTER CITY STATE ZIP ? HARTFORD CT 06105
ENTER NAME - ('END' TO QUIT) ? BILL SMITH
ENTER STREET ADDRESS ? 2 SOUTH STREET
ENTER CITY STATE ZIP ? WEST HARTFORD CT 06195
ENTER NAME - ('END' TO QUIT) ? END
Ok
```

Printed Output

```
"JOHN C. JONES","125 MAIN STREET","HARTFORD CT 06105"
"BILL SMITH","2 SOUTH STREET","WEST HARTFORD CT 06195"
```

FIGURE 9–1
Mailing label program.

The WRITE statement not only saves considerable coding time, but also greatly reduces the errors that often occur when punctuating an output line of data for files. The WRITE statement also places quotation marks around strings that are placed on files, making the inclusion of commas possible in strings.

Retrieving Data from a File

Once files are created, they can be used as data sources for programs much like keyboard input, but without the time-consuming and tedious process of retyping. To access a file created earlier, a variation of the OPEN statement combined with the INPUT # is used. The OPEN statement will contain the name of the file, the number of the channel assigned to the file, and specification that the file is opened for input. This is often hard to remember. Try to think of output as outputting onto a file and input as inputting from a file. (*Out* is "onto," *in* is "in from.") The OPEN statement used to accomplish this looks like this:

```
10 OPEN "I", #1 "MAIL.DAT"
```

or

```
OPEN "MAIL.DAT" FOR INPUT AS FILE #1
```

Again the channel number, #1, is like a nickname. After the OPEN instruction, the computer will refer to MAIL.DAT as #1. To get information from the file to the program, the

316

INPUT # statement is used, where the # reflects the assigned channel number. An INPUT statement would look like this to access the MAIL.DAT file:

```
20    INPUT#1, N$,S$,C$
```

The complete mailing label access program with sample labels appears in figure 9–2. Note the WHILE NOT EOF(1) statement at line 80. This very useful feature in BASIC tells your program to process the data on the MAIL.DAT file until the end of the file is reached.

At the end of the program, the file should be closed, which is accomplished with the following statement:

```
999 CLOSE #1
```

CLOSE places a final marker on the file, which can be used in subsequent programs to detect the End-of-File condition. Most programs will function without the CLOSE, but it is important in many sequential file applications where the end of file needs to be marked.

Input

```
10      REM     MAILING LABEL ILLUSTRATION FOR SEQUENTIAL ACCESS FILE
20      REM     THIS PROGRAM ACCESSES A SEQUENTIAL FILE CALLED
30      REM     MAIL.DAT WHICH WAS CREATED IN THE PREVIOUS PROGRAM AND
40      REM     PRODUCES MAILING LABELS ON STANDARD LABEL FORMS
50              OPEN "I",#1, "MAIL.DAT"
60      REM
80              WHILE NOT EOF(1)
90                      INPUT#1,N$,S$,C$
100                     LPRINT N$
110                     LPRINT S$
120                     LPRINT C$
130                     LPRINT:LPRINT:LPRINT
140             WEND
150             CLOSE #1
160             END
```

Printed Output on Label Forms

```
JOHN C. JONES
125 MAIN STREET
HARTFORD CT 06105



BILL SMITH
2 SOUTH STREET
WEST HARTFORD CT 06195
```

FIGURE 9–2
Mailing label program with sample labels.

Payroll Register Program

CONCEPTS TO BE ILLUSTRATED

This case study takes the principles of sequential file processing and expands upon them to produce a realistic payroll program.

In the final program, the master file data is stored on a sequential file at the beginning. This file is then used in conjunction with timecard records to produce paychecks, to update the master file with revised year-to-date figures, and to produce a number of management reports, including a printout of the updated master file.

Payroll processing provides a perfect example of sequential file use because all records on this file are typically processed in order. Care must be taken to ensure that the transaction records (timecards) are in exactly the same order as the records on the master file and error routines are included to check for disorder or missing timecards. Also included, typically, are provisions for adding, deleting, or simply changing records on the master file. These provisions and error-checking routines have been omitted from the following example, however, to focus attention on the sequential file update logic. If you wish to expand the program to realistic proportions, consider including the features that were omitted.

PROBLEM DEFINITION

Input Specifications

Input consists of two record types. Record type 1 is used to set up a master file of employee data having a variety of characteristics such as employee number and name, address, year-to-date gross, YTD taxes, etc. Record 2 contains a timecard consisting of employee hours worked.

	Field No.	Field Description	Type	Example
Payroll	1	Employee Number	Integer	24311
Master	2	Employee Name	Alphabetic	Mary H. Smith
Record	3	Address	Alphanumeric	2310 Slumber LA
	4	Age	Integer	35
	5	Sex	Alphabetic	F
	6	Hourly Wage Rate	Decimal Number	6.25
	7	Year-to-Date Gross Pay	Decimal Number	800.00
	8	Year-to-Date Federal Tax	Decimal Number	160.00
	9	Year-to-Date FICA Tax	Decimal Number	49.04
Employee	1	Employee Name	Alphabetic	John C. Jones
Transaction	2	Employee Number	Integer	12345
Record	3	Hours Worked	Integer	40

Processing Decisions and Formulas

After the (old) master file is set up and printed for verification, the employee's timecard records and the master file records are input, one of each at a time. Payroll calculations are then performed and a new updated master file is stored. YTD data is accumulated for the management report and a new updated master file is printed for verification.

1. Input five payroll master records and determine the end-of-file with a 'signal' field on the last record. Use the DO UNTIL (trailing decision structure) operation executed, then test condition.
2. Input five employee timecard records and determine the end-of-file during processing with a 'signal' field for either timecard records or payroll master records. Again, use the DO UNTIL (trailing decision structure) operation executed, then test condition.

Payroll Deductions

Federal Tax = .20 of Gross Pay
FICA Tax = .0613 of Gross Pay

Old master file is not updated. New master file is updated. Print directly to file as each input (2 records) is sequentially read.

Optional

Compare key fields on input records; if there is no match print message.

Key Fields = Employee Number and Name

Go to a subroutine to print a message. Develop logic to perform subroutine in such a way as to eliminate the GOTO instruction in your program.

Output

1. The contents of the "old" master file are to be printed with titles and headings.
2. A paycheck is to be printed for each employee.
3. The contents of the updated master file are to be printed with titles and headings.
4. A management report consisting of YTD totals is to be printed with titles and headings.
5. An end of program message is to be printed indicating that program execution has ended.

```
                    OLD PAYROLL MASTER FILE
EMPNO    NAME        ADDRESS        AGE SEX HR WAGE YTDGROSS YTDFED YTDFICA
12345 JOHN C. JONES  123 HIGH ST    30  M   8.50      0.00     0.00    0.00
24311 MARY H. SMITH  2310 SLUMBER LA 35 F   6.25    800.00   160.00   49.04
43212 HARRY R. BROWN 145 FOREST RD  23  M   6.75  5,430.50 1,086.10  332.89
54321 ANNE MENARD    1850 LAUREL ST 28  F  10.40 12,430.00 2,486.00  761.96
32140 CAROL WINTERS  240 SO MAIN ST 47  F  12.50 10,500.00 2,100.00  643.65
****************************************************************************
*   EMPLOYEE RECORD:                                                       *
*                EARNINGS:                    TAX DEDUCTIONS:              *
*  EMP NO.  HOURS  REGULAR  OVERTIME  TOTAL GROSS  FEDERAL  FICA    NET    *
*  12345      40   340.00     0.00      340.00      68.00  20.84  251.16*
*_____*
* PAYROLL CHECK                                                            *
*                                                                          *
*                                                                          *
*    PAY TO THE ORDER OF: JOHN C. JONES            AMOUNT     $251.16      *
*                         _____                  _____     *
*                                                                          *
*                                                                          *
*                                       _____        *
*                                       JOHN SMITH, TREASURER      *
****************************************************************************
```

```
***********************************************************************
*  EMPLOYEE RECORD:                                                   *
*                  EARNINGS:                      TAX DEDUCTIONS:     *
*  EMP NO.  HOURS  REGULAR  OVERTIME  TOTAL GROSS  FEDERAL  FICA   NET *
*                                                                     *
*  24311     10     62.50     0.00       62.50      12.50   3.83  46.17*
*_____ *
*  PAYROLL CHECK                                                      *
*                                                                     *
*                                                                     *
*    PAY TO THE ORDER OF: MARY H. SMITH           AMOUNT    $46.17    *
*                         ----------------                  -------   *
*                                                                     *
*                                                                     *
*                                         ------------------------    *
*                                         JOHN SMITH, TREASURER       *
*                                                                     *
***********************************************************************
```

```
***********************************************************************
*  EMPLOYEE RECORD:                                                   *
*                  EARNINGS:                      TAX DEDUCTIONS:     *
*  EMP NO.  HOURS  REGULAR  OVERTIME  TOTAL GROSS  FEDERAL  FICA   NET *
*                                                                     *
*  43212     48    270.00    81.00      351.00      70.20  21.52 259.28*
*_____ *
*  PAYROLL CHECK                                                      *
*                                                                     *
*                                                                     *
*    PAY TO THE ORDER OF: HARRY R. BROWN          AMOUNT    $259.28   *
*                         ----------------                  -------   *
*                                                                     *
*                                                                     *
*                                         ------------------------    *
*                                         JOHN SMITH, TREASURER       *
*                                                                     *
***********************************************************************
```

```
***********************************************************************
*  EMPLOYEE RECORD:                                                   *
*                  EARNINGS:                      TAX DEDUCTIONS:     *
*  EMP NO.  HOURS  REGULAR  OVERTIME  TOTAL GROSS  FEDERAL  FICA   NET *
*                                                                     *
*  54321     44    416.00    62.40      478.40      95.68  29.33 353.39*
*_____ *
*  PAYROLL CHECK                                                      *
*                                                                     *
*                                                                     *
*    PAY TO THE ORDER OF: ANNE MENARD             AMOUNT    $353.39   *
*                         ----------------                  -------   *
*                                                                     *
*                                                                     *
*                                         ------------------------    *
*                                         JOHN SMITH, TREASURER       *
*                                                                     *
***********************************************************************
```

```
*************************************************************
*  EMPLOYEE RECORD:                                         *
*                EARNINGS:                  TAX DEDUCTIONS:  *
*  EMP NO.  HOURS  REGULAR  OVERTIME  TOTAL GROSS  FEDERAL  FICA    NET  *
*                                                           *
*  32140    35     437.50   0.00      437.50       87.50   26.82  323.18*
*_____*
*  PAYROLL CHECK                                            *
*                                                           *
*                                                           *
*    PAY TO THE ORDER OF: CAROL WINTERS        AMOUNT   $323.18  *
*                       _____           _____  *
*                                                           *
*                                                           *
*                              _____   *
*                              JOHN SMITH, TREASURER        *
*                                                           *
*************************************************************
```

NEW PAYROLL MASTER FILE

EMPNO	NAME	ADDRESS	AGE	SEX	HR WAGE	YTDGROSS	YTDFED	YTDFICA
12345	JOHN C. JONES	123 HIGH ST	30	M	8.50	340.00	68.00	20.84
24311	MARY H. SMITH	2310 SLUMBER LA	35	F	6.25	862.50	172.50	52.87
43212	HARRY R. BROWN	145 FOREST RD	23	M	6.75	5,781.50	1,156.30	354.41
54321	ANNE MENARD	1850 LAUREL ST	28	F	10.40	12,908.40	2,581.68	791.29
32140	CAROL WINTERS	240 SO MAIN ST	47	F	12.50	10,937.50	2,187.50	670.47

PAYROLL REGISTER MANAGEMENT REPORT
YEAR-TO-DATE TOTALS

GROSS PAYROLL	FED WITHHOLDING TAX	TAX	FICA PAYROLL	NET
$ 30,829.90	$ 6,165.98		$1,889.87	$ 22,774.05

END OF PAYROLL REGISTER PROGRAM

Test Data

Test data to be used is shown below.

> 12345, John C. Jones, 123 High St, 30, M, 8.50, 0.00, 0.00, 0.00
> 24311, Mary H. Smith, 2310 Slumber La, 35, F, 6.25, 800.00, 160.00, 49.04
> 43212, Harry R. Brown, 145 Forest Rd, 23, M, 6.75, 5430.50, 1086.10, 332.89
> 54321, Anne Menard, 1850 Laurel St, 28, F, 10.40, 12430.00, 2486.00, 761.96
> 32140, Carol Winters, 240 So Main St, 47, F, 12.50, 10500.00, 2100.00, 643.65

> John C. Jones, 12345, 40
> Mary H. Smith, 24311, 10
> Harry R. Brown, 43212, 48
> Anne Menard, 54321, 44
> Carol Winters, 32140, 35

Error Recovery Routines

None.

Validation Procedure

1. Hand calculate paycheck results to verify that they are correct.
2. Add these calculation results to the old master file figures to verify that master file update is correct.
3. Total all new master file YTD fields to verify totals on management report.

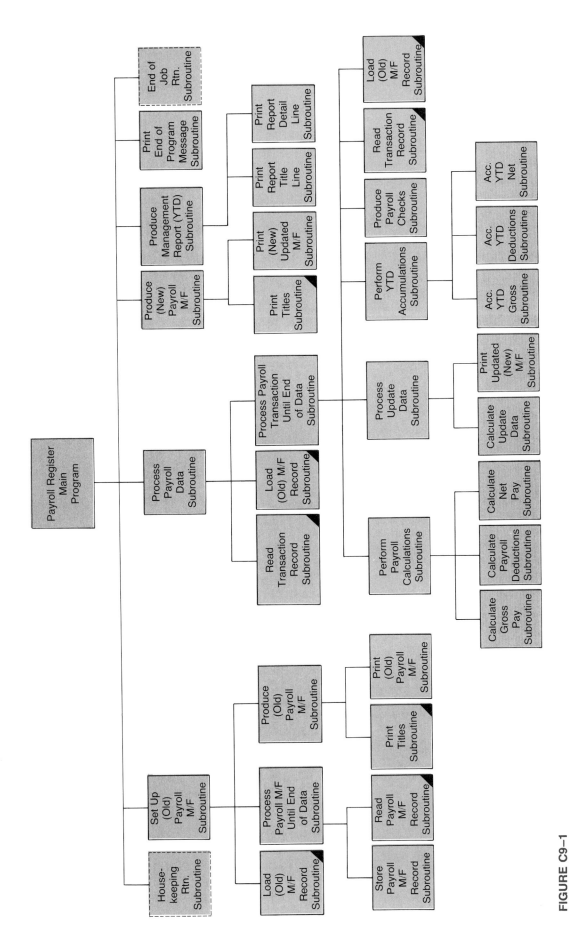

FIGURE C9–1
Visual table of contents—payroll register program.

```
10      REM   ***************************************************
20      REM   *          SEQUENTIAL FILE PROCESSING           *
30      REM   *             CASE STUDY: C9-1                  *
40      REM   *          PAYROLL REGISTER PROGRAM             *
50      REM   *  THIS PROGRAM SETS UP A PAYROLL MASTER FILE,  *
60      REM   *    SEQUENTIALLY PROCESSES A TRANSACTION,      *
70      REM   * UPDATES,AND PRINTS THE NEW MASTER TO A FILE   *
80      REM   *                                               *
90      REM   *              VARIABLE LEGEND                  *
100     REM   *    TABLE DATA:                                *
110     REM   *            EMPNO = EMPLOYEE NUMBER            *
120     REM   *            NAM$ = EMPLOYEE NAME               *
130     REM   *            ADDR$ = ADDRESS                    *
140     REM   *            AGE = AGE                          *
150     REM   *            SEX$ = SEX                         *
160     REM   *            HW = HOURLY WAGE                   *
170     REM   *            YTDGR = YEAR TO DATE GROSS         *
180     REM   *            YTDFED = "      " FED TAX          *
190     REM   *            YTDF =    "      " FICA TAX        *
200     REM   *    TRANSACTION DATA"                          *
210     REM   *            NM$ = EMPLOYEE NAME                *
220     REM   *            ENO = EMPLOYEE NUMBER              *
230     REM   *            HRS = HOURS WORKED                 *
240     REM   *    ACCUMULATION DATA:                         *
250     REM   *            OT = OVERTIME HOURS                *
260     REM   *            OTGR = OVERTIME GROSS PAY          *
270     REM   *            REGRH = REGULAR HOURS              *
280     REM   *            REGR  = REGULAR GROSS PAY          *
290     REM   *            GROSS = TOTAL GROSS PAY            *
300     REM   *            WTAX = FED/WITHHOLDING TAX         *
310     REM   *            FTAX = FICA TAX                    *
320     REM   *            NET = NET PAY                      *
330     REM   *            TOTWT = YTD FED/WITH TAX           *
340     REM   *            TOTFT = YTD FICA TAX               *
350     REM   *            TOTGR  = YTD GROSS PAYROLL         *
360     REM   *            TOTNET = YTD NET PAYROLL           *
370     REM   ***************************************************
380     REM

390           PRINT "COPYRIGHT (C) 1989, BY MERRILL PUBLISHING COMPANY
400           PRINT "FOR USE WITH STRUCTURED BASIC PROGRAMMING
410     REM

420     REM   ***************
430     REM   * MAIN PROGRAM *
440     REM   ***************
450     REM   PERFORM 'OPEN OUTPUT FILES' SUBROUTINE
460           GOSUB 600
470     REM   PERFORM 'SET UP PAYROLL MASTER FILE' SUBROUTINE
480           GOSUB 660
490     REM   PERFORM 'PROCESS PAYROLL DATA' SUBROUTINE
500           GOSUB 1350
510     REM   PERFORM 'PRODUCE NEW PAYROLL MASTER FILE' SUBROUTINE
520           GOSUB 2950
530     REM   PERFORM 'PRODUCE MANAGEMENT REPORT' SUBROUTINE
540           GOSUB 3140
550     REM   PERFORM 'END OF PROGRAM MESSAGE' SUBROUTINE
560           GOSUB 3420
570     REM   PERFORM 'END OF PROGRAM' SUBROUTINE
580           GOSUB 3500
590           END
```

```
600    REM       **********************
610    REM       * OPEN OUTPUT FILES *
620    REM       **********************
630              OPEN "O",#1,"OLD.MAS"
640              OPEN "O",#2,"NEW.MAS"
650              RETURN
660    REM       ****************************
670    REM       * SET UP PAYROLL MASTER FILE *
680    REM       ****************************
690    REM       PERFORM 'LOAD MASTER FILE RECORD' SUBROUTINE
700              GOSUB 760
710    REM       PERFORM 'PROCESS PAYROLL M/F UNTIL END OF DATA' SUBROUTINE
720              GOSUB 870
730    REM       PERFORM 'PRODUCE (OLD) PAYROLL M/F' SUBROUTINE
740              GOSUB 1040
750              RETURN
760    REM       **************************
770    REM       * LOAD MASTER FILE RECORD *
780    REM       **************************
790              READ EMPNO,NAM$,ADDR$,AGE,SEX$,HW,YTDGR,YTDFED,YTDF
800              DATA 12345,JOHN C. JONES,123 HIGH ST,30,M,8.50,0.00,0.00,0.00
810              DATA 24311,MARY H. SMITH,2310 SLUMBER LA,35,F,6.25,800.00,160.00,49.04
820              DATA 43212,HARRY R. BROWN,145 FOREST RD,23,M,6.75,5430.50,1086.10,332.89
830              DATA 54321,ANNE MENARD,1850 LAUREL ST,28,F,10.40,12430,2486.00,761.96
840              DATA 32140,CAROL WINTERS,240 SO MAIN ST,47,F,12.50,10500.00,2100.00,643.65
850              DATA 0,,,,,,,,
860              RETURN
870    REM       ********************************************
880    REM       * PROCESS PAYROLL M/F UNTIL END OF DATA *
890    REM       ********************************************
900              WHILE EMPNO <> 0
910    REM       PERFORM 'STORE PAYROLL MASTER RECORD' SUBROUTINE
920              GOSUB 980
930    REM       PERFORM 'READ MASTER FILE RECORD' SUBROUTINE
940              GOSUB 760
950              WEND
960              CLOSE #1
970              RETURN
980    REM       ****************************
990    REM       * STORE PAYROLL MASTER RECORD *
1000   REM       ****************************
1010             WRITE #1, EMPNO;NAM$;ADDR$;AGE;SEX$;HW;YTDGR;YTDFED;YTDF
1020             NREC = NREC + 1
1030             RETURN
1040   REM       **********************************************
1050   REM       * PRODUCE (OLD) PAYROLL MASTER FILE *
1060   REM       **********************************************
1070   REM       PERFORM 'PRINT M/F TITLES' SUBROUTINE
1080             TSW = 1
1090             GOSUB 1140
1100   REM       PERFORM 'PRINT (OLD) PAYROLL MASTER FILES' SUBROUTINE
1110             GOSUB 1240
1120             CLOSE #1
1130             RETURN
1140   REM       ****************************
1150   REM       * PRINT MASTER FILE TITLES *
1160   REM       ****************************
1170             LPRINT
1180             IF TSW = 1 THEN LPRINT TAB(30);"OLD PAYROLL MASTER FILE"
1190             IF TSW = 2 THEN LPRINT TAB(28);"NEW PAYROLL MASTER FILE"
1200             LPRINT
1210             LPRINT "EMPNO    NAME      ADDRESS              AGE SEX HR WAGE YTD GROSS YTD
       FED YTDFICA"
```

```
1220              LPRINT
1230              RETURN
1240    REM       ***********************************
1250    REM       * PRINT (OLD) PAYROLL MASTER FILE *
1260    REM       ***********************************
1270              OPEN "I",#1,"OLD.MAS"
1280              FOR I = 1 TO NREC
1290              INPUT #1,EMPNO,NAM$,ADDR$,AGE,SEX$,HW,YTDGR,YTDFED,YTDF
1300              F$ =    "##### \                 \ \                 \   ## !  ##.## ##,###.## #,
###.## ###.##
1310              LPRINT USING F$;EMPNO,NAM$,ADDR$,AGE,SEX$,HW,YTDGR,YTDFED,YTDF
1320              NEXT I
1330              CLOSE #1
1340              RETURN
1350    REM       ************************
1360    REM       * PROCESS PAYROLL DATA *
1370    REM       ************************
1380              OPEN "I",#1,"OLD.MAS"
1390    REM       PERFORM 'INPUT TIME CARD' SUBROUTINE
1400              GOSUB 1460
1410    REM       PERFORM 'INPUT OLD MASTER FILE' SUBROUTINE
1420              IF ENDSW <> 1 THEN GOSUB 1640
1430    REM       PERFORM 'PROCESS PAYROLL TRANSACTION UNTIL END OF DATA' ROUTINE
1440              GOSUB 1690
1450              RETURN
1460    REM       ************************
1470    REM       * READ TRANSACTION CARD *
1480    REM       ************************
1490              CLS
1500              PRINT "AS YOU ENTER THE DATA PRESS RETURN AFTER EACH"
1510              PRINT "ENTRY. WHEN YOU ARE FINISHED, TYPE 'EOD' FOR"
1520              PRINT "THE EMPLOYEE'S NAME AND PRESS RETURN FOR THE"
1530              PRINT "NUMBER AND HOURS WORKED."
1540              PRINT:PRINT:PRINT
1550              PRINT "        ENTER EMPLOYEE PAY PERIOD DATA    "
1560              PRINT " ENTER EMPLOYEE NAME......:_____"
1570              PRINT " ENTER EMPLOYEE NUMBER....:_____"
1580              PRINT " ENTER HOURS WORKED.......:_____"
1590              LOCATE 9,28  : INPUT NM$
1600              LOCATE 10,28 : INPUT ENO
1610              LOCATE 11,28 : INPUT HRS
1620              IF NM$ = "EOD" THEN ENDSW = 1
1630              RETURN
1640    REM       ************************
1650    REM       * INPUT OLD MASTER FILE *
1660    REM       ************************
1670              INPUT #1,EMPNO,NAM$,ADDR$,AGE,SEX$,HW,YTDGR,YTDFED,YTDF
1680              RETURN
1690    REM       *****************************************************
1700    REM       * PROCESS PAYROLL TRANSACTION UNTIL END OF DATA *
1710    REM       *****************************************************
1720              ENDSW = 0
1730              WHILE ENDSW = 0
1740    REM       PERFORM 'CALCULATE DATA' SUBROUTINE
1750              GOSUB 1890
1760    REM       PERFORM 'PROCESS UPDATA DATA' SUBROUTINE
1770              GOSUB 2210
1780    REM       PERFORM 'ACCUMULATE YTD DATA' SUBROUTINE
1790              GOSUB 2410
1800    REM       PERFORM 'PRODUCE PAYCHECK' SUBROUTINE
1810              GOSUB 2670
1820    REM       PERFORM 'READ TRANSACTION CARD' SUBROUTINE
1830              GOSUB 1460
```

```
1840    REM      PERFORM 'READ MASTER FILE RECORD' SUBROUTINE
1850             IF ENDSW = 0 THEN GOSUB 1640
1860             WEND
1870             CLOSE #2
1880             RETURN
1890    REM      * * * * * * * * * * * * * * * * * *
1900    REM      * CALCULATE DATA *
1910    REM      * * * * * * * * * * * * * * * * * *
1920    REM      PERFORM 'CALCULATE GROSS PAYROLL' SUBROUTINE
1930             GOSUB 1990
1940    REM      PERFORM 'CALCULATE PAYROLL DEDUCTIONS' SUBROUTINE
1950             GOSUB 2100
1960    REM      PERFORM 'CALCULATE NET PAYROLL' SUBROUTINE
1970             GOSUB 2160
1980             RETURN
1990    REM      * * * * * * * * * * * * * * * * * * * * * * * * *
2000    REM      * CALCULATE GROSS PAYROLL *
2010    REM      * * * * * * * * * * * * * * * * * * * * * * * * *
2020             OT = 0
2030             OTGR = 0
2040             IF HRS > 40 THEN OT = HRS - 40
2050             REGHR = HRS - OT
2060             REGR = REGHR * HW
2070             OTGR = OT * (HW * 1.5)
2080             GROSS = REGR + OTGR
2090             RETURN
2100    REM      * * * * * * * * * * * * * * * * * * * * * * * * * * * *
2110    REM      * CALCULATE PAYROLL DEDUCTIONS *
2120    REM      * * * * * * * * * * * * * * * * * * * * * * * * * * * *
2130             WTAX = GROSS * .2
2140             FTAX = GROSS * .0613
2150             RETURN
2160    REM      * * * * * * * * * * * * * * * * * * * * * *
2170    REM      * CALCULATE NET PAYROLL *
2180    REM      * * * * * * * * * * * * * * * * * * * * * *
2190             NET = GROSS - (WTAX + FTAX)
2200             RETURN
2210    REM      * * * * * * * * * * * * * * * * * * * * *
2220    REM      * PROCESS UPDATE DATA *
2230    REM      * * * * * * * * * * * * * * * * * * * * *
2240    REM      PERFORM 'UPDATE NEW PAYROLL MASTER FILE' SUBROUTINE
2250             GOSUB 2290
2260    REM      PERFORM 'STORE NEW PAYROLL MASTER FILE' SUBROUTINE
2270             GOSUB 2360
2280             RETURN
2290    REM      * * * * * * * * * * * * * * * * * * * * * * * * * * * * * * *
2300    REM      * UPDATE NEW PAYROLL MASTER FILE *
2310    REM      * * * * * * * * * * * * * * * * * * * * * * * * * * * * * * *
2320             YTDGR = YTDGR + GROSS
2330             YTDFED = YTDFED + WTAX
2340             YTDF = YTDF + FTAX
2350             RETURN
2360    REM      * * * * * * * * * * * * * * * * * * * * * * * * * * * *
2370    REM      * STORE NEW PAYROLL MASTER FILE *
2380    REM      * * * * * * * * * * * * * * * * * * * * * * * * * * * *
2390             WRITE #2,EMPNO;NAM$;ADDR$;AGE;SEX$;HW;YTDGR;YTDFED;YTDF
2400             RETURN
2410    REM      * * * * * * * * * * * * * * * * * * * * * * * * * *
2420    REM      * ACCUMULATE YTD PAYROLL DATA *
2430    REM      * * * * * * * * * * * * * * * * * * * * * * * * * *
2440    REM      PERFORM 'ACCUMULATE YTD GROSS' SUBROUTINE
2450             GOSUB 2510
```

```
2460      REM       PERFORM 'ACCUMULATE YTD DEDUCTIONS' SUBROUTINE
2470                GOSUB 2560
2480      REM       PERFORM 'ACCUMULATE YTD NET' SUBROUTINE
2490                GOSUB 2620
2500                RETURN

2510      REM       ************************
2520      REM       * ACCUMULATE YTD GROSS *
2530      REM       ************************
2540                TOTGR = TOTGR + YTDGR
2550                RETURN

2560      REM       *****************************
2570      REM       * ACCUMULATE YTD DEDUCTIONS *
2580      REM       *****************************
2590                TOTWT = TOTWT + YTDFED
2600                TOTFT = TOTFT + YTDF
2610                RETURN

2620      REM       **********************
2630      REM       * ACCUMULATE YTD NET *
2640      REM       **********************
2650                TOTNET = TOTGR - (TOTWT + TOTFT)
2660                RETURN

2670      REM       ********************
2680      REM       * PRODUCE PAYCHECK *
2690      REM       ********************
2700                FOR J = 1 TO 5
2710                LPRINT
2720                NEXT J
2730                LPRINT "************************************************************
********************"
2740                F3$ = "*  #####      ##   #,###.## #,###.## ##,###.##    ####.
## ####.## #,###.##*"
2750                F4$ = "*    PAY TO THE ORDER OF: \                    \     AMO
UNT $$#,###.##    *"
2760                LPRINT "*  EMPLOYEE RECORD:                                       *"
2770                LPRINT "*                         EARNINGS:                  TAX
DEDUCTIONS:      *"
2780                LPRINT "*  EMP NO.  HOURS  REGULAR  OVERTIME  TOTAL GROSS  FEDE
RAL  FICA    NET *"
2790                LPRINT "*                                                        *"
2800                LPRINT USING F3$;EMPNO,HRS,REGR,OTGR,GROSS,WTAX,FTAX,NET
2810                LPRINT "*_____
_____*"
2820                LPRINT "* PAYROLL CHECK                                          *"
2830                FOR J = 1 TO 2
2840                LPRINT "*                                                        *"
2850                NEXT J
2860                LPRINT USING F4$;NAM$,NET
2870                LPRINT "*                               ------------------------ *"
2880                LPRINT "*                                                        *"
2890                LPRINT "*                                                        "*
2900                LPRINT "*                                             -----------
--------------- *"
2910                LPRINT "*                                                  JOHN S
MITH, TREASURER   *"
2920                LPRINT "*                                                        "*
2930                LPRINT "************************************************************
********************"
```

328

```
2940              RETURN
2950      REM     *********************************
2960      REM     * PRODUCE NEW PAYROLL MASTER FILE *
2970      REM     *********************************
2980      REM     PERFORM 'PRINT M/F TITLES' ROUTINE
2990              TSW = 2
3000              GOSUB 1140
3010      REM     PERFORM 'PRINT NEW MASTER FILE' SUBROUTINE
3020              GOSUB 3040
3030              RETURN

3040      REM     *************************
3050      REM     * PRINT NEW MASTER FILE *
3060      REM     *************************
3070              OPEN "I",#2,"NEW.MAS"
3080              FOR I = 1 TO NREC
3090              INPUT #2,EMPNO,NAM$,ADDR$,AGE,SEX$,HW,YTDGR,YTDFED,YTDF
3100              LPRINT USING F$;EMPNO,NAM$,ADDR$,AGE,SEX$,HW,YTDGR,YTDFED,YTDF
3110              NEXT I
3120              CLOSE #2
3130              RETURN

3140      REM     *****************************
3150      REM     * PRODUCE MANAGEMENT REPORT *
3160      REM     *****************************
3170      REM     PERFORM 'PRINT REPORT TITLE' SUBROUTINE
3180              GOSUB 3220
3190      REM     PERFORM 'PRINT REPORT DETAIL LINE' SUBROUTINE
3200              GOSUB 3340
3210              RETURN

3220      REM     **********************
3230      REM     * PRINT REPORT TITLE *
3240      REM     **********************
3250              LPRINT
3260              LPRINT
3270              LPRINT
3280              LPRINT TAB(24);"PAYROLL REGISTER MANAGEMENT REPORT"
3290              LPRINT TAB(31);"YEAR-TO-DATE TOTALS"
3300              LPRINT
3310              LPRINT TAB(13);"GROSS        FED WITHHOLDING    FICA       NET"
3320              LPRINT TAB(12);"PAYROLL        TAX          TAX      PAYROLL"
3330              RETURN

3340      REM     ****************************
3350      REM     * PRINT REPORT DETAIL LINE *
3360      REM     ****************************
3370              LPRINT
3380              LPRINT
3390              F5$ = "$###,###.##        $##,###.##            $#,###.##    $##
#,###.##"
3400              LPRINT USING F5$;TOTGR,TOTWT,TOTFT,TOTNET
3410              RETURN

3420      REM     ********************************
3430      REM     * PRINT END OF PROGRAM MESSAGE *
3440      REM     ********************************
3450              LPRINT
3460              LPRINT
3470              LPRINT
3480              LPRINT TAB (26);"END OF PAYROLL REGISTER PROGRAM"
3490              RETURN

3500      REM     ******************
3510      REM     * END OF PROGRAM *
3520      REM     ******************
3530              CLOSE #1,#2
3540              END
```

ALLOCATING AND PROGRAMMING WITH DIRECT ACCESS FILES

In direct access, any desired record or all of the records on file can be processed randomly because the operating system locates the desired records by their addresses on the disk, and these are related to the key field of the records. Any record, regardless of its location on the file, can be retrieved, processed, or updated without inputting or reading all previous records. Similarly, updating can take place directly in the record being processed without creating a new record on a new file.

However, here are disadvantages of BASIC direct access files. For example, all records must be the same length, regardless of the size of the data fields. And, most troublesome, there are numerous conversion functions needed when data is retrieved and stored.

Principles of Direct Access with I/O Buffer

BASIC actually permits two methods for direct access file processing. These are block I/O (record input/output) and virtual array storage (a feature of DEC's BASIC-Plus® and other mainframe systems). Block I/O is more frequently used on microcomputers, so this section will focus on this technique.

In earlier programs, you used various types of numeric (integer, single-precision, double-precision), alphabetic, or alphanumeric (string) variables. You were able to input, calculate, and output numeric values freely without concern for the binary conversion process that took place "behind the scenes." This is because numeric information was being converted automatically to a binary code (called binary floating point) that uses two, four, and eight bytes of storage, depending on the type of variable (integer, single-precision, or double-precision). The computer, through its operating system, converts numbers from base 10 to base 2 (binary) for storage and for calculations and then back to base 10 for printing and display.

Alphabetic and alphanumeric data, on the other hand, are stored quite differently. First, the computer does not reserve a fixed number of bytes for a string variable. Instead, it allocates the exact number of bytes needed to store all the characters in the string (up to 256, including blanks). For example, the following INPUT instruction causes the computer to first set aside 10 bytes for NM$ and then 20.

```
                  INPUT NM$
        ?         JOHN JONES
                  10 bytes

        ?         JOHN CORNELIUS JONES
                  20 bytes
```

Also, the data for NM$ is stored "as is" and placed anywhere in memory, as determined by the computer's operating system. You have no control over where the value for NM$ goes in memory, nor will you usually care as long as you can retrieve it when needed, which is done simply by using that variable name.

By contrast, information stored on disk files cannot be recalled by individual field names (except with virtual array storage). Instead, the operating system performs the task of retrieving data and giving the data fields the names designated for them in the program using the FIELD statement described later.

When a direct access file is set up, the operating system sets up a block of storage for each record in the file. It also allocates an amount of storage space in memory called an I/O (Input/Output) buffer that corresponds to the record size. When the disk record is read into the buffer or the information in the buffer is written onto the disk sector, there is no conversion on the information being exchanged. This has a number of important implications.

1. All the conversions required for transferring program variables to disk storage format and all the conversions from disk storage format back to program variables for use in the program are up to the programmer. This is a lot of work and the syntax for the required functions is not simple.
2. The layouts of the individual fields of each record on disk and in the buffer must be identical. You must use a special instruction, the FIELD statement, to ensure where data fields in the record are to be stored; how large each field will be; and in what order the fields are to be arranged in the record. Remember that previously the computer's operating system placed variables in memory as programmed.
3. The coding of data for each field in the record must be consistent with how information is stored on disk. For string variables, this presents no problem because the codes are already consistent; however, for numbers it is much more difficult.

For numeric fields, numbers are not stored in the binary floating-point format, but rather in the same format as strings (in the ASCII code). Therefore, before numeric information can be placed in a direct access file, it must first be converted to the string format. Also, before that same numeric information can be used in a program after being input from the disk, it must be converted back from the string format to its true numeric form. The instructions needed to do this are numerous and complex, and many formats vary from system to system.

Opening a Direct Access File

Opening a direct access file and preparing it for use involves two statements (compared to one for sequential file): the OPEN statement and a FIELD statement. The OPEN statement has the same general form as the sequential access file OPEN except for an R which specifies "random" access and an N used to give record size, as shown below.

```
line #      OPEN "R", filenum, "FILENAME", Record length
    100         OPEN "R", #1, "RAN.FIL", 34
```

In these statements, the total length of each record will be 34 bytes on a random file, called a RAN.FIL.

```
 2 bytes for Integer Employee Number
20 bytes for String Employee Name
 4 bytes for Pay Rate
 8 bytes for YTD Gross Pay, a double-precision decimal number
34 bytes total
```

It is the FIELD statement, shown below, that specifies the needed details about the direct file records' fields. In the FIELD statement, only string variables are written since these are the only type that can be written on and retrieved from a direct access disk file.

```
110  FIELD #1, 2 AS DEMPNO$, 20 AS DNAM$, 4 AS DPAYRATE$, 8 AS DYTDGROSS$
```

The numbers that precede the word AS in front in each variable are the bytes allocated, determined by the type of variable being processed. The variable naming convention used here is designed to show that these are direct or random access *disk* variables (preceded with a *D* or *R*) as opposed to usable numeric program variables. As a convention for the direct access programs in this text, any variable preceded with a *D* or *R* (in later illustrations) will have to be converted before use in the program, and any program variable will need to be converted to a *D* (disk string) or *R* variable before it is placed on the direct access file. This convention is only for convenience, as there is complete flexibility in naming variables for a disk or program as long as the disk variables are strings. It is *not a* BASIC syntactical rule!

Although the FIELD statement explains the details of the fields that make up each direct access record (including the number of bytes for each field and the field names on the disk), it is impossible to tell from the FIELD statement alone which variables are numbers (converted to strings) and which are strings since all data is stored on disk in string format. A well-documented program is, therefore, *essential* when dealing with direct access files.

Generally, the size of variables follows these rules:

1. The string is the maximum size (up to 256, numbered 0 to 255) in the program
2. Integers are 2 bytes
3. Single-precision decimal numbers are 4 bytes
4. Double-precision decimal numbers are 8 bytes

But be careful! It is possible to have 2-, 4-, and 8-byte strings in your program. The 2, 4, and 8 do not mean the variable will always become numbers in your program, but numbers *must* be defined as 2-, 4- or 8-byte strings on disk.

Creating a Direct Access File with Conversion Functions and PUT

Since all data on a random access file is stored on disk in ASCII (or string form), every time a direct access file is created, the numeric program variables must be converted to strings of the proper size using these functions, as needed:

MKI$ Make an integer into a string 2 bytes long

MKS$ Make a single-precision number into a string 4 bytes long.

MKD$ Make a double-precision number into a string 8 bytes long

The exact form of these conversion functions and an illustration of how they are used with typical payroll data are shown in figure 9–3.

Notice that in addition to the conversion of numbers to strings, the resulting string representations are left justified in their string variables by a special form of the LET command called LSET. Justification is a convention. There is an RSET statement (which is not used in this text) that right justifies strings in the buffer and on the file. Left justification makes more sense since it facilitates more usual printouts and lists.

The PUT actually places the data (defined in the FIELD statement and stored in the I/O direct access buffer) onto your disk file. Its general form is:

```
line# PUT# FILENUM,RECORDNUMBER
```

where FILENUM is the ''channel'' number assigned in the OPEN statement for the file and RECORDNUMBER is the location (address) where the entire record is located in the range of 1 to 16 megabytes (if that much disk space is available). BASIC and DOS ''block'' as many records as possible (to conserve disk space) into each 512-byte sector; therefore, each PUT statement may not actually write each record, but rather accumulate records until a total of 512 bytes is used. This is called blocking and is *not* critical knowledge for BASIC programmers.

Figure 9–4 is a payroll program showing how fields are input in program format (normal) and then converted to string format for placement on direct access files. In the example, each of the four types of BASIC variables is converted by its appropriate conversion function: integer, employee number (EMPNO%); normal string, employee name

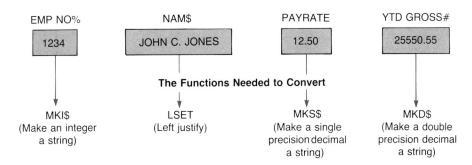

The Variables In a Program

EMP NO%	NAM$	PAYRATE	YTD GROSS#
1234	JOHN C. JONES	12.50	25550.55

The Functions Needed to Convert

MKI$	LSET	MKS$	MKD$
(Make an integer a string)	(Left justify)	(Make a single precision decimal a string)	(Make a double precision decimal a string)

Actual Statements Used

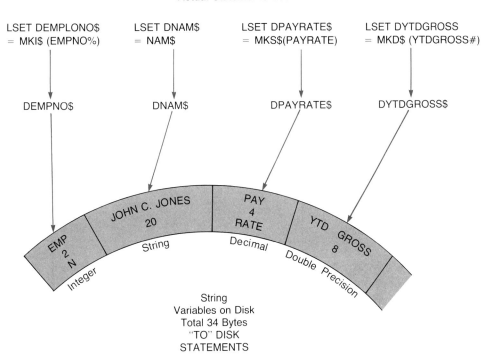

LSET DEMPLONO$ = MKI$ (EMPNO%)	LSET DNAM$ = NAM$	LSET DPAYRATE$ = MKS$(PAYRATE)	LSET DYTDGROSS = MKD$ (YTDGROSS#)
DEMPNO$	DNAM$	DPAYRATE$	DYTDGROSS$

String
Variables on Disk
Total 34 Bytes
"TO" DISK
STATEMENTS

FIGURE 9–3
Data conversions for direct access files.

(NAM&); single-precision decimal, payrate (PAYRATE); and double-precision, year-to-date gross pay (YTDGROSS).

In figure 9–4 lines 40 and 50 declare the file and fields with the OPEN and FIELD statements, respectively. Lines 60 through 220 establish a loop that repeats five times so that five records will be placed on the direct access file. Lines 70 through 100 accept the four fields that make up each record on the file, while lines 140 through 170 convert these to string format so they can be placed on disk. Line 210, the PUT, places the record input onto disk in the location specified by the EMPLOYEE NUMBER input at line 70. This number will correspond exactly to that number, which permits direct access of the record subsequently.

At this point, you can verify that a file called RANDOM.FIL was created by getting back into DOS (type SYSTEM and then DIR) or by issuing the FILES "D: command in BASIC (where D: is your current logged drive).

333

Input

```
10       REM       THIS PROGRAM SETS UP A RANDOM ACCESS FILE BY ACCEPTING
20       REM       DATA FOR 5 EMPLOYEES, NUMBERED 1 THROUGH 5
30       REM
40                 OPEN "R",#1,"RANDOM.FIL",34
50                 FIELD #1,2 AS DEMPNO$,20 AS DNAM$,4 AS DPAYRATE$,8 AS DYTDGROSS$
60                 FOR I = 1 TO 5
70                       INPUT "ENTER EMPLOYEE NUMBER ";EMPNO%
80                       INPUT "ENTER EMPLOYEE NAME    ";NAM$
90                       INPUT "ENTER EMPLOYEE PAY RATE ";PAYRATE
100                      INPUT "ENTER EMPLOYEE YTD GROSS ";YTDGROSS#
110      REM
120      REM       CONVERT THESE TO DISK STRING FORMAT
130      REM
140                      LSET DEMPNO$    = MKI$(EMPNO%)
150                      LSET DNAM$      = NAM$
160                      LSET DPAYRATE$  = MKS$(PAYRATE)
170                      LSET DYTDGROSS$ = MKD$(YTDGROSS#)
180      REM
190      REM       PUT THIS RECORD ON DISK IN LOCATION EMPNO% (EMP. NUMBER)
200      REM
210                      PUT #1,EMPNO%
220                NEXT I
230                END
```

Screen Output

```
EMPLOYEE NUMBER ? 2
EMPLOYEE NAME   ? SMITH
EMPLOYEE PAY RATE ? 10.75
EMPLOYEE YTD GROSS ? 9664.25
EMPLOYEE NUMBER ? 4
EMPLOYEE NAME   ? WILLIAMS
EMPLOYEE PAY RATE ? 10.50
EMPLOYEE YTD GROSS ? 9439.50
EMPLOYEE NUMBER ? 1
EMPLOYEE NAME   ? JONES
EMPLOYEE PAY RATE ? 12.50
EMPLOYEE YTD GROSS ? 11237.50
EMPLOYEE NUMBER ? 3
EMPLOYEE NAME   ? BROWN
EMPLOYEE PAY RATE ? 7.50
EMPLOYEE YTD GROSS ? 6742.50
EMPLOYEE NUMBER ? 5
EMPLOYEE NAME   ? RIVERA
EMPLOYEE PAY RATE ? 13.50
EMPLOYEE YTD GROSS ? 12136.50
```

FIGURE 9-4

Payroll program showing how fields are input into program format and then converted to string format for direct access files.

Retrieving from a Direct Access File with Conversion Functions and GET

When the fields on disk are retrieved for use in a program, the numbers must be reconverted back to usable numeric form. This is accomplished by another set of conversion functions:

CVI   Convert a 2-string to integer

CVS   Convert a 4-string to a single-precision number

CVD   Convert an 8-string to a double-precision number

These functions take the string data from the disk and make the conversions according to the function used, and the variable names conventions, as shown in figure 9–5.

It is always a good idea to print the contents of the entire direct access file to verify that the records that were sent to the file actually arrived. If you try to print the file directly (as in DOS PRINT or TYPE), you will not be able to read the numbers since they too (along with the string variables) are represented in ASCII code, as shown below.

```
SYSTEM
RANDOM.FIL
JONES          H/SMITH                        X? „BROWN
WILLIAMS   p4R   (~RIVERA                          "=
C:\SUB8>
```

This is what happens when you try to print the contents of a random access file directly. Notice numbers do not print out. To read numbers, you need another program, shown in figure 9–6. The GET statement reads a record from the direct access file created in the creation program. Here, the GET works with the OPEN and FIELD statements for the direct access file to retrieve the desired record and subdivide it into its component fields. The data thus obtained is in string form when brought into the I/O buffer and must be converted as described. The general form of the GET statement is

```
line# GET# FILENUM,RECORDNUMBER
```

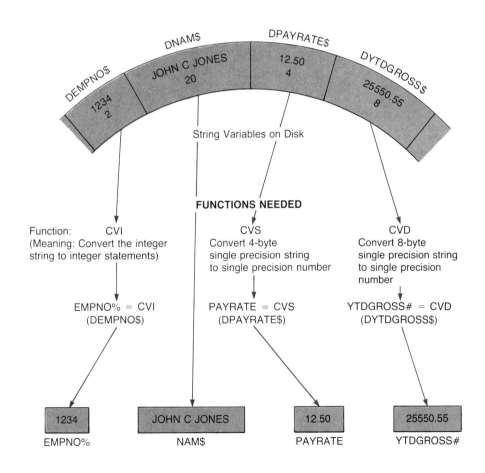

FIGURE 9–5
Data conversions for direct access files—retrieval, disk to program.

335

Input

```
10       REM      THIS PROGRAM ACCESSES THE DIRECT ACCESS FILE
20       REM      CREATED BY THE PREVIOUS PROGRAM.
30       REM      AFTER PRINTING THE ENTIRE FILE TO VERIFY ITS CONTENTS
40       REM      AN EMPLOYEE'S NUMBER IS ENTERED AND USED TO RETRIEVE
50       REM      THAT PERSON'S RECORD FROM THE DIRECT ACCESS FILE.
60                OPEN "R",#1,"RANDOM.FIL",34
70                FIELD #1,2 AS DEMPNO$,20 AS DNAM$,4 AS DPAYRATE$,8 AS DYTDGROSS$
80       REM
90       REM      PRINT THE ENTIRE DIRECT ACCESS FILE FOR VERIFICATION
100               PRINT
110               PRINT
120               PRINT " EMP.NUMBER     NAME                      PAYRATE      YTD GROSS
PAY"
130               FOR N = 1 TO 5
140               GET #1,N
150                   EMPNO%   = CVI(DEMPNO$)
160                   NAM$     = DNAM$
170                   PAYRATE  = CVS(DPAYRATE$)
180                   YTDGROSS# = CVD(DYTDGROSS$)
190                   PRINT EMPNO%,NAM$,PAYRATE,YTDGROSS#
200               NEXT N
210      REM
220      REM      NOW DO A DIRECT ACCESS BY EMPLOYEE NUMBER
230      REM
240               PRINT
250               PRINT
260               PRINT
270               INPUT " ENTER EMPLOYEE NUMBER FOR COMPLETE RECORD ";ENO
280               GET #1,ENO
290                   EMPNO%   = CVI(DEMPNO$)
300                   NAM$     = DNAM$
310                   PAYRATE  = CVS(DPAYRATE$)
320                   YTDGROSS# = CVD(DYTDGROSS$)
330               PRINT
340               PRINT
350               PRINT "             RECORD LOCATION FOR EMPLOYEE NO.  ";ENO
360               PRINT " EMP.NUMBER     NAME                      PAYRATE      YTD GROSS
PAY"
370               PRINT EMPNO%,NAM$,PAYRATE,YTDGROSS#
380               CLOSE #1
390      END
```

Screen Output

```
EMP.NUMBER      NAME                PAYRATE       YTD GROSS PAY
1               JONES               12.5          11237.5
2               SMITH               10.75         9664.25
3               BROWN               7.5           6742.5
4               WILLIAMS            10.5          9439.5
5               RIVERA              13.5          12136.5


ENTER EMPLOYEE NUMBER FOR COMPLETE RECORD ? 3

          RECORD LOCATED FOR EMPLOYEE NO.  3
EMP.NUMBER      NAME                PAYRATE       YTD GROSS PAY
3               BROWN               7.5           6742.5
Ok
```

FIGURE 9-6
Retrieval program.

where FILENUM corresponds to the file number in the OPEN statement and FIELD statement and RECORDNUMBER is the record number to be read. For example,

```
100   GET#1, N
```

Again since DOS blocks records, each GET may not do an actual read for each record; instead, one GET may read a number of records at once, depending on the blocking mentioned previously.

In the retrieval program in figure 9–6, lines 60 and 70, the OPEN and FIELD, respectively specify the file created in the previous program. The file name RANDOM.FIL was created, and this is the one from which records will be retrieved. Lines 100 through 120 print the title for the file fields, while lines 130 through 200 set up a FOR/NEXT loop so that each record can be retrieved in sequence for verification. Line 140, the GET, retrieves one record at a time* as specified by the record number, N, and lines 150 through 180 convert the disk string variables thus retrieved to ''normal'' program variables for printing at line 190.

The direct access logic starts at line 270. First, the desired employee number (ENO) is input at line 270 and this is used to specify the record to be retrieved by the GET statement at line 280.

Once the record is retrieved, lines 290 through 320 convert the fields to program format, and that direct access record is printed with titles and headings at lines 330 through 370. Line 380 closes the file and ends the retrieval program.

Updating a Direct Access File

The program in figure 9–7 combines the retrieval step of the previous illustration with an update of the direct access file created. (The YTD gross pay is increased by the gross pay

FIGURE 9–7
Updated direct access program.

```
Input

10      REM     THIS PROGRAM ACCESSES THE DIRECT ACCESS FILE
20      REM     CREATED BY THE PREVIOUS PROGRAM. IT THEN PRINTS OUT
30      REM     THE ENTIRE FILE TO VERIFY ITS CONTENTS AND THEN USES
40      REM     EMPLOYEE NUMBER TO RETRIEVE AND UPDATE THE RECORD
50      REM     FOR THAT PERSON (YTD GROSS PAY) ON THE DIRECT ACCESS FILE.
60              OPEN "R",#1,"RANDOM.FIL",34
70              FIELD #1,2 AS DEMPNO$,20 AS DNAM$,4 AS DPAYRATE$,8 AS DYTDGROSS$
80      REM
90      REM     PRINT THE ENTIRE DIRECT ACCESS FILE FOR VERIFICATION
100             PRINT
110             PRINT
120             PRINT " EMP.NUMBER     NAME                     PAYRATE        YTD GROSS PAY"
130         FOR N = 1 TO 5
140         GET #1,N
150                 EMPNO%    = CVI(DEMPNO$)
160                 NAM$      = DNAM$
170                 PAYRATE   = CVS(DPAYRATE$)
180                 YTDGROSS# = CVD(DYTDGROSS$)
190                 PRINT EMPNO%,NAM$,PAYRATE,YTDGROSS#
200             NEXT N
210     REM
220     REM     NOW DO A DIRECT ACCESS BY EMPLOYEE NUMBER, BUT ALSO INPUT
230     REM     HOURS WORKED TO CALCULATE CURRENT GROSS PAY AND ADD THIS
240     REM     TO THE PREVIOUS YTD GROSS PAY. THEN PLACE THE UPDATED
```

*See qualification of this above.

```
250      REM      RECORD BACK ON THE DIRECT ACCESS FILE.
260               PRINT
270               PRINT
280               PRINT
290               INPUT " ENTER EMPLOYEE NUMBER FOR COMPLETE RECORD ";ENO
300               INPUT " ENTER THE HOURS WORKED FOR THAT EMPLOYEE ";HOURS
310               GET #1,ENO
320                    EMPNO%    = CVI(DEMPNO$)
330                    NAM$      = DNAM$
340                    PAYRATE   = CVS(DPAYRATE$)
350                    YTDGROSS# = CVD(DYTDGROSS$)
360               PRINT
370               PRINT
380               PRINT "              RECORD LOCATED FOR EMPLOYEE NO. ";ENO
390               PRINT " EMP.NUMBER    NAME                    PAYRATE      YTD GROSS PAY"
400               PRINT EMPNO%,NAM$,PAYRATE,YTDGROSS#
410      REM
420      REM      CALCULATE CURRENT GROSS PAY AND ADD TO YTD GROSS PAY
430      REM
440               GROSS = PAYRATE * HOURS
450               YTDGROSS# = YTDGROSS# + GROSS
460               PRINT
470               PRINT "CURRENT GROSS PAY FOR EMPLOYEE IS ";GROSS
480               PRINT "UPDATED YTD GROSS PAY IS           ";YTDGROSS#
490               PRINT
500      REM
510      REM      CONVERT THE NEW YTD GROSS PAY TO STRING AND PLACE THE WHOLE
520      REM      RECORD BACK ON DISK
530               LSET DYTDGROSS$ = MKD$(YTDGROSS#)
540               PUT #1,ENO
550               CLOSE #1
```

Output

```
EMP.NUMBER      NAME                PAYRATE       YTD GROSS PAY
1               JONES               12.5          11237.5
2               SMITH               10.75         9664.25
3               BROWN               7.5           6742.5
4               WILLIAMS            10.5          9439.5
5               RIVERA              13.5          12136.5
ENTER EMPLOYEE NUMBER FOR COMPLETE RECORD ? 3
ENTER THE HOURS WORKED FOR THAT EMPLOYEE ? 40
              RECORD LOCATED FOR EMPLOYEE NO.  3
EMP.NUMBER      NAME                PAYRATE       YTD GROSS PAY
3               BROWN               7.5           6742.5
CURRENT GROSS PAY FOR EMPLOYEE IS  300
UPDATED YTD GROSS PAY IS        7042.5
Ok
UPDATED FILE
EMP.NUMBER      NAME                PAYRATE       YTD GROSS PAY
1               JONES               12.5          11237.5
2               SMITH               10.75         9664.25
3               BROWN               7.5           7042.5
4               WILLIAMS            10.5          9439.5
5               RIVERA              13.5          12136.5
```

amount for the current period.) This program shows how direct access allows random updating. Any employee record can be processed in any order, and the resulting updated file takes place without creation of a second file, as would be the case with sequential access.

Referring to this multi-step program, in lines 130 through 200 the direct access file is printed, record-by-record, for verification using the FOR/NEXT to retrieve each record by number. Lines 290 and 300 accept as input the employee's number whose record you want to update and the hours worked needed for the update calculation for that employee. At line 310 the GET obtains the desired record because ENO specifies the record number. Once retrieved, the fields in the record are converted to "normal" program format for calculation and printing. This takes place with the conversion functions at lines 320 through 350. Lines 360 through 400 print the located record with titles. Line 440 calculates the current gross pay for the employee located from the file using the hours input at line 300, multiplied by the pay rate from the direct access file. Line 450 adds the current period gross pay to the YTD gross pay from the file. Lines 460 through 490 print these values out, and line 530 converts the YTD Gross Pay back to string format so that it can be stored on disk. Finally, in line 540, the PUT places the entire updated record for the employee in its proper location on the disk.

Charge Account Processing and Updating with Direct Access

CONCEPTS TO BE ILLUSTRATED

This program presents an extension of the concepts illustrated in the previous direct access example. A direct access customer master file is established which contains realistic charge account information, including customer account number, customer name, address, current account balance, year-to-date interest, and current interest for the billing period being processed.

This master file is directly accessed using the customer account number as the key field on a transaction record, which also contains a transaction code (charge purchase, credit return, or payment) and the dollar amount of the transaction described.

The direct access logic is the most significant feature of the case, although the calculations, file update logic, and error routines constitute realistic additions to a popular—although simplified—business system.

Output from the program consists of a realistic charge account monthly statement, which includes the customer's account number, name, address, new balance, current interest, and minimum monthly payment due, all properly edited and titled. In addition, dunning messages are printed on the statement for accounts for which the credit limit has been exceeded.

Additional output includes a register of transactions and typical management reports for a charge account billing system, including an error report for transactions processed with account numbers or transaction codes that are invalid or incorrect.

The processing of coded transactions takes place using input/output buffer direct access file techniques. Each customer master file record is maintained in an account number location on the master file disk, and this same number is used to retrieve the customer's master file data, perform the necessary calculations for the monthly statement, and produce the updated figures, which are then replaced on each processed master file record.

Since transactions are to be processed randomly, the order of transaction data entry is unimportant, a fact that greatly reduces processing time. Printing of monthly statements is usually a sequential process, and this case demonstrates the ease with which a direct access file can be processed both randomly and sequentially.

To simulate more realistic error reporting than in previous case studies, the principles of ''printing'' error results to a file during normal processing and then preparing the actual error reports from that file at the end of normal processing are covered. This involves the use of various file types within one program and introduces you to this widely used concept. Care in the selection of file names, channels, types, and opening and closing statements is emphasized in the problem. Processing logic is shown in general in the following system flowchart:

Step 1 Set up customer direct-access master file

Step 2 Process sales and payments customer records

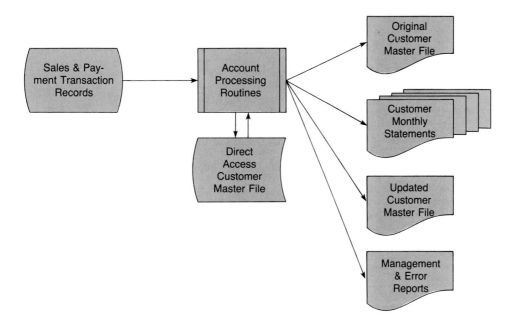

PROBLEM DEFINITION

Input Specifications

Input consists of customer charge account master records containing the customer account number, name, address, current balance, and year-to-date interest. Updated transaction records consist of the account number, charges, payments, and credits.

	Field No.	Field Description	Type	Example
Customer	1	Customer Account Number	Integer	00001
Master	2	Customer Name	Alphabetic	John C. Jones
File	3	Address	Alphanumeric	125 Main Street
Record				Los Angeles
	4	Current Account Balance	Decimal Number	355.00
	5	Year-to-Date Interest	Decimal Number	46.15
	6	Current Interest	Decimal Number	5.32
	7	Zip Code	Integer	90066
Customer	1	Account Number	Integer	00001
Transaction	2	Transaction	Alphabetic	Payment
Record	3	Transaction Amount	Decimal Number	50.00

Processing Decisions and Formulas

Direct access is used to locate the customer's record on the master file. The master file is then updated to reflect the new current balance and YTD interest. Transaction codes are tested.

Transaction Codes

Payment = Subtract transaction amount from balance
Charge = Add transaction amount to balance
Credit = Subtract transaction amount from balance

341

Interest

Compute interest for current period as 0.015 * balance. Add interest to YTD interest and replace new value on m/f.

Calculation of interest takes place only once. Set a switch to insure this or calculate interest before processing transaction records.

For Payments

$$\text{Balance} = \text{Balance} - \text{Payment Amount}$$

For Charges

$$\text{Balance} = \text{Balance} + \text{Charge Amount}$$

For Credit Returns

$$\text{Balance} = \text{Balance} - \text{Credit Amount}$$

In all 3 transactions, the new balance is replaced on the master file record.

Minimum Payment

$$\text{Minimum Payment} = .10 * \text{Balance}$$

Output

Output from the program will consist of a report (file) of all transactions processed plus a monthly bill for every customer on file after all transactions are processed. Error reports for nonexistent account numbers will also be produced.

CUSTOMER MASTER FILE RECORDS

ACNO	NAME	STREET	CITY	STA	BALANCE	YTDINT	INTEREST	ZIP
1	JOHN C. JONES	125 MAIN STREET	LOS ANGELES	CA	355.00	46.15	5.32	90066
2	MARY R. JONES	125 MAIN STREET	LOS ANGELES	CA	166.95	15.22	1.67	90066
3	BOB SMITH	10 SOUTH STREET	SAN JOSE	CA	745.25	76.25	11.18	96131
4	ALICE SMITH	10 SOUTH STREET	SAN JOSE	CA	1615.92	125.65	24.24	95131
5	LOUIS BROWN	25 NORTH AVENUE	HAYWARD	CA	414.18	86.26	6.21	94545
6	BETSY BROWN	25 NORTH AVENUE	HAYWARD	CA	65.11	5.21	0.98	94545
7	BILL LOTT	161 EAST AVENUE	TORRANCE	CA	233.23	14.56	3.35	90503
8	JILL LOTT	161 EAST AVENUE	TORRANCE	CA	11.00	103.92	16.50	90503
9	RICH ROGERS	141 MAIN STREET	ANAHEIM	CA	856.92	98.88	12.85	94088
10	DON ELLSWORTH	ONE ESTATE DRIVE	SUNNYVALE	CA	990.90	144.85	2.17	94086

```
*****************************************************************
*                                                               *
*                   BEST DEPARTMENT STORE                       *
*                                                               *
*                     ONE SOUTH STREET                          *
*                                                               *
*                     LOS ANGELES, CA.                          *
*                                                               *
*                                                               *
*                                                               *
* CUSTOMER ACCOUNT NO:    1            NEW BALANCE:     $  205.33 *
*                                                               *
* CUSTOMER NAME:    JOHN C. JONES      CURRENT INTEREST: $    5.33 *
*                                                               *
* CUSTOMER ADDRESS:  125 MAIN STREET   MINIMUM PAYMENT:  $   20.53 *
*                                                               *
* CITY-STATE-ZIP:    LOS ANGELES    CA    90066                 *
*                                                               *
*****************************************************************
```

```
*****************************************************************
*                                                               *
*                   BEST DEPARTMENT STORE                       *
*                                                               *
*                     ONE SOUTH STREET                          *
*                                                               *
*                     LOS ANGELES, CA.                          *
*                                                               *
*                                                               *
*                                                               *
* CUSTOMER ACCOUNT NO:    2            NEW BALANCE:     $  119.45 *
*                                                               *
* CUSTOMER NAME:    MARY R. JONES      CURRENT INTEREST: $    2.50 *
*                                                               *
* CUSTOMER ADDRESS:  125 MAIN STREET   MINIMUM PAYMENT:  $   11.95 *
*                                                               *
* CITY-STATE-ZIP:    LOS ANGELES    CA    90066                 *
*                                                               *
*****************************************************************
```

```
*****************************************************************
*                                                               *
*                   BEST DEPARTMENT STORE                       *
*                                                               *
*                     ONE SOUTH STREET                          *
*                                                               *
*                     LOS ANGELES, CA.                          *
*                                                               *
*                                                               *
*                                                               *
* CUSTOMER ACCOUNT NO:    3            NEW BALANCE:     $  906.43 *
*                                                               *
* CUSTOMER NAME:    BOB SMITH          CURRENT INTEREST: $   11.18 *
*                                                               *
* CUSTOMER ADDRESS:  10 SOUTH STREET   MINIMUM PAYMENT:  $   90.64 *
*                                                               *
* CITY-STATE-ZIP:    SAN JOSE       CA    95131                 *
*                                                               *
*****************************************************************
```

```
*******************************************************************************
*                                                                             *
*                          BEST DEPARTMENT STORE                              *
*                                                                             *
*                             ONE SOUTH STREET                                *
*                                                                             *
*                             LOS ANGELES, CA.                                *
*                                                                             *
*                                                                             *
*                                                                             *
* CUSTOMER ACCOUNT NO:     4                   NEW BALANCE:      $1,640.16     *
*                                                                             *
* CUSTOMER NAME:      ALICE SMITH              CURRENT INTEREST: $    24.24    *
*                                                                             *
* CUSTOMER ADDRESS:  10 SOUTH STREET           MINIMUM PAYMENT:  $   164.02    *
*                                                                             *
* CITY-STATE-ZIP:     SAN JOSE        CA    96131                             *
*                                                                             *
*******************************************************************************


*******************************************************************************
*                                                                             *
*                          BEST DEPARTMENT STORE                              *
*                                                                             *
*                             ONE SOUTH STREET                                *
*                                                                             *
*                             LOS ANGELES, CA.                                *
*                                                                             *
*                                                                             *
*                                                                             *
* CUSTOMER ACCOUNT NO:     5                   NEW BALANCE:     $   355.39     *
*                                                                             *
* CUSTOMER NAME:      LOUIS BROWN              CURRENT INTEREST: $     6.21    *
*                                                                             *
* CUSTOMER ADDRESS:  25 NORTH AVENUE           MINIMUM PAYMENT:  $    35.54    *
*                                                                             *
* CITY-STATE-ZIP:     HAYWARD         CA    94545                             *
*                                                                             *
*******************************************************************************


*******************************************************************************
*                                                                             *
*                          BEST DEPARTMENT STORE                              *
*                                                                             *
*                             ONE SOUTH STREET                                *
*                                                                             *
*                             LOS ANGELES, CA.                                *
*                                                                             *
*                                                                             *
*                                                                             *
* CUSTOMER ACCOUNT NO:     6                   NEW BALANCE:     $    66.09     *
*                                                                             *
* CUSTOMER NAME:      BETSY BROWN              CURRENT INTEREST: $     0.98    *
*                                                                             *
* CUSTOMER ADDRESS:  25 NORTH AVENUE           MINIMUM PAYMENT:  $     6.61    *
*                                                                             *
* CITY-STATE-ZIP:     HAYWARD         CA    94545                             *
*                                                                             *
*******************************************************************************
```

344

```
**********************************************************************
*                                                                    *
*                    BEST DEPARTMENT STORE                           *
*                                                                    *
*                      ONE SOUTH STREET                              *
*                                                                    *
*                      LOS ANGELES, CA.                              *
*                                                                    *
*                                                                    *
*                                                                    *
*  CUSTOMER ACCOUNT NO:    7          NEW BALANCE:      $   561.73    *
*                                                                    *
*  CUSTOMER NAME:    BILL LOTT        CURRENT INTEREST: $     3.50    *
*                                                                    *
*  CUSTOMER ADDRESS: 161 EAST AVENUE  MINIMUM PAYMENT:  $    56.17    *
*                                                                    *
*  CITY-STATE-ZIP:    TORRANCE       CA   90503                      *
*                                                                    *
**********************************************************************



**********************************************************************
*                                                                    *
*                    BEST DEPARTMENT STORE                           *
*                                                                    *
*                      ONE SOUTH STREET                              *
*                                                                    *
*                      LOS ANGELES, CA.                              *
*                                                                    *
*                                                                    *
*                                                                    *
*  CUSTOMER ACCOUNT NO:    8          NEW BALANCE:      $    11.17    *
*                                                                    *
*  CUSTOMER NAME:    JILL LOTT        CURRENT INTEREST: $     0.16    *
*                                                                    *
*  CUSTOMER ADDRESS: 161 EAST AVENUE  MINIMUM PAYMENT:  $     1.12    *
*                                                                    *
*  CITY-STATE-ZIP:    TORRANCE       CA   90503                      *
*                                                                    *
**********************************************************************



**********************************************************************
*                    BEST DEPARTMENT STORE                           *
*                                                                    *
*                      ONE SOUTH STREET                              *
*                                                                    *
*                      LOS ANGELES, CA.                              *
*                                                                    *
*                                                                    *
*                                                                    *
*  CUSTOMER ACCOUNT NO:    9          NEW BALANCE:      $   569.77    *
*                                                                    *
*  CUSTOMER NAME:    RICH ROGERS      CURRENT INTEREST: $    12.85    *
*                                                                    *
*  CUSTOMER ADDRESS: 141 MAIN STREET  MINIMUM PAYMENT:  $    56.98    *
*                                                                    *
*  CITY-STATE-ZIP:    ANAHEIM        CA   94088                      *
*                                                                    *
**********************************************************************
```

345

```
***********************************************************************
*                                                                     *
*                      BEST DEPARTMENT STORE                          *
*                                                                     *
*                        ONE SOUTH STREET                             *
*                                                                     *
*                        LOS ANGELES, CA.                             *
*                                                                     *
*                                                                     *
*                                                                     *
*  CUSTOMER ACCOUNT NO:   10            NEW BALANCE:    $   755.76     *
*                                                                     *
*  CUSTOMER NAME:     DON ELLSWORTH     CURRENT INTEREST: $   14.86    *
*                                                                     *
*  CUSTOMER ADDRESS:  ONE ESTATE DRIVE  MINIMUM PAYMENT:  $   75.58    *
*                                                                     *
*  CITY-STATE-ZIP:    SUNNYVALE     CA   94086                        *
*                                                                     *
***********************************************************************
```

```
                        _____
                        TRANSACTION REPORT
                        _____

     ACCOUNT NO.              TRANSACTION TYPE         AMOUNT
          1                       CREDIT           $    155.00
          2                       CREDIT           $     50.00
          3                       CHARGE           $    150.00
          5                       PAYMENT          $    100.00
          5                       CHARGE           $     35.00
          7                       CHARGE           $    325.00
          9                       PAYMENT          $    300.00
          10                      PAYMENT          $    250.00

                     END OF TRANSACTION REPORT



                  _____
                  INVALID TRANSACTION REPORT
                  _____

               THE FOLLOWING TRANSACTIONS WERE
             ENCOUNTERED WITH INVALID ACCOUNT NUMBERS

     ACCOUNT NO.              TRANSACTION TYPE         AMOUNT
          14                      CHARGE           $    100.00
          23                      PAYMENT          $     50.00

                END OF INVALID TRANSACTION REPORT
```

```
                       UPDATED MASTER FILE RECORDS
ACNO      NAME              STREET        CITY     STA BALANCE   YTDINT  INTEREST ZIP
   1  JOHN C. JONES    125 MAIN STREET LOS ANGELES CA   205.33   51.48     5.33 90066

   2  MARY R. JONES    125 MAIN STREET LOS ANGELES CA   119.45   17.72     2.50 90066

   3  BOB SMITH        10 SOUTH STREET SAN JOSE    CA   906.43   87.43    11.18 95131

   4  ALICE SMITH      10 SOUTH STREET SAN JOSE    CA  1640.16  149.89    24.24 96131

   5  LOUIS BROWN      25 NORTH AVENUE HAYWARD     CA   355.39   92.47     6.21 94545

   6  BETSY BROWN      25 NORTH AVENUE HAYWARD     CA    66.09    6.19     0.98 94545
```

```
7   BILL LOTT       161 EAST AVENUE TORRANCE    CA  561.73   18.06     3.50 90503

8   JILL LOTT       161 EAST AVENUE TORRANCE    CA   11.17  104.09     0.16 90503

9   RICH ROGERS     141 MAIN STREET ANAHEIM     CA  569.77  111.73    12.85 94088

10  DON ELLSWORTH   ONE ESTATE DRIVESUNNYVALE   CA  755.76  159.71    14.86 94086
```

```
              END OF CHARGE ACCOUNT PROCESSING AND UPDATE PROGRAM
```

Test Data

Test data for the customer master file, as well as all transactions, appear below.

1, John C. Jones, 125 Main Street, Los Angeles, CA, 355.00, 46.15, 5.32, 90066
2, Mary R. Jones, 125 Main Street, Los Angeles, CA, 166.95, 15.22, 1.67, 90066
3, Bob Smith, 10 South Street, San Jose, CA, 745.25, 76.25, 11.18, 95131
4, Alice Smith, 10 South Street, San Jose, CA, 1615.92, 125.65, 24.24, 96131
5, Louis Brown, 25 North Avenue, Hayward, CA, 414.18, 86.26, 6.21, 94545
6, Betsy Brown, 25 North Avenue, Hayward, CA, 65.11, 5.21, 0.98, 94545
7, Bill Lott, 161 East Avenue, Torrance, CA, 233.23, 14.56, 3.35, 90503
8, Jill Lott, 161 East Avenue, Torrance, CA, 11.00, 103.92, 16.50, 90503
9, Rich Rogers, 141 Main Street, Anaheim, CA, 856.92, 98.88, 12.85, 94088
10, Don Ellsworth, One Estate Drive, Sunnyvale, CA, 990.90, 144.85, 2.17, 94086

1, Credit, 155.00
2, Credit, 50.00
3, Charge, 150.00
5, Payment, 100.00
5, Charge, 35.00
7, Charge, 325.00
9, Payment, 300.00
10, Payment, 250.00
14, Charge, 100.00
23, Payment, 50.00

Error Recovery Routines

Invalid customer account numbers are to be output to an "error file" during transaction processing. The "error file" is to be printed after all transactions are processed. Invalid account numbers should not halt program execution.

Validation Procedure

Calculate new account balance and YTD interest values for two customers to verify the program results. Print out the direct access master file before and after transaction processing to verify that updating took place and that invalid account number routines functioned properly.

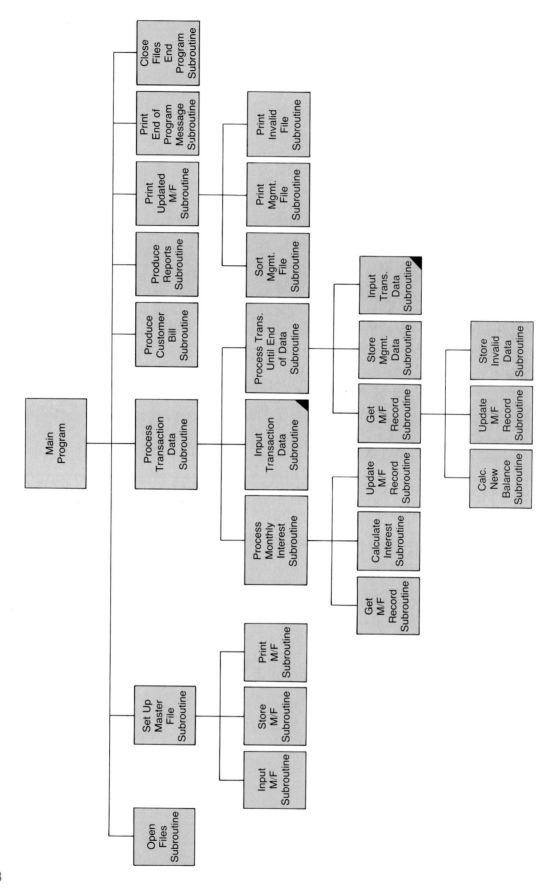

348

FIGURE C9–2
Visual table of contents—charge account processing program.

```
10      REM     ****************************************************
20      REM     *           DIRECT FILE PROCESSING              *
30      REM     *           CASE STUDY: C9-2                   *
40      REM     *  CHARGE ACCOUNT PROCESSING & UPDATE PROGRAM   *
50      REM     * THIS PROGRAM SETS UP A CUSTOMER MASTER FILE   *
60      REM     * USING DIRECT ACCESS TO LOCATE AND UPDATE      *
70      REM     * THE CUSTOMER RECORD IN THE MASTER FILE FOR    *
80      REM     * EACH TRANSACTION. TWO ADDITIONAL FILES ARE    *
90      REM     * SET UP TO STORE INVALID DATA * MGMT DATA      *
100     REM     *                                              *
110     REM     *           VARIABLE LEGEND                    *
120     REM     *  MASTER FILE DATA:                           *
130     REM     *           NBR/RNBR$ = ACCOUNT NUMBER         *
140     REM     *           NAM$/RNAM$ = CUSTOMER NAME         *
150     REM     *           ST$/RSTR$ = STREET ADDRESS         *
160     REM     *           CITY$/RCTY = CITY                  *
170     REM     *           STA$/RSTA$ = STATE                 *
180     REM     *           BAL/RBAL$ = CUSTOMER BALANCE       *
190     REM     *           YTD/RYTD$ = YTD INTEREST           *
200     REM     *           INTR/RINT$ = CURRENT INTEREST      *
210     REM     *           ZIP$/RZIP$ = ZIP CODE              *
220     REM     *  TRANSACTION DATA:                           *
230     REM     *           AN = ACCOUNT NUMBER                *
240     REM     *           CODE = TRANSACTION TYPE            *
250     REM     *           AMT = AMOUNT                       *
260     REM     *  COUNTERS:                                   *
270     REM     *           Z = NUMBER OF FILE RECORDS         *
280     REM     *           TREC = NUMBER OF TRANSACTIONS      *
290     REM     *           IREC = NUMBER OF INVALID TRANS.    *
300     REM     ****************************************************
310             PRINT "COPYRIGHT (C) 1989, BY MERRILL PUBLISHING COMPANY"
320             PRINT "FOR USE WITH STRUCTURED BASIC PROGRAMMING"
330     REM     ****************
340     REM     * MAIN PROGRAM *
350     REM     ****************
360     REM     PERFORM 'OPEN FILES' SUBROUTINE
370             GOSUB 530
380     REM     PERFORM 'SETUP MASTER FILE' SUBROUTINE
390             GOSUB 600
400     REM     PERFORM 'PROCESS TRANSACTION DATA' SUBROUTINE
410             GOSUB 1230
420     REM     PERFORM 'PRODUCE CUSTOMER BILL' SUBROUTINE
430             GOSUB 2410
440     REM     PERFORM 'PRODUCE REPORTS' SUBROUTINE
450             GOSUB 2820
460     REM     PERFORM 'PRINT UPDATED MASTER FILE' SUBROUTINE
470             GOSUB 3590
480     REM     PERFORM 'END OF PROGRAM MESSAGE' SUBROUTINE
490             GOSUB 3780
500     REM     PERFORM 'END OF PROGRAM' SUBROUTINE
510             GOSUB 3860
520             END
530     REM     **************
540     REM     * OPEN FILES *
550     REM     **************
560             OPEN "R",#1,"RAN.FIL",80
570             OPEN "O",#2,"INV.FIL"
580             OPEN "O",#3,"MGT.FIL"
590             RETURN
600     REM     ********************
610     REM     * SET UP MASTER FILE *
620     REM     ********************
630             Z = 10
640             FOR N = 1 TO Z
```

```
650     REM     PERFORM 'LOAD MASTER FILE RECORDS' SUBROUTINE
660             GOSUB 730
670     REM     PERFORM 'STORE MASTER FILE RECORDS' SUBROUTINE
680             GOSUB 890
690             NEXT N
700     REM     PERFORM 'PRINT MASTER FILE RECORDS' SUBROUTINE
710             GOSUB 1030
720             RETURN

730     REM     *****************************
740     REM     * LOAD MASTER FILE RECORDS  *
750     REM     *****************************
760             FIELD #1,4 AS RNBR$, 16 AS RNAM$, 16 AS RSTR$, 13 AS RCTY$,2 AS RSTA$,8 AS RBAL$,8
AS RYTD$,8 AS RINT$,5 AS RZIP$
770             READ NBR,NAM$,ST$,CTY$,STA$,BAL,YTD,INTR,ZIP$
780             DATA 1,JOHN C. JONES,125 MAIN STREET,LOS ANGELES,CA,355.00,46.15,5.32,90066
790             DATA 2,MARY R. JONES,125 MAIN STREET,LOS ANGELES,CA,166.95,15.22,1.67,90066
800             DATA 3,BOB SMITH,10 SOUTH STREET,SAN JOSE,CA,745.25,76.25,11.18,95131
810             DATA 4,ALICE SMITH,10 SOUTH STREET,SAN JOSE,CA,1615.92,125.65,24.24,96131
820             DATA 5,LOUIS BROWN,25 NORTH AVENUE,HAYWARD,CA,414.18,86.26,6.21,94545
830             DATA 6,BETSY BROWN,25 NORTH AVENUE,HAYWARD,CA,65.11,5.21,0.98,94545
840             DATA 7,BILL LOTT,161 EAST AVENUE,TORRANCE,CA,233.23,14.56,3.35,90503
850             DATA 8,JILL LOTT,161 EAST AVENUE,TORRANCE,CA,11.00,103.92,16.50,90503
860             DATA 9,RICH ROGERS,141 MAIN STREET,ANAHEIM,CA,856.92,988.88,12.85,94088
870             DATA 10,DON ELLSWORTH,ONE ESTATE DRIVE,SUNNYVALE,CA,990.90,144.85,2.17,94086
880             RETURN

890     REM     *****************************
900     REM     * STORE MASTER FILE RECORDS *
910     REM     *****************************
920             LSET RNBR$ = MKI$  (NBR)
930             LSET RNAM$ = NAM$
940             LSET RSTR$ = ST$
950             LSET RCTY$ = CTY$
960             LSET RSTA$ = STA$
970             LSET RBAL$ = MKS$  (BAL)
980             LSET RYTD$ = MKS$  (YTD)
990             LSET RINT$ = MKS$  (INTR)
1000            LSET RZIP$ = ZIP$
1010            PUT #1,N
1020            RETURN

1030    REM     *****************************
1040    REM     * PRINT MASTER FILE RECORDS *
1050    REM     *****************************
1060            LPRINT TAB(27);"CUSTOMER MASTER FILE RECORDS"
1070            LPRINT "ACNO     NAME              STREET       CITY    STA BALANCE YTDINT INTEREST
ZIP"
1080            FOR N = 1 TO Z
1090            GET #1,N
1100            NBR = CVI(RNBR$)
1110            NAM$ = RNAM$
1120            ST$ = RSTR$
1130            CTY$ = RCTY$
1140            STA$ = RSTA$
1150            BAL = CVS(RBAL$)
1160            YTD = CVS(RYTD$)
1170            INTR = CVS(RINT$)
1180            ZIP$ = RZIP$
1190            F1$ = "### \          \\            \\          \\ \####.## ####.## ####.##
\    \"
1200            LPRINT USING F1$;NBR,NAM$,ST$,CTY$,STA$,BAL,YTD,INTR,ZIP$
1210            NEXT N
1220            RETURN
```

```
1230    REM     ***************************
1240    REM     * PROCESS TRANSACTION DATA *
1250    REM     ***************************
1260    REM     PERFORM 'PROCESS MONTHLY INTEREST' SUBROUTINE
1270            GOSUB 1330
1280    REM     PERFORM 'INPUT TRANSACTION DATA' SUBROUTINE
1290            GOSUB 1660
1300    REM     PERFORM 'PROCESS TRANSACTION UNTIL END OF DATA' SUBROUTINE
1310            GOSUB 1830
1320            RETURN

1330    REM     ****************************
1340    REM     * PROCESS MONTHLY INTEREST *
1350    REM     ****************************
1360    REM     PERFORM 'GET MASTER FILE RECORD' SUBROUTINE
1370            FOR N = 1 TO Z
1380            GOSUB 1440
1390    REM     PERFORM 'CALCULATE INTEREST' SUBROUTINE
1400            GOSUB 1520
1410    REM     PERFORM 'UPDATE MASTER FILE RECORD' SUBROUTINE
1420            GOSUB 1580
1430            NEXT N

1440    REM     *************************
1450    REM     * GET MASTER FILE RECORD *
1460    REM     *************************
1470            GET #1,N
1480            BAL = CVS (RBAL$)
1490            INTR = CVS (RINT$)
1500            YTD = CVS (RYTD$)
1510            RETURN

1520    REM     *********************
1530    REM     * CALCULATE INTEREST *
1540    REM     *********************
1550            INTR = BAL * .015
1560            YTD = YTD + INTR
1570            BAL = BAL + INTR

1580    REM     ****************************
1590    REM     * UPDATE MASTER FILE RECORD *
1600    REM     ****************************
1610            LSET RBAL$ = MKS$ (BAL)
1620            LSET RINT$ = MKS$ (INTR)
1630            LSET RYTD$ = MKS$ (YTD)
1640            PUT #1,N
1650            RETURN

1660    REM     *************************
1670    REM     * INPUT TRANSACTION DATA *
1680    REM     *************************
1690            CLS
1700            PRINT "PLEASE ENTER THE DATA AS SPECIFIED AND PRESS"
1710            PRINT "RETURN AFTER EACH ENTRY. WHEN YOU ARE FINISHED, "
1720            PRINT "TYPE '0' (ZERO) FOR THE ACCOUNT NUMBER AND PRESS"
1730            PRINT "RETURN FOR THE TRANSACTION TYPE AND THE AMOUNT."
1740            PRINT:PRINT:PRINT
1750            PRINT "ENTER THE ACCOUNT NUMBER....:"
1760            PRINT "ENTER THE TRANSACTION TYPE..:"
1770            PRINT "ENTER AMOUNT OF TRANSACTION.:"
1780            LOCATE  8,30 : INPUT AN
1790            LOCATE  9,30 : INPUT CD$
1800            LOCATE 10,30 : INPUT AMT
1810            IF AN = 0 THEN ENDSW = 1
1820            RETURN
```

```
1830   REM      *****************************************
1840   REM      * PROCESS TRANSACTION UNTIL END OF DATA *
1850   REM      *****************************************
1860            TREC = 0
1870            IREC = 0
1880            ENDSW = 0
1890            WHILE ENDSW = 0
1900   REM      PERFORM 'SEARCH MASTER FILE' SUBROUTINE
1910            GOSUB 2010
1920   REM      PERFORM 'STORE MANAGEMENT DATA' SUBROUTINE
1930   REM                  IF TRANSACTION DATA IS 'VALID'
1940            IF ISW = 0 THEN GOSUB 2350
1950            ISW = 0
1960   REM      PERFORM 'INPUT TRANSACTION DATA' SUBROUTINE
1970            GOSUB 1660
1980            WEND
1990            CLOSE #2,#3
2000            RETURN
2010   REM      *********************
2020   REM      * SEARCH MASTER FILE *
2030   REM      *********************
2040   REM      PERFORM 'STORE INVALID DATA' SUBROUTINE
2050            ISW = 0
2060            IF AN > Z THEN GOSUB 2280
2070            IF ISW = 1 THEN GOTO 2140
2080            GET #1,AN
2090            BAL = CVS (RBAL$)
2100   REM      PERFORM 'CALCULATE NEW BALANCE' SUBROUTINE
2110            GOSUB 2150
2120   REM      PERFORM 'UPDATE MASTER FILE RECORD' SUBROUTINE
2130            GOSUB 2220
2140            RETURN
2150   REM      ************************
2160   REM      * CALCULATE NEW BALANCE *
2170   REM      ************************
2180            IF CD$ = "CHARGE" THEN BAL = BAL + AMT
2190            IF CD$ = "PAYMENT" THEN BAL = BAL - AMT
2200            IF CD$ = "CREDIT" THEN BAL = BAL - AMT
2210            RETURN
2220   REM      ****************************
2230   REM      * UPDATE MASTER FILE RECORD *
2240   REM      ****************************
2250            LSET RBAL$ = MKS$(BAL)
2260            PUT #1,AN
2270            RETURN
2280   REM      *********************
2290   REM      * STORE INVALID DATA *
2300   REM      *********************
2310            PRINT #2,AN;",";CD$;",";AMT
2320            ISW = 1
2330            IREC = IREC + 1
2340            RETURN
2350   REM      *************************
2360   REM      * STORE MANAGEMENT DATA *
2370   REM      *************************
2380            PRINT #3,AN;",";CD$;",";AMT
2390            TREC = TREC + 1
2400            RETURN
2410   REM      **************************
2420   REM      * PRODUCE CUSTOMER BILLS *
2430   REM      **************************
2440            FOR N = 1 TO Z
2460            NBR = CVI (RNBR$)
```

352

```
2470          NAM$ = RNAM$
2480          ST$ = RSTR$
2490          CTY$ = RCTY$
2500          STA$ = RSTA$
2510          BAL = CVS (RBAL$)
2520          INTR = CVS (RINT$)
2530          ZIP$ = RZIP$
2540          IF BAL > 0 THEN MIN = BAL * .1
2550          LPRINT
2560          LPRINT

2570          LPRINT "*************************************************************************************************"
2580          LPRINT "*                                                                                             *"
2590          LPRINT "*                              BEST DEPARTMENT STORE                                          *"
2600          LPRINT "*                                                                                             *"
2610          LPRINT "*                              ONE SOUTH STREET                                               *"
2620          LPRINT "*                                                                                             *"
2630          LPRINT "*                              LOS ANGELES, CA.                                               *"
2640          LPRINT "*                                                                                             *"
2650          LPRINT "*                                                                                             *"
2660          LPRINT "*                                                                                             *"
2670          F3$ = "* CUSTOMER ACCOUNT NO: ####              NEW BALANCE:     $#,###.##       *"
2680          F4$ = "* CUSTOMER NAME:       \               \    CURRENT INTEREST: $ ###.##       *"
2690          F5$ = "* CUSTOMER ADDRESS:    \               \    MINIMUM PAYMENT:  $ ###.##       *"
2700          F6$ = "* CITY-STATE-ZIP:      \          \ \ \ \     \                            *"
2710          LPRINT USING F3$;NBR,BAL                                                              *"
2720          LPRINT "*                                                                                             *"
2730          LPRINT USING F4$;NAM$,INTR                                                            *"
2740          LPRINT "*                                                                                             *"
2750          LPRINT USING F5$;CTY$,ST$,MIN                                                         *"
2760          LPRINT "*                                                                                             *"
2770          LPRINT USING F6$;CTY$,STA$,ZIP$                                                       *"
2780          LPRINT "*                                                                                             *"
2790          LPRINT "*************************************************************************************************"
2800          NEXT N
2810          RETURN

2820   REM    *******************
2830   REM    * PRODUCE REPORTS *
2840   REM    *******************
2850   REM    PERFORM 'SORT MANAGEMENT FILE' SUBROUTINE
2860          GOSUB 2920
2870   REM    PERFORM 'PRINT MANAGEMENT REPORT' SUBROUTINE
2880          GOSUB 3110
2890   REM    PERFORM 'PRINT INVALID DATA REPORT' SUBROUTINE
2900          GOSUB 3320
2910          RETURN

2920   REM    **************************
2930   REM    * SORT MANAGEMENT FILE *
2940   REM    **************************
2950          OPEN "I",#3,"MGT.FIL"
2960          DIM AN(100),CD$(100),AMT(100)
2970          FOR I = 1 TO TREC
2980          INPUT #3,AN(I),CD$(I),AMT(I)
2990          NEXT I
3000          NREC = TREC - 1
3010          SORTSW = 1
3020          FOR K = 1 TO NREC
3030          IF SORTSW = 0 THEN GOTO 3050
3040          SORTSW1 = 0
3050          FOR I = 1 TO NREC
3060          J = I + 1
3070          IF AN(I) > AN(J) THEN SWAP AN(I),AN(J):SWAP CD$(I),CD$(J):SWAP AMT(I),AMT(J):SORTSW = 1
3080          NEXT I
```

353

```
3090          NEXT K
3100          RETURN
3110   REM    ***************************
3120   REM    * PRINT MANAGEMENT REPORT *
3130   REM    ***************************
3140          FOR I = 1 TO 4
3150          LPRINT
3160          NEXT I
3170          LPRINT TAB(31);"_____"
3180          LPRINT TAB(31);"TRANSACTION REPORT"
3190          LPRINT TAB(31);"_____"
3200          LPRINT
3210          LPRINT TAB(14);"ACCOUNT NO.        TRANSACTION TYPE        AMOUNT"
3220          FOR I = 1 TO TREC
3230          F7$ = "              ####                \       \      $#,###.##"
3240          LPRINT USING F7$;AN(I),CD$(I),AMT(I)
3250          NEXT I
3260          LPRINT
3270          LPRINT
3280          LPRINT TAB(21);"        END OF TRANSACTION REPORT"
3290          LPRINT
3300          CLOSE #3
3310          RETURN
3320   REM    *****************************
3330   REM    * PRINT INVALID DATA REPORT *
3340   REM    *****************************
3350          OPEN "I",#2,"INV.FIL"
3360          FOR I = 1 TO 4
3370          LPRINT
3380          NEXT I
3390          LPRINT TAB(28);"_____"
3400          LPRINT TAB(28);"INVALID TRANSACTION REPORT"
3410          LPRINT TAB(28);"_____"
3420          LPRINT
3430          LPRINT TAB(25);"THE FOLLOWING TRANSACTIONS WERE"
3440          LPRINT TAB(21);"ENCOUNTERED WITH INVALID ACCOUNT NUMBERS"
3450          LPRINT
3460          LPRINT TAB(14);"ACCOUNT NO.        TRANSACTION TYPE        AMOUNT"
3470          LPRINT
3480          FOR I = 1 TO IREC
3490          INPUT #2,AN(I),CD$(I),AMT(I)
3500          LPRINT USING F7$;AN(I),CD$(I),AMT(I)
3510          NEXT I
3520          LPRINT
3530          LPRINT TAB(24);"END OF INVALID TRANSACTION REPORT"
3540          LPRINT
3550          LPRINT
3560          LPRINT
3570          CLOSE #2
3580          RETURN
3590   REM    ****************************
3600   REM    * PRINT UPDATED MASTER FILE *
3610   REM    ****************************
3620          LPRINT TAB(27);"UPDATED MASTER FILE RECORDS"
3630          LPRINT "ACNO      NAME            STREET        CITY   STA BALANCE  YTDINT INTEREST
ZIP"
3640          FOR N = 1 TO Z
3650          GET #1,N
3660          NBR = CVI(RNBR$)
3670          NAM$ = RNAM$
3680          ST$ = RSTR$
3690          CTY$ = RCTY$
3700          STA$ = RSTA$
```

```
3710            BAL = CVS(RBAL$)
3720            YTD = CVS(RYTD$)
3730            INTR = CVS(RINT$)
3740            ZIP$ = RZIP$
3750            LPRINT USING F1$;NBR,NAM$,ST$,CTY$,STA$,BAL,YTD,INTR,ZIP$
3760            NEXT N
3770            RETURN
3780    REM     *************************
3790    REM     * END OF PROGRAM MESSAGE *
3800    REM     *************************
3810            LPRINT
3820            LPRINT
3830            LPRINT
3840            LPRINT TAB(14);"END OF CHARGE ACCOUNT PROCESSING AND UPDATE PROGRAM"
3850            RETURN
3860    REM     *****************
3870    REM     * END OF PROGRAM *
3880    REM     *****************
3890            CLOSE #2
3900            RETURN
3910    REM
3920    REM     END OF PROGRAM
```

SUMMARY

File processing is comprised of two main categories: sequential access and direct access. As with tables, both access methods have advantages and disadvantages. In sequential access, all the records on file must be processed in sequence even if only one or just a few of them are needed; this can lead to delays. Updating a sequential file implies that another sequential file must be created record by record (except on disk storage).

In direct access, any desired record or all of the records on file can be processed randomly because the computer's operating system locates the desired records by their addresses on disk, and these in turn are related to the key fields of the records. Any record, regardless of its location in the file, can be retrieved, processed, or updated without inputting or reading all previous records. Similarly, updating can take place directly in the record being processed without creating a new record on a new file.

Sequential access and direct access files must be declared, opened, processed, and closed using special BASIC statements and functions. All files must have a name and should have an extension that follows a period and denotes the type of file. Some examples of file names are EMMPAY.RAT, MASTER.FIL, MAIL.DAT, and BILLING.FYL.

Learning to write programs that use files is important in business applications because main memory is usually limited. Furthermore, main memory is volatile and most business systems require permanent storage for data retrieval and record updating. Loading a computer's main memory with data also limits its usefulness to the program being processed.

Files can be created by editing using a text editor (word processor) or by a file-creation program that accepts data from the keyboard and sends the data to the file. This is the method covered in this text. When data is directed to a file, delimiters must be placed between the fields in the record so that the access program can distinguish between fields. When a file is created by editing, commas are inserted, usually between the data fields, exactly as in a DATA statement. When a file is created in your program, you can place commas in a PRINT statement, or use the WRITE statement, which performs this automatically.

The file created in a program must be opened using the OPEN statement. After a file is opened, data can be input from the keyboard with READ/DATA and then directed to the file with a PRINT # statement. You should remember that opening an existing file for output destroys the contents of that file and after a file is created, it should be closed because on some BASIC systems the file and all the data in it will be lost. This is accomplished by using the CLOSE statement.

A file also can be used as a source of data into a program once it has been created. This is done by opening the file for input using the OPEN statement. After opening the file for input and inputting data in memory with the INPUT #, data can be displayed, printed, or transferred to another file.

Direct access files are somewhat more complex and are not yet standardized on many BASIC systems. Check your system before attempting any of the direct access programs, especially the conversion functions described in the text.

Opening a direct access file involves two statements, not one. After the file has been opened for direct access, the FIELD statement is used to specify the variable type, size, and sequence. In the FIELD statement, the disk variables should be allocated as follows: 2 bytes for integer; 4 bytes for single-precision numbers; 8 bytes for double-precision numbers; and N bytes for a string of size N. All variables on the direct access disk file and those specified in the FIELD statement must be string variables, even program numeric variables. Numeric variables must be converted to string for placement on a direct access file and reconverted back to numbers for use in the program using the 6 special conversion functions described.

To place data onto a direct access file, three operations must be performed: input or read data into your program; convert this "normal" data to a string code, using the special string- conversion functions; and put the coded data onto the direct file in a location corresponding to the key field using the PUT # statement.

To retrieve a direct access file record, the GET statement is used; however, data obtained from the direct access disk file must be converted from its binary code back to program format. The BASIC functions used to accomplish this are described in the chapter.

COMMON ERRORS AND SOLUTIONS

Error	Example	Solution
1. Forgetting to open a file for input, output, or direct access.	10 INPUT #1 A,B, (bad file mode in 10) 20 PRINT #1, A,B,	Remember, every time information is to be placed onto or retrieved from a file, that file must be opened.
2. Opening a file for output when it should be input, or vice versa.	(bad file mode in 10) 10 OPEN ''O'',#1, ''DATA.FIL'' 20 INPUT #1 A,B (bad file mode in 10) 10 OPEN ''I'',#1, ''RESULT.FIL'' 20 PRINT #1,A,B (file not found in 10)	Remember, opening a file for output means your program will be outputting *onto* the file; opening for input implies that your program will be obtaining input data from the file.
3. Assigning an invalid file number channel to a file opened for input or output.	10 OPEN ''O'',#15, ''DATA.FIL'' 20 PRINT #15 A,B (bad file number)	Check your system manual for the permissible range of file numbers, as systems do vary significantly.
4. Trying to open a file for input that has been opened for output in a previous step; i.e., forgetting to close the file before changing the input or output mode.	10 OPEN ''O'',#1, ''DATA.FIL'' 20 PRINT #1 A,B 30 OPEN ''I'',#1, ''DATA.FIL'' 40 INPUT #1,A,B (file already open in 30)	Make sure to close your files before opening for a different mode: e.g.: 25 CLOSE #1
5. Trying to access a file for input that has not been created, or one that is located on a storage device (disk drive, e.g., B:) not specified or currently logged.	10 OPEN ''I'', #1, ''DATA.FIL'' ''DATA.FIL'' is on ''B'' drive 20 INPUT #1, A,B, (file not found)	Make sure that the file to be accessed has been created and that its name contains the name of the device on which it resides, e.g.: 10 OPEN ''I'', #1, ''B:DATA.FIL''
6. Writing over a file that already exists, or naming a file with the same name as a file already created, overwrites the information placed on the file originally. This error can destroy your original data file, so care is needed in the processing of sequential files.	10 OPEN ''O'', #1, ''DATA.FIL'' 20 FOR I = 1 TO 10 30 PRINT #I, I, I^2 40 NEXT I 50 CLOSE #1 60 CLOSE ''O'', #1, ''DATA.FIL'' 70 FOR I = 11 TO 20 80 PRINT #1, I, I^2 90 NEXT I 100 END (change 60 to) 60 OPEN ''O'',#1,''DAT1.FIL''	Results in this case would be DATA.FIL with the following values: $\underline{I}$ $\underline{I^2}$ 11 121 12 144 13 169 . . . . . . 20 400 The original values on the file would be overwritten and lost. To save all data, the second reference to the output file should contain a different file name if you want to save *all* the results.
7. Trying to create a file (data or program) before checking the contents of the disk for available space. You can lose your program and data when this occurs.	10 OPEN ''O'', #1, ''OPEN.FIL'' 20 FOR I = 1 TO 1000 30 PRINT #1, I+1, I+2, etc. 40 NEXT I (disk full at 30)	Always check the space available *before* creating a large data file and calculate how much space you will need before executing your program, as considerable wasted time and effort can be avoided.

357

Error	Example	Solution
8. Trying to input data from a file after the end of the file was reached. Running out of data fields or data records while still trying to input your program.	10 OPEN "O",#1, "DATA.FIL" 20 PRINT #1, A,B 30 CLOSE #1 40 OPEN "I",#1, "DATA.FIL" 50 INPUT #1,A,B 60 PRINT A,B 70 INPUT #1,A,B 80 PRINT AB 90 END (input past END in 70)	Make sure that your program logic does not attempt to read more data from a file than was originally placed on that file. Use an EOF test or last-record test in your logic if you are inputting records in a loop or inputting many records in sequence.
9. Attempting to create a new file with either the OPEN or the SAVE command when all file directory entries are full (not the same as "disk full"). This can cause the loss of a program or a data file.	Too many SAVEs or OPENs on the logged disk file.	Check your manual to determine how *many* files can be stored on your system's auxiliary storage devices.

10. Improper record number specified in a GET or PUT statement used to update, create, or access a direct access file.	10 OPEN "R", #1, "RAND.FIL"
	20 INPUT A
	30 PUT #1, RN
	   where RN > 32767
	   or < = ZERO
	   or
	40 GET #1, RN
		Make sure that the record number used to locate the record on a direct access file falls within the permissible range for your system.

11. Improper coding of the FIELD statement used to allocate space for string variables on a random-access disk file. Improper names used for disk variables, or incorrect number of bytes allocated for numeric variables.	05 OPEN "R", #1, "RAND.FIL' 10 FIELD #1, 20 AS NM$, 4 AS EMPNO$, 8 AS PAYRT$, 8 AS YTDGS$, 20 AS NM*, 3* AS EMPNO$, AND 7* AS PAYRT$ (errors)*	The FIELD statement is a complex one. Make sure that the correct number of bytes are allocated for string variables and for numeric variables (integers, single-precision, and double-precision numbers—if your system supports three), and that the random file variable names are *all* string variables.
12. Improper conversion of strings for placement on a direct access file.	10 DNAM$ = NM$ (should be) 10 DNAM$ = LSET (NM$)	Always left-justify strings before conversion to random access disk file names.
13. Improper conversion of numeric variables to string format for placement on direct access files using the PUT instruction. These work together with the FIELD statement, so check both simultaneously.	10 EMANO = MKI$ (ENO) 20 PAYRT$ = MKS$ (PRATE) 30 YTDG$$ = MKD$ (YTD) (these are correct!)	Check *your* system manual for exact form of these important conversion statements, and be sure the variable *types* and bytes allocated in the FIELD statement correspond.
14. Improper conversion of disk variables (used to store numeric data) back to "normal" numeric values after a GET statement during direct access file data retrieval.	ENO = CVI(EMPNO$) PRATE = CVS(PAYRT$) YTD = CVD(YTDG$) (these are correct!)	Check your system manual for the exact forms of each of these important conversion statements, and make sure that the variable types and numbers of bytes allocated in the FIELD statement correspond.

1. Explain the importance of storing data and information in business data processing applications.
2. Compare and contrast the storage of data on files and in tables in terms of the speed of access and specific limitations.
3. Describe, in general terms, the two methods of retrieving data and information from files.
4. What are the advantages and disadvantages of sequential access and direct access?
5. Name and briefly describe five business systems that use sequential access file processing.
6. Name and briefly describe five business systems that use direct access files. Why do these systems depend on this type of file organization?
7. Name the four steps needed to establish a sequential access file, to input data into it, and to make the file ready for use.
8. Write a BASIC statement for your system to accomplish the steps in question 7.
9. Name the four steps needed to use a sequential file for inputting data into a program.
10. Write the BASIC statements for your system that enable you to use a sequential file in a program, as indicated in question 9.
11. Why is it important to close a file at the end of a program?
12. Referring to the mailing label program in the chapter, why is it desirable to save the data in a file as opposed to setting up an in-memory table with the same information?
13. What type of key field variable is permitted in sequential access file processing? Explain why this is true.
14. In most sequential access file processing programs, the master file is processed after a transaction record has been input. Explain the relationship between these two elements.
15. Sequential files can be accessed to retrieve information or to update information in the file. Explain the differences between the two procedures.
16. On many BASIC systems, the updating of a record that exists in a sequential access file requires creating a new file. Explain why this is true.
17. Referring to the payroll program in the chapter, explain why it is necessary to place the timecard records in the same order as the master records in the file. What would happen if this were not done?
18. Although they were not included in the payroll program, what error routines or error conditions would be reasonable inclusions for the program?
19. Once the master file in the payroll program had been established, was it necessary to set it up again? Explain why or why not.
20. What would limit the number and the size of records placed in the sequential master file in the payroll example previously mentioned?
21. With programming problems that involve sequential files, it is good to print or display the contents of the file before and after processing. Why is this recommended?
22. Explain with examples a transaction document.
23. Describe the advantages and limitations of direct access file processing.
24. Why can't direct access files be used in all business applications?
25. Describe with an analogy the principles of direct access.
26. Name the two most frequently used methods for establishing a direct access file.
27. Consult the reference manual for your system, and then describe, in general terms, the direct access method(s) supported by your system.
28. Why is it necessary on some systems to become familiar with the code used to store data and information on some direct access files?
29. Why must the key field on a direct access file be an integer?
30. On systems that support block input/output, the record size is sometimes fixed as a sector in disk. What are the implications of this, and how does it affect the efficiency of direct access file storage?

31. Describe the concept of a storage buffer, which is used on many BASIC systems in conjunction with direct access file processing. Why is such a buffer important?

32. Why must layouts of the fields in the storage buffer be identical to layouts of the fields in a random access file record?

33. What is the name of the binary code used on many direct access files to store both numeric and string data?

34. Write the OPEN statement used on your system to establish a direct access file.

35. Write the buffer statement (usually FIELD) used in your system to establish an I/O buffer for direct access. Use the following fields: account number, current balance, and customer's name (30 characters maximum).

36. Why is it good practice to precede the variable names in the buffer with the letter D?

37. Why are variable names in the buffer always string variables?

38. Before being placed on a direct access file, data must be converted to ASCII code. Write the instructions used by your system (if applicable) to convert integers and decimal numbers to the format.

39. Why is it necessary to convert string variables like the numeric data in question 38?

40. What is the purpose of the LSET instruction?

41. Write the BASIC statement used in your system to place one record on the direct access file. Explain each of the key parts to this statement.

42. When converting ''normal'' variables in a BASIC program for storage on direct access files, a specific number of bytes must be allocated with the FIELD statement for variables of different types. Consult your manual and list the sizes needed for variables of different types (i.e., for integers, decimal numbers, string, etc.).

43. What statement is used in your system to place data on a direct access file? Explain each of the key parts to this statement.

44. Why is it necessary to convert the buffer fields back to ''normal'' format for use within the program?

45. Write the conversion statements used in your system to accomplish the conversion described in question 44 for integers and decimal numbers (if applicable on your system).

46. In both the simplified and expanded payroll programs presented in this chapter, it was possible to sequentially access the master file and to directly access the same file. Explain why this is true and how it is accomplished.

47. What were the advantages of being able to directly access the master file in the payroll examples in the chapter?

48. The charge account program represents a realistic application of direct access. Explain why it is beneficial to be able to access the customer master file in this program by direct access techniques.

49. The charge account program in the chapter contains an error routine that will execute if the customer's data is not found in the master file. How is this routine accomplished, and why is it important?

PROBLEMS FOR SOLUTION

1. Refer to the problem definition for problem 1 of chapter 7 and convert the telephone directory table to a sequential access file. You may either set up the file from the original table or load the file directly from terminal input. Be sure to print the contents of the file before you attempt to access it to make certain that it exists and that it is correct.

Process inquiries as indicated in problem 1 of chapter 7 and produce the same output as described in the output for the problem.

2. Refer to the problem definition for problem 4 of chapter 7 and convert the inventory master table to a sequential access file. Process sales records with the method described in the problem and remember to print the contents of the file you create to make certain that it exists and that it is correct before you begin the sales-processing logic.

Produce the same reports described in the output for problem 4 of chapter 7, including sales receipts, reorder messages, and the management report. Also, update the master inventory file to reflect the new quantities on hand for each type of pet at the end of the day's sales processing.

3. Using the problem definition for problem 3 in chapter 7, convert the appointment date table to a direct access file if your system supports direct access files. Use the Julian date as the key field to access the appointment file.

You can access, update, and delete entries easily on this type of file, as in table processing, so use test data of your own choice to set up a useful program suited to your needs or preferences.

Consult the output for problem 3 of chapter 7 for typical output formats, and add fields to the direct access file records, as desired, to enhance the program.

4. Using the computer dating program problem definition in problem 1 of chapter 8, convert the master table to a sequential file and process the transaction records exactly as you did for the matching problems in chapter 8. You may wish to add evaluation fields to the master file and transaction records to produce a program that is more realistic and useful.

After evaluating all of the records on your file and computing a match score, load the file records into a table, sort the table, and print out the best five matches in descending order.

5. Referring to problem 2 of chapter 8, convert the disease master table to a sequential access file, and evaluate the symptoms transaction record. As in problem 2 of chapter 8, you may wish to add evaluation fields to the master file; but remember, do not use this program to actually diagnose any diseases—always consult a doctor!

After evaluating a person's symptoms against each disease in your master file, compute a matching score. Save that score on your file and continue the evaluation logic for all diseases in your file.

When the evaluation is complete, the records on file should be loaded into a table for sorting by evaluation score. Then, you print the three most likely diseases (i.e., those with the three highest matching scores).

6. Refer to the job search illustration program in chapter 8 and rewrite the BASIC logic so that the job master table is stored on a sequential access file and so that the fields in each record are increased to include other significant job characteristics.

To obtain records for your job master file, consult your local newspaper's classified advertisements for available programming, systems analyst, and data processing positions. Process job requests as illustrated in the program presented in chapter 8, and print the five best job matches for each applicant's job request. Do this by loading your evaluated jobs into a table, sorting the table by score, and printing the first five records in the table.

7. Convert the appointment calendar from problem 3 of chapter 7 to a direct access file, and access data directly by Julian date, as was done with the table version of this program. With a direct access file, you should be able to store one year's data and retrieve any day's data directly.

CHAPTER TEN

INDEXED SEQUENTIAL ACCESS METHOD

THEORY AND ADVANTAGES OF THE INDEXED SEQUENTIAL
ACCESS METHOD (ISAM)

The sequential access of a large file can be very slow when the records are large and there are many of them. Direct access is very fast, but the key field (the field used to retrieve the desired record) must be a simple integer. Often in business both methods are ruled out: the files are too large and the key field may be a person's name, part description, or airline flight number and/or destination. Yet with a very clever combination of sequential and direct access principles, it is possible to overcome the disadvantages of both methods (i.e., search for and find very quickly any record you want even when the key field is alphabetical and the file is large). The combination of sequential and direct access logic that accomplishes this is called the indexed sequential access method, or ISAM. On large computer systems using COBOL, ISAM logic retrieval is automatic when a file is set up in ISAM. For BASIC programmers (for the time being), ISAM logic and the special files needed must be constructed.

The indexed sequential access method can be compared to the way information is looked up in a textbook. For example, if you want to locate information about looping in this text, you would begin your search by turning to the index and reading through the topics listed until you found the section with words starting with the letter *l*. Continuing your search through the *l*s, you would eventually find the word *looping* and note the page number. After turning to the page referenced, you could read the material of interest to you.

This method obviously is faster than thumbing through all the pages in the book until you locate information on looping (which is analogous to a sequential search procedure). But, it is still not as fast as finding out the page number of the looping material from another person directly so you can turn immediately to the page desired (which is analogous to direct access).

The manual indexed sequential method used above for finding the looping information required a sequential search for an index followed by a direct access (in the text) to the particular page referenced in the index. This process is the basis of ISAM.

Principles of ISAM Logic

Referring back to the simplified direct access payroll program in chapter 9, suppose you wanted to access the master direct access file, but you did not know the employee's number. Is there any way you could modify or add to the program logic so that by just knowing the employee's name, you could quickly find out the employee number and proceed with the direct access?

Clearly, all you would need is another file (or even a table) in which you had saved just the employee names and their respective employee numbers, such as the one shown below:

Employee Name	Employee Number
Jones	01
Smith	02
Brown	03
Williams	04
Rivera	05

This file, called the index file, could be searched quickly and sequentially until a match was found between the name you were looking for and the corresponding name in the file. When it was located, the name in the file would yield the employee number, which could then be used for direct access of a "master" file—the original *complete* direct access file containing *all* the employee's information.

Setting up the Master and Index Files

The first step in designing an indexed file system (ISAM) would be to create an index file. You could add the required logic to figure 9–4 by including another OPEN statement for the sequential index file called INDEX.FIL at line 45 and a WRITE statement at line 215 which would place just the employees' names and numbers on that file. After the program was run, you could return to DOS and print the two files: the INDEX.FIL and RANDOM.FIL. The results of this appear in figure 10–1.

Notice that the index file (INDEX.FIL) contains the employee names and numbers as desired and that the direct access file (RANDOM.FIL) contains the names and lots of strange coded information. (These are the numbers that were converted to strings—payrate and YTD gross pay.)

Searching the Index File

The next step in ISAM logic would be to access the master file. But this is a two-part operation. First, you must input a name and use this name to sequentially search through the much shorter index file until a match is found. Take a look at a modified version of figure 9–4 in figure 10–2 to see what new statements are required.

At line 65 an OPEN statement has been added for the INDEX.FIL. The file is opened for "I" (input) since you will be obtaining data from it in this program. At line 270, an employee's name is entered instead of employee number and the sequential search of the index file (to locate that number) takes place at lines 271 to 274. Line 276 prints out the employee number (and record number) of the record you will want to retrieve by direct access of the RANDOM.FIL.

FIGURE 10–1
Payroll program from figure 9–1 with indexed sequential access features.

```
Input

10      REM     THIS PROGRAM SETS UP A RANDOM ACCESS FILE AND AN INDEX
20      REM     FILE FOR 5 EMPLOYEES, NUMBERED 1 THROUGH 5
30      REM
40              OPEN "R",#1,"RANDOM.FIL",34
45              OPEN "O",#2,"INDEX.FIL"
50              FIELD #1,2 AS DEMPNO$,20 AS DNAM$,4 AS DPAYRATE$,8 AS DYTDGROSS$
60              FOR I = 1 TO 5
70                      INPUT "EMPLOYEE NUMBER ";EMPNO%
80                      INPUT "EMPLOYEE NAME ";NAM$
90                      INPUT "EMPLOYEE PAY RATE ";PAYRATE
100                     INPUT "EMPLOYEE YTD GROSS ";YTDGROSS#
110     REM
120     REM     CONVERT THESE TO DISK STRING FORMAT
130     REM
140                     LSET DEMPNO$ = MKI$(EMPNO%)
150                     LSET DNAM$ = NAM$
160                     LSET DPAYRATE$ = MKS$(PAYRATE)
170                     LSET DYTDGROSS$ = MKD$(YTDGROSS#)
180     REM
190     REM     PUT THIS RECORD ON DISK IN LOCATION EMPNO% (EMP. NUMBER)
200     REM     AND PLACE THE EMPLOYEE'S NAME AND NUMBER ON THE INDEX FILE
210                     PUT #1,EMPNO%
215                     WRITE #2, NAM$,EMPNO%
220             NEXT I
225             CLOSE #1
227             CLOSE #2
230             END
```

Printout of the Sequential Index File

```
"JONES",1
"SMITH",2
"BROWN",3
"WILLIAMS",4
"RIVERA",5
```

Printout of the Direct Access File

Note: **This file is impossible to read because the numbers are stored in code as strings, which do not print as numbers.**

```
TYPE RANDOM.FIL
JONES               H/SMITH              ,BROWN
WILLIAMS     p4R         ~ RIVERA        X " =
```

Data for RANDOM.FIL and INDEX.FIL

```
RUN
EMPLOYEE NUMBER ? 1
EMPLOYEE NAME    ? JONES
EMPLOYEE PAY RATE ? 12.50
EMPLOYEE YTD GROSS ? 11237.50
EMPLOYEE NUMBER ? 2
EMPLOYEE NAME    ? SMITH
EMPLOYEE PAY RATE ? 10.75
EMPLOYEE YTD GROSS ? 9664.25
EMPLOYEE NUMBER ? 3
EMPLOYEE NAME ? BROWN
EMPLOYEE PAY RATE ? 7.50
EMPLOYEE YTD GROSS ? 6742.50
EMPLOYEE NUMBER ? 4
EMPLOYEE NAME ? WILLIAMS
EMPLOYEE PAY RATE ? 10.50
EMPLOYEE YTD GROSS ? 9439.50
EMPLOYEE NUMBER ? 5
EMPLOYEE NAME ? RIVERA
EMPLOYEE PAY RATE ? 13.50
EMPLOYEE YTD GROSS ? 12136.50
```

Accessing the Direct Access Master File

To accomplish the last and most important step in ISAM logic (to get the entire master record from the direct access file), you need only to substitute the located record number from the index file search in the GET statement at line 280 of figure 10–2.

Updating an ISAM File

Updating the direct access file in the ISAM system you have constructed is very similar to the updating shown in figure 9–4. Here, however, the key field input will be the employee name, not number, and the INDEX.FIL will have to be opened for input (''I'') in line 100, as shown in figure 10–3.

The next change in the program involves printing the index file and the master file. Statements 260 through 300 provide logic to read each index record and then print it. Notice that there are no conversions required to print the index file fields since this is a sequential file.

The file is closed in line 310 because you will need to begin reading the index file from the beginning in the access portion of the program. (The CLOSE statement acts like

FIGURE 10–2
Modified version of figure 9–4.

Input

```
10      REM     THIS PROGRAM ACCESSES THE DIRECT ACCESS FILE CREATED
20      REM     BY THE PREVIOUS PROGRAM BUT FIRST SEARCHES AN INDEX FILE
25      REM     TO LOCATE THE RECORD NUMBER TO BE ACCESSED (EMPLOYEE NO.)
30      REM     AFTER PRINTING THE ENTIRE FILE TO VERIFY ITS CONTENTS
40      REM     AN EMPLOYEE'S NAME IS ENTERED AND USED TO SEARCH FOR
50      REM     THAT PERSON'S EMPLOYEE NUMBER (SAME AS RECORD NUMBER)
55      REM     IN THE INDEX FILE. WHEN THE NUMBER IS RETRIEVED, IT IS USED
56      REM     TO LOCATE THE DESIRED MASTER FILE RECORD IN THE RANDOM FILE
60              OPEN "R",#1,"RANDOM.FIL",34
65              OPEN "I",#2,"INDEX.FIL"
70              FIELD #1,2 AS DEMPNO$,20 AS DNAM$,4 AS DPAYRATE$,8 AS DYTDGROSS$
80      REM
90      REM     PRINT THE ENTIRE DIRECT ACCESS FILE FOR VERIFICATION
100             PRINT
110             PRINT
120             PRINT " EMP.NUMBER NAME PAYRATE YTD GROSS PAY"
130             FOR N = 1 TO 5
140             GET #1,N
150                     EMPNO%    = CVI(DEMPNO$)
160                     NAM$      = DNAM$
170                     PAYRATE   = CVS(DPAYRATE$)
180                     YTDGROSS# = CVD(DYTDGROSS$)
190                     PRINT EMPNO%,NAM$,PAYRATE,YTDGROSS#
200             NEXT N
210     REM
220     REM     NOW DO A SEQUENTIAL SEARCH OF THE INDEX TABLE
230     REM
240             PRINT
250             PRINT
260             PRINT
270             INPUT " ENTER EMPLOYEE NAME FOR INDEX SEARCH ";TRXNM$
271             FOR I = 1 TO 5
272                     INPUT #2,INAM$,INO
273                     IF TRXNM$ = INAM$ THEN REC = INO
274             NEXT I
275             PRINT
276             PRINT "THE DESIRED RECORD NUMBER ON THE DIRECT FILE IS ";REC
277             PRINT
280             GET #1,REC
290                     EMPNO%    = CVI(DEMPNO$)
300                     NAM$      = DNAM$
310                     PAYRATE   = CVS(DPAYRATE$)
320                     YTDGROSS# = CVD(DYTDGROSS$)
330             PRINT
340             PRINT
350             PRINT "               RECORD LOCATED FOR EMPLOYEE NO. ";REC
360             PRINT " EMP.NUMBER    NAME              PAYRATE       YTD GROSS PAY"
370             PRINT EMPNO%,NAM$,PAYRATE,YTDGROSS#
380             CLOSE #1
390             CLOSE #2
400             END
```

Output

EMP.NUMBER	NAME	PAYRATE	YTD GROSS PAY
1	JONES	12.5	11237.5
2	SMITH	10.75	9664.25
3	BROWN	7.5	6742.5
4	WILLIAMS	10.5	9439.5
5	RIVERA	13.5	12136.5

```
 ENTER EMPLOYEE NAME FOR INDEX SEARCH ? BROWN

THE DESIRED RECORD NUMBER ON THE DIRECT FILE IS  3


               RECORD LOCATED FOR EMPLOYEE NO.   3


EMP.NUMBER        NAME                     PAYRATE     YTD GROSS PAY
3                 BROWN                        7.5          6742.5
OK
```

FIGURE 10–3
ISAM update.

Input

```
10      REM     THIS PROGRAM ISAM TO UPDATE THE DIRECT ACCESS FILE
20      REM     CREATED BY THE PREVIOUS PROGRAM. FIRST THE ENTIRE INDEX
30      REM     AND MASTER FILES ARE PRINTED FOR VERIFICATION. THEN AN
40      REM     EMPLOYEE NAME IS USED TO RETRIEVE THE RECORD NUMBER ON THE
50      REM     INDEX FILE CORRESPONDING TO THE RECORD ON THE DIRECT ACCESS
60      REM     FILE, BY SEQUENTIAL ACCESS. WITH THIS RECORD NUMBER, THE
70      REM     DIRECT ACCESS FILE RECORD FOR THE DESIRED EMPLOYEE CAN
80      REM     BE LOCATED BY DIRECT ACCESS AND UPDATED.
90              OPEN "R",#1,"RANDOM.FIL",34
100              OPEN "I",#2,"INDEX.FIL"
110              FIELD #1,2 AS DEMPNO$,20 AS DNAM$,4 AS DPAYRATE$,8 AS DYTDGROSS$
120     REM
130     REM      PRINT THE ENTIRE DIRECT ACCESS FILE FOR VERIFICATION
140              PRINT
150              PRINT
160              PRINT " EMP.NUMBER      NAME                     PAYRATE       YTD GROSS PAY"
170              FOR N = 1 TO 5
180              GET #1,N
190                      EMPNO%    = CVI(DEMPNO$)
200                      NAM$      = DNAM$
210                      PAYRATE   = CVS(DPAYRATE$)
220                      YTDGROSS# = CVD(DYTDGROSS$)
230                      PRINT EMPNO%,NAM$,PAYRATE,YTDGROSS#
240              NEXT N
250     REM
260     REM      PRINT THE INDEX FILE
270              FOR I = 1 TO 5
280              INPUT #2,INAM$,INO
290              PRINT INAM$,INO
300              NEXT I
310              CLOSE #2
320     REM
330     REM     NOW DO A SEQUENTIAL SEARCH OF THE INDEX FILE BY NAME.
340     REM     WHEN A MATCH OCCURS, USE THE NUMBER OBTAINED TO DIRECTLY
350     REM     ACCESS THE MASTER DIRECT ACCESS FILE.
360     REM
370     REM     ALSO, INPUT HOURS WORKED TO CALCULATE GROSS PAY AND ADD THIS
380     REM     TO THE PREVIOUS YTD GROSS PAY. THEN PLACE THE UPDATED
390     REM     RECORD BACK ON THE DIRECT ACCESS FILE.
400              PRINT
410              PRINT
420              PRINT
430              INPUT " NAME OF EMPLOYEE WHOSE RECORD IS DESIRED ";TRXNM$
440              INPUT " ENTER THE HOURS WORKED FOR THAT EMPLOYEE ";HOURS
```

368

```
450      REM
460      REM      THE SEQUENTIAL SEARCH OF THE INDEX FILE
470      REM
480           OPEN "I",#2,"INDEX.FIL"
490           FOR I = 1 TO 5
500                INPUT #2, INAM$,INO
510                IF TRXNM$ = INAM$ THEN REC = INO
520           NEXT I
530           GET #1,REC
540                EMPNO%    = CVI(DEMPNO$)
550                NAM$      = DNAM$
560                PAYRATE   = CVS(DPAYRATE$)
570                YTDGROSS# = CVD(DYTDGROSS$)
580           PRINT
590           PRINT
600           PRINT "           RECORD LOCATED FOR EMPLOYEE NO. "; END
610           PRINT " EMP.NUMBER     NAME               PAYRATE     YTD GROSS PAY"
620           PRINT EMPNO%,NAM$,PAYRATE,YTDGROSS#
630      REM
640      REM      CALCULATE CURRENT GROSS PAY AND ADD TO YTD GROSS PAY
650      REM
660           GROSS = PAYRATE * HOURS
670           YTDGROSS# = YTDGROSS# + GROSS
680      REM
690      REM      CONVERT THE NEW YTD GROSS PAY TO STRING AND PLACE THE WHOLE
700      REM      RECORD BACK ON DISK
710           LSET DYTDGROSS$ = MKD$(YTDGROSS#)
720           PUT #1,REC
730           CLOSE #1
740           CLOSE #2
750 END
```

Output

```
EMP.NUMBER      NAME                PAYRATE      YTD GROSS PAY
1               JONES               12.5         11237.5
2               SMITH               10.75        9664.25
3               BROWN               7.5          6742.5      ← Original
4               WILLIAMS            10.5         9439.5
5               RIVERA              13.5         12136.5
JONES           1
SMITH           2
BROWN           3
WILLIAMS        4
RIVERA          5



 NAME OF EMPLOYEE WHOSE RECORD IS DESIRED ? BROWN
 ENTER THE HOURS WORKED FOR THAT EMPLOYEE ? 40



           RECORD LOCATED FOR EMPLOYEE NO.  0
EMP.NUMBER      NAME                PAYRATE      YTD GROSS PAY
3               BROWN               7.5          6742.5      ← Updated
```

Output

```
EMP.NUMBER      NAME                PAYRATE      YTD GROSS PAY
1               JONES               12.5         11237.5
2               SMITH               10.75        9664.25
3               BROWN               7.5          7042.5      ← Updated
4               WILLIAMS            10.5         9439.5
5               RIVERA              13.5         12136.5
```

a rewind for sequential files, so that when it is reopened and read, the first record is retrieved.)

In line 430, the most significant change in the program is apparent. Here, instead of inputting a number for direct access, you are inputting an employee's name. At line 440 you also input hours worked, as before, for the update calculations needed.

The sequential search of the index file begins at line 490, but before the search, you must reopen that file for input since you need to read *all* the records in it again. The search logic consists of reading one index file record containing an employee name and number (line 500) and then comparing the name you are looking for to the name just input *from* the index file. If they match, you save the index number (INO) as variable REC at line 510.

It is the REC value that is used in the GET at line 530 to directly access the desired master record from the RANDOM.FIL. When that record is retrieved, the fields are converted to program variables by the conversions at statements 540 through 570. After that, logic is identical to the direct access update in figure 9–4. The current gross pay is calculated at line 660, the YTD Gross is updated at line 670, and the new YTD Gross Pay value is replaced in the direct access disk in lines 710 and 720 in its disk format. Lines 730 and 740 close both files and end the program.

SAVING TIME WITH ISAM

At this point you may be wondering how much time has been saved by sequentially searching one file and following that with a direct access of another file. Why not simply set up one large sequential file with all the information on it and sequentially search it by name? This question is difficult to answer because it depends on a number of factors, such as the size of each master file record, the number of records on the file, the disk operating system being used, and even your computer system and version of BASIC.

Generally, though, if you consider the time needed for the direct access portion of the search negligible (it is quite fast), then the advantage in speed of ISAM vs. sequential file accessing is a function of the relative record size of the index record and logical size of the direct file record.

The logical size of the direct access file record is not always the same as the actual number of bytes in the record, which is often a sector size of 512 bytes. Therefore, calculations of speed advantage are based on a hypothetical situation where the direct access records *would have been* placed on a sequential file.

In the payroll example, the ratio was about 3:2 (34 bytes for the direct file to 24 on the index file), so the saving was minimal. For a large master file record, say 500 bytes, the ratio improves to about 10:1. There are, in fact, other ways to improve the overall access time, such as bringing the index file into memory as a table and then doing a binary search of the index table, but these are not discussed since the program logic gets very involved. Suffice it to say for large files with large records, the speed advantage warrants using ISAM logic.

Airline Reservation System Simulation

CONCEPTS TO BE ILLUSTRATED

This case study will involve the use of programmer-constructed indexed sequential access files and will illustrate the following principles, techniques, and concepts:

1. Creation of an index file and master file.
2. Sequential search of an index file.
3. Retrieval of a master file record number.
4. Direct access of the master file by record number.
5. Inquiry plus interactive update of the master file.

The information retrieved from the system is realistic, as are the output documents and displays produced. Displayed flight information is patterned after current airline information systems, and tickets also reflect a reasonable subset of the information typically printed on a passenger's airline ticket. Limitations to the case study fall into the following two categories:

1. The master file of available flights is greatly abridged. Examples here represent a mere fraction of the total number of flights existing on a true airline flight and reservation system.
2. The flight information is retrieved by city pair only (as will be explained shortly), not by city pair and date as would normally be the case. This shortens the master file to a reasonable length for purposes of illustrating the system concepts.

The city-pair key field is interesting because it requires the use of indexed sequential access—the field is alphabetic and a sequential search of an entire airline reservations master file would be prohibitively long. Direct access would be impossible because it is alphabetic.

In the city-pair key field, the first three letters indicate the point of departure for the aircraft (a three-letter code established for every airport in the world), and the subsequent three letters denote the arrival airport. Thus, with only six letters you can designate the departure and arrival points for any flight on normally flown commercial routes. The three-letter airport codes used in this case study are as follows:

JFK = John F. Kennedy International Airport, New York, New York
MUC = Munich Airport, West Germany
FRA = Frankfort Main Airport, West Germany
ORD = O'Hare Airport, Chicago, Illinois
LGA = La Guardia Airport, New York, New York

In addition to the standard three-letter airport codes, abbreviations are used for airline names and specific aircraft nomenclature. The following abbreviations are used in this case study because they reflect common airline industry practice:

LH = Lufthansa German Airlines
EA = Eastern Airlines
AA = American Airlines
B747 = Boeing 747 aircraft
DC10 = Douglas DC 10 aircraft

371

In this case study, program logic follows these steps:

1. Set up a master flight information file of all available flights between the selected city pairs, including seats available, fares, movies, meals, aircraft type, departure and arrival times, etc., using direct access file techniques. At the same time, extract an index file that contains the key field (city pair) and the record number of the master record on the direct access master file.
2. Input an inquiry (i.e., a request for flight information), a booking request (i.e., a ticket issue), or a combination of the two transactions using the keyboard as the input medium.
3. Use the city pair specified in the inquiry or ticket-request transaction as the key field to perform a search of the index file which locates the record number of the master record for the flight on the direct access master file.
4. Retrieve that record number for the master record from the index file and use it to directly access the master record on the direct access master flight information file. Then display the information retrieved on the display screen.
5. Input a code that indicates additional flight information or a ticket purchase is desired for that flight. (If additional flight data is desired for the city pair, search the index file again for another flight with the same city-pair key field and repeat direct accessing of the master file.) If a flight is to be booked (i.e., a ticket purchased), enter the appropriate passenger information so that the ticket output on the printer is complete.
6. Print the passenger's ticket.
7. Update the flight master file to reflect the number of seats remaining in each seat class for the flight retrieved by the inquiry if a ticket is actually sold.
8. Repeat this procedure with a DO UNTIL construct until the appropriate code is entered to end the inquiries, the ticket purchases, and the file updates.

These steps are shown schematically in figure C10–1. Figure C10–2 gives an overview of the processing.

Instructors or students who wish to enhance the realism of this case need only enter the master file flight information indicated on the test data worksheet and add the data to the city pair key field. Thus, instead of inquiring by JFK MUC with no date specified, the new key field entered would be JFKMUCSEPT05.

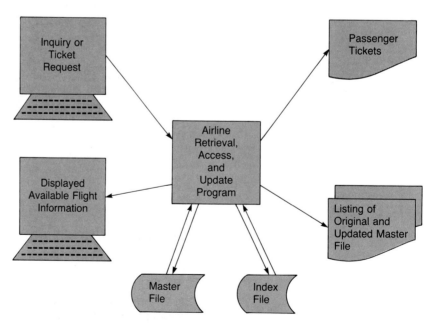

FIGURE C10–1
Airline reservation system flowchart—ISAM processing.

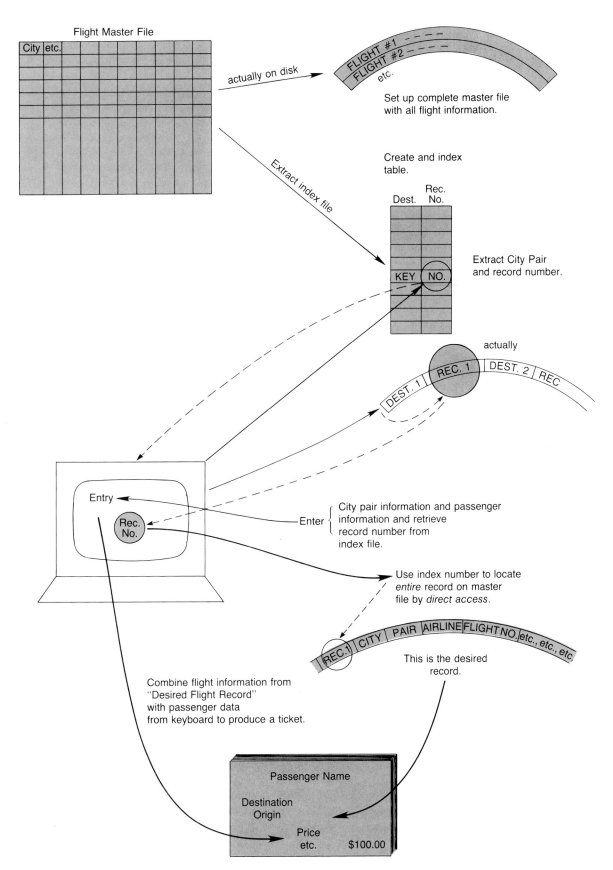

Flight Master File

City | etc.

actually on disk

FLIGHT #1 - - - - -
FLIGHT #2 - - - - -
etc.

Set up complete master file
with all flight information.

Create and index
table.

Extract index file

Dest. | Rec. No.

KEY | NO.

Extract City Pair
and record number.

actually

DEST. 1 | REC. 1 | DEST. 2 | REC

Entry

Rec. No.

Enter { City pair information and passenger
information and retrieve
record number from
index file.

Use index number to locate
entire record on master
file by *direct access.*

REC.1 | CITY | PAIR | AIRLINE | FLIGHT NO. | etc., etc., etc.

This is the desired
record.

Combine flight information from
"Desired Flight Record"
with passenger data
from keyboard to produce a ticket.

Passenger Name

Destination
Origin

Price
etc. $100.00

FIGURE C10–2
Airline reservations system—processing overview.

PROBLEM DEFINITION

Input Specifications

	Field No.	Field Description	Type	Size	Example
Master File Record Description	1	City Pair (Origin/Dest.)	Alphanumeric	6	LGAORD
	2	Airline Name	Alphanumeric	2	EA
	3	Flight Number	Numeric	4	101
	4	Seats Avail. in First Class	Numeric	4	8
	5	Seats Avail. in Bus. Class	Numeric	4	0
	6	Seats Avail. in Tour. Class	Numeric	4	138
	7	Fare in First Class	Numeric	8	240.00
	8	Fare in Business Class	Numeric	8	0.00
	9	Fare in Tourist Class	Numeric	8	130.00
	10	Departure Time	Alphanumeric	4	0935
	11	Arrival Time	Alphanumeric	4	1145
	12	Meals Served	Alphabetic	16	B
	13	Aircraft Type	Alphanumeric	8	B-727
	14	Movie Title	Alphanumeric	8	None
	15	International Tax	Numeric	8	0.00
	16	Domestic Tax	Numeric	8	0.08
Inquiry and Ticket Request Records	**Inquiry**				
	1	City Pair (Origin/Dest.)	Alphanumeric	6	LGAORD
	Ticket Request				
	1	City Pair (Origin/Dest.)	Alphanumeric	6 max.	LGAORD
	2	Seat Class Requested	Alphabetic	8 max.	FIRST
	3	Passenger Name	Alphanumeric	20 max.	JOHN C JONES
	4	Passenger Address	Alphanumeric	30 max.	125 MAIN ST.
	5	Type of Payment	Alphanumeric	10 max.	CASH
	6				

Processing Decisions and Formulas

Decisions

1. Use transaction for inquiry and/or ticket purchase by city-pair keyfield.
2. Update master file according to tickets issued (i.e., seat type on appropriate flight).
3. Issue tickets.
4. Produce updated master file listing after processing is finished.

Formulas

$$\text{International Tax} = \$3.00 \text{ added to Fare}$$
$$\text{Domestic Tax} = 8\% \text{ of Fare}$$

Output

Output—Original Master File Listing

```
RUN
COPYRIGHT (C) 1989, BY MERRILL PUBLISHING COMPANY
FOR USE WITH STRUCTURED BASIC PROGRAMMING
 NUMBER OF RECORDS IN FILE : 10
----------------------- RECORD NUMBER  1 ---------------------------------
City Pair: LGAORD Airline:EA:101 Seats    8    0 138 Fares    $240   $0 $130    Times:0935-
1145 Meals:SNACK    Aircraft:B727   Movie:NONE    Tax:$0.00/.08
```

```
--------------------------- RECORD NUMBER   2 ----------------------------------
City Pair: LGAORD Airline:AA:900 Seats    8    0 138 Fares    $240    $0 $130    Times:1300-
1530 Meals:SNACK    Aircraft:B727    Movie:NONE    Tax:$0.00/.08
--------------------------- RECORD NUMBER   3 ----------------------------------
City Pair: ORDLGA Airline:EA:102 Seats    8    0 138 Fares    $240    $0 $130    Times:1710-
1950 Meals:SNACK    Aircraft:B727    Movie:NONE    Tax:$0.00/.08
--------------------------- RECORD NUMBER   4 ----------------------------------
City Pair: ORDLGA Airline:AA:901 Seats    8    0 138 Fares    $240    $0 $130    Times:2030-
2300 Meals:SNACK    Aircraft:B727    Movie:NONE    Tax:$0.00/.08
--------------------------- RECORD NUMBER   5 ----------------------------------
City Pair: JFKFRA Airline:LH:401 Seats   33  134 212 Fares  $1,514 $735 $275    Times:1830-
0755 Meals:DIN-BREA Aircraft:B747    Movie:ARTHUR    Tax:$3.00/.00
--------------------------- RECORD NUMBER   6 ----------------------------------
City Pair: JFKFRA Airline:LH:403 Seats   24   76 136 Fares  $1,514 $735 $275    Times:2120-
1050 Meals:DIN-BREA Aircraft:DC10    Movie:ARTHUR    Tax:$3.00/.00
--------------------------- RECORD NUMBER   7 ----------------------------------
City Pair: FRAJFK Airline:LH:404 Seats   33  132 212 Fares  $1,514 $735 $275    Times:1330-
1555 Meals:LUN-DIN  Aircraft:B747    Movie:KLUTE     Tax:$3.00/.00
--------------------------- RECORD NUMBER   8 ----------------------------------
City Pair: FRAJFK Airline:LH:400 Seats   24   76 136 Fares  $1,514 $735 $275    Times:1000-
1230 Meals:BREAK-LU Aircraft:DC10    Movie:KLUTE     Tax:$3.00/.00
--------------------------- RECORD NUMBER   9 ----------------------------------
City Pair: JFKMUC Airline:LH:409 Seats   33  134 212 Fares  $1,531 $757 $294    Times:1730-
0855 Meals:DIN-BREA Aircraft:B747    Movie:ARTHUR    Tax:$3.00/.00
--------------------------- RECORD NUMBER  10 ----------------------------------
City Pair: MUCJFK Airline:LH:408 Seats   33  134 212 Fares  $1,531 $757 $294    Times:1110-
1535 Meals:LUN-DIN Aircraft:B747     Movie:KLUTE     Tax:$3.00/.00
PRESS RETURN TO CONTINUE
```

Screen Outputs

```
READY TO ACCEPT INQUIRY OR TICKET REQUEST
TO RETRIEVE INFORMATION, ENTER THE CITY-PAIR
AS JFKFRA (JFK=ORIGIN,FRA=DESTINATION)
-------------------------------------------------
ENTER CITY PAIR SUCH AS 'JFKMUC', 'END' TO QUIT  :? LGAORD
THERE ARE  2
FLIGHTS TO MEET YOUR NEEDS - DISPLAY FOLLOWS - JOT DOWN THE RECORD NUMBER OF
THE FLIGHT YOU MAY WANT TO BOOK
PRESS ANY KEY TO CONTINUE THEN RETURN ?
  ******** FLIGHTS AVAILABLE *******
-------------------------------------
RECORD NUMBER           : 1
CITY-PAIR               :LGAORD
AIRLINE                 :EA
FLIGHT NUMBER           : 101
DEPARTURE TIME          :0935
ARRIVAL TIME            :1145
MEALS SERVED ON BOARD   :SNACK
MOVIE SHOWN             :NONE
AIRCRAFT TYPE           :B727
AIR FARE INFORMATION IN U.S. DOLLARS
        FIRST CLASS : 240
     BUSINESS CLASS : 0
      TOURIST CLASS : 130
SEAT AVAILABILITY INFORMATION :
    OPEN IN FIRST CLASS     : 8
    OPEN IN BUS. CLASS      : 0
    OPEN IN TOURIST CLASS   : 138
-------------------------------------
  PLEASE CHECK FARE RESTRICTIONS BEFORE
    PROCESSING TICKET REQUEST !!
-------------------------------------
```

Inquiry request on screen

**Screen after inquiry
showing first available flight**

375

```
PRESS RETURN TO CONTINUE
DO YOU WISH TO BOOK A FLIGHT NOW ? (ANSWER YES OR NO)? NO
 ******* FLIGHTS AVAILABLE *******
    RECORD NUMBER              : 2
    CITY-PAIR                  :LGAORD
    AIRLINE                    :AA
    FLIGHT NUMBER              : 900
    DEPARTURE TIME             :1300
    ARRIVAL TIME               :1530
    MEALS SERVED ON BOARD      :SNACK
    MOVIE SHOWN                :NONE
    AIRCRAFT TYPE              :B727
    AIR FARE INFORMATION IN U.S. DOLLARS
          FIRST CLASS : 240
       BUSINESS CLASS : 0
        TOURIST CLASS : 130
    SEAT AVAILABILITY INFORMATION :
        OPEN IN FIRST CLASS       : 8
        OPEN IN BUS. CLASS        : 0
        OPEN IN TOURIST CLASS     : 138
-----------------------------------------
    PLEASE CHECK FARE RESTRICTIONS BEFORE
      PROCESSING TICKET REQUEST !!
-----------------------------------------
PRESS ANY KEY TO CONTINUE THEN RETURN ?
 DO YOU WISH TO BOOK A FLIGHT NOW ? (ANSWER YES OR NO)? NO
 NOW ENTER THE NUMBER OF THE FLIGHT YOU MAY WANT ? 1

    ******* FLIGHTS AVAILABLE *******
-----------------------------------------
    RECORD NUMBER              : 1
    CITY-PAIR                  :LGAORD
    AIRLINE                    :EA
    FLIGHT NUMBER              : 101
    DEPARTURE TIME             :0935
    ARRIVAL TIME               :1145
    MEALS SERVED ON BOARD      :SNACK
    MOVIE SHOWN                :NONE
    AIRCRAFT TYPE              :B727
    AIR FARE INFORMATION IN U.S. DOLLARS
          FIRST CLASS : 240
       BUSINESS CLASS : 0
        TOURIST CLASS : 130
    SEAT AVAILABILITY INFORMATION :
        OPEN IN FIRST CLASS       : 8
        OPEN IN BUS. CLASS        : 0
        OPEN IN TOURIST CLASS     : 138
-----------------------------------------
    PLEASE CHECK FARE RESTRICTIONS BEFORE
      PROCESSING TICKET REQUEST !!
-----------------------------------------
PRESS ANY KEY TO CONTINUE THEN RETURN ?
 DO YOU WISH TO BOOK A FLIGHT NOW ? (ANSWER YES OR NO)? YES
 ------ BEGIN ENTERING INFORMATION FOR TICKET  ------
 SEAT STATUS REPORT FOR RECORD : 1  LGAORD
 FIRST CL      BUSINESS CL    TOURIST CL
 8                0              138
 ABBREVIATIONS ; FIRST,BUS,TOUR
 ENTER TYPE SEAT REQUESTED ? FIRST
 PASSENGER NAME :? JOHN C. JONES
 PASSENGER ADDRESS :? 125 MAIN STREET
 TYPE OF PAYMENT OR CHARGE NO. :? CASH

 **************TICKET ISSUED**************
    AIRLINE      : EA
    FLIGHT NUMBER : 101
    SEAT CLASS   : FIRST
```

Screen after inquiry showing second available flight

Screen after entering record number of flight to be booked

Screen for entry of passenger information for booked flight

Screen showing ticket purchase confirmation

```
PASSENGER NAME: JOHN C. JONES                                    AIRLINE
AIR FARE + TAX: 259.2                                        RESERVATION
-----------------------------------------                        SYSTEM
TYPE OF PAYMENT - CREDIT CARD NO. IF CHARGE CASH             SIMULATION

PICK UP TICKET AND BOARDING PASS AT PRINTER
-----------------------------------------------
          END OF PASSENGER TRX


*******************************************
*                                         *
*      TRAVEL AGENT ISSUED TICKET     *       Printed
*                                         *   ticket
*   AIRLINE : EA         FLIGHT NO:   101 *
*                                         *
*                 FROM-TO: LGAORD         *
*                 DEPARTURE TIME: 0935    *
*                 ARRIVAL TIME :  1145    *
*   PASSENGER NAME: JOHN C. JONES         *
*   SEAT CLASS     : FIRST                *
*   BASIC FARE     : $  240.00            *
*   TAX            : $   19.20            *
*   TOTAL FARE     : $  259.20            *
*                                         *
*******************************************
PRESS ANY KEY TO CONTINUE -THEN RETURN ?
READY TO ACCEPT INQUIRY OR TICKET REQUEST
TO RETRIEVE INFORMATION, ENTER THE CITY-PAIR
AS JFKFRA (JFK=ORIGIN,FRA=DESTINATION)
-----------------------------------------------
ENTER CITY PAIR SUCH AS 'JFKMUC', 'END' TO QUIT :? JFKFRA    Similar outputs
THERE ARE  2                                                 for second inquiry
FLIGHTS TO MEET YOUR NEEDS - DISPLAY FOLLOWS -
JOT DOWN THE RECORD NUMBER OF THE FLIGHT YOU MAY WANT TO BOOK
PRESS ANY KEY TO CONTINUE THEN RETURN ?

   ******** FLIGHTS AVAILABLE *******
   ------------------------------------
RECORD NUMBER              : 5
CITY-PAIR                  :JFKFRA
AIRLINE                    :LH
FLIGHT NUMBER              : 401
DEPARTURE TIME             :1830
ARRIVAL TIME               :0755
MEALS SERVED ON BOARD      :DIN-BREAK
MOVIE SHOWN                :ARTHUR
AIRCRAFT TYPE              :B747
AIR FARE INFORMATION IN U.S. DOLLARS            Screen showing first
        FIRST CLASS : 1514                      available flight
     BUSINESS CLASS : 735
      TOURIST CLASS : 275
SEAT AVAILABILITY INFORMATION :
    OPEN IN FIRST CLASS       : 33
    OPEN IN BUS. CLASS        : 134
    OPEN IN TOURIST CLASS     : 212
-----------------------------------------
 PLEASE CHECK FARE RESTRICTIONS BEFORE
    PROCESSING TICKET REQUEST !!
-----------------------------------------
PRESS ANY KEY TO CONTINUE THEN RETURN ?
DO YOU WISH TO BOOK A FLIGHT NOW ? (ANSWER YES OR NO)? NO

   ******** FLIGHTS AVAILABLE *******
   ------------------------------------                  Screen showing
RECORD NUMBER              : 6                            second available flight    377
CITY-PAIR                  :JFKFRA
```

```
AIRLINE                   :LH
FLIGHT NUMBER             : 403
DEPARTURE TIME            :2120
ARRIVAL TIME              :1050
MEALS SERVED ON BOARD     :DIN-BREAK
MOVIE SHOWN               :ARTHUR
AIRCRAFT TYPE             :DC10
AIR FARE INFORMATION IN U.S. DOLLARS
         FIRST CLASS : 1514
        BUSINESS CLASS : 735
          TOURIST CLASS : 275
SEAT AVAILABILITY INFORMATION :
     OPEN IN FIRST CLASS    : 24
     OPEN IN BUS. CLASS     : 76
     OPEN IN TOURIST CLASS  : 136

-----------------------------------------
  PLEASE CHECK FARE RESTRICTIONS BEFORE
     PROCESSING TICKET REQUEST !!
-----------------------------------------

PRESS ANY KEY TO CONTINUE THEN RETURN ?
  DO YOU WISH TO BOOK A FLIGHT NOW ? (ANSWER YES OR NO)? YESNO
NOW ENTER THE NUMBER OF THE FLIGHT YOU MAY WANT ? 5

    ******* FLIGHTS AVAILABLE *******
-----------------------------------------
  RECORD NUMBER             : 5
  CITY-PAIR                 :JFKFRA
  AIRLINE                   :LH
  FLIGHT NUMBER             : 401
  DEPARTURE TIME            :1830
  ARRIVAL TIME              :0755
  MEALS SERVED ON BOARD     :DIN-BREAK
  MOVIE SHOWN               :ARTHUR
  AIRCRAFT TYPE             :B747
  AIR FARE INFORMATION IN U.S. DOLLARS
           FIRST CLASS : 1514
          BUSINESS CLASS : 735
            TOURIST CLASS : 275
  SEAT AVAILABILITY INFORMATION :
       OPEN IN FIRST CLASS    : 33
       OPEN IN BUS. CLASS     : 134
       OPEN IN TOURIST CLASS  : 212

-----------------------------------------
  PLEASE CHECK FARE RESTRICTIONS BEFORE
     PROCESSING TICKET REQUEST !!
-----------------------------------------

PRESS ANY KEY TO CONTINUE THEN RETURN ?
  DO YOU WISH TO BOOK A FLIGHT NOW ? (ANSWER YES OR NO)? YES
  ------ BEGIN ENTERING INFORMATION FOR TICKET ------
  SEAT STATUS REPORT FOR RECORD : 5  JFKFRA
  FIRST CL     BUSINESS CL    TOURIST CL
  33             134            212
  ABBREVIATIONS ; FIRST,BUS,TOUR
  ENTER TYPE SEAT REQUESTED ? TOUR
  PASSENGER NAME :? MARY SMITH
  PASSENGER ADDRESS :? 12 SOUTH STREET
  TYPE OF PAYMENT OR CHARGE NO. :? CASH

   ***************TICKET ISSUED*************
     AIRLINE      : LH
     FLIGHT NUMBER :  401
     SEAT CLASS    : TOUR
     PASSENGER NAME: MARY SMITH
     AIR FARE + TAX: 278
-----------------------------------------
```

Screen showing flight to be booked

Screen showing passenger information entered

TYPE OF PAYMENT - CREDIT CARD NO. IF CHARGE CASH

PICK UP TICKET AND BOARDING PASS AT PRINTER

                END OF PASSENGER TRX

AIRLINE
RESERVATION
SYSTEM
SIMULATION

```
*******************************************
*                                         *
*     TRAVEL AGENT ISSUED TICKET          *
*                                         *
*  AIRLINE : LH        FLIGHT NO:  401    *
*                                         *
*            FROM-TO: JFKFRA              *
*            DEPARTURE TIME: 1830         *
*            ARRIVAL TIME :  0755         *
*  PASSENGER NAME: MARY SMITH             *
*  SEAT CLASS   : TOUR                    *
*  BASIC FARE   : $  275.00               *
*  TAX          : $    3.00               *
*  TOTAL FARE   : $  278.00               *
*                                         *
*******************************************
```

Second passenger's ticket

Updated Master File Listing

PRESS ANY KEY TO CONTINUE -THEN RETURN?

READY TO ACCEPT INQUIRY OR REQUEST
TO RETRIEVE INFORMATION, ENTER THE CITY-PAIR
AS JFKFRA (JFK=ORIGIN,FRA=DESTINATION)

Updated master file listing showing seats updated for 2 flights booked

```
-----------------------------------------------
ENTER CITY PAIR SUCH AS 'JFKMUC', 'END' TO QUIT :? END
_____ RECORD NUMBER  1 _____
City Pair: LGAORD Airline:EA:101 Seats (7)  0 138 Fares    $240   $0 $130   Times:0935-1145 Meals:SNACK    Aircraft:B727
Movie:NONE   Tax:$0.00/.08
_____ RECORD NUMBER  2 _____
City Pair: LGAORD Airline:AA:900 Seats  8   0 138 Fares    $240   $0 $130   Times:1300-1530 Meals:SNACK    Aircraft:B727
Movie:NONE   Tax:$0.00/.08
_____ RECORD NUMBER  3 _____
City Pair: ORDLGA Airline:EA:102 Seats  8   0 138 Fares    $240   $0 $130   Times:1710-1950 Meals:SNACK    Aircraft:B727
Movie:NONE   Tax:$0.00/.08
_____ RECORD NUMBER  4 _____
City Pair: ORDLGA Airline:AA:901 Seats  8   0 138 Fares    $240   $0 $130   Times:2030-2300 Meals:SNACK    Aircraft:B727
Movie:NONE   Tax:$0.00/.08
_____ RECORD NUMBER  5 _____
City Pair: JFKFRA Airline:LH:401 Seats 33 134 (211) Fares $1,514 $735 $275  Times:1830-0755 Meals:DIN-BREA Aircraft:B747
Movie:ARTHUR  Tax:$3.00/.00
_____ RECORD NUMBER  6 _____
City Pair: JFKFRA Airline:LH:403 Seats 24  76 136 Fares  $1,514 $735 $275   Times:2120-1050 Meals:DIN-BREA Aircraft:DC10
Movie:ARTHUR  Tax:$3.00/.00
_____ RECORD NUMBER  7 _____
City Pair: FRAJFK Airline:LH:404 Seats 33 132 212 Fares  $1,514 $735 $275   Times:1330-1555 Meals:LUN-DIN  Aircraft:B747
Movie:KLUTE   Tax:$3.00/.00
_____ RECORD NUMBER  8 _____
City Pair: FRAJFK Airline:LH:400 Seats 24  76 136 Fares  $1,514 $735 $275   Times:1000-1230 Meals:BREAK-LU Aircraft:DC10
Movie:KLUTE   Tax:$3.00/.00
_____ RECORD NUMBER  9 _____
City Pair:JFKMUC Airline:LH:409 Seats  33 134 212 Fares  $1,531 $757 $294   Times:1730-0855 Meals:DIN-BREA Aircraft:B747
Movie:ARTHUR  Tax:$3.00/.00
_____ RECORD NUMBER 10 _____
City Pair: MUCJFK Airline:LH:408 Seats 33 134 212 Fares  $1,531 $735 $275   Times:1110-1535 Meals:LUN-DIN  Aircraft:B747
Movie:KLUTE   Tax:$3.00/.00
```

END OF AIRLINE INFORMATION PROGRAM

Test Data

Test Data for Master File Records

Field	Size	Type											
City Pair	6	AN	LGAORD	LGAORD	ORDLGA	ORDLGA	JFKFRA	JFKFRA	FRAJFK	FRAJFK	JFKMUC	MUCJFK	P$
Airline Name	2	AN	EA	AA	EA	AA	LH	LH	LH	LH	LH	LH	A$
Flight Number	4	I	101	900	102	901	401	403	404	400	409	408	N
Seats in F/C	4	I	8	8	8	8	33	24	33	24	33	33	F
Seats in B/C	4	I	0	0	0	0	134	76	134	76	134	134	B
Seats in T/C	4	I	138	138	138	138	212	136	212	136	212	212	T
Fare in F/C	8	F	240.00	240.00	240.00	240.00	1514.00	1514.00	1514.00	1514.00	1531.00	1531.00	FF
Fare in B/C	8	F	0.00	0.00	0.00	0.00	735.00	735.00	735.00	735.00	757.00	757.00	FB
Fare in T/C	8	F	130.00	130.00	130.00	130.00	275.00	275.00	275.00	275.00	294.00	294.00	FT
Departure Time	4	AN	0935	1300	1710	2030	1830	2120	1330	1000	1730	1110	DT$
Arrival Time	4	AN	1145	1530	1950	2300	0755	1050	1555	1230	0855	1535	AT$
Meals Served	16	A	B	L	D	D	D-B	D-B	L-S	L-S	D-B	L-S	M$
Aircraft Type	8	AN	B727	B727	B727	B727	B747	DC10	B747	DC10	B747	B747	T$
Movie Title	8	AN	NONE	NONE	NONE	NONE	ARTHUR	ARTHUR	KLUTE	KLUTE	ARTHUR	KLUTE	MO$
Internat. Tax	8	F	0.00	0.00	0.00	0.00	3.00	3.00	3.00	3.00	3.00	3.00	IT
Domestic Tax Rate	8	F	0.08	0.08	0.08	0.08	0.00	0.00	0.00	0.00	0.00	0.00	DT

Test Data—Inquiry and Ticketing

LGAORD, FIRST, John Jones, 125 Main St, CASH

JFKFRA, TOUR, Mary Smith, 12 South St, CASH

Error Routines

Although no error recovery routines were included in this version of the program for length considerations, sensible error routines would include provisions for non-existent city-pair entries, invalid seat class specification, and nonavailability of seats in any class. Program these for extra challenge, if you wish.

Validation Procedure

This program relies on proper index and master file organization. Be sure to print or display all files before processing to insure their accuracy. Check the inquiry results displayed on the screen for city-pair inquiries used to be sure the proper records are being retrieved from the master file for printing tickets. After printing tickets, verify that all information reproduced on the ticket is correct and properly edited where needed and that titles and headings are correct in location and wording.

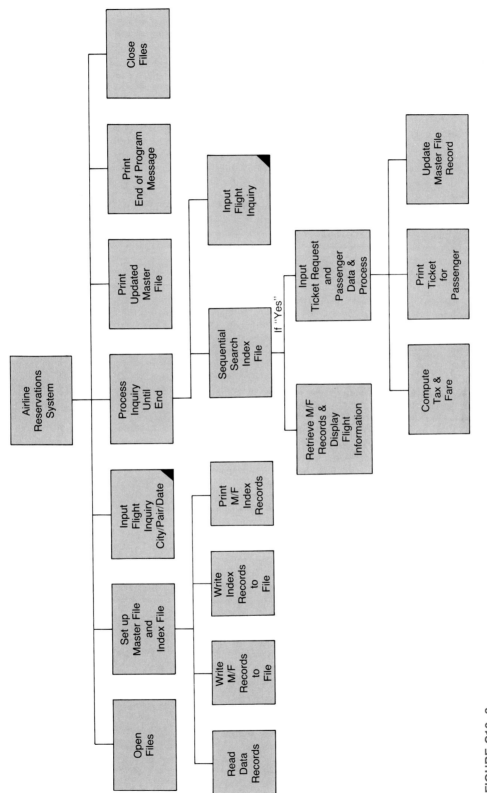

FIGURE C10–3
Visual table of contents—airline reservations program.

381

```
10      REM     *************************************************************
20      REM     *              INDEXED SEQUENTIAL FILE PROCESSING            *
30      REM     *                     CASE STUDY: C10-1                      *
40      REM     *                  AIRLINE RESERVATION SYSTEM               *
50      REM     * THIS PROGRAM SETS UP A FLIGHT MASTER FILE AND             *
60      REM     * AN INDEX FILE SO THAT PASSENGER FLIGHT INQUIRIES          *
70      REM     * AND/OR TICKET REQUESTS CAN BE PROCESSED USING             *
80      REM     * INDEXED SEQUENTIAL ACCESS.                                *
90      REM     * FLIGHT INQUIRY INFORMATION IS DISPLAYED ON THE            *
100     REM     * CRT, WHILE PASSENGER TICKETS, ORIGINAL AND UP-            *
110     REM     * DATED FLIGHT MASTER RECORDS ARE PRINTED ON THE            *
120     REM     * PRINTER.                                                  *
130     REM     *                                                          *
140     REM     *                        VARIABLE LEGEND                   *
150     REM     *   PROGRAM      FILE             MEANING                   *
160     REM     *    CTPR$      RCTPR$    CITY PAIR FOR FLIGHT (FROM-TO)    *
170     REM     *    ALIN$      RALIN$    AIRLINE CODE (TWO LETTERS)        *
180     REM     *    NO         RNO$      FLIGHT NUMBER                     *
190     REM     *    FC         RFC$      FIRST CLASS SEATS AVAILABLE       *
200     REM     *    BC         RBC$      BUSINESS CLASS SEATS AVAILABLE    *
210     REM     *    TC         RTC$      TOURIST CLASS SEATS AVAILABLE     *
220     REM     *    FCFA       RFCFA$    FIRST CLASS AIRFARE               *
230     REM     *    BCFA       RBCFA$    BUSINESS CLASS AIRFARE            *
240     REM     *    TCFA       RTCFA$    TOURIST CLASS AIRFARE             *
250     REM     *    ETD$       RETD$     DEPARTURE TIME                    *
260     REM     *    ETA$       RETA$     ARRIVAL TIME (AT DESTINATION)     *
270     REM     *    ML$        RML$      MEALS SERVED ON FLIGHT            *
280     REM     *    TYP$       RTYP$     AIRCRAFT TYPE                     *
290     REM     *    MOV$       RMOV$     MOVIE SHOWN IN FLIGHT             *
300     REM     *    TX         RTX$      TAX ON INTERNATIONAL FLIGHT       *
310     REM     *    Z                    NUMBER OF FLIGHT RECORDS          *
320     REM     *    I                    FLIGHT RECORD COUNTER             *
330     REM     *    CPDA$                INDEX FILE CITY PAIR              *
340     REM     *    IR                   INDEX FILE RECORD NUMBER          *
350     REM     *    TAX                  TAX ADDED TO AIRFARE              *
360     REM     *    TOTAL                TOTAL COMPUTED AIRFARE            *
370     REM     *                                                          *
380     REM     *************************************************************
390             PRINT "COPYRIGHT (C) 1989, BY MERRILL PUBLISHING COMPANY"
400             PRINT "FOR USE WITH STRUCTURED BASIC PROGRAMMING"
401             KEY OFF '"TURNS FUNCTION KEY LINE ON SCREEN OFF"
402             CLS
410     REM     ****************
420     REM     * MAIN PROGRAM *
430     REM     ****************
440     REM     PERFORM "OPEN FILES" ROUTINE
450             GOSUB 580
460     REM     PERFORM "SET-UP MASTER FILE/INDEX TABLE" ROUTINE
470             GOSUB 650
480     REM     PERFORM "INPUT FLIGHT INQUIRY" ROUTINE
490             GOSUB 1600
500     REM     PERFORM "PROCESSING INQUIRY DATA UNTIL END" ROUTINE
510             GOSUB 1720
520     REM     PERFORM "PRINT UPDATED MASTER FILE" ROUTINE
530             GOSUB 1320
540     REM     PERFORM "END OF PROGRAM MESSAGE" ROUTINE
550             GOSUB 3400
560     REM     PERFORM "CLOSE FILES" ROUTINE
570             GOSUB 3480
575             END
580     REM     *************
590     REM     * OPEN FILES *
600     REM     *************
610             INQ$ = "START"
```

```
620          OPEN "R",#2,"RAN.FIL",80
630          OPEN "O",#3,"IND.FIL"
640          RETURN
650   REM    ********************************
660   REM    * SET UP MASTER FILE/INDEX FILE  *
670   REM    ********************************
680          Z = 10 'CHANGE THIS VALUE FOR MORE RECORDS
690          PRINT "NUMBER OF RECORDS IN FILE :";Z
700          FIELD #2,6 AS RCTPR$, 2 AS RALIN$,4 AS RNO$,4 AS RFC$,4 AS RBC$,4 AS RTC$,4 AS
RFCFA$,4 AS RBCFA$,4 AS RTCFA$,4 AS RETD$,4 AS RETA$,16 AS RML$,4 AS RTYP$,8 AS RMOV$,4 AS RTX$,4 AS
RSTX$
710          DIM CPDA$(100),IR(100)
720          FOR I = 1 TO Z
730   REM    PERFORM "READ INPUT RECORD" ROUTINE
740          GOSUB 840
750   REM    PERFORM "WRITE MASTER FILE RECORD" ROUTINE
760          GOSUB 990
770   REM    PERFORM "WRITE INDEX FILE RECORD" ROUTINE
780          GOSUB 1240
790          NEXT I
800   REM    PERFORM "PRINT MASTER FILE RECORDS" ROUTINE
810          GOSUB 1320
820          CLOSE #3
830          RETURN
840   REM    *********************
850   REM    * READ INPUT RECORDS *
860   REM    *********************
870          READ CTPR$,ALIN$,NO,FC,BC,TC,FCFA,BCFA,TCFA,ETD$,ETA$,ML$,TYP$,MOV$,TX,STX
880          DATA LGAORD,EA,101,8,0,138,240,0,130,0935,1145,SNACK,B727,NONE,0,.08
890          DATA LGAORD,AA,900,8,0,138,240,0,130,1300,1530,SNACK,B727,NONE,0,.08
900          DATA ORDLGA,EA,102,8,0,138,240,0,130,1710,1950,SNACK,B727,NONE,0,.08
910          DATA ORDLGA,AA,901,8,0,138,240,0,130,2030,2300,SNACK,B727,NONE,0,.08
920          DATA JFKFRA,LH,401,33,134,212,1514,735,275,1830,0755,DIN-BREAK,B747,ARTHUR,3,0
930          DATA JFKFRA,LH,403,24,76,136,1514,735,275,2120,1050,DIN-BREAK,DC10,ARTHUR,3,0
940          DATA FRAJFK,LH,404,33,132,212,1514,735,275,1330,1555,LUN-DIN,B747,KLUTE,3,0
950          DATA FRAJFK,LH,400,24,76,136,1514,735,275,1000,1230,BREAK-LUN,DC10,KLUTE,3,0
960          DATA JFKMUC,LH,409,33,134,212,1531,757,294,1730,0855,DIN-BREAK,B747,ARTHUR,3,0
970          DATA MUCJFK,LH,408,33,134,212,1531,757,294,1110,1535,LUN-DIN,B747,KLUTE,3,0
980          RETURN
990   REM    *****************************
1000  REM    * WRITE MASTER FILE RECORDS *
1010  REM    *****************************
1020  REM    THIS ROUTINE PLACES PROGRAM VARIABLES
1030  REM    INTO THE I/O BUFFER AS STRINGS
1040         LSET RCTPR$=CTPR$
1050         LSET RALIN$=ALIN$
1060         LSET RNO$=MKI$(NO)
1070         LSET RFC$=MKI$(FC)
1080         LSET RBC$=MKI$(BC)
1090         LSET RTC$=MKI$(TC)
1100         LSET RFCFA$=MKS$(FCFA)
1110         LSET RBCFA$=MKS$(BCFA)
1120         LSET RTCFA$=MKS$(TCFA)
1130         LSET RETD$=ETD$
1140         LSET RETA$=ETA$
1150         LSET RML$=ML$
1160         LSET RTYP$=TYP$
1170         LSET RMOV$=MOV$
1180         LSET RTX$=MKS$(TX)
1190         LSET RSTX$=MKS$(STX)
1200         PUT #2,I
1210  REM    THE PUT STATEMENT PLACES THE I/O BUFFER ONTO DISK
1220         PRINTSW = 1
1230         RETURN
```

```
1240     REM       ****************************
1250     REM       * WRITE INDEX FILE RECORDS *
1260     REM       ****************************
1270               CPDA$    = CTPR$
1280               IR    = I
1290     REM       * PRINT TO SEQUENTIAL INDEX FILE *
1300               PRINT #3,CPDA$;",";IR
1310               RETURN


1320     REM       ****************************
1330     REM       * PRINT MASTER FILE RECORDS *
1340     REM       ****************************
1350     REM       IF PRINTSW = 1 THEN LPRINT "    ORIGINAL MASTER FILE RECORDS BEFORE UPDATE " ELSE LPR
INT "        UPDATED MASTER FILE RECORDS AFTER TICKET PROCESSING"
1360               FOR I = 1 TO Z
1370               PRINT "_____ RECORD NUMBER " ;I;" _____
_____"
1380               GET #2,I
1390     REM       BRING DISK RECORD INTO THE I/O BUFFER, CONVERT TO PGM VARIABLES
1400               CTPR$ = RCTPR$
1410               ALIN$ = RALIN$
1420               NO = CVI(RNO$)
1430               FC = CVI(RFC$)
1440               BC = CVI(RBC$)
1450               TC = CVI(RTC$)
1460               FCFA = CVS(RFCFA$)
1470               BCFA = CVS(RBCFA$)
1480               TCFA = CVS(RTCFA$)
1490               ETD$ = RETD$
1500               ETA$ = RETA$
1510               ML$ = RML$
1520               TYP$ = RTYP$
1530               MOV$ = RMOV$
1540               TX = CVS(RTX$)
1550               STX = CVS(RSTX$)
1560               F10$="City Pair: \         \Airline:\\:### Seats ### ### ### Fares $$#, ###$$###$$###
Times:\ \-\ \ Meals:\      \ Aircraft:\   \ Movie:\   \ Tax:$#.##/.##"
1570               PRINT USING F10$;CTPR$, ALIN$, NO, FC, BC, TC, FCFA, ETD$, ETA$, ML$, TYP$, MOV$, TX,
STX
1580               NEXT I
1590               RETURN


1600     REM       ***********************
1610     REM       * INPUT FLIGHT INQUIRY *
1620     REM       ***********************
1630               CLS
1640               INPUT " PRESS RETURN TO CONTINUE "; AA$
1650               PRINT
1660               PRINT " READY TO ACCEPT INQUIRY OR TICKET REQUEST"
1670               PRINT " TO RETRIEVE INFORMATION, ENTER THE CITY PAIR"
1680               PRINT " AS JFKFRA (JFK=ORIGIN,FRA=DESTINATION)"
1690               PRINT "_____"
1700               INPUT " ENTER CITY PAIR SUCH AS 'JFKMUC', 'END' TO QUIT :";INQ$
1710               RETURN


1720     REM       ******************************
1730     REM       * PROCESS INQUIRY DATA UNTIL END *
1740     REM       ******************************
1750               WHILE INQ$ <> "END"
1760     REM           PERFORM "SEARCH INDEX FILE" ROUTINE
1770               GOSUB 1820
1780     REM           PERFORM "INPUT FLIGHT INQUIRY" ROUTINE
1790               GOSUB 1600
1800               WEND
1810               RETURN
```

384

```
1820    REM       ********************************
1830    REM       * SEQUENTIALLY SEARCH INDEX FILE *
1840    REM       ********************************
1850          IR=0:C=0
1860          OPEN "I",#3,"IND.FIL"
1870          FOR N = 1 TO Z
1880          INPUT#3,CPDA$,IR
1890          IF INQ$ = CPDA$ THEN C = C + 1
1910          NEXT N
1915          IF C > 1 THEN PRINT " THERE ARE " ;C ;"FLIGHTS TO MEET YOUR NEEDS - DISPLAY FOLLOWS -
JOT DOWN THE RECORD NUMBER OF THE FLIGHT YOU MAY WANT TO BOOK"
1917          INPUT " PRESS ANY KEY TO CONTINUE THEN RETURN ";A3$
1920          CLOSE#3
1925          OPEN "I" ,#3,"IND.FIL"
1928          FOR N = 1 TO Z
1929          INPUT#3,CPDA$,IR
1930          IF INQ$ = CPDA$ THEN GOSUB 2010
1932          NEXT N
1934          CLOSE#3
1940          INPUT " NOW ENTER THE NUMBER OF THE FLIGHT YOU MAY WANT ";IR
1945          OPEN "I",#3,"IND.FIL"
1950          IF IR > 0 THEN GOSUB 2010
1955          CLOSE#3
1960    REM
2000          RETURN


2010    REM       ******************************
2020    REM       * RETRIEVE MASTER FILE RECORD *
2030    REM       ******************************
2040          GET #2,IR
2050               FC = CVI(RFC$)
2060               BC = CVI(RBC$)
2070               TC = CVI(RTC$)
2080               FCFA = CVS(RFCFA$)
2090               BCFA = CVS(RBCFA$)
2100               TCFA = CVS(RTCFA$)
2110               CTPR$ = RCTPR$
2120               ALIN$ = RALIN$
2130               NO = CVI(RNO$)
2140               ETD$ = RETD$
2150               ETA$ = RETA$
2160               ML$ = RML$
2170               TYP$ = RTYP$
2180               MOV$ = RMOV$


2190          CLS:PRINT "  ******* FLIGHTS AVAILABLE *******"
2200          PRINT "_____"
2210          PRINT " RECORD NUMBER           :";IR
2220          PRINT " CITY-PAIR               :";CTPR$
2230          PRINT " AIRLINE                 :";ALIN$
2240          PRINT " FLIGHT NUMBER           :";NO
2250          PRINT " DEPARTURE TIME          :";ETD$
2260          PRINT " ARRIVAL TIME            :";ETA$
2270          PRINT " MEALS SERVED ON BOARD   :";ML$
2280          PRINT " MOVIE SHOWN             :";MOV$
2290          PRINT " AIRCRAFT TYPE           :";TYP$
2300          PRINT " AIR FARE INFORMATION IN U.S. DOLLARS"
2310          PRINT "          FIRST CLASS :";FCFA
2320          PRINT "       BUSINESS CLASS :";BCFA
2330          PRINT "        TOURIST CLASS :";TCFA
2340          PRINT " SEAT AVAILABILITY INFORMATION :"
2350          PRINT "       OPEN IN FIRST CLASS    :";FC
2360          PRINT "       OPEN IN BUS. CLASS     :";BC
2370          PRINT "       OPEN IN TOURIST CLASS  :";TC
```

```
2380            PRINT "_____"
2390            PRINT " PLEASE CHECK FARE RESTRICTIONS BEFORE"
2400            PRINT "    PROCESSING TICKET REQUEST !!"
2410            PRINT "_____"
2415            INPUT "PRESS RETURN TO CONTINUE ";A4$
2420            INPUT " DO YOU WISH TO BOOK A FLIGHT NOW ? (ANSWER YES OR NO)";A$
2430            IF A$ = "YES" OR A$ = "Y" THEN GOSUB 2470
2440    REM     TO BOOK A FLIGHT
2450            IF A$ = "NO" OR A$ = "N" THEN INPUT " PRESS ANY KEY FOR OTHER FLIGHTS TO SAME DESTINAT-
ION "; X$ ELSE PRINT " OTHER AVAILABLE FLIGHTS - FOR YOUR INFORMATION "
2460            RETURN

2470            ***********************
2480    REM     * INPUT TICKET REQUEST *
2490    REM     ***********************
2500    REM     PRINT INFORMATION REQUESTS FOR TICKET PREPARATION
2510            PRINT " _____  BEGIN ENTERING INFORMATION FOR TICKET _____"
2520            PRINT " SEAT STATUS REPORT FOR RECORD :";IR;" ";CTPR$
2530            PRINT " FIRST CL","BUSINESS CL","TOURIST CL"
2540            PRINT FC,BC,TC
2550    REM
2560            PRINT " ABBREVIATIONS ; FIRST,BUS,TOUR "
2570            INPUT " ENTER TYPE SEAT REQUESTED ";CLAS$
2580            INPUT " PASSENGER NAME :";NAM$
2590            INPUT " PASSENGER ADDRESS :";ADDR$
2600            INPUT " TYPE OF PAYMENT OR CHARGE NO. :";PMT$
2610    REM     PERFORM "COMPUTE TAX" ROUTINE
2620            GOSUB 2680
2630    REM     PERFORM "PRINT TICKET" ROUTINE
2640            GOSUB 2800
2650    REM     PERFORM "UPDATE MASTER FILE" ROUTINE
2660            GOSUB 3280
2670            RETURN

2680    REM     ***************
2690    REM     * COMPUTE TAX *
2700    REM     ***************
2710            STX = CVS(RSTX$) ' INTERNATIONAL TAX
2720            TX  = CVS(RTX$) ' DOMESTIC TAX RATE
2730            IF CLAS$ = "FIRST" THEN FARE = FCFA:TAX = (FCFA * STX) + TX
2740            IF CLAS$ = "BUS" THEN FARE = BCFA:TAX = (BCFA * STX) + TX
2750            IF CLAS$ = "TOUR" THEN FARE = TCFA:TAX = (TCFA * STX) + TX
2760    REM     FOR INTERNATIONAL FLIGHTS THE TAX IS #3.00
2770    REM     FOR DOMESTIC FLIGHTS THE TAX IS 8% OF FARE
2780            TOTAL = FARE + TAX
2790            RETURN

2800    REM     **************************
2810    REM     * PRINT TICKET SUBROUTINE *
2820    REM     **************************
2830            PRINT
2840            PRINT
2850            PRINT "*************TICKET ISSUED*************"
2860            PRINT " AIRLINE      :";ALIN$
2870            PRINT " FLIGHT NUMBER : ";NO
2880            PRINT " SEAT CLASS    : ";CLAS$
2890            PRINT " PASSENGER NAME: ";NAM$
2900            PRINT " AIR FARE + TAX: ";TOTAL
2910            PRINT "_____"
2920            PRINT " TYPE OF PAYMENT - CREDIT CARD NO. IF CHARGE ";PMT$
2930            PRINT " "
2940            PRINT " PICK UP TICKET AND BOARDING PASS AT PRINTER"
2950            PRINT "_____"
2960            PRINT "          END OF PASSENGER TRX"
2970            PRINT
2980    REM     PRINT PASSENGER TICKET
```

```
2990          F1$="*****************************************"
3000          F2$="*                                       *"
3010          F3$="*   AIRLINE : \        \ FLIGHT NO: #### *"
3020          F4$="*                 FROM-TO: \          \  *"
3030          F5$="*               ARRIVAL TIME :   \    \*"
3040          F6$="*   PASSENGER NAME: \                 \*"
3050          F7$="*   SEAT CLASS    : \          \        *"
3060          F8$="*_____*"
3070          F9$="*   BASIC FARE    : $#,###.##            *"
3080          F10$="*  TAX           : $  ###.##            *"
3090          F11$="*  TOTAL FARE    : $#,###.##            *"
3100          F12$="*                 DEPARTURE TIME: \   \*"
3110          LPRINT F1$
3120          LPRINT F2$
3130          LPRINT "*        TRAVEL AGENT ISSUED TICKET        *"
3140          LPRINT F2$
3150          LPRINT USING F3$;ALIN$,NO
3160          LPRINT F2$
3170          LPRINT USING F4$;CTPR$
3180          LPRINT USING F12$;ETD$
3190          LPRINT USING F5$;ETA$
3200          LPRINT USING F6$;NAM$
3210          LPRINT USING F7$;CLAS$
3220          LPRINT USING F9$;FARE
3230          LPRINT USING F10$;TAX
3240          LPRINT USING F11$;TOTAL
3250          LPRINT F2$
3260          LPRINT F1$
3270          RETURN
3280  REM    **********************
3290  REM    * UPDATE MASTER FILE *
3300  REM    **********************
3310          IF CLAS$ = "FIRST" THEN FC = FC - 1
3320          IF CLAS$ = "BUS" THEN BC = BC - 1
3330          IF CLAS$ = "TOUR" THEN TC = TC - 1
3340               LSET RFC$ = MKI$(FC)
3350               LSET RBC$ = MKI$(BC)
3360               LSET RTC$ = MKI$(TC)
3370          PUT #2,IR
3380          PRINTSW = 0
3390          RETURN
3400  REM    *******************************
3410  REM    * PRINT END OF PROGRAM MESSAGE *
3420  REM    *******************************
3430          PRINT
3440          PRINT
3450          PRINT
3460          PRINT " END OF AIRLINE INFORMATION PROGRAM"
3470  REM    **************
3480          CLOSE #1,#2,#3
3490          RETURN
3500  REM    **************
3510  REM    END OF PROGRAM
```

SUMMARY

Indexed sequential access field programming overcomes the disadvantages of sequential and direct access file processing. In ISAM, the key field used for file searching and data retrieval can be any type: numeric, alphabetic, or alphanumeric. The access time is much faster than in sequential access. ISAM logic and syntax are complex in BASIC because the operating systems do not automatically create the index file for the master file, as is done in languages like COBOL. As a result, BASIC programmers must create and use their own ISAM files and must have a thorough understanding of the principles underlying ISAM.

In creating and accessing an ISAM file, you first read in master file records. The fields in these records are then converted to string format so that they can be written to the random (direct access) file, which becomes the master file. Unconverted key fields and the assigned number of each record on the master file are written at the same time to a sequential file. This file is called the index file because it will be sequentially searched to locate the record number of the record in the direct access master file. Since it *is* an index file, it need only contain two fields: the key field and the record number of the corresponding record in the master file.

After the index file and the master file have been created, both should be printed or displayed to verify that all the desired is present on both files; otherwise, hours of debugging can follow. (Remember, a direct access file like the master file MUST be printed with a proper conversion function. It cannot be displayed like a sequential file can using TYPE or PRINT from DOS.)

When accessing an ISAM file pair, the next step involves inputting an inquiry record (a record having a key field and transaction data), which is used to search sequentially through the index file. The key field on the inquiry or transaction record (as well as the index file) can be any type, since this file will be searched until a character-by-character match is found. Once the match is found, the record number that corresponds to that record's location in the direct master file is retrieved from the index file. This number is used as a locator to find the complete master record by direct access of the direct access master file using the GET statement.

Once brought into the program, the numeric fields in the direct access file record must be converted to computational numbers, since they were stored as strings (ASCII format) when originally placed on the random file (review chapter 9, conversion functions).

REVIEW QUESTIONS

1. Indexed sequential file processing overcomes many of the limitations encountered with both direct and sequential access file processing. Explain some of these limitations and how they can be circumvented by the use of indexed sequential access methodology.
2. Name and briefly describe five business systems that rely on indexed sequential access. Why is this access method important to these systems?
3. Name and briefly describe the key steps in setting up an indexed sequential access file.
4. The index file is merely a fast method of locating a record number on a master file so that it can be retrieved from the master file directly. Explain with an example.
5. What familiar manual operation can be used to explain indexed sequential access performed in computer programs?
6. The index file can be loaded into main memory for later access. What are some of the advantages of this compared to placing the index data on a disk storage as a sequential file?
7. What information must the index file or table contain and why?
8. After bringing an index file into main memory as a table, sorting that index table by key field in alphabetic or numeric order improves the speed of the indexed sequential access method if a binary search is used to locate the desired record in the index table. Explain why this is true.
9. In the airline reservation program, inquiries were used to retrieve information from the master file and also to book tickets on flights. Explain the significance of both operations and the importance of indexed sequential access in this application.

PROBLEMS FOR SOLUTION

1. Set up indexed sequential access files with the input data provided as follows (each master file will have its index file with Field 1 as the key field in both cases).

	Customer Master File	Inventory Master
Field 1:	Customer's name	Item description
Field 2:	Customer's address	Item selling price
Field 3:	Customer's current balance	Item wholesale cost
Field 4:	Customer's credit limit	Current quantity on hand

After the files are set up, a sales entry will be read in at the terminal (which will simulate a point-of-purchase cash register). This sales entry will contain the customer's name, the description of the item purchased, and the discount code.

Test Data

1. Customer Master File

    ALAN BROWNING,210 NORTH AVENUE,AVON,CONN, 150 , 1000
    ALICE GRAYSON,77 FOREST STREET,MANCHESTER, CONN, 0 , 1000
    CAROLYN MULLER,25 WOODLAND ROAD,E HARTFORD, CONN, 600 , 750
    MARY SMITHFIELD,5 SUNNYVALE LANE,W HARTFORD, CONN, 200, 1000
    PETER WHITMORE,12 EAST STREET,HARTFORD, CONN, 500 , 1000

2. Inventory Master File

    SONY TV, 600 , 300 , 4
    RCA STEREO, 1000 , 650 , 6
    GE CASSETT, 89 , 45 , 11
    PAN VIDEO REC, 875 , 525 , 3
    MAG COLOR CAMERA, 490 , 275 , 1

3. Sales Transaction Records

    ALAN BROWNING,210 NORTH
    AVENUE,AVON,CONN, *150 , 1000*
    MAG COLOR CAMERA
    MARY SMITHFIELD,5 SUNNYVALE
    LANE,W HARTFORD, CONN, _____ , _____
    RCA STEREO
    ALICE GRAYSON,77 FOREST
    STREET,MANCHESTER, CONN, _____, _____
    PAN VIDEO RE

```
             Output Customer Bills Specifications
* * * * * * * * * * * * * * * * * * * * * * * * * * * * * * * * * * * * * * *
*                                                              *
*                    CUSTOMER BILL                            *
*                                                              *
*       SOLD TO:   ALAN BROWNING                              *
*                  210 NORTH AVENUE                           *
*                  AVON, CONN                                 *
*                                                              *
*       ITEM DESCRIPTION      MAG COLOR CAMERA                *
*                                                              *
*             LIST PRICE           490.00                     *
*             DISCOUNT              98.00                     *
*             SALE PRICE           392.00                     *
*                                                              *
*             NEW BALANCE         $542.00                     *
* * * * * * * * * * * * * * * * * * * * * * * * * * * * * * * * * * * * * * *
```

Sales Transaction Record

```
MARY SMITHFIELD 5 SUNNYVALE LANE W HARTFORD, CONN , 200 , 1000
ITEM DESCRIPTION SOLD: RCA STEREO
```

Bill

```
***************************************************************
*                                                             *
*                     CUSTOMER BILL                           *
*                                                             *
*       SOLD TO:   MARY SMITHFIELD                            *
*                  5 SUNNYVALE LANE                           *
*                  W HARTFORD, CONN                           *
*                                                             *
*     ITEM DESCRIPTION                   RCA STEREO           *
*                                                             *
*            LIST PRICE          1,000.00                     *
*            DISCOUNT              250.00                     *
*            SALE PRICE           750.00                      *
*                                                             *
*            NEW BALANCE         $950.00                      *
*                                                             *
***************************************************************
```

Sales Transaction Record

```
ALICE GRAYSON 77 FOREST STREET MANCHESTER, CONN, 0 , 1000
ITEM DESCRIPTION SOLD: PAN VIDEO REC
```

Bill

```
***************************************************************
*                                                             *
*                     CUSTOMER BILL                           *
*                                                             *
*       SOLD TO:   ALICE GRAYSON                              *
*                  77 FOREST STREET                           *
*                  MANCHESTER, CONN                           *
*                                                             *
*     ITEM DESCRIPTION         PAN VIDEO REC                  *
*                                                             *
*            LIST PRICE            875.00                      *
*            DISCOUNT              218.75                      *
*            SALE PRICE            656.25                      *
*                                                             *
*            NEW BALANCE          $656.25                      *
*                                                             *
***************************************************************
```

Sales Transaction Record (Leading to Exception Routine)

```
PETER WHITMORE 12 EAST STREET HARTFORD, CONN, 500 , 1000
CREDIT LIMIT EXCEEDED
```
No bill produced; customer credit maximum reached

2. This program uses the principles of indexed sequential access programming with files, including a master file, index file, inputting an inquiry record, searching the index file, and direct accessing of the master file.

The master file in this program contains information about the owner of a vehicle parked in a collegé campus lot. The information includes the owner's location (by room number) during the day and his or her position at the college (i.e., faculty, student, or staff). From this master file, two index files are to be created that contain the key field to be used for inquiry and the record location of the entire master record in the master file. Inquiries will be made by using either the vehicle's license plate number or the owner's name; therefore, the two separate index files must be created.

When the master record number has been retrieved from the index file, the desired master table record is then accessed directly using the record number attained from the index file. Finally, the entire master record will be printed to provide the schedule, location, position, or name of the vehicle's owner.

Input Specifications

Master file input consists of a license plate number, car owner's name, and room location of the car owner for each class period. To get an entire schedule of times and locations, codes are used to represent room numbers. The transaction inquiry record consists of the *license plate number* or the *name of car owner,* and a code number that determines whether the search is to be done on the name or plate number.

	Field No.	Field Description	Type	Size	Example
Master Information File	1	Vehicle License Plate Number	Alphanumeric	6	1 2 3 A B C
	2	Owner's Name	Alphabetic	20 max.	Carolyn Smith
	3	Monday Room Schedule (coded)	Alphanumeric	8	A B O O B O C O
	4	Tuesday Room Schedule (coded)	Alphanumeric	8	A D O D F F O A
	5	Wednesday Room Schedule (coded)	Alphanumeric	8	A B O O B O C O
	6	Thursday Room Schedule (coded)	Alphanumeric	8	A D O D F F O A
	7	Friday Room Schedule (coded)	Alphanumeric	8	A B O O B O C O
	Field No.	Field Description	Type	Size	Example
Inquiry Record	1	License Number	Alphanumeric	8	432 EGH
	2	Name	Alphabetic	20 max.	James Carson
	3	Type of Inquiry (2 = by Name, 1 = by License No.)	Numeric	1	2

Processing Decisions and Formulas

The master file is set up with *two* index files, one for name and one for license plate number. These are printed for verification. An inquiry record is then input. The code number on this record determines which index table is to be searched. When the name is located in the name index table, or the license plate number is located in the license index table, the index table acts as a "pointer" to retrieve the master file record number that contains the location of the entire record, which is then retrieved by direct access to yield the schedule of the car owner.

Input light inquiry records and determine end of file during processing with a signal field for the last record.	Do until. . .(trailing decision structure). Operation executed. Then test condition.
Search the correct index file for match.	Code will determine which index table is to be searched.
	If code is 1, then lic. no. index table search.
	If code is 2, then name index table search.
When match is found, index file record number will act as a 'pointer' to the correct record in the master table and retrieve it.	Record number field is located at the end of master file record.

Output

The master file and both index files should be printed for verification before inquiries are processed. Inquiry data is also printed. A schedule for each car owner is printed,

391

and an End of Program message is printed to indicate that all inquiries have been processed and program run is normally terminated. Error routines for no matching records in index files are optional.

Output Specifications

```
                                    MASTER FILE

1  LIC. PLATE      CAR OWNER'S                 ROOM LOCATION SCHEDULE              RECORD
      NUMBER          NAME        MONDAY    TUESDAY  WEDNESDAY  THURSDAY   FRIDAY   NUMBER
      XXXXX   XXXXXXXXXXXXXXXXXXX XXXXXXXXX XXXXXXXXX XXXXXXXXX XXXXXXXXX XXXXXXXXX   99


      XXXXX   XXXXXXXXXXXXXXXXXXX XXXXXXXXX XXXXXXXXX XXXXXXXXX XXXXXXXXX XXXXXXXXX   99

   LIC. PLATE INDEX FILE

2   LIC. PLATE  RECORD
       NUMBER    NUMBER
       XXXXX      99


       XXXXX      99

3  NAME INDEX FILE

       CAR OWNERS     RECORD
          NAME        NUMBER
   XXXXXXXXXXXXXXXXXXX   99

   XXXXXXXXXXXXXXXXXXX   99



                                  INQUIRY REPORT

                    INQUIRY DATA:  XXXXXXXXXXXXXXXXXXX

                              MASTER TABLE RECORD

   LIC.NO       NAME          MONDAY     TUESDAY      WEDNESDAY  THURSDAY    FRIDAY      SATURDAY   REC.NO
   XXXXX   XXXXXXXXXXXXXXXXXXX XXXXXXX   XXXXXXXXX    XXXXXXXXX  XXXXXXXX   XXXXXXXXX   XXXXXXXX      99



                    ALL INQUIRIES HAVE BEEN PROCESSED.
               END OF PARKING INFORMATION RETRIEVAL PROGRAM.
```

Test Data

Six records will be input to the Master File. Eight inquiry transaction records are input. Two inquiry transaction records will contain the same name and license plate number—but different codes—to illustrate the advantage of dual access retrieval in the event that only one data field is available for an inquiry.

```
123ABCCAROLYN SMITH      0000ABBCA0000ADDAF0000ABBCB0000ADDAF0000ABBCA0000000
236BAIALICE JONES        ABBACCOOOFFAEEA000ABBACC000FFAEEA000ABBACC0000000000
987CDFJOHN BROWN         DDBEEA0000000000000DDAEEA00000000000000DDAECA000BBCA000
645VIPROBERT WHITE       ACCA0DD00AGGBA0000ACCA000000AGGBA0000ACCA0000000000000
432EGHJAMES CARSON       0000AEEAB000000000000AEEAB000000000000AEEAB0000000
723ABGSUSAN GRANT        FFABBA000CCADDA000FFABBA000CCADDA000FFABBA000CCGA000
```

```
432EGHJAMES CARSON        1
645VIPROBERT WHITE        2
236BAIALICE JONES         1
452EGHJAMES CARSON        2
723ABGSUSAN GRANT         2
123ABCCAROLYN SMITH       1
987CDFJOHN BROWN          2
723ABGSUSAN GRANT         1
END    END                0
```

Validation Procedure

Index files can be visually verified. Retrieved schedules can be visually compared to the inquiry data and further checked against the master file records.

3. The National Crime Information Center computer system is a sophisticated data base and retrieval system that is used by federal, state, and municipal law enforcement agencies to locate and retrieve information about criminals and missing or stolen goods. The system's central computer is located in Washington, D.C.; its terminals and other related computer systems are located throughout the nation. File access is based on ISAM.

Features and capabilities of the NCIC system include:

1. Location of persons by description, fingerprints, voiceprints, and other physical characteristics.
2. Location of owner, place of origin, and related characteristics of stolen articles by item serial number.
3. Location of vehicle owner, place of origin, and status by license plate number, vehicle identification number, etc.

While no attempt can be made to simulate all the features of the comprehensive NCIC system, the principles of indexed sequential access permit you to program some of the system's characteristics, such as identification of items by description or serial numbers, and determination of criminals' histories by name or aliases.

Consult the problem definition worksheets on the following pages for a description of characteristic data that can be used to set up an NCIC-type master file. From this file, set up a number of relevant index files that might be used to retrieve data from the master file according to any of the desired key fields specified.

If you like, research some of the additional capabilities of the NCIC system, and include some other fields in your program logic. Enhancements such as identification by fingerprint analysis might prove to be an interesting programming challenge.

Input Specifications

Field No.	Field Description	Type	Size
Master	Suspect Name	String	20
File	Last Known Address	String	30
Records	M/O	String	10
(Persons)	Current Address	String	30
1	Status	String	40
2			
3			
4			
5			
Master	Item Description	String	20
File	Item Serial Number	String	20

Field No.	Field Description	Type	Size
Records	Owner's Name	String	20
(Items)	Owner's Address	String	30
1	Date Lost/Stolen	String	12
2			
3			
4			
5			
Inquiry	Type Inquiry	Numeric	1
Records	Transaction Inquiry Field**	String	20
1	* 1 = Person 2 = Item		
2	**Person's Name or		
	Item Serial Number		

Processing Decisions and Formulas

This program is an inquiry only program in its present version. Index sequential access should be used to retrieve data from the master file which simulates an NCIC file.

Since inquiry can be by either a person's name or item's description, two index files are appropriate. Set these up and print them out to verify correctness.

Processing inquiries involves determining the type of inquiry (code), searching the appropriate index file, and then directly accessing the master file for the complete record. Since no file updating takes place, there are no formulas or file update decisions. (Incorporate these if you wish to alter master ''file'' data.)

Typical Output

```
(PRINT THE ENTIRE MASTER FILE FIRST TO CHECK IT        }  Master Table, Output 1
          INQUIRY FOR:xxxxxxxxxxxxxxxxxxxxx
SUSPECT NAME
LAST KNOWN ADDS:xxxxxxxxxxxxxxxxxxxxxxxxxxxxxxxxxxx
SUSPECT'S MO:xxxxxxxxxxxx                                  Inquiry Retrieval Output
CURRENT ADDRESS:xxxxxxxxxxxxxxxxxxxxxxxxxxxxxxxxx          for Suspect Name,
                                                          Output 2

STATUS:xxxxxxxxxxxxxxxxxxxxxxxxxxxxxxxxxxxxxxxxxx
          INQUIRY FOR:xxxxxxxxxxxxxxxxxxxxx
ITEM DESCRIPTION:xxxxxxxxxxxxxxxxxxxxxxxxxxxxxxxxxxx       Inquiry Retrieval Output
ITEM SERIAL NO.:xxxxxxxxxx                                 for Item Description,
OWNER'S NAME:xxxxxxxxxxxxxxxxxxxx                          Output 3
OWNER'S ADDRESS:xxxxxxxxxxxxxxxxxxxxxxxxxxxxxxxxx

END  OF  PROGRAM MESSAGE                                   End of Program Message,
                                                          Output 4
```

Test Data

To avoid lawsuits, no test data is provided. Make up your own names, crimes, and stolen items for this program.

APPENDIX A

SUMMARY OF BASIC STATEMENTS, FUNCTIONS, AND OPERATING COMMANDS FOR SOME POPULAR BASIC-SUPPORTING SYSTEMS

The following tables are presented in order to give you an overview of BASIC statements, functions, and operating commands for many operating systems supporting the BASIC programming language. For more detailed explanation of their use, consult the user's manual for your particular system.

BASIC Statements	ANSI Proposed Standard BASIC (1985)	ANSI Minimal BASIC	APPLESOFT BASIC
Allows branch to REMARK statement	Yes	Yes	Yes
Allows quotes within strings	Yes	No	Yes*
Allows for direct access files	Yes (option)	Yes	No
Allows for indexed/sequential access files	Yes (option)	No	No
Allows for option BASE of zero or one for array	Yes	Yes	No
Allows for sequential file processing	Yes	Yes	Yes
Assign an expression or value to a variable	LET ex = or =	LET or =	Let or =
Branch on CASE to statement	ON ex GOTO ln	ON ex GOTO	ON ex GOTO ln
Branch on CASE to subroutine	ON ex GOSUB ln SELECT*	ON ex GOSUB	ON ex GOSUB ln
Branch on error condition to statement	(structured error handling via WHEN blocks)*	ON ERROR GOTO ln	ONERR GOTO ln
Branch on error condition to subroutine	(Structured error handling)	—	—
Branch to a subroutine	GOSUB ln call*	GOSUB ln	GOSUB ln
Clear the CRT screen	CLEAR (graphics package)	—	HOME
Close disk files	CLOSE #fnum	—	PRINT CHR$(4)*
Decimal variable naming convention	31 char	2 char	2 char
Define a user function	FUNCTION*	DEF FN	DEF FN
Define fields in a random file buffer	NO	—	No
Dimension space for subscripted variables (arrays)	DIM (N)	—	DIM
End a program	END	END	END
Erase specified arays	Yes (through matrix package)	—	CLEAR*
Exchange two variables (contents)	—	—	—
Exponential variable form notation	E	E	E
Field the I/O buffer for random file	No	—	—
Flash output on CRT	(Print ESC sequence)	—	FLASH
Format for PRINT USING statement	F$ or IMAGE	String	—
IF conditional branch	IF cond THEN ex or ln	IF cond THEN ex or ln	IF cond THEN ex or ln
If conditional branch with ELSE option	IF cond THEN ex ELSE ex or ln	IF cond THEN ex or ln ELSE ex or ln	—
Input data from a file	—	—	Print CHR$(4); ''READ filename'' INPUT X (DOS command)
Input data from the terminal	INPUT	INPUT	INPUT
Input entire matrix	MAT INPUT V	—	—
Input an entire line (string) from terminal	LINE INPUT A$	—	INPUT
Input an entire line from file	LINE INPUT #fnum: STRING-VARIABLE LIST	—	INPUT*
Integer variable naming convention	No	—	2 char %
Left-justify data in a random file buffer	No	—	—
Line continuation symbol	Yes*	—	(not needed)
Logical AND operator	AND	AND	AND

*For details see your operating manual.

APPLE Business BASIC	Commodore BASIC	DIGITAL (DEC) BASIC PLUS BASIC PLUS-2 VAX-11 BASIC	IBM Advanced BASIC	TRS-80 Model II, 12 BASIC
Yes	Yes	Yes	Yes	Yes
Yes	—	Yes	Yes (with function)*	Only single*
Yes*	Yes	Yes	Yes	Yes
No	Yes	(User defined)	(User defined)	No
No	—	Yes	Yes	Yes
Yes	Yes	Yes	Yes	Yes
LET or =	LET or =	LET or =	LET or =	LET or =
ON ex GOTO ln	ON ex GOTO ln	ON ex GOTO ln	ON ex GOTO	ON EX GOTO ln, ln, ln, etc.
ON ex GOSUB ln	ON ex GOSUB ln	ON ex GOSUB ln	ON ex GOSUB ln	ON ex GOSUB ln,
ONERR GOTO ln	—	ON ERROR GOTO ln	ON ERROR GOTO ln	ON ERROR GOTO ln
ONERR GOSUB ln	—	ON ERROR GOSUB ln	ON ERROR GOTO ln	ON ERROR GOSUB ln
GOSUB ln	GOSUB ln	GOSUB ln	GOSUB ln	GOSUB ln
HOME	PRINT (heart symbol) ?CHR$(147)	—	CLS	CLS
CLOSE #fnum	CLOSE lfn	CLOSE or CLOSE #fnum	CLOSE or CLOSE #fnum	CLOSE
63 char	2 char	6 char	40 char normal (DEFDBL V for extended)	8 char
DEF FN	DEFFN(X) = expression	DEF FN	DEF FN (R = real, etc.) DEF FNR	DEF FN
CREATE fname*	—	FIELD #fnum, N as A$,M as B$	FIELD fnum, N as A$, M as B$, etc.	FIELD fnum, N as A$, M as B$, etc.
DIM	DIM	DIM	DIM	DIM
END	END	END	END	END
—	—	MAT A = ZER A$ = NUL	—	ERASE V(N)
SWAP V1, V2	—	—	SWAP V1, V2	SWAP V1, V2
E	E	E	E	E
—	—	FIELD #fnum, N as A$, M as B$, etc.	FIELD fnum, N as A$, M as B$, etc.	FIELD fnum, N as A$, M as B$, etc.
No	—	(Print ESC sequence)	—	—
String	—	String	String	String
IF cond THEN ex or ln	IF cond THEN ex or ln	IF cond THEN ex or ln	IF cond THEN ex or ln	IF cond THEN ex or ln
IF cond THEN ex or ln: ELSE ex or ln	No	IF cond THEN ex or ln ELSE ex or ln	IF cond THEN ex or ln ELSE ex or ln	IF cond THEN ex or ln ELSE ex or ln
INPUT #fnum; V, V INPUT #fnum, N; V, V*	INPUT# fnum V, V	INPUT# fnum, V, V, V	INPUT# fnum, V, V, V	INPUT # fnum, V, V, V
INPUT	INPUT	INPUT	INPUT	INPUT
—	—	MAT INPUT	—	No
INPUT	INPUT A$	LINE INPUT	LINE INPUT	LINE INPUT
INPUT*	INPUT# lfn, A$	LINE INPUT# fnum	LINE INPUT# fnum	LINE INPUT#
63 char %, long integer &	2 char %	6 char %	40 char (DEFINT V)	8 char %
—	—	LSET	LSET	LSET
(not needed)	—	&	(not needed)	*
AND	AND	AND	AND	AND

BASIC Statements	ANSI Proposed Standard BASIC (1985)	ANSI Minimal BASIC	APPLESOFT BASIC
Logical NOT operator	NOT	NOT	NOT
Logical OR operator	OR	OR	OR
Looping with FOR/NEXT loop	For V = ex to ex STEP + or − ex	FOR V = ex to ex STEP + or − ex	FOR V = ex to ex STEP + or − ex
Multiple statements per line symbol	Yes*	—	:
Open a random file	Yes*	—	PRINT CHR$(4); ''OPEN filename, L length''*
Open a sequential disk file for input	Yes*	—	PRINT CHR$(4); ''READ filename''*
Open a sequential disk file for output	Yes	—	PRINT CHR$(4); WRITE filename*
Place remarks in program listing	REM	REM	REM
Place remarks in program listing (Method 2)	!	!	!
Print formatted results to a file	PRINT #fnum USING F$*	—	—
Print formatted results to the CRT	PRINT USING ''F$''*	—	—
Print output on the printer	Yes*	—	PR# fnum*
Print results on the CRT	PRINT	PRINT	PRINT
Print results to a file	PRINT #fnum: output list WRITE #fnum: ex list	—	PRINT CHR$(4); ''WRITE filename''* PRINT X
Print statement abbreviation	—	—	?
Random file byte size for real numbers	*	—	*
Random file byte size for integers	*	—	*
Random file maximum record size	*	—	*
Random file variable record size permitted	*	—	—
Read data into variables from within program	READ	READ	READ
Read entire matrix	MAT READ	—	—
Read a record from a random disk file	No	—	PRINT CHR$(4); ''READ filename, R recnum'' INPUT X
Restore data list pointer for the READ statement	RESTORE	—	RESTORE
Resume program execution after error	(Structured?) Yes*	RESUME	RESUME
Return from a subroutine	RETURN	RETURN	RETURN
Set up data within a program	DATA	DATA	DATA
Step increment for FOR/NEXT loop	STEP ex or − ex	STEP ex or − ex	STEP ex or − ex
Stop program execution	STOP	STOP	STOP
Store right-justified data for random file buffer	No	—	—
String variable naming convention	31 char $	2 char $	2 char $
Tab the output on the CRT or printer	TAB(N)	TAB	TAB
Unconditional branch to a statement	GO-TO ln	GOTO ln	GOTO ln
WHILE loop beginning	DOWHILE	—	—
WHILE loop end	LOOP	—	—
Write data from I/O buffer to random file	—	—	—

*For details see your operating manual.

APPLE Business BASIC	Commodore BASIC	DIGITAL (DEC) BASIC PLUS BASIC PLUS-2 VAX-11 BASIC	IBM Advanced BASIC	TRS-80 Model II, 12 BASIC
NOT	NOT	NOT	NOT	NOT
OR	OR	OR	OR	OR
FOR V = ex to ex STEP + or − ex	FOR V = ex TO ex STEP + or − ex	FOR V = ex TO ex STEP + or − ex	FOR V = ex to ex STEP + or − ex	FOR V = ex to STEP + or − ex
:	:	\	:	:
CREATE 'fname', TEXT. N OPEN # fnum as ''INPUT''*, 'fname'	OPEN fn. dn, sa,''#*	OPEN ''fname'' AS FILE fnum%	OPEN ''R'', #N, ''fname.ext'', No*	OPEN ''R'', fnum, fname/dat, rel
OPEN #fnum AS INPUT. fname*	OPEN lfn, dn, sa, ''0: filename, S, W'' R	OPEN ''fname'' FOR INPUT AS FILE fnum	OPEN ''I''#N, ''fname.ext''	OPEN ''I'', fnum, 'fnam'
OPEN #fnum AS OUTPUT, fname*	*	OPEN ''fname'' FOR OUTPUT AS FILE fnum	OPEN ''O'', #N, ''fname.ext''	OPEN ''O'', fnum, 'fnam
REM	REM	REM	REM	REM
!	—	!	*	*
PRINT # fnum USING F$; V, V, etc	—	PRINT # fnum USING F$; V, V	PRINT #fnum USING F$; V, V, etc.	PRINT #fnum USING F$; V, V, etc.
PRINT USING ln; A$, V, etc.	—	PRINT USING F$	PRINT USING F$; V, V, etc.	PRINT USING
PRINT USING F$; A$; etc.	PRINT # lfn	PRINT# fnum— QU, fname	LPRINT	LPRINT
PRINT	PRINT	PRINT	PRINT	PRINT
PRINT# fnum;V,V,etc. or PRINT# fnum, N; V, V	PRINT# fnum V1, V2	PRINT# fnum V1, V2	PRINT# fnum V1, V2	PRINT# fnum V1, V2
?	?	No	?	?
5	—	4 for single precision 8 for double precision	Varied automatically by system	4, 8 bytes overhead
3, 9 for long integer	—	2	—	2
—	—	512	—	256
—	—	Yes*	—	Yes
READ	READ	READ	READ	READ
—	—	MAT READ	—	No
*	—	GET fnum, R%*	GET fnum, R%*	GET fnum, R%*
RESTORE	RESTORE	RESTORE	RESTORE	RESTORE
RESUME	No	RESUME ln	RESUME	RESUME
RETURN	RETURN	RETURN	RETURN	RETURN
DATA	DATA	DATA	DATA	DATA
STEP ex or − ex	STEP*	STEP ex or − ex	STEP ex or − ex	STEP ex or − ex
STOP	STOP	STOP	STOP	STOP
—	—	RSET	RSET	RSET
63 char $	2 char $	6 char $	40 char $	8 char $
TAB (N); or SPC (N);	TAB	TAB (N)	TAB (N)	TAB
GOTO ln	GOTO ln	GOTO ln	GOTO ln	GOTO ln
—	—	WHILE	WHILE	WHILE
—	—	NEXT	WEND	WEND
—	—	PUT #fnum, R%	PUT #fnum, R%	PUT #fnum, R%

Built-In Functions	APPLE Business	APPLESOFT
ASCII string equivalent of a numeric value	CHR$(X)	CHRS(X)
ASCII value of a string expression	ASC(X$)	ASC(X$)
Absolute value of a numeric expression	ABC(X)	ABS(X)
Arctangent of an angle in radians	ATN(X)	ATN(X)
Available free memory	FRE	FRE(X)
Check for end-of-file in file processing	EOF	—
Convert argument to double precision	—	—
Convert decimal number to integer	—	—
Convert double-precision number to string for random file	—	—
Convert integer to decimal number	—	—
Convert integer to string for random file	—	—
Convert single-precision number to string for random file	—	—
Convert string to double-precision number (random files)	—	—
Convert string to single-precision number (random files)	—	—
Convert string to an integer (random files)	—	—
Convert a number to a string	STR$(X)	STR$(X)
Convert a string to a real number	VAL(X$)	VAL(X$)
Convert to single-precision number	—	—
Cosine of an angle in radians	COS(X)	COS(X)
Current date	DATE$	—
Current time	TIME$	—
Exponentiate a number to the power x	EXP(X)	EXP(X)
Integer portion of a decimal number	INT(X)	INT(X)
Natural logarithm of argument	LOG(X)	LOG(X)
Random number generation	RND(X) or	RND(0)
Sign of a number ($+1$ or -1)	SGN(X)	—
Sine of an angle in radians	SIN(X)	SIN(X)
Square root of a positive number	SQR(X)	SQR(X)
String of blanks	—	—
Tangent of an angle in radians	TAN(X)	TAN(X)

Operating System Commands	APPLE APPLESOFT APPLE Business BASIC	Commodore
AUTOMATIC line numbering of program statements	AUTO	*
CLEAR memory for new program	CLEAR	NEW
CONTINUE execution of a program within program	CONT	CONT
CONTINUE scrolling display on CRT	CONTROL-7	—
CURSOR control commands	Arrow keys	↑ ↓ →←
DELETE a disk file from disk storage	DELETE (many options)	OPEN 15, 8, 15, "SCRATCH 0: filename"
DELETE current program from memory	NEW	NEW
DELETE program lines	DEL ln or ln, ln	type line no. CR
EDIT a program in special edit mode	Yes (many commands)	none
ENTER data or statements on the CRT	RETURN	RETURN
EXECUTE a program (all or at specific line number)	RUN or RUN ln	RUN or RUN ln or GO TO ln
HALT the execution of a program	CONTROL-C	RUN-STOP key
LIST a directory of files on disk	CATALOG	LOAD "$",8 LIST
LIST a program on the CRT	LIST (many options)	LIST (many options)
LIST a program on the printer	OPEN #fnum "driver" OUTPUT #fnum LIST	OPEN4,4:CMD4:LIST
LOAD a program into memory from disk	LOAD	LOAD "pname",8
RENAME a file with a new name	RENAME	OPEN 15, 8, 15 "R: newname = oldname"
RESUME execution of program after command stop	RESUME, CONT*	CONT
SAVE a program on disk	SAVE	SAVE "pname",8
STOP display from scrolling on CRT	CONTROL-7	RUN-STOP key
TERMINATE BASIC programming session	—	—
TRACE execution of a program OFF	NOTRACE	—
TRACE execution of a program ON	TRACE	—

401

APPENDIX B

MICROSOFT QUICKBASIC

With the development of QuickBASIC, the BASIC programming language has evolved into a full-fledged professional programming language. Here are some of the features of QuickBASIC that have made this possible:

1. Programs run 4 to 10 times faster than interpreted BASIC.
2. Program logic in machine code is not easily copied (logically).
3. True independent subroutines and functions are now possible without the global variable limitations. Global variables can be declared for convenience, if desired.
4. Subroutines and functions can be independently written, compiled, and tested, and then placed in program libraries.
5. Program and data area sizes are not limited to 64 K, as is the case with many previous versions of BASIC.
6. The QuickBASIC programming environment is menu driven and mouse supported for very fast program development, testing, debugging, and compiling. With the mouse, it is possible to issue most commands without typing. These include loading, saving, running, tracing, editing, compiling, linking, and printing.
7. The editor in QuickBASIC is very powerful; it is based on WordStar keystrokes and permits the copy, cut, and paste capabilities not often found in program language editors.
8. There is a DOS shell for convenient file transfer, directory access, and any DOS-based application (such as formatting a disk if you forget to do it, but need to save your program).
9. A command, compile, and link operation (which leads you to DOS, if desired) makes conversion of BASIC programs to machine code quick and easy.
10. Powerful debugging aids such as Trace and Watchpoint can be invoked to examine the contents of variables and trace program execution step by step. In addition, you can make changes in program source code and resume execution from the change on.

Additionally, enhanced statement syntax include:

1. **CALL**—This replaces the GOSUB and refers to a true subroutine to be executed at that point in the logic. The subroutine reference can now be a routine name, not just a number, making for much clearer program documentation. The actual subroutine is now identified by a keyword SUB followed by the name of the referenced subroutine.
2. **FUNCTION**—Similar to a subroutine and replacing the previous DEF FN, the FUNCTION can now be independently compiled and placed in any program library.
3. **TYPE...END TYPE**—Variables can now be typed implicitly or explicitly instead of relying on variable name endings to differentiate type of variables.
4. **SELECT CASE**—For decisions with many alternatives, the CASE select permits easy selection, compressed syntax, and easy error trapping. The QuickBASIC interpreter/compiler even allows for case selection on string variables.

5. **DO Loop**—True DO UNTIL and DO WHILE loops can be written directly, without resorting to programming "tricks" to convert WHILE structures to UNTIL structures. Leading or trailing decisions are syntactically and logically very clear.

6. **Screen View Ports**—The screen can be divided into sections for partitioning program output and source code or any other desired function.

7. **32-Bit Long Integers**—Financial calculations can be done with assurance of accuracy in dollars and cents with 32-bit integers.

Converting BASICA Case Studies to QuickBASIC

USING THE QUICKBASIC BUILT-IN EDITOR

The QuickBASIC case studies that follow were obtained by modifying the last case in each chapter (except for Case 3–3). For the short cases, the QuickBASIC editor was used as described below. For the longer, more involved, cases that contain many subroutines, the modifications were done in the non-document mode using WordStar, which is described in the next section.

1. Load the program to be modified into BASICA and save it with the A option to produce ASCII code—for example, LOAD''CASE3-2, then SAVE''CASE3-2.BAS'',A.
2. Load the program into QuickBASIC with the LOAD command.
3. Edit out the line numbers.
4. Convert all GOSUBs to CALLs and all referenced GOSUB line numbers to subroutine names.
5. Delete the remarks that identified the GOSUB and the subroutines (since the subroutine names are adequate).
6. Use the editor to cut and paste logic for each subroutine into the real subroutines established by QuickBASIC with each CALL. (This is explained in detail with the case description in chapter 2).
7. Enter the appropriate ''subroutine support'' statement, such as parameter and argument lists, variable typing, and/or common and shared variable statements.
8. Convert logic and syntax into QuickBASICS's fully structured syntax, such as SELECT CASE, DO, SUB, FUNCTION, CALL, etc.

A QUICKBASIC BASICA CONVERSION SESSION

1. Type QB after the DOS prompt, and the QuickBASIC welcome screen will appear. There are 7 main menu choices. The first 5 will be used in this first example program.

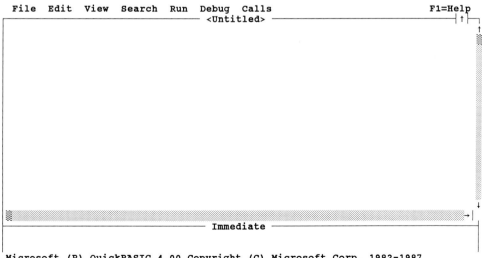

```
File  Edit  View  Search  Run  Debug  Calls                    F1=Help
──────────────────────── <Untitled> ──────────────────────────┤↑├┐
```

```
Microsoft (R) QuickBASIC 4.00 Copyright (C) Microsoft Corp. 1982-1987
```

2. Select the File main menu choice to begin. The pull down menu will display the choices. Start with New Program by typing in N or by selecting New Program with the mouse.

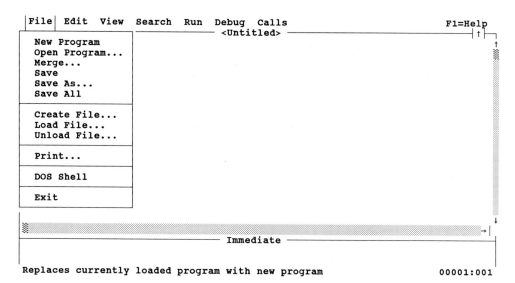

3. Type in your program. Remember, you can now leave off the line numbers. Replace the REM with ' and indent the program lines for an easier-to-follow and neater-looking program.

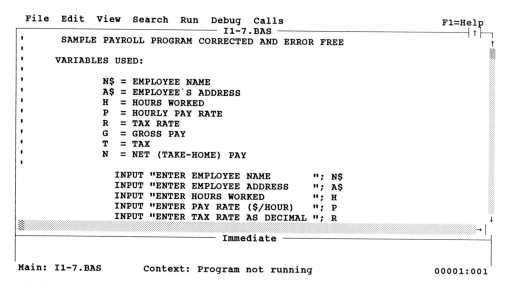

4. If you make any errors, use the arrow, insert, and delete keys to correct mistakes. Later you will see some of the powerful WordStar-like editing commands that are available in the EDIT mode. When you finish typing in the program, look it over for errors and correct them.

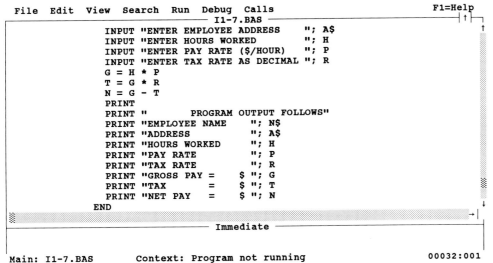

```
 File  Edit  View  Search  Run  Debug  Calls                        F1=Help
─────────────────────── I1-7.BAS ───────────────────────
         INPUT "ENTER EMPLOYEE ADDRESS      "; A$
         INPUT "ENTER HOURS WORKED          "; H
         INPUT "ENTER PAY RATE ($/HOUR)     "; P
         INPUT "ENTER TAX RATE AS DECIMAL "; R
         G = H * P
         T = G * R
         N = G - T
         PRINT
         PRINT "          PROGRAM OUTPUT FOLLOWS"
         PRINT "EMPLOYEE NAME      "; N$
         PRINT "ADDRESS            "; A$
         PRINT "HOURS WORKED       "; H
         PRINT "PAY RATE           "; P
         PRINT "TAX RATE           "; R
         PRINT "GROSS PAY =     $ "; G
         PRINT "TAX        =    $ "; T
         PRINT "NET PAY    =    $ "; N
         END
──────────────────────── Immediate ────────────────────────

Main: I1-7.BAS        Context: Program not running                 00032:001
```

5. When you have finished typing in your program, save it using the SAVE option of the file menu choice. Use standard file-naming conventions, but omit the .BAS extension.

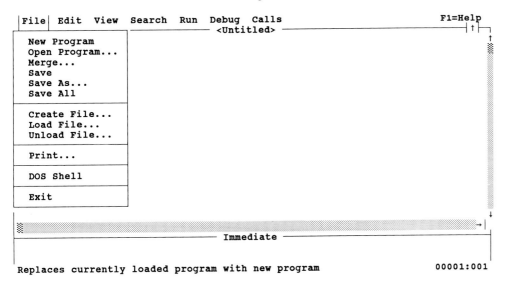

```
|File| Edit  View  Search  Run  Debug  Calls               F1=Help
──────────────────── <Untitled> ────────────────────
 New Program
 Open Program...
 Merge...
 Save
 Save As...
 Save All
 ───────────────
 Create File...
 Load File...
 Unload File...
 ───────────────
 Print...
 ───────────────
 DOS Shell
 ───────────────
 Exit
──────────────────────── Immediate ────────────────────────

Replaces currently loaded program with new program            00001:001
```

6. Select the TEXT option and save your program. Use the SAVE AS option if you wish to rename the program (a good idea when converting from BASICA to QuickBASIC) or the SAVE option to save your program with the same name you loaded it as.

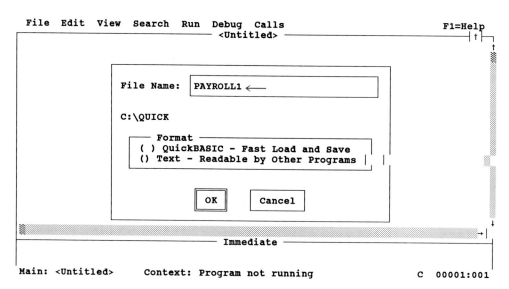

7. If you want to see your program after saving, select the VIEW menu choice, and highlight the program name in the view window. Then, place the program in the active window with the W command or mouse. Begin any editing you need to do using the powerful built-in editor.

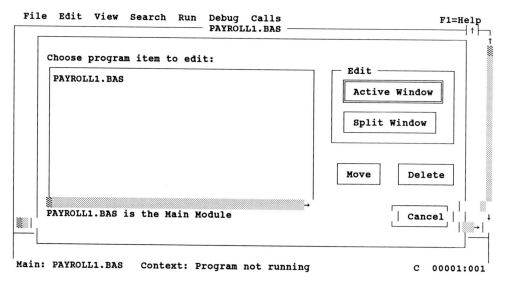

8. Now select the RUN menu choice followed by start. The program screen will clear, and the program execution can be viewed on the full screen. In this example, after entering data, the results were printed to the screen.

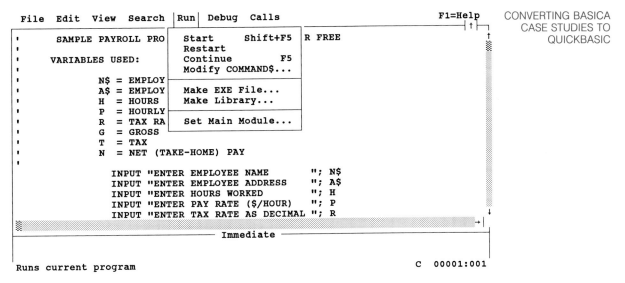

```
File  Edit  View  Search │Run│ Debug  Calls                        F1=Help
┌──────────────────────────────────┬─────────────────────────┐────┤↑├─┐
│ '    SAMPLE PAYROLL PRO│ Start      Shift+F5 │R FREE            │    ↑
│ '                      │ Restart             │                  │ ▓
│ '    VARIABLES USED:   │ Continue         F5 │                  │ ▓
│ '                      │ Modify COMMAND$...  │                  │
│ '          N$ = EMPLOY ├─────────────────────┤                  │
│ '          A$ = EMPLOY │ Make EXE File...    │                  │
│ '          H  = HOURS  │ Make Library...     │                  │
│ '          P  = HOURLY ├─────────────────────┤                  │
│ '          R  = TAX RA │ Set Main Module...  │                  │
│ '          G  = GROSS  └─────────────────────┘                  │
│ '          T  = TAX                                             │
│ '          N  = NET (TAKE-HOME) PAY                             │
│ '                                                               │
│           INPUT "ENTER EMPLOYEE NAME       "; N$                │
│           INPUT "ENTER EMPLOYEE ADDRESS    "; A$                │
│           INPUT "ENTER HOURS WORKED        "; H                 │
│           INPUT "ENTER PAY RATE ($/HOUR)   "; P                 │
│           INPUT "ENTER TAX RATE AS DECIMAL "; R                 │ ↓
│▓▓▓▓▓▓▓▓▓▓▓▓▓▓▓▓▓▓▓▓▓▓▓▓▓▓▓▓▓▓▓▓▓▓▓▓▓▓▓▓▓▓▓▓▓▓▓▓▓▓▓▓▓▓▓▓▓▓▓─→│
└───────────────────────── Immediate ─────────────────────────────┘
 Runs current program                              C  00001:001
```

NCD-NORTON Change Directory, Version 4.00, (C) Copr 1984-87, Peter Norton

```
C:\QUICK>
C:\QUICK>qb
ENTER EMPLOYEE NAME        ? John C. Jones
ENTER EMPLOYEE ADDRESS     ? 125 Main Street
ENTER HOURS WORKED         ? 40.00
ENTER PAY RATE ($/HOUR)    ? 12.50
ENTER TAX RATE AS DECIMAL  ? 0.25

        PROGRAM OUTPUT FOLLOWS
EMPLOYEE NAME    John C. Jones
ADDRESS          125 Main Street
HOURS WORKED     40
PAY RATE         12.5
TAX RATE         .25
GROSS PAY  =  $ 500
TAX        =  $ 125
NET PAY    =  $ 375

Press any key to continue
```

9. Press any key to return to the QuickBASIC main menu.
10. Next, you can compile your program by selecting the RUN menu choice followed by the MAKE EXE FILE selection. The .EXE file is a machine language version of your original BASIC source program. It will run 4 to 10 times faster, but in this example, because of the input and output operations (and no calculations or data manipulation), you won't see the improvement in execution speed.

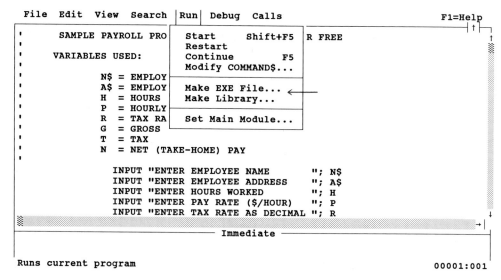

Runs current program   00001:001

11. QuickBASIC reminds you to save your program before the compile and link steps (make the EXE file) since that process erases your original program from memory.

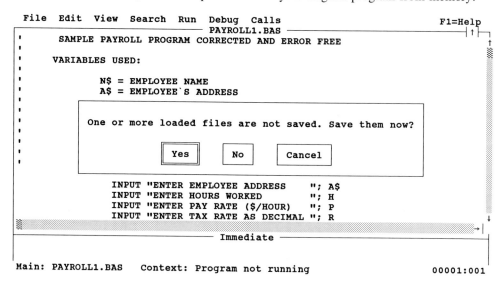

Main: PAYROLL1.BAS   Context: Program not running   00001:001

12. When you create the EXE file, you have a choice between creating the file and exiting QuickBASIC to try it out immediately, or staying in QuickBASIC. In this example, EXIT is chosen to illustrate the commands used to run the program from DOS.

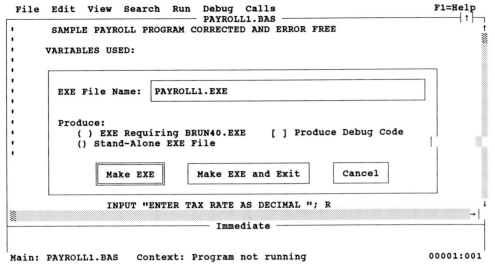

```
File   Edit   View   Search   Run   Debug   Calls                    F1=Help
                            PAYROLL1.BAS
'     SAMPLE PAYROLL PROGRAM CORRECTED AND ERROR FREE
'
'     VARIABLES USED:
'
'
'
'        EXE File Name:    PAYROLL1.EXE
'
'
'        Produce:
'           ( ) EXE Requiring BRUN40.EXE      [ ] Produce Debug Code
'           () Stand-Alone EXE File
'
'
'              Make EXE           Make EXE and Exit          Cancel
'
'
                    INPUT "ENTER TAX RATE AS DECIMAL "; R

                              Immediate
```

Main: PAYROLL1.BAS   Context: Program not running   00001:001

13. The compile and link steps look like this. When these are completed, your program is
    a ''stand-alone'' module, which can be run directly from DOS.

```
BC C:\QUICK\PAYROLL1.BAS/O;
Microsoft (R) QuickBASIC Compiler Version 4.00
Copyright (C) Microsoft Corp. 1982-1987. All rights reserved.

44092 Bytes Available
44048 Bytes Free

    0 Warning Error(s)
    0 Severe  Error(s)
BC A:\PAYROLL1.BAS/O;
Microsoft (R) QuickBASIC Compiler Version 4.00
Copyright (C) Microsoft Corp. 1982-1987. All rights reserved.

44108 Bytes Available
42249 Bytes Free

    0 Warning Error(s)
    0 Severe  Error(s)
LINK /EX PAYROLL1+PAYROLL1,C:\QUICK\PAYROLL1.EXE,NUL,;

Microsoft (R) Overlay Linker Version 3.61
Copyright (C) Microsoft Corp 1983-1987. All rights reserved.
```

14. Run the EXE version of your program simply by typing the file name (without the
    .EXE) after the DOS prompt. You may see slightly faster screen displays when you
    run the .EXE file.

411

```
C:\QUICK>payroll1
ENTER EMPLOYEE NAME        ? John C. Jones
ENTER EMPLOYEE ADDRESS     ? 125 Main Street
ENTER HOURS WORKED         ? 40.00
ENTER PAY RATE ($/HOUR)    ? 10
ENTER TAX RATE AS DECIMAL  ? .25

          PROGRAM OUTPUT FOLLOWS
EMPLOYEE NAME     John C. Jones
ADDRESS           125 Main Street
HOURS WORKED       40
PAY RATE           10
TAX RATE             .25
GROSS PAY  =    $   400
TAX        =    $   100
NET PAY    =    $   300
```

15. Last, look at the directory of your disk and you will see the new file(s) created by QuickBASIC.

```
            dir payroll1.*

Volume in drive C is DRIVE C
Directory of C:\QUICK

PAYROLL1  BAS      166    7-19-88    1:11p
PAYROLL1  MAK       31    7-19-88    1:11p
PAYROLL1  OBJ     1986    7-19-88    1:13p
PAYROLL1  EXE    31183    7-19-88    1:13p
        4 File(s)    3012608 bytes free

C:\QUICK>
```

Converting More Complex BASICA Programs to QuickBASIC

USING WORDSTAR (OR ANY TEXT EDITOR OR WORD PROCESSOR WITH A ASCII OPTION)

1. Load the program to be modified into BASICA and save it with the A option to produce ASCII code. For example—LOAD"CASE3-2, then SAVE"CASE3-2.BAS",A.
2. Load the program into WordStar (or your word processor) in the non-document, ASCII mode.
3. Edit out the line numbers and change REMs to '.
4. Convert all GOSUB statements to CALLs and all referenced GOSUB line numbers to subroutine names.
5. Delete the remarks that identified the GOSUB and the subroutines (since the subroutine names will be adequate for documentation.
6. Change the REM statement at the beginning of each subroutine to an actual SUB statement, and change the RETURN at the end of the subroutine to END SUB. Leave the subroutine logic in place, but delete the line numbers and superfluous remarks. Also, substitute QuickBASIC syntax for statements that were not permitted in BASICA (for example, in QuickBASIC you can branch to a name, not just a line number. (This will be illustrated in the case for chapter 5 in this appendix.).
7. Enter the appropriate "subroutine support" statements such as COMMON SHARED, variable typing, etc., at the beginning of the main program module.
8. Convert logic and syntax into QuickBASIC's fully-structured syntax, such as SELECT CASE (chapter 6), DO loop (chapter 5), SUB, FUNCTION, CALL, etc.
9. When editing is complete, save your non-document file and print it out to check that you did all the required editing, but don't worry too much about whether your program is perfect. You will be able to clean it up and improve it in the QuickBASIC environment.
10. Load your modified program into QuickBASIC the same way you would for a BASIC program. You will notice something interesting as soon as you view your program. QuickBASIC will divide your program into one main module (your main logic) and separate subroutines (one for each GOSUB that you replaced). To view and/or edit these separate subroutines now, you will have to select them in the view window.
11. Next, run your program as shown previously. If it needs editing, select the EDIT from the menu and correct or modify the main program or subroutines that need alteration. When the program is working perfectly, create the .EXE file as shown.

CONVERTING BASICA PROGRAMS TO QUICKBASIC USING WORDSTAR—A SESSION

Remember before doing any editing on a program created in BASICA, you have to convert it into ASCII format. Do this by loading the program into BASICA and then saving it with the A option like this:

```
LOAD"I2-1.BAS"
SAVE"I2-1.BAS",A
```

List or print the converted program. It should look exactly the same. However, you will probably notice that it takes longer to load and save a basic program in this form. (Another

413

way to check to see if your program is in ASCII is to try to display it directly in DOS like this:

```
A>TYPE I2-1.BAS
```

If the program is in ASCII code, you will be able to read it on the screen. If it is in the original "tokenized form," there will be a lot of graphics characters on the screen.

1. Load program into QB as shown before.
2. With your program in ASCII, enter QuickBASIC and select the FILE menu option; then load file. Your program will appear in the QB window.

```
File  Edit  View  Search  Run  Debug  Calls                    F1=Help
┌──────────────────────────── I2-1.BAS ───────────────────────────┤↑├─┐
│ 10      REM  **************************************************** │↑│
│ 20      REM  *        ILLUSTRATION OF STRUCTURED DESIGN        *  │ │
│ 30      REM  *                                                 *  │ │
│ 40      REM  *  A SIMPLIFIED CHECKING ACCOUNT BALANCE PROGRAM  *  │ │
│ 50      REM  *  THIS PROGRAM ACCEPTS DATA FROM THE KEYBOARD,   *  │ │
│ 60      REM  *  CALCULATES NEW BALANCE, AND PRINTS THE RESULT  *  │ │
│ 70      REM  *  ON THE PRINTER.                                *  │ │
│ 80      REM  *                                                 *  │ │
│ 90      REM  *        VARIABLE LEGEND                          *  │ │
│ 100     REM  *        PB = PREVIOUS BALANCE                    *  │ │
│ 110     REM  *        TD = TOTAL DEPOSITS MADE DURING THE MONTH *  │ │
│ 120     REM  *        TC = TOTAL AMOUNT OF CHECKS WRITTEN      *  │ │
│ 130     REM  *        NB = NEW BALANCE                         *  │ │
│ 140     REM  **************************************************** │ │
│ 150     CLS                                                       │ │
│ 160     PRINT "COPYRIGHT (C) 1989, BY MERRILL PUBLISHING COMPANY" │ │
│ 170     PRINT "FOR USE WITH STRUCTURED BASIC PROGRAMMING"         │ │
│ 180     REM  * MAIN PROGRAM *                                     │↓│
│                                                                  →│
├──────────────────────────── Immediate ───────────────────────────┤
│                                                                   │
└───────────────────────────────────────────────────────────────────┘
Main: I2-1.BAS        Context: Program not running        C  00018:012
```

Proceed through the program, changing all GOSUBs to CALL and all referenced GOSUB line numbers to subroutine names. Use meaningful names. Although they take longer to type, they are very helpful when tracing and documenting your program.

3. As soon as you name a subroutine, QB places you in the subroutine EDIT screen, expecting you to enter the subroutine's logic. Since the logic is already present in the original program, all you have to do is "move" those statements to the SUBROUTINE window (later in chapter 3 appendix you will see a different and easier procedure for long programs).

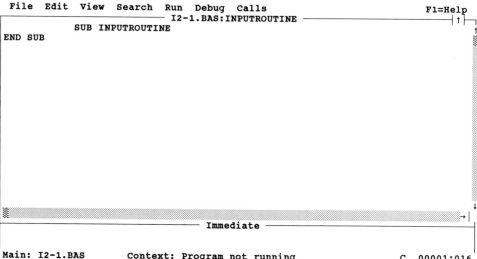

```
File  Edit  View  Search  Run  Debug  Calls                    F1=Help
┌────────────────────── I2-1.BAS:INPUTROUTINE ─────────────────────┤↑├─┐
│        SUB INPUTROUTINE                                           │↑│
│ END SUB                                                           │▒│
│                                                                   │ │
│                                                                   │ │
│                                                                   │ │
│                                                                   │ │
│                                                                   │ │
│                                                                   │ │
│                                                                   │ │
│                                                                   │ │
│                                                                   │ │
│                                                                   │ │
│                                                                   │ │
│                                                                   │↓│
│                                                                  →│
├──────────────────────────── Immediate ───────────────────────────┤
│                                                                   │
└───────────────────────────────────────────────────────────────────┘
Main: I2-1.BAS        Context: Program not running        C  00001:016
```

```
 File  Edit  View  Search  Run  Debug  Calls                    F1=Help
─────────────────────────── I2-1.BAS ──────────────────────────────┤↑├──┐
│ '    *         VARIABLE LEGEND                          *              ↑
│ '    *         PB = PREVIOUS BALANCE                    *
│ '    *         TD = TOTAL DEPOSITS MADE DURING THE MONTH *
│ '    *         TC = TOTAL AMOUNT OF CHECKS WRITTEN      *
│ '    *         NB = NEW BALANCE                         *
│ '    ***************************************************
│                CLS
│                PRINT "COPYRIGHT (C) 1989, BY MERRILL PUBLISHING COMPANY"
│                PRINT "FOR USE WITH STRUCTURED BASIC PROGRAMMING"
│ '              * MAIN PROGRAM *
│                CALL INPUTROUTINE
│                CALL CALCULATIONROUTINE
│                CALL OUTPUTROUTINE
│                END
│ 300     REM        ********************
│ 310            INPUT "ENTER PREVIOUS BALANCE "; PB
│ 320            INPUT "ENTER AMOUNT OF DEPOSITS "; TD
│ 330            INPUT "ENTER AMOUNT OF CHECKS WRITTEN "; TC             ↓
│                                                                      →│
│█──────────────────────────── Immediate ─────────────────────────────────
│
│
 Main: I2-1.BAS       Context: Program not running        C  00023:001
```

4. To do this, select the VIEW menu choice and choose the main module (your original program). Then select the subroutine statements you want to move by highlighting them with the shift and arrow keys.

```
 File  Edit  View  Search  Run  Debug  Calls                    F1=Help
─────────────────────────── I2-1.BAS ──────────────────────────────┤↑├──┐
│ '    *         TC = TOTAL AMOUNT OF CHECKS WRITTEN      *              ↑
│ '    *         NB = NEW BALANCE                         *
│ '    ***************************************************
│                CLS
│                PRINT "COPYRIGHT (C) 1989, BY MERRILL PUBLISHING COMPANY"
│                PRINT "FOR USE WITH STRUCTURED BASIC PROGRAMMING"
│ '              * MAIN PROGRAM *
│                CALL INPUTROUTINE
│                CALL CALCULATIONROUTINE
│                CALL OUTPUTROUTINE
│                END
│ 300     REM        ********************
│ 310            INPUT "ENTER PREVIOUS BALANCE "; PB
│ 320            INPUT "ENTER AMOUNT OF DEPOSITS "; TD
│ 330            INPUT "ENTER AMOUNT OF CHECKS WRITTEN "; TC
│ 340            RETURN
│ 350     REM        *************************
│ 360     REM        * CALCULATION SUBROUTINE *                          ↓
│                                                                      →│
│█──────────────────────────── Immediate ─────────────────────────────────
│
│
 Main: I2-1.BAS       Context: Program not running        C  00029:001
```

5. "Cut" these statements from the main program module by selecting the EDIT menu choice; then CUT.

415

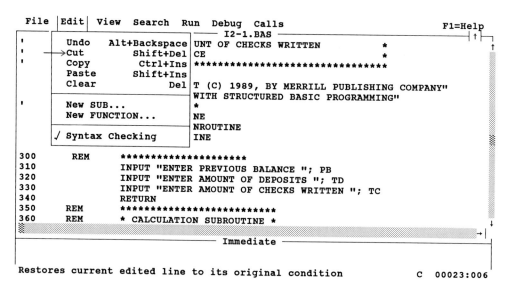

6. Select VIEW from the main menu, and view the subroutine in which you want to place the "cut" statements. Place the subroutine in the active window so you can work on it again.

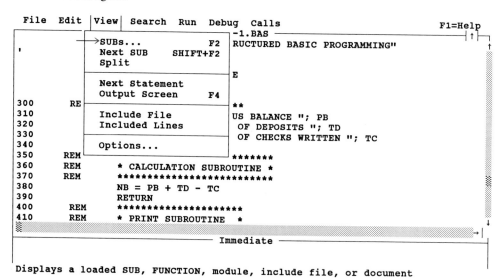

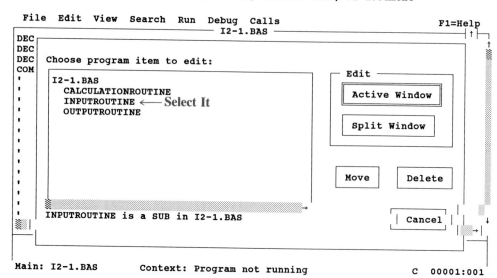

7. Next select EDIT from the main menu and choose paste. This will put the subroutine logic where it belongs, but now in a truly separate subroutine.

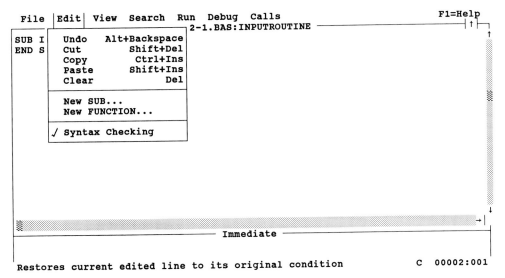

```
 File |Edit| View  Search  Run  Debug  Calls                          F1=Help
                          2-1.BAS:INPUTROUTINE                          | ↑ |
SUB I| Undo    Alt+Backspace                                                ↑
END S| Cut           Shift+Del
     | Copy          Ctrl+Ins
     | Paste         Shift+Ins
     | Clear             Del
     |
     | New SUB...
     | New FUNCTION...
     |
     |√ Syntax Checking



                                                                            ↓
                                                                         →|
                              Immediate
Restores current edited line to its original condition      C  00002:001
```

8. After the cut and paste, you will still want to do some editing to eliminate the line numbers and the RETURN statement. You may also wish to delete the REMARKS that identified the subroutine in the original program because these are really superfluous now.

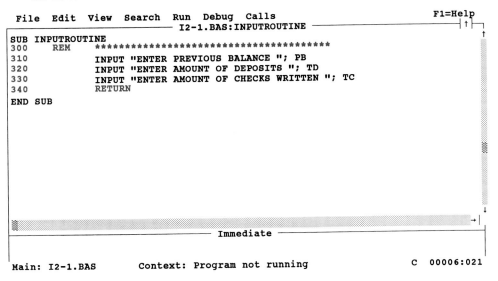

```
 File  Edit  View  Search  Run  Debug  Calls                           F1=Help
                          I2-1.BAS:INPUTROUTINE                          | ↑ |
SUB INPUTROUTINE                                                            ↑
300      REM    ************************************
310            INPUT "ENTER PREVIOUS BALANCE "; PB
320            INPUT "ENTER AMOUNT OF DEPOSITS "; TD
330            INPUT "ENTER AMOUNT OF CHECKS WRITTEN "; TC
340            RETURN
END SUB




                                                                            ↓
                                                                         →|
                              Immediate
Main: I2-1.BAS       Context: Program not running           C  00006:021
```

9. The complete and cleaned up subroutine will look like this, and it will now appear in the VIEW option window with the name that you gave it. This is important to remember because you won't find the logic in your main program any longer.

417

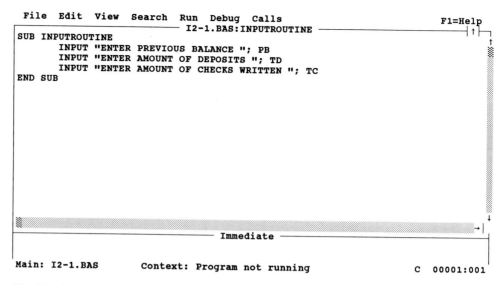

```
 File  Edit  View  Search  Run  Debug  Calls                    F1=Help
 ─────────────────── I2-1.BAS:INPUTROUTINE ───────────────────────
SUB INPUTROUTINE
        INPUT "ENTER PREVIOUS BALANCE "; PB
        INPUT "ENTER AMOUNT OF DEPOSITS "; TD
        INPUT "ENTER AMOUNT OF CHECKS WRITTEN "; TC
END SUB




 ──────────────────────────── Immediate ─────────────────────────

Main: I2-1.BAS       Context: Program not running         C  00001:001
```

10. Continue this process of converting subroutines until each GOSUB is removed and you have a new, real subroutine in its place.

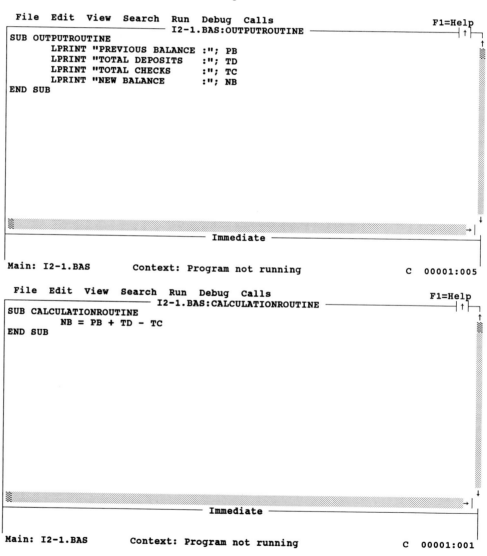

```
 File  Edit  View  Search  Run  Debug  Calls                    F1=Help
 ─────────────────── I2-1.BAS:OUTPUTROUTINE ──────────────────────
SUB OUTPUTROUTINE
        LPRINT "PREVIOUS BALANCE :"; PB
        LPRINT "TOTAL DEPOSITS   :"; TD
        LPRINT "TOTAL CHECKS     :"; TC
        LPRINT "NEW BALANCE      :"; NB
END SUB




 ──────────────────────────── Immediate ─────────────────────────

Main: I2-1.BAS       Context: Program not running         C  00001:005
```

```
 File  Edit  View  Search  Run  Debug  Calls                    F1=Help
 ───────────────── I2-1.BAS:CALCULATIONROUTINE ───────────────────
SUB CALCULATIONROUTINE
        NB = PB + TD - TC
END SUB




 ──────────────────────────── Immediate ─────────────────────────

Main: I2-1.BAS       Context: Program not running         C  00001:001
```

418

11. When you're done with the conversion, add the common shared statement as shown, and then save your program (perhaps with a different name than the original so you can compare the two later). Then, print the entire program, main module, and subroutines by selecting PRINT ALL from the file menu choice. Note that QB adds DECLARE SUB statements automatically at the top of your program for each subroutine that you created. This only happens if you use the QB EDITOR to create or convert a BASIC program. Remember that as you experiment with the next method for converting BASICA programs to QuickBASIC.

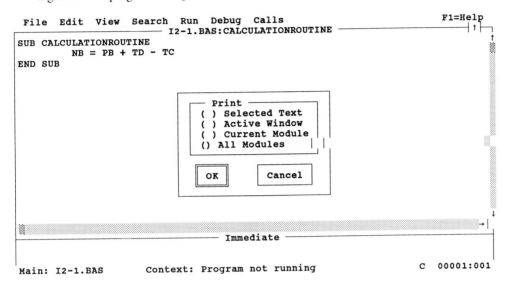

Here is the complete chapter 2 case study.

```
DECLARE SUB OUTPUTROUTINE ()
DECLARE SUB INPUTROUTINE ()
DECLARE SUB CALCULATIONROUTINE ()
COMMON SHARED PB, TD, TC, NB
'    *********************************************************
'    *        ILLUSTRATION OF STRUCTURED DESIGN              *
'    *                                                       *
'    *   A SIMPLIFIED CHECKING ACCOUNT BALANCE PROGRAM       *
'    *   THIS PROGRAM ACCEPTS DATA FROM THE KEYBOARD,        *
'    *   CALCULATES NEW BALANCE, AND PRINTS THE RESULT       *
'    *   ON THE PRINTER.                                     *
'    *                                                       *
'    *        VARIABLE LEGEND                                *
'    *        PB = PREVIOUS BALANCE                          *
'    *        TD = TOTAL DEPOSITS MADE DURING THE MONTH      *
'    *        TC = TOTAL AMOUNT OF CHECKS WRITTEN            *
'    *        NB = NEW BALANCE                               *
'    *********************************************************
'            CLS
             PRINT "COPYRIGHT (C) 1989, BY MERRILL PUBLISHING COMPANY"
             PRINT "FOR USE WITH STRUCTURED BASIC PROGRAMMING"
'        * MAIN PROGRAM *
             CALL INPUTROUTINE
             CALL CALCULATIONROUTINE
             CALL OUTPUTROUTINE
             END
```

```
SUB CALCULATIONROUTINE
        NB = PB + TD - TC
END SUB


SUB INPUTROUTINE
        INPUT "ENTER PREVIOUS BALANCE "; PB
        INPUT "ENTER AMOUNT OF DEPOSITS "; TD
        INPUT "ENTER AMOUNT OF CHECKS WRITTEN "; TC
END SUB


SUB OUTPUTROUTINE
        LPRINT "PREVIOUS BALANCE :"; PB
        LPRINT "TOTAL DEPOSITS   :"; TD
        LPRINT "TOTAL CHECKS     :"; TC
        LPRINT "NEW BALANCE      :"; NB
END SUB
```

12. It's a good idea to run the program after conversion to verify that it still works. Remember, you can run any QuickBASIC program in the interpreter mode (before compiling) to quickly test and debug it. In fact, this procedure is recommended to take full advantage of the debug options which are available in the debug menu choice and not available when running the compiled program.

13. If the program runs perfectly, producing the correct results in the proper format, you are ready to compile it. To do this, follow the same steps illustrated in chapter 1 appendix. Again, make sure you have enough room on your disk to compile and link your program.

The case study from chapter 3 was prepared using the procedure described. Notice the clear, compact code.

```
DECLARE SUB INPUTSUBROUTINE ()
DECLARE SUB OUTPUTSUBROUTINE ()
'      ********************************************************
'      *            INPUT/OUTPUT OPERATION                   *
'      *               CASE STUDY: 3-1C                      *
'      *    NAME & PHONE NUMBER LISTING PROGRAM              *
'      *    THIS PROGRAM READS IN FROM THE TERMINAL          *
'      *    A PERSON'S NAME AND PHONE NUMBER, AND            *
'      *    PRINTS THEM OUT ON THE PRINTER.                  *
'      *                                                     *
'      *                                                     *
'      *          NM$ = NAME                                 *
'      *          PHO$ = PHONE NUMBER                        *
'      ********************************************************
'      CLS
'    * MAIN PROGRAM *
        COMMON SHARED NM$, PHO$
        CALL INPUTSUBROUTINE
        CALL OUTPUTSUBROUTINE
        END
```

```
SUB INPUTSUBROUTINE
          PRINT "COPYRIGHT (C) 1989, BY MERRILL PUBLISHING COMPANY"
          PRINT "FOR USE WITH STRUCTURED BASIC PROGRAMING"
          PRINT
          PRINT
          PRINT "PLEASE MAKE SURE THAT THE PRINTER IS ON. "
          PRINT
          PRINT "ENTER NAME AND PHONE NUMBER, SEPATATED BY A COMMA."
          PRINT
          PRINT "PRESS RETURN WHEN DATA IS ENTERED PROPERLY. "
          LOCATE 9, 45: INPUT NM$, PHO$
          CLS
END SUB

SUB OUTPUTSUBROUTINE
       LPRINT NM$, PHO$
END SUB
```

Calculations with QuickBASIC Subroutines

One of the previous limitations of BASIC that kept professionals from using it was the global nature of variables. If a variable was named in your program, that variable was the same memory location for every "subroutine" in the program. If the value of that variable was changed, it was changed in the main program and every subroutine that referenced it. Therefore, there was no such thing as a true subroutine that could be considered of general purpose.

In contrast, variables in QuickBASIC do not have to be global if you elect not to have them global. Since subroutines are independent, the values of the variable passed to the subroutine in a parameter list are passed by reference to their address, not their name. This means the subroutine need not use the same variable names as the main program module.

A good example of this is a simple subroutine that averages two numbers passed to it and returns the result, as follows:

```
SUB AVERAGE (N1,N2,AVG)
AVG=(N1+N2)/2
END SUB
```

If we call this subroutine, we can pass it two numbers that represent test scores, for example, in the main program, and the subroutine will return the average of the two tests. If we call this very same subroutine from another part of our main program (or even from another program), and pass two numbers representing the company income for the past two years, the subroutine will return the average income for two years.

The CALL statements from both cases would be:

```
CALL AVERAGE (TEST1,TEST2,AVGTEST)
CALL AVERAGE (INCOME1,INCOME2,AVGINCOME)
```

Notice that the variable names do not have to be the same in the CALL and in the subroutine. In fact, that's what makes the subroutine a true general purpose subroutine!

Subroutines can be thought of more like complex, built-in functions like SQRT,SIN although subroutines are generally written by the programmer. (In the future, don't be surprised to see libraries of prorating subroutines that you can call into your programs. This has been done in many other high-level languages for years, and is now possible in QuickBASIC.)

```
DECLARE SUB INPUTROUTINE (ACNO, NM$, OBAL, CHG, CRT)
DECLARE SUB CALCULATIONS (OBAL, CHG, CRT, INTR, NBAL, MINPAY)
DECLARE SUB OUTPUTROUTINE (ACNO, NM$, OBAL, CHG, CRT, NBAL, MINPAY)

'    *****************************************************
'    *                 SIMPLE CALCULATIONS               *
'    *                   CASE STUDY: 4-2                  *
'    *                MONTHLY STATEMENT PROGRAM           *
'    *           THIS PROGRAM CALCULATES INTEREST ON A    *
'    *    CUSTOMER'S OLD BALANCE, ADDS THE CHARGES FOR    *
'    *    THE MONTH, SUBTRACTS THE CREDITS AND PAYMENTS   *
'    *    AND PRINTS A MONTHLY STATEMENT FOR THE ACCOUNT  *
'    *                                                    *
```

```
'    *              VARIABLE LEGEND              *
'    *  ACNO = ACCOUNT NO.     NM$ = NAME        *
'    *  AD$ = ADDRESS          OBAL = OLD BALANCE *
'    *  CHG = CHARGES          CRT = CREDITS      *
'    *  INTR = INTEREST        NBAL = NEW BALANCE *
'    *  MINPAY = MINIMUM PAYMENT DUE              *
'    ****************************************************
          CLS
          PRINT "COPYRIGHT (C) 1989, BY MERRILL PUBLISHING COMPANY"
          PRINT "FOR USE WITH STRUCTURED BASIC PROGRAMMING"
          PRINT
          PRINT
          PRINT
          PRINT "THIS PROGRAM WILL CALCULATE INTEREST ON CUSTOMER'S"
          PRINT "OLD BALANCE, ADD THE CHARGES FOR THE MONTH,"
          PRINT "SUBTRACT THE CREDITS AND BILLS THE CUSTOMER FOR"
          PRINT "THE NEW BALANCE AMOUNT."
          PRINT
' MAIN PROGRAM *
          CALL INPUTROUTINE(ACNO, NM$, OBAL, CHG, CRT)
          CALL CALCULATIONS(OBAL, CHG, CRT, INTR, NBAL, MINPAY)
          CALL OUTPUTROUTINE(ACNO, NM$, OBAL, CRT, CHG, NBAL, MINPAY)
          END


SUB CALCULATIONS (OBAL, CHG, CRT, INTR, NBAL, MINPAY)
          INTR = .01 * OBAL
          NBAL = OBAL + INTR + CHG - CRT
          MINPAY = .1 * NBAL
END SUB

SUB INPUTROUTINE (ACNO, NM$, OBAL, CHG, CRT)
          PRINT "PLEASE MAKE SURE THE PRINTER IS ON"
          PRINT
          PRINT
          PRINT
          PRINT "ACCOUNT NUMBER......._____"
          PRINT "NAME................._____"
          PRINT "ADDRESS.............._____"
          PRINT "OLD BALANCE..........____.__"
          PRINT "CHARGES..............____.__"
          PRINT "PAYMENTS + CREDITS...____.__"
          LOCATE 15, 21: INPUT ACNO
          LOCATE 16, 21: INPUT NM$
          LOCATE 17, 21: INPUT ADDR$
          LOCATE 18, 21: INPUT OBAL
          LOCATE 19, 21: INPUT CHG
          LOCATE 20, 21: INPUT CRT
END SUB

SUB OUTPUTROUTINE (ACNO, NM$, OBAL, CHG, CRT, NBAL, MINPAY)
          LPRINT
          LPRINT "                    MONTHLY STATEMENT"
          LPRINT "                    ABC DEPARTMENT STORE"
```

```
          LPRINT "                        HARTFORD CONN  06105"
          LPRINT
          LPRINT "ACCOUNT NO.        NAME       OLD BAL  CHARGES  CREDITS  NEW BAL MIN PAYMENT"
          F1$ = "  #####    \                 \ $###.##  $###.##  $###.##  $###.##  $###.##"
          LPRINT USING F1$; ACNO, NM$, OBAL, CHG, CRT, NBAL, MINPAY
  END SUB
```

Looping DO WHILE and DO UNTIL

BASICA does not contain a true DO UNTIL construct. Once a loop is started, it will finish unless you put in an unconditional or conditional branch (GOTO, IF, etc.) which is not considered good structured programming practice.

Because of this, intricate logic was used in the cases in chapters 5 through 10 to "fabricate" a DO UNTIL construct from the WHILE loop. Recall that we rearranged the operations in the WHILE loop from INPUT-PROCESS-OUTPUT to INPUT-WHILE-PROCESS-OUTPUT INPUT-WEND. The INPUT before the WHILE was needed to "prime the pump" so that the loop could begin with actual data. The INPUT at the end of the loop triggered the termination condition so that the loop was not executed again.

With QuickBASIC, we have a true DO UNTIL construct with the DO loop. Inside the loop, when we wish to terminate based on the trigger condition we establish, we write EXIT DO. You can see that this enhancement makes looping logic straightforward. There is nothing tricky about it. When the test condition such as

```
DO UNTIL CUR$="EOD"
```

is encountered, the loop is immediately terminated. No extra routines are processed, and logic need not be rearranged within the loop.

Refer to the subroutine PROCESSUNTILEND in the following QuickBASIC Case 5, and compare it to the GOSUB and the original "subroutine" in the original Case 5–3.

```
DECLARE SUB READINPUTDATA ()
DECLARE SUB PROCESSUNTILEND ()
DECLARE SUB PRINTTITLELINES ()
DECLARE SUB PREPARETABLES ()
DECLARE SUB CALCULATEVALUESANDPRINT ()
DECLARE SUB ENDOFTABLEMESSAGE ()
DECLARE SUB ENDOFPROGRAMMESSAGE ()
COMMON SHARED CUR$, RATE, CNTRY$, D, EXCH
'       *****************************************
'       *              LOOPING              *
'       *          CASE STUDY: 5-3          *
'       *     CURRENCY EXCHANGE TABLE PROGRAM     *
'       *       THIS PROGRAM DEMONSTRATES THE     *
'       *       DO WHILE AND DO UNTIL CONSTRUCTS.  *
'       *                                    *
'       *              VARIABLE LEGEND       *
'       *     CUR$ = CURRENCY NAME            *
'       *     RATE = EXCHANGE RATE TO US DOLLAR    *
'       *     CNTRY$ = COUNTRY NAME           *
'       *     D = LOOP COUNTER FOR US DOLLAR  *
'       *     EXCH = AMOUNT EQUAL TO US DOLLAR     *
'       *                                    *
'       * MAIN PROGRAM *
           CALL PROCESSUNTILEND
           CALL ENDOFPROGRAMMESSAGE
           END
```

```
        SUB CALCULATEVALUESANDPRINT
                EXCH = D * RATE
                F5$ = "                              ###.##              ##,###.##"
                LPRINT USING F5$; D, EXCH
        END SUB


        SUB ENDOFPROGRAMMESSAGE
                LPRINT
                LPRINT "                        END OF CURRENCY EXCHANGE PROGRAM      "
        END SUB


        SUB ENDOFTABLEMESSAGE
                LPRINT
                F6$ = "                        END OF DOLLARS TO \              \ "
                LPRINT USING F6$; CUR$
        END SUB


        SUB PREPARETABLES
                        FOR D = 1 TO 10
        REM                 PERFORM 'CALCULATE VALUES AND PRINT' SUBROUTINE
                        CALL CALCULATEVALUESANDPRINT
                        NEXT D
        REM                 PERFORM 'END OF TABLE MESSAGE' SUBROUTINE
                        CALL ENDOFTABLEMESSAGE
        END SUB


        SUB PRINTTITLELINES
                LPRINT
                LPRINT
                F1$ = "                    CURRENCY EXCHANGE TABLE - \              \"
                F2$ = "                       DOLLARS TO \                      \"
                F3$ = "                 EXCHANGE RATE = ##,###.## \       \ PER DOLLAR"
                F4$ = "                    DOLLARS              \                \"
                LPRINT USING F1$; CNTRY$
                LPRINT USING F2$; CUR$
                LPRINT USING F3$; RATE, CUR$
                LPRINT
                LPRINT USING F4$; CUR$
                LPRINT
        END SUB


        SUB PROCESSUNTILEND
                DO UNTIL CUR$ = "EOD"
                    CALL READINPUTDATA
                IF CUR$ = "EOD" THEN EXIT DO
                    CALL PRINTTITLELINES
                    CALL PREPARETABLES
                LOOP
        END SUB


        SUB READINPUTDATA
                CLS
                PRINT "COPYRIGHT (C) 1989, BY MERRILL PUBLISHING COMPANY"
                PRINT "FOR USE WITH STRUCTURED BASIC PROGRAMMING"
```

```
          PRINT
          PRINT "TO END PROGRAM, TYPE IN 'EOD' FOR CURRENCY NAME,"
          PRINT "FOLLOWED BY ZERO FOR EXCHANGE RATE AND ANY "
          PRINT "CHARACTER FOR COUNTRY NAME - PRESS RETURN AFTER"
          PRINT "EVERY DATA ENTRY."
          PRINT
          PRINT
          PRINT "ENTER CURRENCY NAME......................"
          PRINT "ENTER EXCHANGE RATE IN UNITS PER DOLLAR.."
          PRINT "ENTER NAME OF COUNTRY...................."
          LOCATE 10, 41: INPUT CUR$
          LOCATE 11, 41: INPUT RATE
          LOCATE 12, 41: INPUT CNTRY$
END SUB
```

Decision Making

BASICA has good selection constructs with the IFTHEN, IFTHENELSE, ON...GOTO, and ON...GOSUB, but selecting from a large number of alternatives that are not simple, continuous, or low-valued integers such as strings is very cumbersome in BASICA.

QuickBASIC addresses this problem with the new SELECT CASE which allows the selection of many alternatives, numeric integers, decimal numbers, and even strings. Note in Case 6 the simple numeric selection using this contruct subroutine CALCULATECOMMISSION and the outstanding new string CASE SELECT in subroutine DETERMINECARDESCRIPTION. In both cases, the CASE SELECT is used. Notice the added feature of a built-in error-trapping provision by including a CASE ELSE phase in the construct. This error trapping logic has traditionally been difficult in BASICA.

The illustration QCASE6 also shows the defined function called FUNCTION COMMISSION. This is similar to the BASICA DEF FN, but the new function can be compiled separately and linked to other programs, thereby making it a true function, usable by any BASIC program that you write.

```
DECLARE SUB CALCULATECOMMISSION ()
DECLARE SUB PROCESSSALESDATA ()
DECLARE SUB PRODUCEMANAGEMENTREPORTS ()
DECLARE SUB ENDOFPROGRAMMESSAGE ()
DECLARE SUB PROCESSINITIALINVENTORY ()
DECLARE SUB SETUPINITIALINVENTORY ()
DECLARE SUB ENDOFSETUPMESSAGE ()
DECLARE SUB READIQOHDATA ()
DECLARE SUB PRINTIQOHDATA ()
DECLARE SUB INPUTSALESDATA ()
DECLARE SUB PROCESSSALESUNTILENDOFDATA ()
DECLARE SUB ENDOFSALESDATAMESSAGE ()
DECLARE SUB DETERMINECARDESCRIPTION ()
DECLARE SUB DETERMINESALESMANCOMMISSION ()
DECLARE SUB PROCESSBUICK ()
DECLARE SUB PROCESSFORD ()
DECLARE SUB PROCESSPONTIAC ()
DECLARE SUB CALCULATEBUICKSTATISTICS ()
DECLARE SUB OUTOFSTOCKMESSAGE ()
DECLARE SUB CALCULATEFORDSTATISTICS ()
DECLARE SUB CALCULATEPONTIACSTATISTICS ()
DECLARE SUB CALCULATESALESMAN1COMMISSION ()
DECLARE SUB CALCULATESALESMAN2COMMISSION ()
DECLARE SUB CALCULATESALESMAN3COMMISSION ()
DECLARE SUB CALCULATEMANAGEMENTSTATISTICS ()
DECLARE SUB PRODUCEAUTOMOBILESALESREPORT ()
DECLARE SUB PRODUCESALESMANCOMMISSIONREPORT ()
COMMON SHARED IQOHB, IQOHF, IQOHP, QOHB, QOHF, QOHP, SMAN, DES$, PRC, CST, COMM
COMMON SHARED PROFITB, PROFITF, PROFITP, NUMB, NUMF, NUMP, COMM1, COMM2, COMM3
COMMON SHARED SOLD1, SOLD2, SOLD3, ENDSW, CARSW, TNUM
COMMON SHARED TPROFIT, TPROFB, TPROFF, TPROFP
COMMON SHARED TSOLD, TCOMM, TIQOH, TQOH
```

```
'      ********************************************************
'      *         CALCULATIONS WITH LOGICAL DECISIONS         *
'      *                   CASE STUDY 6-2                    *
'      *              AUTOMOBILE DEALERSHIP PROGRAM          *
'      * THIS PROGRAM CALCULATES THE CURRENT INVENTORY       *
'      * LEVEL, PRODUCES AN 'OUT OF STOCK' MESSAGE, AN       *
'      * AUTOMOBILE SALES REPORT AND A SALESMANS REPORT      *
'      *                                                     *
'      *                   VARIABLE LEGEND                   *
'      *         IQOH = INITIAL QUANTITY ON HAND             *
'      *         QOH = QUANTITY ON HAND                      *
'      *         SMAN = SALESMAN CODE                        *
'      *         DES$ = CAR DESCRIPTION                      *
'      *         PRC = SALE PRICE                            *
'      *         CST = DEALER COST                           *
'      *         COMM = SALESMAN COMMISSION                  *
'      *         PROFIT = PROFIT ON SALE                     *
'      *         TPROF = TOTAL PROFIT ALL SALES              *
'      *         NUM = NUMBER OF CARS SOLD                   *
'      *         SOLD = NO. OF CARS SOLD BY SALESMAN         *
'      *         TIQOH = TOTAL INITIAL QUANTITY ON HAND      *
'      *         TNUM = TOTAL ALL NUMBER OF CARS SOLD        *
'      *         TQOH = TOTAL ALL QUANTITY ON HAND           *
'      *         TPROFIT = TOTAL PROFIT ALL CARS SOLD        *
'      *         TCOMM = TOTAL ALL COMMISSIONS PAID          *
'      *         TSOLD = TOTAL CARS SOLD BY SALESMEN         *
'      *         B = BUICK                                   *
'      *         F = FORD                                    *
'      *         P = PONTIAC                                 *
'      *         ENDSW = END OF DATA SWITCH                  *
'      *         CARSW = PROCESS SALE SWITCH                 *
'      ********************************************************

'      COPYRIGHT (C) 1989, BY MERRILL PUBLISHING COMPANY
'      FOR USE WITH STRUCTURED BASIC PROGRAMMING

'      *****************
'      * MAIN PROGRAM *
'      *****************

              CALL PROCESSINITIALINVENTORY
              CALL PROCESSSALESDATA
              CALL PRODUCEMANAGEMENTREPORTS
              CALL ENDOFPROGRAMMESSAGE
              END


SUB CALCULATEBUICKSTATISTICS
              CALL CALCULATECOMMISSION
              PROFITB = PRC - CST - COMM
              TPROFB = TPROFB + PROFITB
              NUMB = NUMB + 1
              CARSW = 1
              QOHB = QOHB - 1
END SUB
```

```
SUB CALCULATECOMMISSION
    SELECT CASE SMAN
        CASE 1
                COMM = .1 * PRC
        CASE 2
                COMM = .15 * PRC
        CASE 3
                COMM = .2 * PRC
        CASE ELSE
                COMM = 0
                LPRINT " ERROR ----SORRY, NO SUCH SALESPERSON !!! "; SMAN
    END SELECT
END SUB


SUB CALCULATEFORDSTATISTICS
            CALL CALCULATECOMMISSION
            PROFITF = PRC - CST - COMM
            TPROFF = TPROFF + PROFITF
            NUMF = NUMF + 1
            CARSW = 1
            QOHF = QOHF - 1
END SUB


SUB CALCULATEMANAGEMENTSTATISTICS
            TIQOH = IQOHB + IQOHF + IQOHP
            TNUM = NUMB + NUMF + NUMP
            TQOH = QOHB + QOHF + QOHP
            TPROFIT = TPROFB + TPROFF + TPROFP
            TCOMM = COMM1 + COMM2 + COMM3
            TSOLD = SOLD1 + SOLD2 + SOLD3
END SUB


SUB CALCULATEPONTIACSTATISTICS
            CALL CALCULATECOMMISSION
            PROFITP = PRC - CST - COMM
            TPROFP = TPROFP + PROFITP
            NUMP = NUMP + 1
            CARSW = 1
            QOHP = QOHP - 1
END SUB


SUB CALCULATESALESMAN1COMMISSION
            COMM1 = COMM1 + COMM
            SOLD1 = SOLD1 + 1
END SUB


SUB CALCULATESALESMAN2COMMISSION
            COMM2 = COMM2 + COMM
            SOLD2 = SOLD2 + 1
END SUB


SUB CALCULATESALESMAN3COMMISSION
            COMM3 = COMM3 + COMM
            SOLD3 = SOLD3 + 1
END SUB
```

```
SUB DETERMINECARDESCRIPTION
    SELECT CASE DES$
        CASE "BUICK"
            CALL PROCESSBUICK
        CASE "FORD"
            CALL PROCESSFORD
        CASE "PONTIAC"
            CALL PROCESSPONTIAC
        CASE ELSE
            LPRINT " ERROR ---- WRONG CAR DESCRIPTION - TRY AGAIN ";
            LPRINT " WE DO NOT STOCK  "; DES$
    END SELECT
END SUB


SUB DETERMINESALESMANCOMMISSION
'    PERFORM 'CALCULATE SALESMAN COMMISSION' SUBROUTINE
    IF SMAN = 1 THEN CALL CALCULATESALESMAN1COMMISSION
    IF SMAN = 2 THEN CALL CALCULATESALESMAN2COMMISSION
    IF SMAN = 3 THEN CALL CALCULATESALESMAN3COMMISSION
END SUB


SUB ENDOFPROGRAMMESSAGE
        LPRINT : LPRINT : LPRINT
        LPRINT "                    END OF AUTOMOBILE DEALERSHIP PROGRAM"
END SUB


SUB ENDOFSALESDATAMESSAGE
        LPRINT
        LPRINT "                    ALL SALES DATA HAS BEEN PROCESSED"
        LPRINT
END SUB


SUB ENDOFSETUPMESSAGE
        LPRINT
        LPRINT
        LPRINT "                    INITIAL QUANTITY ON HAND HAS BEEN PROCESSED"
        LPRINT
        LPRINT
        LPRINT
END SUB


SUB INPUTSALESDATA
        CLS
        PRINT "COPYRIGHT (C) 1989, BY MERRILL PUBLISHING COMPANY"
        PRINT "FOR USE WITH STRUCTURED BASIC PROGRAMMING"
        PRINT
        PRINT "ENTER INFORMATION, WHEN COMPLETE PRESS RETURN"
        PRINT "WHEN ALL SALES HAVE BEEN RECORDED TYPE 0 FOR SALESMAN"
        PRINT
        PRINT "SALESMAN #...."
        PRINT "DESCRIPTION..."
        PRINT "PRICE........."
        PRINT "COST.........."
        LOCATE 7, 15: INPUT SMAN
        LOCATE 8, 15: INPUT DES$
```

431

```
                              LOCATE 9, 15: INPUT PRC
                              LOCATE 10, 15: INPUT CST
                              IF SMAN = 0 THEN ENDSW = 1
                              CARSW = 0
          END SUB


          SUB OUTOFSTOCKMESSAGE
              LPRINT : LPRINT : LPRINT
              F1$ = "                              OUT OF STOCK \           \"
              LPRINT USING F1$; DES$
              LPRINT
          END SUB


          SUB PRINTIQOHDATA
                       LPRINT
                       LPRINT "                    BEGINNING INVENTORY"
                       LPRINT "                    INITIAL QUANTITY ON HAND"
                       LPRINT
                       LPRINT "              BUICK      FORD      PONTIAC"
                       F$ = "                ##        ##         ##"
                       LPRINT USING F$; IQOHB, IQOHF, IQOHP
          END SUB


          SUB PROCESSBUICK
          '    IF "AVAILABLE" PERFORM 'CALCULATE BUICK STATISTICS'
          '    IF "OUT OF STOCK" PERFORM 'OUT OF STOCK MESSAGE'
           IF QOHB > 0 THEN CALL CALCULATEBUICKSTATISTICS ELSE CALL OUTOFSTOCKMESSAGE
          END SUB


          SUB PROCESSFORD
          '    IF "AVAILABLE " PERFORM 'CALCULATE FORD STATISTICS'
          '    IF "OUT OF STOCK" PERFORM 'OUT OF STOCK MESSAGE'
           IF QOHF > 0 THEN CALL CALCULATEFORDSTATISTICS ELSE CALL OUTOFSTOCKMESSAGE
          END SUB


          SUB PROCESSINITIALINVENTORY
                       CALL SETUPINITIALINVENTORY
                       CALL ENDOFSETUPMESSAGE
          END SUB


          SUB PROCESSPONTIAC
          '    IF "AVAILABLE " PERFORM 'CALCULATE PONTIAC STATISTICS'
          '    IF "OUT OF STOCK " PERFORM 'OUT OF STOCK MESSAGE'
           IF QOHP > 0 THEN CALL CALCULATEPONTIACSTATISTICS ELSE CALL OUTOFSTOCKMESSAGE

          END SUB


          SUB PROCESSSALESDATA
                       CALL INPUTSALESDATA
                       CALL PROCESSSALESUNTILENDOFDATA
                       CALL ENDOFSALESDATAMESSAGE
          END SUB
```

432

```
SUB PROCESSSALESUNTILENDOFDATA
            ENDSW = 0
            WHILE ENDSW = 0
                CALL DETERMINECARDESCRIPTION
                IF CARSW = 1 THEN CALL DETERMINESALESMANCOMMISSION
                CALL INPUTSALESDATA
            WEND
END SUB


SUB PRODUCEAUTOMOBILESALESREPORT
            LPRINT "                       AUTOMOBILE SALES REPORT"
            LPRINT "      DESCRIPTION         IQOH      SOLD      QOH        PROFIT"
            LPRINT
            F2$ = "        BUICK             ##        ##        ##       $ #,###.##"
            F3$ = "        FORD              ##        ##        ##       $ #,###.##"
            F4$ = "        PONTIAC           ##        ##        ##       $ #,###.##"
            F5$ = "                 TOTAL    ###       ###       ###      $##,###.##"
            LPRINT USING F2$; IQOHB, NUMB, QOHB, TPROFB
            LPRINT USING F3$; IQOHF, NUMF, QOHF, TPROFF
            LPRINT USING F4$; IQOHP, NUMP, QOHP, TPROFP
            LPRINT USING F5$; TIQOH, TNUM, TQOH, TPROFIT
            LPRINT : LPRINT : LPRINT
END SUB


SUB PRODUCEMANAGEMENTREPORTS
            CALL CALCULATEMANAGEMENTSTATISTICS
            CALL PRODUCEAUTOMOBILESALESREPORT
            CALL PRODUCESALESMANCOMMISSIONREPORT
END SUB


SUB PRODUCESALESMANCOMMISSIONREPORT
            LPRINT "                      SALESMAN COMMISSION REPORT"
            LPRINT "               SALESMAN      COMMISSION     NUMBER SOLD"
            LPRINT
            F6$ = "                  1        $ #,###.##          ##"
            F7$ = "                  2        $ #,###.##          ##"
            F8$ = "                  3        $ #,###.##          ##"
            F9$ = "                TOTAL      $##,###.##          ###"
            LPRINT USING F6$; COMM1, SOLD1
            LPRINT USING F7$; COMM2, SOLD2
            LPRINT USING F8$; COMM3, SOLD3
            LPRINT USING F9$; TCOMM, TSOLD
            LPRINT : LPRINT : LPRINT
END SUB


SUB READIQOHDATA
            CLS
            PRINT "COPYRIGHT (C) 1989, BY MERRILL PUBLISHING COMPANY"
            PRINT "FOR USE WITH STRUCTURED BASIC PROGRAMMING"
            PRINT
            PRINT "ENTER STARTING INVENTORY FOR ALL MAKES"
            PRINT
            PRINT "PLEASE MAKE SURE PRINTER IS ON"
            PRINT
```

433

```
                    PRINT "BUICK...."
                    PRINT "FORD....."
                    PRINT "PONTIAC.."
                    LOCATE 8, 10: INPUT IQOHB
                    LOCATE 9, 10: INPUT IQOHF
                    LOCATE 10, 10: INPUT IQOHP
                    QOHB = IQOHB
                    QOHF = IQOHF
                    QOHP = IQOHP
          END SUB

          SUB SETUPINITIALINVENTORY
                    CALL READIQOHDATA
                    CALL PRINTIQOHDATA
          END SUB
```

Table Processing

Allocating memory for tables in QuickBASIC can be done dynamically or at compile time. This saves memory and/or improves program execution depending on the application. If the size of the table is known ahead, then the static allocation will occur at compile time, resulting in quicker execution. If the table size is not known, then dynamic allocation will save memory.

In both cases, tables can be passed as arguments or in common to subroutines so that table processing subroutines can truly be of general purpose. You can now have true sort utilities, matrix algebra routines, or any table processing application by passing values via arguments, not global variables. The translation program in chapter 7 could be written now as a general purpose translation program, with table routines that perform translations of words, do data look-ups, convert numbers in different bases, or any application where there is a key field and related field in the table.

```
DECLARE SUB SETUPDICTIONARY ()
DECLARE SUB PROCESSTRANSLATIONTABLE ()
DECLARE SUB PRINTENDOFPROGRAMMESSAGE ()
DECLARE SUB READDICTIONARY ()
DECLARE SUB PRINTDICTIONARY ()
DECLARE SUB INPUTENGLISHSENTENCE ()
DECLARE SUB PROCESSTRANSLATIONUNTILENDOFDATA ()
DECLARE SUB TRANSLATESENTENCE ()
DECLARE SUB SEARCHDICTIONARY ()
DECLARE SUB PRINTTRANSLATION ()
COMMON SHARED ENG$(), SPA$(), SENT$(), SPAWD$(), NREC, ENDSW, I, J, K

'      ********************************************************
'      *                      TABLES                         *
'      *                 CASE STUDY: 7-2                      *
'      *                TRANSLATION PROGRAM                   *
'      *     THIS PROGRAM SETS UP A DICTIONSRY TABLE OF       *
'      *     ENGLISH AND SPANISH WORDS AND TRANSLATES         *
'      *     THE ENGLISH SENTENCES INTO SPANISH.              *
'      *                                                      *
'      *                  VARIABLE LEGEND                     *
'      *         ENG$ = ENDLISH WORD INPUT TABLE              *
'      *         SPA$ = SPANISH WORD INPUT TABLE              *
'      *         SENT$ = ENGLISH SENTENCE WORD                *
'      *         SPAWD$ = SPANISH WORD OUTPUT                 *
'      *         NREC = NUMBER OF RECORDS                     *
'      *         ENDSW = END OF DATA SWITCH                   *
'      *         I,J,K = SUBSCRIPTS                           *
'      ********************************************************

       PRINT "COPYRIGHT (C) 1989, BY MERRILL PUBLISHING COMPANY"
       PRINT "FOR USE WITH STRUCTURED BASIC PROGRAMMING"
'   NOTE: WHEN RUNNING THIS PROGRAM ON SOME SYSTEMS, IT IS
'         NECESSARY TO ENTER THE 'BLANK' SENTENCE WORDS IN
```

```
'               QUOTATION MARKS TO BE COMPATIBLE WITH THE BLANK IN
'               THE DATA STATEMENT DICTIONARY.
'
'     * MAIN PROGRAM *
               CALL SETUPDICTIONARY
               CALL PROCESSTRANSLATIONTABLE
               CALL PRINTENDOFPROGRAMMESSAGE
               END
DATA THIS,ESTO
DATA A,UN
DATA IS,ES
DATA LANGUAGE,LENGUAJE
DATA TRANSLATION,TRADUCCION
DATA PROGRAM,PROGRAMA
DATA SET-UP,CREACION
DATA TABLE,TABLA
DATA AND,Y
DATA ENABLED,PERMITIDO
DATA US,NOSOTROS
DATA SEARCH,BUSQUEDA
DATA OF,DE
DATA THE,LA
DATA TO,A
DATA TRANSLATE,TRADUCIR
DATA SENTENCE,FRASE
DATA SPANISH,ESPANOL
DATA HAS,HA
DATA ENGLISH,ENGLES
DATA ".","."
DATA " "," "


SUB INPUTENGLISHSENTENCE
               PRINT "ENTER AN ENGLISH SENTENCE"
               PRINT "WITH A MAXIMUM OF 8 WORDS"
               FOR I = 1 TO 8
               PRINT "ENTER WORD "; I
               INPUT SENT$(I)
               IF SENT$(I) = "EOD" THEN ENDSW = 0
               NEXT I
END SUB


SUB PRINTDICTIONARY
               LPRINT TAB(32); "DICTIONARY TABLE"
               FOR I = 1 TO 22
               LPRINT TAB(25); ENG$(I); TAB(45); SPA$(I)
               NEXT I
               LPRINT : LPRINT
END SUB


SUB PRINTENDOFPROGRAMMESSAGE
               LPRINT
               LPRINT
               LPRINT
               LPRINT TAB(27); "END OF TRANSLATION PROGRAM"
END SUB
```

436

```
SUB PRINTTRANSLATION
        LPRINT TAB(30); "ENGLISH SENTENCE"
        FOR I = 1 TO 8
        LPRINT SENT$(I); " ";
        NEXT I
        LPRINT
        LPRINT TAB(30); "SPANISH SENTENCE"
        FOR I = 1 TO 8
        LPRINT SPAWD$(I); " ";
        NEXT I
        LPRINT
END SUB


SUB PROCESSTRANSLATIONTABLE
        DIM SENT$(8), SPAWD$(8)
        CALL INPUTENGLISHSENTENCE
        CALL PROCESSTRANSLATIONUNTILENDOFDATA
END SUB


SUB PROCESSTRANSLATIONUNTILENDOFDATA
        ENDSW = 1
        WHILE ENDSW = 1
        CALL TRANSLATESENTENCE
        CALL INPUTENGLISHSENTENCE
        WEND
END SUB


SUB READDICTIONARY
        DIM ENG$(22), SPA$(22)
        FOR I = 1 TO 22
        READ ENG$(I), SPA$(I)
        PRINT ENG$(I), SPA$(I)
        NEXT I
END SUB


SUB SEARCHDICTIONARY
        FOR I = 1 TO 8
        NREC = 22
        FOR J = 1 TO NREC
        IF SENT$(I) = ENG$(J) THEN SPAWD$(I) = SPA$(J)
        NEXT J
        NEXT I
END SUB


SUB SETUPDICTIONARY
        CALL READDICTIONARY
        CALL PRINTDICTIONARY
END SUB


SUB TRANSLATESENTENCE
        CALL SEARCHDICTIONARY
        CALL PRINTTRANSLATION
END SUB
```

437

Advanced Table Processing

The program illustration for chapter 8 makes use of line labels instead of line numbers to simplify the complex logic of the original BASICA program. What was a difficult program to follow becomes easier with the descriptive subroutine names and CALL statements, which are self-documenting. Using labels instead of numbers make for easier reading. In the BUBBLESORTSCORES subroutine, notice how much clearer the sort switch logic becomes with these labels replacing the previous line numbers. IF SORTSW = 0 THEN GOTO ENDSORT makes the statement purpose obvious.

```
DECLARE SUB MATCHDATAANDCALCULATESCORE ()
DECLARE SUB PRINTCOLUMNHEADINGS ()
DECLARE SUB SETUPMASTERTABLE ()
DECLARE SUB INPUTTRANSACTION ()
DECLARE SUB PROCESSMATCH ()
DECLARE SUB ENDOFPROGRAMMESSAGE ()
DECLARE SUB READTABLEDATA ()
DECLARE SUB PRINTTABLEDATA ()
DECLARE SUB BUBBLESORTSCORES ()
DECLARE SUB PRINTPREFERENCERECORDS ()
DECLARE SUB PRINTHEADINGS ()
DECLARE SUB PRINTDATALINES ()
COMMON SHARED ADR$(), TWN$(), PHON$(), RMS(), ACR(), BDRM(), BTH(), GAR(), MRTG(), PRC(), SCORE()
COMMON SHARED TN$, PNE$, RM, AC, BR, BA, GA, MGT, PRCE, REPSW, NM$, NREC, SORTSW, I, J, K
'    **********************************************
'    *              ADVANCED TABLE HANDLING       *
'    *                  CASE STUDY: 8-1           *
'    *              REAL ESTATE MATCHING PROGRAM  *
'    *                                            *
'    *    THIS PROGRAM SETS UP A TABLE OF AVAILABLE *
'    *    HOMES AND THEIR CHARACTERISTICS.  IT THEN *
'    *    PERFORMS A SEQUENTIAL COMPARISON (MATCH)  *
'    *    COMPARING A CLIENT'S PREFERENCES TO THE   *
'    *    CHARACTERISTICS OF THE HOMES IN THE TABLE *
'    *                                            *
'    *    THE BEST MATCH IS INDICATED BY AN        *
'    *    EVALUATION SCORE FOR EACH HOME, WHICH IS *
'    *    THEN USED AS THE KEY FIELD TO SORT (RANK) *
'    *    THE HOMES FROM BEST MATCH TO WORST.       *
'    *                                            *
'    *    THE RESULTS ARE THEN PRINTED AS A CLIENT *
'    *    REPORT FOR THE BEST THREE MATCHES.       *
'    *                                            *
'    *                    VARIABLE LEGEND         *
'    *       TABLE DATA:                          *
'    *                ADR$ = ADDRESS              *
'    *                TWN$ = TOWN                 *
'    *                PHON$= PHONE NUMBER         *
'    *                RMS  = NUMBER OF ROOMS      *
'    *                ACR$ = NUMBER OF ACRES      *
'    *                BDRM = NUMBER OF BEDROOMS   *
'    *                BTH  = NUMBER OF BATHS      *
'    *                GAR  = GARAGE               *
'    *                MRTG = ASSUMABLE MORTGAGE   *
'    *                PRC  = PRICE                *
'    *                SCORE= EVALUATION SCORE     *
'    *       CLIENT PREFERENCE DATA:              *
'    *                TN$  = TOWN PERFERRED       *
'    *                PNE$ = CLIENT PHONE NUMBER  *
'    *                RM   = NUMBER OF ROOMS      *
'    *                AC   = NUMBER OF ACRES      *
'    *                BR   = NUMBER OF BEDROOMS   *
'    *                BA   = NUMBER OF BATHS      *
'    *                GA   = GARAGE               *
'    *                MGT  = ASSUMABLE MORTGAGE   *
'    *                PRCE = MAXIMUM PRICE        *
'    **********************************************
     PRINT "COPYRIGHT (C) 1989, BY MERRILL PUBLISHING COMPANY"
     PRINT "FOR USE WITH STRUCTURED BASIC PROGRAMMING"
'        * MAIN PROGRAM *
```

```
                CALL PRINTCOLUMNHEADINGS
                CALL SETUPMASTERTABLE
                CALL INPUTTRANSACTION
'               'PROCESS MATCH' SUBROUTINE WHILE NOT END OF DATA
                CALL PROCESSMATCH
                CALL ENDOFPROGRAMMESSAGE
                END
DATA 125 MAIN STREET,HARTFORD,232-4040,6,.5,3,2,2,0,75000
DATA 60 SOUTH DRIVE,AVON,677-1111,1,1,4,3,2,0,178000
DATA 10 NORTH AVENUE,W. HARTFORD,563-1234,7,.5,3,1,1,0,86000
DATA 15 EAST STREET,E. HARTFORD,569-6666,6,.3,2,1,0,1,68000
DATA 12 ARGOSY DRIVE,MANCHESTER,644-1313,8,.4,2,2,1,1,92000
DATA 1020 FOREST LANE,SIMSBURY,678-4131,9,2,2,2,2,0,96000
DATA 4 WOODSTOCK AVE.,HARTFORD,522-6100,5,.2,2,1,0,1,48000
DATA 1336 CHURCH ST.,S. WINDSOR,644-8080,7,.5,3,2,2,0,95000
DATA 45 SPRING STREET,BLOOMFIELD,244-1600,8,.3,3,1,1,0,72000
DATA 300 ROSE DRIVE,HARTFORD,232-1652,5,.3,2,1,0,1,49000


SUB BUBBLESORTSCORES
            NREC = 10 - 1
            SORTSW = 1
            FOR K = 1 TO NREC
            IF SORTSW = 0 THEN GOTO ENDSORT
                SORTSW = 0
                FOR I = 1 TO NREC
                    J = I + 1
                    IF SCORE(I) < SCORE(J) THEN SWAP ADR$(I), ADR$(J)
                    IF SCORE(I) < SCORE(J) THEN SWAP TWN$(I), TWN$(J): SWAP PHON$(I), PHON$(J): SWAP RMS(I), RMS(J): SWAP ACR(I), ACR
                    IF SCORE(I) < SCORE(J) THEN SWAP BDRM(I), BDRM(J): SWAP BTH(I), BTH(J)
                    IF SCORE(I) < SCORE(J) THEN SWAP GAR(I), GAR(J): SWAP MRTG(I), MRTG(J): SWAP PRC(I), PRC(J): SWAP SCORE(I), SCORE
                    SORTSW = 1
                NEXT I
            NEXT K
            I = 1
ENDSORT:    IF SCORE(I) >= 10 THEN REPSW = 1
END SUB


SUB ENDOFPROGRAMMESSAGE
            LPRINT : LPRINT : LPRINT
            LPRINT TAB(23); "END OF REAL ESTATE MATCHING PROGRAM"
END SUB


SUB INPUTTRANSACTION
            CLS
            PRINT "COPYRIGHT (C) 1989, BY MERRILL PUBLISHING COMPANY"
            PRINT "FOR USE WITH STRUCTURED BASIC PROGRAMMING"
            PRINT
            PRINT "PLEASE ENTER YOUR PREFERENCES.  PRESS RETURN AFTER EACH ENTRY"
            PRINT "TYPE 'EOD' INSTEAD OF CLIENT NAME, TO END THE PROGRAM"
            PRINT
            PRINT "PLEASE MAKE SURE THAT THE PRINTER IS ON"
            PRINT
            PRINT "NAME......"
            PRINT "TOWN......"
            PRINT "PHONE #..."
            PRINT "ROOMS....."
            PRINT "ACRES....."
            PRINT "BEDROOMS.."
            PRINT "BATHS....."
            PRINT "GARAGE...."
            PRINT "MORTGAGE.."
            PRINT "PRICE....."
            LOCATE 9, 11: INPUT NM$
            LOCATE 10, 11: INPUT TN$
            LOCATE 11, 11: INPUT PNE$
            LOCATE 12, 11: INPUT RM
            LOCATE 13, 11: INPUT AC
            LOCATE 14, 11: INPUT BR
            LOCATE 15, 11: INPUT BA
            LOCATE 16, 11: INPUT GA
            LOCATE 17, 11: INPUT MGT
            LOCATE 18, 11: INPUT PRCE
            REPSW = 0
END SUB

SUB MATCHDATAANDCALCULATESCORE
    FOR I = 1 TO 10
        IF PRCE > PRC(I) THEN SCORE(I) = SCORE(I) + 20
        IF TN$ = TWN$(I) THEN SCORE(I) = SCORE(I) + 20
        IF RM <= RMS(I) THEN SCORE(I) = SCORE(I) + 10
        IF AC <= ACR(I) THEN SCORE(I) = SCORE(I) + 10
        IF BR <= BDRM(I) THEN SCORE(I) = SCORE(I) + 10
```

439

```
                    IF BA <= BTH(I) THEN SCORE(I) = SCORE(I) + 10
                    IF GA <= GAR(I) THEN SCORE(I) = SCORE(I) + 10
                   IF MGT = MRTG(I) THEN SCORE(I) = SCORE(I) + 10
              NEXT I
         END SUB


    SUB PRINTCOLUMNHEADINGS
              LPRINT TAB(28); "TABLE OF AVAILABLE HOMES"
              LPRINT TAB(28); "------------------------"
              LPRINT "RECORD    ADDRESS     TOWN       PHONE NO  RMS ACRE  BDRM BATH GAR MRTG PRICE"
    END SUB


    SUB PRINTDATALINES
              FOR I = 1 TO 3
              F3$ = "         #          \           \      \      \        ###           $###,###"
              IF SCORE(I) > 0 THEN LPRINT USING F3$; I, ADR$(I), PHON$(I), SCORE(I), PRC(I)
              NEXT I
    END SUB


    SUB PRINTHEADINGS
              LPRINT : LPRINT : LPRINT
              LPRINT TAB(30); "CLIENT INQUIRY REPORT"
              LPRINT TAB(32); "A.D.P. REALTY CO."
              LPRINT
              F2$ = "            CLIENT: \                \ PHONE:\        \"
              LPRINT USING F2$; NM$, PNE$
              LPRINT
              IF REPSW = 1 THEN LPRINT TAB(6); "RATING"; TAB(15); "PREFERRED HOME ADDRESS"; TAB(39); "PHONE NO"; TAB(49); "EVALUATION S
              IF REPSW = 1 THEN LPRINT TAB(6); "------"; TAB(15); "----------------------"; TAB(39); "--------"; TAB(49); "-----------
              IF REPSW = 0 THEN LPRINT TAB(14); "THERE ARE NO HOMES AVAILABLE THAT MEET YOUR PREFERENCE"
    END SUB


    SUB PRINTPREFERENCERECORDS
              CALL PRINTHEADINGS
              IF REPSW = 1 THEN CALL PRINTDATALINES
    END SUB


    SUB PRINTTABLEDATA
              FOR I = 1 TO 10
              F$ = " ## \          \ \        \ \       \## #.##   #   #   #   # $###,###"
                   LPRINT USING F$; I, ADR$(I), TWN$(I), PHON$(I), RMS(I), ACR(I), BDRM(I), BTH(I), GAR(I), MRTG(I), PRC(I)
              NEXT I
    END SUB


    SUB PROCESSMATCH
              WHILE NM$ <> "EOD"
                   CALL MATCHDATAANDCALCULATESCORE
                   CALL BUBBLESORTSCORES
                   CALL PRINTPREFERENCERECORDS
                   CALL INPUTTRANSACTION
                      FOR I = 1 TO 10
                         SCORE(I) = 0
                      NEXT I
              WEND
    END SUB


    SUB READTABLEDATA
              FOR I = 1 TO 10
                   READ ADR$(I), TWN$(I), PHON$(I), RMS(I), ACR(I), BDRM(I), BTH(I), GAR(I), MRTG(I), PRC(I)
                   SCORE(I) = 0
              NEXT I
    END SUB


    SUB SETUPMASTERTABLE
              DIM ADR$(100), TWN$(100), PHON$(100), RMS(100), ACR(100), BDRM(100), BTH(100), GAR(100), MRTG(100), PRC(100), SCORE(100)
              CALL READTABLEDATA
              CALL PRINTTABLEDATA
    END SUB
```

Direct Access File Processing

The most striking and time-saving enhancement in QuickBASIC is in direct access field processing syntax. Now the FIELD statement is replaced by a TYPE statement which groups and declares all variables to be stored on the direct access file. There are no longer two types of variables in direct access file programs—one for the program and one for the file. This means there is no longer the need for the cumbersome and complex conversion functions that were needed to convert from program variables to file variables and vice-versa. Those conversions were difficult to remember and time-consuming to code. Now, the same type variables are used in the program and on the direct access file. Any conversions and behind-the-scenes operations to actually get the data on the direct access file is taken care of by the QuickBASIC system.

Notice how this shortens Case 9–2 when compared to the original in chapter 9. Notice also how much more staightforward the new program version is. This improvement alone opens the door for many professional applications of BASIC in serious business programming applications using files.

```
DECLARE SUB PRODUCECUSTOMERBILLS ()
DECLARE SUB OPENFILES ()
DECLARE SUB SETUPMASTERFILE ()
DECLARE SUB PROCESSTRANSACTIONDATA ()
DECLARE SUB PRODUCEREPORTS ()
DECLARE SUB PRINTUPDATEDMASTERFILE ()
DECLARE SUB ENDOFPROGRAMMESSAGE ()
DECLARE SUB ENDOFPROGRAM ()
DECLARE SUB LOADMASTERFILERECORDS ()
DECLARE SUB STOREMASTERFILERECORDS ()
DECLARE SUB PRINTMASTERFILERECORDS ()
DECLARE SUB PROCESSMONTHLYINTEREST ()
DECLARE SUB INPUTTRANSACTIONDATA ()
DECLARE SUB PROCESSTRANSACTIONUNTILENDOFDATA ()
DECLARE SUB GETMASTERFILERECORD ()
DECLARE SUB CALCULATEINTEREST ()
DECLARE SUB UPDATEMASTERFILERECORD ()
DECLARE SUB SEARCHMASTERFILE ()
DECLARE SUB STOREMANAGEMENTDATA ()
DECLARE SUB STOREINVALIDDATA ()
DECLARE SUB CALCULATENEWBALANCE ()
DECLARE SUB SORTMANAGEMENTFILE ()
DECLARE SUB PRINTMANAGEMENTREPORT ()
DECLARE SUB PRINTINVALIDDATAREPORT ()
COMMON SHARED ENDSW, Z, ISW, N, NBR, AN, NAM, ST, CTY, STA, BAL, YTD, INTR, ZIP
COMMON SHARED CD$(), AMT(), AN(), CD$, AMT, IREC, TREC
TYPE RECORDTYPE
    NBR AS INTEGER
    NAM AS STRING * 16
    ST  AS STRING * 16
    CTY AS STRING * 13
    STA AS STRING * 2
    BAL AS SINGLE
    YTD AS SINGLE
```

```
      INTR AS SINGLE
      ZIP AS STRING * 5
END TYPE
COMMON SHARED R AS RECORDTYPE
Z = 10 ' THE NUMBER OF DIRECT ACCESS FILE RECORDS
'          CHANGE THIS NUMBER FOR MORE RECORDS, OR INPUT
'          AS A VARIABLE.

'     *********************************************
'     *             DIRECT FILE PROCESSING          *
'     *               CASE STUDY: 9-2               *
'     *   CHARGE ACCOUNT PROCESSING & UPDATE PROGRAM *
'     * THIS PROGRAM SETS UP A CUSTOMER MASTER FILE  *
'     * USING DIRECT ACCESS TO LOCATE AND UPDATE     *
'     * THE CUSTOMER RECORD IN THE MASTER FILE FOR   *
'     * EACH TRANSACTION. TWO ADDITIONAL FILES ARE   *
'     * SET UP TO STORE INVALID DATA * MGMT DATA     *
'     *                                              *
'     *                VARIABLE LEGEND               *
'     *  PROGRAM AND FILE VARIABLE    MEANING        *
'     *  ------------------------     -------        *
'     *              NBR       = ACCOUNT NUMBER      *
'     *              NAM       = CUSTOMER NAME       *
'     *              ST        = STREET ADDRESS      *
'     *              CTY       = CITY                *
'     *              STA       = STATE               *
'     *              BAL       = CUSTOMER BALANCE    *
'     *              YTD       = TYD INTEREST        *
'     *              INTR      = CURRENT INTEREST    *
'     *              XIP       = ZIP CODE            *
'     *  TRANSACTION DATA:                           *
'     *              AN = ACCOUNT NUMBER             *
'     *              CODE = TRANSACTION TYPE         *
'     *              AMT = AMOUNT                    *
'     *  COUNTERS:                                   *
'     *              Z = NUMBER OF FILE RECORDS      *
'     *              TREC = NUMBER OF TRANSACTIONS   *
'     *              IREC = NUMBER INVALID TRANS.    *
'     *********************************************
          PRINT "COPYRIGHT (C) 1989, BY MERRILL PUBLISHING COMPANY"
          PRINT "FOR USE WITH STRUCTURED BASIC PROGRAMMING"
          NBR = 1
'         * MAIN PROGRAM *
          CALL OPENFILES
          CALL SETUPMASTERFILE
          CALL PROCESSTRANSACTIONDATA
          CALL PRODUCECUSTOMERBILLS
          CALL PRODUCEREPORTS
          CALL PRINTUPDATEDMASTERFILE
          CALL ENDOFPROGRAMMESSAGE
          CALL ENDOFPROGRAM
          END
DATA 1,JOHN C. JONES,125 MAIN STREET,LOS ANGELES,CA,355.00,46.15,5.32,90066
DATA 2,MARY R. JONES,125 MAIN STREET,LOS ANGELES,CA,166.95,15.22,1.67,90066
DATA 3,BOB SMITH,10 SOUTH STREET,SAN JOSE,CA,745.25,76.25,11.18,95131
```

```
DATA 4,ALICE SMITH,10 SOUTH STREET,SAN JOSE,CA,1615.92,125.65,24.24,96131
DATA 5,LOUIS BROWN,25 NORTH AVENUE,HAYWARD,CA,414.18,86.26,6.21,94545
DATA 6,BETSY BROWN,25 NORTH AVENUE,HAYWARD,CA,65.11,5.21,0.98,94545
DATA 7,BILL LOTT,161 EAST AVENUE,TORRANCE,CA,233.23,14.56,3.35,90503
DATA 8,JILL LOTT,161 EAST AVENUE,TORRANCE,CA,11.00,103.92,16.50,90503
DATA 9,RICH ROGERS,141 MAIN STREET,ANAHEIM,CA,856.92,98.88,12.85,94088
DATA 10,DON ELLSWORTH,ONE ESTATE DRIVE,SUNNYVALE,CA,990.90,144.85,2.17,94086


SUB CALCULATEINTEREST
            R.INTR = R.BAL * .015
            R.YTD = R.YTD + R.INTR
            R.BAL = R.BAL + R.INTR
END SUB


SUB D
END SUB


SUB ENDOFPROGRAM
        CLOSE #2
        PRINT "FILES CLOSED PROGRAM CONCLUDED "
END SUB


SUB ENDOFPROGRAMMESSAGE
        LPRINT : LPRINT : LPRINT
        LPRINT TAB(14); "END OF CHARGE ACCOUNT PROCESSING AND UPDATE PROGRAM"
END SUB


SUB GETMASTERFILERECORD
        GET #1, N, R
END SUB


SUB INPUTTRANSACTIONDATA
        CLS
        PRINT "PLEASE ENTER THE DATA AS SPECIFIED AND PRESS"
        PRINT "RETURN AFTER EACH ENTRY.  WHEN YOU ARE FINISHED, "
        PRINT "TYPE '0' (ZERO) FOR THE ACCOUNT NUMBER AND PRESS"
        PRINT "RETURN FOR THE TRANSACTION TYPE AND THE AMOUNT."
        PRINT : PRINT : PRINT
        PRINT "ENTER THE ACCOUNT NUMBER....:_____"
        PRINT "ENTER THE TRANSACTION TYPE..:_____"
        PRINT "ENTER AMOUNT OF TRANSACTION.:_____"
        LOCATE 8, 30: INPUT AN
        LOCATE 9, 30: INPUT CD$
        LOCATE 10, 30: INPUT AMT
        CALL STOREMANAGEMENTDATA
        IF AN = 0 THEN ENDSW = 1
END SUB


SUB LOADMASTERFILERECORDS
        READ R.NBR, R.NAM, R.ST, R.CTY, R.STA, R.BAL, R.YTD, R.INTR, R.ZIP
END SUB
```

443

```
SUB OPENFILES
          OPEN "RAN.FIL" FOR RANDOM AS #1 LEN = LEN(R)
          OPEN "O", #2, "INV.FIL"
          OPEN "O", #3, "MGT.FIL"
END SUB


SUB PRINTINVALIDDATAREPORT
          OPEN "I", #2, "INV.FIL"
          LPRINT : LPRINT : LPRINT
          LPRINT TAB(28); "-------------------------"
          LPRINT TAB(28); "INVALID TRANSACTION REPORT"
          LPRINT TAB(28); "-------------------------"
          LPRINT
          LPRINT TAB(25); "THE FOLLOWING TRANSACTIONS WERE"
          LPRINT TAB(21); "ENCOUNTERED WITH INVALID ACCOUNT NUMBERS"
          LPRINT
          LPRINT TAB(14); "ACCOUNT NO.          TRANSACTION TYPE          AMOUNT"
          LPRINT
          FOR I = 1 TO IREC
              INPUT #2, AN(I), CD$(I), AMT(I)
              F7$ = "       #####              \              \   $$###,###.##"
              LPRINT USING F7$; AN(I), CD$(I), AMT(I)
          NEXT I
          LPRINT
          LPRINT TAB(24); "END OF INVALID TRANSACTION REPORT"
          LPRINT : LPRINT : LPRINT
          CLOSE #2
END SUB


SUB PRINTMANAGEMENTREPORT
          FOR I = 1 TO 4
              LPRINT
          NEXT I
          LPRINT TAB(31); "------------------"
          LPRINT TAB(31); "TRANSACTION REPORT"
          LPRINT TAB(31); "------------------"
          LPRINT
          LPRINT TAB(14); "ACCOUNT NO.          TRANSACTION TYPE          AMOUNT"
          FOR I = 1 TO TREC
              F7$ = "              ####                 \        \     $ #,###.##"
              LPRINT USING F7$; AN(I), CD$(I), AMT(I)
          NEXT I
          LPRINT : LPRINT
          LPRINT TAB(21); "     END OF TRANSACTION REPORT"
          LPRINT
          CLOSE #3
END SUB


SUB PRINTMASTERFILERECORDS
          LPRINT TAB(27); "CUSTOMER MASTER FILE RECORDS"
          LPRINT "ACNO     NAME          STREET       CITY   STA BALANCE YTDINT INTEREST ZIP"
          FOR N = 1 TO Z
          GET #1, N, R
```
444

```
'   HERE AGAIN, NO CONVERSIONS ARE NEEDED FOR DISK VARIABLES
'   WHEN BROUGHT BACK INTO THE PROGRAM !!
          F1$ = "### \            \\               \\          \\ \####.## ####.## ####.## \    \"
          LPRINT USING F1$; R.NBR, R.NAM, R.ST, R.CTY, R.STA, R.BAL, R.YTD, R.INTR, R.ZIP
          NEXT N
END SUB


SUB PRINTUPDATEDMASTERFILE
          LPRINT TAB(27); "UPDATED MASTER FILE RECORDS"
          LPRINT "ACNO       NAME      STREET       CITY    STA BALANCE  YTDINT  INTEREST ZIP"
          FOR N = 1 TO Z
            GET #1, N, R
            F1$ = " ### \            \\            \\        \\ \ ####.## ####.## ####.## \    \"
            LPRINT USING F1$; R.NBR, R.NAM, R.ST, R.CTY, R.STA, R.BAL, R.YTD, R.INTR, R.ZIP
            LPRINT
          NEXT N
END SUB


SUB PROCESSMONTHLYINTEREST
            FOR N = 1 TO Z
               CALL GETMASTERFILERECORD
               CALL CALCULATEINTEREST
               CALL UPDATEMASTERFILERECORD
            NEXT N
END SUB


SUB PROCESSTRANSACTIONDATA
          CALL PROCESSMONTHLYINTEREST
          CALL INPUTTRANSACTIONDATA
          CALL PROCESSTRANSACTIONUNTILENDOFDATA
END SUB


SUB PROCESSTRANSACTIONUNTILENDOFDATA
          ENDSW = 0
          WHILE ENDSW = 0
          CALL SEARCHMASTERFILE
          CALL INPUTTRANSACTIONDATA
          WEND
          CLOSE #2, #3
END SUB


SUB PRODUCECUSTOMERBILLS
        FOR N = 1 TO Z
        GET #1, N, R
        IF R.BAL > 0 THEN MIN = R.BAL * .1
        LPRINT
        LPRINT
        LPRINT "***********************************************************************************"
        LPRINT "*                                                                     *"
        LPRINT "*                      BEST DEPARTMENT STORE                          *"
        LPRINT "*                                                                     *"
        LPRINT "*                       ONE SOUTH STREET                              *"
        LPRINT "*                                                                     *"
        LPRINT "*                       LOS ANGELES, CA.                              *"
        LPRINT "*                                                                     *"    445
```

```
            LPRINT "*                                                                    *"
            LPRINT "*                                                                    *"
            F3$ = "* CUSTOMER ACCOUNT NO: ####              NEW BALANCE:     $#,###.##    *"
            F4$ = "* CUSTOMER NAME:      \              \   CURRENT INTEREST: $  ###.##   *"
            F5$ = "* CUSTOMER ADDRESS:  \              \   MINIMUM PAYMENT: $  ###.##     *"
            F6$ = "* CITY-STATE-ZIP:    \          \ \ \ \      \                         *"
            LPRINT USING F3$; R.NBR, R.BAL
            LPRINT "*                                                                    *"
            LPRINT USING F4$; R.NAM, R.INTR
            LPRINT "*                                                                    *"
            LPRINT USING F5$; R.ST; MIN
            LPRINT "*                                                                    *"
            LPRINT USING F6$; R.CTY, R.STA, R.ZIP
            LPRINT "*                                                                    *"
            LPRINT "****************************************************************************"
        NEXT N
END SUB


SUB PRODUCEREPORTS
            CALL SORTMANAGEMENTFILE
            CALL PRINTMANAGEMENTREPORT
            CALL PRINTINVALIDDATAREPORT
END SUB


SUB SEARCHMASTERFILE
'      PERFORM 'STORE INVALID DATA' SUBROUTINE
            ISW = 0
            IF AN > Z THEN CALL STOREINVALIDDATA
            IF ISW = 1 THEN GOTO EXIT1
            PRINT " THE VALUE OF AN IS "; AN
            IF AN = 0 GOTO EXIT1
            GET #1, AN, R
'      CALCULATENEWBALANCE
            IF CD$ = "CHARGE" THEN R.BAL = R.BAL + AMT
            IF CD$ = "PAYMENT" THEN R.BAL = R.BAL - AMT
            IF CD$ = "CREDIT" THEN R.BAL = R.BAL - AMT
'      UPDATEMASTERFILERECORD
            PUT #1, AN, R
EXIT1:
END SUB


SUB SETUPMASTERFILE
            Z = 10
            FOR N = 1 TO Z
                CALL LOADMASTERFILERECORDS
                CALL STOREMASTERFILERECORDS
            NEXT N
            CALL PRINTMASTERFILERECORDS
END SUB


SUB SORTMANAGEMENTFILE
            OPEN "I", #3, "MGT.FILE"
            DIM AN(100), CD$(100), AMT(100)
            FOR I = 1 TO TREC
            INPUT #3, AN(I), CD$(I), AMT(I)
```

446

```
          PRINT AN(I), CD$(I), AMT(I)
          NEXT I
          NREC = TREC - 1
          SORTSW = 1
          FOR K = 1 TO NREC
          IF SORTSW = 0 THEN GOTO EXIT2
          SORTSW = 0
          FOR I = 1 TO NREC
          J = I + 1
          IF AN(I) > AN(J) THEN SWAP AN(I), AN(J): SWAP CD$(I), CD$(J): SWAP AMT(I), AMT(J): SORTSW = 1
          NEXT I
          NEXT K
EXIT2:    PRINT
END SUB


SUB STOREINVALIDDATA
          WRITE #2, AN, CD$, AMT
          ISW = 1
          IREC = IREC + 1
END SUB


SUB STOREMANAGEMENTDATA
          WRITE #3, AN, CD$, AMT
          TREC = TREC + 1
END SUB


SUB STOREMASTERFILERECORDS
'    THE MOST DRAMATIC DIFFERENCE IS IN THIS SUBROUTINE
'    NOTE THAT NO CONVERSIONS ARE NECESSARY TO PLACE VARIABLES
'    ON THE DIRECT ACCESS FILE, AS IN THE ORIGINAL CASE 9-2 !!
          PRINT "RECORD GOING IN POSITION "; R.NBR
          PUT #1, R.NBR, R
END SUB


SUB UPDATEMASTERFILERECORD
          PRINT "Updating Record N : "; N
          PUT #1, N, R
END SUB
```

447

Indexed Sequential File Processing

QuickBASIC does not as yet support ISAM directly. You still have to create your own index file or table and search it sequentially or with the binary search before doing the direct access of the "master" file. However, the program logic is so much simplified and shortened with the new direct access features that eliminate the nasty conversion functions that ISAM becomes a practical reality.

The logic of the modified airline reservation program is still not easy to follow without the VTOC chart. However, the QuickBASIC version is much shorter, better documented, and better designed with the true QuickBASIC subroutines that use labels and not numbers. The direct access file syntax is shorter and clearer but you must remember to include the prefix for the direct access file record with the large number of variables that make up the direct access record. Until QuickBASIC supports ISAM directly (as COBOL does), this improvement in the direct access portion of the ISAM algorithm should encourage many programmers to write their own ISAM algorithms.

```
DECLARE SUB OPENFILES ()
DECLARE SUB INPUTFLIGHTINQUIRY ()
DECLARE SUB PROCESSINQUIRYDATAUNTILEND ()
DECLARE SUB PRINTMASTERFILERECORDS ()
DECLARE SUB READINPUTRECORDS ()
DECLARE SUB WRITEMASTERFILERECORDS ()
DECLARE SUB WRITEINDEXFILERECORDS ()
DECLARE SUB SEQUENTIALLYSEARCHINDEXFILE ()
DECLARE SUB RETRIEVEMASTERFILERECORDS ()
DECLARE SUB INPUTTICKETREQUEST ()
DECLARE SUB COMPUTETAX ()
DECLARE SUB PRINTTICKET ()
DECLARE SUB UPDATEMASTERFILE ()
DECLARE SUB PRINTENDOFPROGRAMMESSAGE ()
DECLARE SUB SETUPMASTERFILEINDEXFILE ()
'     ******************************************************
'     *           INDEXED SEQUENTIAL FILE PROCESSING       *
'     *                  CASE STUDY: 10-1                  *
'     *               AIRLINE RESERVATION SYSTEM           *
'     *  THIS PROGRAM SETS UP A FLIGHT MASTER FILE AND     *
'     *  AN INDEX FIE SO THAT PASSENGER FLIGHT INQUIRIES   *
'     *  AND/OR TICKET REQUESTS CAN BE PROCESSED USING     *
'     *  INDEXED SEQUENTIAL ACCESS.                        *
'     *  FLIGHT INQUIRY INFORMATION IS DISPLAYED ON THE    *
'     *  CRT, WHILE PASSENGER TICKETS, ORIGINAL AND UP-    *
'     *  DATED FLIGHT MASTER RECORDS ARE PRINTED ON THE    *
'     *  PRINTER.                                          *
'     *                                                    *
'     *                  VARIABLE LEGEND                   *
'     *    NAME    TYPE           MEANING                  *
'     *    ----    ----           -------                  *
COMMON SHARED CTPR, ALIN, NO, FC, BC, TC, FCFA, BCFA, TCFA, ETD, ETA
COMMON SHARED ML, TYP, MOV, TX, Z, I, CPDA, IT, TAX, TOTAL, IR
COMMON SHARED NAM$, CLASS$, FARE, CPDA$, INQ$
TYPE RECORDTYPE
        CTPR AS STRING * 6 ' CITY PAIR FOR FLIGHT (FROM-TO)   *
        ALIN AS STRING * 2 ' AIRLINE CODE (TWO LETTERS)       *
        NO   AS INTEGER    ' FLIGHT NUMBER                    *
        FC   AS INTEGER    ' FIRST CLASS SEATS AVAILABLE      *
        BC   AS INTEGER    ' BUSINESS CLASS SEATS AVAILABLE   *
        TC   AS INTEGER    ' TOURIST CLASS SEATS AVAILABLE    *
        FCFA AS SINGLE     ' FIRST CLASS AIRFARE              *
        BCFA AS SINGLE     ' BUSINESS CLASS AIRFARE           *
        TCFA AS SINGLE     ' TOURIST CLASS AIRFARE            *
        ETD  AS STRING * 5 ' DEPARTURE TIME                   *
        ETA  AS STRING * 5 ' ARRIVAL TIME (AT DESTINATION)    *
        ML   AS STRING * 10 'MEALS SERVED OF FLIGHT           *
        TYP  AS STRING * 8 ' AIRCRAFT TYPE                    *
        MOV  AS STRING * 8 ' MOVIE SHOWN IN FLIGHT            *
        TX   AS SINGLE
        STX  AS SINGLE
END TYPE
```

```
COMMON SHARED R AS RECORDTYPE
'    Z              '    NUMBER OF FLIGHT RECORDS        *
'    I              '    FLIGHT RECORD COUNTER           *
'    CPDA$          '    INDEX FILE CITY PAIR            *
'    IR             '    INDEX FILE RECORD NUMBER        *
'    TAX            '    TAX ADDED TO AIRFARE            *
'    TOTAL          '    TOTAL COMPUTED AIRFARE          *
'    ********************************************************
            PRINT "COPYRIGHT (C) 1989, BY MERRILL PUBLISHING COMPANY"
            PRINT "FOR USE WITH STRUCTURED BASIC PROGRAMMING"
            KEY OFF
            CLS
'    ***************
'    * MAIN PROGRAM *
'    ***************
            CALL OPENFILES
            CALL SETUPMASTERFILEINDEXFILE
            CALL INPUTFLIGHTINQUIRY
            CALL PROCESSINQUIRYDATAUNTILEND
            CALL PRINTMASTERFILERECORDS
            CALL PRINTENDOFPROGRAMMESSAGE
        END
            Z = 10 'CHANGE THIS VALUE FOR MORE RECORDS
            PRINT " NUMBER OF RECORDS IN FILE :"; Z
            FOR I = 1 TO Z
                CALL READINPUTRECORDS
                CALL WRITEMASTERFILERECORDS
                CALL WRITEINDEXFILERECORDS
            NEXT I
            CALL PRINTMASTERFILERECORDS
            CLOSE #3
DATA LGAORD,EA,101,8,0,138,240,0,130,0935,1145,SNACK,B727,NONE,0,.08
DATA LGAORD,AA,900,8,0,138,240,0,130,1300,1530,SNACK,B727,NONE,0,.08
DATA ORDLGA,EA,102,8,0,138,240,0,130,1710,1950,SNACK,B727,NONE,0,.08
DATA ORDLGA,AA,901,8,0,138,240,0,130,2030,2300,SNACK,B727,NONE,0,.08
DATA JFKFRA,LH,401,33,134,212,1514,735,275,1830,0755,DIN-BREAK,B747,ARTHUR,3,0
DATA JFKFRA,LH,403,24,76,136,1514,735,275,2120,1050,DIN-BREAK,DC10,ARTHUR,3,0
DATA FRAJFK,LH,404,33,132,212,1514,735,275,1330,1555,LUN-DIN,B747,KLUTE,3,0
DATA FRAJFK,LH,400,24,76,136,1514,735,275,1000,1230,BREAK-LUN,DC10,KLUTE,3,0
DATA JFKMUC,LH,409,33,134,212,1531,757,294,1730,0855,DIN-BREAK,B747,ARTHUR,3,0
DATA MUCJFK,LH,408,33,134,212,1531,757,294,1110,1535,LUN-DIN,B747,KLUTE,3,0


SUB COMPUTETAX
            IF CLAS$ = "FIRST" THEN FARE = R.FCFA: TAX = (R.FCFA * R.STX) + R.TX
            IF CLAS$ = "BUS" THEN FARE = R.BCFA: TAX = (R.BCFA * R.STX) + R.TX
            IF CLAS$ = "TOUR" THEN FARE = R.TCFA: TAX = (R.TCFA * R.STX) + R.TX
'    FOR INTERNATIONAL FLIGHTS THE TAX IS #3.00
'    FOR DOMESTIC FLIGHTS THE TAX IS 8% OF FARE
            TOTAL = FARE + TAX
END SUB

SUB INPUTFLIGHTINQUIRY
            CLS
            INPUT " PRESS ANY KEY TO CONTINUE -THEN RETURN "; AA$
            PRINT
            PRINT " READY TO ACCEPT INQUIRY OR TICKET REQUEST"
            PRINT " TO RETRIEVE INFORMATION, ENTER THE CITY-PAIR"
            PRINT " AS JFKFRA (JFK=ORIGIN,FRA=DESTINATION)"
            PRINT "-------------------------------------------"
            INPUT " ENTER CITY PAIR SUCH AS 'JFKMUC', 'END' TO QUIT   :"; INQ$
END SUB

SUB INPUTTICKETREQUEST
'    PRINT INFORMATION REQUESTS FOR TICKET PREPARATION
            PRINT " ------ BEGIN ENTERING INFORMATION FOR TICKET ------"
            PRINT " SEAT STATUS REPORT FOR RECORD :"; IR; " "; R.CTPR
            PRINT " FIRST CL", "BUSINESS CL", "TOURIST CL"
            PRINT R.FC, R.BC, R.TC
'
            PRINT " ABREVIATIONS ; FIRST,BUS,TOUR "
            INPUT " ENTER TYPE SEAT REQUESTED "; CLASS$
            INPUT " PASSENGER NAME :"; NAM$
            INPUT " PASSENGER ADDRESS :"; ADDR$
            INPUT " TYPE OF PAYMENT OR CHARGE NO. :"; PMT$
            CALL COMPUTETAX
            CALL PRINTTICKET
            CALL UPDATEMASTERFILE
END SUB

SUB OPENFILES
            INQ$ = "START"
            OPEN "RAN.FIL" FOR RANDOM AS #1 LEN = LEN(R)
            OPEN "O", #3, "IND.FIL"
```

449

```
END SUB

SUB PRINTENDOFPROGRAMMESSAGE
          PRINT : PRINT : PRINT
          PRINT " END OF AIRLINE INFORMATION PROGRAM"
          CLOSE #1, #2, #3
END SUB

SUB PRINTMASTERFILERECORDS
       IF PRINTSW = 1 THEN LPRINT "   ORIGINAL MASTER FILE RECORDS BEFORE UPDATE " ELSE LPRINT "        UPDATED MASTER FILE RECORDS AF
          FOR I = 1 TO Z
             LPRINT "------------------------ RECORD NUMBER "; I; " ------------------------------"
             GET #1, I, R
             F10$ = "City Pair: \     \Airline:\\:### Seats ### ### ### Fares $$#,###$$###$$###      Times:\ \·\ \ Meals:\       \ A
             LPRINT USING F10$; R.CTPR, R.ALIN, R.NO, R.FC, R.BC, R.TC, R.FCFA, R.BCFA, R.TCFA, R.ETD, R.ETA, R.ML, R.TYP, R.MOV, R.T
          NEXT I
END SUB

SUB PRINTTICKET
          PRINT
          PRINT
          PRINT "**************TICKET ISSUED**************"
          PRINT " AIRLINE       : "; R.ALIN
          PRINT " FLIGHT NUMBER : "; R.NO
          PRINT " SEAT CLASS    : "; CLAS$
          PRINT " PASSENGER NAME: "; NAM$
          PRINT " AIR FARE + TAX: "; TOTAL
          PRINT "----------------------------------------"
          PRINT " TYPE OF PAYMENT - CREDIT CARD NO. IF CHARGE "; PMT$
          PRINT " "
          PRINT " PICK UP TICKET AND BOARDING PASS AT PRINTER"
          PRINT "----------------------------------------------"
          PRINT "            END OF PASSENGER TRX"
          PRINT " "
      PRINT PASSENGER TICKET
          F1$ = "*****************************************"
          F2$ = "*                                       *"
          F3$ = "*  AIRLINE : \      \ FLIGHT NO: #### *"
          F4$ = "*                FROM-TO: \        \   *"
          F5$ = "*               ARRIVAL TIME :  \     \*"
          F6$ = "*  PASSENGER NAME: \                  \*"
          F7$ = "*  SEAT CLASS    : \            \      *"
          F8$ = "*---------------------------------------*"
          F9$ = "*  BASIC FARE    : $#,###.##           *"
          F10$ = "*  TAX           : $ ###.##           *"
          F11$ = "*  TOTAL FARE    : $#,###.##          *"
          F12$ = "*               DEPARTURE TIME: \     \*"
          LPRINT F1$
          LPRINT F2$
          LPRINT "*       TRAVEL AGENT ISSUED TICKET      *"
          LPRINT F2$
          LPRINT USING F3$; R.ALIN, R.NO
          LPRINT F2$
          LPRINT USING F4$; R.CTPR
          LPRINT USING F12$; R.ETD
          LPRINT USING F5$; R.ETA
          LPRINT USING F6$; NAM$
          LPRINT USING F7$; CLAS$
          LPRINT USING F9$; FARE
          LPRINT USING F10$; TAX
          LPRINT USING F11$; TOTAL
          LPRINT F2$
          LPRINT F1$
END SUB

SUB PROCESSINQUIRYDATAUNTILEND
          PRINT " INQ IS EAUAL TO "; INQ$
          WHILE INQ$ <> "END"
               CALL SEQUENTIALLYSEARCHINDEXFILE
               CALL INPUTFLIGHTINQUIRY
          WEND
END SUB

SUB READINPUTRECORDS

          READ R.CTPR, R.ALIN, R.NO, R.FC, R.BC, R.TC, R.FCFA, R.BCFA, R.TCFA, R.ETD, R.ETA, R.ML, R.TYP, R.MOV, R.TX, R.STX
END SUB

SUB RETRIEVEMASTERFILERECORDS

          GET #1, IR, R
          CLS : PRINT " ******** FLIGHTS AVAILABLE ********"
          PRINT "------------------------------------"
```

```
             PRINT " RECORD NUMBER           :"; IR
             PRINT " CITY-PAIR               :"; R.CTPR
             PRINT " AIRLINE                 :"; R.ALIN
             PRINT " FLIGHT NUMBER           :"; R.NO
             PRINT " DEPARTURE TIME          :"; R.ETD
             PRINT " ARRIVAL TIME            :"; R.ETA
             PRINT " MEALS SERVED ON BOARD   :"; R.ML
             PRINT " MOVIE SHOWN             :"; R.MOV
             PRINT " AIRCRAFT TYPE           :"; R.TYP
             PRINT " AIR FARE INFORMATION IN U.S. DOLLARS"
             PRINT "          FIRST CLASS :"; R.FCFA
             PRINT "       BUSINESS CLASS :"; R.BCFA
             PRINT "        TOURIST CLASS :"; R.TCFA
             PRINT " SEAT AVAILABILITY INFORMATION :"
             PRINT "      OPEN IN FIRST CLASS    :"; R.FC
             PRINT "      OPEN IN BUS. CLASS     :"; R.BC
             PRINT "      OPEN IN TOURIST CLASS  :"; R.TC
             PRINT "------------------------------------"
             PRINT " PLEASE CHECK FARE RESTRICTIONS BEFORE"
             PRINT "    PROCESSING TICKET REQUEST !!"
             PRINT "------------------------------------"
             INPUT "PRESS ANY KEY TO CONTINUE THEN RETURN "; A4$
             INPUT " DO YOU WISH TO BOOK A FLIGHT NOW ? (ANSWER YES OR NO)"; A$
             IF A$ = "YES" OR A$ = "Y" THEN CALL INPUTTICKETREQUEST
'     TO BOOK A FLIGHT
'     IF A$ = "NO" OR A$ = "N" THEN INPUT " PRESS ANY KEY FOR OTHER FLIGHTS TO SAME DESTINATION "; X$ ELSE PRINT " OTHER AVAILABLE FL
END SUB

SUB SEQUENTIALLYSEARCHINDEXFILE
             CLOSE #3
             IR = 0: C = 0
             OPEN "I", #3, "IND.FIL"
             FOR N = 1 TO Z
                 PRINT INQ$, CPDA$, " THIS IS IS SEQUENTIAL SEARH INDEX"
                 INPUT #3, CPDA$, IR
                 IF INQ$ = CPDA$ THEN C = C + 1
             NEXT N
             IF C > 1 THEN PRINT " THERE ARE "; C; " FLIGHTS TO MEET YOUR NEEDS - DISPLAY FOLLOWS - JOT DOWN THE RECORD NUMBER OF THE
             INPUT " PRESS ANY KEY TO CONTINUE THEN RETURN "; A3$
             CLOSE #3
             OPEN "I", #3, "IND.FIL"
             FOR N = 1 TO Z
                 INPUT #3, CPDA$, IR
                 IF INQ$ = CPDA$ THEN CALL RETRIEVEMASTERFILERECORDS
             NEXT N
             CLOSE #3
             INPUT " NOW ENTER THE NUMBER OF THE FLIGHT YOU MAY WANT "; IR
             OPEN "I", #3, "IND.FIL"
             IF IR > 0 THEN CALL RETRIEVEMASTERFILERECORDS
             CLOSE #3
END SUB

SUB SETUPMASTERFILEINDEXFILE
         PRINT
         Z = 10
         PRINT " NUMBER OF RECORDS ON FILE IS "; Z
         FOR I = 1 TO Z
             CALL READINPUTRECORDS
             CALL WRITEMASTERFILERECORDS

             CALL WRITEINDEXFILERECORDS
         NEXT I
         CALL PRINTMASTERFILERECORDS
END SUB

SUB UPDATEMASTERFILE
             IF CLAS$ = "FIRST" THEN R.FC = R.FC - 1
             IF CLAS$ = "BUS" THEN R.BC = R.BC - 1
             IF CLAS$ = "TOUR" THEN R.TC = R.TC - 1
             PUT #1, IR, R
             PRINTSW = 0
END SUB

SUB WRITEINDEXFILERECORDS
             CPDA$ = R.CTPR
             IR = I
'     * PRINT TO SEQUENTIAL INDEX FILE *
             WRITE #3, CPDA$, IR
END SUB

SUB WRITEMASTERFILERECORDS
             PUT #1, I, R
             PRINTSW = 1
END SUB
```

451

INDEX

Standard design programming, versus structured design programming, 33–34
Statements. *See* Looping statements; Reserved words, for BASIC
STEP statement, 57
STOP statement, 10, 57
String data, comparing, 180–81
String too long error code, 80
Structure
  charts and charting, 16, 18
  iteration flowchart, 99
  selection flowchart, 99
  sequence, 99–100, 101–03
  flowchart, 99
Structured design
  advantages of, 33
  applying with VTOCs to problem solving, 34–42
Structured design programming, 30–42
  calculations in, 98–99
  outline for, 30, 31
    using cue cards, 30, 32
  versus standard design programming, 33–34
Subscripts
  use of counters to vary, 224, 225
  use of FOR/NEXT to vary, 224, 225
SWAP statement, 57
Syntax
  errors, 22
  statements for QuickBASIC
    CALL, 403
    DO loop, 404
    FUNCTION, 403
    Screen view ports, 404
    SELECT CASE, 403
    Thirty-two bit integers for, 404
    TYPE . . . END TYPE, 403
SYSTEM statement, 57

TAB statement, 57
Table processing
  errors and solutions in (table), 300
  with QuickBASIC, 435–37, 438–40
Tables, 222–29
  and business programming, 223
  DIM statement for, 224, 225, 226
  errors and solutions for (table), 258–59
  general concepts of, 222–23

key facts about, 223
matching with programs, 283–89
sequential data search in, 225, 226–29
setting up, 223–25, 226
TAN(X) function, 114
TERMINATE BASIC system command, 10
Thirty-two bit integers, for QuickBASIC, 404
TIME system command, 9
TIMER statement, 57
TIME$ statement, 57
Titles, printing, 68
TROFF statement, 10, 57
TRON statement, 10, 57
Tutorial, computerized. *See* Computer-assisted instruction
TYPE . . . END TYPE statement, for QuickBASIC, 403
Type mismatch error code, 80

UNTIL loop. *See* DO UNTIL loop
User friendly programs, 115–18
USING statement, 57

Variable names, 59–60
Variables, 59–60
Video display terminal (VDT). *See* CRT display
Virtual array storage, 330
VTOC (visual table of contents) chart, 18, 30, 32–33
  application to problem solving, 34–42

WAIT statement, 57
Welcome message and instructions, 116–18
WEND statement, 57
WHILE loop, 134–37, 425–27
  with FOR/NEXT statement, 136, 137
  with WHILE/WEND statement, 134–36, 138
WHILE statement, 57
WHILE/WEND statement, 134–36, 138
  and nested loops, 136, 138
WIDTH statement, 57
WordStar, converting BASICA programs to QuickBASIC using, 413–21
WRITE statement, 57
WRITE# statement, 57